NEW CENTURY BIBLE COMMENTARY

General Editors

RONALD E. CLEMENTS
(Old Testament)

MATTHEW BLACK
(New Testament)

Joshua, Judges, Ruth

THE NEW CENTURY BIBLE COMMENTARIES

EXODUS (J. P. Hyatt)
LEVITICUS AND NUMBERS (N. H. Snaith)*
DEUTERONOMY (A. D. H. Mayes)
JOSHUA, JUDGES, RUTH (John Gray)
1 AND 2 KINGS (Gwilym H. Jones)
1 AND 2 CHRONICLES (H. G. Williamson)
EZRA, NEHEMIAH, AND ESTHER (D. J. Clines)
JOB (H. H. Rowley)
PSALMS Volumes 1 and 2 (A. A. Anderson)
ISAIAH 1–39 (R. E. Clements)
ISAIAH 40–66 (R. N. Whybray)
EZEKIEL (John W. Wevers)
THE GOSPEL OF MATTHEW (David Hill)
THE GOSPEL OF MARK (Hugh Anderson)
THE GOSPEL OF LUKE (E. Earle Ellis)
THE GOSPEL OF JOHN (Barnabas Lindars)
THE ACTS OF THE APOSTLES (William Neil)
ROMANS (Matthew Black)
1 AND 2 CORINTHIANS (F. F. Bruce)
GALATIANS (Donald Guthrie)
EPHESIANS (C. Leslie Mitton)
PHILIPPIANS (Ralph P. Martin)
COLOSSIANS AND PHILEMON (Ralph P. Martin)
PASTORAL EPISTLES (A. T. Hanson)
1 AND 2 THESSALONIANS (I. Howard Marshall)
1 PETER (Ernest Best)
JOHANNINE EPISTLES (K. Grayston)
JAMES, JUDE AND 2 PETER (E. M. Sidebottom)
THE BOOK OF REVELATION (G. R. Beasley-Murray)

** Not yet available in paperback*
Other titles are in preparation

NEW CENTURY BIBLE COMMENTARY

Based on the Revised Standard Version

Joshua, Judges, Ruth

JOHN GRAY

WM. B. EERDMANS PUBL. CO., GRAND RAPIDS
MARSHALL MORGAN & SCOTT PUBL. LTD., BASINGSTOKE

First published 1986 by Marshall Morgan & Scott, England

Printed in the United States of America
for
Wm. B. Eerdmans Publishing Company
255 Jefferson Av. S.E., Grand Rapids, Mich. 49503
and
Marshall Morgan & Scott
3 Beggarwood Lane, Basingstoke, Hants RG23 7LP, England

British Library Cataloguing in Publication Data:–
Gray, J.
Joshua, Judges, Ruth.—(New Century Bible commentary)
1. Bible. O.T. Judges—Commentaries. 2. Bible.
O.T. Ruth—Commentaries
I. Title II. Series
222′.2077 BS1305.3

ISBN 0–551–01215–3

The Bible references in this publication are taken from the Revised Standard Version of the Bible, copyrighted 1946 and 1952 by the Division of Christian Education, National Council of the Churches of Christ in the U.S.A., and used by permission.

CONTENTS

INTRODUCTION TO RUTH 365

COMMENTARY ON RUTH 383

ABBREVIATIONS

BIBLICAL

OLD TESTAMENT (*OT*)

Gen.	Jg.	1 Chr.	Ps.	Lam.	Ob.	Hag.
Exod.	Ru.	2 Chr.	Prov.	Ezek.	Jon.	Zech.
Lev.	1 Sam.	Ezr.	Ec.	Dan.	Mic.	Mal.
Num.	2 Sam.	Neh.	Ca.	Hos.	Nah.	
Dt.	1 Kg.	Est.	Isa.	Jl	Hab.	
Jos.	2 Kg.	Job	Jer.	Am.	Zeph.	

APOCRYPHA (*Apoc.*)

1 Esd.	Tob.	Ad.Est.	Sir.	S.3 Ch.	Bel	1 Mac.
2 Esd.	Jdt.	Wis.	Bar	Sus.	Man.	2 Mac.
			E.Jer.			

NEW TESTAMENT (*NT*)

Mt.	Ac.	Gal.	1 Th.	Tit.	1 Pet.	3 Jn
Mk	Rom.	Eph.	2 Th.	Phm.	2 Pet.	Jude
Lk.	1 C.	Phil.	1 Tim.	Heb.	1 Jn	Rev.
Jn	2 C.	Col.	2 Tim.	Jas	2 Jn	

GENERAL

AASOR	*Annual of the American Schools of Oriental Research*
AB	Anchor Bible
AJSL	*American Journal of Semitic Languages*
ALUOS	*Annual of the Leeds University Oriental Society*
ANEP	*The Ancient Near East in Pictures*, ed. J. B. Pritchard, 1954; 3rd ed., 1969
ANET	*Ancient Near Eastern Texts relating to the Old Testament*, ed. J. B. Pritchard, 3rd ed., 1969

Ant.	Josephus, *Antiquities of the Jews*
AOTS	*Archaeology and Old Testament Study*, ed. D. W. Thomas, 1967
ATD	Das Alte Testament Deutsch
AV	*Authorised Version* (*King James*), 1611
BA	*Biblical Archaeologist*
BASOR	*Bulletin of the American Schools of Oriental Research*
BAT	Die Botschaft des Alten Testaments
BBB	Bonner Biblische Beiträge
Bib	*Biblica*
BJ	La Bible de Jérusalem
BJPES	*Bulletin of the Jewish Palestine Exploration Society*
BJRL	*Bulletin of the John Rylands Library*
BKAT	Biblischer Kommentar Altes Testaments
BWANT	Beiträge zur Wissenschaft vom Alten und Neuen Testament
BZAW	Beihefte zur Zeitschrift für die alttestamentliche Wissenschaft
CambB	Cambridge Bible
CAH	*Cambridge Ancient History*, 12 vols, 1923–39; rev. ed., 1970–
CB	Century Bible
CBQ	*Catholic Biblical Quarterly*
E	Elohistic source
EAT	J. Knudtzon, *Die El-Amarna Tafeln*, 1915
EB	Die Heilige Schrift in deutscher Übersetzung
ET	English translation
EV(V)	English version(s)
ExpT	*Expository Times*
F. und F.	Forschungen und Fortschritte
FRLANT	Forschungen zur Religion und Literatur des Alten und Neuen Testaments
GK	Gesenius' Hebrew Grammar, ed. E. Kautzsch; rev. A. E. Cowley, 1898
GP	*Géographie de la Palestine*, F. M. Abel I, 1933; II, 1938
HAT	Handbuch zum Alten Testament
HDB	*Dictionary of the Bible*, ed. J. Hastings, 5 vols, 1898–1904
HKAT	Handkommentar zum Alten Testament
HTR	*Harvard Theological Review*
HUCA	*Hebrew Union College Annual*
IB	Interpreter's Bible
ICC	International Critical Commentary
IEJ	*Israel Exploration Journal*

J	Yahwistic source
JAOS	*Journal of the American Oriental Society*
JB	*Jerusalem Bible*
JBL	*Journal of Biblical Literature*
JCS	*Journal of Cuneiform Studies*
JEA	*Journal of Egyptian Archaeology*
JNES	*Journal of Near Eastern Studies*
JPOS	*Journal of Palestine Oriental Society*
JRAS	*Journal of Royal Asiatic Society*
JSS	*Journal of Semitic Studies*
KHCAT	Kurzer Hand-Commentar zum Alten Testament
Kn	J. Knudtzon, *Die El-Amarna Tafeln*, 1915
KS	A. Alt, *Kleine Schriften zur Geschichte des Volkes Israel*, I–III, 1953–9
LXX	Septuagint, Codex Sinaiticus
LXX[A]	Codex Alexandrinus
LXX[B]	Codex Vaticanus
MS(S)	manuscript(s)
MT	Massoretic Text of the Old Testament
NEB	*New English Bible*
NGT	*Norsk Geografisk Tidsskrift*
NSI	G. A. Cooke, *A Text-book of North Semitic Inscriptions*, 1903
P	Priestly source
PEFQS	*Palestine Exploration Fund Quarterly Statement*
PEQ	*Palestine Exploration Quarterly*
PJB	*Palästinajahrbuch des deutschen evangelischen Institut für Altertumswissenschaft des heiligen Landes zu Jerusalem*
RB	*Revue Biblique*
RGG	*Die Religion in Geschichte und Gegenwart*, ed. K. Galling et al., 1st ed., 1909–13 2nd ed., 1927–32; 3rd ed., 1957–62.
RSV	*Revised Standard Version*
RV	*Revised Version*
SANT	Studien zum Alten and Neuen Testament
SAT	Die Schriften des Alten Testaments in Auswahl
SOTS	Society for Old Testament Studies
ThLZ	*Theologische Literaturzeitung*
UF	*Ugarit-Forschungen*
UT	C. H. Gordon, *Ugaritic Textbook*, 1965
VT	*Vetus Testamentum*
Vulg.	Vulgate
ZAW	*Zeitschrift für die Alttestamentliche Wissenschaft*
ZDPV	*Zeitschrift des deutschen Palästinavereins*

SELECT BIBLIOGRAPHY

Note In the text, commentaries and some monographs are cited by author's name alone, and other works listed here by an abbreviated title. Works not included in this select bibliography are cited in full in the text.

COMMENTARIES

F.-M. Abel, *Le Livre de Josué* (BJ), 1950; 2nd ed., 1958.

R. G. Boling, *Judges* (AB), 1975.

J. Bright, 'Judges' (IB), 1953.

K. Budde, *Das Buch der Richter* (KHCAT), 1897.

C. F. Burney, *The Book of Judges*, 1919; rp 1970, with introd. by W. F. Albright.

E. F. Campbell, *Ruth* (AB), 1975.

G. A. Cooke, *The Book of Joshua* (CambB), 1918.

—*The Book of Judges* (CambB), 1913.

—*The Book of Ruth* (CambB), 1913.

G. Gerleman, *Ruth* (BKAT), 1960.

H. Gressmann, *Die Anfänge Israels* (SAT), 1922.

M. Haller, *Ruth: Die Fünf Megillot* (HAT), 1940.

A. W. Hertzberg, *Die Bücher Josua, Richter, Ruth* (ATD), 1953; 2nd ed., 1959.

P. Joüon, *Ruth Commentaire Philologique et Exégétique*, 1924; 2nd ed., 1935.

A. R. S. Kennedy, *The Book of Ruth*, 1928.

M. J. Lagrange, *Le Livre des Juges*, 1903.

H. Lamparter, *Das Buch der Sehnsucht. Das Buch Ruth. Das Hohelied. Die Klagelieder* (BAT), 1962.

C. Lattery, *The Book of Ruth* (Westminster Version of the Sacred Scriptures), 1935.

H. G. May, 'Joshua', *Peake's Commentary on the Bible*, ed. M. Black and H. H. Rowley, 1962.

G. F. Moore, *A Critical and Exegetical Commentary on Judges* (ICC), 1895; 2nd ed., 1908.

J. M. Myers, *The Book of Judges* (IB), 1953.

M. Noth, *Das Buch Josua* (HAT), 1938; 2nd ed., 1953.

F. Nötscher, *Josua* (EB), 1950.

—*Das Buch der Richter* (EB), 1950; 2nd ed., 1955.

W. Nowack, *Richter* (HKAT), 1902.

H. W. Robinson, *Deuteronomy and Joshua* (CB), 1907.
W. Rudolph, *Das Buch Ruth* (KAT), 1939; 2nd ed., 1962.
J. Sasson, *Ruth. A New Translation with a Philological Commentary and a Formalistic-Folkloristic Interpretation*, 1979.
J. N. Schofield, 'Judges', *Peake's Commentary on the Bible*, ed. M. Black and H. H. Rowley, 1962.
J. A. Soggin, *Le Livre de Josué,* 1970.
—*Judges*, ET 1981.
C. Steuernagel, *Josua* (HKAT), 1902.
G. W. Thatcher, *Judges and Ruth* (CB), 1904.
A. Vincent, *Le Livre des Juges* (BJ), 1952.
E. Würthwein, *Ruth* (HAT), 1969.

OTHER WORKS

F.-M. Abel, *Géographie de la Palestine*, 2 vols, 1933, 1938.
Y. Aharoni, *The Land of the Bible*, 1967.
M. Avi-Yonah, *Encyclopaedia of Archaeological Excavations in the Holy Land*, 4 vols, 1975–8.
D. Baly, *The Geography of the Bible*, 1957.
A. Bentzen, *Introduction to the Old Testament*, 6th ed., 1961.
J. Bright, *A History of Israel*, 1960.
O. Eissfeldt, *The Old Testament: An Introduction*, 1965.
A. D. H. Mayes, *Israel in the Period of the Judges*, 1978.
S. Mowinckel, *Israels opphav og eldste historie*, 1967.
M. Noth, *The History of Israel*, 1960.
W. Richter, *Die Bearbeitung des 'Retterbuches' in der deuteronomistischen Epoche* (BBB), 1964.
—*Traditionsgeschictliche Untersuchungen zum Richterbuch* (BBB), 1963.
H. Rösel, '*Studien zur Topographie der Kriege in den Büchern Josua und Richter*', *ZDPV* 91, 1975, pp. 159–90; 92, 1976, pp. 10–46.
H. H. Rowley, *The Servant of the Lord*, 1965.
R. Smend, *Jahnwekrieg und Stämmebund* (FRLANT), 1963.
J. A. Soggin, *Introduction to the Old Testament*, 2nd ed., 1980.
G. A. Smith, *The Historical Geography of the Holy Land*, 26th ed., 1935.
E. Täubler, *Biblische Studien. Die Epoche der Richter*, ed. H.-J. Zobel, 1958.
D. W. Thomas (ed.), *Archaeology and Old Testament Study* (SOTS Jubilee Vol., 1917–67), 1967.

R. de Vaux, *Ancient Israel: Its Life and Institutions*, 1961.
—*The Early History of Israel. II, From the Entry into Canaan to the Period of the Judges*, 1978.
A. Weiser, *Introduction to the Old Testament*, 1961.
H. M. Witzenrath, *Das Buch Ruth. Ein Literatur-wissenschaftliche Untersuchung* (SANT), 1975.

GENERAL INTRODUCTION

to

Joshua and Judges

1. PLACE IN THE CANON

The books of Joshua and Judges, so called after their respective protagonists, belong with Samuel and Kings in Jewish tradition to the Former Prophets. They are recognised as distinct from the Law, with which nevertheless many have associated Joshua in literary criticism. The Pentateuch, which Noth (*Überlieferungsgeschichte des Pentateuchs*, 2nd ed., 1957, pp. 13ff.) considered apart from Deuteronomy, really the introduction to Joshua, Judges, Samuel and Kings, is concerned with what was believed to be the genesis and growth of Israel to a religious confederacy expressed in the covenant-sacrament, and elaborates on the salvation experience, the Exodus, which was the basis of Israel's common faith. In Deuteronomy the drama of salvation (*Heilsgeschichte*) is recalled in the context of the covenant-sacrament (Dt. 26–28) in the literary framework of Moses' speech on the eve of the occupation of the Promised Land, recapitulating the history of the desert period (Dt. 1:1–3:29; 29:2–9), stating the religious and social implications of the covenant as the principles of the life of the historical Israel as the distinctive people of God (Dt. 4:1–30:20), and concluding with the assurance of God's presence in the occupation of Palestine beyond Jordan (Dt. 31:3ff.), with the injunction 'Be strong and of good courage', the note resumed in Jos. 1, and committing to Joshua the charge to lead the people into the Promised Land (Dt. 31:3, 23). Joshua and Judges deal with the two centuries of settlement in Palestine after the decisive penetration *c.* 1225 BC, the former recounting the occupation of the Promised Land (Jos. 2–12), mainly from aetiological traditions associated with the sanctuary of Gilgal and the vicinity (chs 2–11), and describing the sacrament of the covenant at Shechem (Jos. 23; 24) as anticipated in Dt. 11:29f.; 27f.; cf. the redactional note in Jos. 8:30–35.

Joshua, however, is but the prelude to Judges. The former depicts the successful fulfilment of the programme of the occupation of the land in Dt. in the strength of the presence of God, who directly overbore all opposition, while as yet the influence of Moses and his successor Joshua was strong on the people. In the latter, traditions of local communities chiefly and hero-legends which reflect the fluctuations of the fortunes of Israelite groups, are used to illustrate the conditional nature of God's grace to Israel in terms of the stern admonition in the paraenetic conclusion to the covenant-sacrament in Dt. 28:15ff. The blessings and curses in this context respectively in Dt. 28:1–14 and vv. 15ff. are in fact the key to the understanding of Jos., Jg., Sam. and Kg., thus justly recognised by Noth (*op. cit.*) as the Deuteronomistic History. In agreement with the Jewish classification of those books as 'the Former Prophets', this work may be appreciated as a theological interpretation of the history of Israel from the settlement in the Promised Land to the Exile, and illustration in the traditions of the people of the living force of the Word of God in history according to the paraenesis in the covenant-sacrament in Dt. 28.

This work, like the Pentateuch a compilation of sources, differs entirely in its literary framework. Whereas the structure of the Pentateuch is the post-Exilic redaction, that of Jos., Jg., Sam. and Kg. is the Deuteronomistic compilation from the end of the monarchy with, we believe, a post-exilic redaction from the same Deuteronomistic circles. The redaction naturally reflects conceptions characteristic of the roughly contemporary Priestly redaction of the Pentateuch. But in no sense is the influence of P strong in Jos., Jg., Sam. and Kg., being in fact confined to comparatively few passages and easily isolated glosses.

Theology apart, the stylistic characteristics of the Deuteronomistic History are evident throughout in the redundant, repetitive, rhetorical style, where the same phraseology is used in the same subjects without any attempt at variation, and the impression is that the element of admonition is being adapted from a familiar liturgy. Though large portions of the work are obviously from earlier sources which served the purpose of the compiler with little or no comment, there is no doubt that it is he who gives unity to the whole. This is particularly apparent from the punctuation of the history at significant crises by passages in the Deuteronomic style, reviewing the past and adumbrating the future, as in Moses' address in Deuteronomy. These may be either in narrative form, as the summary of Joshua's conquests (Jos. 12), the programme of the book of Judges (Jg. 2:11–3:6) and the review of the tragic past of the northern Kingdom at its fall (2 Kg. 17:7ff.), or in speeches from the protagonists, e.g. of Yahweh to Joshua on the eve of the occupation (Jos. 1:2–9), the address of Joshua on the eve of the occupation (Jos. 23), which anticipates the problems of the next phase, the speech of Samuel, which marks the end of the period of the judges (1 Sam. 12), and the prayer of Solomon at the dedication of the Temple (1 Kg. 8:14ff.).

The unity of Jos., Jg., Sam. and Kg. with Dt. as an introduction is further indicated by overlaps in subject-matter, indicating that certain of the books at least were not divided as now. 1 Kg. 1–2, for instance, continues the theme of the Davidic succession which occupies much of 2 Sam., and the Philistine oppression, stated in Jg. 13:1 to have lasted forty years, is still the theme of 1 Sam., at least until the victory in 1 Sam. 7:10 of Israel under the leadership of Samuel, who is regarded as the last of the judges of Israel (1 Sam. 7:15; 12:11). Similarly, forty-five years span the time between Joshua's reconnaissance of Canaan, envisaged as immediately after the Exodus, and his apportionment of the land, allowing five years for the conquest east and west of Jordan.

This impression of unity is confirmed by the schematic chronology, which is so marked a feature of Jos., Jg., Sam. and the reigns of David and Solomon in the beginning of Kg. The statement that the Temple was begun in the end of Solomon's fourth year, 480 years after the Exodus (1 Kg. 6:1) has demonstrably some connection with the periods of forty, twenty and eighty years which are characteristic of the chronology of Jg., and Noth has used this as an argument for the unity of those books in the Deuteronomistic History according to the following chronological scheme (*op. cit.*, pp. 21–7):

The address and death of Moses 'in the fortieth year' (*sc.* after the Exodus, Dt. 1:3)	40 years
The completion of the 'conquest' under Joshua, 45 years after his reconnaissance of Canaan, represented as immediately after the Exodus (Jos. 14:10)	5
8 years of oppression from which Othniel delivered the people (Jg. 3:8) and subsequently 40 years 'rest'	48
18 years of Moabite oppression (Jg. 3:14) and 80 years 'rest' (Jg. 3:30)	98
20 years oppression under Sisera (Jg. 4:3) and subsequently 40 years 'rest' (Jg. 5:31)	60
7 years of Midianite oppression (Jg. 6:1) and subsequently 40 years 'rest' (Jg. 8:28)	47
Abimelech's 3-year reign (Jg. 9:22)	3
Tola as judge, 23 years (Jg. 10:2)	23
Jair as judge, 22 years (Jg. 10:3)	22
18 years of Ammonite oppression (Jg. 10:8)	18
Jephthah as judge, 6 years (Jg. 12:7)	6
Ibzan as judge, 7 years (Jg. 12:9)	7
Elon as judge, 10 years (Jg. 12:11)	10
Abdon as judge, 8 years (Jg. 12:14)	8
40 years Philistine oppression (Jg. 13:1) including the latter part of Eli's forty-year office	

(1 Sam. 4:18), Samson's career (Jg. 16:31) and that of Samuel until the elevation of Saul or until his death (time unspecified)	40
Saul's reign of '2 years' (1 Sam. 13:1)	2
David's reign of 40 years (1 Kg. 2:11)	40
The foundation of the Temple in Solomon's fourth year (1 Kg. 6:1), his first year coinciding with David's last (1 Kg. 1)	3
Total	480 years

Here we are not concerned with the historical probability of this chronology, which has obvious limitations, but only with its schematic character. The preoccupation with chronology, which is characteristic of P in the Pentateuch, may indicate the post-Exilic redactor, who obviously recognised the unity of Jos., Jg., Sam. and Kg. But in the sources of the Deuteronomic History, the saga affinities of the stories of the great judges would accord with the round numbers in this part of the work, while in the notices of the office of the minor judges the odd numbers have the ring of authenticity. In the assumption that they were consecutive rather than in part contemporary, we may have an indication of selection of those figures whose duration of authority fitted the chronology which accepted the period from the Exodus to the foundation of the Temple as 480 years.

2. DATE OF THE DEUTERONOMISTIC HISTORY

It has been held that this was a post-Exilic work, a frank self-scrutiny imposed by the discipline of the Exile. On the other hand, it is maintained that there was a pre-exilic compilation by the Deuteronomic circle about the end of the Monarchy, with a continuation from the same circle until 561 BC, as indicated by 2 Kg. 25:27, and a redaction. This is suggested by the repeated statement of the abiding divine covenant with the House of David in Sam. and Kg., which would seem to indicate a date before 586 BC, and other references to the Exile and later events, which suggest a post-Exilic redaction. The evidence of those two stages, though not of their respective dates, is clear in Jos. and Jg., especially in the *two* farewell addresses of Joshua (Jos. 23 by the Deuteronomistic compiler and ch. 24 by the redactor, though reflecting a genuine early tradition) and in the appendix on the outrage at Gibeah and its sequel (Jg. 20–21), which disrupts the pattern of the Deuteronomistic compilation and, though based on older sources, is strongly impregnated with post-Exilic language and theology. Such a major redaction and also minor Priestly adjustments, mainly quite obvious glosses, especially in Jos., might be the more readily made since the Former Prophets did not become canonical Scripture till about the beginning of the second century BC.

3. THEOLOGY OF THE DEUTERONOMIC HISTORY

The theology of the work is straightforward and is conveyed by the tradition which classified it as 'the Former Prophets'. It is history presented as a commentary on the Word of God. 'God is not mocked'; he declared his will for Israel in the religious and moral principles communicated in the sacrament of the covenant and endorsed by Israel with solemn adjuration (Dt. 28:15–26). Those principles were developed in their practical application in the literary context of Moses' address in Deuteronomy and the consequences of obedience or apostasy, the blessings or curses elaborated in Dt. 28. The Deuteronomistic History develops the theme of the operation of God's Word in blessing and curse in the history of Israel in Palestine. Jos., somewhat ideally, dwells on the theme of God's blessing in the triumphal establishment of Israel in the Promised Land while yet the strong hands of Moses and Joshua held her in the path of obedience; from Jos. onwards the vicissitudes of Israel are cited in Jg. as evidence of the operation of the Word of God in judgment though tempered by his mercy.

4. SOURCES AND COMPOSITION

The Deuteronomistic History, though conceived and executed as a whole dominated by this single main theme, is none the less a compilation from earlier sources, which were often used as the sources of the Pentateuch were used, i.e. in such a way that doublets and discrepancies occasionally emerge. Under the influence of traditional Pentateuchal criticism, older critics like Wellhausen, Budde, Moore, H. W. Robinson and Burney, related those, particularly in Jos., to the narrative sources J and E in the Pentateuch, and this was still done by Eissfeldt with his refinement of a J and earlier L source in addition to the later E (*Einleitung in das Alte Testament*, 1934, pp. 288–301; 3rd ed., 1964, pp. 321–57, Hölscher (*Geschichtsschreibung in Israel*, 1952, pp. 336–64), Weiser (*Introduction to the Old Testament*, 1961, pp. 144ff.) and C. A. Simpson (*The*

Early Traditions of Israel, 1948; *Composition of the Book of Judges*, 1957). As is well known, von Rad in his fine study, *Das formgeschichtliche Problem des Hexateuchs*, BWANT 78, 1938, distinguished as the subject of the J source of the Pentateuch the originally independent tradition of the covenant eventually combined with the independent tradition of the Exodus as a preliminary and that of the occupation of the Promised Land, the occupation having its antecedents in patriarchal tradition in the promise to Abraham of land and national status. There is little doubt then that the Pentateuchal source J envisaged the occupation. The question is whether J elaborated the theme in detail as is done in Jos.

Simpson would distinguish in the account of the conquest from Num. 13:1 to Jg. 2:5 three main bodies of tradition, which crystallised in the literary sources J^1, the southern tradition (Eissfeldt's L source), J^2 from the north, to which the covenant tradition was proper, and which developed and incorporated J^1, and the third, the conflation of those two sources in E, which introduced traditions from a northern group different from those which crystallised in J^2. No analysis of Jos. on those lines, however, has compelled general assent, and here, where evidence of the narrative sources of the Law has been claimed, critics are usually content to assign certain narrative portions, chiefly in the first half of the book, to JE without attempting further analysis. Modern criticism, however, since Noth's work (*op. cit.*; *Das Buch Josua*, 1937, 2nd ed., 1953) is less sure of the possibility of such analysis, a mood which is reflected by Bentzen (*Introduction to the Old Testament*, vol. 2, 1949, pp. 83, 90), who admits variant tradition-complexes but is still doubtful of evidence for the documentary sources J and E in Jg.

In a more recent view of the situation, Mowinckel (*Tetrateuch-Pentateuch-Hexateuch*, BZAW 90, 1964) shared the view that the J tradition of the Pentateuch with a secondary variant (JV), which corresponds to the traditional E source, culminated in an account of the occupation of the land, which, he agreed, was the substance of Jos. and Jg. 1 in the Deuteronomistic History recognised by Noth with its introduction in Dt. 1–4, with a pre-Deuteronomic compilation in Jos. 2–11. According to Mowinckel, whatever the J tradition of the occupation of the land may have amounted to, it survived in the pre-Deuteronomic compilation and in the Deuteronomistic History mainly in *oral* tradition. It is indeed significant that in his latest study Mowinckel claimed to recognise J only in one account of the crossing of Jordan (Jos. 3f.) and the taking of Jericho (Jos. 6) besides the summary survey of the extent of the occupation in Jg. 1 (*Israels opphav og eldste historie*, 1967, pp. 87f.). This does not suggest a fully developed J tradition of the settlement with initial success (Jos.) and subsequent checks (Jg.). This is in fact the direct development of the admonition of Moses in Dt., the actual preface to Jos. and Jg. in the context of the Deuteronomistic History rather than of the older narrative sources of the Pentateuch. The Deuteronomist certainly had sources, but those were not directly J or E, but were tradition-complexes independent of those compilations, some of which, especially in the first half of Jos., had already been given literary form in the early Monarchy roughly simultaneously with or soon after J. The compilation of traditions in J and E might even have suggested the compilation of local traditions of the penetration and settlement of Israel, especially those in Jos. 2–11 and the stories of the great judges.

In Jos., Noth discerned the work of such a collector (*der Sammler*), which he dated between the disruption of Solomon's kingdom and the death of Ahab (see below, pp. 40ff., 62); and in Jg., W. Beyerlin ('Gattung und Herkunft des Rahmens im Richterbuch', *Tradition and Situation*, ed. by E. Würthwein and O. Kaiser, 1963, pp. 1–29) has distinguished a similar collection of stories of deliverance by the great judges within the pattern of apostasy, suffering, public penitence, appeal to God, God's mercy and deliverance through the divinely called leader expressed in the liturgical convention of the divine contention with his people, which was an important element in the sacrament of the covenant. W. Richter (*Traditionsgeschichtliche Untersuchungen zum Richterbuch*, 1963) also postulates such a pre-Deuteronomistic literary work on the deliverances by the great judges. This most recent development of the critical study of Jg. freely admits variant sources, but those are not explained on the hypothesis of the documentary sources of the Pentateuch J and E. The narrative complexes in Jos. 2–11 and Jg. 3:7–12:7 on the contrary are compositions in their own rights no less than J and E in the Pentateuch but with a quite different motivation. If Jos. 2–11 stands closer to J and E in its theme of the occupation of the Promised Land, its theme is more accentuated, and like the stories of the great judges it is dominated by the motif of the holy war. The stories of the great judges, however, are even more sharply differentiated from J and E by their strong and consistent theological motivation, which the Deuteronomist found so congenial to his own. Richter is probably right in detecting a controversial note in the collection of the stories of the great judges (*op. cit.*, pp. 336–9), evincing criticism of the Monarchy in the context of charismatic leadership of the judges and the assumed effectiveness of the sacral confederacy of the tribes of Israel. The polemical character of the stories of the great judges for which Richter has contended may of course be given by the Deuteronomist's careful selection and presentation of his sources, and this we consider to be notably so in the story of Abimelech (Jg. 9). But the fact remains that the Deuteronomist has such matter to draw upon, and so clearly did it speak that it required the minimum of retouching to suit his theology. Meanwhile we reserve discussion of those and other sources of Jos. and Jg. in the Deuteronomistic History for our introduction to each of those books.

5. THE HISTORICAL VALUE OF JOSHUA AND JUDGES

The Deuteronomistic History and its main sources in Jos. and Jg. represent Israel as an effective polity of twelve tribes which had already achieved unity on the first impact on Palestine, with tribal identity according to their familiar names even before their entrance into Palestine. This corresponds to nothing in the two centuries of settlement between *c.* 1225 and *c.* 1010 BC. It is a later idealization of the Deuteronomistic compiler and his sources from the early monarchy. The earliest expression of the idea apart from J in the Pentateuch is the Blessing of Jacob (Gen. 49). But in the citation of the groups of Israel in the Song of Deborah (Jg. 5:13–18) the northern groups are named according to those in the Blessing of Moses (Dt. 33), which notices Ephraim and Manasseh as components of Joseph (Dt. 33:17). In the Song of Deborah the southern groups Judah and Simeon are not mentioned, nor Levi, nor indeed Joseph, but Ephraim and Machir. The priority of Judah in Gen. 49, by contrast, indicates that that tradition is from after the time of David, to whose monarchy Gen. 49:10 clearly alludes. This, incorporated in the J strand of the Pentateuch, reflects David's unification of the Israel of the Song of Deborah in the north and east of Jordan and Judah and associated groups in the south. This was facilitated by the fact that the southern group and the most dynamic element in the north, the Rachel group, Ephraim, Manasseh and Benjamin, were all worshippers of Yahweh with associations at one time or another with his sanctuary at Kadesh. David's ideal of a greater Israel was based on this fact, and was so firmly implanted in his reign that in the Blessing of Moses from north Israel after the disruption of the kingdom, when Joseph has the priority, the return of Judah to the community was desired (Dt. 33:7).

If we must dismiss the twelve-tribe confederacy of all Israel as effective in the time of the judges on the evidence of Jg. 5:13–18, is there any sense in which we can still admit a sacral confederacy of Israel which was politically effective according to the representation of the settlement in Jos. and Jg. in the Deuteronomistic History and its main sources?

The fact that the twelve-tribe community reflecting David's unification was designated 'Israel' despite David's rule over Israel *and* Judah suggests that at least something corresponding to the ideal realised in David's reign had evolved by his time. This we find in the enumeration of the ten groups, or 'tribes', in the Song of Deborah (Jg. 5:13–18) united in faith in 'the God of Israel' (vv. 3, 5), 'the Lord of Sinai' (v. 5) and 'the champion of Israel' (v. 11). The celebration of Yahweh's vindication of his people (v. 11) in the well-attested exploit of Zebulun and Naphtali and probably Issachar (see below, pp. 273ff.) indicates a well-developed sense of solidarity by *c.* 1150 BC, when the event is most likely dated. But it is likely that this was only gradually achieved. The process whereby the ten groups in the Israel of the Song of Deborah were drawn together into a sacral community with some political potential is bound up with the nature of the settlement of each group, and here a consideration of the various groups concerned in the light of the traditional material used in the Blessing of Jacob (Gen. 49) and the patriarchal traditions of Gen. 12–50 seems to provide clues.

If we are to reject the Deuteronomistic presentation of the settlement of Palestine as an invasion by Israel as a twelve-tribe confederacy, and with it the apportionment of the land by Moses and Joshua after a totally successful combined operation under Joshua, there is no reason to reject the importance in Palestine of a virile group committed to the exclusive worship of Yahweh expressed in simple terms of faith and worship and a social ethic, the obligations of the covenant, however that may have been celebrated. This is surely the militant group which penetrated the hill-country of Ephraim ('the well-wooded country') from which the group eventually took its name, with local elements which joined them. With this the tradition of the warlike Joshua the Ephraimite who mediates the covenant at Shechem (Jos. 24) would accord. With Ephraim, traditionally the son of Joseph, Benjamin is associated in patriarchal tradition and in worship at the sanctuaries of Gilgal by Jericho and Bethel. In the association of those two groups at those boundary sanctuaries in the worship of Yahweh at least we may find the early elements of the sacral community of the Israel attested in the Song of Deborah. Those groups are reckoned as the sons of Rachel in the list of the family of Jacob, which reflects the Monarchic conception of Israel as a twelve-tribe community.

Despite the relatively late schematisation reflecting David's unification of Israel and Judah, the patriarchal tradition clearly distinguishes two groups, the younger Rachel group and the earlier

Leah group Reuben, Simeon, Levi, Judah, Issachar and Zebulun, with Gad and Asher reckoned as concubine tribes. Of those the most dynamic element was Ephraim of the Rachel group, with her southern neighbour Benjamin and those to the north, Manasseh, or Machir. The southern elements of the Leah group Judah and Simeon are significantly omitted in Jg. 5:13–18, and with them Levi, which was probably specifically associated originally with Kadesh in north Sinai. With Ephraim in Jg. 5:13–18 are associated Naphtali in Galilee and their neighbour Dan, which patriarchal tradition reckons as the sons of Jacob by Rachel's maid. This may be the crystallisation of the historical tradition that Dan, originally settled south-west of Ephraim, was either of the same kindred or a neighbouring group of different origin which had embraced Yahwism and made common cause with Ephraim before it had been forced out by Philistine pressure to emigrate to the headwaters of Jordan, where it was the neighbour of Naphtali. The patriarchal tradition that Naphtali was the son of the same handmaid of Rachel was in turn probably occasioned by the geographical proximity of Naphtali to Dan in north Galilee, as Mowinckel proposed (*Israels opphav*, p. 127). To the north of Ephraim Machir, mentioned in Jg. 5:14, is reckoned as a clan of Manasseh, the brother of Ephraim in patriarchal tradition, in Jos. 17:3.

We find the last passage significant. Associating settlements in the hills of central Palestine of such antiquity as Shechem and Tirzah with Machir, it indicates a long period of assimilation of a significant element of the later Israel with the natives of this region, which patriarchal tradition recognises in the settlement of Jacob by Shechem (Gen. 33:18–20) and his covenant with the natives (Gen. 34). Furthermore, the narrative sources of the Pentateuch recognise the significance of this early settlement for the growth of the later Israel by the tradition of the adoption by Jacob of the name Israel on the eve of his settlement here (Gen. 32:27f.) and his founding of the sanctuary of 'El the God of Israel' (Gen. 32:20). At this sanctuary in the district of Machir/Manasseh near the district of Ephraim, Ephraim and Machir/Manasseh realised their solidarity on the basis of common faith in Yahweh. This may be the historical kernel of the tradition of Jacob's covenant at Shechem which the Deuteronomistic redactor has elaborated in Jos. 24.

However this may be, the sanctuary of Yahweh at Shechem, originally a boundary sanctuary of Ephraim and their southern neighbour and confederate Benjamin and Machir/Manasseh, was probably the sanctuary where the groups of the north and east mentioned in Jg. 5:13–18 realised solidarity with the southern neighbours Machir/Manasseh and their confederates Ephraim and

Benjamin. This enlargement of the sacral community may well have been facilitated by the original affinity or association of Dan with Ephraim before their northern migration, if we may adopt the suggestion of Mowinckel, and by the common cause of Machir/ Manasseh with their northern neighbours Issachar, Zebulun and probably Naphtali at the sanctuary of Yahweh at Tabor, the sanctuary common to Issachar and Zebulun (Dt. 33:19).

The recognition of the earlier settlement by Machir and the Leah groups Reuben, Gad, Issachar, Zebulun and Asher of those mentioned in Jg. 5:13–18 permits certain opinions about the settlement which are at variance with the representation of 'conquest' in Jos. 2–11.

Reuben was isolated, living as semi-nomads in the south part of Transjordan and was not free even to be present at the sacral occasion to which, we consider, Jg. 5:2ff. relates (see below, pp. 204f.). It is surprising to find that so small and ineffective a group (cf. Gen. 49:3f.; Dt. 33:6) as Reuben should have been accorded the status of the eldest son of Jacob by tradition. This may possibly be explained by the fact that in the advance of the Rachel group through Transjordan Reuben was the first group to adopt the new faith.

Like Reuben Gad was traditionally pastoral. As the tradition of their descent from Jacob by a concubine suggests, together with the name Gad ('Good Luck'), which is most likely the hypocoristicon of a compound with a divine name (cf. the deity Gad in Isa. 65:11), this group was only later attracted to Yahwism and reckoned a member of the sacral community Israel. Actually, Gad is designated 'Gilead' in Jg. 5:16, which seems to reflect the wider community of non-Israelite inhabitants who were drawn into the confederacy in course of time. Like Reuben they were noticed in Jg. 5:17 as absent.

Issachar, situated in the east part of the Great Central Plain where the hills of Galilee approach those of the centre of Palestine like converging fold-walls of a corral, and including Mount Tabor, betrays its origin in the name ('hireling'). Both geographical situation and menial status are implied in the Blessing of Moses (Gen. 49:14ff.):

Issachar, a gelded ass,
Crouching down between the converging fold-walls,
. . . .
He bent his back to the burden
And submitted to perpetual forced labour.

The origin of this group may have been as *ḫabiru* recruited as serfs on lands in the region depopulated by Egypt in her suzerainty of Palestine after the suppression of native revolt mentioned in the Amarna Tablets (so Alt, 'Neues über Palästina aus der Archiv

Amenophis IV', *KS* III, 1959, pp. 169–75). The burial place of the minor judge Tola of Issachar in the hill-country of Ephraim (Jg. 10:11) is adduced by Mowinckel (*Israels opphav*, pp. 129ff.) for the view that the serfs in the Great Central Plain were supplemented by *ḫabiru* from the hills south of the plain. Issachar then would be composed of the underprivileged *ḫabiru* who were attracted by the success and the social ethic of the Rachel group and the nascent Israel, which offered them for the first time independent status in Palestine.

Zebulun was contiguous with Issachar in the west part of the Great Central Plain and with Machir, later Manasseh, to the south and extended to the western foothills of southern Galilee. The group was thus settled about the nexus of trade-routes between Egypt and Mesopotamia and from the Phoenician seaports which the Blessing of Moses on Issachar and Zebulun notices (Dt. 33:19):

They shall suck the abundance of the seas,
And draw out the hidden wealth of the sand . . .

cf. Gen. 49:13:

Zebulun dwells by the sea-shore,
His shore is a haven for ships,
And his frontier rests on Sidon.

Whatever the original significance of Zebulun, this element of the Leah group may have been *ḫabiru* from the Amarna period employed by the Canaanite city-states bordering on the Great Central Plain like Taanach, Megiddo and Acco to transport or convoy merchandise along the trade-routes. The name in fact in its present passive form may be adapted from an active participle ('porter'), being derived from a verb *zbl*, which means in Arabic 'to take up, carry' and in Hebrew 'to exalt'. The service of the forebears of the Israelite groups Issachar and Zebulun to the Canaanite cities about the Great Central Plain probably enabled them to have unmolested a common sanctuary at Tabor, noticed in Dt. 33:19, which eventually served as a rallying-point for Zebulun, and probably Issachar, and their northern neighbour Naphtali in the campaign in Jg. 4:6ff.; cf. 5:19ff., when those groups had attained status in the sacral community of Israel with their neighbours to the south and to the east of Jordan.

The extent of Asher above the narrow coastal strip from Achzib southwards to the Nahr Zerqa (Jos. 19:26, 29) suggests that Asher is the name primarily of a district rather than an ethnic term, recalling the place-name Asaru in the Egyptian Papyrus Anasti I (late thirteenth cent. BC). As suggested by the Arabic *'asr* ('tube'), it might denote a long restricted area. Asher's reputation for producing 'royal dainties' in the Blessing of Jacob (Gen. 49:20), though from the early Monarchy, might originate from the pre-Israelite period when the forebears of Israelite Asher were tolerated by the coastal city-states as cultivators, like the *ḫubšu* in the Amarna letters of Ribaddi of Byblos (Kn. 77:36; 85:12; 125:27ff., etc.). Again, the reputed descent of Asher from Jacob through Leah's maid suggests the pre-Israelite origin of the group and their status as a social group like their neighbours Zebulun and Machir and Issachar, who found a new status in the community of worshippers of Yahweh under the initial impetus of the Rachel group.

Like Issachar and Zebulun, Machir, their neighbour to the south, may have been *ḫabiru* before the emergence of Israel, being so named ('hireling' or 'mercenary') from their employment by the Canaanite city-states Megiddo, Taanach, Ible-am and Shechem, with the last of which Machir was particularly involved (Jos. 17:3).

Naphtali, the neighbour of Issachar and Zebulun on the north and of Asher on the east, was reputedly one of the younger tribes of Israel whom tradition regarded as a son of Jacob not by Rachel or Leah, but, like Dan, by Rachel's maid. The affinity of Naphtali with Dan, whose affinity with the Rachel group is indicated by Dan's original settlement south-west of Ephraim, may have been suggested by the geographical proximity of Dan and Naphtali in historical times, as Mowinckel proposed (*Israels opphav*, p. 157). Naphtali as a group in the sacral community of Israel in Jg. 5:13–18 also took its origin possibly as *ḫabiru* in the convoluted hill-country of Upper and Lower Galilee, Naphtali being a Niphal formation from the verb *pātal* ('to plait, intertwine'). The group was probably associated with its southern neighbours and probably also with Asher at Tabor as a boundary shrine before they and those associates realised a firmer solidarity with the southern and eastern group of worshippers of Yahweh mentioned in Jg. 5:13–18.

From the foregoing survey it is highly improbable that the sacral community of the ten groups mentioned in Jg. 5:13–18 made the violent impact on Palestine as the Israel represented in the Deuteronomistic History of its early Monarchic sources. Thus we have probably to reckon with the irruption into Palestine by Gilgal of groups and clans from Sinai and ultimately Egypt who after settlement in the hills of central Palestine achieved identity as Ephraim and their southern confederate Benjamin and their neighbours or kindred Manasseh first possibly settled in the Jordan Valley and later about Shechem and northwards, where they absorbed or displaced Machir. This development involved not only the consolidation of groups of kinsmen into the familiar tribes, but the incorporation of local social groups of hitherto underprivileged persons, *ḫabiru*, as Mendenhall has proposed ('The Hebrew Conquest of

Palestine', *BA*, 25, 1962, pp. 66–87), indicated by such names as Machir and Issachar ('hireling') and Zebulun (possibly originally 'porter'). But the nucleus round which the community of Israel gradually grew by force, persuasion or attraction was the elements of the later Ephraim and Benjamin fresh from their commitment to the worship of Yahweh in north Sinai. In the conflict with Sisera, as Jg. 5 indicates, those groups who had had no part in the Exodus and covenant in Sinai or the penetration of Palestine by the forebears of Ephraim and Benjamin were sacramentally associated with Ephraim and Benjamin in faith in Yahweh at the sanctuary of Tabor, though probably not then for the first time.

As to how and to what extent this solidarity was effected we consider that the significance of boundary sanctuaries is the vital clue. Here it may well be that in the order Gilgal (Jos. 4:19; 5), Bethel (Jg. 1:22; 2:1) and Shechem (Jos. 24; cf. 8:30–35) the Deuteronomist has preserved the tradition of the actual progress towards the sacral community of Israel in the north.

Gilgal, about two miles north-east of old Jericho and either in Benjamin (so Noth, *PJB* 37, 1941, p. 82, n. 1) or Ephraim (so K. D. Schunck, *Benjamin*, BZAW 86, 1963, p. 43) and at any rate about the boundary between those two groups, was frequented by both in daily transactions which involved the mutual recognition of social standards and oaths by the God respected by each, namely Yahweh. The early association of Ephraim and Benjamin is expressed in patriarchal tradition which derived both from Jacob and Rachel. Both are associated too with Egypt, and in the pre-Monarchic period Ephraim was the custodian of the ark at Gilgal, Bethel and eventually at Shiloh. Since the ark is traditionally associated with the desert wandering (Num. 10:35, J), the Rachel group were distinctively among the groups of north Palestine the worshippers of Yahweh, to whom they had committed themselves at Sinai. The solidarity of Ephraim and Benjamin, whatever its ultimate origin, was cemented at their common sanctuary of Gilgal, in which the Transjordanian groups Reuben and Gad possibly also shared (so Möhlenbrink, *ZAW* N.F. 15, 1938, pp. 246ff.), and possibly also Manasseh, traditionally Ephraim's nearest kin, who may have been settled in the valley west of the Jordan before expanding north-east of Shechem, where they absorbed or displaced the earlier Machir. Those groups, united in the cult of Yahweh at Gilgal, may well have been the germinal Israel.

The sanctity of Bethel is indicated in the name. This was in Ephraim but was also a boundary sanctuary (Jos. 16:2; 18:13), less than five miles from the eventual north boundary of Benjamin (Bethel in the list of towns in Benjamin in Jos. 18:22 reflects the realm of Josiah in the late seventh century; see below, p. 154). As a boundary sanctuary between Ephraim and Benjamin, Bethel was of little significance for the expansion of the sacral community of worshippers of Yahweh in the period of the judges. For antecedents of the sacral community of the ten groups of Jg. 5:13–18, we must look to Shechem.

Shechem, in the valley between the mountains to the north and those to the south of Palestine and at the head of a pass from the Jordan Valley and the lands beyond Jordan, was obviously the natural place for a boundary sanctuary. It was here that Israelite tradition located the altar of El the God of Israel which Jacob set up on his return from north Mesopotamia by agreement with the rulers of Shechem (Gen. 34:18–20), and indeed the local sanctuary of Baal-berith, the Lord of the Covenant, suggests a boundary sanctuary where relations between neighbouring groups could be ratified. Such an agreement between the forebears of Israel and the local inhabitants seems to be implied in the name of the altar, which implies recognition of Canaanite El, with his social concern (J. Gray, 'Social Aspects of Canaanite Religion', *VT Suppl.* 15, *Congress Vol.*, Geneva, 1965, 1966, pp. 170–92), with the God of the Jacob group. The sanctuary traditionally associated with Jacob was a natural boundary sanctuary for Ephraim and Manasseh, or originally Machir. Since Ephraim and Manasseh were both traditionally associated with Egypt their deliverance from Egypt and subsequent emergence as a sacral community defined by the covenant at Kadesh may have been sacramentally celebrated here by Ephraim and their southern associates Benjamin together with Machir, which was closely associated with Shechem and its neighbourhood and was actually more significant than Manasseh in Jg. 5:13–18. Since the undoubtedly early Song of Deborah (*c.* 1150 BC) clearly implies a confederacy of Ephraim, Benjamin and Machir with Machir's northern neighbour Issachar and their neighbours Zebulun and Naphtali and the inhabitants of Gilead (Gad) and Reuben, Asher and Dan, it would seem that this ten-member community had already effected some degree of solidarity, though, we think, religious rather than political, probably at Shechem. This is the natural sanctuary at which the solidarity of Ephraim, Benjamin and Machir (Manasseh) on the basis of the covenant would be extended to include the northern and eastern groups, both those more nearly related to Ephraim, Benjamin and Manasseh for whom Jacob's altar of El the God of Israel was meaningful, and other under-privileged groups who were attracted by the social ethic of the covenant and by the driving force of the Rachel group which seemed to betoken the divine favour. In view of the pretentions of Ephraim (Jg. 8:1–3;

12:1–6) and their practical hegemony realised in the time of Samuel, when the ark was housed in their territory in the sanctuary of Shiloh, the role of the Ephraimite Joshua as mediator of the covenant at Shechem (cf. Jos. 24) gains historical feasibility.

Here we must consider more closely the historical worth of the tradition of the covenant mediated by Joshua at Shechem in Jos. 24, which has been questioned and indeed absolutely dismissed (e.g. E. Auerbach, *VT Suppl.* 1, 1953, p. 3). Though this passage is probably a late redactional elaboration of the Deuteronomistic farewell address of Joshua in Jos. 23, prompted particularly by the reference to the covenant in Jos. 23:16, it is not likely that Shechem in north Israel should be gratuitously introduced by the redactor. Moreover, such a novel feature as the proposal to worship Yahweh alone rather than the gods (*sic*) of the forefathers in Mesopotamia and Egypt (Jos. 24:15) as an option rather than a categorical demand indicates that under the very free reconstruction of the sacrament of the covenant there is a germ of history. The fact of the option indicates that those addressed had not yet committed themselves to the worship of Yahweh, like Joshua and the Ephraimites and their associates Benjamin, perhaps Manasseh while still in the Jordan Valley, possibly Reuben and Gad from Transjordan, with whom Ephraim had possibly already realised solidarity at Gilgal, and Machir in whose territory Shechem lay. The reference moreover to the gods worshipped by the forefathers in Mesopotamia points to older elements than Ephraim and her first associates, namely, the northern group, Zebulun, Issachar, Asher, with the 'concubine tribes' Naphtali and Dan, as de Vaux suggested (*Histoire ancienne d'Israël* I, 1971, pp. 613f.).

The key to the situation seems to be 'Yahweh the God of Israel' in Jos. 24:2, 23, to whose exclusive worship those addressed by Joshua now commit themselves. The identification of Yahweh with the God of Israel is again associated with the covenant at Shechem in the redactional Jos. 8:30 and, significantly according to Noth (*Das System der zwölf Stämme Israels*, BZAW 52, 1930, p. 139), also with Shechem or its immediate neighbourhood in Gen. 33:20, where the name El the God of Israel indicates the assimilation of the 'God of the fathers' of the Jacob-Israel group with El the senior god of the Canaanite pantheon with his distinctive social concern. The commitment to Yahweh God of Israel indicated the mediation by Ephraim and her associates, with their traditions of the sole worship of Yahweh and their deliverance from Egypt, to the northern group who had already recognised the assimilation of the God of Israel to the Canaanite El. This is probably, we think, Israel 'the people of Yahweh' of the Song of Deborah, which, according to de Vaux, took its genesis at Shechem in the covenant in Jos. 24, *c.* 1200, half a century before the Battle of the Kishon.

At all stages of the development of the sacral confederacy of the ten tribes of north Israel Ephraim was involved, at Gilgal, Bethel, Shechem and in the action at Gibeon (Jos. 10). In Jg. 5:13–18 it is highly significant that, where the ten groups are enumerated from south to north, the list begins not with Benjamin, but with their northern neighbours Ephraim, with whom, however, Benjamin is closely associated (Jg. 5:14). While no argument for the historicity of the ubiquitous Joshua in the 'conquest' of Israel (Jos. 2–11), in the allotment to the tribes (Jos. 13–19) and Levites (Jos. 21) and the appointment of cities of asylum (Jos. 20) and the covenant at Shechem (Jos. 24), the involvement of Ephraim in all significant stages of the growth of Israel supports the tradition of the leadership of the Ephraimite Joshua, particularly in the penetration from Gilgal to the plateau by Bethel and Gibeon (Jos. 2:1–8:29) and in the successful resistance to Amorite opposition at Gibeon (Jos. 10:1–12). The dynamic role of Ephraim in the development of Israel by the time of te campaign celebrated in Jg. 5 is supported by the tradition of the resentment of the initiative of Gideon and his clan of Abiezer and their neighbours (Jg. 8:1–3) and of Jephthah and the Israelites of Gilead (Jg. 12:1–6), and, beyond Jos. and Jg., by the practical leadership of Ephraim under Samuel in the war against the Philistines (1 Sam. 4ff.). Significantly at that time the sanctuary at Gilgal, the boundary sanctuary of Ephraim, Benjamin and possibly Manasseh in the Jordan Valley, was where the resistance of Ephraim and Benjamin crystallized in the anointing of Saul of Benjamin as king on the initiative, or at least with the acquiescence, of the Ephraimite Samuel (1 Sam. 10:8; 11:14f.).

In the appendix to Jg., the war against Benjamin in chs. 19–21, which is much elaborated by post-Exilic redaction, the fact that the injured Levite was a resident in Ephraim and the outrage occurred at the house of an Ephraimite resident in Gibeah of Benjamin makes it feasible that the incident concerned only Ephraim and Benjamin and reflected an attempt on the part of Ephraim's southern associates to assert their independence. The statement that in those days the ark 'of the covenant' with Aaronid priests was at Bethel (Jg. 20:27), though a Deuteronomistic gloss, may nevertheless be a matter of fact, and the deposit of the ark, the symbol of Yahweh militant, at Shiloh (1 Sam. 3:3; 4:3), not a boundary sanctuary but deep in Ephraimite territory, was possibly the assertion of Ephraimite supremacy in consequence of the Benjaminite war, as Schunck feasibly proposes (*Benjamin*, p. 47, n. 171).

On the question of the significance of the ark in the days of the judges, the most reliable tradition is that which associates it with Shiloh in 1 Sam. 1–4 in the last phase before Saul in the time of Samuel. There, however, we have not sufficient evidence for Shiloh as the central sanctuary of all Israel, since we do not know the extent of the Israelite opposition to the Philistines when the ark was taken, evidently as an exceptional measure, to the fighting force in the field after the defeat at Aphek in the foothills of the district of Ephraim. It is doubtful if more of Israel was involved than Ephraim and Benjamin, so that the ark may have been peculiarly associated only with Ephraim. Indeed the only authentic notice of the role of the ark in war involving all Israel is the Ammonite campaign under David (2 Sam. 11:11).

The ark to be sure, the visible token of the presence of God, as Num. 31:10 suggests, was a kind of mobile sanctuary, probably with the Tent of Meeting (Exod. 33:7–11), though this association is not explicitly made before P. Those who have argued for an effective sacral community of all Israel in the days of the judges assume that the ark was moved from sanctuary to sanctuary. Actually this is rather poorly supported in Jos.-Jg., where it is associated, besides Shiloh, with Gilgal (Jos. 7:6), Bethel (Jos. 2:1–5; 20:27) and Shechem (Jos. 8:33). Of those passages, Jos. 8:33 is late and redactional. But since both Gilgal and Bethel were boundary sanctuaries for Ephraim and Benjamin the tradition of the ark at both places may have a nucleus of historical fact. In the case of Gilgal, however, in the association of the ark with the crossing of the Jordan by Gilgal (Jos. 3:13ff.) its original association with the components of the later Ephraim in the occupation of Gilgal and central Palestine is elaborated by the tradition of the celebration of the tradition of the occupation in pageant and dramatic narrative familiar in the early monarchy from the cult at Gilgal, which continued to be an objective of pilgrimage until the eighth century at least (Am. 4:4; 5:5). The opening of Ps. 68, however, invoking the presence of Yahweh in the ark by citing Num. 31:10, if we take the extant psalm to be elaborated from the liturgy of the sacral community of ten tribes at Tabor (so Mowinckel, *Der achtundsechszigste Psalm*, ANVA II, Hist. Filo. Klasse, 1953, No. 1; H. J. Kraus, *Die Psalmen* I, BK XV, 1960, p. 471; J. Gray, 'A Cantata of the Autumn Festival: Psalm LXVIII', *JSS* 22, 1977, pp. 2–26), may well indicate the association of the ark also with Tabor when the solidarity of the ten northern groups was celebrated there.

Here we should again notice that in Jg. 5:13–18 Ephraim is mentioned first of the groups. The presence of the dynamic Ephraim at Shechem also implies the presence of the ark here, despite our reserve over the redactional Jos. 8:30–35. It has been thought that the fact that Saul was able to conduct a campaign against the Amalekites in north Sinai (1 Sam. 15:1–10) implies that Judah by that time was a member of the sacral community of Israel. But in this passage no more is implied than that the various elements which composed the tribe of Judah in David's time had not yet coalesced sufficiently to offer Saul either effective support or opposition. Like the northern group they were of course worshippers of Yahweh and so sympathetic to Saul's enterprise, especially as it was against their inveterate enemy Amalek, in which we may see an effort on the part of Saul and Samuel to extend the sacral community effectively to include Judah.

The fact that the elders of Saul's kingdom in Israel in the north accepted David, already king of Judah, as king of Israel also by covenant 'before Yahweh' at Hebron (2 Sam. 5:3) confirms that Judah worshipped Yahweh and that Hebron was an important sanctuary of his. Indeed there is no hint of any other sanctuary of Yahweh in the geographical region of Judah. Previous to this transaction David was anointed king of Judah in Hebron (2 Sam. 2:4). We find it significant that in this passage special mention is made of his two wives Abinoam of Jezreel and Abigail of Carmel (2 Sam. 2:2), both localities east of Hebron in the region occupied by the Kenizzites, the group to which Caleb, who settled Hebron (Jos. 14:13f.; 15:13; Jg. 1:20) and Othniel, who settled Debir (Kiriath-sepher) (Jos. 15:16; Jg. 1:12f.) belonged. Hebron then was evidently an important boundary sanctuary where Judah from their centre in Bethlehem and the Kenizzites, both worshippers of Yahweh, could ratify agreements. Indeed the notion of confederacy might be implied in the name Hebron, the very *ḥāḇar* meaning 'to unite' (intransitive). We are told that the name of the place was formerly Kiriath-arba ('the City of Four'). This may have been Amorite groups in the nineteenth century BC such as are noted in the Execration Texts from Luxor, where several chiefs are occasionally mentioned in the same locality.

But it may also indicate Hebron as a focal sanctuary for four main groups at the end of the Late Bronze Age, Judah and the Kenizzites and two other southern groups of worshippers of Yahweh, possibly Simeon and either Yeraḥmeel, traditionally 'the brother of Caleb' (1 Chr. 2:42), or the more mobile Kenites, or Midianites, whose main sanctuary was at Kadesh, which they shared with those other southern groups and with the group Moses led out of Egypt (Exod. 17; cf. Num. 10:29–32). All indications are that this southern group remained for all intents and purposes independent of the northern group Israel until the eighth year of David's reign. This is supported by the war between David and the northern group for the first seven years of his reign in Hebron (2 Sam. 2:12–3:1). Both groups, however, were worshippers of Yahweh and both looked to the cradle of their faith at Sinai, specifically, we think, at Kadesh.

To complete the list of boundary sanctuaries conducive to the ultimate unification of Israel before the political unification under David, Beer-sheba, possibly 'the sanctuary of Isaac' of Am. 7:9 (cf. 5:5; 8:14), in the district of Simeon was probably frequented by Kenites, their associates in the occupation of this region in Jg. 1:16f., and Yeraḥmeelites, while the Israelite temple from Solomon's time at Tell Arad may well have had Kenite or Yeraḥmeelite antecedents, as B. Mazar has suggested (*JNES* 24, 1965, p. 301, n. 17), being possibly Ḥormah ('the sanctuary') of Jg. 1:17 and Num. 21:1–3. The itinerant habits of the Kenite smiths incidentally explains the presence of Jael the wife of Heber the Kenite in proximity to the battle of the Kishon (Jg. 5:24), and their Yahwism accounts in some degree for her dispatch of Sisera.

From this survey of the evidence it seems clear that, though the sources of Jg. do not support the view of Israel as the political force, which the compilations, pre-Deuteronomistic and Deuteronomistic, and the recension of the latter present, various neighbouring groups found solidarity on the basis of a common faith in Yahweh. In the north, thanks evidently to Ephraim's fresh experience of the commitment to this faith and their physical impulse, the neighbouring groups at the boundary sanctuaries of Gilgal, Bethel and Shechem were bound together into a larger sacral community. On the evidence of the source material in Jg., however, we are not entitled to say that the sacral community was more than that, though in their successful defensive campaign against Sisera we can see the germ of political potential. But the specification of Ishbosheth's inheritance of Saul's kingdom as Gilead, Geshur (so Syriac Version; cf. MT and Targam, 'the Asherites'), Jezreel, Ephraim and Benjamin (2 Sam. 2:9) indicates how fragile Israel was as a political force about a century after the events of Jg. 5.

Regarding the cult of Yahweh at those sanctuaries in the time of the judges, it is reasonable to conclude that the three great agricultural festivals were observed, at least in the settled land, namely, the festivals of Unleavened Bread and Weeks, respectively at the beginning and end of the grain harvest, and the Ingathering of all crops to winter storage, the great autumn festival. It is not without significance that the early festal calendars in Exod. 23:14–17 (E) and 34:22–24 (J) specify that those must be occasions of pilgrimage 'before Yahweh'. *Ipso facto* they were effective means of expressing the solidarity of the devotees of Yahweh, and it is natural that each new generation of worshippers should be empathetically inducted into the basis of their common faith, the Covenant at Sinai whereby God who had delivered the fathers from Egypt had claimed them for his people and they in turn committed themselves to him as exclusively their God, with religious and social implications such as are reflected in the Decalogue. Those occasions were opportunities for fresh commitment to Yahweh. With such commitment and the recognition of the founding of the community of Yahweh's people, the boundary sanctuaries became more than common sanctuaries where daily transactions between neighbours could be confirmed by a mutually binding oath. They promoted a really effective solidarity between neighbours and, by harking back to the origins of the faith, fostered a sense of solidarity with more remote worshippers of Yahweh.

We have more than a vague hint of the sacramental significance of such occasions in the Song of Deborah, where no fewer than ten members, all the tribes of north Israel in fact, are included in the sacral community, the people of 'the God of Israel' (Jg. 5:2f.), of 'him of Sinai' (Jg. 5:5). The Song gives further indication of the content of those solemn occasions of pilgrimage to the sanctuaries of Yahweh in the admission of demoralisation of the community in the days of its struggle for existence:

They chose new gods,
Gods they had not hitherto known (Jg. 5:8; see below, ad loc.).

This most likely reflects fast and confession before fresh commitment and renewal in God's favour, illustrated in the assembly of the people that Samuel convoked at Mizpah in the resistance to the Philistines (1 Sam. 7:5f.). This experience supplied an apt framework to the pre-Deuteronomistic compilation of the stories of the great judges in Jg. 3:7–12:6, and was congenial to the thesis of the compiler of the Deuteronomistic History.

If we give up Noth's theory of a sacral community, his 'amphictyony', of the twelve tribes of Israel in the time of the judges with a central sanctuary, what of the minor judges, whom he regarded as the regular custodians of the law of the community and its expounders in the changing situation during the settlement, which Alt (*Die Ursprünge des israelitischen Rechts*, 1934, pp. 31–3) and Noth ('Das Amt des "Richters Israel"', *Bertholet Festschrift*, 1950, pp. 407–17) admitted as the only regular office in the community?

This view assumes that the root *šāpaṭ* means exclusively 'to judge' in the juridical sense, for which O. Grether ('Die Bezeichnung "Richter" fur die charismatischen Helden der vorstaatlicher Zeit', *ZAW* 57, 1939, pp. 110–21) has contended. In the light of usage in the Mari texts, the Rās Shamra texts and Phoenician inscriptions, this is no longer tenable. Jurisdiction is not excluded, but the cognate verb and its participle in those texts denotes 'rule' or 'government', of which jurisdiction is but one function. Indeed, in the Old Testament itself *šôpᵉṭîm* is parallel to *mᵉlākîm* ('kings') in Ps. 2:10, and to *mᵉlākîm* and *śārîm* in Ps. 148:11. Thus it is feasibly proposed (W. Richter, 'Zu den "Richtern Israels"', *ZAW* 77, 1965, pp. 140–72; G. Fohrer, 'Altes Testament – "Amphiktyonie" und "Bund"?', *Studien zur alttestamentlichen Theologie und Geschichte* (1949–66), 1969, pp. 117–19; R. de Vaux, *Histoire ancienne*, II, 1973, pp. 71–86; C. H. J. de Geus, *The Tribes of Israel*, 1976, pp. 205–7) that the minor judges were actually local rulers and not merely judges in the juridical sense. Emphasising the local association of the 'judges' in question, Richter regards them as regularly invested by the tribal elders with administration, hence the specification of the duration of their office in Jg. 10:1–5; 12:7–15. Richter concludes that this marked a transition between the authority of tribal elders and the monarchy. On this view, the main difference between 'minor' and 'great judges' is that in the case of the former the circumstances of their rise to power are not noticed, while the authority of the latter was the result of their success in some spectacular act of commitment which indicated their possession of the divine favour (*bᵉrākâll*).

The notice in most cases of the local as well as the tribal association of the minor judges in particular reflects the sedentarisation of Israel and perhaps the shift to authority independent of that within kindred or strictly local units. In view of the reference to the specific periods of office of the minor judges, it is difficult not to credit the note that they bore office in Israel. We do not believe nevertheless that 'Israel' is as comprehensive as Noth maintained. Indeed, we notice that they derived from, and were buried in, Issachar, Zebulun, Ephraim and Gilead, the 'Israel' in fact of Jg. 5:13–15. We find it significant that the offices of the minor judges, with the duration of rule of each, are mentioned after the expression of the solidarity of the ten northern tribes after the battle of the Kishon in Jg. 5 and the career of Gideon of Abiezer in Manasseh. According to Jg. 8:22, the latter was invited by virtue of his act of deliverance from the Midianites to 'rule' (*māšal*) over Israel. Whatever his reaction, Gideon was able to levy the spoils of the campaign and dedicate them at the sanctuary of Yahweh at Ophrah. The actual duration of Gideon's office is not specified, but in agreement with the notices of the minor judges the place of his burial is given (Jg. 8:32). If we may date the battle of the Kishon *c.* 1150 BC, which is generally agreed, the 76 years of office of the minor judges and the period of the authority of Gideon and Samuel would practically span the period from then until the reign of Saul, so that Richter may well be right in seeing in the rule of the minor judges some small anticipation of centralised rule before the actual Monarchy.

The office of Gideon, like that of Jephthah, was accorded as a result of his success in war. The same may possibly be inferred of Tola' from the statement that he 'delivered (*hôšîa'*) Israel'; cf. the description of Othniel, Ehud, Shamgar and Gideon as preeminently 'deliverers' (*môšî'îm*). We may then infer that the *berākâh*, of which their victory was the evidence, designated Gideon and Jephthah and possibly Tola' for office. But other factors were involved. In the case of Jephthah, outcast from his own community, his success and potential menace as a brigand chief suggested his appointment as commander (*qāṣîn*, Jg. 11:6, 10, 11) and 'head' (*rô'š*), his promotion being confirmed by his victory against the Ammonites. This is an instructive example and is significantly analogous to David's rise from the status of successful and dreaded brigand chief (1 Sam. 25–26), feudatory of Achish of Gath (1 Sam. 27) and allied by marriage with the powerful Kenizzites in and near Hebron before he was anointed king by the men of Judah in Hebron (2 Sam. 2:3f.).

The authority of Jair in Gilead may have been similarly recognised in virtue of his power in the north of that region (Jg. 10:3f.) on the border with the Aramaeans, where Jephthah was initially active. Jair's success and consequent status was palpably, and perhaps intentionally, betokened by his thirty sons, each mounted on a probably prestigious ass (cf. Jg. 5:10), like Abdon of Pirathon in Ephraim (Jg. 12:14). The thirty strongpoints (*'ārîm*), if not a tradition developed from the 'tent-agglomerations of Jair', a clan of Manasseh (see on Jos. 13:30; Jg. 10:4), may indicate the settlement of the frontier area in northern Transjordan which was the basis of the rule of the judge Jair. The thirty sons and thirty daughters of Ibzan of Bethlehem, probably in Zebulun, indicate a person of more than average substance, and the marriages he could effect beyond his own locality and kinship (Jg. 12:8f.) indicate, like David's marriages with Kenizzite women, his aspirations and the respect in which he was held, resulting in his recognition as a ruler (*šôpēṭ*).

While the minor judges may have emerged with an authority beyond their own locality or kinship through an aptitude for rule, like Gideon or Jephthah, or through notable juridical ability, as Noth proposed, personal ambition also may have led to the exploitation of a situation. In the case of Abimelech this appears to have been so, and the accumulation of wealth and influence may be reflected in the case of Ibzan with his thirty sons and thirty daughters (Jg. 12:9) and Abdon with his forty sons and thirty grandsons (Jg. 12:14). After all for the Israelite settlers and the local inhabitants who had joined them there was the precedent of the kings of the small city-states of Palestine in the Amarna age.

We would, however, emphasise in conclusion that the rule of Jephthah and possibly Jair was localised in Gilead. Jephthah was a Gileadite called and invested with office by the elders of the community at a local sanctuary Mizpah to deal with the local menace from Ammon. The other minor judges were signalised first by local preeminence before they were more widely recognised in Israel. This 'Israel', we would stress, was that both east and west of Jordan which had found its solidarity after the battle of the Kishon in Jg. 5, which, by and large, was commensurate with the kingdom Ishbosheth inherited from Saul, which consisted of Gilead, the Geshurites (MT Asherites), Jezreel, Ephraim, and Benjamin, the regions associated also with Gideon, Samuel, and Saul, the first king of Israel.

The Deuteronomistic History and its early monarchic narrative sources in Jos. and Jg. give the superficial impression that the various conflicts were the expression of Israel in the holy war. This impression is strongest in Jos. 2–11, and in Jg. the conflicts are represented as following periods of apostasy and oppression which affected all Israel and from which they were delivered by the heroic initiative and leadership of a great 'judge', or 'saviour' (*môšîa'*). It has been maintained that the sacred war was the most characteristic expression of the solidarity of the sacral community of all Israel (e.g. Wellhausen, *Skizzen und Vorarbeiten* I, 1884, p. 10; *Israëlitische und jüdische Geschichte*, 1914, p. 23; G. von Rad, *Der heilige Krieg im alten Israel*, 1951, p. 20). When, however, we discount the redactional character of the schematic narrative in Jos. 2–11 and Jg. 3:1–12:15 and focus attention rather on the earliest sources, we find no support for this view. If support could be expected anywhere, it would be in the Song of Deborah, which von Rad emphasised. Yet as R. Smend observes, if the campaign there described a holy war of the sacral community of all the groups named, then those who did not take part would have been cursed like Meroz (*Jahwekrieg und Stämmebund. Erwägungen zur ältesten Geschichte Israels*, FRLANT 84, 1963, p. 13). This is always supposing that Jg. 5:13ff. describes the campaign. If, as we believe, the enumeration of the tribes in vv. 13–18 is a kind of roll-call of the members of the sacral community where Reuben, Gilead, Dan and Asher are excused for their absence at a sacral occasion, then the conflict, which was inspired by Deborah, though still a holy war (vv. 23, 31), was not one which involved the ten members of the sacral community, though the success of Zebulun and Naphtali, and possibly Issachar, strengthened the bond of the faith and led eventually to at least an increased measure of political unity under Saul.

From what we have noticed of the independent settlement of districts in Palestine by various groups at sundry times, culminating in the settlement of those comprising Ephraim and their kindred and immediate neighbours to the south and north of central Palestine, and of the gradual growth of a sacral community Israel, that of Jg. 5, *c.* 1150 BC, it is extremely precarious to seek to match archaeological data from Palestinian sites to the narrative in the Deuteronomistic History in Jos. and Jg. Such evidence is not to be ignored, but must only be considered after source-analysis. The appreciation of the often anachronistic presentation of the settlement as a sweeping conquest and consolidation as in the Deuteronomistic History and the pre-Deuteronomistic compilations in Jos. 2–11 and Jg. 3:2–12:6 and of the nature of the source-traditions of those, liturgical and aetiological, as in most of Jos. 2–8; 9; 10:16–27, leaves a residue of sober history which, for the most part, proves much less spectacular than in the compilations. Here we are in close agreement with the methods of source-analysis and form-criticism as a prior discipline applied by Alt ('The Settlement of Israel in Palestine', *Essays in Old Testament History and Religion*, ET 1966, pp. 175–21), Noth (*The History of Israel*, ET, 2nd ed., 1960, pp. 68ff.) and more recently M. Weippert (*The Settlement of the Israelite Tribes in Palestine*, SBT, 2nd ser., 21, ET 1971) in contrast to the priority of archaeological facts and the assumption of their relevance to the Deuteronomistic account of the 'conquest', emphasised by Albright (*The Biblical Period from Abraham to Ezra*, 1963, pp. 23–34), Wright (*JNES* 5, 1946, pp. 105–14; *Biblical Archaeology*, 2nd ed., 1962, pp. 69–84) and, with more reserve, by Bright (*A History of Israel*, 2nd ed., 1972, pp. 126–35).

The evidence to be considered is the archaeological findings at Jericho, Ai (at-Tell), Bethel (Beitin) in the region on which Jos. 2–8 concentrates, Tell Beit Mirsim, Tell ad-Duwair (Lachish), Tell-al-Ḥesi (Eglon) and other sites in the south-west in the region where Jos. 10:28ff. depicts a campaign of Joshua and Hazor (Tell al-Qedaḥ) in Galilee (Jos. 11:1–11).

In Jos. 2–8 everything is concentrated about Gilgal where pilgrims on the road to that sanctuary travelled past Ai. These chapters are largely composed of aetiological traditions which helped to actualise the occupation of the Promised Land for worshippers. Though this fact does not necessarily preclude a historical origin, it certainly obscures it. In any case the fall of Late Bronze Age Jericho, dated by Kenyon (*Digging up Jericho*, 1957, pp. 63ff.), so far as erosion permitted a decision, *c.* 1350 BC, cannot be relevant to the same situation as the destruction of Tell Beit Mirsim, Lachish, Hazor and other sites destroyed *c.* 1225 BC or to the destruction of Late Bronze Age Bethel, for which the latest date proposed is 1250 BC (Wright, *JNES* 5, 1946, p. 108), while Ai was derelict between *c.* 2500 and 1100 BC (J. Marquet-Krause, *Syria* 16, 1935, p. 326; J. A. Callaway, *BASOR* 178, 1965, pp. 13–40).

In the south-west, Aharoni (*The Land of the Bible*, 1967, p. 197, n. 64) well emphasised the development of the doubtless historical tradition of the occupation of Hebron and Kiriath-sepher, or Debir, by the Kenizzites Caleb and Othniel (Jos. 15:13–19; Jg. 1:12–15) to the attribution of the exploit to Judah (Jg. 1:10f.) and finally to Joshua and all Israel (Jos. 10:36–39). We may note a similar development in Jos. 10. Here the battle with the king of Jerusalem and his Amorite allies was occasioned by the alliance between the Israelites and the people of Gibeon (al-Jīb). The pursuit of the defeated Amorites, significantly limited, to Azekah (Jos. 10:1–11), may well contain a sound historical tradition, in which the figure of Joshua as a military leader may have been properly at home (so Alt, *KS* i, 1953, pp. 189ff.). However, this has no archaeological support beyond the general evidence of new village settlements in the central hill country in the Early Iron Age. *Pace* G. E. Wright, it is more than doubtful if the destruction of Lachish, *c.* 1220 BC (J. L. Starkey, *PEFQS* 1935, p. 239), Tell Beit Mirsim *c.* 1225 BC (Albright, *AASOR* 17, 1938, pp. 78ff.), Tell al-Ḥesi (F. J. Bliss, *A Mound of Many Cities*, 1898, pp. 71ff., 147), Ashkelon (W. J. Phythian-Adams, *PEFQS* 1921, p. 163; 1923, p. 60) and Ashdod (D. N. Freedman, *BA* 26, 1963, p. 139) is relevant to Jos. 10:28ff., a secondary development of Jos. 10:1–11.

After the battle about Gibeon (Jos. 10:1–11) and the return of 'Joshua and all Israel' to Gilgal (Jos. 10:15), we detect the incorporation of the local tradition in Jos. 10:1–11 into the secondary one of a holy war of the sacral confederacy of all Israel derived by the pre-Deuteronomistic compiler from the cult at Gilgal. The Makkedah incident (Jos. 10:16–27), with its obvious character as topographic aetiology, coming after the return to Gilgal, is surely an accretion, and the sweeping conquest of the south-west (Jos. 10:33ff.) has been developed from the Makkedah incident by local association. If there is any connection between the fall of Late Bronze Age Lachish and Tell al-Ḥesi and the Israelite occupation, that may rather be the result of the expansion of Judah from Bethlehem down the Wādī Naṭṭīf and the Wādī 's-Sanṭ and the southern Shephelah, or of the Kenizzites from Hebron and Kiriath-sepher, or possibly of both together. But, since the Philistines settled this region almost simultaneously with the decisive phase of Israelite penetration of Palestine, and characteristic Philistine remains are found in the twelfth-century settlement of Lachish, it is impossible to associate the destruction of Lachish with one group or another.

Moreover, in his Hamada stele, Merneptah mentions Bedouin aggression from Palestine as far as the Delta (Breasted, *Ancient Records of Egypt* iii, 1906–7, p. 606; A. Youssuf, *Annales du service des antiquités de l'Égypte*, viii, 1964, pp. 273–80). The destruction of Late Bronze Ashkelon and Ashdod could be the result of such raids, whether elements of Israel were involved or not, but in view of Merneptah's claim that he took Ashkelon and Gezer, devastating the former, in 1220 BC (*ANET*, p. 378), it was more likely that he was responsible for the destruction of Ashdod and Ashkelon. Merneptah's mention of Israel in the same inscription, with the determinative for 'people', indicates that some, probably sacral, confederacy so designated was already established in Palestine.

The extent of 'Israel' here is problematic, but its inclusion after Yenoam may be significant. Yenoam, mentioned in an account of the campaign of Seti I from his base at Beth-shan (*ANET*, p. 253), indicates south Galilee or the Jordan Valley just south-west of the Lake of Galilee. This was possibly a confederacy of the forebears of the later Israelite tribes of Galilee about the sanctuary of Tabor (see above, p. 13) or of the older elements of the later Israel indicated by the name of Jacob's altar by Shechem, 'El, the God of Israel', but it might include the dynamic Ephraim and Benjamin in the consolidation of the community at Shechem possibly reflected in Jos. 24. However this may be, it is significant for the correspondence between Jos. and Jg. and independent archaeological data that the reverse claimed by Merneptah is quite unsuspected in the Deuteronomistic History or its sources.

The incidental mention of the fall of Bethel to 'the house of Joseph' (Jg. 1:22–26), significantly not all Israel, merits serious consideration and might be associated with the destruction at Beitīn in the first half of the thirteenth century BC and its resettlement, like elsewhere in the hill-country at this time, on a poorer scale with new and cruder pottery and building.

The relevance of the archaeological data from Arad to the biblical account of the destruction of the place in Jg. 1:16f. must be viewed with the same caution. According to Jg. 1:16f., Arad was settled by the Kenites and Judah after its destruction, hence the name Ḥormah, understood as 'put to the ban'; cf. Num. 21:1–3, where 'the place' was called Hormah; cf. the banning of Zephath ('Watch-post') in the Negeb of Arad (Jg. 1:17). The destruction of Arad at this time is not supported by excavations at Tell Arad, which like Ai was unoccupied from *c.* 2500 to the eleventh century BC (Y.

Aharoni, 'The Negeb', *Archaeology and Old Testament Study*, ed. D. W. Thomas, 1967, p. 392). This suggested to Aharoni that Canaanite, or Late Bronze, Arad, may have been elsewhere in the neighbourhood. The apparent discrepancy between Jg. 1:16f. and the archaeological data from Tell Arad is probably owing to the misunderstanding of the name Ḥormah attached to Arad. Actually the name might have meant 'sanctuary' (cf. Arabic *ḥaram*), denoting possibly an original Kenite sanctuary (so Aharoni, *op. cit.*, p. 401: *JNES* 24, 1965, pp. 297–303), probably a simple open-air holy place prior to the Israelite temple of the tenth century on the site. In the tradition of the banning (*ḥerem*) of Arad we may suspect aetiology under the assumption of the holy war in the Deuteronomistic History and its source from the tradition of the sanctuary at Gilgal. The association of Judah with the Kenites from the base at 'the City of Palm-trees' (Jg. 1:16), by which the Deuteronomist understood Jericho (Dt. 24:3; Jg. 3:13; cf. 2 Chr. 28:15), further indicates the influence of this cultic tradition, the source of the pre-Deuteronomistic narrative of the 'conquest'. We may thus reduce the scriptural tradition to its historical nucleus, the occupation of Arad and district east of Beersheba by the Kenites, who like Israel were worshippers of Yahweh. This is neither proved nor disproved by the excavation of Tell Arad, though the Israelite temple from the tenth century may indicate the earlier sanctity of the place, which the name Ḥormah suggests.

In his critical assessment of archaeological evidence for the 'conquest' in Jos. 2–11, Noth (*VT Suppl.* VII, Congress Vol., Oxford, 1959, 1960, pp. 262–82) admitted only the data from Hazor as relevant to Jos. 11:1–11. This passage, without any element of aetiology or sacral tradition, is purely historical, apart from its association with Joshua and all Israel. The destruction of the city with its Late Bronze Age temples was certainly the work of an enemy, dated by Yigael Yadin and his colleagues as *c.* 1225 BC. It is unlikely that this was the result of Merneptah's campaign in Palestine, since it is unmentioned by him in his relevant inscription, nor was there any local rival strong enough to overthrow this great city, which was paramount in Galilee (Jos. 11:1f., 10). After the destruction of the Late Bronze Age city there were two levels of occupation of the citadel in the Early Iron Age (*c.* 1200–950 BC), before its rebuilding under Solomon (Yadin, 'Hazor', *AOTS*, p. 254). These Yadin considers as settlements of semi-nomads, the remains consisting of storage-pits, hearths and the stone foundations for huts or windbreaks for tents. Is it possible that those squatters were responsible for the destruction of the great city of Hazor? Aharoni maintained that the occupation of a city does not register the whole situation of the country, and so he emphasised the importance of an extensive regional survey to supplement the excavation of a given site. Such a survey of sites throughout northern Galilee revealed that the Early Iron Age pottery at Hazor had no affinities with that of the new settlements of the period in the centre and south of Palestine, but was paralleled in new village settlements in east Galilee northwards from the great central plain (*Antiquity and Survival* ii, 1957, pp. 142ff.).

This settlement of eastern Galilee northwards, up to the point at which Hazor and her allies vainly attempted to stem the penetration, was not likely to be suddenly achieved, and this movement may be connected with the *'prw* whom Seti I mentions in his stele at Beth-shan as active in the mountains of Yarmuth (*ANET*, p. 255), which may be Remeth in Issachar (Jos. 19:21). This would give a date some time after 1313 BC for the beginning of the new settlement in the uplands of Lower Galilee south of Meirun, allowing almost a century for the clearance of scrub and the thick settlement which Aharoni discovered, until they eventually expanded to menace the Canaanite settlements of the Late Bronze Age on the plateau of Upper Galilee.

The second-last destruction of Bronze Age Hazor, in the fourteenth century BC, may have been associated with Seti's campaigns. The deposit of bronze weapons and a figurine of Canaanite type at what was evidently a cult place in the Early Iron Age settlement at Hazor (Yadin, *op. cit.*, p. 256) certainly does not suggest the Israel of Jos. 2–11, but a group independent so far of the sacral community of Yahwists. Here it may be noted that Naphtali, the settlers in this region who were incorporated in Israel, were traditionally regarded as a concubine tribe (Gen. 30:8). Such a group could only have succeeded in destroying Hazor after success in the open field, as indeed Jos. 11:5ff. represents.

Generally, the indication of a new element in the land which may be identified with Israel or their forebears is the settlement of hitherto unpopulated areas attested by new pottery types of the Early Iron Age. Biblical traditions of the settlement of Israel and their forebears may on the other hand be supported by negative evidence. Thus the tradition of the symbiosis of Jacob with the people of Shechem and the inclusion of local settlements like Tirzah and Shechem in the family of Manasseh (Jos. 17:2–4; cf. Num. 26:28–34; 27:1) accords with the fact that excavations at Shechem (Tell Balaṭa) and Tirzah (Tell al-Far'a) attest no destruction of the Late Bronze strata that would correspond with a new settlement in the Early Iron Age (Wright, *Shechem*, 1965, pp. 101f.; de Vaux, 'Tirzah', *AOTS*, pp. 376ff.). The same may be said for the excavation of Gibeon (al-Jīb), where settlement begins in the thirteenth century, with earlier settlement in the Late Bronze Age attested in tombs, but with no indication of violent disruption, thus according with the tradition of a *modus vivendi* between Gibeon and her Israelite neighbours in Jos. 9 (without aetiological embellishments).

Such evidence could support Alt's view that the penetration of Israel was effected not by the dramatic conquest represented in the Deuteronomistic History and its early monarchic source in Jos. 2–11, but by the gradual settlement of the less populous hills by seasonal immigrants, who eventually settled and only latterly came into conflict with the inhabitants of the fortified settlements in the plains, as Jg. describes. The same evidence accords with Mendenhall's view of the assimilation of underprivileged persons (*ḫabiru*) including groups recognised traditionally as progenitors of Israel, who were attracted by the new faith and egalitarian social ethic of the more immediate forebears of Israel, the Rachel group.

The Deuteronomistic representation of Joshua as the successful leader of all Israel in the swift conquest of all Palestine, the allotment of land to the twelve tribes and the mediation of the Covenant at Shechem, must be viewed in the context of the introduction to the Deuteronomistic History in Moses' resumé and paraenesis in Dt. 1:1–4:49; 31:1–30, which emphasises the role of Joshua, the attendant of Moses in the desert wandering (Dt. 1:38), to whom he gave the charge of the occupation of Palestine (Dt. 31:7f., 23). Like the farewell address and the paraenesis of Moses, the farewell address of Joshua is predominantly paraenetic, and like Moses he recalls what God had so far done for Israel. This theme, in the tradition of the historical prelude to the covenant, is continued in Jos. 24:3–13, and, like Moses' specific admonition to worship Yahweh alone without the use of images under pain of the forfeiture of the land (Dt. 4:15–25), Joshua is represented as calling upon the people to put away all strange gods under the same pain of forfeiture (Jos. 24:20). Both passages emphasise the mandatory obligation to Yahweh in the 'statutes and ordinances' (Dt. 4:14; Jos. 24:26), the obligations of the covenant (Dt. 4:13), duly inscribed upon the two tablets of stone (Dt. 4:19, and the Deuteronomistic Jos. 8:32), and in Jos. 24:26 in 'the book of the Law of Yahweh'. Joshua's covenant at Shechem, moreover, is the fulfilment of Moses' programme in Dt. 11:29f.; 27:2–8. Are we on that account to dismiss Joshua as a figment of the imagination of the pre-Deuteronomistic compiler of Jos. 2–11 and of the Deuteronomistic History lacking any historical significance?

Since the pre-Deuteronomistic compilation in Jos. 2–11 is just after the J narrative in the Pentateuch and just before E (see below,

p. 62) the question arises whether Joshua was original in the J narrative from which the pre-Deuteronomistic compiler borrowed him, or whether he was 'borrowed' by the compiler of E from the pre-Deuteronomistic compilation or some local tradition upon which he drew.

We would emphasise that, in contrast to Num. 13:8, 21–29; 14:6–10, 30 (JE), the optimistic and realistic report of Caleb and Joshua on their reconnaissance of Canaan, Num. 13:30 and 14:24 (JE) and Dt. 1:36, mention only Caleb. This suggests either that Caleb was exclusively from J and Joshua from E, so after the pre-Deuteronomistic compilation, or that Joshua is secondary in the Pentateuch and original in the local sources of the pre-Deuteronomistic compilation. Apart from the tradition of Joshua as the young acolyte of Moses in the cult of the Tent of Meeting (Exod. 33:11, JE) and at variance with it, the older tradition in J in Exod. 17:6ff. (J^1, Eissfeldt's L source), like Jos. 2–11, represents Joshua as a mature warrior, indeed as the commander of the fighting men of his people in the campaign against Amalek, which had barred direct access to Palestine, as envisaged by Caleb and Joshua after the reconnaissance from North Sinai (Num. 13–14, JE), thus necessitating the advance by way of the Gulf of Aqaba (Num. 14:25; cf. 39–45; JE). Since there is no reliable indication of the sequence of events in the Exodus and Desert Wandering, nor indeed of the duration of the Wandering beyond the conventional forty years, or a generation, the tradition of Joshua as military commander in the Amalekite campaign and its sequel is historically feasible (so K. Mohlenbrink, 'Josua im Pentateuch', *ZAW* 59, 1942–3, pp. 14ff.) and no fiction evolved from the figure of Joshua as represented in the early Monarchic compilation and the Deuteronomistic History in Jos. 2–11. Equally feasible, in our opinion, is the penetration of Palestine by Joshua and those who later constituted the nucleus of Ephraim in Palestine by Jericho and Gilgal, having been joined beyond Jordan by Reuben and Gad and Benjamin west of the Jordan, their solidarity being consolidated at the sanctuary of Gilgal and resulting in the penetration of the central highlands of Palestine by armed conflict where necessary, as the tradition of the fall of Bethel to 'the house of Joseph' (Jg. 1:22ff.) may reflect.

In view of the fact that the source-traditions of Jos. 2–11, with the exception of that of the Hazor campaign, are attached to sanctuaries in Ephraim or where Ephraim was involved with their neighbours, it must be admitted that Joshua the Ephraimite is a figure of historical verisimilitude, even though we do not admit him as the generalissimo of all Israel of the scope represented in the Deuteronomistic History or its narrative source in Jos. 2–11 from the early

Monarchy. This is supported by the notice of his burial-place in his patrimony, probably that of his heirs in Ephraim (Jos. 24:29). This was probably as well known as the burial-places of the minor judges and was a living tradition in his family.

It would be indeed odd, in view of the essential role of the group comprising Ephraim in the settlement in Palestine and in the expansion of the sacral confederacy and their hegemony indicated by their mention at the head of the tribes of Israel in Jg. 5:13–18 and in the time of Samuel, that the group provided no great political leader until Samuel except Deborah. Thus the balance of historical probability supports the view that Joshua was such a leader when the settlement was effected from Gilgal to Bethel and in the successful resistance to the Amorite reaction to the Gibeonite alliance (Jos. 10:1–11). In virtue of his possession of the divine favour (*berākâh*) it may well be that Joshua, the leader of Ephraim, mediated the covenant to the northern groups, who with Ephraim, Benjamin, Machir/Manasseh, with Reuben and Gad from Transjordan, comprised the Israel of Jg. 5:13–18.

In the covenant at Shechem in Jos. 24, Noth recognised the historical Joshua (*Geschichte Israels*, 3rd ed., 1956, p. 91) rather than in the events at Gilgal and Gibeon. But when we admit the boundary sanctuaries of Gilgal and Bethel, some seven miles from Gibeon, as Ephraimite sanctuaries and not, as Noth claimed, Benjaminite, and when we consider the growing strength of the confederacy of Ephraim and Benjamin and Manasseh/Machir in whose district Shechem lay, the role of Joshua at Shechem in Jos. 24 may be admitted as the natural consequence of his role in the penetration of the Rachel group from Gilgal to the plateau by Gibeon, as Alt proposed ('Josua', *KS* I, 1953, pp. 189ff.). The event at Shechem, moreover, might not be long after that at Gibeon, where the Amorite opposition was broken. Indeed, such progress northwards was easy and natural considering the fact that since the fall of Bethel there was no urban settlement or organised opposition between Gibeon and Shechem, where Machir was ready to join Ephraim and her southern associates. Given the role of Joshua in the mediation of the covenant to the growing confederacy of northern groups, the nucleus of the Israel of Jg. 5:13–18, it is feasible that in the Deuteronomistic representation of his allotment of tribal lands in Jos. 13–19, we may have the Deuteronomistic development of a historical tradition of Joshua's authority, as Alt proposed (*op. cit.*, pp. 198ff.), not indeed of allotting the tribal territories to all Israel, but of resolving the disputes of the various local groups, which often involved rights of water and grazing and responsibility for manslaughter, involving the recognition of boundaries, recognised by Alt ('Das System der Stammes grenzen im Buche Josua', *op. cit.*, p. 196) as the most ancient element in the tradition of the allotment in Jos. 13–19. This role, important and yet far more limited than in the Deuteronomistic History or its early Monarchic narrative source in Jos. 2–11, may well have suggested the representation of Joshua there as the commander-in-chief of all Israel, the Israel of the twelve tribes which the early Monarchic compiler and the Deuteronomist assumed.

6. TEXT

The Massoretic, or traditional, text (MT) of Jos. and Jg., like the rest of the Old Testament, is attested fully vocalised in the Leningrad Codex of 1008, the basis of Kittel's *Biblia Hebraica* (3rd ed.), which is the basis of our study, and in the Aleppo Codex from the first half of the tenth century. The tradition of a vocalised text goes back to the middle of the first millennium AD, before which only consonants were used, certain consonants being occasionally used for vowels to avoid ambiguity. The consonantal text was standardised by *c.* AD 100. Vowels, where not indicated by consonants, were supplied by the reader according to a well-established tradition, which is substantially that of the Leningrad and Aleppo Codices. The biblical manuscripts from Qumran are of tremendous significance for the history of the text of the Old Testament in so far as they attest in fragments, both more and less extensive, practically all books of the Old Testament almost half a millennium before the great uncial manuscripts of the Septuagint (LXX) and even, in the case of a manuscript of Samuel (4QSam[a]) in the third century BC (F. M. Cross, *BASOR* 132, 1953, pp. 15–26; *JBL* 74, 1955, pp. 165–72). While it is significant that this text and certain later manuscripts from Qumran support LXX where it notably diverges from the standard Hebrew text, the bulk of the evidence indicates that, if the Hebrew text was not standardised by *c.* AD 100, there was at least a definite trend in this direction. The few fragments of Jg. from Qumran exhibit this tendency, though giving the following variants:

Jg. 9:31 *ṣārîm ʿal-hā(ʿîr)* ('they are besieging the city') for MT *ṣārîm ʾet-hāʿîr*, where the difficulty of this particular verb with the direct object has suggested a conjectural emendation of *ṣārîm* to *mēʿîrîm* ('they are stirring up');

Jg. 9:40 *wayyirdᵉpēm* ('and he pursued them') for MT *wayyirdᵉpēhû* ('and he pursued him');

Jg. 9:42 *wayyaggēd* ('and one told') for MT *wayyaggîdû* ('and they told').

None of these affects seriously the general sense of MT except the first, where MT has prompted a conjectural emendation.

In passages in the traditional Hebrew text where the sense has broken down through obvious scribal corruption the clue to an earlier Hebrew text may be found in the early versions, notably the Greek translation, LXX, made in Alexandria between *c.* 250 BC (Law) and *c.* 190 BC (Prophets) and attested *in extenso* in the great uncial codices Sinaiticus (A) and Vaticanus (B) from the first part of the fourth century AD and in earlier fragments such as the John Rylands Papyrus of parts of Dt. (*c.* 150 BC). Other Greek translations later than LXX are those of Aquila, a proselyte to Judaism (*c.* AD 130), Symmachus, probably an Ebionite, or Jewish Christian sectary, (*c.* AD 170) and Theodotion, a proselyte to Judaism (*c.* AD 200), which was really the revision of one of the current Greek translations, either LXX (so A. Rahlfs) or another Greek translation (so Kahle), of which examples have come to light from caves in the Wadi Murabbaʿāt south of Qumran. Of those versions that of Aquila, best known from a fourth-century palimpsest from the Karaite Geniza in Old Cairo, deserves special consideration. Literal to the extent of barbarism, it is a very faithful witness to its original Hebrew text, and indeed its very inelegance is its chief merit for the textual criticism of the Old Testament. It is furthermore of greater value than LXX as evidence of MT, which had been standardised about half a century before. This fact, according to Kahle (*The Cairo Geniza*, 1947, p. 117) occasioned Aquila's translation.

While valuable as a key to the Hebrew text of the Old Testament and as a translation for making the Old Testament intelligible to congregations no longer familiar with ancient Hebrew idiom, whose thought-world was far removed from that of the biblical writers, LXX had inevitable limitations. Both the importance and the limitations of LXX were recognised by the great Alexandrine scholar Origen, who in Caesarea in Palestine *c.* AD 240 prepared his great Hexapla, including the Hebrew text, by then standardised (MT), a transliteration into Greek letters, the Greek translations by Aquila, Symmachus and Theodotion. Fragments of other Greek translations, Quinta, Sexta, Septima, were also included, so far as they were available. Disturbed by the number of variants of LXX, Origen set out in this work to collate variants and produce a version which should directly reproduce the standard Hebrew text. His resultant recension of LXX notes additions and deficiencies of LXX *vis-à-vis* MT by signs used in textual criticism of classical texts in Alexandria, the omissions being supplemented by Origen chiefly from Theodotion.

Hexaplar LXX is attested in the Codex Colberto-Sarravianus from the fourth or fifth century containing Gen. 31:5–Jg. 13:12. A similar work, the Tetrapla, in four columns, comprising Aquila, Symmachus, another recension of LXX by Origen, and Theodotion, was produced, probably later (Rahlfs). Here Origen treated LXX even more critically, with further emendations on the basis of MT. This recension of LXX is known in a Syriac translation made in 617 by Paul, Bishop of Tello, and is termed, not quite correctly, the Hexaplar Syriac (S^h).

The LXX of Origen's Hexapla was only one recension current in contemporary Christendom, and Jerome, writing *c.* 400 AD, mentions three authoritative recensions of LXX, that of Hesychius, which was esteemed in Egypt, that of Origen in Palestine and that of Lucian in North Syria (Antioch) and Asia Minor. Of these the Hesychian recension is known only by name, but the Lucianic recension (LXX^L) is known and is of value in the restoration of the Hebrew text. Owing, however, to a tendency to simplification, smoothing out the language according to the canons of Greek grammar and style and expansion to facilitate understanding, it must be used with care and never independently of other textual evidence. The recension of Lucian, who was martyred in AD 312, has peculiarities in common with several early citations from the Greek translation of the Old Testament, particularly in Philo of Alexandria, Josephus and Justin Martyr in the first century AD, the John Rylands Papyrus 458, and now in fragments of the Minor Prophets from Qumran (P. Kahle, *ThLZ* 79, 1954, cols. 83ff.). The early date of these and the fact that they were made by Jews before the standardisation of the Hebrew text give the variants in LXX^L a quite peculiar value.

The need for the Old Testament in the vernacular, which necessitated the LXX in Egypt, occasioned the Syriac translation (Peshitta) in North Mesopotamia, where the native royal family of the Aramaean kingdom of Adiabene became proselytes to Judaism in the middle of the first century AD. The value of this version, especially where it diverges from LXX, is that Syriac is a cognate Semitic language with Hebrew, and might reasonably be supposed to be more sensitive to the idiom and ethos of the Hebrew original.

Related to LXX, but a translation of the Hebrew, is the Vulgate, made by Jerome between AD 390 and 405, which has a peculiar value in that Jerome lived and worked in Bethlehem and so was familiar with local customs and topography.

Divergences from MT in LXX raise the question of the relative reliability of MT and the Hebrew text from which LXX was translated.

For instance additions in LXX raise the question as to whether those are amplifications and explanations necessitated by the presentation of the Old Testament to a later age and environment. Alternatively there is the possibility that such readings may indicate an actual Hebrew revision older than MT, such as is attested in the manuscript of Samuel from Qumran (4QSam).

On the other hand LXX may give a shorter text than MT, especially where MT is pleonastic. This has been taken by S. Holmes (*Joshua, the Hebrew and Greek Texts*, 1914) as an indication of an original Hebrew text varying from MT and preferable to it. Again this may indicate a Hebrew revision older than MT. But, when the pleonastic style of the Hebrew original according to MT is of less significance than the subject matter a shortening of the text may be expected in its presentation to a Greek-speaking, Greek-thinking congregation in the synagogue in Egypt, for which LXX was designed. A case in point is Jos. 5:4–6, where LXX confines the circumcision at Gilgal to the males born in the forty years wandering, omitting the statement in MT that all the men fit for war who left Egypt had died (v. 4), which is in fact repeated in MT at v. 6, which is rendered by LXX. The statement in MT that all the people who left Egypt were circumcised and that those born subsequently were uncircumcised (v. 5) is significantly omitted in LXX. This is an obvious expansion to the Hebrew text before its standardisation in accordance with the Priestly tradition of the covenant with Abraham involving circumcision (Gen. 17:9–14) and the tradition, also Priestly, that all males in the first Passover in Egypt were circumcised (Gen. 12:43).

Occasionally, where the sense of MT breaks down, LXX suggests an obviously correct Hebrew original. Often the difference is owing to a scribal error in the transcription of the Hebrew text at one stage or another in the development of the Hebrew script in the transmission of the text from the earliest literary element, in the case of Jos. and Jg. *c.* tenth century BC, to the extant MT in the early Christian era.

In restoring the Hebrew text in the light of variant readings in the versions we must test the feasibility of such variations in the context, reckoning with the possibility of scribal corruption. We must not limit our study of the Hebrew text to that in the script familiar in the manuscripts, but envisage it in its various stages of palaeographic development attested fully in inscriptions of various length from archaeological stations and from the whole period during which the books of the Old Testament were written and transmitted. In restoring the picture of the ancient Near East, archaeology, even in its more material aspects, has made its contribution to textual criticism, and even more so in the ancient literature to which it has introduced us. Many words in the Old Testament, occurring only once and on that account suspect and often misunderstood or corrupted by later Jewish scribes no longer familiar with ancient dialects, are now elucidated in those other literatures, Akkadian and Canaanite chiefly, where their cognates occur more often and in contexts which fix their meanings beyond doubt. The recovery of those literatures, notably the Canaanite literature from Rās Shamra, has stimulated a new interest even in Semitic languages so well known as Arabic, and has opened the way for new insights into the nuances of words and phrases in cognate Semitic languages and in the older sources of the Old Testament to which later scribes were strange.

INTRODUCTION

to

Joshua

1. CONTENTS

The book of Joshua, so called after its chief character whose work it describes and in whose death it culminates, falls into three sections:

FIRST SECTION. 1–12. NARRATIVES OF THE CONQUEST introduced by the divine exhortation to Joshua (1:2–9, Deuteronomistic) and terminated by a summary of his conquests (12, Deuteronomistic).

SECOND SECTION. 13–21. APPORTIONMENT OF THE LAND to the tribes (13:1–19:51), apportionment of cities of refuge (20) and Levitical settlements (21:1–42), and summary note on the occupation of the Promised Land (21:43–45, Deuteronomistic).

THIRD SECTION. 22–24. CONCLUSION: the dismissal of the Transjordanian tribes to their homes (22:1–9), the controversy on the altar in the Jordan Valley (22:10–34), the farewell address of Joshua in the context of the covenant at Shechem (23, the original conclusion by the Deuteronomistic compiler), and 24, an elaboration by the later redactor (see above, p. 17) summarising the general historical theme of the Law, but reflecting the ancient tradition of the covenant at Shechem and probably a decisive step in the consolidation of early Israel.

2. SOURCES AND COMPOSITION

The sporadic, local penetration and gradual consolidation of the components of the historical Israel in Palestine, noticed in Jg. 1 and Jos. 15:63; 16:10 and 17:12, contrasts strongly with the general representation of the occupation as a conquest by all Israel which proceeded practically without check under Joshua's leadership in fulfilment of the ineluctable purpose of God, who enervated the opposition usually without a struggle. It is therefore obvious that Jos. 2–11 is generally the stylisation of the occupation as a conquest by a compiler familiar with the ideal of a united Israel of twelve tribes, as in the J source of the Pentateuch, which was realised only under David over two centuries after the decisive penetration of Palestine by the Rachel group and the dynamic activity of Ephraim. This was evidently, like J, a literary work in narrative style by one who collected and combined traditions which he considered relevant to his main theme, as Noth proposed. The evidence of such literary compilation is to be detected in the editorial notes by which separate local traditions are artificially drawn together, e.g. 'when . . . the kings of the Amorites . . . and the kings of Canaan . . . heard that the Lord had dried up the waters of Jordan' (5:1); 'so the Lord was with Joshua; and his fame was in all the land' (after the fall of Jericho) (6:27), 'when the inhabitants of Gibeon heard what Joshua had done to Jericho and to Ai (9:3–4), 'when Adonizedek . . . heard how Joshua had taken Ai . . . and how the inhabitants of Gibeon had made peace . . .' (10:1). The campaign against Hazor is similarly introduced (11:1). Noth would include with these the summaries of Joshua's conquests in the south (10:40–42) and the whole country (11:20) (*Das Buch Josua*, 1953, pp. 12f.), but in our opinion those summaries have been very much elaborated by the Deuteronomist. The date of this compilation according to Noth's feasible reckoning (*op. cit.*, p. 13) was the early Monarchy. The ruin of Hazor, which was rebuilt under Solomon (1 Kg. 9:15), is a living memory, but nothing is known of the rebuilding of Jericho (6:26) under Ahab (874–853 BC) according to 1 Kg. 16:34. The reference to 'the hill-country of Israel' (11:16) obviously reflects a date after the Disruption of the kingdom, so that this work may be dated at the outside limits between 931 and 853 BC. The reference to 'the hill-country of Israel' and the detail in the traditions of the south in comparison with the few and rather vague references to details in the occupation of the north indicate an origin in Judah, probably in Jerusalem. This literary assembling of local traditions may in fact have been conceived as a supplement to the J source of the Pentateuch possibly within half a century or less later than that work.

The main source used by the early monarchic compiler is indicated by the fact that, with the exception of the battle of Gibeon (10:1–15) and the fall of Hazor (11:1–9) and the later, redactional passage on the covenant at Shechem (8:30–36), all the action is concentrated about Gilgal or on the road pilgrims would take to that sanctuary. In the themes of the cult at Gilgal (see above, p. 15) the early monarchic compiler found a source which conditioned his presentation of the occupation as a conquest in a holy war. In his presentation of the Ephraimite Joshua as commander-in-chief in the advance from Gilgal to the central plateau he may have utilised an element from the historical traditions of the dominant Ephraim and their neighbours and confederates Benjamin, but the theme of the occupation of the Promised Land in the cult of Gilgal was the main source, which presented the compiler with a unified theme and conditioned the nature of his work.

Particularly associated with Gilgal was the miraculous crossing of the Jordan (4–5) and the fall of Jericho (6), both of which by their nature indicate their source in ritual observance in the cult at Gilgal, 2½ miles distant from Jericho. Also associated with Gilgal and its vicinity and the road taken by pilgrims from the north are aetiological, or explanatory, legends concerning certain localities, the Hill of Foreskins, the scene of the circumcision (5:2–9), the scene of a theophany authenticating a holy site near or at Jericho (5:13–15), the derelict site of Ai, 'the Ruin' (8:24–29), with a conspicuous tree on which, tradition told, the king of Ai had been hanged (8:28), and a pile of stones at the gate, reputedly heaped over his dead body and visible 'to this day' (8:29). The unfailing location of incidents in the life of our Lord by the Christian Church as a stimulus to the faith of pilgrims is a not unapt analogy to the development of such traditions in the cult of Gilgal. The aetiological legend of the cairn of Achan, however, in the Valley of Achor (al-Buqei'a) a few miles south-west of Gilgal (7:10–26) and of the curse on Jericho (6:26), still practically derelict, with the exception of a family (that of Rahab), were probably secular traditions which were incorporated with the compiler's account of the 'conquest' and adapted to his theological theme.

The tradition of the covenant with the Gibeonites and the hostile reaction of the Amorite kings of Jerusalem, Hebron, Yarmuth, Lachish and Eglon and their subsequent defeat (9:1–10:15) was originally independent of events at Gilgal, with which they were combined by the early monarchic compiler. As evidenced by 2 Sam. 21:1–10, the relations between Gibeon and her Israelite neighbours were a historical fact, the Gibeonites being evidently a non-Semitic, probably Hurrian, community (9:7; see below, on 9:3), who, for security or commercial advantage, proposed and secured a defensive alliance with the Rachel group. The ruse by which the Gibeonites secured this relationship (9:3–15), however, may be the contribution of the compiler, for whom such rapprochement modified his presentation of the occupation as a resounding success for intransigent Israel in the holy war. The probably Deuteronomistic elaboration of the servile status of the Gibeonites in the cult of Yahweh (9:26f.) is a further aetiological tradition similarly motivated.

The subsequent battle about Gibeon has historical verisimilitude, and in the poetic citation from the Book of Yashar (10:12; see below, ad loc.) we have more than a hint of an important source of the pre-Deuteronomistic compiler's account of the 'conquest' in Jos. 2–11. The title, which may be a variant of 'the Book of the Wars of Yahweh' (Num. 21:14f.), indicates the theme of the occupation as a holy war, and to this extent it was theologically conditioned like the work of the compiler of Jos. 2–11. But it seems none the less to have incorporated secular historical traditions of the local groups which consolidated as the later Israel. The pursuit of the defeated Amorites to Azekah in the foothills south-west of Gibeon (10:13–27) is probably a genuine historical tradition, though embellished by local aetiological legend concerning five conspicuous trees and a cave blocked by a rock-fall at Makkedah (5:26f.), which recalls the legend of the tree and stone-heap at Ai. The original independence of the Makkedah incident (10:16–27) is indicated by the note in 10:15 that after the rout and death of the Amorite kings to Azekah 'Joshua and all the Israelites returned to the camp at Gilgal'.

The association of the Gibeonite campaign with Gilgal and all Israel is the work of the early monarchic compiler, to whom by the same token (10:43) Joshua's sweeping 'conquest' of the south-west (10:33–39, 43) is also due, though in the account of general massacre in this region as far as Kadesh-barnea and Gaza (10:41), the inclusion of the latter seems to indicate the Deuteronomistic Historian, reflecting conditions of Josiah's time rather than the pre-Deuteronomistic compilation in the early Monarchy.

Another local historical tradition, which, like that of the Gibeonite campaign as distinct from those about Gilgal, is quite free of cultic influence, is that of the surprise defeat of the forces of Hazor and their allies in the open country in north Galilee and the subsequent destruction of Hazor (11:1–11). This is incorporated in the compiler's account of the 'conquest' by Joshua and all Israel, to which he goes on to attribute the total and bloody subjugation of the whole of the north, corresponding to the subjugation of the south after the battle of Gibeon (10:28–39).

This then was the first main literary source incorporated in the Deuteronomistic History, the account of the occupation of the Promised Land, which he introduced by the divine command to Joshua (1:2–9) and Joshua's summons to the tribes east of Jordan (1:12–18), by which the connection with Dt. is effected (cf. Dt. 3:18–20), and concluded with the comprehensive list of conquered kings in Jos. 12. In accordance with the tradition of the sacrament of the covenant at Shechem in the programme of the occupation of the Promised Land (Dt. 11:29–32), the Deuteronomist inserts a passage on this theme (8:30–35), though in this case he probably reflects the decisive step in the founding of the community of the ten groups comprising the Israel of Jg. 5:13–18. Since the Deuteronomistic History, or Former Prophets, was not yet canonical Scripture for practically four centuries, other adjustments and glosses were made, particularly reflecting the doctrinal susceptibilities and interests of Priestly circles. Those are comparatively few and rather obvious, and will be noted in the commentary.

The second part of Jos. (13–21), dealing with the apportionment of the land, and being largely geographical lists, differs in character from the narrative of chs. 1–12. The matter is threefold, concerning tribal territories (14:1–19:49*a*), prefaced by a recapitulation of the land of Reuben and Gad and the half-tribe of Manasseh in Transjordan (18:8–33), cf. Num. 32:34ff. (JE), and concluded by a note on the inheritance of Joshua (19:49*b*–50), a list of cities of refuge (20), and of Levitical settlements (21:1–42).

In the list of tribal territories the heading 'These are the inheritances which the people of Israel received . . . which Eleazar . . . and Joshua . . . distributed to them' (14:1*a*), and the conclusion 'So they finished dividing the land . . .' (19:51), mean just what they say. The section is pragmatic, as distinct from the preceding, where the predominating view is that of the pre-Deuteronomistic compiler, who renders the cultic theme of the occupation of the Promised Land by God's invincible agency. In Jos. 13–21 the theme of the guidance and agency of God is conserved to be sure by the representation of the apportionment of the land by lot at the sanctuaries of Gilgal and Shiloh, by Joshua and the priest Eleazar, but the actual sources are factual descriptions of tribal boundaries supplemented by administrative town-lists. There are also traditions of the independent settlement of certain groups, such as the Kenizzites under Caleb and Othniel, who were affiliated to Judah, and the expansion of 'Joseph', which are conserved in certain narrative passages, and as such are exceptional in this section (e.g. 14:6–15; 15:13–19; cf. Jg. 1:10; Jos. 15:15–19 = Jg. 1:11–15; Jos. 15:63 cf. Jg. 1:21; Jos. 16:10 cf. Jg. 1:29; and Jos. 17:14–18; cf. Jg. 1:27f.). The ultimate source of those passages is the same historical traditions of tribal initiative and struggle as emerge in Jg. 1. The association of those narrative traditions with the boundary descriptions reflects on the authority and antiquity of the latter.

Jos. 13–21 has generally been assigned to P. Eissfeldt (*Einleitung in Das Alte Testament*, 3rd ed., 1964, p. 335) emphasised the analogy of a similar, ideal division in the reconstruction of the new Israel in Ezek. 48. But the analogy is superficial, and the division of tribal lands in Ezek. is ideal and quite vague, showing none of the odd projections and indentations of the division in Jos. (e.g. 15:5; 16:7) which give the tribal boundaries there the stamp of originality (Alt, *Das System der Stämmesgrenzen . . .*, *KS* I, 1953, p. 196). Alt argued that if the lists in Jos. had been the artificial reconstruction of an exilic redactor they would have conformed to the twelve-tribe system assumed by the redactor. On the contrary, the omission of boundaries for Simeon and Dan, and the practical omission of a boundary for Issachar, indicates that the compiler was using older material conditioned by the actual historical situation (*op. cit.*, p. 194). With the Galilean territories, too, he must have been working with older, though deficient, material, otherwise those areas would have been treated like the others had he been applying his own artificial scheme. Here, however, instead of the description of boundaries followed by town-lists, town-lists and boundary points are generally not distinguished, and in the case of Issachar there is no systematic description of the boundary at all. Obviously the compiler was limited by his sources. The acceptance of old local divisions too in the fiscal organisation of Solomon's administration (1 Kg. 4:7–19), though these are considerably modified, corroborates the view that the description of tribal boundaries in Jos. 13–19 rests on a genuine historical tradition in the main, though it reflects the situation in the time of David or Solomon rather than earlier. Alt further feasibly contended that the separation of the fortified settlements of Tappuah (17:8) and Jerusalem (15:8) from their arable lands is quite inconceivable after the Monarchy, and must refer to the resistance and eventual fall of the city-states in the time of the penetration and settlement of Israel (*op. cit.*, p. 200).

Von Rad ('Das formgeschichtliche Problem des Hexateuch', *Gesammelte Studien*, 1958, pp. 79f.) regarded tribal boundaries as the subject of claim and argument at the central sanctuaries of the sacral community, which were confirmed after David's conquests and incorporation of the Canaanite lands. We doubt the role of a central sanctuary of all Israel, as represented in the account of the allotment in Jos. 13–19, but admit that the occasionally meticulous detail in the tribal boundaries may reflect local arbitration at some time in the settlement of the components of the later Israel in disputes over water (cf. the matter of the sources of water between Caleb and Othniel), grazing and cultivation and responsibility for crime, which was settled by proximity to settlements (cf. Dt. 21:1–8). This was quite possibly settled at boundary sanctuaries, like Gilgal, Bethel, Shechem and Tabor, though not, as Jos. 18–19 represents, at Shiloh, which was not a boundary sanctuary, but exclusively in Ephraim. We doubt if written documents from the period of the settlement were used as source material, but believe that we may assume at least a well-established local tradition.

Alt went on to emphasise discrepancies in the description of those tribal boundaries and the list of towns named in each territory, which led him to the conclusion that, though the description of tribal territories by boundary points was genuinely old, and possibly a feature of the period of the judges, the towns are generally enumerated from administrative lists in the Monarchy. The fact that settlements in Judah, Benjamin, Simeon and Dan in that tribe's original settlement in the south are fully listed in contrast to the incomplete lists of Galilean settlements, and that there is no town-list at all for the territory of the Joseph tribes suggested to him the period of

Josiah in his extension of the realm in the last decade before the collapse of Assyria in 612 BC, while the north was still organised as an Assyrian province. While official documents of Josiah's time were doubtless used, especially for the districts claimed for Judah in the Philistine plain and immediately north of Jerusalem, evidence of the wilderness settlements of Middin, Secacah, Nibshan and the City of Salt, which have been identified in the vicinity of Qumran, and Engedi (ninth–seventh centuries BC) suggest that for this district at least official records of the reign of Jehoshaphat (871–847 BC) may have been used (F. M. Cross and G. E. Wright, 'The Boundary and Province Lists of the Kingdom of Judah', *JBL* 75, 1956, pp. 202–26; see below, pp. 142f.). While this archaeological evidence does not exclude Alt's dating of the source as an administrative list in the time of Josiah, the dating of Cross and Wright at this point is the more probable. In any case a date before *c.* 900 BC or after *c.* 600 BC is excluded, and with it the P authorship of the section.

The location of the allotment by Joshua at the assembly of all Israel at the sanctuaries of Gilgal and Shiloh is the contribution of the Deuteronomistic Historian, while the role of the priest Eleazar at Shiloh may indicate a Priestly redactor.

The literary history of Jos. 20 and 21 is rather more complicated. In ch. 20 the prescription of six cities of refuge in the event of unpremeditated homicide (vv. 1–6, 9) immediately suggests a connection with Num. 35:9–34 (P), which prescribes three cities east and three west of Jordan, though not naming them; with Dt. 4:41–43, where three cities are appointed for this purpose in Transjordan, namely, Bezer, Ramoth Gilead and Golan; and with Dt. 19:1–13, where three cities (unnamed) are to be set apart for this purpose in three districts (also unnamed) west of the Jordan, and another three in a region unspecified, where the elders are to guarantee sanctuary or, in the case of murder, to hand the guilty party over to the avenger of blood. In Jos. 20:7–8 the regions and cities both east and west of the Jordan are specified. The four passages have been influenced in transmission one by the other. Dt. 4:41–43, unconnected with the context and naming the three cities in Transjordan, which are unnamed in Dt. 19:1–13, is an interpolation suggested by Jos. 20:8. The omission of vv. 1–5, and v. 6 except 'until he stand before the congregation for judgment' from LXX suggests that this is a later expansion, and the mention of the term of office of the high priest (v. 6) indicates the influence of Num. 35:9–34 in the post-Exilic redaction of the Deuteronomic History in Jos. The fact that Dt. 19:7–9 mentions six cities indicates, according to de Vaux (*Ancient Israel: its Life and Institutions*, ET 1961, p. 162), familiarity with the tradition in Jos. 20, though the specification of cities in Transjordan was unrealistic in the time of the Deuteronomist, when the extension of Jewish influence to this area was at the best only a prospect. De Vaux argues that since the organisation was not on a tribal but a regional basis, this indicates a date not before the time of Solomon, in whose administrative division of the kingdom tribal boundaries were not strictly followed. This, we think, does not follow. The regional basis seems to us rather to be designed to avoid complications between neighbouring groups in the rights of asylum, still a matter of some delicacy among Arab tribes. In essence then the Deuteronomistic compiler in Jos. 20 has preserved a genuine old tradition, though this has received redactional retouching, reflected in the passages already cited, to which, 'of which I spoke to you through Moses' (v. 2) probably points. The note on the tribal location of the three cities of refuge in Transjordan in Reuben, Gad and Manasseh (v. 8) may be, as Noth suggested (*Das Buch Josua*, 3rd ed., p. 125), by the redactor, who misunderstood the significance of Naphtali, Ephraim and Judah in v. 7, which, though tribal names, were probably earlier, as here, geographical terms (see above, pp. 10, 13, 14).

The list of settlements for Levites (Jos. 21) according to the prescription of Num. 35:1–8 (P) was also taken by the older critics as an unrealistic reconstruction reflecting the Priestly interest of the post-Exilic redactor. This view, when critically considered, raises more problems than it solves. The Levitical settlement in Hebron and the south has no relevance in the post-Exilic period, when that region was occupied by the Edomites, as Yehezkel Kaufmann observes (*The Biblical Account of the Conquest of Palestine*, 1953, p. 41). Generally the area covered is much more extensive than that occupied by the Jews in the post-Exilic period, except briefly in the time of Judas the Maccabee, as W. Rudolph has observed (*Chronikbücher*, 1955, p. 179) and under Alexander Jannaeus (103–76 BC), by which time the references to the system in the Law (Num. 35:1–8) and in Jos. were crystallised in Holy Scripture. This applies particularly to the Levitical settlements in Transjordan, such as Golan and Ashtaroth (Be-eshterah of Jos. 21), which were lost to the Syrians after *c.* 900 BC and recovered only temporarily under Jeroboam II, and the region north-east of the Dead Sea, where such settlements as Heshbon and Jazer (v. 39) passed out of Israelite hands, certainly by *c.* 830 BC. This militates also against Alt's view that the list relates to Josiah's removal of provincial Levites to Jerusalem in 2 Kg. 23:8 ('Bemerkungen zu einigen jüdaïschen Ortslisten', *KS* II, 1953, pp. 297ff.), or his later view that it relates to the resettlement of Levites in the vicinity of places in Judah which Josiah refortified in his reorganisation of the realm after the curtailment of the kingdom of Hezekiah by Sennacherib ('Festungen und Levitenorte im Lande Juda', *KS* II, pp. 310–15).

Noth regarded the Levitical settlement indicated in Jos. 21 as post-Exilic. He suggested that the fact that in Num. 35:6f. the Samaritan Pentateuch shows a knowledge of Jos. 21 indicates that this passage, even though post-Exilic, cannot post-date the Samaritan schism, though the omission of certain districts in central Palestine suggests, he submitted, a time when there was already tension between the Jews and their neighbours in the district of Samaria (*Das Buch Josua*, 3rd ed., p. 131). This view strangely ignores the inclusion of Shechem in the list of the Levitical settlements. Noth would explain the omission of Jerusalem and regions in the neighbourhood on the grounds that the passage is really interested in Levitical settlements after the Exile, when Jerusalem was the administrative capital of imperial powers. But Noth clearly felt uneasy about this explanation, and the obvious objection to this view is that Levitical settlements so near Jerusalem as Gibeon, Geba and Anathoth (vv. 17f.) are mentioned. Noth's strongest argument for a post-Exilic date is the organisation of the Levites by the families of Kohath, Gershon and Merari, which is unknown to the Chronicler in Ezr. 2:4–Neh. 7:43 (but cf. 1 Chr. 6:1), though accepted in P. This, however, may be a redactional adjustment to a list which, we think, goes back much earlier.

Against the representation in Jos. 21 and Num. 35:1–8 of the Levitical settlement as an ideal to be realised at the occupation, the obvious objection, unless we admit the Levitical settlement as 'an ancient Priestly utopia' (Kaufmann, *op. cit.*, p. 44), is that when particular localities, many quite obscure, are specified it is natural to relate the lists to periods when those were actually under Israelite control and had been settled by Levites. So the inclusion of places such as Gibbethon, Elteke and Gath-rimmon (Jos. 21:23f.), all west of Gezer, must reflect a time at the earliest after Gezer had passed into Solomon's possession by a gift of the Pharaoh, and indeed the list includes many cities that, according to the realistic statement of Jg. 1, remained Canaanite enclaves after the main phase of the Israelite penetration of Palestine. Apart from the confirmation of archaeology, which is considerable at such sites as Beth-shemesh and Tell Jerīsheh (Gath-rimmon, according to Mazar) there is enough to suggest to critical scholarship that those lists, like the town-lists in Jos. 13–19, reflect conditions of the Monarchy, and possibly rest on official lists. Alt, as we have seen, proposed the reign of Josiah. Albright (*Archaeology and the Religion of Israel*, 1953, pp. 123ff.), on the other hand, after S. Klein, contended for a Davidic date, which the evidence of the text, topography and archaeology seems rather to support. This view had already been advanced by M. Lohr (*Das Asylwesen im Alten Testament*, 1930).

Albright made an important advance in demonstrating by the use of LXX that Jos. 21 was a variant of the same tradition as in 1 Chr. 6:54ff. (MT, vv. 39ff.), which attributes the actual settlement of Levites to David.

B. Mazar goes further and proposes that the section is based on an official document from the archives of the Jerusalem priesthood ('The Cities of the Priests and Levites', *VT Suppl.* 7, Congress Vol., 1960, pp. 193–205). He dates the Levitical settlement specifically in the end of David's reign, when Solomon was co-regent, citing 1 Chr. 26:30–32, which refers to the installation of Levites of Hebron in office throughout the realm in the fortieth year of David, the town of Jazer being specifically mentioned as a Levitical centre in southern Transjordan both in Jos. 21:39 and 1 Chr. 26:31. The statement that the Levites were 'in royal service' (1 Chr. 26:30) is highly significant, since it is not likely that this would have been mentioned gratuitously in a post-Exilic reconstruction. Mazar emphasises the pre-eminence of the Kohathite family of Hebron in the Levitical settlement. Hebron was the first centre to acclaim David as king, and Mazar regards the Levites of Hebron as his loyal supporters. 1 Chr. 26:31, however, suggests that the Levitical settlement had already been made before the fortieth year of David, when a certain Levitical family of Hebron already settled in Jazer was selected for a new Levitical settlement, doubtless connected with the constitutional innovation of the dynastic succession of Solomon. We suggest that the intensive settlement of Levites in Hebron and the Kenizzite district south and east of Hebron (21:11, 13f.) may rather represent measures taken by David after the suppression of Absalom's revolt, which had been organised from Hebron (2 Sam. 15:10). Mazar goes on most plausibly to demonstrate that the Levites were settled in border areas in the west of the Shephelah (Jos. 21:13–16) and in Transjordan (vv. 27, 36–39) and in Canaanite enclaves recently annexed in the coastal and central plains (vv. 23–25, 28–35). There their role was defensive, but Mazar feasibly suggests that, as 1 Chr. 26:30 indicates, it was also fiscal, to collect revenues and to administer royal estates which now passed from the Canaanite local rulers to David and Solomon. Mazar further particularises, arguing that the mention of Gibbethon as a Levitical settlement must predate the two-years' reign of Nadab the son of Jeroboam I, when it passed to the Philistines (1 Kg. 15:27); and indeed the settlement of Elteke, Gibbethon and Gath-rimmon on the north frontier of Philistine territory (vv. 23f.), if for strategic purposes as the association with Aijalon (v. 24) and Libnah (v. 13) suggests, would be quite pointless except in the early Monarchy. The same applies to the settlements in Moab and north Transjordan, which were lost to Moab and Damascus within fifty years of the death of Solomon, and Mahanaim in Gilead, which disappears from the records after its destruction by Sheshonk (Mazar, 'The Campaign of Pharaoh Shishak to Palestine', *VT Suppl.* IV, Congress Vol., 1957, p. 63).

The remarkable lacuna in the Levitical settlements in the hill-country of Ephraim and Manasseh and about Jerusalem was singled out by Noth as an outstanding problem, and Mazar feasibly suggests that this was in deference to the strong tribal tradition and sense of Israelite solidarity and also, we would suggest, to the absence of Canaanite elements in any strength in the hill-country except at Shechem, where there was a Levitical settlement (v. 21). A further reason for the settlement at Shechem may have been to safeguard the interests of the House of David at this ancient sanctuary of the Israel of Jg. 5:13–15. In Judah, too, between Jerusalem and Hebron, there were no Levitical settlements. In the restricted territory of Benjamin, however, immediately north of Jerusalem, there were four within a radius of two miles (vv. 17f.). This settlement may date from the elevation of Jerusalem to the status of the central sanctuary of Israel, and may have served the purposes of counteracting the influence of the local sanctuary at Gibeon and of protecting David against a possible rising of the family of Saul in Benjamin and in North Israel, which was more than a mere possibility (witness the cursing of Shimei, 2 Sam. 16:5–14, and the revolt of Sheba, 2 Sam. 20:1–22). It may be thought that the relatively dense Levitical settlement in the restricted area of Benjamin reflects post-Exilic conditions, but the association of Jeremiah and his priestly family with Anathoth (Jer. 1:1) is but another indication that the lists of Levitical settlements in Jos. 21 actually reflect pre-Exilic conditions.

Using Alt's data for the view that the Pharaohs from the fifteenth century secured their interest in vital parts of Palestine (such as the south of the coastal plain) by the award of confiscated lands to Egyptian temples ('Ägyptische Tempel in Palästina und die Landnahme der Philister', *KS* I, 1953, pp. 216–30), as at Gaza, possibly 'the City of Canaan' (in an inscription of Seti I from Karnak, *ANET*, 3rd ed., p. 254) and Ashkelon (in an inscription on an ivory from Megiddo, *c.* 1350–1150 BC), Mazar suggests that the system of control of areas of doubtful loyalty by a priestly caste was suggested by Egyptian practice in the reign of Solomon, who was in other respects open to the influence of the higher culture and organisation of Egypt (E. W. Heaton, *Solomon's New Men*, 1974). We might even hazard the conjecture that this may have been suggested to Solomon at Gezer when this place was handed over to him by the Pharaoh. In the strengthening of his frontiers and approaches after the Disruption of David's kingdom Rehoboam may have continued the policy of settling Levites in his south-western approaches in the Shephelah, especially such as were ejected from the northern kingdom by Jeroboam I, as is specifically stated in 2 Chr. 11:13–17.

Thus, while the basis of the lists of Levitical settlements in Jos. 21 may have been David's organisation of his kingdom after the incorporation of Canaanite districts and crown properties, possibly recorded on official documents, later adjustments also under Solomon and Rehoboam may be reflected, though the organisation by the families of Kohath, Gershon and Merari is probably a Priestly adjustment.

The matter in Jos. 13–21 was adapted for incorporation in Jos. by the attribution to Joshua of the apportionment of tribal lands, cities of refuge and Levitical settlements, which in the extent to which it is depicted in the Deuteronomistic History is probably unhistorical, though the apportionment of tribal boundaries may preserve the historical tradition of the role of supra-tribal judges in arbitration in disputes regarding privileges and responsibilities which involved the boundaries of distinct local groups. The section is also introduced by a preface, which notes in retrospect the apportionment of land to the tribes east of Jordan (13:8–33), already depicted in Dt. as apportioned by Moses (Dt. 3:8ff.; Num. 32:33ff. (P)). The apportionment of the territory of Judah is prefaced by a digression on Caleb's claim to Hebron, which is drawn from Dt. 1:22–46. However, the repetition that Joshua was 'old and advanced in years' in the preface to the apportionment of the land (Jos. 13:1) and to his valedictory address (23:1) indicates that 13:1–21:45 was a secondary addition to the original Deuteronomistic book of Joshua, of which ch. 23 is the natural conclusion. The post-Exilic redactor probably made the qualifications on the occupation in 15:63; 16:10; 17:12f., in agreement with Jg. 1:21, 27ff. The role of Eleazar the priest in the apportionment alongside Joshua at the Tent of Meeting at Shiloh (18:1; 19:51) is probably the only substantial contribution of P to this section, besides the Priestly retouching of the chapter on the cities of refuge and the note on the families of Kohath, Gershon and Merari in Jos. 21. The section is rounded out by a Deuteronomistic epilogue on the Occupation, represented as the fulfilment of the word of God in blessing, probably a reflection of the conditional blessing of God in Dt. 28:1–14, which, with the curses in Dt. 28:15ff., is the leading motif of the Deuteronomistic History.

The dismissal of the Transjordanian tribes (22:1–9) is probably also a secondary Deuteronomistic addition. The passage on the controversy on the altar in the Jordan Valley (vv. 9ff.), as the role of Shiloh and Phineas the son of Eleazar indicates, may also be a Priestly elaboration, though probably of an earlier tradition. It possibly reflects the local rivalry of Shiloh, peculiarly an Ephraimite sanctuary housing the ark (see above, p. 18), and Gilgal, the provincial boundary sanctuary shared by Ephraim, Benjamin, possibly Manasseh in its earlier settlement in the Jordan Valley and certainly the Transjordanian groups Reuben and Gad.

In the third section of Jos. we encounter the problem of *two* formal valedictory addresses by Joshua (Jos. 23; 24). Jos. 23, a homiletic admonition, well impregnated with characteristic Deuteronomistic phraseology and theology, finds its natural conclusion in Joshua's dismissal of the people and his death and burial in Jg. 2:6–9. This suggests that Jos. 24 is a later redactional expansion, and indeed patriarchal traditions from the Pentateuchal sources J, E and P support this conclusion, though the problem of the insertion of Jos. 24 is best solved by the recognition that it reflects an actual situation on which ch. 23 was modelled. In Jos. 23 the Deuteronomistic compiler has drawn upon the tradition of an admonitory address at the conclusion of the sacrament of the covenant (e.g. Dt. 28) for an appropriate valedictory address by Joshua in accordance with his custom of punctuating his history by a speech from one of the protagonists, which was both recapitulation and prospectus (see above, p. 3). In Jos. 24 the post-Exilic Deuteronomistic redactor, mindful of the association of the homiletic admonition with the covenant-sacrament, amplifies by a more formal rendering of that ceremony, though with modifications which reflect the tradition of a decisive stage in the expansion of the Rachel group to or towards the proportions of the sacral community of Israel in Jg. 5:13–18 (see above, p. 16). Why the redactor amplified Jos. 23, we can only speculate. Perhaps he felt that an important step in the growth of Israel in Palestine had been omitted, a lacuna which the redactional Jos. 8:30–35 was designed to fill; perhaps Jos. 24 was suggested by the incidental mention of the covenant in 23:16; or perhaps, as the references to patriarchal traditions from J, E and P suggest, he may have felt it appropriate to associate the historical theme of the Law with that of the occupation of the Promised Land in Jos. as the historical prelude to the covenant. Formally the covenant in Jos. 24 conforms closely, though not absolutely, to the pattern of Hittite vassal-treaties from the fourteenth and thirteenth centuries BC, as first recognised by V. Korošec (*Hethitische Staatsverträge, ein Beitrag zu ihrer juristischen Wertung*,

Leipziger Rechtswissenschaftliche Studien, Heft 60, 1931) and more recently applied to Old Testament criticism by G. E. Mendenhall (*Law and Covenant in the Ancient Near East*, 1955, reprinted from *BA* 17, 1954) and particularly with relation to Jos. 24 by K. Baltzer, (*Das Bundesformular*, 1960). The form of the Hittite vassal-treaties, which evidently reflected a common form in international law and was still substantially reflected in later treaties imposed by Assyrian kings on their Aramaean vassals in the ninth–seventh centuries BC, is as follows:

(1) The preamble, where the suzerain declares his identity; cf. Jos. 24:2: 'Thus says the Lord, the God of Israel.'

(2) The historical prelude, reviewing the relations of the suzerain with his vassals and declaring his benefactions with the hint of his power to punish, often mentioning and describing the land with which the suzerain has invested his vassal or which he confirms in his possession; cf. Jos. 24:2–13, a summary statement of Israel's Story of Salvation culminating in the occupation of the Promised Land. The fact that Jos. 24:13 shows such a close verbal agreement with Dt. 6:10*b*f. may indicate a common origin within the covenant-form familiar to the Deuteronomist in the covenant-renewal.

(3) The basic declaration, stating the relationship demanded of the vassal, introduced like the main business of ancient letters by the phrase 'and now . . .' (*wᵉʿattāh* . . .) (Jos. 24:14), which states the main demand of the suzerain in consequence of the situation described in the historical prelude. So Yahweh demands through the mediator of the covenant, 'Now therefore fear the Lord, and serve him in sincerity and faithfulness; put away the gods which your fathers served beyond the River and in Egypt, and serve the Lord.' This claim on exclusive loyalty is a regular feature of the Hittite vassal-treaties, where the vassal is expressly forbidden to contract agreements with any other than the suzerain (cf. Jos. 24:23).

(4) The more detailed conditions, which are a feature of the Hittite treaties, are lacking in Jos. 24, but it is plausibly conjectured (Steuernagel, Noth) that at the sacrament of the renewal of the covenant bodies of laws like those included in the Book of the Covenant (Exod. 20:22–23:33) and certainly apodictic laws like the Decalogue in its primitive form were presented. The 'statutes and ordinances' (v. 25) or 'the words' (vv. 26, 27) may have such a reference in the intention of the redactor, if they do not refer to ritual details, as in the Ritual Code in Exod. 34:10–26, as suggested by G. Schmitt (*Der Landtag von Sichem*, 1964, pp. 45ff., 64ff., 80ff., 85).

(5) The treaty was formally endorsed by the vassal, either the

king or some other representative of the subject community; cf. Jos. 24:15, where Joshua declared 'as for me and my house, we will serve the Lord', and vv. 17–18*a*, where the people formally admit that God has done for them what the historical prelude describes, and admit the obligations which that implies. In the vassal-treaties it was important that the vassal accepted the treaty of his own free will; cf. the voluntary acceptance of the covenant by the people in Jos. 24:16, 18, 21.

(6) An appeal to the gods as witnesses and guarantors of the bond. In monotheistic Israel, where God was himself a party to the covenant, such an appeal was impossible, hence 'heaven and earth' are called to witness (Dt. 4:26; 30:19; 31:28); cf. the invocation of natural features along with the gods in Hittite vassal-treaties. Alternatively, in Israel the people might invoke themselves as witnesses (Jos. 24:22), implying the adjuration.

(7) The treaty is laid under the sanction of the curse, of which the best example in Israel, in the context of the covenant-sacrament, is the Twelve Adjurations in Dt. 27:15–26. Formally the adjuration is omitted in Jos. 24, but it is implicit in the engagement of the people, 'Far be it from us that we should forsake the Lord' (which is more obvious in Hebrew than in EVV), in the threefold pledge to allegiance (vv. 16, 18, 21) and the solemn warning of the dire consequences of the broken bond (Jos. 24:20), with its obvious reference to the Twelve Adjurations and the admonitory elaboration of this theme in the address which follows in Dt. 28.

(8) The recording of the treaty, without which it was not valid; cf. Jos. 24:25f., 'So Joshua made a covenant with the people . . . and Joshua wrote these words in the book of the law of God'; cf. Neh. 9:38 (MT, 10:1). The 'book of the law of God' may be a late feature, as Gressmann thought (*Die Anfänge Israels*, SAT, 1922, p. 162); but the record of the covenant reflects genuine ancient usage. The record might be on a stele, as at Sujin in north Syria; cf. Jos. 24:27; 8:32).

(9) Provision was made for the deposit of the record, usually at a sanctuary under the feet of the god's image; cf. the tradition of the ark as the receptacle of the covenant and the footstool or throne of God. Provision was also made for the regular reading of the treaty, which had its counterpart in Israel in the stereotyped liturgy of the sacrament of the covenant with the public acknowledgement of the sovereignty of Yahweh and of his historical salvation of Israel, and the public declaration of the law in its compendious form, e.g. the Decalogue in its original form, and its public endorsement by the people with solemn adjuration (e.g. Dt. 27:15–26).

But despite the attested antiquity of the vassal-treaty convention in the ancient Near East, the fact remains that in the Old Testament it is distinctive of the Deuteronomistic passages, where the covenant theology prevails, as D. J. McCarthy (*Treaty and Covenant*, Analecta Biblica 21, 1963) has demonstrated. The formal correspondence with the covenant convention in Jos. 24 is, we think, clear indication of the Deuteronomistic redaction. We cannot, however, on that account dismiss the passage as having no relevance to any historical situation, as E. Auerbach has done (*VT Suppl.* I, Congress Vol., 1953, p. 3, quoted with approval by K. D. Schunck, *Benjamin*, BZAW 86, 1963, p. 481). The influence of the tradition of the vassal-treaties on that of the covenant is, in our opinion, to be assumed earlier than the Deuteronomistic writings, to judge from the reflection in Isa. and Mic. of the tradition of the divine contention (*rîb*) on the basis of the covenant, where the analogies with the vassal-treaties of the second and first millennia are noticed by J. Harvey ('Le "*Rîb*-Pattern" requisatoire prophétique sur le rupture d'alliance', *Biblica* 43, 1962, pp. 172ff.). We may well question Israel's familiarity with the protocol of the vassal-treaty before the modest empire of David and Solomon. But while the *form* of the covenant in Jos. 24 may be the fiction of the Deuteronomistic redactor, a covenant whereby Ephraim and other members of the Rachel-group already committed to dynamic faith in Yahweh effected solidarity with other northern groups on the basis of that faith is, we think, historically feasible in the days of the settlement, and indeed probable in view of the solidarity of the ten groups in Israel in Jg. 5:13–18 (see above, p. 16). The historical germ in Jos. 24 is indicated by comparison with the redactional passage on the covenant at Shechem, Jos. 8:30–35. This envisages the mediation of the covenant to all Israel already a covenant community; Jos. 24 envisages the incorporation into the community of worshippers of Yahweh represented by Joshua and his group of people not yet familiar with the covenant nor even worshippers of Yahweh, to whom commitment of the new faith is presented not mandatorily but as an option, as de Vaux has stressed (*Histoire ancienne*, I, p. 611).

The book ends with a note on the death and burial of Joshua (vv. 29f.), which the Deuteronomistic redactor here evidently repeats from the Deuteronomistic compiler at Jg. 2:8f. The notices of the burial of the bones of Joseph (v. 32), reflecting Gen. 50:25 and Exod. 13:19 (both E), and of the death of Eleazar and his burial on the hill (or 'at Gibeah', RSV) of Phineas (v. 33) may reflect a local tradition of Shechem.

COMMENTARY

on

Joshua

1. THE CONQUEST OF CANAAN 1–12

DEUTERONOMISTIC INTRODUCTION

1:1–18

This effects the transition to a new phase of history by the familiar Deuteronomistic convention of speeches by way of recapitulation and introduction. The theological character of Jos. in the Deuteronomistic History is forthwith emphasised in the address of God to Joshua as the representative of his people (vv. 1–9), and in Joshua's address to Reuben, Gad and Manasseh in Transjordan (vv. 12–15) and their response (vv. 16–18). Such historical details as are incorporated in the sequel are subsidiary to the theme of the fulfilment of the divine promise to Israel through Moses, which is conditional upon Israel's fidelity to the covenant. Joshua too in this context is subsidiary to Moses, his 'servant' (v. 1; cf. Dt. 31:1–8), fulfilling Moses' programme (vv. 5; 7f., 12–18; cf. Dt. 31:1–8), though from this he derives his courage (vv. 5f.; 9), strength (vv. 16–18) and authority (vv. 16–18). The engagement of Reuben, Gad and eastern Manasseh (vv. 12–18; cf. Dt. 3:12f., 18–20) emphasises the view of the Deuteronomistic compiler that what is to follow is the occupation of the Promised Land as the culmination of the Drama of Salvation from Egypt and the engagement of Israel in God's covenant. The full rhetorical style and the hortatory and admonitory tone of the Deuteronomist is unmistakable, especially in vv. 3–9, 11*b*–18. In contrast vv. 1f., 10–11*a* are in narrative style, giving the historical context as envisaged by the Deuteronomist. Those passages are the Deuteronomist's free adaptation of an older tradition, possibly derived from the liturgy of the sacramental crossing of the Jordan as an element in the cult at Gilgal. The tradition of the role of the Transjordanian tribes as an advance guard (v. 14*b*) in military formation, if not actually in arms (v. 14; cf. Dt. 3:18–20), differs so widely from the pre-Deuteronomistic compiler's representation of the occupation as an unhindered and miraculous crossing of the Jordan that it is either the Deuteronomist's ideal reconstruction or the reflection of a ritual procession in the cult at Gilgal.

Divine Address to Joshua **1:1–9**

1. the servant of the LORD: the stock title of Moses, and also applied to Joshua (24:29). It was applied to David and the kings of Judah; cf. 'the servant of El' as a royal title in the royal legends from Ras Shamra. It thus denotes a leader of the sacral community, especially here in his sacral function as mediator of the covenant.
Joshua . . . Moses' minister: cf. Exod. 24:13; 33:11; Num. 11:28, which probably reflect the later tradition of Joshua as leader of all Israel in the occupation of the Promised Land, enhancing his significance by the association with Moses, though his role in the battle against Amalek (Exod. 17:9–11, 14*b*, 16) and in the reconnaissance of Palestine may be historical (see above, p. 32). The name signifies 'Yahweh is Deliverance', the Greek form through Aramaic being 'Jesus' (Ac. 7:45; Heb. 4:8, Greek text).

2. this Jordan: The demonstrative may indicate that *yardēn* is actually a common noun 'river'. The reading of the demonstrative, however, is uncertain, and is omitted in LXX.

3. I have given it to you: the verb is in the declaratory, or prophetic perfect. Though the land remains to be occupied the occupation is already as good as effected, being decided in the divine purpose.
as I promised to Moses: cf. Dt. 11:24ff. (see above, p. 1), recalling specifically Moses' threefold exhortation of Joshua in Dt. 31:6–8, 23.

4. this Lebanon: the demonstrative reads strangely and may agree with 'wilderness', **Lebanon** being an interpolation. The regular Deuteronomist description of the Promised Land, however, assumes the extent of the land from the steppes on the south and east (the **wilderness**) to, but not including, the western slopes of Lebanon and thence north-east to the **Euphrates**. This reflects the extent of the influence of David and his control of the trade-routes after his defeat of the Aramaeans (1 Kg. 4:21, 24, MT 5:1, 4; 2 Chr. 9:26). While realistic in the time of David and Solomon, it remained an ideal in the time of the Deuteronomist, e.g. Ezek. 47:15–23.
all the land of the Hittites: probably a later interpolation, being omitted in LXX and the Vulgate. The ethnic significance of **Hittites** cannot be pressed. The term is regularly used in Assyrian inscriptions to describe Syria and Palestine long after the collapse of the Hittites of Anatolia, and reflects the former Hittite domination of North Syria, now so well illustrated by Hittite political correspondance from the palace of Rās Shamra (*c.* 1365–1190 BC). Before **as far as the great river** and **to the Great Sea** the Hebrew text reads 'and'.

6. Be strong and of good courage: lit. 'be strong and rally (*sc.* your heart)', a feature of the hortatory style of the Deuteronomistic introduction, being repeated four times in the chapter. This emphasises the Deuteronomist's theological view of the occupation: God effects the fulfilment of his promise; man's part is to hold fast to his faith.

which I swore to their fathers to give them: the theme of the promise to the patriarchs (Gen. 12:7ff., J) is combined with the occupation of the land as the culmination of the drama of salvation (*Heilsgeschichte*), as already in the older narrative sources of the Pentateuch.

the law: an interpolation, as indicated by its omission in LXX; cf. the sequel 'do not depart from it' (masc. sing. pronominal suffix), which does not agree with the feminine antecedent 'law' (*hattôrâh*). The MT, though true to the tradition which associated **the law** with the drama of salvation, reflects a legalistic view later than the Deuteronomistic compilation, associating Moses particularly with the law. The conception of the law is developed further in v. 8, which reflects the later Deuteronomistic view of the history of Israel as a response to God's precept and submission to his guidance. The conception of the law, actually **this book of the law**, as the object of study and the key to practical success, recalls Ps. 1:2f.

be not frightened, neither be dismayed: both strong words, lit. 'be not struck with awe (or terror), neither be shattered'. Those verbs are the antithesis of 'be strong and of good courage', indicating the Deuteronomistic view of the history of Israel as under God's control, demanding that man should keep his morale in confidence in God's effective power, manifested in the break in the enemy's morale (e.g. 2:9, 11, 24).

Preparation to Cross the Jordan 1:10–11

In this brief narrative fragment, probably rounded out by Deuteronomistic phraseology in v. 11*b*, the only note of preparation is for three days' provisions. Rather than indicating a military movement, it seems more likely to be based on statutory ritual instructions for a procession from the sanctuary at Gilgal to Shittim (2:1) beyond Jordan, a token sojourn in tents there and a sacramental crossing of the Jordan.

10. officers (*šôṭᵉrîm*) may signify either field officers or, as in Dt. 20:5, officials who had charge of conscription and exemption from service. The word has a wide connotation in the Old Testament; cf. 'foremen' associated with the Pharaoh's task-masters (Exod. 5:6,

10) and of civil officials associated with judges (Dt. 16:18). It means 'policemen' in modern Hebrew.

11. provisions: generally signifying for a journey.
three days: if it has not the ritual significance suggested above, this may be suggested by the three days' absence of the spies at Jericho.

Joshua's Appeal to the Tribes of Israel in Transjordan; Their Ready Response **1:12–18**

Cf. Dt. 3:18–20, with close verbal correspondence. The section is mainly motivated by the conception that all Israel took part in the occupation, but may preserve the tradition of an early penetration by Reuben and Gad, suggested by the seniority of these groups in the Blessings of Jacob (Gen. 49) and Moses (Dt. 33), and particularly in Num. 26:5,15. The long history of Reuben is suggested by the fact that, though traditionally associated with Transjordan, they had once been settled west of Jordan, as indicated by the Stone of Bohan the son of Reuben, south of Jericho (15:6; 18:17). Before its wider significance in the growing community of Israel, Gilgal may have been the boundary sanctuary of Reuben, Gad, Ephraim, Benjamin and Manasseh in the Jordan Valley.

14. beyond the Jordan: from the standpoint of the Deuteronomistic historian, forgetting the scene was set east of the river. An aggressive penetration was envisaged, whether on any sound basis of traditions of Reuben, Gad and the Rachel group (see above, p. 12) or not is uncertain, by the engagement of **all the** mighty **men of valour** (*kol gibbôrê haḥayil*).
gibbôr has the Arabic cognate *jabbār*, with the nuance of 'giant' or 'bully'. Primarily meaning a freeborn Israelite, able and liable to defend the community in arms, it comes to mean in the historical period those able by their property to equip themselves and their dependants for war, and eventually, under David's adaptation of the feudal system indicated in 1 Sam. 8:11, those who were enabled to do so by the royal grant of property.
armed in this context is rather a guess at the meaning of *ḥ^{a}mûšîm*. The word is used in Num. 32:17 and Jos. 4:12, referring to the same incident. In Jg. 7:11 it refers to the Midianites in Gideon's reconnaissance, and in Exod. 13:18 it describes the conditions in which the Hebrews left Egypt. In the last passage LXX renders 'in the fifth generation', but since it translates the word in Jg. 7:11 as 'fifties' it is likely that the Greek translator was ignorant of the precise meaning of the word, which he connects, not unnaturally, with the Hebrew word for 'five'. In the context of Jos. 1:14; 4:12

it may be cognate with Arabic *ḥamisa* ('to be courageous, or aggressive'), but as it is a passive participle it is more likely to be connected with Arabic *ḫamsa*, 'five', and may mean 'in battle order'; cf. Arabic *ḫamīs* ('in five-formation', of an army, i.e. centre, vanguard, rearguard and two wings).

THE RECONNAISSANCE OF JERICHO AND THE INCIDENT OF RAHAB

2:1–24

This narrative has the ring of historical verisimilitude in contrast to a number of aetiological traditions in narrative style attached to Jericho (ch. 6) and places in the vicinity of, or on the way to, Gilgal (Jos. 3; 4; 5; 7; 8), e.g. the crossing-place of the Jordan and the stones commemorating this event (3:1–5; 4:1–9, 20–22), the traditional place of circumcision (5:2–9), the theophany of the Captain of the Lord's Host (5:13–15), all of which were developed in connection with the ritual celebration of the occupation of the Promised Land at the sanctuary of Gilgal, with the story of the destruction of Ai, 'the Ruin' (7:1–8:29), into which is inserted the story of Achan in the Valley of Achor (7:11–26). Those were combined by a collector at an earlier literary stage (see above, pp. 41ff.), having received some unity with the theme of the occupation of the land through their association as edifying stories for pilgrims to the sanctuary of Gilgal. Their artificial unity and their original independence is indicated, as Noth observed (*Das Buch Josua*, 1953, p. 21) by the fact that there is no essential connection between the fall of Jericho in chapter 6 and the reconnaissance in chapter 2, though to be sure the conclusion of the Rahab story (2:1–24) is inserted in chapter 6 (vv. 22–25), with the note on the survival of a Canaanite family in Jericho 'to this day' (v. 25), which betrays an aetiological tradition. The pre-Deuteronomistic narrative has been incorporated *en bloc* into the Deuteronomistic History, with amplifications characterised by Deuteronomistic sentiment and language at various stages since the Deuteronomistic compilation. An outstanding example of Deuteronomistic amplification is the recapitulation of the drama of salvation and the monotheistic declaration by Rahab in 2:10f.

In the incident as a whole, the reconnaissance of Jericho is inconsistent with the pre-Deuteronomistic compiler's view of the occupation as the fulfilment of the divine promise by his sovereign power, as exemplified in the miraculous collapse of the walls of Jericho (ch. 6), except perhaps that in noticing the anxiety of the king of Jericho (2:2f.) the story stresses the low morale of the

Canaanites, which 1:5 implies. Behind the story of the spies there may be an independent historical tradition of the capture of Jericho by treachery (so Mohlenbrink, *op. cit.* p. 258; Noth, *Das Buch Josua*, 1953, p. 22), the red thread in the window of a house on the wall perhaps really denoting a weak point, or at least one at which the Hebrews could expect collaboration. The tradition of the fall of Jericho by treachery, if that were really the situation, has been suppressed in its conclusion through the theological emphasis on the direct divine activity in the miraculous collapse of the walls in chapter 6, where incidentally no further mention is made of the red thread. The incident of Rahab, the oath of the spies and the arrangement for the display of the red thread, on the other hand, may simply be elaborated as an aetiological legend explaining the survival of a Canaanite family at the derelict site of Jericho in the historical period, as indicated in Jos. 6:22–25. The text translated by LXX seems to have been aware of two distinct traditions since only the oath is mentioned as a safeguard for Rahab in v. 12 without any reference to a sign, the sign of the scarlet cord being noted as something distinct from the oath in vv. 17–20. The combination of the motif of the red thread and the survival of Rahab's 'house' may have been suggested by the prophylactic significance of the red cord; cf. the crimson cord attached to the door of the Temple in the interim before the scapegoat was destroyed in the desert (Mishnah, Yoma 6.8), the use of blood as a prophylactic on the doorposts of Arab peasants (S. A. Curtiss, *Primitive Semitic Religion Today*, 1902, p. 191), and of course the blood-rite of the Passover. The tradition of the betrayal of Jericho is not developed, and after the tradition of the miraculous collapse of the walls in 6:1–21, the aetiological account of the survival of Rahab's 'house' is appended (6:22–25).

1. Shittim (*haššiṭṭîm*, 'the Acacias'): here the Israelites cohabited with Moabite women. It is also called Abel-shittim ('the Stream of the Acacias', Num. 33:49), probably to be identified with Tell al-Ḥammām, where the Wadi 'Shuweib breaks from the hills on the road over the Allenby bridge from Amman to Jericho (N. Glueck, *Explorations in Eastern Palestine* IV, 1951, pp. 378–82).

especially Jericho may be displaced from after 'they went', where LXX has it in addition to its position in MT. In view of the role of Jericho in the sequel, however, it should certainly be retained as in MT. With its strong spring **Jericho** and its lands were a conspicuous oasis in an otherwise desolate plain, *c.* 5 miles west of the Jordan, and had been occupied and fortified since *c.* 7000 BC. The site (Tell as-Sulṭān) is so badly eroded that the reconstruction of the Late Bronze Age settlements is hazardous, but with reserve K. M. Kenyon, the most recent excavator, suggested that it was destroyed *c.* 1350–1325 BC (*Digging up Jericho*, 1957, pp. 261f.). The tradition of its fall by treachery, if that is historical, may perhaps be connected with a penetration by Reuben and Gad from beyond Jordan, perhaps activated by the penetration of the Rachel group later known as Ephraim and Manasseh in the Jordan Valley, 'the house of Joseph', with which the fall of Bethel *c.* 1250 BC was associated (Jg. 1:22–25; see above, pp. 12, 61; cf. Jos. 24:11). The city was again occupied, less extensively, in the Early Iron Age (*c.* 1200–*c.* 900 BC), when the king of Moab had his seat there (Jg. 3:13) before his assassination by Ehud. Perhaps the meagre settlement in the interim of a favourable site which ought to have been much more heavily fortified gave rise to the tradition of the miraculous collapse of the walls (ch. 6), a tradition which would certainly not be discouraged in the theme of God's settlement of his people in the Promised Land in the cult at Gilgal.

the house of a harlot whose name was Rahab: Rahab is designated *'iššâh zônâh*, which almost certainly means a secular prostitute and not, as G. Hölscher ('Zum Ursprung der Rahabsage', ZAW 38, 1919–20, pp. 54ff.) and Mowinckel (*Tetrateuch*, *Pentateuch*, *Hexateuch*, BZAW 90, 1964, pp. 13ff.) proposed, a devotee of the fertility cult (*qᵉdēšâh*). The presence of strange men in the house of such would attract no undue attention. 'The house of Rahab', on the other hand may mean 'the family of Rahab', possibly the name of the sole Canaanite inhabitants of the derelict site of Jericho, who had special privileges among the Israelites. Another possibility is that the tradition of Rahab as a harlot was an elaboration of the term *bêt raḥab*, which, Noth suggests, may mean 'a brothel' (cf. Isa. 57:8; Ezek. 16:24).

2. **the king of Jericho** is envisaged as just another minor local ruler like those attested in the Amarna Tablets (*c.* 1411–1358 BC). His alarm at two men from the Hebrews is designed to reflect the defensive mood of the Canaanites, emphasised by the Deuteronomist at vv. 9, 11.

4. **hidden them:** certainly to be read with LXX for Hebrew 'hid him', which has the wrong pronominal suffix with the imperfect. This is an obvious scribal error of *w* for *m*, which closely resemble each other in the proto-Hebraic script.

6. **the roof** is the familiar flat roof of the oriental house, which is used for the entertainment of guests (1 Sam. 9:25), for social parties, and also for storage of fuel. The laying out of the flax stalks to dry before being beaten out for the fibres is natural since they were safe there from animals.

7. **the fords:** there are several within range of Jericho. The

Jordan, though not wide, runs deep and swift over a muddy bed, so that fords are important.

9. Rahab's admission that **the Lord** (Yahweh) had given Israel the land and had sent panic among the Canaanites is probably a reflection of the liturgy from the sacrament of the occupation of the land in a holy war from the cult at Gilgal; **melt** (*nāmôgû*) means 'lose coherence'; cf. the Arabic cognate in the Qur'an, which describes the confusion and incoherence of waves and the weltering of the helpless bodies of the damned in a sea of fire.

10. A Deuteronomistic abbreviation of the traditional drama of salvation, the triumph over **Sihon and Og** being a Deuteronomistic peculiarity; the confession of monotheism is a later theological amplification (cf. Dt. 4:39).

utterly destroyed: i.e. devoted to total destruction as sacrosanct, as Jericho in 6:17, on which see.

11. hearts: i.e. reason and will in Hebrew idiom.

there was no courage left: lit. 'spirit no longer stood', i.e. maintained itself. The spirit (*rûaḥ*) is the invasive divine influence which nerves and enables a man to achieve more than is natural. It was manifest in leadership as in the case of the judges in Jg., who could inspire to dare and do. The passage directly recalls Dt. 2:25.

12. deal kindly with: better, 'deal loyally with'; lit. 'make *ḥesed* with'. *ḥesed* expresses dealings between God and man which imply loyalty to the covenant. Here it expresses the mutual loyalty of Rahab and the spies, which is confirmed by the oath. It is significant that **and give me a sure sign** is omitted in LXX, which suggests two independent traditions; cf. v. 18, where the preservation of Rahab and her family is associated with the red thread and not with the oath. It is nevertheless natural to expect a token, here 'a trustworthy sign', in connection with the oath; cf. the pledge in Gen. 38:17ff.

13. lives renders the basic meaning of *nepeš*, often mistranslated 'soul'.

14. if you do not tell this business of ours: the stipulation for Rahab's discretion suggests that she was involved in treachery. The phrase is omitted in LXX.

15. The verse seems parenthetical, interrupting the conversation between Rahab and the spies. It is possibly an indication of the composite nature of the narrative, belonging to the tradition of the oath to Rahab as distinct from that of the red thread (vv. 18, 21).

16. into the hills, i.e. the desolate hill-country west of Jericho, which, being in the rain-shadow, is still largely uninhabited and rough, therefore well adapted for concealment and for observation of events around Jericho.

17. We will be guiltless: better 'quit of' (cf. Gen. 24:41, also of quittance from an oath). In vv. 17–20 three conditions are apparently imposed upon Rahab, the fixing of the red thread in the window (v. 18), the gathering of her family into the house (vv. 18f.) and secrecy (v. 20).

18. scarlet cord: see above, Introduction to chapter 2, p. 63. In early Christian tradition Rahab became an eminent example of faith (Heb. 11.31) and of good works (Jas. 2:25), cf. Jewish tradition, which made her the ancestress of eight prophets and priests, of which tendency her inclusion in the genealogy of our Lord (Mt. 1:5) after 1 Chr. 2:11 is a reflection. So the **scarlet cord** in the allegorical interpretation of the Church Fathers became the prototype of atonement.

The display of the red cord in the window, here obviously facing *out* from the city wall, indicates that it was represented as a sign not of the house to be spared but of the point of attack at which the assailants could expect collaboration.

19. his blood shall be on our head: blood, peculiarly associated with life (Dt. 12:23), had for ancient Israel a mysterious quasi-automatic potency, which demanded and exacted vengeance (Gen. 4:10), a conception expressed by the covering of shed blood with earth or salt (Jg. 9:45; cf. A. M. Honeyman, 'The Salting of Shechem', *VT* 3, 1953, pp. 192–5.

THE CROSSING OF THE JORDAN

3:1–17 (see also 4:1–24)

In the Deuteronomistic History and probably in the pre-Deuteronomistic compilation this is noted as the achievement of God and not of Israel, thus the element of miracle prevails (3:6, 8, 13, 15–17; 4:18) and the significant role of the ark (3:5, 6, 8, 11, 13, 15, 17; 4:18), which may reflect a ritual enactment (so H. J. Kraus, *VT* 1, 1951, pp. 190, 194–8; but cf. Noth, *op. cit.*, p. 53, and de Vaux, *Histoire ancienne*, I, pp. 556ff.), as suggested by the ritual preparations (3:5) and the stipulation for keeping a safe distance from the holy object (3:4).

The passage is a notorious complex of repetitions, overlappings, parentheses and variant traditions, which sadly impairs the dramatic effect of the older narrative source. Here earlier critics assumed the customary variety of literary sources familiar in the Law. J and E, however, could not be distinguished, so a JE redaction was postulated; P was not thought to be extensively represented, but D was easily distinguished by diction, style and theology. The free composition of the Deuteronomist and his retouching of the older narrative source is still to be noted in the D elements recognised by the earlier critics. P is represented less than was once thought, being confined to ritual particularities, e.g. 3:4*b*; 4:15–17, 19. In the older narrative sources which remain there is evidence of variants and redundancies. This may be explained to a certain extent by variant traditions in the sources, and Möhlenbrink has suggested a Shiloh tradition of a crossing at Admah, which ignores the stones at Gilgal, and a Gilgal tradition, to which this is fundamental (*ZAW* N.F. 15, 1938, pp. 256–8). More recent critics (e.g. Noth, H. W. Hertzberg, J. Dus and J. Maier), see these rather as the result of the continued elaboration of one basic tradition which developed through the intense interest of pilgrims in connection with the cult at Gilgal, when it became a sanctuary for the northern confederacy of Israel after the destruction of Shiloh in the Philistine oppression (Herzberg, *op. cit.*, p. 26), reflecting a ritual re-enactment of the passage of the river.

The later literary elaboration is most apparent in the terminology of the ark, which reflects respectively the older narrative source ('the ark' or 'the ark of Yahweh'), the Deuteronomist ('the ark of the covenant') and the Priestly redactor ('the ark of the Testimony'), which shows the developing theological conception of the ark as the symbol of Yahweh's presence (older narrative source), the receptacle of the covenant document (D), and a synthesis of the two conceptions of the ark as a place where God met men at his own discretion in revelation in the law and in mercy, as in the atonement (G. von Rad 'Zelt und Lade', *Gesammelte Studien zum Alten Testament*, 1958, pp. 109–29). There is further evidence of revisions in the agents involved, 'those who bore the ark' (3:15*a*), 'the priests bearing the ark'; cf. 'the Levitical priests' (3:3) and Joshua, who directs the priests (3:6, 8 etc.).

There is similar variation, with similar explanation, in the traditions of the setting up of the stones commemorating the crossing of the Jordan, which are also of an aetiological character. According to 4:3–8, twelve stones were set up, apparently on the west bank of the ford but possibly at Gilgal (cf. v. 20), in the river bed (vv. 9f.) and definitely at Gilgal (v. 20). The number twelve certainly reflects a later stage than the phase of penetration to which it purports to refer, reflecting as it does Gilgal as the sanctuary of all Israel, at least all the northern groups. The tradition of stones in the bed of the Jordan is possibly the reminiscence of a stone causeway, much needed in the muddy bed of the river, or stones marking a ford (so Steuernagel), possibly associated with the ceremonial crossing in the ritual of the cult at Gilgal. The number twelve in this case may have been attached to those stones at the ford through the influence of the twelve memorial stones at Gilgal, the number possibly being the contribution of the pre-Deuteronomistic compiler from Judah in the early Monarchy.

The crossing of the Jordan had a high significance in the historical consciousness of Israel, emphasised in the passage by the word *'ābar* 22 times. The Jordan, despite its deep, swift and muddy stream and soft bed between jungle growth (Arabic *zawr*) bordered by broken marly land (Arabic *qattara*), was frequently crossed at several fords during the history of Israel, so that the miracle indicates either the literary influence of the crossing of the Red Sea or the ritual commemoration of this. Theologically and in its present context the crossing of Jordan marks a decisive juncture, heralding the consummation of God's gracious acts in the fulfilment of the promise of settlement, or 'rest' in the Deuteronomistic idiom. Historically considered, however, the crossing of the Jordan had the significance emphasised in the pre-Deuteronomistic compilation and in the Deuteronomistic History in so far as, associated with the aggressive elements of the Hebrews of the centre of Palestine, who had found identity in the worship of Yahweh in Sinai, it marked the beginning of a movement which eventually resulted in the effective realisation of the historical Israel.

1. **lodged:** Hebrew 'passed the night', implying one night; but cf. vv. 2f., which connect with 1:1, which depicts the preparation for crossing after three days.

2f. the ark of the covenant of the LORD your God and **the Levitical priests** (cf. Dt. 18:1) are certainly Deuteronomistic conceptions (see Introduction to chs 3 and 4, p. 67), but the tradition of the encampment on the east bank for **three days** (cf. 1:11; 2:16, 22) before crossing under the direction of stewards (**officers**; cf. 1:11) may go back to the ritual of the cult at Gilgal (Hos. 2:14f.).

4. **there shall be a space between you and it:** this is in form parenthetical. The specification of the exact distance is a Priestly contribution, but the demand for a respectful distance may well reflect the cultic ordinance; cf. the incident of Uzzah in an early monarchic source (2 Sam. 6:7).

two thousand cubits: cf. Num. 35:5 (P), over 900 yards, the distance of the boundaries of the Levitical lands from the actual settlements.

5. **Sanctify yourselves:** i.e. condition yourselves ritually for the presence of God; cf. before the covenant ceremony in Exod. 19:10, 14, 15 (E), which involved washing of clothes and abstention from sexual intercourse. God's presence is betokened by the ark and by the supernatural (*niplā'âh*) in the crossing of the Jordan (v. 11). In

vv. 5f. the instructions are given by **Joshua**, and not, as in vv. 2–4, by the 'officers'. The instructions in vv. 2–4 probably go back to the ritual in the cult at Gilgal, but the role of Joshua reflects the pre-Deuteronomistic compilation, where various local traditions were subsumed under the activity of Joshua. Verse 5 was probably immediately followed by v. 11.

7. The Deuteronomist repeats the divine commission to Joshua as the successor of Moses (1:5, 17), but this is no pointless redundance. What is stated generally in 1:5, 17, is now particularised, hence **This day I will begin to exalt you . . .**

10. the living God: Hebrew *'ēl ḥay* (Hos. 1:10, MT 2:1; Pss. 42:2, MT 1; 8:19, etc.; or 'As I (Yahweh) live', Dt. 32:40), which the term here probably reflects.

drive out: better 'dispossess', lit. to cause to inherit (by depriving others of their inheritance), hence used in the sense of 'dispossess' with the dispossessed as the direct object. The phrase and the list of the seven peoples is Deuteronomistic. The list nevertheless reflects the demographic diversity of the inhabitants of Palestine when the Israelites made their decisive impact, to the success of which, though social rather than military, it contributed in no small degree.

Canaanites refers primarily to the inhabitants of the cities of the Phoenician coast (Jos. 13:4. Isa. 23:11), *kinaḫna*, the source of purple dye (*kinaḫḫu*), then secondarily to those in regions of Palestine and southern Syria under their cultural influence (e.g. Num. 13:29; Jos. 5:1; Jg. 5:19), then generally, as in Egyptian inscriptions from just before *c.* 1200 BC, to Palestine as a whole. The **Amorites**, whom Num. 13:29 locates specifically in the hills, refers primarily to the descendants of tribal invaders from the north-eastern steppes whose settlement is evidenced at archaeological stations at the end of the third millennium BC and in lists of their names and settlements in Egyptian execration texts from the nineteenth century BC. **Canaanites** and **Amorites** were the Semitic elements in the population. There is no evidence of the **Hittites** of Anatolia in force in Palestine, and the term probably loosely refers to non-Semites from the north, mostly Hurrians, attested by their peculiar names in documents and by seal designs from Palestine in the fourteenth century BC. The **Hivites**, for which LXX occasionally reads Chorraioi, are probably also Hurrians, like the Girgashites. The name Perizzi in the Amarna Tablets suggests that **Perizzites** may be a genuine ethnic term, but *pᵉrāzôt*, denoting unwalled open villages as distinct from walled town in Dt. 3:5 and 1 Sam. 6:18, suggests that the term may be really appellative. The **Jebusites** are particularly associated with Jerusalem; but the ethnic significance of the term, if there is any, is uncertain.

11. This is the natural sequel to v. 5 in the narrative source, though later worked over by the Deuteronomistic Historian.

the covenant, in the absolute with the ungrammatical definite article before 'the LORD' is an obvious Deuteronomistic interpolation, as 'the covenant of the LORD' in v. 17 indicates, following, as it does, 'the ark' with the definite article where a construct would be used. **the Lord of all the earth** is peculiar to late passages (Mic. 4:13; Zech. 4:14; Ps. 97:5) and is probably a Deuteronomistic elaboration of Dt. 10:14.

12. This sentence hangs in the air, being resumed in its natural context in 4:2f., describing the setting up of the memorial stones, which is suspended in favour of the narrative account of the miraculous passing of the Jordan (vv. 14–17*a*), introduced by Joshua's speech, where the miracle described in v. 16 is anticipated in v. 13.

13. in one heap: (Hebrew *nēd*), used only of the dammed-up waters of the Jordan here and at v. 16, and significantly for the development of the tradition, the dammed-up waters of the Reed Sea (Exod. 15:8; Ps. 78:13). Exod. 15:8 is the first representation of the 'fishtank' conception of the passage of the Reed Sea, from which Exod. 14:22 (P) was developed, as distinct from the sober, naturalistic account of the event in J. The mention in Exod. 15:17f. of the Temple as the palace of the Divine King indicates a date in or after the reign of Solomon, so that the pre-Deuteronomistic narrative may reflect this tradition.

14. set out: (*nāsa'*) the term, like so much in Hebrew, goes back to desert usage and means originally 'pulled up the tent-pegs' in migration.

15. overflows all its banks throughout the time of harvest: the time is late April by Jericho. The parenthesis has respect to the time of crossing, which is fixed by its sacramental celebration at Gilgal 'on the tenth day of the first month', i.e. Nisan, or April, on post-Exilic reckoning. The river was swollen at this time by the melting snows on Hermon and its massif, where it rises. The banks refer to *az-zawr* (see Introduction to ch. 3, p. 68), which, because of the flood-water, supports a luxuriant jungle growth which was proverbial (Jer. 49:19; 50:44; Zech. 11:3). This is explicitly stated to enhance the miracle; but see on v. 16.

16. MT states that the damming of Jordan took place at **Adam**, far north of the traditional place of crossing nearer Gilgal. Mowinckel (*Israels opphav*, p. 117) took this to refer to a variant version of the crossing of Jordan, citing Hos. 6:7, which refers to the breaking of Yahweh's covenant 'at Admah' (MT *kᵉ'ādām*), which seems precarious evidence for his theory. Adam or Admah is Tell ad-Dāmiyeh, just over a mile from the confluence from the east of the Wadi 'z-Zarqā (Jabbok) with Jordan, about sixteen miles from Jericho. **Zarethan** is of uncertain location, near Abelmeholah (1 Kg. 4:12). If the latter place is correctly located at Tell Abu Sifrī, *c.* ten miles south of Bethsaan, and so twelve miles north of ad-Dāmiyeh, this would agree with its location by Rabbi Johanan (third century AD) as twelve miles from Adama. However, the damming of Jordan may have been coloured by cultic celebration and the tradition of the crossing of the Reed Sea. F.-M. Abel (*Géographie de la Palestine* I, 1933, p. 481) has cited the Arab historian an-Nawairī, who attests the damming of the Jordan about ad-Dāmiyeh for some ten hours on the night of 7 December 1267, through the undermining of the high marl banks by flood and by natural collapse or local earthquake. A similar phenomenon, also about ad-Dāmiyeh, for 21½ hours occurred in 1929. The high, dry marl banks, unprotected by turf, in the exceptionally tortuous course of the swift Jordan, might easily collapse with this effect, especially in flood time. However this may be, the tradition of the miracle prevailed thanks to the cultic tradition of Gilgal.

the Salt Sea: the Dead Sea, from which there is no outlet. Through heavy evaporation it is saturated with a considerable solution of all the chemicals brought down by the Jordan, to such an extent that no life is possible in it.

opposite Jericho: rather vague. If Gilgal is to be located north-east of the old site of Jericho (see on 4:19) the place of crossing may be about the Allenby Bridge, and not the traditional crossing-place and place of the baptism of our Lord shown to pilgrims since Byzantine times south-east of Jericho.

17. of the covenant: a Deuteronomistic elaboration, as suggested by the preceding word **ark** in the absolute with the definite article instead of the construct. For the earlier sources the ark was either 'the ark' simply or 'the ark of Yahweh'; for the Deuteronomist it was 'the ark of the covenant', not a symbol of God's presence, nor his throne or footstool thereof, but simply a receptacle for the covenant-contract. The agency of God in the miracle is emphasised here in the ark being held in the river bed until the crossing was complete.

THE MEMORIAL OF THE CROSSING

4:1–24

This is a composite tradition (see Introduction to ch. 3–4, pp. 66f.) presumably introduced by 3:12.

3. **from the very place where the priests' feet stood:** lit. 'from the place of standing . . .', which is ambiguous as to time, and may denote where their feet should stand. In v. 5 twelve men are sent on ahead of the ark with instructions to take each a stone on his shoulder, which rather suggests that the stones were envisaged as taken from the east bank and laid in the river bed to give a firm footing in the ford. There is obviously a confusing complication of traditions here, but the twelve stones carried by a representative from each tribe reflect the conception of all Israel of twelve tribes not realised until the reign of David, when the stones were regarded as a memorial, so represented in the pre-Deuteronomistic compilation. The threefold narration with verbal repetition is familiar in the Rās Shamra myths and legends in epic style, and may be designed to inculcate the significance of the stones, 'when your children ask in time to come . . .' (vv. 6ff.). The theme is repeated in vv. 20–23 in the form of question and answer, which relates the crossing of the Jordan to the passage of the Reed Sea, indicating an important element in the cult. *RSV* treats the infinitive *hākēn* (MT) as a dittograph after *hakkôh*^{a}*nîm*.

5. **in time to come:** lit. tomorrow; cf. Exod. 13:14 (regarding the Passover cult-legend) and Dt. 6:20 (of the Law as a whole). The practice of systematic instruction in the symbolism of the cult as related to Israel's historical faith was well established in ancient Israel (cf. Dt. 6:7), and, as here, conditioned the development of cult-legend to recorded history.

7. **the waters . . . were cut off before the ark of the covenant of the LORD:** the Divine agency is clearly emphasised. 'The covenant' is probably a Deuteronomistic expansion.

8. **the place where they lodged:** lit. 'spent the night'. Close by the west bank may be envisaged, as in early Christian tradition, by the ford associated with the Baptism; but Gilgal, near Khirbet al-Mafjār, *c.* five miles west of the ford by the Allenby Bridge (cf. v. 20), is not excluded.

9. **in the midst of the Jordan:** a variant tradition, probably later than the account of the twelve memorial stones in vv. 2–8, and related to a feature known at the time of the compiler 'to this day'. A foundation of the ford is here definitely envisaged. The introduction of **stones** without the definite article, if textually genuine, indicates an independent tradition, though the number **twelve** indicates the influence of the tradition of the twelve memorial stones of Gilgal.

11. **before the people:** *coram populo*, since the people had already all passed over.

12. The specific notice of Reuben, Gad and eastern Manasseh

is probably a Deuteronomistic amplification (cf. 1:12–18; Num. 32:20ff.).

13. about forty thousand is usually taken as a Priestly addition, but in that case we should expect closer agreement with the numbers of the tribes in Num. 1:21, 25, 35, which is about three times as great. **Forty** is simply the conventional indefinite number of Semitic folklore, and the passage, though a later amplification, is from another hand than P.

ready armed for war: lit. 'girt' for active service, perhaps reflecting the realisation of the sacral community as those ready to fight in the holy war, ability for military service qualifying one for the status of a member of the community of the people of God. Possibly underlying this verse is the historical fact of an earlier armed attack on Jericho from east of the Jordan by Reuben and Gad (Manasseh being a Deuteronomistic anachronism), belonging to the same tradition as the reconnaissance of Jericho in ch. 2, cf. the reference to the battle of Jericho in Jos. 24:11, as proposed by J. A. Soggin (*Josua*, 1970, pp. 53f.).

the plains of Jericho: cf. 2 Kg. 25:5. The steppe-land between the depression of Jordan and the oasis of Jericho, which for lack of water is semi-desert.

14. The Deuteronomistic Historian or the redactor notes the completion of the crossing as the authentication of the divine commission to Joshua (cf. 3:7), who on this tangible evidence of the divine favour (*b^e^rākâh*) merits the respect which the people accorded to Moses (cf. 1:17).

15–17. This is certainly later than the narrative source in v. 11, where the priests with the ark had already come out of the river bed. As **the ark of the testimony** (v. 16) indicates, this is from the post-Exilic redactor, reflecting P, as an introduction to the return of the water (v. 18).

were lifted up: Hebrew 'drawn out', i.e. of the mud in the bed of Jordan. The same verb (*nātaq*) is used of the drawing away of the defenders of Ai in 8:16.

19. the tenth day of the first month: i.e. on Babylonian reckoning, the pre-exilic month Abib, post-exilic Nisan, our April. Such accurate dates usually indicate P in the Pentateuch, and here may indicate the post-exilic redactor rather than the Deuteronomistic Historian. The date may reflect the association of this public sacrament with the tradition of the selection of Passover lambs on the tenth day of the first month (Exod. 12:2f., P) in connection with the preparation for the Exodus.

Gilgal: on the east edge of the oasis of Jericho. In Byzantine times it was commemorated by a church, and has been until recently located at Khirbet an-Niṭleh, just over two miles south-east of Jericho, although there is no trace of ancient occupation before Byzantine times. Surface exploration by J. Muilenburg, however, revealed Iron Age remains just north of Khirbet al-Mafjār, which fits Josephus' location, ten stades from Jericho and fifty from Jordan (*Ant.* v.i.4), i.e. from the ford by the Allenby Bridge. Pillars inscribed with crosses in the Umayyad winter palace near by are probably from the Christian church noticed by early mediaeval pilgrims north (actually north-east) of Jericho. Arabic *jiljūlīyeh* means a stone circle, evidently a feature of the sanctuary of Gilgal, probably from before Israelite times. However, no conspicuous evidence of Iron Age occupation need be expected. Gilgal was only a sanctuary, and that probably of the simplest, not an occupied settlement but frequented only at festal seasons, like the Muslim sanctuary of Nebī Mūsā south-west of Jericho, which is occupied at times other than the Nebī Mūsā festival only by the custodian and his family. On the significance of the sanctuary of Gilgal in Israel, see above, p. 15. The representation of Gilgal as the first sanctuary of all Israel in Palestine is an anachronism of the pre-Deuteronomistic compiler.

21–24: probably from the Deuteronomistic redactor, as suggested by the monotheism of v. 24 (vocalising the Hebrew text to read *l^ema'an yir'ātām*, 'that they might stand in awe of' for the ungrammatical MT *l^ema'an y^erā'tûm*, 'that you may fear', *RSV*), recalling the triumphant monotheism of Isa. 52:13–53:12.

AT GILGAL

5:1–15

This is prefaced by a statement (v. 1) of the effect on the morale of the 'Amorites' and 'Canaanites' (see on 3:10), a Deuteronomistic note which closes the first episode in the occupation of the land and emphasises the omnipotent divine activity in the occupation, which is to be characterised by a series of miracles.

There are apparently three independent traditions here, the circumcision of the people (vv. 2–9), the first celebration of the Passover and the Festival of Unleavened Bread in the Promised Land (vv. 10–12) and the theophany of the Captain of the Lord's Host (vv. 13–15). The first is a topographical aetiological tradition explaining the name 'the Hill of Foreskins', presumably by Gilgal. The second seems at first sight a ritual interpolation, with an antiquarian note on the cessation of the manna. Older critics assigned this to P, but a genuine old tradition of a rite of Unleavened Bread associated with the beginning of harvest, thus inaugurated at the sanctuary of Gilgal in the early days of the settlement by those who constituted the later Ephraim and Benjamin and possibly the forebears of Reuben and Gad from Transjordan, may have survived. The desacralisation rite of Unleavened Bread was associated with the Exodus in the old ritual codes (Exod. 23:15, E; and 34:18, J), with which the Passover was also associated (Exod. 12:21–17, J), the two festivals, which coincided in time, being associated in Dt. 16:1–8.

The association of the festivals in Jos. 5:10f. in conjunction with their links both in time and in connection with the Exodus in the early monarchic J is highly significant in view of the statement in 2 Kg. 23:22 that the Passover, which was celebrated in the Temple by Josiah, had not been so celebrated since the days of the judges. In the present context the association of Passover and Unleavened Bread with circumcision may indicate the hand of the Deuteronomist, familiar with the restriction of the Passover to circumcised persons (Exod. 12:44, P). As Passover marked the break with Egypt, the rite of Unleavened Bread, suitably for the pre-Deuteronomist compiler or the Deuteronomistic Historian, inaugurated the occupation of the Promised Land with its fruits, which, as the Lord's, are fittingly made available by this rite of desacralization. The association of the festival of Unleavened Bread with sanctuaries of Yahweh ('before the Lord') in the early festal calendar in Exod. 23:15 (E) and 34:18 (J) and with the drama of salvation from Egypt indicates that the tradition of the festival of Unleavened Bread at Gilgal was known to the pre-Deuteronomistic compiler. The date (v. 10) and the phrase 'on that very day' (v. 11) are usually assigned to P (Noth, *op. cit.*, p. 39). But Herzberg (*Die Bücher Josua, Richter, Ruth*, ATD, 2nd ed., 1959, p. 34, n. 1) objects that P would have been more specific, 'the fourteenth day of the month' simply indicating the full moon. Our view (see below) is that there are more indications of P than Noth admitted. The third tradition, the theophany of the Captain of the Lord's Host, is a local aetiological legend authenticating a holy place, perhaps Gilgal itself, as Wellhausen considered (*Die Composition des Hexateuchs*, 2nd ed., 1889, p. 123) or a sacred place in the immediate neighbourhood (see below, *ad loc.*); cf. Möhlenbrink (*op. cit.*, pp. 263ff.), who takes the passage either as the introduction to the fall of Jericho (Jos. 6) or, as he prefers, the authentication of the central sanctuary in 8:30ff., which he regards as Shiloh, Shechem in that tradition being taken by him as secondary.

The Circumcision **5:2–9**

The circumcision, later performed in infancy on the eighth day, was probably originally done at puberty, signalising fitness for marriage (cf. Exod. 4:24–26), war (warriors are twice mentioned in vv. 4 and 6, as noted by Hertzberg, *op. cit.*, p. 32), and membership of the religious community. Hence in the association with the sanctuary of Gilgal the tradition here may have a genuine historical basis. The passage, however, is complex. LXX continues the statement of the circumcision of the Israelites at Gilgal: 'Thus Joshua purified the children of Israel, those who were born on the way and those who were uncircumcised.' This is amplified by the statement of the forty years wandering in the desert (v. 6), LXX stating that most of the survivors of this period were uncircumcised, and MT stating that the generation which had come out of Egypt were consumed in this period. In v. 5 MT states that all those who came out of Egypt were circumcised. This is omitted in LXX, and is evidently an amplification in MT in consideration of the tradition of circumcision in the Priestly tradition of the covenant with Abraham (Gen. 17:9–14) and of the restriction of those participating in the first Passover to the circumcised. LXX either deliberately omitted the amplification in the interests of clarity, or represents a Hebrew original before the Priestly amplification (see above, p. 37).

The tradition of the circumcision at the Hill of Foreskins at **Gilgal** is unskilfully combined with the popular etymology of Gilgal. **This day I have rolled away** (*gālal*) **the reproach of Egypt from you** (v. 9)..The reproach of Egypt was not being uncircumcised, since it is stated that the Hebrews while in Egypt were circumcised (vv. 4f.), as for that matter were also the Egyptians. Whatever the tradition was that concluded with v. 9, it was lost or omitted when the conclusion was unskilfully combined with the tradition of the circumcision, a different aetiological tradition explaining 'the Hill of Foreskins' (**Gibeath-haaraloth**, v. 3). We consider that the reproach of Egypt was the servile status of the Hebrews there, who were not yet a religious community, the people of Yahweh, first realised by the Rachel group in Sinai and later expressed at various sanctuaries including Gilgal where that community communicated their experience to others, whereby the sacral community Israel developed. The Hill of Foreskins by Gilgal may have been associated with circumcision as a rite of initiation into the sacral community, hence the association of the two traditions. The detail of the use of flint blades in the circumcision at Gilgal (cf. Moses' circumcision, Exod. 4:25) may indicate the relics of a stone-age workshop, as Dhorme suggested. Whatever the historical basis of the tradition may have been, it subserved the Deuteronomist's presentation of history by signifying, in accordance with the significance of circumcision in his time, an initial act of dedication prior to the occupation of the Promised Land.

2. flint knives: evidently *de rigueur*, cf. the circumcision of Moses' son and of Moses by token (Exod. 4:25) and an Egyptian sculpture (*ANEP*, Fig. 329). The flint, as well as being antiseptic, reflects the inhibition against metal, the secret of an exclusive smith caste, whom early superstition suspected as being able to invest it with a baneful influence; cf. the ban on metal-hewn stones in the altar (Exod. 20:25. Dt. 27:5; Jos. 8:31), and *per contra*, iron as a prophylactic in dealing with the fairies or vanished races in folklore. The Egyptian sculpture just cited and probably, we think, Exod. 4:24–26, indicate that circumcision was a rite of puberty in preparation for marriage and for full responsibilities and rights in the community, including war service and membership in the sacral community. It is significant that among those circumcised in the Egyptian period and the sequel, warriors are twice mentioned in the Deuteronomistic expansion (vv. 4, 6).

seat yourself, and make Israel a circumcised people again: 'sit' is the rendering of LXX, reading Hebrew *šēb* for *šûb* ('do again'). LXX also omits 'a second time' (MT *šēnît*). The Egyptian sculpture already cited shows the ministrant seated.

3. Gibeath-haaraloth: either the pre-Israelite name of a local feature near Gilgal, which is explained by popular etymology ('the Hill of Foreskins') or a place where circumcision actually took place as a rite of dedication in the sacral community, like the consecration of first-fruits.

4–7. Explanatory note by the Deuteronomistic Historian and by the later redactor (see above, pp. 37 and 76).

8. till they were healed: an excellent example of the range of meaning of the verb *ḥāyāh*, which means generally 'to live'. Here, as regularly in the Syriac version of the healing miracles in the Gospels, it means 'restoration to full health'. Texts concerning 'life' and 'death' in the Old Testament must be handled with great care by systematic theology.

9. I have rolled away (Hebrew *gallôtî*: the popular and quite unsound etymology of **Gilgal**, which denoted stones rolled up into position at the sanctuary (4:19f.), possibly in a circle as at various Palestinian sites named *Jiljūlīyeh* in Arabic.

The Passover and the Festival of Unleavened Bread **5:10–12**

10. at sunset on the fourteenth day of the month: i.e. Nisan; cf. 4:19. Dt. 16:7f. specifies the slaughter of the Passover lamb, kid or calf and the meal at sunset at the sanctuary; cf. Exod. 12:1–10 (P) where the slaughter of *a lamb* is specified on the tenth of the month, the meal being eaten *roasted* at sunset **on the fourteenth day of the** first **month** (Nisan). It is the latter tradition that this passage reflects, so that it may be redactional.
the passover (Hebrew *pesaḥ*): the etymological significance of which is still uncertain, was a nomad rite probably associated with the annual migration to grazings on the aftermath of the harvest in the settled land. It was eventually invested with a historical significance as a memorial of the Exodus (Exod. 12:21–27, JE; Dt. 16:1–6), an association which was deliberately inculcated in the religious community of Israel (Exod. 12:27).
the plains of Jericho: the specification of the lowlands, plains or steppes, of Jericho (see above, on 4:13) instead of the actual sanctuary of Gilgal may conserve the significance of the rite in the seasonal migration of nomads.

11. unleavened cakes, Hebrew *maṣṣôt*, were eaten for seven days after the fourteenth day of the first month (Exod. 12:15–20; cf. Dt. 16:8, which prescribes eating of unleavened bread at Passover and for six days after, and Lev. 23:6–8, which reckons the eating of the unleavened bread seven days from the fifteenth of the month). The apparent discrepancy may be explained by the fact that in ancient Hebrew reckoning a day began at sunset. The abstaining from a regular element in the daily diet is a rite of separation associated with the transitional period between growth and harvest and with the desacralisation of the new crop, so that it might be safely used by the community. Parched grain at this time was an item in the rite of desacralisation of the new crop in Israel (Lev. 2:15, P) and in Canaan as reflected in the Baal myth of Rās Shamra (Gordon, *UH* 49; II; 30–7; J. Gray, *Documents from Old Testament Times*, ed. D. W. Thomas, 1958, pp. 130f.). **produce** (*ʿabûr*) occurs in the Old Testament only here and at v. 12, but it is well attested in its Akkadian and Syriac cognates.

12. manna: cf. Exod. 16:35 (JE); the secretion of plant-lice on desert bushes, valued by the Bedouin for its sugar content, in which their diet is markedly deficient. Thus the Deuteronomistic Historian emphasises the transition from the desert to the Promised Land.

The Theophany of the Commander of the Army of the Lord **5:13–15**

The significance of this obscure and truncated episode is further obscured by *bîrîḥô* (**by Jericho**), which may mean 'in' or 'by' Jericho, either the town or the oasis. The reference may be to the authentication of any holy place near Jericho or, for that matter, Gilgal, or even to a tree or rock of traditional sanctity, which, for the benefit of pilgrims and in the interests of orthodoxy, was thus invested with significance in the cult of Gilgal, itself probably a pre-Israelite cult-place with its great stones, now appropriated to the worship of Yahweh. Noth (*op. cit.*, p. 23) supposed that the incident concerned a sanctuary actually *in* Jericho, the details being suppressed by the pre-Deuteronomistic compiler through motives of orthodoxy. Soggin (*op. cit.*, p. 63) also relates the incident to the appropriation for the cult of Yahweh of a local sanctuary *in* Jericho, being associated with the tradition of the taking of Jericho by forcee (cf. Jos. 2; 24:11). Though such a theophany is usually associated with the authentication of a holy site (cf. Bethel, Gen. 28:12), it may also authenticate a commission to the recipient, as the theophany to Moses at the burning bush (Exod. 3:5), of which there are verbatim echoes in v. 15. In agreement with this view the drawn sword (v. 13) recalls the symbolic pointing of Joshua's javelin towards the doomed Ai at 8:18. The tradition may have been developed from a rite in the cult of Gilgal commemorating the divine destruction of Jericho as the inauguration of the occupation of the Promised Land.

13. before him: possible, or 'opposite', or 'at some distance' (Pss. 10:5; 38:11, MT 12). **Are you for us or for our adversaries?:** the question supports our view that the object of the theophany was Joshua's mission.

14. the army of the LORD: cf. 1 Kg., the heavenly court. In accordance with the conception of Yahweh militant in the cause of Israel his angelic attendants are depicted as an army. The conception of the stars as 'the heavenly host' (Gen. 2:1, P) is as early as the Deuteronomistic History (2 Kg. 21:5; 23:4f.); but probably the idea of the army of the Lord was a projection of the conception of Yahweh militant as peculiarly manifest in the ark and the sacral community in arms (cf. Von Rad, *Theology of the Old Testament*, I, 1962, pp. 18f.).

I have now come: the Hebrew formula (*'attāh bā'tî*) is familiar in the epistolary style, where it introduces the substance of the message after preliminaries. This, however, is abruptly supplanted by the note of Joshua's obeisance and the sanctity of the place, which surely indicates the fragmentary nature of the tradition.

15. Put off your shoes . . .: as in Exod. 3:5 this indicates the revelation of the sanctity of the place, sanctuaries being entered barefoot (Exod. 29:20, P) as still among the Samaritans at Nablus and the Muslims in their mosques. But here as in Exod. 3:5 it may rather acknowledge the divine presence or authority and his commission to the person addressed.

THE FALL OF JERICHO

6:1–27

This incident, like so much in Jos. 2–6, is described in duplicate, first in the divine instructions and then in the event, certain details being communicated in triplicate, Joshua transmitting the divine command. This had a mnemonic value, perhaps being instructions for ritual celebration. The episode is introduced by a note on the fortification of Jericho, alert and in a state of siege, which might well defy semi-nomads, who lacked the experience, equipment and temperament to reduce such a place.

What was once no doubt a strikingly dramatic narrative in the pre-Deuteronomistic compilation is ruined by continual accretions, to the bewilderment of the reader and even the critic. According to one version, the people marched round the city on the decisive seventh day in silence until at the seventh circuit on the word of command they raised a shout (vv. 5, 10, 16, 20), at which the wall fell down in its place (v. 20), while according to another account the march round the city was accompanied by the priests with horns blowing possibly at each daily circuit and certainly during the seven circuits on the seventh day (v. 4). Verse 11 may even indicate yet another tradition in which the ark alone was carried round the city by its bearers. In v. 5 the priests blow their horns apparently only on the seventh day, but according to vv. 8, 9, 13 they blow the horns during the whole march round. In the march round the city the warriors only are mentioned in vv. 3 and 7, priests and ark being introduced, apparently as a later accretion, in v. 4. They were inserted here, no doubt, with respect to Joshua's instructions to the priests with the ark in v. 6 (obviously a later version than his instructions to the people in v. 3). The variants, however, are dovetailed in the course of composition and redaction till they cannot be separated with certainty.

With this reserve we may propose a secular and a sacred tradition. The former, which represents a march round the city by warriors in arms in silence till they raise the shout at a given signal, when the walls collapse and the city is taken and put under the ban, is possibly the tradition of the Rachel group, later Ephraim and

Benjamin. It may reflect their surprise at finding such a site as Jericho by its strong spring and with ample evidence of its former strength virtually an open settlement, if not actually derelict. Here we recall Kenyon's tentative dating of the fall of Late Bronze Age Jericho *c.* 1350–1325 BC. This version would then be an aetiological saga. The tradition of the ban on Jericho (vv. 16, 17, 21, 24), if not part of this account, may be part of a historical tradition of an earlier hostile penetration, possibly by Reuben and Gad, as is suggested by the tradition of the seniority of Reuben in Israel and the association with the Stone of Bohan, the son of Reuben, south of Jericho (15:6; 18:17), and perhaps by the tradition of those elements in the van of Israel in the passage of the Jordan (1:12–18). This tradition would also be conserved at Gilgal, the boundary sanctuary of those eastern groups and Ephraim, Benjamin and Manasseh in the Jordan Valley before its prominence as a sanctuary of the northern confederacy of Israel in the time of Saul.

The role of the priests with the ark and the horns and the daily procession round the city, culminating in the sevenfold circuit on the seventh day, has every appearance of an aetiological account of a ritual, like the crossing of the Jordan, where the priests with the ark play a similar role. This was no doubt part of the ritual celebration of the occupation of the Promised Land at the nearby sanctuary of Gilgal. This may be indicated by the note that after the daily circumambulation the people returned to the camp for the night (v. 11*b*), the 'camp' being the conventional description of the temporary lodging of pilgrims to the central sanctuary. The circumambulation of territory to symbolise possession is well known in royal ritual in Egypt and among the Hittites, and in the Baal myth from Rās Shamra, where at the apogee of his royal power Baal makes a round of '77 towns, 88 cities'. More specifically, it is tempting to see in the sevenfold procession culminating in the sevenfold circumambulation and in the use of the ram's horn trumpet (*yôbēl*) a reflection of the Jewish ritual of the Jubilee Year, when there was a reversion of land to its owners, and which was inaugurated by the blowing of the *yôbēl*, from which the word Jubilee is derived. Details of the Jubilee Year are from P (Lev. 25:1–55), so that here we may have elaboration from the Deuteronomistic Historian or, more probably, we think, the post-Exilic redactor.

The mention of the ban on Jericho in vv. 17 and 24 suggests to the pre-Deuteronomistic compiler of the sundry local traditions the preservation of Rahab and her family (vv. 17, 23, 25) and, in v. 18 anticipates the incident of Achan (ch. 7).

Both the secular and sacred traditions of the fall of Jericho served the purpose of the Deuteronomistic Historian in emphasising after the pre-Deuteronomistic compiler the divine agency in the occupation of Canaan.

1. **shut up from within and from without:** 'shutting in and shut', shutting in the inhabitants and itself shut in.

2. **I have given:** prophetic, or declaratory, perfect, used of the divine promise, which is considered effective when it is resolved upon. This is probably from the oracle in the tradition of the Holy War (so Noth, *op. cit.*, p. 137). **and mighty men of valour:** actually without the conjunction in MT, which indicates that perhaps this is a gloss on 'men of war' in v. 3, displaced from the margin.

4. **seven:** the number had a magical significance in the ancient Near East and generally in popular religion and superstition. It is also a motif of folklore and saga as a literary convention. In the present context it probably reflects the sacramental celebration of the fall of Jericho in the cult at Gilgal, but it could as well be a feature of secular saga. The secondary nature of the tradition is indicated by the premature introduction of the facts formally communicated by Joshua in v. 6.
trumpets of rams' horns: (*šôpᵉrôt hayyôbᵉlîm*). *yôbēl* ('ram's horn') may be connected with Assyrian *šapparu*, a kind of wild goat or sheep; cf. Arabic *sawāfir* ('wild sheep', pl.).

5. The verse shows evidence of the fusion of the tradition of the final shout of the people after their silent circumambulation at the signal of a long-drawn blast on the ram's horn and the later version of the procession in which the priests sustain the blowing of the horns.
flat: Hebrew 'in its place'.

7. **and he said:** correctly with the Syriac version, the Targum and Vulgate for MT, 'and they said'.
the ark of the LORD: from the pre-Deuteronomistic tradition as distinct from 'the ark of the covenant of the Lord'. The mention of the ark here after the warriors indicates a fusion of secular and sacred traditions, and occasions further literary adjustment of the two traditions in the arrangement of the procession in v. 9. Since the ark was captured by the Philistines *c.* 1050 BC and played no role in the cult until its restoration by David to Jerusalem *c.* sixty years later, the tradition of its role in the taking of Jericho either reflects the cult at Gilgal among Ephraim and her confederates before 1050 BC or is a reflection of its role in festal processions in the Temple in Jerusalem familiar to the pre-Deuteronomistic compiler in the early Monarchy (e.g. Pss. 68:1, MT 2; 132:8).

9. **armed men:** Hebrew *hehālûṣ*, collective singular, 'girt up', or 'kilted', so free for action. Hertzberg (*op. cit.*, p. 41n.) aptly cites

the use of the term for young pioneers in the Zionist settlement of Palestine.

13. blowing the trumpets continually: reading *hālōk wᵉtāqôaʿ* for MT *hālōk wᵉtāqᵉʿû*.

17. devoted to the LORD for destruction: Hebrew *ḥerem*, lit. 'sacrosanct', which has an Arabic cognate, e.g. *ḥaram*, 'sacred precinct of a holy place', *ḥarīm*, 'women', as sacrosanct to the husband. The Hebrew term denotes what is renounced to God either in consequence of a vow or of a divine command in the Holy War (1 Sam. 15:3ff.). The institution is described as an ideal in Dt. 20:16f., but it was an actual practice in the ancient Semitic world, being attested in the inscription of Mesha of Moab in the second half of the ninth century BC where it involved the slaughter of all the 7,000 inhabitants of the Israelite town of Nebo and the appropriation of the cult-equipment of Yahweh for Chemosh, the god of Moab (G. A. Cooke, *NSI*, nos. 1, 11, 17f.) (cf. v. 19). In the context of the Holy War the explanation of this wanton and wasteful practice may be that, as the warriors and their weapons were dedicated to God (1 Sam. 21:5; 2 Sam. 11:11), all with which they came into contact, including the spoils of the captured city, would be infected by their 'holiness', hence unsafe for common use.

18. keep yourselves: so with the versions for MT 'keep'.

lest when you have devoted them: read with LXX (cf. 7:21; Dt. 7:25) 'lest you appropriate them' (*pen taḥmᵉdû* for MT *pen taḥᵃrîm*). The verb *ḥāmad* means 'to covet', but also, as the Karatepe inscription indicates, 'to appropriate', which is probably the meaning in the Decalogue (Exod. 20:17; cf. v. 15, 'thou shalt not steal, *lôʾ tignôb*, i.e. kidnap) and certainly in Exod. 34:24.

19. sacred to the LORD: Hebrew *qōdeš*, denoting an exclusive ritual relationship with God, 'holy' with the moral connotation being secondary and later.

the treasury of the LORD: see above, on v. 17; cf. David's consecrated spoils (1 Kg. 7:51), and also the armour of Saul deposited by the Philistines in the temple of Ashtaroth, probably at Beth-shan (1 Sam. 31:10). See further, v. 24, where the deposit in 'the house' of Yahweh is likely to be a later anachronistic expansion, as indicated by its omission in LXX. This prepares for the incident of Achan's sacrilege and punishment in ch. 7.

21. utterly destroyed: Hebrew 'put to the ban', as prescribed in v. 17.

26. laid an oath upon them: MT requires the direct object. Better, with a change of vowels, 'swore an oath'.

Jericho: probably a gloss, as indicated by its omission in LXX.

Cursed: Hebrew *ʾārûr*, the Akkadian cognate of which means 'bound', physically or by incantation, the form the curse often takes in Hebrew. The curse in ancient Israel was thought to operate automatically, and was effective on all associated with the person cursed; cf. *per contra* the blessing, e.g. on Jacob (Gen. 27:27ff.) (cf. J. Gray, 'Blessing and Curse', *HDB*, one vol., 2nd ed., 1963). The curse is said to be fulfilled on Hiel of Bethel (1 Kg. 16:34), as LXX here adds, but with a different name. The fact that the passage does not envisage the rebuilding of Jericho under Ahab with the curse on Hiel indicates the date of the pre-Deuteronomistic compilation before this time. There was actually a small settlement at Jericho in the interim, as revealed by Kenyon's excavations; but this was not extensive and probably not heavily fortified if at all.

27. On the conclusion, which signifies the pre-Deuteronomistic narrative, see Introduction, p. 31f.

THE INCIDENT OF ACHAN

7:1–26 (*see also* 8:1–29)

Here the pre-Deuteronomistic compiler of the traditions of Gilgal and the neighbourhood has combined two independent tradition-complexes, that of the campaign of Ai, where a historical tradition is combined with an aetiological one concerning the name of Ai ('the Ruin'), and the aetiological tradition of the sin and punishment of Achan, which primarily explained the significance of the stone-heap near the Plain of Achor (7:26). Apart from the location of the Plain of Achor in Judah (15:7), the fact that Achan belonged to a sept of Judah (7:18) may indicate that this was a tradition of Judah, particularly of the Zarhites, the sept to which Achan belonged (7:17), through whom it may have been associated with Gilgal in the Jordan Valley, with which the inhabitants of the Plain of Achor had a natural connection. On the other hand, in view of the discredit on a clan of Judah, it may have been a tradition of the neighbouring group Benjamin, who were familiar with the cairn as a boundary point. However this may be, the tradition was originally distinct from those of the Ai campaign, which were located probably along the comparatively open Wādī Makkūk, west of ancient Jericho, hence well north of the northern end of al-Buqei'a, the Plain – not Valley – of Achor (7:26; 15:7). The instance of God's anger provoked by the sin of Achan in the original Achan tradition was probably other than the reverse at Ai, in favour of which it has been suppressed in the pre-Deuteronomistic compilation (Noth, *op. cit.*, p. 45; Hertzberg, *op. cit.*, p. 50).

In the pre-Deuteronomistic compilation the infringement of the tabu by Achan at Jericho (7:11*a*-25) is associated with the reverse in the first attack on Ai in an obviously artificial way, vv. 5*b*–10 being the work of the pre-Deuteronomistic compiler, as is indicated by the fact that in the independent Ai tradition the reason for the reverse is already given as over-confidence and miscalculation (vv. 3–5*a*).

The main impression of the Ai incident is also of an aetiological tradition, explaining the name and condition of the place and various features in the vicinity, such as the large conglomeration of stones at the gate, explained as the place where the body of the king was thrown out (8:29) and a certain conspicuous tree where he was hanged (*ibid.*). The details of the local contours (esp. 8:3ff.) suggested to Noth a tradition from the time when the citadel area of the ruined site, ruined since *c.* 2000 BC, was reoccupied by a limited settlement of Benjaminites from the twelfth century to the end of the tenth century BC, as the excavations of J. Marquet-Krause demonstrated (*Les fouilles de 'Ai (et-Tell), 1933–35*, 1939), confirmed by the excavations of J. A. Callaway ('New Evidence on the Conquest of 'Ai', *JBL* 87, 1968, pp. 312–20; 'The 1966 'Ai (et-Tell) Excavations', *BASOR* 196, 1969, pp. 2–16).

Noth's explanation of the detailed knowledge of local topography, however, is not the only possible one. Ai was just over a mile from Bethel, and may well have played a part in the tradition of the occupation of the land at the sanctuary at Bethel, which according to Jg. 20:26–28 housed the ark, just as the traditions of the crossing of the Jordan, the taking of Jericho and possibly the Achan incident were conserved in connection with the tradition of the occupation at the sanctuary of Gilgal (Hertzberg, *op. cit.*, p. 60). Ai, however, was on the main road taken by pilgrims from the hill-country of Ephraim to Gilgal (Alt, 'Josua', *KS* I, 1953, p. 183), and nothing was more natural than that its ruin and features in the vicinity should be connected with the cult-tradition of the occupation at Gilgal. But the close association of the tradition of the taking of Ai with nearby Bethel *and* with the pilgrimage to Gilgal might explain the two variants, apparent particularly in the numbers of the men in ambush (thirty thousand, according to 8:3f.; five thousand, according to 8:12).

A further possible explanation of this double tradition is that a genuine historical tradition of the defeat of the men of Bethel at the ruined site of Ai by the Rachel group ('the men of Joseph' of Jg. 1:22–26), conserved by them as a local tradition, was combined with an accretion of traditions developed in connection with the cult of Bethel and the pilgrimage to Gilgal. Noth, on the other hand, contended for two stages in the development of the Ai tradition, the first associated with the Benjaminite settlement of the place from the twelfth to the late tenth centuries, which conserved the significance of local features, and the second after that settlement, which knew Ai as 'for ever a heap of ruins unto this day' (8:28). Among those various explanations of the variant traditions of the Ai incident it is not possible to dogmatise, though obviously Noth is right in dating the tradition of the perpetual desolation of Ai after the abandonment of the place in the latter half of the tenth century, always provided that Ai is correctly located at et-Tell.

In the pre-Deuteronomistic compilation the calculating reconnaissance and subsequent rash attack without specific divine direction and the discomfiture, contrast with the divinely directed crossing of the Jordan, on which the compiler animadverts (7:7) in the passage which is recognised as the link he forged between the originally independent traditions of Achan and Ai (vv. 5*b*–11). The contrast with the fall of Jericho is also striking. By contrast the successful phase of the campaign against Ai is heralded by God's direct command and assurance in the declaratory perfect: 'See, I have given into your hand the king of Ai' (8:1). This language recalls that of the tradition of the fall of Jericho: 'See, I have given into your hand Jericho, with its king and mighty men of valour' (6:2). The stereotyped phraseology suggests a regular literary type, the oracle in the Holy War of the invincible God, the theme of the cult at Gilgal as transmitted by the pre-Deuteronomistic compiler. He was also responsible for the explanation of the initial reverse at Ai as the result of Achan's breach of the tabu at Jericho. The explanation of the first failure as the result of the miscalculation of the opposition (7:3f.) belongs to the independent Ai tradition, perhaps that variant which may be the local secular tradition reflected in Jg. 1:22–26.

The Achan story, probably originally quite a trivial aetiological tradition relating to the cairn between Judah and Benjamin dominating the Plain of Achor (al-Buqei'a) from the north-west (Jos. 15:7; 18:17), once it was associated by the pre-Deuteronomistic compiler with the ban on Jericho, pointedly illustrates the conception of the occupation of the Promised Land as God's conditional grace to Israel, a theme elaborated by the Deuteronomistic Historian, who relates it to the covenant with its moral and religious implications.

1. broke faith: the verb *mā'al*, being confined to the late parts of the Old Testament, particularly P, may indicate a redactional gloss, and this is supported by the proleptical character of the verse, which violates the essentially dramatic character of the pre-Deuteronomistic narrative.

Achan: modified to *Achar* in LXX[BA], and Josephus (*Ant.* V.i.10). On the paranomasia, see on v. 25. In the genealogy of the clans of Judah in 1 Chr. 2:7, Achar (*sic*) is probably a clan of Judah rather than an individual, intertribal affinites being described as individual relationships, as still among Bedouin tribes. The association with Zerah the brother of Perez (Gen. 38:29f.) is interesting in view of the association of Perez with Bethlehem (Ru. 4:12, 18), with which the Ta'amira Bedouin of the Buqei'a still have associations.

2. Ai: this place, actually *hā'ay* ('the Ruin'), is usually identified with et-Tell ('the burial-mound of an ancient settlement'), *c.* 1½ miles south-east (cf. v. 2, 'east') of Bethel and is cut off on the north and east by a deep ravine (8:11) and bounded on the west by an open valley (8:13). Two modern village tracks during the British Mandate ran east and west of the ridge on which the settlement stood, to meet in more open country south-east of the ridge, 'the descent' (better, 'meeting-place') 'toward the Arabah' (8:14), from which the easiest access to Jericho is by way of the Wādī Makkūk. The valley on the east and its northern extension may be the place where Joshua is depicted as sending his main advance force (8:13), himself remaining apparently with his main force where he could control both approaches east and west of the ridge. (On the relevance of archaeological data, see Introduction to chs 7 and 8, p. 85.) **Beth-aven** may be the Jewish parody of Bethel, 'House of Vanity', in which case either 'which is near Beth-aven' or 'east of Bethel' is a late gloss.

3. about two or three thousand: in view of the statement that the people are but few, Eissfeldt is surely right in assuming a scribal error for 'three hundred', which is more in accordance with the casualties, 'about thirty-six men' (v. 5).

5. Shebarim: lit. 'breakings'; either 'quarries' or 'cliff-faces'. Like 'the descent', a precipitous part of the valley east of Ai, a local feature, indicating the intense elaboration of the local tradition.

the hearts of the people melted: 'heart' in Hebrew idiom means thought or resolution. In the presentation of the pre-Deuteronomistic compiler or the Deuteronomistic Historian, the Israelites in their attack on Ai on their own initiative suffer the same experience as the Canaanites when God directed Israel in the occupation of the Promised Land (2:9).

6. rent his clothes: a mourning rite; e.g. of Jacob for Joseph (Gen. 37:34), David for Absalom (2 Sam. 13:31), etc. This is probably the modification of the laceration of the skin (Dt. 14:1), now attested as a rite of mourning for the dead in the Rās Shamra texts.

and the elders of Israel: the pre-Deuteronomistic compiler represents the reverse as affecting all Israel, hence Joshua's associ-

ation with the elders and the rite before the ark of the Lord. This is the only reference to the ark in this incident, significantly occurring in the section from the pre-Deuteronomistic compiler, which suggests that the earlier, independent tradition of the Ai incident in the variant to which vv. 2–5*a* belong was a secular tradition of a limited number of the Israelites (see Introduction to chs 7 and 8).
dust upon their heads: this is also attested as a rite of mourning for the dead in the Rās Shamra texts, as indicative of the suspension of normal behaviour and appearance in the transitional period experienced by the community at the death of one of its members. This rite came to have the general significance of normal humiliation in the fast.

7. **why hast thou brought this people over Jordan . . .?:** this points the contrast between Israel's triumph under divine leadership and the present reverse under her own initiative. It reflects further the paradox of Israel's sacramental experience of the grace of God in the drama of salvation and the occupation of the Promised Land and her political reverses during the settlement and later.
Amorites: perhaps specific here, referring to the inhabitants of the hills (Num. 13:29). On Amorites and Canaanites (v. 9), see further, on 3:10.

9. **our name . . . thy great name:** the implication here is that the name, which often denoted the character and destiny of the bearer, had substance as the extension of the personality (cf. Dt. 7:24; 9:14; Isa. 55:13). This is admirably illustrated in the Egyptian Execration Texts, where pottery vessels and figurines were inscribed with the names of various enemies of the Pharaohs of the Twelfth Dynasty and broken or buried with magical ritual and incantation to impair the evil potential of the enemies or to divest them of their personality (K. Sethe, *Die Ächtung feindlicher Fürsten, Völker und Dinge auf altägyptischen Tongefäss-scherben des mittleren Reiches*, 1926; G. Posener, *Princes et Pays d'Asie et de Nubie, Textes Hiératiques sur des Figurines d'Envoûtement du Moyen Empire*, 1939). In the Deuteronomic theology the name of God often signifies his presence, which may be realised in time or place, e.g. in the Temple (Dt. 12:11; 1 Kg. 8:29). This extension of the divine personality is what Christian theology terms a person of the Godhead. In this passage, however, **what wilt thou do for thy great name?** may mean 'What of thy reputation?' But it may envisage the impairing of God and his being deprived of his people among whom he was invoked by name and his presence thus realised. For the identification of the interests of Israel with the honour of God, cf. Dt. 9:28.

10–11. The pre-Deuteronomistic compiler completes the transition from the reverse at Ai to the story of Achan with the stimulating thought that man cannot remain prostrate under the stroke of disaster, but must seek the moral cause of it in his own conduct. This anticipates the attitude of the Deuteronomistic Historian and is characteristic of the moral fibre of ancient Israel.

11. Achan's sin is Israel's by the old Semitic principle of corporate responsibility, as Jonathan's breach of the tabu imposed by Saul involved the whole force (1 Sam. 14:24–45); see further, below, on v. 14. It is emphasised that Achan's sin is no case of unwitting infringement of ritual, which sinned (*ḥāṭā'*) might signify, but deliberate sin. The appropriation of the banned property was sacrilege and was aggravated by deceit and dissembling.

12. **backs:** actually the 'back of the neck'.

a thing for destruction: under the infectious influence of the banned property which they held. Sacrilege might be a moral fault, but for ancient Israel it effected automatic retribution.

13. **sanctify:** condition by ceremonial purification for a sacred transaction, namely, the divine arbitration by the casting of the sacred lots (cf. 3:5, and note).

the LORD, God of Israel: Yahweh, the God of Israel was probably the specific title of God in the sacral assembly of Israel.

14. **brought near:** i.e. into the presence of God, symbolised by the ark or at the sanctuary for divine arbitration, as in Exod. 22:8, where the same verb is used.

takes: cf. 1 Sam. 14:41ff., which gives the fullest information on the manipulation of the sacred lots Urim and Thummim. These were apparently shaken, as in the Roman manipulation of lots, until one 'went out', clearing the party represented. That which was 'contained' or 'taken' (Hebrew *nilkād*) indicated the guilty party. The process was continued by elimination (vv. 16–18), here by **tribes** (*šᵉbāṭîm*), Judah, etc.; septs (*mišpāḥôt*), Zarhi, etc.; smaller kinship groups (*bāttîm*), Zabdi, etc.; by houses under fathers of families, Carmi etc.; then by individual heads of families under the authority of their father or oldest member, so arriving at Achan. Lots as the means of divine arbitration were well known in antiquity in Israel, Mesopotamia and Arabia, in classical antiquity and even in the early Church (Ac. 1:26).

burned: the method of utter extinction (Am. 2:1), the penalty of adultery in certain cases (Gen. 38:24; Lev. 20:14; 21:9). This need not exclude stoning in the case of Achan, a rite in which all the community might participate (v. 25; cf. Dt. 17:5; 22:21), though the stoning here was demanded as the explanation of the cairn of Achan in the Plain of Achor, and by its mention both before and after the burning in v. 25 it seems either a variant tradition or probably, as indicated by the 'transgression of the covenant of the Lord', a Deuteronomistic feature; see above, on v. 11.

a shameful thing: cf. Gen. 34:7. Dt. 22:21 (adultery); Jg. 20:6 (rape). From its recurrence 'a shameful thing in Israel' (*nᵉbālâh bᵉyiśrā'ēl*) is a technical term, but *nᵉbālâh* is also used generally of the presumptuous contention of Job's friends (Job 42:8) and of thoughtless speech (Is. 9:17, MT 16). The classical example of one *nābāl* by name and nature is Nabal (1 Sam. 25:25), who could not govern his indignation by discretion. The lack of control or wilful failure to govern one's temper, desire or whim is *nᵉbālâh* in the Old Testament. *nᵉbālâh bᵉyiśrā'ēl*) denotes indulgence of one's personal desires or impulses in defiance of the standards and sanctions of the community.

17. families: correctly with some ancient MSS for MT 'men'.

was taken: correctly with LXX, Syriac and Targum for MT 'he took'.

19. give glory: lit. 'acknowledge the weight' (*kābôd*), or the effective power (of God). *kābôd* is the opposite of *qᵉlālâh*, 'lightness', also 'curse', the natural reaction of the condemned man.

render praise: i.e. for the vindication of God's justice and omnipotence revealed by the sacred lots. The phrase reflects the solidarity of the ancient society. As the sinner had involved the community in sin and so impaired its effectiveness he was now required to give it the advantage of his auspicious word as by his punishment he delivered it from sin.

21. mantle from Shinar: Shinar is Mesopotamia in Gen. 10:10, where it denotes Sumer, South Mesopotamia. Nothing is known of any such special product associated with Mesopotamia, but inventories from the palace of Ugarit (Rās Shamra) mention vestments trimmed with jewels, some of which are valued at ten shekels of silver (C. Virolleaud, *Le Palais Royal d'Ugarit* II, 1957, pp. 137ff.). The mantle taken by Achan may have been represented, like those, for ceremonial or cultic purposes (cf. 2 Kg. 23:7). The recurrence of the term *š'r* ('wool') in the Rās Shamra inventories, however, may indicate that *n* in *šin'ar* is a scribal error.

two hundred shekels of silver: the shekel here is a weight, coinage being introduced from the mercantile cities of Asia Minor in the seventh century BC, though shekel pieces, probably metal rings of that weight and fractions of it told off on a stick, are mentioned in the Rās Shamra legends (fourteenth century BC). There were two systems of weight in use in Palestine: the Babylonian, of 3,600 shekels to the talent, and the Canaanite, attested at Rās Shamra, of 3,000 shekels to the talent (e.g. Exod. 38:25f., P). Comparison of ancient weights found in excavations in Palestine and Mesopotamia suggests that the talent in pre-exilic Palestine contained 2,500 shekels. This may be the biblical 'shekel after the king's weight' (2 Sam. 14:26) as distinct from 'the shekel of the sanctuary'. See further, R. B. Y. Scott, 'Weights, Money, Measures and Time', *Peake's Commentary on the Bible*, ed. M. Black and H. H. Rowley, 1962, p. 38.

a bar of gold: lit. 'a tongue'.

coveted: rather, 'desired and appropriated' (see on 6:18).

23. laid them down: lit. 'poured them out'. This would be appropriate of shekel weights, but not of the objects in question. Possibly, with LXX and the Syriac version, we should read *wayyaṣṣîgûm* ('and they set them down') for MT *wayyaṣṣîqûm*.

24. This is a classic example of the solidarity of the community. It is not clear if Achan's family (**tent**) actually perished, but their presence indicated their involvement, and, suffering from the curse on their kinsman, they would at least be excommunicated. This principle of communal responsibility underlies the clause in the Decalogue 'visiting the iniquity of the fathers upon the children . . .' (Exod. 20:5), and operates in the law of blood-revenge among the Bedouin. It may be a defective ethic, but is practically a wholesome deterrent. Its operation to comparatively late in the history of Israel is indicated by its particular modification in Dt. 24:16. Stoning was a public act (Ac. 7:58).

Valley of Achor: Hebrew *'ēmeq*, lit. 'deepening', indicates perhaps the soil of the valley bottom rather than the depression of the contour, and is used of open cultivable valleys, like Jezreel, Elah and Hebron, as distinct from the torrent bed (*naḥal*) and ravine (*gay*). The description of the tribal boundary of Judah in 15:7 indicates that the Plain of Achor must lie south of the Wādī Qilt, with which it is occasionally identified. Noth is right in identifying it with al-Buqei'a, the upland plain cultivable in a season of good rainfall, west of the cliffs above Qumran, which gives access from the lower Jordan valley to Bethlehem. It was one of those regions which serve Bedouin as a stepping-stone in their penetration to the more desirable land, as in the case of the Ta'amira, who have now penetrated to Bethlehem and Tekoa, but still have an interest in al-Buqei'a.

25. bring trouble: from Hebrew *'ākar*, a word-play on Achor. The verb means 'to vitiate'; cf. the Arabic cognate, 'to pollute with mud'. The rhythm of Joshua's reply to Achan may indicate a metric couplet, the proper name standing before 'Why did you bring trouble on us?', with a further word-play between Achan, *'ākar* and Achor (cf. n. on v. 1).

26. a great heap of stones: perhaps an actual grave-cairn (Hebrew *bāmâh*; *EVV*, 'high place') which may have been traditionally associated with an accursed person on whose grave passers by cast stones, as they did until recently at the reputed tomb of Absalom in the Kidron Valley at Jerusalem. Alternatively this cairn, traditionally associated with Achan, may have been a boundary cairn between Judah and Benjamin (cf. 15:7).

THE CAMPAIGN OF AI

8:1–29

1. **Do not fear or be dismayed:** probably originally part of the formula of the oracle of assurance in the war of Yahweh, this was used by the Deuteronomistic compiler to give unity to his compilation.

I have given: the declaratory perfect (see on 6:2) and also part of the oracle in the tradition of the Holy War.

2. So far nothing has been said of the death of the **king** of **Jericho**, so that this may be assumption of the pre-Deuteronomistic compiler. **only its spoil and its cattle you shall take as booty for yourselves:** cf. v. 27. This may be a note from the Deuteronomistic Historian, mindful of the modification of the ban in Dt. 2:34ff.; 3:6ff.

3. The representation of the action about **Ai** or Bethel as based on Gilgal about sixteen miles distant is probably the contribution of the pre-Deuteronomistic compiler, though Saul and Jonathan operated between those two localities with great mobility (1 Sam. 13:4ff.). The germ of history in the tradition is probably the solidarity of the forebears of Ephraim and her associates at the boundary sanctuary of Gilgal which conditioned the occupation of Bethel, Ai and its vicinity.

thirty thousand: much too large a number for the unobtrusive movement into an ambush, and probably a scribal error for 'three thousand'; cf. 'five thousand' in v. 12.

4. **behind it:** i.e. west of Ai, as v. 9 and the variant tradition in v. 12 say more specifically.

6. **drawn them away:** the same verb is used of the priests' feet drawn out of the bed of Jordan in 4:18.

9. **among the people:** *bā'ām*, perhaps a scribal error for *bā'ēmeq*, 'in the plain', agreeing with v. 13. This would be the comparatively open valley, south and east of the ridge on which Ai stands.

10. The fact that Joshua is already said to have gone on his campaign to Ai, where he sets an ambush of thirty thousand (probably three thousand) men (vv. 3–9), suggests that v. 10, where he sets an ambush of about five thousand (v. 12) in the same position, is from a different source.

11. all the fighting men of *RSV* assumes the emendation of MT *kol-hā'ām hammilḥāmâh*, which is grammatically impossible. *milḥāmâh* should probably be omitted, reading 'all the people'.

13. the rear guard: Hebrew *'aqēbô*, lit. 'its heel'.

14. the descent towards the Arabah: better 'the meeting place . . .' (see on 7:2). The **Arabah**, which denotes the Jordan Valley, is still used in Arabic to describe the depression from the southern end of the Dead Sea to the Gulf of Aqaba. The phrase is omitted in LXX[BA].

15. the wilderness: the uncultivated land east of Ai. The land east of the watershed of the hills of south Palestine lies in the rain-shadow, and cultivation deteriorates sharply, being largely abandoned to Bedouin, who hazard a harvest in odd pockets of earth in hope of sufficient rain. Such areas were those first settled by the Hebrews in their penetration from the east and south.

17. Bethel: this may indicate that the action was really associated with the penetration indicated in Jg. 1:22–26, of which the destruction of Bethel, attested by archaeology in the late fourteenth or early thirteenth centuries, may be evidence. As Ai was derelict at that time, the site may have been chosen by the men of Bethel as a strategic point at which to resist the invaders. This might explain the ease with which the Israelite commandos occupied the site.

18–19. stretched out the javelin: Hebrew *kîdôn*, for casting, not thrusting as the spear (*ḥanît*). According to v. 19, this was a signal from Joshua with the main body to the commandos in ambush in the western wadi. This may be according to one tradition; but v. 26, which depicts Joshua as stretching forth the javelin until the victory was complete, obviously treats the act as one of imitative magic, possibly influenced by the tradition of Moses' rod upraised at the battle of Rephidim (Exod. 17:9ff., E).

19. set the city on fire: if Ai was a ruin occupied in the campaign by the men of Bethel, the origin of this tradition may be the burning of the equipment of the defenders. The smoke, rather than Joshua's javelin, was the signal to the main body east of the ridge that the ruse had succeeded.

20. no power: lit. 'hands', as in Dt. 16:17; 32:36; 34:12; Ps. 76:5, MT v. 6; etc.

to flee this way or that: back to Bethel by the valleys east or west of Ai, where their retreat was cut off by the commandos in control of their camp in Ai.

23ff. Here the tradition of the slaughter of the king of Ai and the inhabitants is an amplification of the tradition of the battle of Ai influenced by the tradition of the ban on Jericho, perhaps developed through pilgrimage past Ai to Gilgal. Actually Ai had no king at this time. Local Benjaminite tradition may also have made its contribution, explaining a significant tree as that on which the king was hanged, and a large heap of stones as the place where his body was thrown. So Arab folk-legend identifies conspicuous rocks at the derelict settlement at Medain Ṣāliḥ in the northern Hejaz as the petrified bodies of the ancient king and his notables.

27. Only: the adverb suggests an addition to the original tradition by the Deuteronomistic Historian (see on vv. 2 and 29*b*).

28. heap: 'ruin-mound' (Hebrew *tēl*, Arabic *tell*, hence the modern name et-Tell.

29. hanged . . . until evening: after having been killed (10:26; Dt. 21:22, 23). The latter passage enjoins the taking down of the body by sunset. This punctilio probably indicates a note by the Deuteronomist. LXX, doubtless reflecting the later practice of crucifixion, reads 'on a pair of pieces of wood'.

THE BUILDING OF THE ALTAR AND THE COVENANT AT SHECHEM

8:30–36

The passage comes directly from the Deuteronomistic Historian, as is clear from the phraseology and the emphasis on such details as the unhewn stones untouched by iron, 'as is written in the book of the law of Moses' (v. 31; cf. Dt. 27:5–7*a*; Exod. 20:25), the inscribing of the 'copy of the law of Moses' (v. 32; cf. Dt. 27:2ff., 8) and the covenant-sacrament in general, though there are differences in detail (vv. 33ff.; cf. Dt. 27). Significantly, too, this is the only explicit mention in Jos.–Jg. of the ark 'of the covenant' at Shechem. The passage seems quite out of context even as presented in the schematic account of the 'conquest', coming as it does between the campaign at Ai and the Gibeonite campaign, which is the natural sequel to the campaign about Ai. The Deuteronomistic Historian seems anxious to represent Joshua as carrying out Moses' instructions for the keeping and proclamation of the Law (Dt. 11:29ff.; 27:1ff.) to the letter, even to the localisation at Shechem (Dt. 11:29f.; 27:4), a theme which is elaborated by the Deuteronomistic redactor in Jos. 24. This passage is the amplification of the Deuteronomist's general theme in 1:1–9.

Though introducing the covenant at Shechem prematurely, the Deuteronomistic Historian may nevertheless reflect the significance of Shechem in the consolidation of the sacral community of the Israelite groups of the south central hills and groups of the north, the event possibly underlying Jos. 24. Without some such historical tradition it seems unlikely that the Deuteronomist would have gratuitously introduced the covenant at Shechem when he was interested in the centralisation of the cult in Jerusalem. The pattern of a public reading, or recitation, of the law, or at least an epitome of it, such as the Decalogue in its original form or the Twelve Adjurations (Dt. 27:15–26), which recurs in the Deuteronomistic History (Jos. 8:30–35; 2 Kg. 22–23), but also in the older narrative sources of the Pentateuch (Exod. 19:3–8; 24:3, 4*a*; 7) as demonstrated by K. Baltzer (*Das Bundesformular*, 1960) and W. Beyerlin (*Herkunft und Geschickte der ältesten Sinaitraditionen*, 1961), has a long history and finds its formal prototype in vassal-treaties, best illustrated by documents from the Hittite chancellery at Boghazkoi in the fourteenth and thirteenth centuries BC (see Introduction, pp. 52ff.).

30. Mount Ebal: north of Shechem opposite Mount Gerizim, which lies south of the town. As in Dt. 27:4, the altar is on Ebal. The Samaritan Pentateuch in both passages places it on Gerizim. The question of whether the Samaritans altered the text, or whether Jewish orthodox scribes did so in disagreement with the Samaritan sectaries, seems to be decided in favour of the latter by the fact that, in both orthodox and Samaritan versions at Dt. 11:29, Ebal is associated with the curse and Gerizim with the blessing.

31. as Moses the servant of the LORD had commanded . . .: cf. Dt. 27:2–6. The specification of stones dressed by iron tools is explicitly noted by the Deuteronomist after Dt. 27:5f., though it is an old ordinance, being included in the Book of the Covenant (Exod. 20:25).

iron: until *c.* 1200 BC worked by subjects of the Hittites in Anatolia and in the state of Mitanni, who had also subjects from Anatolia, and jealously guarded as a monopoly; hence the prejudice against its use in cultic installation as the product of an alien smith caste, who through it might have put a curse upon the installations (cf. 5:2).

burnt offerings: (*'ôlôt*) in which the whole victim was burnt in token of whole commitment to God or of acknowledgement of total dependence upon him, as distinct from communion-offerings (*šelāmîm*, *RSV* **peace-offerings**), in which the blood, fat and vital parts were offered to God and the rest eaten by the worshippers, who thus in the convention of commensality effected solidarity with one another and all with God. This was an important element in the covenant ceremony (Exod. 24:11).

32. he wrote upon the stones a copy of the law of Moses: the conception of a written record of the law or terms of the covenant is well established in Deuteronomistic tradition (cf. Dt. 27:3; Jos. 24:26), which must surely reflect a usage familiar to the Deuteronomistic Historian from the end of the Monarchy (so Beyerlin, *op. cit.*, pp. 52f.). That those passages reflect an older tradition is indicated by Exod. 24:3 4 7 (probably E) and by the fact that in the Hittite vassal-treaties of the fourteenth and thirteenth centuries it was the written record which gave a treaty validity. **a copy of the law** (cf. Dt. 17:18) is rendered in LXX *to deuteronomion* ('the second law'), hence 'Deuteronomy'. 'The law', or obligations of the covenant, expanded in Deuteronomic interpretation to include the whole Deuteronomic 'law of Moses' (Dt. 31:9–13, 24–29), was the development of an original tradition of the epitome of such obligations, religious and social, such as the Twelve Adjurations (Dt. 27:15–26) or the original form of the Decalogue or similar statements, to which smaller groups of apodictic laws in the Book of the covenant probably belong (Alt, 'Die Ursprunge des israelitischen Rechts', *KS* I, 1953, pp. 278–332).

33ff. The public assembly for the reading or recitation of the law, though based on a ceremony such as that described in Dt. 27:11–26, reflects rather the development of this practice as envisaged in the late Deuteronomistic passage Dt. 31:11ff., which also mentions 'resident aliens' (*RSV* **sojourner**), **women** and **the little ones**. The resident alien (Hebrew *gēr*; Arabic *jār*, usually *jāru 'llāhi*, as under the protection of God and so acknowledging his authority) is admitted to the divine assembly. The **elders**, **officers** and **judges** are mentioned also with the tribal heads in 23:2 and 24:1 as the representatives of the people at the sacrament of the covenant at Shechem, implying an organisation envisaged by the Deuteronomist as distinct from the historical situation of the consolidation of groups of the Israel of the north, which the passage may reflect, with ample and specific Deuteronomistic elaboration. The **elders** had real significance as the representatives of Israel before the Monarchy (cf. 1 Sam. 4:3ff.; 8:4; 15:30; 2 Sam. 5:3), fulfilling this function for the last time at Solomon's dedication of the Temple (1 Kg. 8:1, 3). Thereafter, with the development of the Monarchy, the elders had a merely local significance; see further, de Vaux, *Ancient Israel*, ET 1961, pp. 137f., 152f. On the **officers**, see on 1:10. The mention of **the Levitical priests**, who bless the people and pronounce the solemn curse and the division of the people towards Ebal and Gerizim reflects the usage described in Dt. 27:9–26.

THE COVENANT WITH GIBEON

9:1–27

This incident, though connected with the battle against the Amorites at Gibeon (ch. 10) in the pre-Deuteronomistic compilation and possibly also in historical fact, is transmitted in a separate tradition, or rather two traditions combined in the pre-Deuteronomistic compilation. The tradition of an agreement between the Israelites, probably originally Benjamin, and the 'Hivites', or Horites (see on v. 7) of Gibeon and their associates of Chephirah, Beeroth and Kiriath-jearim (v. 17) in the upland plain neighbouring Benjamin and the strategic passes to it at Beeroth and Kiriath-jearim may well be historical. This was a natural development of the settlement of Israelite groups in the region, and an agreement may well have been made at Gilgal (v. 6), the boundary sanctuary of the groups later to emerge as Ephraim and Benjamin. Such an agreement may have been subsequently ratified at the sanctuary at Gibeon, which continued as a notable sanctuary until the time of Solomon (1 Kg. 3:4ff.). The somewhat humorous account of the Gibeonite ruse in vv. 1–15 may be the Gibeonite version of the tradition, as Hertzberg suggests (*op. cit.*, p. 68). Possibly the whole tradition stems from Gibeon, being transferred to Gilgal by the pre-Deuteronomistic compiler (so Herzberg, *ibid.*). The tradition of the covenant between the Gibeonites and neighbouring Israelites (Benjamininites) is strikingly corroborated by the incident in 2 Sam. 21:2ff., where the Gibeonites were able to appeal to such an agreement against the Benjaminite house of Saul. One of the main sources of ch. 9 may be an aetiological tradition explaining this situation.

This relationship poses a theological difficulty for the pre-Deuteronomistic compiler in that it seriously qualifies his ideal of the intransigent implementation of the divine promise in the occupation promoted in the cult at Gilgal. Historically it reflects a situation which must have recurred in the incorporation of Canaanite districts into the national state under David and Solomon, the beginnings of which we may detect in the incident of Saul and the Gibeonites (2 Sam. 21:2ff.), where this present passage is cited. Many ties between hitherto independent elements of Israel and their non-Israelite neighbours must have been severely strained in competition with aggressive nationalism directed from Jerusalem. Those problems are reflected in Joshua's stern dealing with the Gibeonites in grudging concession to the convention of the formal agreement on the representation of the chiefs of the people (vv. 18–23), and on the emphasis given to the deception whereby the Gibeonites secured the covenant. That this issue of compromise should be so fresh in the mind of the pre-Deuteronomistic compiler supports Noth's dating of this work between the disruption of the Monarchy and the reign of Ahab (see above, p. 41).

The account of the reaction of Joshua to the agreement with the Gibeonites serves as a link with the other tradition, the menial service of the Gibeonites at the sanctuary, of which the former may be adapted as an aetiological legend by the pre-Deuteronomistic compiler. In v. 20, 'This will we do to them . . .', where the demonstrative is followed by nothing in the statement, we seem to have the vestige of an earlier tradition. The statement that they were to be 'hewers of wood and drawers of water' may originally have had the general sense (Dt. 29:11), a relationship of convenience and dependence without privilege or integration in the community of Benjamin. The definition of this as a menial office *in the sanctuary* is probably a later development by, or nearer the time of, the Deuteronomistic compiler. It may, as v. 23 seems to suggest, refer to a minor part assigned to the Gibeonites in the cult, possibly at Gilgal, which had evidently a special significance in the time of Saul or just before. This, though a minor service, may have been a privilege in recognition of the agreement with the Gibeonites, which was given a pejorative interpretation by the pre-Deuteronomistic compiler and his literary successor the Deuteronomistic Historian.

On the other hand, the tradition may relate to service in the sanctuary of Gibeon, which was well known as a sanctuary in Israel in the time of Solomon before the building of the Temple (1 Kg. 3:4ff.). This sanctuary was associated with 'the tent of meeting' by the Chronicler (1 Chr. 16:39; 21:29), who is not likely to have invented the sacred association. Gibeon (lit. 'little hill') may have been 'the hill of God', where Saul met the prophets (1 Sam. 10:5ff.). The tradition of the menial service of the Gibeonites in the sanctuary may reflect the relegation of the natives in the cult after the appropriation of this sanctuary by Israel. There is nothing in the text which definitely localised the tradition at Gilgal or Gibeon, though the pre-Deuteronomistic compiler probably envisaged Gilgal. The Deuteronomistic Historian and the later redactor in vv. 21*b* and 27*b* adapted the tradition to the cult in Jerusalem, where, at least in the Second Temple, there was such temple-servitude, 'the servants of Solomon' (Ezr. 2:55ff.; Neh. 7:57ff.), probably, as the name suggests, a relic of an institution going back to compulsion or concession in Temple service in the early Monarchy (M. Haran, 'The Gibeonites, the Nethinim and the Sons of Solomon's Servants', *VT* 11, 1961, pp. 159–69, esp. pp. 161f.; J. Liver, 'The Literary History of Joshua IX', *JSS* 8, 1963, pp. 227–43).

Thus the pre-Deuteronomistic compiler who represents the occupation as the triumph of Yahweh who demanded the co-operation of Israel to the point of intransigence, admitted the tradition of the agreement with the Gibeonites and their associates neighbouring Benjamin but frowned on it. He represents the agreement as not spontaneous and cordial, but as the result of a trick which laid Israel under the obligation of the oath which could not be revoked. The menial position of the Gibeonites in the sanctuary is also cited to emphasise this protest. This expressed also the view of the Deuteronomistic Historian, who used the earlier compilation practically as he found it.

1–2. A redactional introduction of the Deuteronomistic Historian before the introduction to the pre-Deuteronomistic compilation (v. 3), which related the incident to those of Jericho and Ai. It marks a new part of the book, anticipating the campaigns against the Amorites (ch. 10) and the Canaanites under Hazor in Galilee (ch. 11).

The sharply marked contour of south Palestine is here denoted **the hill country**, rising to just over 3,000 feet at Bethel and Hebron, **the lowland** (Shephelah), the foothills divided by a valley of Senonian chalk running north to south parallel to the mountains, and **the coast**, or coastal plain, which is here extended northwards to **Lebanon**. For the various peoples, see on 3:10. Here the Girgashites are omitted.

with one accord: this is a new element in the account of the occupation, which the pre-Deuteronomistic compiler and the Deuteronomistic Historian represent as the triumph of God before whom the natives are enervated by terror.

3. Gibeon: almost certainly al-Jib, *c.* six miles north-west of Jerusalem, as suggested by the excavation of J. B. Pritchard, especially by the many handles of wine-jars stamped 'Gibeon', and certainly associated with installations for wine-making and storing on a large scale. (Pritchard, *Gibeon: Where the Sun Stood Still*, 1962). From the size of the *tell*, Gibeon was credibly the chief member of a league of four settlements of 'Hivites', better Horites (so LXX) (v. 7). These, or at least the ruling caste, were probably non-Semitic Hurrians, who came ultimately from north Mesopotamia and Anatolia, and are attested in Palestine by their distinctive names on tablets from Taanach and Shechem and in the Amarna Tablets in the fifteenth and fourteenth centuries. Their influence in the upland plain about Gibeon with its passes to the west and south-west by Kiriath-jearim (by Qiryat al-'Ainab or Abu Ghōsh) probably roused the hostility of the Amorite king of Jerusalem and his Amorite allies in the south-west, and may have occasioned the alliance of the 'Hivite' tetrapolis and possibly their overtures to the Hebrews. The tradition of the treaty between the Israelites and Gibeon, if not supported, is not contradicted by the archaeological evidence of a peaceful transmission from the Late Bronze Age (tombs) to the Iron Age (city) at al-Jib (Pritchard, *BA* 24, 1961, p. 23).

4. made ready provisions: Hebrew *yiṣṭayyādû* ('made ready provisions for the way'), *ṣēdâh*, with certain MSS for the variant *yiṣṭayyārû*, *AV* 'made as if they had been ambassadors' (*ṣîrîm*, Isa. 18:2; 57:9; Jer. 49:14; Prov. 13:17).

wine-skins: skins are still used in the east for water.

mended: lit. 'bound up'.

5. mouldy: also in v. 12; better, after Vulgate, 'crumbly', Hebrew *niqqûdîm*, the root of which was used of granulated silver-work (Ca. 1:11).

6. make a covenant with us: the preposition (*l*[e]) indicates the form of a vassal-treaty for the advantage of the inferior party, the Israelites guaranteeing to spare (lit. 'let live') the Gibeonites (v. 15), binding themselves by oath (v. 15). This may reflect the convention of such a treaty known to the pre-Deuteronomistic compiler from the imperial period of Solomon.

7. men of Israel: the collective singular: note the parties to the agreement here as formally distinct from Joshua and the Gibeonites, neither of whom, however, is necessarily excluded. This may indicate a pre-literary source, Joshua being a feature of the pre-Deuteronomistic compilation.

Hivites: LXX *Chorraioi*, 'Hurrians' (biblical 'Horites'): see on v. 3.

covenant: the same word as for the divine covenant (*b*[e]*rît*), cognate with Akkadian *birtu* ('bond'). 'To make a covenant' in Hebrew is lit. 'to cut a covenant', referring to the accompanying sacrifice, which either served as an example of what the parties invoked upon themselves if they broke the covenant (cf. Jer. 34:18f.), or the sacrifice divided, between which the parties then passed as a symbol of communion (Gen. 15:7–18).

8. We are your servants: the customary deferential address, as in v. 9, but developed in vv. 9f., which cites the drama of salvation culminating in the victories in Transjordan, as in the speech of Rahab to the spies (2:10); cf. a further Deuteronomistic echo of the Rahab speech in vv. 24f. No mention is made of the recent successes of the Israelites west of Jordan, to maintain the fiction of the remote home of the Gibeonites.

10. Heshbon: Khirbet Ḥisbān, *c.* twelve miles south-west of Ammān, or perhaps the adjacent mound of al-'al, occupied till *c.* 1200 BC by an Amorite enclave between the Arnon and Jabboq (12:2); cf. Num. 21:21–26, with an ancient poem celebrating a former success of Heshbon against Moab (vv. 27–30). The early monarchic tradition which derives the poem from the statement in Num. 21:21–26 (J) that the Israelites defeated the Amorite king Sihon of Heshbon is, *per contra*, a secondary reconstruction from the poem, which connects Sihon with Heshbon. The description of him as 'the Amorite' is suspect as secondary, being omitted in the variation of the poem on Heshbon's victory over Moab in Jer. 48:45ff.

Og king of Bashan: cf. Num. 21:31–35. This king is lengendary as a giant whose huge 'bedstead of iron', probably a black basalt sarcophagus, was long an ancient monument. This may be one of the many megalithic dolmens in the region, which perhaps suggested the name *'ôg*, 'circle', as Mowinckel proposed (*Israels opphav* . . ., p.134). **Ashtaroth** was probably Ashtaroth Karnaim ('Ashtaroth of the Horns'; cf. Am. 6:13), which is mentioned in the Amarna Tablets.

11. No king of Gibeon is mentioned but only **elders**, as in certain cases also in the Amarna Tablets.

14. **men:** Hebrew *'ᵃnāšîm*, LXX with metathesis of two consonants reads 'leaders' (*nᵉśî'îm*), i.e. representatives of the people, cited as protagonists in the transaction in vv. 15*b*, 18*a* and 19.

did not ask direction from the LORD: lit. 'asked not the mouth of Yahweh' (Isa. 30:2). 'Mouth' here, however, may denote 'word', as in one of the most recently discovered texts from Rās Shamra. The reference is to the oracle by the sacred lots. This suggests that the eating of the provisions was a covenant rite; cf. Gen. 31:44, 54 (E), in the case of Jacob and Laban; Gen. 26:26–31 (J), Isaac and Abimelech; and Exod. 24:11, the communion meal which consummated the covenant (E. Auerbach, *Moses*, 1953, p. 166). In popular narrative, however, it becomes the means whereby the Israelites tested the truth of the statement of the Gibeonites and thereby, by the Gibeonite ruse, the means by which relationships were established which forbade violence; cf. the request of the captive Renauld de Chatillon for a drink of water in the tent of *Salāḥ ad-Dīn* after the battle of Qurn Ḥaṭṭîn (1187), which, however, the Sultan was careful enough not to give personally. The statement that they **did not ask direction from the LORD** expresses the view of the Deuteronomistic compiler that the transaction was a presumptuous modification of the principles of the Holy War.

15. The pre-literary traditions of the role of **the leaders of the congregation** and that of the pre-Deuteronomistic compiler, which assigns the role to Joshua, are awkwardly combined here, and a further complication, which indicates post-exilic retouching, is 'the congregation' (*hā'ēdâh*), which, though not peculiar to, is characteristic of, P in the Pentateuch. The designation of the representatives of the people as *nᵉśî'îm* is also a feature of P; hence W. Rudolph assumed without question that v. 15*b* is from P. The noun, however, 'those raised up', is found in older Pentateuchal sources also, e.g. Exod. 22:28, MT 27 (E); thus we prefer to limit the contribution of

the post-exilic redactor here to the description of Israel as 'the congregation'.

peace: (Hebrew *šālôm*, lit. 'wholeness', 'integration'), signifies a personal relationship, 'concord' rather than 'peace', which is only one aspect of *šālôm*.

16. At the end of three days: an indefinite interval, common in saga and folklore. The theme, however, is elaborated in detail in v. 17, obviously a later redactional expansion.

17. Kireath-jearim: ('Fortress of the Maquis') is located at Qiryat al-'Ainab, also called Abu Ghōsh, *c.* ten miles west of Jerusalem on the Jaffa road, actually Tell al-Azhār, the site of the Church of Our Lady of the Ark (cf. 1 Sam. 7:1; 2 Sam. 6:2ff.), where Bronze Age sherds have been found. **Chephirah** is probably Tell Kefīreh, *c.* five miles west of al-Jīb (Gibeon), and **Beeroth** ('Wells') is probably Rās aṭ-Ṭahūneh, just north of al-Bīreh by Bethel.

18–21: This section gives the substance of the covenant with the Gibeonites, and probably with others of the tetrapolis which they represented, and conditions imposed on them by Joshua in the pre-Deuteronomistic compilation. But as it stands, it is the post-Deuteronomistic elaboration of the pre-literary tradition, where the representatives of the people mediated the covenant. Verse 20 stops short of the conditions imposed (see introduction to ch. 9), which are then abruptly introduced as menial service by the pre-Deuteronomistic compiler, or even by a later redactor. LXX obviates this difficulty somewhat by omitting 'and the leaders said to them'. Possibly the Gibeonites and their associates were simply relegated to the dependent status of 'hewers of wood and drawers of water', 'for all the congregation' being added to adapt the pre-literary tradition of the oath with the Gibeonites to the aetiological tradition explaining the minor role of the Gibeonites in the cult (vv. 23, 26–27).

21. hewers of wood and drawers of water: a menial status (Dt. 29:11), expressing the age of girls among the Arabs and possibly in the Rās Shamra Legend of King Krt, but here later (vv. 23, 26f.) taken as denoting a minor cultic office.

22–26. Note that the initiative and decision to spare the Gibeonites is Joshua's, surely the contribution of the pre-Deuteronomistic compiler. In vv. 16–21 the leaders of the people had already established covenantal relationship with the Gibeonites, which they declare to be binding in v. 20, though on condition of lower status (v. 21). Thus it was they who upheld the Gibeonites against the clamour of the people for vengeance, so that the same office by Joshua was superfluous; hence we conclude that vv. 16–21 was the pre-literary tradition as distinct from the pre-Deuteronomistic compilation with Joshua as protagonist in vv. 22–27, with Deuteronomistic and redactional retouching in vv. 24 and 27*b*.

23. cursed: reflecting a later, and more specific, application of the version of the oath to the Gibeonites fixing their status as 'hewers of wood and drawers of water'.

for the house of my God: probably Gilgal in the pre-Deuteronomistic compilation, but Jerusalem in the Deuteronomist's retouching (v. 27*b*).

THE BATTLE OF GIBEON AND ITS SEQUEL

10:1–41

For the main lines of literary analysis, see above, p. 42f.

In vv. 1–27 the pre-Deuteronomistic compiler has combined two main tradition-complexes, that of the battle of Gibeon and the rout of the Amorites (vv. 1–14, 15) and that connected with the Cave of Makkedah (vv. 16–17), the first based on historical events in the Israelite settlement of the plateau north of Jerusalem and the second a local aetiological tradition regarding the cave of Makkedah in the north part of the Shephelah. The two are combined on the basis of the rout of the Amorites after the battle of Gibeon in the general direction of the Shephelah, where Makkedah lay. Thus Makkedah is the link which served the turn of the pre-Deuteronomistic compiler, as indicated in vv. 10 and 16. There is, however, historical verisimilitude in the combination of those traditions. The alliance between the Israelites and the Hurrians on the plateau, besides menacing Jerusalem on its most vulnerable side, gave Israel access to the Shephelah by the Wādī 'ṣ-Ṣurār (Vale of Sorek), a tributary of which was dominated by Kiriath-jearim, and so cut communications between Jerusalem and her Amorite allies in the Shephelah.

In the five Amorite cities in question, however, Jerusalem, Hebron, Yarmuth, Lachish and Eglon, we cannot tell certainly which properly belonged to the former tradition and which to the latter. The number five may have been suggested by the five trees at Makkedah (v. 26), to which the aetiological tradition was attached, or the number five in both cases may have had a mnemonic value in folk-narration, like the five kings in Gen. 14. Or it may be, as Noth suggested, that the kings of those places is a secondary particularisation of 'all the Amorite kings of the hill-country' of v. 6. We should expect the cities of the five kings of the Makkedah tradition to be within immediate range of that place in the southern Shephelah, south or south-east of Azekah (see on v. 10), and it may be that in Libnah and Gezer, which are mentioned together in vv.

29–33, but not in the traditions of the battle of Gibeon or the incident at Makkedah, we have elements of the original Makkedah tradition, together with Yarmuth, Lachish and Eglon. The destruction of the city of Debir (vv. 38f.) may represent a confusion in tradition with Debir, the name of the king of Eglon (v. 3). Those being the five kings of the Makkedah tradition, the elements common to both traditions which suggested the syncretism were Jarmuth, Lachish and Eglon. If we are right in assuming the confusion in the name Debir, this may have suggested Hebron among the Amorite protagonists at Gibeon and the extension of Joshua's reprisals throughout the south in vv. 28ff.

In the account of the battle of Gibeon the pre-Deuteronomistic compiler evidently worked with two main traditions. One concerned the repulse of the Amorite king of Jerusalem and his allies in their reaction to the accommodation of Gibeon with the Israelites on the plateau at the head of vital passes to the south-west (vv. 1–11), with possibly secondary elaboration of the enemies involved. The other concerned the decisive factor in the Israelite victory at Gibeon. Here the compiler evidently had two traditions at his disposal, the one depicting the activity of God in a hail-storm during the rout (v. 11) and the other where the pre-Deuteronomistic compiler understands a passage from the Book of Jashar as depicting the divine activity in a preternaturally long day (vv. 13*b*f., elaborated from vv. 12–13*a*). Despite the prayer of Agamemnon in the Iliad (II.412ff.) that the sun might not set until the victory of the Achaeans, the actual citation from the ancient poem may refer to a prolongation of darkness rather than of daylight, as proposed by B. J. Alfrink ('Het "stil staan" van zon en maan in Jos. 10:12–15', *Studia Catholica* 24, 1949, pp. 238–69), and may refer to a night march and sudden strike before daylight, as v. 9*a* seems clearly to suggest, though here the assumption that the advance was from a base at Gilgal is probably the contribution of the pre-Deuteronomistic compiler. The historical situation may rather have been the advance of Ephraim from north of the Valley of Aijalon to the support of their southern allies Benjamin rather than the pursuit of the Amorites down the valley, as the compiler assumed in v. 13*b*. Unfortunately, the brief citation from the Book of Jashar does not give details of the battle, which, like the incident by the Waters of Merom (11:6–9) seems to have been rather a surprise and rout than a pitched battle.

The scale of the operations, even if we discount all the Amorite cities in the Shephelah as an accretion in the pre-Deuteronomistic compilation from the aetiological tradition of the Cave of Makkedah, suggests native reaction to Ephraimite expansion from the north southwards, conceivably under an Ephraimite leader like Joshua, whose home was traditionally at Timnah, *c.* fifteen miles north of Gibeon, and here Alt proposed to find the historical Joshua ('Josua', *KS* I, 1953, p. 188).

In the Makkedah incident also two pre-literary traditions are discernible. One explains what was probably a massive rock-fall at a cave there by the tradition that the stones were laid by the Israelites to immure the fugitives, and the other that the stones were cast upon the corpses of the five kings who had been hanged on five trees, which were probably conspicuous landmarks in the neighbourhood, or perhaps an ancient holy place. One notices the repetition in both details of the tradition of the end of the king of Ai in 8:29.

The fusion of the historical and aetiological tradition-complexes here is an interesting instance of the mutual influence of such traditions at the literary level and also, even to a larger degree, in the pre-literary stage.

The hand of the compiler in the fusion of the two main traditions is evident in the addition of Makkedah to Azekah as the extent of the pursuit of the Amorites defeated at Gibeon (v. 10), the fixing of the Israelite camp at Makkedah (v. 21) and the statement of the ban on the king of Makkedah (v. 28), besides the linking of the whole tradition with operations from a base at Gilgal (vv. 6, 9, 15, 43). The fact that the account of the sweeping and comprehensive 'conquest' of the south is later modified, Hebron (vv. 36f.) and Debir (vv. 38f.) falling respectively to Caleb (15:14) and Othniel (15:16–19; Jg. 1:11–15), and the coastal plain and possibly also the Shephelah being beyond Judah's power to subdue, according to the significant exception made in Jg. 1:19, suggests that vv. 28–39 do not reflect, as is often suggested, the advance of Josiah into the Philistine Plain on the decline of Assyria, which was a living memory to the Deuteronomist, but are the summary of Joshua's 'conquest' in the south corresponding to the summary of his conquests in the north in 11:12–14 by the Deuteronomistic compiler, reflecting the extent of the realm under David and Solomon with which he was familiar.

The Campaign about Gibeon **10:1–15**

1. **Adoni-zedek:** 'My Lord is Zedek', Zedek (*ṣedeq*), found in the form Zuduk (*ṣuduq*) as a divine name in sources relating to Phoenician religion (Philo of Byblos), was an Amorite deity particularly associated with Jerusalem, as indicated by the name Melchizedek,

the king of (Jeru)salem in Gen. 14. LXX gives the name as Adonib-ezek, as in Jg. 1:5ff.; on which, see below.

Jerusalem: the first certain mention of the city in the Old Testament, at least by this name, is attested as Urušalimu in the Egyptian Execration Texts (*c.* 1850 BC), which means probably '(the god) Šalim has founded'. In the Amarna Tablets, from seven letters from its king, it appears as a major Egyptian fief in Palestine under its ruler Abdi-Khepa. On the historical verisimilitude of the alliance of Amorites under Jerusalem against the Israelite penetration of the plateau to the immediate north of the city and the alliance with the Gibeonites, see Introduction to ch. 10, p. 103. It should be noted that after the execution of the king of Jerusalem with the kings of Hebron, Jarmuth, Lachish and Eglon at Makkedah (vv. 24ff.) there is no reference to an attack on Jerusalem.

as he had done to Jericho and its king: cf. 8:2; 10:28, 29, a linking phrase of the pre-Deuteronomic compiler, citing the ban on Jericho in 6:2, though the king is not mentioned there.

2. all its men were mighty: this may refer to the status of the men of Gibeon as a feudal garrison (originally under Egypt), there being no mention of a king; cf. its elders (see on 9:11).

3. Hebron: also called Kiriath-arba (15:13); cf. the ruined site called al-Arba'in on the hill of ar-Rumeideh at Hebron, where there are Late Bronze and Early Iron sherds. The ancient city lay on the south-west slope of the depression occupied by the modern Arab town of al-Khalīl ('The Friend', *sc.* of God; namely, Abraham). Hebron controlled the road south to Beersheba and the head of two passes to the coastal plain, the Wādī 'l-Afranj and the Wādī 's-Sanṭ (Vale of Elah).

Jarmuth: sixteen miles south-west of Jerusalem and *c.* two miles north of the Vale of Elah.

Lachish: Tell ad-Duweir, fifteen miles west of Hebron identified by J. L. Starkey by its location by Eusebius on the Roman road, which runs past the site, and almost certainly confirmed by military and political dispatches to its governor found there in early sixth century debris.

Eglon: not Khirbet 'Ajlun, two miles north-west of Tell al-Ḥesy, which was not occupied before Byzantine times. Verses 34–36 suggest a location between Lachish and Hebron, but it may have lain to the south-east of Lachish, in which case it may be the conspicuous mound of Tell 'Eiṭūn (Noth, *op. cit.*, p. 95), *c.* seven miles south-east of Tell ad-Duweir and ten miles south-west of Hebron. Of other localities conjectured, the most likely is Tell al-Ḥesy seven miles west-south-west of Tell ad-Duweir, where a tablet found in the excavations of F. J. Bliss mentions the king of Lachish.

The kings named are unknown, and **Hoham** is a suspect form and may be a corruption of Horam, given in v. 33 as the king of Gezer.

4. made peace: better, 'established concord'.

5. went up: i.e. from the foothills for the most part to the high plateau. The Old Testament is very punctilious in describing movement in Palestine with its sharply diversified contour.

6–7. The appeal to Joshua at Gilgal indicates the pre-Deuteronomistic compiler.

8. The regular formula of assurance from the oracle in the holy war, recurring in the pre-Deuteronomistic compilation (6:2; 8:1; 11:6) and re-echoed in the Deuteronomistic introduction in 1:1–9.

9. suddenly . . . all night: the Israelite success was owing to movement by night and surprise attack, which suggests that the standing still of the sun and moon (v. 12*b*) of the poetic citation really refers to the anxiety of the Israelites to arrive before daylight rather than for a preternaturally long day to exploit the rout of the enemy, as the prose comment in v. 13*b* adds (see ad loc.).

10. the LORD threw them into a panic: the regular instrument of God in the Holy War (cf. Exod. 14:24; 1 Sam. 7:10). Indeed most of the conflicts in the settlement of Israel in Palestine are represented as being settled by this psychological factor rather than by bitter hand-to-hand fighting.

by way of the ascent of Beth-horon: also called the 'descent' (v. 11). This was one of the few means of access from the north part of the Shephelah and the coastal plain to the plateau north of Jerusalem, where Gibeon lay. The name **Beth-horon** denotes the sanctuary of a god Ḥoron, known from theophoric names in the Execration Texts and from the Rās Shamra texts.

Azekah: Tell az-Zakarīyeh, where the Wādī 's-Sant (the lower part of the Vale of Elah) crosses the north-south depression of the Shephelah.

and unto Makkedah: probably added by the pre-Deuteronomistic compiler to adjust the historical tradition of the pursuit to Azekah to the local aetiological tradition of the Cave of Makkedah (vv. 16–27). The location is uncertain, but probably not at al-Mughār ('the Cave') near Ekron in the Philistine plain, but rather in the foothills east of the main north-south depression, where Eusebius' location ten Roman miles from Eleutheropolis (Beit Jibrīn) and eight miles from Bethshemesh, would suggest the vicinity of Beit Jamāl, where the cave might be identical with any of the large limestone caves of the region.

11. great stones: hailstones as divine weapons (cf. Job 38:22; Rev. 8:7). The pre-Deuteronomistic compiler, consistently with his presentation of the action as the triumph of God, emphasises that more died by the hail than by the sword, not reckoning with the fact that such hail would be as deadly to the pursuers. Such a narrative must be used very carefully as a historical source.

12ff. The pre-Deuteronomistic compiler cites a fragment from a poetic epic no longer extant. Here we must carefully distinguish between poetic citation (vv. 12*b*–13*a*) and the prose, and prosaic, interpretation of the compiler in v. 13*b*. In the former we have a warrior's dramatic appeal, either for more time (more daylight) to exploit the victory, like Agamemnon in the *Iliad* II.412ff., cited by Soggin, *op. cit.*; or, we think, for more darkness to make a surprise attack before sunrise, a common stratagem; cf. v. 9 and the attack of Mesha of Moab on Nebo (E. Ullendorff, *Documents from Old Testament Times*, ed. D. W. Thomas, 1958, p. 197). Here **stand . . . still** means 'be inactive'. The metre seems to demand that **stayed** ought to be omitted in v. 13*a*. The reference might then be to an atmospheric obscuration which masked the advance of the Israelites, as Thothmes III exploited a summer morning mist in his advance on Megiddo in 1479 BC. The hail in v. 11 suggests a dark, cloudy winter morning. Thus the oldest source, the fragment of the Book of Jashar, implies no miracle. This element is only introduced in the prose interpretation of the pre-Deuteronomistic compiler, who emphasises the miraculous throughout to emphasise God's immediate activity in the occupation of the land.

12. Aijalon: modern Yālū, *c.* four miles south of the western end of the pass of Beth-horon, where the Wādī Salmān gives direct and easy access from Gibeon to the Shephelah.

13. until the nation took vengeance on their enemies: better, with Delitzsch, 'until he had avenged himself on the nation of his enemies', positing the omission of *m* (prepositional) after the final *m* of *yiqqôm* ('had avenged').

the Book of Jashar: from this citation, and from David's lament for Saul and Jonathan (2 Sam. 1:18), we see that this work was devoted to warlike exploits, and was probably a national epic, like the Book of the Wars of Yahweh (Num. 21:14f.), with which it may be identical, *yašar* being the first word of the work, by which ancient books were often known (as, for example, the books of the Pentateuch in Jewish tradition). The poetic citation concerning the building of the Temple in 1 Kg. 8:12f. is from 'the Book of the Song' (Hebrew *sēper haššîr*), according to LXX, which may be a scribal corruption of *sēper hayyāšār* ('the Book of Jashar'), by the transposition of two consonants. Thus the Book of Jashar, which contained so many martial exploits, probably culminated in the foundation of the Temple. In the earlier passages it developed the theme of the occupation of the Promised Land, which was represented as the exploit of Yahweh, as the title 'the Book of the Wars of Yahweh' indicates. The theme was rendered into prose by the pre-Deuteronomistic compiler with local aetiological amplifications, coloured by the theme of the occupation of the Promised Land from the cult at Gilgal, at least so far as concerned Jos. 2–10. The citation in 1 Kg. 8:12f., if we are right in our assumption regarding the Book of Jashar, in conjunction with 2 Sam. 1:18, dates the pre-Deuteronomic compilation from at least after the early part of David's reign and probably from after the foundation of the Temple in Solomon's fourth year.

15. This verse is omitted in certain MSS of LXX, presumably because it was felt to be out of place if the following incident at Makkedah was a unity with the story of the campaign at Gibeon. In MT it indicates the fusion of two independent traditions (see introduction to ch. 10).

The Cave of Makkedah **10:16–27**

18. The rock-fall at the cave is explained as evidence of the immurement of the kings; cf. v. 27, where the stones are explained alternatively as being cast on the corpses.

20. fortified cities: lit. 'cities of fortification', the last word indicating that which is cut off abruptly, an impression given by the high crenellated walls about ten feet thick surmounting the steep slopes around the settlement, often reinforced, as at Lachish, by a glacis of stone and earth work faced by limestone plaster at an angle of 29°, a technique introduced in the Hyksos period (*c.* 1750–1600 BC) to counteract the battering-ram (so Y. Yadin). The semi-nomad Israelites had neither the experience or the temperament to make any impression on such defences. With such security, it is preposterous that the kings should have taken refuge in a cave, and this reveals the essentially popular aetiological tradition.

21. moved his tongue: lit. 'sharpened . . .', a figurative expression for 'objected' (cf. Exod. 11:7).

23. On the five towns, see on v. 3 and Introduction, pp. 42f.

24. chiefs: singular *qāṣîn*. Here a military commander (cf. Jg. 11:6, 11, Jephthah); but it is used of a ruler in general (Isa. 1:10, etc.). The assumption that *qāṣîn* is cognate with Arabic *qāḍī* ('judge', lit. 'decider') may be unwarranted since Hebrew *qāṣîn* seems rather a passive participle of a verbal root *qāṣan*.

feet upon the necks: an act of imitative magic which engaged the power of the supernatural to effect the result so depicted, hence operating as potently upon the mind of the ancient Oriental, here the subjects of the kings, as the verbal counterpart, the curse. It was a widespread gesture of domination in antiquity; cf. Assyrian sculpture and the throne of Tutankhamun, with his enemies so represented on the footstool (cf. Ps. 110:1).

25. Cf. the Deuteronomistic introduction 1:1–9, which may nevertheless reproduce the ancient oracle-form.

26. The **five trees** were probably a holy place in popular local religion; cf. an Arab *wēlī*, sometimes a historical person once noted for piety or success, but often a local *numen* associated with springs, rocks or trees, generally conspicuous. Such a feature may have suggested the five kings here and in the Gibeon incident after the fusion of the two tradition-complexes in the pre-Deuteronomistic compilation.

27. at the time of the going down of the sun: see on 8:29. The ritual observance indicates Deuteronomistic elaboration of the pre-Deuteronomistic narrative.

Other Campaigns in the south 10:28–41

28ff. The pre-Deuteronomistic elaboration of the aetiological tradition in vv. 16–27; so Mowinckel (*Tetrateuch, Pentateuch, Hexateuch*, BZAW 90, 1964, p. 39), who regarded the involvement of the five kings in the Gibeonite campaign as the further elaboration of the aetiological tradition of Makkedah. On the relevance or otherwise of local archaeology to this passage, see above, pp. 27f. The fortification of frontier fortresses in the south and west of Judah under Rehoboam (2 Chr. 11:5–10) may have suggested to the pre-Deuteronomistic compiler the devastation that he assumed in vv. 28ff.

utterly destroyed: Hebrew 'laid under the ban' (*ḥerem*), a feature of the tradition of the Holy War, and part of the pre-Deuteronomistic schematisation.

29. Libnah: in the Shephelah (15:42), but of disputed location. The name ('White') suggests Tell aṣ-Ṣāfī ('the Gleaming Mound'), Blanchegarde of the Crusaders, on a limestone bluff where the Wadi 's-Sanṭ debouches on the coastal plain *c.* ten miles north of Lachish. An alternative suggestion is Tell Burnāt in a similar position in the Wādī Jibrīn, six miles further south (Albright, *BASOR* 15, 1924, p. 19; K. Elliger, *PJB* 30, 1934, pp. 58ff.). The archaeological remains at both sites would suit the reference here to Libnah as between Lachish and Makkedah, near Beit Jamāl by Bethshemesh.

33. Horam: the name is exceptional in this section, and may suggest the original of Hoham in v. 3.

Gezer: Tell Jezer, *c.* six miles south of Lydda, excavated by R. A. S. Macalister and latterly by W. Dever. In 16:10 and Jg. 1:29 it is stated that Ephraim could not take Gezer; but this does not contradict the present statement, since the reduction of the place is not stated, but simply the defeat of the forces of Gezer before Lachish. Gezer was probably part of the original local tradition of the five kings associated with the five trees at Makkedah, all of whom would naturally be in the vicinity.

36f. Hebron: belongs properly to the tradition of the battle of Gibeon. The destruction of the place by Joshua is evidently at variance with 15:14, where it is taken by Caleb; so also in the case of Debir (v. 38), taken by Othniel according to 15:16–19; Jg. 1:11–15; but G. E. Wright (*JNES* 5, 1946, pp. 105–114) emphasises the stormy history of most Palestinian sites, including Tell Beit Mirsim, Tell al-Ḥesy and Bethshemesh in the south, between the last quarter of the thirteenth century and the middle of the eleventh century, during which Tell Beit Mirsim, which Albright identified with Debir (most recently in *Archaeology and Old Testament Study*, ed. D. W. Thomas, 1967, pp. 207ff.; but see on vv. 38f.), was destroyed three times.

38f. Debir: located by Albright at Tell Beit Mirsim *c.* thirteen miles south-west of Hebron. Jos. 15:16 and Jg. 1:10–15, however, suggest a location nearer Hebron. Noth (*op. cit.*, p. 90) proposed Khirbet Tarrāmeh in a small well-water plain five miles south-west of Hebron as the region of the 'upper sources, or basins of water' of Jos. 15:19; Jg. 1:15, and Khirbet Rabūḍ, a Late Bronze and Early Iron Age settlement, *c.* three miles further to the south-west as the actual city. On the other hand, there is no mention of Debir (also called Kiriath-sepher) in the Hebron district in the town-lists in Judah (15:52–54), whereas Debir, alternatively named 'Kiriath-sannah', is mentioned in the district of Goshen, where Tell Beit Mirsim is (15:48–51, on which see). The present incident is unlikely in view of the capture of Debir by Othniel and may be a secondary tradition in the pre-Deuteronomistic schematisation suggested by Debir the name of the king of Eglon (v. 3).

40–43. The account of the 'conquest' of south-west Palestine in the pre-Deuteronomistic compilation to which the statement of Joshua's return to Gilgal (v. 43) belongs, is rounded out by the Deuteronomist's summary of the unlikely extermination of 'all that breathed'.

40. Negeb: (etymology unknown) refers to the southern foothills of Judah and the plains about Beersheba to north Sinai, hence generally to the south. It was a common noun for semi-arid country, or steppe, hence its qualification as the Negeb of Arad (Jg. 1:16),

the Negeb of Judah (1 Sam. 27:10) and the Negeb of the Cherethites and the Negeb of Caleb (1 Sam. 30:14).
the slopes: (Hebrew *'ašēdôt*) are 'cliffs', according to G. B. Gray (*Numbers*, ICC, 1903, p. 286), qualified in 12:3 and 13:20 by 'Pisgah', and in Num. 21:15 parallel to 'the valley' by Arnon. It may mean 'off-flow'; cf. the root *šd* ('effluence') in the Rās Shamra texts and *'ašād* ('to flow, pour off') in Aramaic. In the comprehensive description of south Palestine here the term must refer to the land draining to the Dead Sea, which falls steeply away to the east to plunge finally in high cliffs to the Dead Sea.
all that breathed: Hebrew 'all breath', 'all life' or 'every living soul', a Deuteronomistic phrase (cf. Dt. 20:16).

41. Kadesh-barnea (Dt. 1:2): the district in north Sinai around 'Ain Qudeirāt with its *tell*, with remains from the eighth–seventh centuries BC, but probably occupied earlier. A spring in the oasis, about three miles from 'Ain Qudeirāt and called 'Ain Qadeis, preserves the ancient name.
Gaza: the most southerly of the cities occupied in the first half of the twelfth century BC by the Philistines, about two miles from the Mediterranean with outlying fiefs in the foothills of Judah. It was an important post on the trunk highway to Egypt as the last considerable settlement before the desert stages southwards to the Delta. It was the metropolis of north Sinai and the terminal of desert-borne trade with south Arabia.
the country of Goshen: not the marginal land north-east of the Nile Delta (Gen. 46:28). Noth (*JPOS* 15, 1935, pp. 35–44) would identify it with the settlement of Goshen in 15:51, for which he proposed Tell Beit Mirsim, which he regarded as the capital of a city-state Goshen. The use of the definite article before Goshen in 11:16 indicates that it is a common noun, and so it may describe a certain type of country, as often in the local terminology of Palestine, e.g. 'the hill country, the steppe, the lowland and the "off-flow"' (on the subject of regional geography, see D. Baly, *Geographical Companion to the Bible*, 1963, pp. 60ff).

THE CAMPAIGN AT THE WATERS OF MEROM AND THE REDUCTION OF THE NORTH

11:1–23

As in the account of the occupation of the south (ch. 10), the pre-Deuteronomistic compiler has related one incident in the occupation of the north, perhaps in each case the most significant, to present his picture of the occupation of the Promised Land by the direct agency of God. The pattern of his account is the same as in ch. 10, a native coalition (vv. 1–5; cf. 10:1–5) here under a conspicuous leader Jabin of Hazor (cf. Adonizedek of Jerusalem), a reassuring oracle (v. 6; cf. 10:8), a sudden and decisive attack (vv. 7–9; cf. 10:9–14), the over-running of the country and the general destruction of certain towns under the ban (vv. 10–15; cf. 10:28–39) in the convention of the Holy War. The pre-Deuteronomistic compiler closes his account with a general resume of the districts over-run (vv. 16–17; cf. 10:40–42) after which both accounts are rounded out by a general review of the whole land occupied. Here significantly it is admitted that 'Joshua made war a long time with all those kings' (v. 18), by which the compiler indicates that he has not given a detailed account of the occupation, but has selected for detailed treatment what he regarded as the most significant events, or what were emphasised in the celebration of the occupation of the Promised Land in the cult at Gilgal. This prepares us for the hint of the partial and piecemeal nature of the occupation which is given in 15:3; 16:10 and 17:12, which may be adjustments by the Deuteronomistic redactor in harmony with Jg. 1, though citing genuine old traditions. This obviously presented a theological problem to the Deuteronomistic Historian in view of the pre-Deuteronomistic compiler's presentation of the cultic conception of the triumph of God in the occupation of the Promised Land. A solution is offered as in the case of Pharaoh's opposition in the drama of salvation: the resistance of the Canaanites was inspired by Yahweh in order to destroy them more thoroughly (v. 20), which we regard as an expansion by the Deuteronomistic Historian.

Underlying the pre-Deuteronomistic compilation there is what is probably the most reliable historical tradition in the compiler's source material. The tradition is not attached to a sanctuary nor schematised and embellished in the cult nor are there any aetiological features such as are so conspicuous in Jos. 2–10. It is rather a tribal tradition, probably of Naphtali, in whose territory the action is set, at the Waters of Merom. The leading role of Naphtali in the defeat of Sisera (Jg. 4:6–10; 5:18) suggests that at the Waters of Merom, too, they played a leading, if not even the sole, part. The role of Joshua and all Israel is of course a feature of the pre-Deuteronomistic compilation, and the leader was probably a local hero of Naphtali, whose name is now lost, as Noth suggested (*op. cit.*, p. 67). On the historical situation as it may be constructed from biblical evidence and archaeological data, see above, pp. 29f.

The closing section (vv. 21–23) in the comprehensive statement of Joshua's extermination of the Anakim in the south (v. 21) seems to be a late appendix to the pre-Deuteronomistic compilation, further elaborated by the Deuteronomistic Historian in the qualification of his statement in v. 22*b*, the statement of Joshua's fulfilment of Moses' divine commission, the proleptic statement of the apportionment of the land, and the statement that 'the land had rest from war' (v. 23), which recalls the familiar pattern of the Deuteronomistic History in Jg.

1. **Jabin king of Hazor:** 'the king of Canaan' in Jg. 4:2, which is secondary. The prominence of the king of Hazor is supported by the role the city plays in the Amarna Tablets, which show it dominating eastern Galilee and allied with Tyre against Sidon, and in the Mari texts from Mesopotamia (eighteenth–seventeenth centuries BC) it is the only city to be named in Palestine, with one possible exception. This impression is confirmed by the size of the city excavated by Yadin and his colleagues at Tell al-Qadāḥ on the Wādī Waqqās (Y. Yadin, *Hazor* I, 1958; *Hazor* II, 1960). Occupying about 200 acres, this is by far the largest antiquities site in Palestine.
Madon: identified by Albright (*BASOR* 29, 1928, pp. 5ff.) with the Late Bronze and Early Iron Age settlement at Qurn Ḥaṭṭīn above Tiberias, the scene of the decisive victory of Salāh ad-Dīn in 1187. The name survives in Khirbet Madīn, about half a mile south of the site. *mdn* is mentioned in the Karnak lists of Thothmes III with Saruna, Arab Sarūniyeh, the Jewish colony of Sharona, *c.* five miles further south, on the old trade-route east of Tabor to the Great Central Plain. It is also mentioned in the Egyptian stele from Tell al-'Oreimeh (Chinnereth) by the Sea of Galilee, *c.* four miles north-east of Ḥaṭṭīn (Albright and Alan Rowe, *JEA* 14, 1928, pp. 281ff.)
Shimron . . . Achshaph: may be secondary, suggested by Shimron-meron and Achshaph of 12:19ff., like the comprehensive reference to all the districts of Galilee and even 'the heights of Dor' (*RSV*, **Naphoth-dor**) in v. 2. **Achshaph** is generally taken as being near Acco, from the Karnak inscriptions of Thothmes III, either Tell Keisan, *c.* four miles south-south-east of Acco, or at-Tell on the Nahr Mafšūḥ, which may be a metathesis of Achshaph. But if **Shimron** is identical with Shimron-meron, this may be Mārūn ar-Rās, *c.* ten miles north-west of Ṣafad, in which case Achshaph here may be Tell Iksīf, *c.* five miles east of this site.

2. **the Arabah south of Chinneroth:** the depression by the Sea of Galilee, south of the town of Chinnere(o)th (Tell al-'Oreimeh), which dominates the small harp-shaped Plain of Chinnereth at the mouth of the Wādī 'l-Hammām and the Wādī 'l-'Amūd (possibly the Waters of Merom) from the north. Chinnereth was occupied from the Late Bronze Age and is listed by Thothmes III at Karnak. The Arabah proper is the Jordan Valley (cf. 8:14), the northern

part of which is probably included here, as in 12:3, and which, from the evidence of two of the Amarna Letters from the king of Piḫili (modern Fiḥl, Pella beyond Jordan, east of Bethshan), was dominated by Hazor (Alt, 'Neues Über Palästine aus dem Archiv Amenophis IV', *KS* III, 1959, pp. 166–8).

Naphoth-dor: 'the heights of Dor', i.e. the foothills of Carmel. Dor, located at Khirbet Burj atṬanṭūra, with Late Bronze Age remains, was a settlement of the Ṯekel, a people associated with the Philistines *c.* 1100 BC. It is probably secondary here after 12:23.

3. the Canaanites in the east and the west: i.e. the Jordan Valley and the coastal plain, where Num. 13:29 specifically locates them. The **Jebusites** in this context indicates that the list is automatically cited by the Deuteronomistic Historian as descriptive of the pre-Israelite inhabitants of Palestine, since the Jebusites are associated only with Jerusalem.

the Hivites, in view of LXX *Chorraioi* (though not here), must always be problematical. Their location **under Hermon** may suggest a non-Semitic people, the Hurrians from the far north-east.

the land of Mizpah: not certainly known in this district (east of Jordan). Mizpah ('Watchpost') is a common name in Palestine and beyond.

4. chariots: the light war-chariot and horse were introduced to Asia by the Aryans *c.* 1800 BC., becoming thereafter the basis of tactical warfare. They were associated with a king in a feudal system, now well illustrated in the administrative texts from Rās Shamra, in which *mariannu* (equestrian feudatories—an Aryan word), have special privileges and duties under the king. The Rās Shamra texts also show that the Canaanite chariots had two horses and one reserve, and Egyptian and Hebrew texts indicate that the chariot team consisted of the driver and a warrior, as distinct from the Hittite team which included a third man as shield-bearer. An Egyptian text reveals that in rough country, such as the mountains of Galilee, the chariot was dismantled and reassembled in suitable terrain (Papyrus of Hori, thirteenth century BC.; J. A. Wilson, *ANET*, ed. Pritchard, 1950, p. 477).

5. the waters of Merom: not Lake Hūleh, but either Meirūn, *c.* four miles west of Safad, on the edge of the plain of Upper Galilee, where there is Late Bronze and Early Iron Age debris (Albright, *BASOR* 35, 1929, p. 8), or the more conspicuous *tell* of Mārūn ar-Rās, *c.* nine miles further north (Y. Aharoni, 'Problems of the Israelite Conquest', *Antiquity and Survival* II, 1957, pp. 142–50); cf. *mrm* of Thothmes' Karnak lists. If Merom is Meirūn, **the waters of Merom** may be the Wadi which runs from there to the Sea of Galilee in the Plain of Chinnereth; but as this is a mere winter-torrent, 'the waters' are possibly permanent springs about Meirūn or Mārūn ar-Rās. The occasion for hostilities was probably the emergence of the Israelites or their forebears in their penetration from the scrub-land on the escarpment to the south to the fertile plateau of Upper Galilee, to which Meirūn is the gateway (see General Introduction, p. 30).

6. Note again the reassuring oracle as a feature of the Holy War (cf. 6:2; 8:18; 10:8), with the declaratory, or prophetic, perfect of divine certainty.

hamstring: a denominative verb, 'to cut the sinew' (Gen. 49:6). So Israel dealt with the horses of the Aramaeans at Rabbath-Ammon (2 Sam. 8:4).

7. suddenly: probably a genuine tradition, in spite of the general conformity of the description of the northern campaign to that of the south in ch. 10 (esp. 10:9–15). In terrain probably chosen by the Canaanites for chariot warfare, surprise would be necessary, probably a night attack, when the chariots could not be used and the horses could be put into a panic. Perhaps the hamstringing of the picketed horses and the burning of the chariots at night was the main part of the Israelite strategy. Significantly no actual battle is described.

8. chased them as far as Great Sidon: this locates the action on the plateau of Upper Galilee (see on v. 5), from which access to the territory of Sidon was relatively easy. The line of flight was towards Sidon, the great Phoenician seaport and to Mishrephoth-maim, Khirbet al-Musheirifeh, a Bronze Age site just south of Rās an-Nāqūra at the present Lebanese–Israeli frontier. In **Mishrephoth-maim**, 'maim', with a change of vowel, may mean 'from the west' (lit. 'from the sea'), indicating for the pre-Deuteronomistic compiler the extent of Israelite domination 'from the sea' **and eastward as far as the valley of Mizpah** (east of the upper Jordan); cf. v. 3.

9. This may be an editorial epilogue, which apparently misunderstands the hamstringing of the Canaanites' horses and the burning of their chariots as *after* the action at the Waters of Merom (cf. on v. 6).

10–20. In the over-running of the country and the general destruction, schematised on the pattern of 10:29–39, the nucleus of historical fact is the destruction of Hazor, which is attested by Yadin's excavations as *c.* 1225 BC, being followed by two very modest settlements on the citadel in the eleventh and twelfth centuries, before the rebuilding of the city under Solomon. In v. 10 **turned back** is significant. The capture of the enormous site of Hazor within its revetted perimeter by direct assault was beyond the men of Naphtali. In representing the fall of the place as in consequence of defeat in the field at some distance from the city the tradition is surely true to historical fact; cf. the view of Noth that the tradition of the ruin of Hazor has arisen from the known fact of its dereliction from the end of the Bronze Age till its resettlement under Solomon.

13. on mounds: Hebrew sing. *tēl* (cf. Arabic *tell* in place-names), signifying a mound built up of the debris of ancient settlements. In view of the statements on the general destruction of the associates of Hazor in accordance with the divine commission through Moses in vv. 12 and 15 (the exception being vv. 13 and 14, which state that only Hazor was actually destroyed and emphasise the modified ban; cf. on 8:27), we regard vv. 10, 11, 13 and 14 as being from the pre-Deuteronomistic compiler and vv. 12 and 15 from the Deuteronomistic Historian.

14. *RSV* involves a slight textual emendation.

16. The description of **all that land** begins with the districts of the south, **the hill country and all the Negeb and all the land of Goshen and the lowland** referring to Judah (see on 10:40f.). The **Arabah** might, as at the present time, be the depression from the Dead Sea to the Gulf of Aqaba; but, as usual in the Old Testament, it refers to the Jordan Valley, hence it is to be considered with the hill country of Israel and its lowland (i.e. foothills in the west). 'The hill country of Israel', as distinct from 'hill country' in v. 16*a*, refers to north Israel, and dates the passage and the pre-Deuteronomistic compilation, to which it belongs, after the Disruption of Solomon's kingdom in 931 BC. (see General Introduction, p. 8).

17. Mount Halak: *ḥālāq* is actually an adjective, 'slippery, bare'. This is an undefined feature in the south of Palestine (**that rises towards Seir**), and may be the modern Jebel Ḥalāq, *c.* forty miles south-west of the south end of the Dead Sea. Seir, however, may also denote Edom, which occasionally extended west of the Arabah, as in Dt. 1:44.

Baal-gad in the valley of Lebanon (cf. 12:7) **below Mount Hermon** (cf. 13:5): this seems the fusion of the traditions of two places Baal-gad, that below Hermon (13:5), possibly at Bāniās, later the shrine of Pan, and the other at Ba'albek in the Biq'a ('Plain') between Lebanon and Antilebanon (Eissfeldt, *F. und F.* 12, 1936, pp. 51ff.). Both were notable shrines in the Graeco-Roman period and probably much earlier. The inclusion of Ba'albek, if that location is correct, may reflect the extent of David's influence 'to the approaches to Hamath'. The other would correspond to Dan as the northern limit of Israel in the conventional description 'from Dan to Beersheba'.

20. harden their hearts: 'make strong, obdurate' (cf. Exod. 4:21).

On the character of this verse as theological apologetic on the part of the Deuteronomistic Historian, see Introduction to ch. 11, p. 113.

21–23. *General appendix*, vv. 21–22*a* being an earlier appendix to the pre-Deuteronomistic compilation, from the divided Monarchy, as indicated by the distinction between the hill-country of Judah and the hill-country of Israel, and the rest from the Deuteronomistic Historian (see Introduction to ch. 11, pp. 113f).

Anakim: according to Arabic etymology, 'tall men'; according to Hebrew etymology, possibly 'necklace-' or 'pendant-folk' (cf. Ca. 4:9; Jg. 8:26; Prov. 1:9). In this case the appellative, usually *bᵉnê hāʿᵃnāqîm*, has become a pseudo-gentilic. A possible connection with the rulers of Iy-ʿanaq in the Egyptian Execration Texts from the nineteenth century BC, an unknown locality in the south of Palestine, has been suggested by J. A. Wilson, *ANET*, p. 328*b*. In the Old Testament they are usually associated with Hebron, as here and in 14:12; 15:13f. (cf. Dt. 1:28; Num. 13:22, 28, 33).

22. Gaza . . . Gath . . . Ashdod: three of the five Philistine cities in the south of the coastal plain of Palestine. **Gaza** and **Ashdod** (Isdūd) retain their ancient names. The location of **Gath** is uncertain and complicated by the fact that Gath was a compound in several place-names, indicating that it was a common noun, like *gt* in country properties listed in the administrative texts from Rās Shamra. One of those places was associated with Ashdod, Ekron and Yabneh in an inscription of Sargon II of Assyria (D. D. Luckenbill, *Ancient Records of Assyria* II, 62) and was evidently at a point where an expedition might deviate from the coastal plain to Jerusalem (2 Kg. 12:17). Mazar identifies this Gath with an Early Iron Age site Rās Abū Ḥamīd by Ramleh, which is probably Gath-rimmon, north of Jaffa, in the territory allocated to Dan in Jos. 19:45. The Gath in the list of Rehoboam's fortifications in the Shephelah (2 Chr. 11:8), associated with Adullam and Mareshah suggests the Iron Age site Tell Burnāt (see above, on 10:29) two miles north-west of Beit Jibrīn (Mareshah), which would suit the association with Gaza in the Philistine domination. The location of Philistine Gath to Gaza near the coast would thus correspond to the inland site of Ekron on a pass to the interior by the Wādī 's-Surār *vis-à-vis* Ashdod. The association of those places with the survivors of **the Anakim** in v. 22 may have been suggested to the Deuteronomistic Historian by the taller Philistine race, which included Goliath of Gath (1 Sam. 17:4; cf. 2 Sam. 21:18–11).

23. This verse summarises the two halves of the book of Jos., the Conquest (Jos. 1–12) and the Apportionment of the Land (Jos. 13–24). The writer therefore knew the book as a whole and integrated it with Dt.; hence he was the Deuteronomistic Historian, as indeed the representation of Joshua's work as the fulfilment of God's word to Moses indicates.

A SUMMARY OF THE CONQUEST WITH A LIST OF THE CONQUERED KINGS

12:1–24

This section is from the Deuteronomistic Historian, partly from materials in the pre-Deuteronomistic compilation, as in 10:23–39 and 11:16–20. Thus the superscription to the list of conquered kings west of the Jordan (vv. 7–8*a*) is based on events in 11:16*a*, 17*a*, 23*a* (with 10:40), while vv. 9–13*a* summarise the result of events described in Jos. 6–10. For the rest of the conquered kings, the Deuteronomist either depends on an independent list, possibly an administrative town-list, such as a fiscal list from the time of the Monarchy like that used in 1 Kg. 4:7–19, or he supplements in free composition in vv. 14–24. In the list of conquests beyond Jordan in vv. 1–6 and in his description of the general extent of the land he reconstructs from matter incorporated in Dt.

The Occupation beyond Jordan **12:1–6**

The extent of the land occupied beyond Jordan is described **from the valley of the Arnon**, the deep gorge of the Wādī Mūjib, the natural, but always disputed, northern boundary of Moab (v. 2), to **Hermon** and the eastern part of the Jordan Valley (**the Arabah**), including the Amorite kingdom of Sihon, whose capital was at Heshbon (see on 9:10).

2. Aroer: Khirbet 'Arā'ir on the north bank of the precipitous Wādī Mūjib, a canyon in places *c.* 1,700 feet deep and two miles wide, which drains into the Dead Sea.

and from the middle of the valley: the text is probably defective; cf. in the same context in 13:16 and Dt. 2:36, '. . . and the city that is in the middle of the valley', always with the conjunction, which suggests that a separate place from Aroer is indicated, namely, the south-west boundary point, probably half-way between Aroer and the mouth of the Arnon. The fact that no name is given to such a well-defined place suggests that *'ir* in 13:16 and Dt. 2:36, which may have dropped out of v. 2, means not city, but 'fortified watch-post'. This being so, the identification of the place is difficult; but it would be one of the few crossing-places on the lower Arnon, possibly about 'Ain al-Buṣeileh, where the Wadi enters its precipitous gorge *c.* six miles west of Khirbet 'Arā'ir and *c.* ten miles from its mouth; or, as Noth suggested (*op. cit.*, p. 79), about Khirbet al-Ḥušreh, *c.* two miles from the mouth of the Arnon, where a ford is just possible.

Gilead: a district, and probably a geographical term, as the definite article here and occasionally elsewhere suggests; cf. Arabic *jal'ad* ('hard, strong'). The name survives in Jebel Jal'ad, sixteen miles north-west of Amman. The region was divided by the lower course of the **Jabbok** (Nahr Zarqā). The Jabbok, as the boundary with the Ammonites, refers to the upper course of the wadi, which rises west of Ammān and runs through the city north-east, then north-west until it runs west to the Jordan.

On **Sihon**, the Amorite king of Heshbon, and Og of Bashan (v. 4), see above, on 9:10.

Ammonites: always referred to by the tribal designation 'sons of Ammon', they developed a kingdom with its capital at Rabbath-Ammon (modern Ammān); but beyond this they never developed an urban civilisation.

3. Arabah: the Jordan Valley.

the Sea of Chinneroth: better, 'Chinnereth', after LXX (see above, on 11:1).

the sea of the Arabah, the Salt Sea: the Dead Sea (see on 3:16).

Beth-jeshimoth: (cf. 13:20; Num. 33:49), located by Eusebius (*Onomasticon*) ten Roman miles south-east of Jericho, near the Dead Sea. Its name may have survived in Suweimeh, north-east of the northern end of the Dead Sea, where a low tell, Tell al-'Azaimeh, has debris of the Early and Late Bronze and of the Iron Ages (F. M. Abel, *GP* II, p. 272).

slopes of Pisgah: perhaps 'off-flow', see on 10:40. **Pisgah**, the massif, of which Nebo (Rās as-Siyāghah) is the summit, dominates the northern end of the Dead Sea from the east.

4. Bashan: a common noun, as the definite article indicates. Possibly from a root cognate with Arabic *baṯana* ('to be smooth'), referring to the fertile upland plains of the Hauran about Der'ā (**Edrei**) and **Ashtaroth** (Tell 'Ashtara; see on 9:10; cf. Dt. 1:4) *c.* fifteen miles north of Der'ā. The kingdom of **Og** is envisaged as extending to the south-east slopes of Hermon, which dominates the Hauran, and to the broken lava country to the east (Jebel Druze). It is not certain that it extended as far as the strongly fortified city of Salkhad (biblical **Salecah**), actually high up in the Jebel Druze to the north-east. What is meant is that this kingdom bordered that region.

the Rephaim: probably not an ethnic term. It is known from Phoenician inscriptions and from the Rās Shamra texts as 'the shades of the dead', from which the conception of a vanished race may be developed. In a ritual text from Rās Shamra defunct kings are termed *rp'um*, and the ancient king Dn'il is termed *mt rp'i*, exercising rites to restore fertility (cf. the Hebrew verb *rāpā'*, Gen. 20:17; 2 Kg. 2:21).

5. Geshurites . . . and . . . Maacathites: Aramaean tribal groups east of the land settled by the Israelites from the Hauran to the lower Jabbok, though there was apparently no fixed boundary, those groups probably having seasonal grazings among the Israelites (13:13). From the former came the mother of Absalom (2 Sam. 3:3). The latter fought with other Aramaean groups against Israel at Rabbath-Ammon (2 Sam. 10:6) and left their name in the site of Abel Beth-maacah (Tell Ibl al-Qamḥ), under two miles south of Metullah, on the present Israeli-Lebanese border.

6. the Reubenites and the Gadites and the half-tribe of Manasseh: see on 13:15–32.

Comprehensive Description of the Land west of the Jordan, by Regions **12:7–8**

For details, see on 11:16f.

8. the wilderness: i.e. of Judah, the land sloping from Bethlehem and Tekoa to the Dead Sea (15:61) and apparently also the slopes east of Beersheba and the Arabah (Jg. 1:16). This region, lying in the rain-shadow, is mainly abandoned to seasonal grazing. Verse 8*b* is a late addition to the passage.

Catalogue of the Defeated Kings **12:9–24**

Not all of these were killed; 'smote' (v. 7) in Hebrew means **defeated** (so *RSV*) as well as 'killed'.

9–13*a*. The kings are mentioned in chs. 6–10, i.e. of **Jericho** (6:1ff.), **Ai** (7:2ff.), **Jerusalem** (10:3, not itself taken), **Hebron** (10:36; but cf. 15:13f., where it was taken by Caleb, and Jg. 1:10, where it was the objective of an attack by Judah), **Jarmuth** (10:3), **Lachish** (10:31), **Eglon** (10:34), **Gezer** (10:33, not itself taken), and **Debir** (10:38; but cf. 15:15–19 and Jg. 1:11–15, which attribute its fall to Othniel).

13*b*–16*a*. The south-east and the Shephelah ('the lowland'), which includes **Libnah** (10:29) and **Makkedah** (10:28) from the passage on the sequel to the battle of Gibeon, and, from an unknown source or from free composition, **Geder** (unknown, and possibly a corruption of Gezer), **Hormah** (Num. 14:45; Jg. 1:16f.; on which, see below), **Arad** (Num. 21:1; Jg. 1:16f., on which see below), Tell 'Arad, *c.* 23 miles east of Beersheba, and **Adullam** (Gen. 38:1; 1 Sam. 22:1), Tell Sheikh Madhkūr by Khirbet 'Id al-Mā, which may preserve the ancient name, *c.* ten miles east-north-east of Beit Jibrīn.

16*b*–18. the central highlands and coastal plain, including **Bethel** (8:17, but not mentioned as taken, except in Jg. 1:22ff.), **Tappuah** (16:18, Tell Sheikh Abū Zarad by Yasūf (cf. 17:7, LXX, *c.* eight miles south-south-west of Nāblus, **Hepher**, aṭ-Ṭayibeh, under four miles south of Ṭulkarm, according to Alt, *KS* I, 1953, p. 128n.), but probably secondary, being found as a clan in 17:2 (cf. Num. 26:32ff.); cf. 'the land of Hepher' in Solomon's third fiscal district (1 Kg. 4:10), **Aphek**, the Philistine base in their advance against Israel in the central highlands in 1 Sam. 4:1, usually identified with Rās al-'Ain, as the name Aphek ('Spring') suggests, where Israeli excavations have revealed a Canaanite city destroyed, possibly by the Philistines. This may be the Aphek mentioned in Egyptian inscriptions of the fifteenth century BC. (*ANET*, pp. 243, 246). **Lasharon** ('belonging to Sharon') is not the seat of a king, but, as LXX implies, it defines Aphek, which, being a fairly common place-name, requires such definition.

19–23. Galilee, including **Madon, Hazor, Shimron-meron** and **Achshaph** from 11:1f., **Taanach** (17:11; 21:25), Tell Ta'anek, 24 miles south-east of Haifa at the north-east end of a pass through the south-east extension of the Carmel ridge, **Megiddo (17:11)**, Tell al-Mutasallim, commanding a main pass through the same hills from the coastal plain to the Great Central Plain, *c.* five miles north-west of Taanach, **Kedesh** (19:37), Qedeis in Upper Galilee, eleven miles north of Safad, and so out of context here, like Tirzah (v. 24), **Jokneam in Carmel** (19:11; 21:34), Tell Qeimūn, commanding the most westerly pass through the hills from the coastal plain to the Great Central Plain, six miles north-west of Megiddo, **Dor** on the coast in the north of the Plain of Sharon (see on 11:2), **Goim in Galilee** ('nations in Galilee'), possibly a scribal corruption of 'Harosheth Haggoiim' (cf. Jg. 4:2ff.) at the western end of the Great Central Plain, possibly Tell al-'Amāṛ or Tell al-Harbāj by al-Ḥārithīyeh, *c.* eight miles south-east of Haifa, which may have preserved the ancient name. On Galilee, see on 15:7.

24. Tirzah (Tell al-Far'a, *c.* seven miles north-east of Nablus) stands strangely at the end of the list, quite out of context, and is obviously secondary. Here, and in Jos. 2–11, Shechem is a notable exception, which agrees with archaeological data, Shechem being undisturbed at the end of the Late Bronze Age.

2. THE APPORTIONMENT OF THE LAND

13:21

See Introduction, pp. 44–46. This, the second section of Jos., is presented as the development of the role of Joshua in carrying out Moses' design for the partition of the land in Dt. 1:38; 3:28 and in the Priestly tradition in Num. 27:18–23; 32:17 and 34:17, where, as in Jos. 14:1 from the post-Exilic redaction of the Deuteronomistic History, Joshua is subordinate to the priest Eleazar. This, however, does not exclude earlier sources. There was a strong tradition of tribal boundaries well defined in pre-Monarchical times and probably applied in local arbitration. Those were to a considerable extent recognised in Solomon's administrative division of the realm (1 Kg. 4:7–19). Where those were non-existent or indefinite, as in the case of Simeon in the Negeb, the former territory of Dan after their northward migration, and the lands of the Galilean tribes, the Deuteronomistic Historian supplemented by town-lists from administrative documents from the Monarchy, certainly from the time of Josiah (so Alt) and probably also from the time of Jehoshaphat (see Cross and Wright) and in Galilee, possibly from lists in the Assyrian provinces in the late eighth and seventh centuries BC. The lists of cities of refuge (Jos. 20), though probably not based on such a documentary source, preserve a tradition which could be as old as the settlement of Israel, and the lists of Levitical settlements (Jos. 21) may be based on the settlement of Levites throughout the realm under David, Solomon and Rehoboam (see Introduction, pp. 47–51). The priority of Judah (14:6–15:63) and Joseph (16:1–17:18) reflects the status of those two groups as the main elements of the south and north Kingdoms when that was a recent memory, which might suggest the end of the Monarchy, when we should date the compilation of the Deuteronomistic History as distinct from its post-Exilic continuation and redaction (see General Introduction, pp. 6–9).

Traditions of the tribal settlement are also incorporated in circumstantial narrative style, e.g. 14:6–13; 15:13–19 (cf. Jg. 1:11–15) and 17:14–18. This is quite exceptional in Jos. 13–21 and may represent adjustments by the redactor, drawing partly on Jg. 1 and partly on ancient local traditions of the settlement.

Those various elements were combined by the Deuteronomistic Historian, but editorial activity continued until the redaction of the work in the Exile, and certain of the more obvious interpolations, such as the role of Eleazar the priest in the apportionment, may be from this time.

INTRODUCTION TO THE APPORTIONMENT OF THE LAND

13:1–33

The Deuteronomistic Historian is well aware that certain districts within the ideal limits of the Promised Land which were included in his documentary sources from the administrative lists of the Monarchy were not occupied by Israel in the days of the settlement, and this is specially mentioned (vv. 1–6) in the context of a general introduction to the apportionment west of Jordan.

1. advanced in years: the same verb is used of the setting of the sun. In 24:29 Joshua is said to have been 110 at his death.
remains: this may have referred to districts within Palestine yet to be subdued (cf. 15:14–19; cf. Jg. 1:10–15; Jos. 15:63; 16:10; 17:11–13, and generally in Jg. 1:19ff.). The inclusion of cities in the Philistine Plain in administrative texts from the time of Josiah used by the Deuteronomist for his description of the territory of Judah suggests the inclusion of this district as yet to be conquered in vv. 2–4, excluding the asyndetic 'it is reckoned as Canaanite' and 'those of the Avvim in the south (cf. Dt. 2:23), all the land of the Canaanites' (vv. 3*b*–4*a*). A later expansion mentioned **Me-arah** ('the Cave') **which belongs to the Sidonians** (v. 4), perhaps the port of Athlit, behind which is the Wādī 'l-Mughāreh ('Valley of the Cave'). This may have suggested **Aphek** beyond the Carmel Head in the Plain of Acco (cf. 19:30 = Jg. 1:31), perhaps confused with another Aphek, Tell al-Mukhmār by Rās al-'Ain, the limit of Philistine rule. A later redactor misunderstood this Aphek in conjunction with 'the Sidonians' as 'Afqā at the source of the River Adonis (Nahr Ibrāhīm) between Beirut and Byblos (Gebal), hence the reference to Lebanon and adjacent districts in vv. 5f. The southern border of Lebanon at 'Mishrephoth-maim' is possibly suggested by the representation of the occupation of Galilee in 11:8 (on which see). The primary reference of this passage to the Philistine country is indicated by the specific enumeration of their cities. The definition of Aphek with regard to the boundary of the Amorites suggests the boundary between the Philistines and the Amorites in the foothills of the mountains of central Palestine, where the Amorites are specifically located (Num. 13:29; Jg. 1:34–36, on which see).

2. regions: Hebrew *gᵉlîlôt*, possibly 'circuits', from the root *gālal* ('to roll'), but possibly from some unknown root; cf. 'Galilee', or 'Galilee of the nations', possibly so called from the Great Central Plain 'ringed' about with great Canaanite fortresses, and secondarily including the hills to the north.
Philistines: Pulusatu, mentioned among the 'Sea Peoples' in Egyp-

tian records from the fifteenth to the thirteenth centuries, who were halted in their great trek through Syria and Palestine towards Egypt in the early part of the twelfth century by Ramses III and settled in the coastal plain of Palestine, possibly as Egyptian vassals in a feudal system based on five great fiefs, Gaza, Ashkelon, Ashdod, Gath and Ekron, where they were settled before the consolidation of Israel, whom they effectively barred from the coastal plain.
Geshurites: probably a tribal name; cf. 1 Sam. 27:8, where they are located south-east of Gaza. They are not to be confused with the Geshurites of Hauran (v. 11; 12:5; Dt. 3:14).

3. **the Shihor:** an Egyptian word denoting a lagoon, or part of the eastern branch of the Nile delta, perhaps 'the Pool of Horus' on the Egyptian military road to Palestine (L. Koehler, *ZAW*, N.F. 13, 1936, pp. 289–91; J. A. Wilson, *ANET* 1950, p. 471).
rulers: Hebrew *s^eränîm*. Used in the Old Testament only of the Philistines, hence probably a Philistine loanword, thought to be the Greek *tyrannos* ('tyrant', 'autocrat'), which would accord with the probable provenance of the Philistines and certain of their associates among the Sea Peoples from the Balkans, which a certain amount of archaeological evidence supports.
Avvim: cf. Dt. 2:23, where they are said to have been dispossessed by the Philistines in the vicinity of Gaza. There they are said to be associated with 'enclosures' (*RSV*, 'villages'), possibly drystone sheepfolds common in a region exposed to desert raiders. Such folds with converging entry-walls are illustrated in the Egyptian Narmer palette together with a walled fortress, from both of which Semites flee naked (*ANEP*, Fig. 296; see further, on v. 23).

4. **south:** lit. 'right hand', implying orientation to the east; cf. Yemen.
Me-arah: see on v. 1.
Aphek: see on v. 1.

5. A secondary expansion. See on v. 1.
Baal-gad below Hermon: see on 11:17.
the entrance of Hamath: the conventional description of the northern boundary of Israel (cf. 1 Kg. 8:65; Am. 6:2); cf. Num. 13:21, 'from the wilderness of Zin to Rehob towards Hamath'. This definition probably originated with the description of the area controlled by David, who subjugated the Aramaeans about Damascus and in the Valley (al-Biq'a) between Lebanon and Antilebanon, but excluding Hamath on the Orontes, whose king Toi made a timely peace (2 Sam. 8:10). It is suggested that **the entrance** (Hebrew *l^ebô'*) should be rendered as a place-name, i.e. Lebweh, *c.* seventy miles south-west of Ḥamā; but this may be a coincidence, and we prefer to render more generally 'the Hamath approaches'.

Except in the time of David this description of the northern extent of Israel was more ideal than real.

6. I myself will drive them out: 'Will dispossess', thus causing others to possess.

Digression on Moses' Apportionment of the Land East of Jordan **13:8–32**

This is prompted by the reference to Joshua's apportionment of the land west of Jordan to the nine tribes and the half-tribe of Manasseh west of Jordan (v. 7), the main theme of the second part of Jos. (chs. 14–19). LXX indicates a different reading from MT, reading after 'the half-tribe of Manasseh' at the end of v. 7, 'From the Jordan to the Great Sea in the direction of the sunset will you give it. The Great Sea shall be the boundary. To the (two) tribes and to the half of the tribe of Manasseh, to Reuben and to Gad Moses gave (their portion) beyond Jordan . . .'. This implies an omission in MT. The nucleus of the passage may be from the Deuteronomistic Historian, but it is probably expanded by redactional glosses. Verses 8–13 give a general summary of the regions in the whole of Transjordan occupied by Reuben, Gad and eastern Manasseh, followed by vv. 15–23, describing the land occupied by Reuben, and by vv. 24–28, the land occupied by Gad, and by vv. 29–31, the land attributed to eastern Manasseh. The particular allotments in vv. 15–31 include rough boundaries, lacking the detail of the tribal allotments in chs. 14–19, and settlements, which recall Num. 32:33–42 (JE). The note on Levi in v. 33, which is omitted in LXX, may be a redactional, possibly Priestly, interpolation being added after the notice on Levi in v. 14. This verse also seems redactional from the abrupt introduction and the exceptive particle and the treatment of Levi as a tribe. This is further suggested by the emphasis in v. 14 on the purely priestly prerogatives of Levi and their perquisites from the cult, and by the theologoumenon in v. 33, 'the Lord, the God of Israel, is his inheritance' (cf. Num. 18:20 (P); Dt. 10:9; 18:2 (redactional); Ezek. 36:12 (of all Israel).

For topographical details in vv. 1–14 and affinities with the Pentateuch, see on 9:10 and on vv. 15–32.

14. offerings by fire: Hebrew *'iššîm*, the priests' perquisites (Dt. 18:1; 1 Sam. 2:28). The word is assumed in *RSV* to be derived from 'fire' (*'ēš*); but the double consonant makes this doubtful.

The Particular Apportionment to Reuben, Gad and Half (east) Manasseh **13:15–32** (cf. Num. 32:34–38)

see Introduction to 13:8–32

Reuben **13:15–23**
See General Introduction to Jos. and Jg., p. 12.

The tribal boundaries are incomplete (vv. 16–17*a*, 23), and are supplemented by a town-list from the early Monarchy (vv. 17*b*–20), with redactional expansion (vv. 21f., after Dt. and Num. 31:8ff.).

16. Aroer, which is on the edge of the valley of the Arnon: apparently the south-eastern boundary point (see on 12:2).
the city that is in the middle of the valley: probably the south-west boundary point; see on 12:2.
Medeba . . . Heshbon (v. 17): define the eastern boundary, **Heshbon** being the north-eastern boundary point, as v. 26 indicates. **Medeba** is the populous Arab town of Mādabā, twenty miles south-west of Ammān, and **Heshbon** is at or by Hesban, six miles farther north.

17. all its cities that are in the tableland: i.e. the large fertile plain on the plateau between the escarpment above the Dead Sea and the desert. This envisages Heshbon as the capital of Sihon's kingdom, and may indicate the adaptation of town-lists from the Monarchy to tribal boundary-lists by the Deuteronomist (so Noth, *op. cit.*, p. 79).

17–20. Dibon: cf. Num. 32:34; in the south of the plain south of Heshbon, the native place of Mesha king of Moab, whose inscription (*c.* 835 BC) was found there. Of the other settlements, few are conspicuous. **Beth-baal-meon** is probably Mā'īn, *c.* five miles south-west of Mādāba, being mentioned with Qiryathān (Kiriathaim, v. 19) in Mesha's inscription (l.10), which is thus not Khirbet al-Qureiyāt (Qeriyot), Mesha's capital south of the Arnon, mentioned in his inscription (l.13), but in the vicinity of Mādabā, where Eusebius locates it ten Roman miles westward. **Sibmah** (v. 19) is located by A. Musil at Khirbet Sūmīyeh *c.* five miles north-west of Heshbon, which is the proper direction but not the proper site, as the archaeological debris indicates; cf. Noth's location (*op. cit.*, pp. 7f.), after N. Glueck, at Khirbet Qurn al-Kibš, *c.* 6½ miles north-west of Mādabā.

19. Zareth-shahar on the hill of the valley: the hill of the valley (Hebrew, *hā'ēmeq*) is probably the mountain overlooking the Jordan Valley, to which only the word *'ēmeq* in this region is applicable.

This would be the Pisgah massif (cf. v. 20), of which the highest point is Mount Nebo, identified traditionally with Rās as-Siyāghah. This and the association with **Kiriathaim** and Sibmah, suggests the location of Zareth-shahar there.

20. Beth-peor: located by Eusebius six Roman miles above Livias (Tell ar-Ramah) in the Jordan Valley, east of the lower Jordan; hence in the plain watered by the 'off-flow from Pisgah' (see on 10:40), with which it is associated in Moses' death and burial (Dt. 34:6). It was probably on the slopes of the mountain mass, from which it overlooked the valley of the lower Jordan (Num. 23:28). It was also a sanctuary (Num. 25:1–3), where the Israelites cohabited with the women of Moab. This indicates perhaps its significance as a boundary-sanctuary in the early days of the Hebrew settlement. **Beth-jeshimoth:** probably Tell al-'Azeimeh, two miles east-north-east of Khirbet as-Suweimeh in the plain, east of the lower Jordan (see on 12:3).

21f. Redactional after Num. 31:8. **The leaders of Midian** are *n^{e}śī'îm* (lit. 'those raised up'), the term describing tribal headmen in Israel in Numbers (P), the king in Ezekiel's sketch of the new Israel and, as here, the chiefs of Ishmael (Gen. 25:13–26

23. villages: 'enclosures', sheepfolds or the like, from a root better known in this sense in Arabic (see on v. 3). These folds with converging entry-walls to facilitate gathering in raids from the desert are still a feature of the region (Eissfeldt, 'Gabelhürden im Ostjordanland', *F. und F.* 25, 1949, pp. 9–11).

Gad **13:24–28**

See above, p. 12.

The town-list of Gad is not at all full, except in the Jordan Valley (v. 27*a*), in spite of the notice of 'all the cities of Gilead', which may have headed such a list. Here the tribal land is described first by districts. **Jazer** (v. 25) is probably a district rather than a town (cf. Num. 21:32) in the region, probably south of as-Salṭ (cf. 2 Sam. 24:5). **Gilead** (v. 25) is here, as the definite article indicates, a common noun, a geographical term, conserved in the Jebel Jil'ād, sixteen miles north-west of Ammān. In this context, **Aroer** (v. 25), which is defined as **east of Rabbah** ('Ammān), which is in this case 'opposite' rather than 'east' (and is actually to the west), as distinct from the Aroer on the edge of the Arnon gorge, defined the border between Ammon and Gad in the south-east. **Heshbon** (v. 26) is given as a boundary-point between Reuben and Gad. **Ramath-mizpah** (v. 26) seems another such boundary-point, probably just west of Ammān, hence not far from Aroer, and **Betonim** (v. 26), is feasibly identified with Khirbet Baṭneh, *c.* three miles south-south-west of as-Salṭ, where archaeological debris supports the location (de Vaux, *RB* 47, 1938, p. 404). **Mahanaim** (v. 26) is probably the seat of Saul's family, after Gilboa, and the place to which David retreated at Absalom's revolt (2 Sam. 17:24ff.), hence not far east of the Jordan Valley (2 Sam. 18:23; 26), so possibly Tell Ḥajjāj, *c.* two miles south of Tulūl edh-Dhahab, south of the lower Jabbok. **Debir** (v. 26) (*RSV* after LXX, Syriac and the Vulgate for MT *Lidᵉbîr*) is unknown in the Old Testament in this region. If MT is read, the place may be Lodebar of 2 Sam. 9:4ff. and 17:27, which was closely associated with Mahanaim.

The valley (*hā'ēmeq*) (cf. on v. 19) refers to the middle Jordan Valley east of the river. Here the compiler uses the town list, the items running from south to north. **Beth-nimrah** (v. 27) seems to be preserved in the Wādī Nimrīn, the lower part of the Wādī 'š-Šuweib, followed by the road from Jericho to Ammān over the Allenby Bridge, where Tell Nimrīn is the successor to Beth-nimrah at Tell Buleibil, as archaeological debris indicates (Glueck, *Explorations in Eastern Palestine* 4, 1951, pp. 347ff.). **Succoth** (v. 27) may be Khirbet Deir Allā, seven miles north of the mouth of the Jabbok, associated with bronze-casting in the time of Solomon (1 Kg. 7:46). The excavations of H. J. Franken (*VT* 10, 1960, pp. 286–93) have revealed traces of metallurgy here and at other sites in the vicinity. **Zaphon** (v. 27) must be still further north, probably at Tell as-Sa'īdīyeh, on the south bank of the Wādī Kufrinjī. No northern boundary is described, which indicates that the area ascribed to Gad ran to a narrow point at the southern end of the Sea of Galilee (**the Sea of Chinnereth**, v. 27; cf. Dt. 3:17).

the rest of the kingdom of Sihon king of Heshbon is vague in the context and is probably a redactional gloss.

East Manasseh 13:29–31

The only fixed boundary-point is **from Mahanaim** (v. 30), the boundary with Gad, and there is no town-list, perhaps because none was available to the compiler. The lack of a boundary-list may be due to the fact that the Israelite settlement here was not effected in the pre-Monarchic period, when tribal jurisdictions were important, but in the Monarchy as a colonising movement to relieve congestion west of the Jordan; cf. Elijah as 'one of the settlers of Gilead' (1 Kg. 17:1). Again, the fluctuation of fortunes in the Syrian wars may explain the lack of fixed boundaries and town-lists in this area.

Otherwise the land is described rather in regions, **all Bashan** (v. 30; cf. Dt. 3:13), to which **the whole kingdom of Og king of Bashan and Ashtaroth and Edrei, the cities of the kingdom of Og in Bashan** are probably redactional glosses, and **half Gilead** (v. 31), presumably the hill-country north of the lower Jabbok.

30. towns of Jair: better 'tent-agglomerations of Jair', who is reckoned as the son of Manasseh in Dt. 3:14. Twenty-three cities are assigned to Jair in 1 Chr. 2:22 (cf. Jg. 10:4, where Jair is associated with Gilead with thirty cities called 'the tent-agglomerations of Jair'). Perhaps there is fortuitous and confused association here between the judge and the place-name.

31. for half of the Machirites: perhaps indicates that only part of the ancient group Machir (see above, pp. 10f.) migrated east of Jordan, some remaining in lands in the Wādī Kanah, west of Jordan, partly assimilated by Manasseh to whom they were mainly affiliated (cf. Machir as **the son of Manasseh**, v. 31), and partly by Ephraim (see further, on 16:9).

33. See above, p. 14.

THE INTRODUCTION TO JOSHUA'S PARTICULAR APPORTIONMENT OF THE LAND WEST OF THE JORDAN, AND CALEB'S CLAIM TO HEBRON

14:1–15

The chapter emphasises very clearly the theological purpose of the Deuteronomistic Historian. Parts of an older tradition are incorporated which depict the occupation as on the initiative of Israel and even of the tribes acting independently, as in Jg. 1, e.g. 'these are the inheritances which the people of Israel took' (v. 1*a*; cf. v. 5*a*). This is already evidenced in Caleb's exploit against Hebron, which is implied in v. 12*b* and explicitly narrated in 15:14–15, with its sequel in Othniel's occupation of Debir (15:16–19; Jg. 1:12–15). Caleb's exploit, however, is deliberately and somewhat artificially related to the allotment by Joshua at Gilgal in congruity with the theological conception of the occupation of the Promised Land by the power and grace of God, which the Deuteronomistic Historian inherited from the cult at Gilgal.

The passage on Caleb's occupation of Hebron has a manifold significance, especially if, as seems feasible, Noth (*op. cit.*, p. 85) was right in seeing it in its present context detached from the passage on the Anakim of Hebron and district in 11:21 in Jos. or from what seems its proper context in Jg. 1. As Jos. 14:6*b*–15 it is partly an aetiological tradition explaining how Hebron, with its intimate associations with the Hebrew patriarchs and with David, should be 'the inheritance of Caleb the son of Jephunneh the Kenizzite to this day' (v. 14). The mention of the fact that Caleb was a Kenizzite is not fortuitous. This people, partly affiliated with the Israelites (1 Chr. 4:13, LXX), was also affiliated with the Edomites (Gen. 36:11, 42). Thus there is an apologetic aspect to the aetiological narrative. The Kenizzite is invested with his title by Joshua at the Israelite sanctuary of Gilgal. This, like the awkward ascription of the same exploit to Judah (Jg. 1:10f.; cf. Jos. 15:14f.), satisfied Israelite pride and orthodoxy. That is why the Deuteronomistic Historian subsumes the incident here, again awkwardly, under the allotment to Judah (ch. 15). The tradition of Caleb's occupation of Hebron is associated with the reconnaissance of Canaan from Kadesh (Num. 13, esp. vv. 30ff.), which may well be a Kenizzite hero-legend, to emphasise that the inheritance of the Promised Land involved responsibilities and merits, as Dt. 1:36 emphasises. By steadfast faith and courage, such as Caleb's, it was merited; and by the same virtues under divine economy, it would be held. The Deuteronomistic History of Israel's inheritance and forfeiture of the Promised Land is largely dominated by that theme.

General Introduction to Joshua's Apportionment **14:1–5**

The original tradition that the various elements of Israel themselves took their lands (vv. 1*a*; 5*b*) has been overworked by the Deuteronomistic Historian to assign that role to Joshua. Eleazar the priest, the son and successor of Aaron (Dt. 10:6) is further added, after the tradition which assigns him the task of dividing the land with Joshua (Num. 27:18–23; 34:17, P), as envisaged by Moses in Dt. 1:38; 3:28, with representatives from each tribe (Num. 34:16–29, P), by lot (Num. 26:53–56; 33:54, P). On a variant, and more specific, account of the apportionment of the land to all the western tribes but Judah and Joseph at Shiloh, see on ch. 18, esp. vv. 6, 8–10). The specification of the nine and a half tribes, the statement of the apportionment in Transjordan, and the notes on the division of Joseph and on Levi (v. 4) are added out of respect to the tradition of the twelve-tribe convention.

1. the heads of the fathers' houses: The phrase is characteristic of P in the Pentateuch (cf. 22:14), where they are called *n^e^śî'îm*, on which see 9:18. This does not mean the head of every household, but the senior representative of the family in its wide extent under its distinctive name.

2. as the LORD commanded Moses: as in Num. 34:13ff. This and the role of Eleazar indicates the post-Exilic redaction of the Deuteronomistic History.

4. to the Levites . . . cities to dwell in: see below, on ch. 21, and Introduction, pp. 47–51.

Caleb's Claim to Hebron **14:6–15**

See Introduction to ch. 14. The incident is recorded in Num. 13:1–14:38 (JE).

6. Kadesh-barnea: 'Ain Qudeirāt in north Sinai (see on 10:41).

7. forty is the conventional indefinite number in Semitic folklore. It indicates a man in his prime. Presuming that Caleb was forty at his reconnaissance of Palestine and allowing for forty years wandering in the desert (v. 40) and five for the occupation of Palestine according to Jos., Caleb's age at this point is given as eighty-five (v. 10).

as it was in my heart: what he really thought (cf. Ps. 15:2; *NEB*, 'an honest report').

8. made the heart of the people melt: reading *hēmassû* (cf. Dt. 1:28) for MT *hmsyw*. The phrase is typical of the Deuteronomist (cf. 2:11).

11. for going and coming: lit. 'for going out and coming in', perhaps an idiom for war service, as the sequel to the phrase in Dt. 28:6 indicates. Totality, here of active service, is expressed according to Hebrew idiom by the two extremes.

12. this hill country: i.e. about Hebron, immediately north of which the land rises to just over 3,000 feet above sea-level. The demonstrative indicates that the passage is out of its context at Gilgal and supports Noth's contention (*op. cit.*, pp. 83–5) that originally it was the sequel to 11:21f., noting the further point that both 11:23*b* and 14:15 end rather oddly in their context in Jos. with the statement that 'the land had rest from war'. This suggests that the source-material so arranged by the Deuteronomist belonged to hero-legends like the sources of Jg.; cf. Jos. 15:14–19; Jg. 1:10–15.

Anakim: a pseudo-gentilic (see on 11:21).

fortified cities: see on 10:20.

14. Caleb . . . the Kenizzite: see Introduction to ch. 14.

to this day: the hall-mark of the aetiological tradition (see Introduction to ch. 14).

15. Kiriath-arba: Hebrew, 'the City of Four' (see on 10:3). The Massoretic tradition assumed an eponymous hero **Arba**, the chief man among the Anakim (*hā'ādām haggādôl bā'ᵃnāqîm*); cf. LXX 'the metropolis of the Anakim' (reading *ha'em*, lit. 'the mother [city]

. . .', for MT *hā'ādām*. This tradition of the occupation of Hebron contradicts that of 10:36ff. and is more true to fact. An alternative tradition to the origin of Hebron here associates Arba with three other chiefs Sheshai, Ahiman and Talmai (15:14; cf. Num. 13:22), whose names suggest Aramaeans; cf. Talmai of Geshur (2 Sam. 3:3; 13:37). Underlying this tradition there may be such a situation as that implied in the Egyptian Execration Texts, which indicate a stage before the sedentarisation of Amorite ('proto-Aramaean', according to Noth) tribes, and note three chiefs associated with Ashkelon and two with Jerusalem. Further we might suggest that the name implies the importance of Hebron as a boundary sanctuary where four groups were associated, i.e. Kenizzites, Kenites, Jerahmeelites and the inhabitants of Judah to the north. Recent excavations at Hebron have revealed no trace of occupation between the sixteenth century BC and a date in the Israelite Monarchy; P. C. Hammond, *RB* 72, 1966, pp. 267–70; 73, 1966–7, pp. 566–9; 75, 1968, pp. 253–8.

THE INHERITANCE OF JUDAH

15:1–63

On sources, see Introduction, pp. 44–46. The allotment of Judah's territory by Joshua in the apportionment of the twelve tribes is late and redactional in view of the independent history of Judah, which is not mentioned in the ten-member confederacy of Israel in Jg. 5:13–18; cf. the repeated mention of Israel *and* Judah in David's monarchy and subsequently. Both 'Judah' and the northern group Israel were worshippers of Yahweh, with antecedents in his sanctuary at Kadesh in north Sinai, so that, whatever the political situation, the north and south kingdoms could be termed from a religious point of view 'Israel'. The boundary-points (vv. 1–12), like those of the other tribal territories, are based on local tradition recognised to a considerable extent in Solomon's fiscal administration (1 Kg. 4:7–19); but in the case of Judah those reflect later conditions in the time of Josiah, when the Philistine plain was incorporated. Within the realm of Judah, and with respect to the affiliation of the Kenizzites and Judah in pre-Monarchic times, the occupation of Hebron by Caleb and of Debir (Kiriath-sepher) by Othniel is described in what is really an aetiological saga, explaining a land-settlement between two Kenizzite clans, represented by Caleb of Hebron and Othniel of Debir. Town-lists are grouped according to the four physical regions, the south, or Negeb (vv. 21*a*–32), the foothills, or the Shephelah (vv. 33–47), the hill country (vv. 48–60), the wilderness east of the watershed to the Dead Sea, and the lower Jordan Valley (vv. 61f.), and according to twelve fiscal districts in the realm of Judah, probably reflecting a regional division under Solomon, with later adjustments under Jehoshaphat (vv. 61f.) and under Josiah. This is indicated especially by the home district (v. 60); here only Kiriath-jearim and Rabbah are mentioned, but included are the towns in the district immediately north of Jerusalem reckoned to Benjamin, which includes Kiriath-jearim (18:28, LXX and Syriac versions). Those administrative districts also were to a certain extent based on physical regions, as Alt recognised ('Judas Gaue unter Josia', *KS* II, 1959, pp. 276–88).

The Boundaries of Judah 15:1–12

1. **Edom:** the district of Mount Seir, west of the Arabah (Dt. 1:2), as the town-lists indicate, probably reflecting the period of Josiah, by which time Judah had lost control of Edom, east of the Arabah, and of Ezion-geber on the Gulf of 'Aqaba.
the wilderness of Zin: between the watershed to the Arabah, which was 'Mount Seir', and Kadesh, which was in Zin (Dt. 32:51).

2. **bay:** lit. 'tongue' (Cf. v. 5; 18:19; Isa. 11:15).

3. **the ascent of Akrabbim:** Num. 34:4; 'Scorpion Pass', giving access from the Arabah by the important and rare spring of 'Ain Ḥuṣb, south-east of Qurnub (Byzantine Mampsis). For illustration, see D. Baly, *The Geography of the Bible*, 1957, pl. 9. As far back as the fourth millennium BC, this was the pathway of caravans which transported raw copper from Feinān (Byzantine Punon), on the east side of the Arabah, to Tell Abū Maṭar, the Chalcolithic site by Beersheba (N. Glueck, *Rivers in the Desert*, 1959, p. 89). The importance of this pass, modern Naqb Sefei, is attested by three stations from the Nabataean, Roman Imperial and Byzantine periods (Glueck, *op. cit.*, pp. 205–7).
Kadesh-barnea: probably the district rather than the particular settlement of 'Ain Qudeirāt (see on 10:41).
Hezron . . . Addar: probably a scribal corruption or misunderstanding of Hazar-Addar, 'the Folds of Addar' (Num. 34:4), *ḥ^{a}ṣar* being a common element in place-names in the steppe (see further, on 13:3, 23).
Karka: Hebrew *qarqa'*. Actually, as the definite article indicates, this is a common noun, lit. 'floor'; cf. the sea-bottom in Am. 9:3, which suggests to us mud-flats (Arabic *qa'qa'*), a feature of basins in the southern steppe, well illustrated in B. Rothenberg, *God's Wilderness*, 1961, pl. 30.

4. **Azmon:** modern Quṣeimeh, an important watering-station between Beersheba and Egypt, *c.* five miles west of ʻAin Qudeirāt. **the Brook of Egypt:** (Hebrew *naḥal miṣrayim*), the Wādī ʼl-ʻArîsh, south of Gaza, where the Assyrian records mention a place Naḥalmuṣur.

The extent of the southern border of Judah from the south end of the Dead Sea and west to the Mediterranean, if it refers to conditions before the Monarchy, must refer to areas occupied by semi-nomads like the Jerahmeelites, Kenites and Kenizzites (Noth, *op. cit.*, p. 89), who were affiliated with Judah. If it is intended to include the Philistine plain, it would reflect the extent of Josiah's realm between the decline of Assyria and his death in 609 BC.
Beth-hoglah: ʻAin Hajla, by the ford of that name, *c.* six miles south-east of modern Jericho.
Beth-arabah: probably ʻAin al-Gharbeh, north of the Wādī Qilt, which runs south-east from Jericho (Alt, *PJB* 22, 1926, pp. 34ff.).
the stone of Bohan the son of Reuben: This may indicate a former settlement of Reuben, west of the lower Jordan (see on 1:12–18). **The stone of Bohan**, unknown, may have been a natural pinnacle of rock which suggested a thumb (*bōhen*). Such a conspicuous natural feature is often considered by the Arabs as the abode of a *wēlī*, or numen. There is such a *wēlī* at the desert sanctuary of Nebī Mūsā, near where the stone of Bohan is to be located, *c.* six miles south-south-west of modern Jericho.

7. **Debir:** not certainly known, but possibly associated with grazings, as the etymology may suggest, was in the same region south-south-west of Jericho.
the Valley of Achor: al-Buqeiʻa: see on 7:24.
Gilgal: certainly not the sanctuary north-east of Jericho, but by **Adummim** (Talʻat ad-Damm), on the modern road from Jericho to Jerusalem and south of the Wādī Qilt. The reading **Gilgal** is questionable; cf. 18:17, which reads *geIîlôt*, a common noun expressing a physical feature, the significance of which is uncertain (cf. 13:2).
the waters of En-shemesh: probably ʻAin al-Ḥuḍ, the strong spring just east of al-ʻAzariyeh (Bethany).
En-rogel: (cf. 2 Sam. 17:17; 1 Kg. 1:9). Bīr ʼAyyūb, south of ancient Jerusalem, below the confluence of the Kidron Valley and the Valley of the Son of Hinnom (Wādī ʼr-Rabābī).

8. **at the southern shoulder of the Jebusite (that is, Jerusalem):** the south-west hill, divided from Jerusalem proper by the central valley (Josephus' Tyropoeon Valley). The inclusion of the whole south-west hill in the fortified area of Jerusalem cannot be demonstrated before the time of Hezekiah (N. Avigad, ʻExcavations in the

Jewish Quarter of the Old City, 1969–1971', *Jerusalem Revealed*, ed. Y. Yadin, 1975, pp. 41f.). The careful delimitation between Jerusalem and the tribal territory of Judah at this point might seem to reflect the distinction which persisted throughout the Monarchy, as repeated references to 'Jerusalem and Judah' indicate, i.e. the city as the crown possession of David and the territory of Judah. The unnatural separation of Jerusalem from the arable land in the Plain of the Rephaim, west of the Valley of Hinnom, however, may indicate penetration of worshippers of Yahweh from Judah from the south-west before the fall of the city itself to David's kinsman Joab; cf. the case of Tappuah (17:7f.), where the occupation of the settlement by Ephraim and the lands by Manasseh indicates the resistance and eventual fall of the Canaanite principality after the Israelite tribes had first infiltrated into and then occupied the lands, as Alt proposed ('Das System der Stammesgrenzen in Buche Josua', *KS* I, 1953, p. 200). The precise significance here and the ethnic connotation, if any, of **Jebusite** is unknown. The word is glossed by **that is Jerusalem**. The view of Dalman ought to be cited that 'Jerusalem' specifically applied to the south-west hill as distinct from Zion, which was the south-east hill and its Solomonic extension northwards.

the mountain that lies over against the valley of Hinnom, on the west, at the northern end of the valley of Rephaim: the high ground now occupied by the King David Hotel and the Y.M.C.A. building.

the valley of Rephaim, the only appreciable tract of arable land in the immediate vicinity of Jerusalem, is the plain around the modern railway station, the Biq'a.

9. the spring of the Waters of Nephtoah: (Hebrew *ma'yan mê neptôaḥ*); cf. 18:15; 'Ain Liftā, just beyond the north-west edge of modern Jerusalem, on the upper course of the Wādī 'ṣ-Ṣurār (Vale of Sorek). It may be 'the Wells of Merneptah (or Mineptah), which is in the mountain range' in a thirteenth-century Egyptian papyrus (J. A. Wilson, *ANET*, p. 258).

Mount Ephron: not certainly known. The direction is roughly that of the modern highway from Jerusalem to Jaffa, above the south bank of the Wādī 'ṣ-Ṣurār, towards Qiryat al-'Ainab (Kiriath-jearim). On our reading 'it went out to Moṣa, a city of Mount Ephron', for **to the cities of Mount Ephron**, see on 18:15.

Baalah: possibly a scribal corruption of a compound place-name introduced by Baalath- ('goddess of . . .') at or near Kiriath-jearim, as is suggested by the gloss **that is Kiriath-jearim**.

10. Beth-shemesh: Tell ar-Rumeileh by 'Ain Shems, south of the lower course of the Wādī 'ṣ-Ṣurār.

Timnah: Khirbet al-Tibneh, lower down the Wādī. See on Jg. 14:1.

11. Ekron: 'Aqir, *c.* sixteen miles south-east of Jaffa.

Shikkeron . . . Mount Baalah: unknown, and textually doubtful.

Jabneel: Yibneh, Roman Jamnia on the Mandatory railway, *c.* twelve miles south of Jaffa. The inclusion of the north part of the Philistine plain to the sea (v. 12) indicates a date after Josiah's nationalist revival on the decline of Assyria.

The Kenizzite Occupation of Hebron and Debir (Kiriath-sepher) **15:13–19**

Cf. Jg. 1:10–15. See Introduction to chs. 14 and 15. On place-names and personalities, see on 14:6–15.

15. Debir (Kiriath-sepher): see on 10:38. *sēper* in Hebrew means generally 'a book' or 'record', and there may be a reference to registration in the Egyptian or Solomonic administration or to a boundary-stone with an inscription. Alternatively, the word may be the corruption of a Canaanite cognate of Akkadian *sippur* ('copper'), so far unattested. *d^ebir* generally signifies 'inmost shrine', but not 'shrine in general', so that in a place-name (cf. 13:26) it may rather signify 'grazing-grounds': cf. *dōber*, Mic. 2:12.

16. Achsah: possibly represents a local or tribal dependent of the powerful Caleb clan of Hebron, which was affiliated with the kindred clan of Othniel after the occupation of Debir.

18. The tribal history here takes the form of popular saga, with charming personal touches, such as the bride's persuasion of her father. The verb *ṣānaḥ*, rendered 'alighted', occurring only here and at Jg. 1:14 and Jg. 4:21, may mean rather 'clapped her hands' to attract attention; cf. Arabic *ṣaḥana*, cited by Koehler, *Lexicon in Veteris Testamenti Libros*, p. 808.

19. present: Hebrew *b^erākâh*, lit. 'a blessing', but also 'a present', a tangible manifestation of goodwill on the communication of the blessing of God in which a gift associates the two parties (cf. Gen. 33:11; 1 Sam. 25:27; 30:26; 2 Kg. 5:15). See the writer's article, 'Blessing and Curse', *HDB*, one volume ed., 2nd ed., 1963, pp. 109f.).

Negeb: root unknown. See on 10:40. The meaning is 'the dry steppe', as the present passage suggests.

springs: Hebrew *gullôt*, lit. 'bowls', e.g. on the top of the pillars Jachin and Boaz before the Temple (1 Kg. 7:41f.), and in Ugaritic. Here 'basins' would be a better translation. LXX adds 'and Caleb gave her (them)'; cf. Jg. 1:15, which adds after 'and Caleb', 'according to her heart's desire' (*k^elibbāh*), with a pun on the name.

Settlement of Judah **15:20–63**

20. This verse reminds the reader that in spite of the digression on Caleb and Othniel occasioned by the incorporation *en bloc* of a narrative source, the subject is the settlement of Judah.

The town-lists of Judah are grouped in physical regions and administrative districts from the Monarchy (see Introduction to ch. 15). The inclusion of settlements in this list south of Beersheba in the tribal territory ascribed to Simeon in 19:2–9, indicates that this is not from a tribal boundary-list, but from an official list of administrative districts in the Kingdom of Judah.

21–32. *District I. The Negeb, or extreme south.* Many of those places, few of which can be certainly located, are no more than wells, or pockets of earth where the rain-bearing wind from the Mediterranean might afford a slight rainfall, in places where contour and exposure were favourable on the western steppe between Beersheba and Kedesh in the south, north and west of a line roughly between Kurnub and 'Ain Qudeirāt (see map in D. Baly, *op. cit.*, pp. 260–3, fig. 47). The semi-sedentary life of the district is indicated by the number of names compounded with Hazor ('enclosure'; here 'sheepfold'); see on 13:3, 23. The best-known of the places are **Kedesh** ('Ain Qudeirāt; see on 13:3, 23); **Beer-sheba** (v. 28), which may have been the administrative centre of the district in the Monarchy, as the note 'and her daughter-settlements' may indicate (reading *b^{e}nôtêhā* by the very slight amendation of **Biziothiah**); **Hormah** (v. 30); **Ziklag** (v. 31); and **Shilhim** (v. 32). **Beer-sheba** was the conventional southern limit of the settled land, as Dan was recognised as the northern limit, the reference here being possibly to the significance of those places as sanctuaries. **Hormah**, which Noth regarded as possibly the district capital, according to Num. 21:1–3 (cf. Jg. 1:16f.) was so called following its destruction under the ban on the advance of Israel or Judah from the south after an initial defeat (Num. 14:45). The name may rather mean a cult-place on the Arabic etymology (so A. von Gall, *Altisraëlitische Kultstätten*, *BZAW* 3, 1898, p. 37). B. Mazar (*JNES* 24, 1965, pp. 298–303) has proposed that the sanctuary may have been a sacral area of the Kenites, the antecedent of the tenth century temple of Yahweh at Tell Arad, *c.* twenty miles east-north-east of **Beer-sheba**, which is identified with Hormah in Jg. 1:16f. (see below, pp. 238f.). **Ziklag** is best known as David's heritable fief when he was a feudal vassal of Achish of Gath (1 Sam. 27:6). It is feasibly located by Alt (*KS* III, 1959, pp. 429f.) at Tell al-Khuweilefeh *c.* eleven miles north-north-east of Beer-sheba. **Shilhim** is possibly Sharuhen in the tribal territory of Simeon (19:6), which is probably to be located at Tell al-Fār'a, the great revetted fortress in the Wādī Ghazzeh, *c.* twenty miles south of Gaza, excavated by Sir W. Flinders Petrie, where the Hyksos maintained themselves stubbornly after their expulsion from Egypt in 1580 BC. With the passing of Egyptian power in Palestine this place lost significance as a frontier fortress, and so was abandoned to semi-nomadic squatters. The whole district is also reckoned to Simeon in 19:2–6.

32. **in all, twenty-nine cities with their villages:** the enumeration is characteristic of the town-lists in the various administrative districts, not always agreeing with the towns listed, which, in defect of names, indicates deficiency in the source, and in the surplus of names, as in this district, indicates later redactional interpolation. The difference between **cities** and **villages** is noteworthy. The former are fortified, not necessarily urban, settlements; the latter open, no more than concentrations of sheepfolds, or, in the settled land, farm-buildings and small villages.

33–36. *District II; in the Shephelah*, particularly east and west of the north–south depression in the foothills of Judah from Zorah (Ṣar'a) and nearby **Eshtaol** (cf. Jg. 13:25), just north of the Vale of Sorek (Wādī 'ṣ-Ṣurār) to Azekah (Tell az-Zakarīyeh), which dominates the Vale of Elah (Wadi 's-Sanṭ), just west of the great depression, and the heights north (Jarmuth) and south of the Wādī 's-Sanṭ (**Socoh, Adullam**).

The most significant of those places was **Zorah**, known as Samson's birthplace (Jg. 13:2), Arab Ṣar'a, two miles north of Beth-shemesh; **Jarmuth**, Arab Yarmūk (see on 10:3); **Adullam** (see 12:13–16*a*); **Socoh**, Arab Khirbet 'Abbād, an Iron Age site just before the Wādī 's-Sanṭ forks towards Adullam and Hebron and north-east to Bethlehem, the name surviving in the adjacent Khirbet aš-Šuweikeh and **Azekah**. Beth-shemesh is a significant omission from this list, by which we may conclude that the list stems from a time when Beth-shemesh was derelict, which G. E. Wright dated towards the end of the tenth century BC (*JBL* 75, 1956, pp. 215f.). We are not convinced by his dating of stratum IIa to the time of David rather than Solomon, but Rehoboam's fortification of the neighbouring **Zorah** (2 Chr. 11:10) suggests that Beth-shemesh was neglected in his time and probably also in the latter part of Solomon's reign. Other sites in this list fortified by Rehoboam (2 Chr. 11:5–10) are **Adullam, Socoh** and **Azekah**, in apprehension therefore of an attack from Egypt. The regional capital would therefore be one of those places.

Eshtaol and **Zorah** are assigned also to Dan (19:41), including

Ir-shemesh ('the City of the Sun', probably Bethshemesh). This either reflects traditional tribal associations of Dan in their earlier settlement or an ideal reconstruction based on administrative lists after Josiah's expansion to the district.

The cities are enumerated as fifteen, but only fourteen are listed; LXX omits **Adithaim** (v. 36).

37–41. *District III, also in the Shephelah*, particularly in the south-west, probably at one time in Solomon's administrative district with the capital at **Lachish** (Tell ad-Duweir; see on 10:3). This, with **Cabbon**, probably the neighbouring Arab village of Qubeibeh, is the only certain location. In view of the probable location of **Makkedah** in the north of the Shephelah near Bethshemesh (see on 10:11), its inclusion here is suspect. On **Eglon**, see on 10:3.

42–44. *District IV, central Shephelah.* This was between the Wādī 's-Sanṭ and the Wadi 'l-Afranj, with the capital probably at **Mareshah**. The places most notable in the Old Testament are **Libnah** (v. 42; see on 10:29); **Keilah** (v. 44), plausibly located by Alt, who proposed that it was the regional capital (*KS* II, 1959, p. 304), at Tell Qīla, on the southern tributary of the Wādī 's-Sanṭ, *c.* nine miles north-west of Hebron, and **Mareshah**, best known as the home of the prophet Micah (Mic. 1:1). The site was in the vicinity of Beit Jibrīn, five miles north-east of Lachish, where a small Roman site Khirbet Mar'aš preserves the name. This is near Tell as-Sanda-ḥanna, just over one mile south-south-east of Beit Jibrīn, which was certainly Marissa of the Hellenistic period, with traces of occupation back to *c.* 800 BC. It is doubtful if this was the site of Mareshah fortified by Rehoboam (2 Chr. 11:8), which should rather be located at Tell al-Judeideh two miles north of Beit Jibrīn. In Micah's punning reference to places in the vicinity, **Achzib** (v. 44) is mentioned (Mic. 1:14).

45–47. *District V, the Philistine Plain.* There is no mention of Ashkelon or Gath, which in the latter case may support the view that Gath and Libnah (v. 42) were identical. The fact that so few, and only Philistine, cities are named, may be owing to the fact that other settlements were enumerated artificially in the territory of Dan (19:41–46). Those, however, are only north of Ekron, and we suggest that the passage reflects a division made soon after Josiah had taken advantage of the defeat of Assyria to claim the Philistine Plain proper, which, however, his death in 609 BC prevented him from organising. Here significantly the settlements are not enumerated.

48–51. *District VI, in the hill country.* In view of the mention of a whole district 'the land of Goshen', which is apparently adjacent to, but distinct from, the Shephelah and the Negeb (11:16), **Goshen**, as Noth suggested (*op. cit.*, p. 97) was probably the capital of the district. The place-names survive in a remarkable degree in the district west of adh-Dhaharīyeh, twelve miles south-west of Hebron in the southern foothills of Judah, and one would expect Goshen to be located at one of the more conspicuous tells in the region, such as Tell 'Eiṭūn, *c.* six miles north-west of Tell adh-Dhaharīyeh, or Tell Beit Mirsīm, *c.* two miles south-west of that, which Noth (*op. cit.*, p. 97) proposed. **Debir**, which Alt suggested was the regional capital, was apparently included in this district (v. 49), here being called also **Kiriath-sannah**, which by homoeoteleuton after **Dannah**, may be a scribal corruption of Kiriath-sepher, with which Debir is repeatedly identified.

52–54. *District VII, also in the hill country.* This includes **Hebron**, the centre of the Kenizzites, an important sanctuary of Yahweh (2 Sam. 5:3), and one of the cities fortified by Rehoboam (2 Chr. 11:10), obviously the capital of the district, and which was especially associated with the Kenizzites. Noth (*op. cit.*, p. 98), after Elliger, explains the omission of Debir, which he would locate within eight miles of Hebron, by supposing that the lists reflect the ravages of Sennacherib in 701. If Debir were here, its omission need not unduly surprise us, as Adoraim (Dūrā, five miles south-west of Hebron) is also omitted, though its significance is indicated by its fortification by Rehoboam (2 Chr. 11:9).

55–57. *District VIII, in the hill country, east of the watershed and south-east of Hebron.* The district capital is uncertain, though Rehoboam's fortification of **Ziph** and the name among the four jar-handle stamps of the period of the Jewish Monarchy may indicate Ziph as the administrative centre. This may have been the district particularly associated with the Kenites, as Alt suggested (*KS* II, 1959, p. 286), cf. **Kain** in the list of settlements (v. 57), or more probably with the Kenizzites. Here David maintained himself as an outlaw from Saul, and four of the places listed are mentioned in the narrative of his escapades: **Maon**, the home of Nabal and Abigail, whom David married (1 Sam. 23:24ff.; 25:2), **Carmel** (1 Sam. 25:2ff.), **Ziph** (1 Sam. 23:14ff.) and **Jezreel**, the home of another of David's wives (1 Sam. 25:43).

58–59. *District IX, the hill country north of Hebron.* The capital was **Beth-zur** (Khirbet aṭ-Ṭubeiqeh; cf. O. R. Sellers, *The Citadel of*

Bethsur, 1939), commanding the head of the important branch of the Wādī 's-Sanṭ, which gives access from the coastal plain to Hebron, was fortified by Rehoboam (2 Chr. 11:7). The largest surviving settlement is **Halhul**, still in the British Mandate a prosperous village amidst extensive orchards and vineyards, *c.* three miles north of Hebron.

District X, the hill country round Bethlehem. For this we depend on LXX, which gives the addition to MT: 'Thekō and Ephratha, that is Bethlehem, and Phagor and Aitan and Koulon and Tatam and Eōbēs and Karem and Galem and Thēther and Manochō, eleven cities and their villages.' The district capital was probably Bethlehem, the tribal centre of Judah proper. The Hebrew text translated by LXX permits a restoration of the system of twelve administrative districts in the kingdom of Judah. Besides Bethlehem, the places best known in the Old Testament lie to the east of the watershed, such as Tekoa, the home of Amos (Am. 1:1), and of modern interest are Beth-Gallim (Beit Jāla, one mile northwest of Bethlehem) and Kerem ('Ain Kārim, two miles west of Jerusalem, or perhaps Ramat Raḥēl).

60. *District XI, comprising apparently two isolated sites, Kiriath-jearim and the unknown Rabbah.* The inclusion of **Kiriath-jearim** in the town-list of Benjamin (18:28) indicates that the list of places in the administrative district of Jerusalem was attached to Benjamin, which reflects the inclusion of Benjamin in the kingdom of Judah after the disruption of David's kingdom at the death of Solomon.

61–62. *District XII, 'the wilderness' of Judah.* This was the steppe south-east of Jerusalem towards the Dead Sea and the lower Jordan Valley, in the rain-shadow and so rapidly deteriorating in fertility. The region is extended southwards to **Engedi**. Under Josiah the administrative centre would be Jericho, which is not named here, which suggests that the list comes from a time when the northern Kingdom held Jericho. A date may be suggested by the inclusion of **Middin**, **Secacah**, **Nibshan** and **the City of Salt**, which are to be identified with Khirbet Abū Ṭabaq, Khirbet as-Samrā, Khirbet al-Maqārī in the Buqei'a beyond the escarpment west of Qumrān, and the Iron Age settlement at Khirbet Qumrān. Those places were not settled before the ninth century and were abandoned *c.* 600 BC (J. T. Milik and F. M. Cross, 'Explorations in the Judaean Buqê'ah', *BASOR* 142, 1956, pp. 5–17; F. M. Cross and G. E. Wright, 'The Boundary and Province Lists of the Kingdom of Judah', *JBL* 75, 1956, pp. 223–6). The settlement may be connected with the building of fortresses and store-cities by Jehoshaphat (2 Chr. 17:12) in the second quarter of the ninth century. The relation of this section in the administrative lists to this date would account for the omission of Jericho, which had been abandoned until the time of Ahab, when it was rebuilt by one of his subjects, Hiel of Bethel (1 Kg. 16:34). The settlement of such places in an area like the Buqei'a, where profitable cultivation is possible perhaps once in several years, indicates the intensive development forced upon Judah after the disruption of David's kingdom and that the settlement had a strategic significance, related perhaps to the restlessness of Moab under the yoke of Omri and Ahab and her eventual revolt (2 Kg. 3). The settlement of **Engedi**, which was a fertile oasis, now revived in the state of Israel, where Tell al-Jurn has Iron Age debris, was possibly connected with the menace from Moab across the Dead Sea, which was fordable until just over a century ago from the Lisān peninsula to a point *c.* ten miles south of Engedi (T. J. Salmon and G. T. McCaw, 'The Level and Cartography of the Dead Sea', *PEQ* 1936, pp. 103–11).

63. *Note on the symbiosis of Judah and the Jebusites of Jerusalem* (cf. the exclusion of Jerusalem from Judah in 15:8, and from Benjamin in 18:16). This may be redactional, but is true to conditions of the settlement, if by Jerusalem the lands as well as the fortified settlement on the south-east hill are meant.

THE INHERITANCE OF JOSEPH

16:1–17:18

Joseph is particularised as Ephraim (16:5–10) and Manasseh (17:1–13). See General Introduction, pp. 16ff.

After the description of the boundary-points of Joseph (16:1–3), the boundaries of Ephraim (vv. 5–8) and Manasseh (17:1–13) are described, with a note on the settlement of certain groups within the latter and on the settlement in Transjordan. The section on Manasseh is much more circumstantial, and may originally have preceded the section on Ephraim. It has received secondary expansions. First, there is the note on the settlement of part of the tribe, Machir, beyond Jordan (17:1), which is probably motivated by the exception to the convention of the eldest son receiving the whole heritage, as Noth suggested (*op. cit.*, p. 102), occasioned in this case by the settlement of Machir in the northern part of north Transjordan. Then, after a note on the settlement of certain clans of Manasseh (17:2), there is a digression on certain minor clans, 'the daughters of Zelophehad' (vv. 3f.), after Num. 27:1–11, which is an aetiological tradition. Those lists differ from the description of Judah in that boundary-lists are used, but there is no systematic listing of towns. The note on the few towns in, and bordering upon, the Great Central Plain, and Dor in the Plain of Sharon (17:11) probably reflects the incorporation of those towns in the realm of David or Solomon.

The names of the clans of Manasseh probably all eventually became the names of settlements, or perhaps rather settlements which had thrown in their lot with Israel gave their names to the group they had joined. Such cases are Shechem (17:2), Tirzah (17:3) and Abi-ezer, Helek, Shemida, Hoglah and Mahlah, all of which but Tirzah are mentioned as places on the fiscal ostraca from Samaria, dated by S. Birnbaum (*Samaria-Sebaste*, III, 1957, ed. J. W. and G. M. Crowfoot and K. M. Kenyon, pp. 9–25) *c.* 750–725 BC. Beyond this there is no definite note of the towns of Manasseh.

The section closes with the narrative of an episode in the expansion of Joseph (17:14–18). Hertzberg (*op. cit.*, p. 104) sees an aetiological tradition explaining how Joseph alone of the sons of Jacob had a double lot, but, however it may have been adapted in Jos., the tradition probably rests on a historical basis of the penetration of the hitherto uninhabited land as the result of tribal arbitration, where Alt proposed to find the actual significance of the historical Joshua ('Josua', *KS* I, 1953, pp. 190f.). Here two variant accounts are indicated, in 17:14f., where the congestion of the land occupied by the group 'Joseph' prompts the desire for more land, and again in vv. 16–18, where the Canaanite fortresses in the Great Central Plain limit the settlement. Probably those factors contributed to the expansion of Manasseh over Jordan, but that is not certainly envisaged here. We find no necessary reference to Transjordan in 'the land of the Perizzites and the Rephaim', which Noth claimed (*op. cit.*, p. 107), and this phrase is lacking in LXX. Both elements, as Hertzberg pointed out (*op. cit.*, p. 104), 'dwellers in open villages and aborigines', are mentioned as often west of the Jordan as east (Gen. 13:7; 34:30; Jos. 11:3), the Perizzites being regularly mentioned in the conventional list of pre-Israelite inhabitants of Palestine (Dt. 7:1; Jos. 3:10).

The South Boundary of Joseph **16:1–3**

The same points are named as in the description of the north boundary of Benjamin from the Jordan to Beth-horon (18:12–14*a*). This may indicate the north boundary of the kingdom of Judah as it was eventually stabilised. In any case the fact that only this boundary of 'the sons of Joseph' is described besides the more specific south boundary of Ephraim suggests that the redactor had the kingdom of Israel in view. The antiquity of the tradition of the boundary may be indicated by the mention of the **Archites** (v. 2) and the **Japhletites** (v. 3), probably tribes, the latter being such in 1 Chr. 7:32ff. and the former probably so in 2 Sam. 15:32.

1. the allotment . . . went: lit. 'the lot went out', referring to the lot falling out of the receptacle in which it was shaken (see on 7:4), though 'lot' might mean portion, as understood by LXX ('the border . . . was from . . .'). LXX reading 'border' (Hebrew *gebûl*) may indicate that MT 'lot' (Hebrew *gôrāl*) was a scribal corruption in the palaeo-Hebraic script.

by Jericho: It is not certain from this passage if Jericho is included. According to 18:21, Jericho was in Benjamin, but this may reflect the incorporation of Benjamin in the southern kingdom after the Disruption.

east of the waters of Jericho: omitted in LXX. If original, it refers either to the outflow of the Wādī Dūq, called in its winter torrent bed in its lower course Wādī Nu'eimeh, or to the general water system of Jericho from the point where it was exhausted in irrigation to the east of the town.

2. Bethel . . . Luz: Cf. Jg. 1:23; Gen. 28:19, where **Luz** is given as the older name of **Bethel**. If, as the present passage suggests, the two are distinct, the first may be Burj Beitīn between Ai (et-Tell) and Beitīn village, where early Christian tradition located the place of Abraham's altar, perhaps the site of the sanctuary of historical Israel, and Luz the settlement on the site of Bethel at Beitīn village, where J. L. Kelso found settlements from *c.* 2000 BC, through the later Bronze Ages and the Israelite period. Certain MSS of LXX, however, omit 'Luz'. The name **Ataroth** survives in Khirbet 'Aṭṭāra, *c.* four miles south-south-west of Beitīn. As this is a Roman–Byzantine site, **Ataroth** of v. 2 must be sought elsewhere in the vicinity, possibly at Tell an-Naṣbeh (Israelite Mizpah) on a ridge *c.* two miles south-south-west of Beitīn.

3. Beth-horon: see on 10:10. The south-west boundary-point was Gezer on a low hill commanding access from the coastal plain to the Valley of Aijalon, *c.* ten miles south-west of the Lower Beth-horon, which Israel occupied only under Solomon (1 Kg. 9:16).

the sea, as the western extremity of the boundary of Joseph, is unrealistic until the time of David or even Solomon, and may reflect the revision of an earlier tradition of the southern boundary-points of Joseph in the light of the administrative division of the Kingdom of Judah, which included Benjamin.

The Settlement of Ephraim **16:4–10**

This section is possibly transposed by a redactor under the influence of the tradition of the junior branch of the Joseph group (cf. Gen. 48:20, J and E); cf. the hegemony of Ephraim in Israel of the north under Samuel. It might naturally be assumed that, the south border of **Joseph** including **Ephraim** and **Manasseh** having been already described, there is no need to describe the south boundary of Ephraim, and in fact it is not described. Nevertheless, **Upper Beth-horon** is mentioned (16:5), with the addition that the boundary goes thence to the sea (v. 6). Since Lower Beth-horon has already been given as a point in the south boundary of **Joseph**, from which the boundary ran west to the sea, this can only mean that the south border of 'Joseph' really envisages the boundary between the kingdoms of Judah and Israel after the Disruption, or the boundary between the kingdom of Judah and the Assyrian province of Samaria after the fall of the northern kingdom. The territory of **Ephraim**, on the other hand, reflects the much more limited occupation of that group before the Monarchy, when the south-west boundary-point was on the edge of the plateau at the Upper Beth-horon, 'and the boundary goes thence to the sea' being a redactional expansion.

Another difficulty seems to be the statement: **the boundary of their inheritance on the east was Ataroth-addar as far as Upper Beth-horon** (16:5). We may understand that the boundary-point on the south-west was Upper Beth-horon, Ataroth-addar being added as an after-thought to indicate that there (Ataroth in the description of the south border of 'the descendants of Joseph', 16:2) the boundary of Ephraim westwards deviated from the southern boundary ascribed to 'Joseph' in vv. 1–3.

Michmethath is the pivotal boundary-point of Ephraim in the north, possibly Khirbet Juleijil in the plain of Makhneh south-east of Shechem ('east of Shechem', 17:7). **Taanath-shiloh** was located by Eusebius at Roman Thena ten miles south-east of Nablus (Arab Khirbet Ta'na al-Fawqa), and **Janoah** at Yanūm twelve miles south-east of Nablus, and **Naarah**, which he notes as a Jewish settlement five Roman miles from Jericho, might indicate 'Ain Duq, where the explosion of a shell in 1918 revealed the mosaic floor of a synagogue (E. L. Sukenik, *Ancient Synagogues in Palestine and Greece*, Schweich Lectures 1930, 1934, pp. 28–31). West from Michmethath the boundary runs some six miles to **Tappuah** (Khirbet Sheikh Abu Zarad by Yasūf) and **westward to the brook Kanah** (still called Wādī Qānā), which drains this vicinity to the River Aujā (Jarkon), nine miles north-east of Jaffa.

9. This evidently has regard to the situation literally exemplified in the case of Tappuah, which was in Ephraim, though the lands of the Canaanite settlement fell to Manasseh (17:8). A list of such places may once have been extant, as 17:9 suggests. Those irregular divisions of land between Ephraim and Manasseh may indicate remnants of Machir in that region after their migration east of Jordan, suggested by the reference in Jos. 13:31 to half of Machir in Transjordan.

10. An adjustment by the post-Exilic redactor with regard to Jg. 1:29. The note that **the Canaanites** became **slaves to do forced labour** (cf. 17:13) reflects Solomon's adaptation of the corvée, now well attested as a Canaanite institution in the administrative texts from the palace at Rās Shamra (C. Virolleaud, *Syria* 21, 1940, pp. 123–51; 247–76; *Le palais royale d'Ugarit* II, ed. C. F. A. Schaeffer, 1955, pp. 23–176). This suggests to the Deuteronomist a satisfactory explanation of the survival of the Canaanites in the divinely directed occupation of the Promised Land.

The Settlement of Manasseh 17:1–13

Prefaced by a note on the settlement of Gilead by **Machir**, stated to be 'the eldest son' of Manasseh (v. 1), that is the oldest group to be assimilated by Manasseh; cf. Num. 26:28ff., where he is apparently the *only* son (cf. Gen. 50:23). On the warlike Machir in north Transjordan (v. 1), see above on 13:31. The description of Machir as **'a man of war'** (v. 1) indicates a situation like that of Jephthah and his retinue in Jg. 11:3. Further on **Machir**, see above, pp. 11, 14.

2. *The 'families' of Manasseh*, of which **Abiezer**, the clan of Gideon (Jg. 6:11), **Helek, Shechem** and **Shemida** are named as settlements near Samaria in the Samarian ostraca. The fact that certain of these, e.g. Shechem and Helek, are mentioned in the Egyptian Execration Texts (nineteenth century BC) either indicates that Israelite clans took their names from those localities and not *vice versa*, or probably reflects agreements between natives and newcomers of the Rachel group which eventually resulted in full assimilation.

3–4. *The inheritance of the daughters of Zelophehad* (see Introduction to chs. 16–17). The redactor, who introduced the episode from Num. 26:33; 27:1ff., adapts it to the secondary tradition of the apportionment by **Eleazar the priest and Joshua** and tribal representatives (**the leaders**; see on 9:15). The role of the priest Eleazar is a Priestly redaction after Num. 26:52–56; 33:54; 34:16–29; cf. Jos. 18:6, 8–10, where Joshua is the sole arbiter in the allotment.

5. ten portions, besides . . . Gilead and Bashan: i.e. without Hepher, whose land was divided among his 'daughters'. Here their inheritance is severally equal to that of each of the other clans. The debate seems to concern not so much land as status in a sacral confederacy of the various groups in Manasseh, perhaps the reorganisation of such a confederacy at Shechem. Note the definite article with Gilead, which is thus a district rather than a tribe (see further, below, on Jg. 5:17; 11:1).

7–10. *Fragmentary description of the boundary of Manasseh.* The north-east limit is given vaguely as **Asher**, and there are only three fixed boundary-points, **Michmethath, which is east of Shechem,** the pivotal boundary-point of Ephraim (see on 16:4–10), Yasib (so LXX for MT **the inhabitants**, Hebrew *yôšᵉbê*) **of En-tappuah**, which may be located at Yasūf, eight miles south of Shechem by Tell Sheikh Abū Zarad, the probable site of **Tappuah**, and **the brook Kanah**, the western part of the northern boundary of Ephraim. There is no description of the eastern border of Manasseh beyond the vague statement that it was contiguous with Issachar (v. 10), surely on the north-east rather than the east. The occupation by Manasseh of the lands of **Tappuah** and by Ephraim of the settlement, sufficiently odd to warrant a special note in the text (v. 8), is rightly emphasised by Alt ('Das System der Stämmesgrenzen im Buche Josua', *KS* I, 1953, p. 200) as an indication of the early date of the boundary-lists of the tribes, preserving, as it does, the memory of the old Canaanite unit of central fortified town and surrounding country and villages, which were occupied piecemeal by the various elements of Israel. The situation at **Tappuah** might indicate the revolt of peasants, possibly part of the original Machir (see above, p. 14), later assimilated to Manasseh, and the subsequent occupation of the settlement by force by the warlike Ephraim.

The abrupt note in v. 9*b*: **The cities here, to the south of the brook** (Kanah) **among the cities of Manasseh, belong to Ephraim** agrees with nothing in the context, and a list of settlements may have been lost. The composite nature of the passage is indicated by the reiteration that the northern border of Manasseh reached to **Asher** (v. 10). The eastern part of the northern border of Manasseh, quite vague here, may be supplemented from the list of the southern settlements of Issachar in 19:18–22.

11–13. *Canaanite settlements surviving the occupation.* The reckoning of cities in **Issachar** and **Asher** to Manasseh may indicate that Manasseh, more recent arrivals, made a stronger and more effective claim to lands on which the older groups had merely rights of grazing and sojourn (see on 19:17–23 on the settlement of

Zebulun and Asher possibly as part of the land-settlement policy of Egypt in the fourteenth century). Neither **Beth-shean** nor **Ible-am** is mentioned in the settlement of Issachar (19:17–23), nor **En-dor**, **Taanach** or **Megiddo** in the settlement of Asher (19:24–31). In the case of Asher, this may indicate that the name may primarily describe a physical region (see on 19:24–31). Verse 12 is an awkward admission of the failure to make any impression on the fortified cities at the edge of the Great Central Plain (Jg. 1:27ff.). Those were Canaanite city-states commanding the passages through the hills from the coast to the Great Central Plain which carried the bulk of the traffic from Egypt to Damascus and beyond; e.g. **Beth-shean** (Tell al-Ḥusn by Arab Beisān) at the eastern end of the plain, **Ible-am** (Khirbet Bel'āmeh) in the central foothills near the southern pass from the Great Central Plain to the coastal plain by the Plain of Dothan *c.* two miles south of Arab Jenīn. **En-dor** (Arab 'Ain Dūr) *c.* seven miles south-east of Nazareth, seems too far north of Manasseh, and is possibly a corruption suggested by **Dor** (Khirbet Burj aṭ-Ṭanṭura; cf. Jg. 1:27) on the coast south of the Carmel head.

12. persisted in dwelling: lit. 'were pleased to dwell', i.e. 'settled as they pleased'.

13. forced labour: see on 16:10.

14–18. *Two variant traditions of the expansion of 'Joseph'* (vv. 14f. and 16f.).
See Introduction to chs. 16–17, especially on the area occupied east and west of the Jordan. H.-J. Zobel (*Stammesspruch und Geschichte*, 1965, p. 116) relates the situation in vv. 14f. to the blessing on Joseph in Gen. 43:22: 'Joseph is a fruitful *ben*-tree by a spring with branches climbing over the wall.'

15. forest: the word may mean either the evergreen forests of the northern part of Transjordan ('the forest of Ephraim', 2 Sam. 18:6) or the scrub, or *maquis*, of Palestine.
clear: correct, though the verb in MT is *bārā'*, which is used of creation in Gen. 1:1, and in Isa. 41:28 of Jerusalem being 'transformed' into gladness. It may be a homonym meaning in the intensive 'to clear', which has an Arabic cognate meaning 'to cut (into shape)'.

16. chariots of iron: i.e. plated with iron, an indication of the gradual penetration by Israel to the Great Central Plain from the time of the decisive incursion west of Jordan by the Rachel group, *c.* 1225 BC, when iron, hitherto a Hittite monopoly, used in Syria, Palestine and Egypt in small luxury goods, was introduced in weapons to Palestine by the Philistines, who retained its working as a monopoly for a century, as is implied in 1 Sam. 13:19ff.

Jezreel (Arab Zer'īn) is near the low watershed of the Great Central Plain, and gave its name either to the whole plain both east and west or specifically to the lower part eastwards where it slopes to below sea-level at Beisān.

18. to its farthest borders: (lit. 'its goings out'). Possible, but a paraphrase. The Hebrew word, *tôṣᵉ'ôtāyw*, is possibly cognate with Arabic *wāṣā*, 'to be contiguous'. The eventual annexation of the Canaanite cities on the edge of the Great Central Plain is envisaged after the Israelites have cleared settlements in the *maquis* in the hills between Shechem and that region.

THE APPORTIONMENT TO THE OTHER TRIBES

18:1–19: 48

This is represented in the introduction (18:1–10) as being effected by Joshua by means of the sacred lots before 'the whole congregation' (Hebrew *'ēdâh*) at Shiloh as a central sanctuary. In contrast to the occupation of the south by Judah (ch. 15; Jg. 1:2ff.) and the Kenizzites (15:14–19; Jg. 1:11–15) on their own initiative, like Joseph in the central highlands (17:14–18), the formality of the transaction is surprising, and there is much that suggests artificial reconstruction at a late date together with Priestly influence. The conception of the transaction before 'the whole congregation' convened *ad hoc* before 'the tent of meeting' (v. 1) and the technical language, suggests the influence of P, and the needless repetition of Moses' apportionment to Reuben, Gad and eastern Manasseh (v. 7) and the special case of the Levites (v. 7), the reiteration of the settlement of Judah and Joseph (v. 5), and indeed the whole unrealistic conception of a systematic survey and apportionment by lot in the case of groups already settled in their regions, as in the case of Issachar and Zebulun at least, (see on 17:11–13, and p. 123), is certainly redactional.

The result is a definite theological schematisation: the Promised Land is conquered by the sovereign power of God, who distributes it to the twelve tribes by lot. Though Judah and Joseph had taken the initiative in occupying their lands, they too, with the Transjordan tribes, are sacramentally associated with this transaction, which is before 'the whole congregation of the people of Israel'. Shiloh, in Ephraim and the repository of the ark in the latter days of the pre-Monarchic period (1 Sam. 1–4) and of 'the tent of meeting' (1 Sam. 2:22), is assumed to be the sanctuary where the lots were cast, obviously being inserted after the occupation of the territory of 'Joseph', where Shiloh was. In point of fact if at that time a central sanctuary of the various elements of Israel in the north is to be assumed that was probably at Shechem, which is envisaged in Dt. 11:29–32; 27:4, 11ff.; Jos. 24; and the redactional 8:30–35. If there is a nucleus of historical fact in 18:1–10, that may be the role of a figure like Joshua, if not indeed Joshua himself, as Alt proposed, as the supreme arbiter in boundary disputes and other cases in contention between the component groups of Israel of the north, as in the claim of 'Joseph' in 17:14–18. The survey of the land before apportionment by three men from each tribe is so novel a feature as to suggest some degree of originality, despite the assumption of the twelve-tribe confederacy and its artificiality, especially as it modifies the theological conception of the apportionment by the divine lot before Joshua, Eleazar the priest and the representatives of the tribes (Num. 34:16–28). The factual origin of the tradition may have been boundary commissions—not indeed to survey the land to be apportioned by lot, but to settle disputed claims in the case of groups already settled. The importance of such local boundaries is fully apparent from the case of responsibility for manslaughter in Dt. 21:1–9. The written account of the various districts, on which the passage repeatedly insists (vv. 4, 6, 8, 9), may refer to written and attested records of evidence in such arbitrations for future reference, which Alt admitted among the sources for the boundary-lists of the various groups in Jos. 13–19.

The secondary, redactional character of the Shiloh tradition of the apportionment is clearly indicated by the fact that after the natural conclusion of the transaction, 'so they finished distributing . . .' (1:50), a further formal conclusion is added, explicitly mentioning the apportionment by lot by Eleazar the priest, Joshua and the tribal heads in that order 'at Shiloh before the Lord' (19:51).

The tribal territories are described with varying fullness. That of Benjamin (18:11–28) is composed of the same elements as that of Judah (ch. 15), a list of boundary-points (18:11–20) and town-lists (vv. 21–28), both very full, as we should expect since Benjamin was incorporated in the kingdom of Judah, from which administrative lists were available to the Deuteronomist. The boundaries of Simeon (19:1–9), semi-nomadic in the southern steppe, are not described, since the southern border of Judah at its greatest extent included Simeon, and the deficiency is supplemented by the use of the town-list (vv. 2ff.) of District I of Judah (15:21ff.). In the case of the tribes in the Great Central Plain and Galilee (19:10–39) local data regarding boundary-points and town-lists must have been very inadequate, partly because the Central Plain and the Plain of Acco were not effectively occupied until the early Monarchy, with David's incorporation of Canaanite districts into the realm, and partly because of the fluctuations of the northern frontier after the disruption of Solomon's kingdom. When we consider that for the description of Judah the Deuteronomist depended on administrative lists in a kingdom whose frontier never drastically fluctuated for over three hundred years, except for an interlude of some twenty years under Assyria and on such lists from as late as the end of Josiah's reign, by which time north Israel had been recognised for over a century as Assyrian provinces, this deficiency is not surprising.

Preliminaries to the Apportionment at Shiloh **18:1–10**

1. congregation: (Hebrew *'ēdâh*), i.e. 'those who keep tryst (*mô'ēd*). A religious assembly is denoted, though the word may be used generally of a gathering, e.g. of the wicked (Pss. 22:16, MT 17; 86:14; Job 15:34), or a swarm of bees (Jg. 14:8). P in the Pentateuch employs by preference *qāhāl*, which is used here in the verbal root assembled.
Shiloh: the addition of a later, Priestly redactor (see Introduction to chs 18–19), as is also probably **the tent of meeting**, which is probably suggested by the sacred lot; cf. the oracle lot in the E tradition of the tent of meeting in the desert wandering (Exod. 33:7–11). The sanctuary here, probably the first built sanctuary of Yahweh (1 Sam. 1:9; 3:15), was associated with the settlement of Ephraim, in the middle of whose territory it was situated, as distinct from other sanctuaries at or near the boundaries of different groups (see above, pp. 15f.). It was the repository for the ark (1 Sam. 3:3), which may thus have been associated specifically with Ephraim. The origin of the sanctuary is uncertain. In the sequel to the Benjaminite war (Jg. 21:15ff.), it was certainly not envisaged as a central sanctuary, and the possibility of the Benjaminites getting wives as the girls danced in the vineyards at the yearly 'feast of Yahweh' despite the ban, indicates the local fertility cult either before the cult of Yahweh or the survival of such among natives not yet integrated into Ephraim. Its significance as the repository of the ark may date from the nearly successful attempt of Ephraim's southern neighbours Benjamin to assert their independence (Jg. 20–21). The destruction of the sanctuary at Shiloh is not mentioned before Jer. 7:12, 14; 26:9, nor is it attested by the most recent Danish excavations at Khirbet Seilūn (M. C. Buhl and S. Holm-Nielsen, *Shilo*, 1969, pp. 56–9) contrary to earlier claims by H. Kjaer (*JPOS* 10, 1930, p. 103), nor indeed has the sanctuary been certainly identified.

4. writing a description of it: if genuine, this might reflect the recording of decisions in boundary disputes (see Introduction to chs 18–19, p. 151). Alt ('Das System der Stämmesgrenzen im Buche Josua', *KS* I, 1953, p. 201n) cites works by Wilhelm and Tod for Greek analogies, and boundary records were duly attested and filed in Mesopotamia. The linear alphabet of twenty-two signs was already in use in Palestine in the thirteenth century BC and would have facilitated such records, which would normally be deposited in a sanctuary, but, it must be said, in a boundary sanctuary.

7. Redactional note explaining why only seven portions are assigned, the settlement of Judah and Ephraim and Manasseh having been mentioned already (v. 5).

the priesthood of the LORD: cf. Dt. 10:8; 18:1ff., where the office of the Levites as a priestly caste is defined in the service of Yahweh in sacrifice and worship according to the Deuteronomic conception before the degradation of the Levites to menial office in the cult. In Dt. 10:8 they are particularly associated with the ark, as in redactional expansions in chs 3 and 4.

9. **by towns:** probably redactional, suggested by the town-lists, which are used to supplement the deficiency of the boundary-lists.

The Settlement of Benjamin **18:11–28**

11–20. *List of boundary-points*; cf. the southern border of 'Joseph' (see on 16:1–3), coinciding with the northern border of Benjamin from the high ground (lit. 'shoulder') north of Jericho to the Lower Beth-horon (vv. 11–14), where it turned south, then east to the outskirts of Kiriath-jearim (Qiryat al-'Ainab; see on 9:16). From there the southern boundary coincides with the northern border of Judah (see on 15:5*b*–9, in the opposite direction).

12. the shoulder north of Jericho: the ridge north of the Wādī Dūq ('the waters of Jericho', 16:1) and its dry lower course, the Wadi Nu'eimeh. The description **shoulder** befits the last spur of this ridge before the plain in the Jordan Valley.

the wilderness of Beth-aven: i.e. 'pasture-land', lying on the dry slopes east of Bethel and vicinity (cf. 8:20, 24). Beth-aven is probably an orthodox parody ('house of Vanity') of Bethel as the description of the southern border of 'Joseph' at this point (16:2) suggests.

14–15. The details of the boundary between Kiriath-jearim and the Spring of the Waters of Nephtoah are unclear and ambiguous. *RSV* rightly takes the last clause of v. 14 (Hebrew *zô't p^e'at-yam*) as a summary statement: **This forms the western side**. The southern border begins at the (presumably northern edge of) the lands of Kiriath-jearim. Literally, MT *w^{e}yāṣā' hagg^{e}bûl yammāh* *w^e^yāṣā' 'el ma'yan mê neptôaḥ* means 'and the border used to go out westwards and it went out to the Spring of the Waters of Nephtoah', which is absurd. *RSV* suggests reading 'Ephron' for 'westwards' after the description of the northern boundary of Judah at this point (15:9). This passage, however, reads not 'Ephron' but 'the cities of Mount Ephron'. We propose to keep closer to MT, and suggest, on the reading of LXX 'to Gasein' for 'westwards', that *môsā'* has dropped out, Moṣa' being the well-known settlement Mozah in the Wādī 'ṣ-Ṣurār, north-east of Qiryat al-'Ainab (18:26). We restore the text: *w^e^yāṣā' hagg^e^bûl yammāh l^e^moṣā' w^e^yāṣā' 'el-ma'yan mê neptôaḥ* ('and the border went out west of Mozah to the Spring of the Waters of Nephtoah') or *w^e^yāṣā' hagg^e^bûl 'el-moṣā' w^e^yāṣā 'el-ma'yan mê neptôaḥ* ('and the border went out to Mozah and went out to the Spring of the Waters of Nephtoah'). This suggests the reading at 15:9, *w^e^yāṣā' 'el-moṣā' 'ir har-'eprôn* ('and it went out to Mozah, a city of Mount Ephron'), instead of the vague *w^e^yāṣā' 'el 'ārê har-'eprôn* ('and it went out to the cities of Mount Ephron').

21–28. *Town-list in Benjamin.* The settlements fall into two groups, vv. 21–24 and vv. 25–28, each ending with an enumeration as the various district-lists of Judah. The latter is District XI of the administrative division of the kingdom of Judah, which is defective in 15:60, listing only Kiriath-jearim and the unknown Rabbah, for the simple reason that the centres were fully noted in the description of the portion of Benjamin, in whose tribal district indeed those regions fell, at least north of the Wādī 'ṣ-Ṣurār. The former town-list has a peculiar interest in including **Bethel** (v. 22) and **Ophrah** (v. 23). Bethel is mentioned as a point in the southern boundary of Ephraim, hence was probably the boundary-sanctuary where the solidarity of Ephraim and Benjamin, reflected in the story of Joseph and Benjamin in the Pentateuch, was expressed; see further, on Jg. 2:1; 20:23–28; and pp. 15f. Ophrah also is included in Ephraim, and, if to be located at aṭ-Ṭayibeh, four miles north of Bethel, would be quite irrelevant to the situation before Josiah's expansion to the north on the decline of Assyria in the last decade of his life (622–609 BC), as Alt argued (*KS* II, 1953, pp. 281ff.). Another such place is **Ophni** (v. 24), if this is identical with Jiphneh just north-west of Bethel, the modification of the initial guttural in the Arabic place-name being due to the rendering of the initial Hebrew consonant ' in LXX by *g*. With this exception those localities, as distinct from those in vv. 25–28, were east of the watershed of the central highlands, hence in the climatic region to which District XII (the wilderness) of the kingdom of Judah belonged. Certain sites in this list have already been discussed in ch. 15, on which see.

The groupings are hard to understand, e.g. **Parah**, identified by

Dalman (*PJB* 10, 1914, p. 22ff.) with Tell Fāra by 'Ain Fāra, six miles north-east of ancient Jerusalem, which we expect rather to be grouped with Geba (Arab Jeba'), *c.* three miles north of 'Ain Fāra. The fact that **Geba** falls into a different district from Ramah (ar-Ram, *c.* two miles westwards) indicates how strictly the division is determined by the watershed, with one exception, **Ophni**, if that is identical with Jifneh. This surely relates to fiscal divisions, places with similar rainfall and agricultural potential being carefully grouped together to facilitate fair assessment. In 18:28 *RSV* reading 'Kiryath-jearim' depends on LXX; cf. MT 'Kiryath'.

The Lot of Simeon, Zebulun, Issachar, Asher, Naphtali and Dan 19:1–48

With conclusion (v. 49), additional notes on the inheritance of Joshua (vv. 49*b*–50) and the conclusion by the post-Exilic redactor of the whole episode (v. 51).

This matter varies considerably in content and treatment and in the fullness of source material available. The description of the territory of Simeon (vv. 1–9), like Levi of no political significance in Israel of historical times, omits boundary-points, and lists settlements only, which are based on the second part of the town-list of the first administrative district of Judah (15:21–32). In support of the artificial reconstruction of the settlement of Simeon in the Negeb, it may be noted that there was no sedentary settlement from the Early Iron Age south and west of Beersheba until the eleventh century, just before Solomon's administrative division of his realm, as Y. Aharoni has noticed (*Archaeology and Old Testament Study*, ed. D. W. Thomas, 1967, pp. 389f.).

2. Sheba: probably the dittograph of the second element in the preceding place-name Beer-sheba, as the enumeration of settlements in v. 6 suggests. For the text the lists should be checked against 1 Chr. 4:28–32, which depends on the present passage.

Simeon: Gen. 34:25–31 depicts Simeon and Levi in a much more active, and indeed aggressive, role by Shechem, which, however, resulted in their dispersal (Gen. 49:5–7) and decline in political significance, Levi to be a priestly caste and Simeon to live a semi-nomadic life in the steppes about Beer-sheba and southwards. Politically and economically overshadowed by Judah (v. 9; Jg. 1:1–3), Simeon retained recognition among the groups composing Israel probably as custodians of the sanctuary of Beer-sheba, which we believe to be 'the high places of Isaac' (Am. 7:9), which was a place of pilgrimage until at least the eighth century (Am. 5:5).

10–16. *The Lot of Zebulun*, contiguous in the south-west and north-west and in the north and north-east with Naphtali, and on the south-east with Issachar. On the original significance of Zebulun, see above, p. 13.

Here, as in the other tribal areas in Galilee, there is a marked difference of treatment. Instead of the enumeration of boundary-points followed by a list of settlements, the list of settlements generally coincides with the boundary-points. Besides eleven towns as boundary-points, v. 15 lists five towns, then mentions twelve in all. This surely indicates an incomplete town-list, probably supplemented by redactional accretions; cf. 21:34f.; Jg. 1:30. Here the boundary-points of Zebulun are listed from **Sarid**, probably to be read after certain MSS of LXX and the Syriac versions Sadid, Tell Šadūd in the foothills of Galilee five miles south-east of Nazareth, **westwards . . . to the brook that is east of Jokneam** (Tell Qeimūn), that is probably the wadi that breaks through the foothills of Galilee by **Bethlehem** (v. 15) seven miles west of Nazareth. From 'Sarid', or Sadid, the border runs eastwards along the foothills to **Chisloth-tabor** (v. 12), probably near Arab Iksal, two miles south-east of Nazareth and three miles west of Dabbūriyeh (**Daberath**, v. 12). If **Japhia** is Yāfā, this boundary-point may be displaced from after 'Sarid', since it lies west of the places previously mentioned in v. 12. It is in fact the first point in the boundary going north and up the foothills (note that it went *up*) in a north-easterly direction (**on the east toward the sunrise) to Gath-hepher**, the reputed home of Jonah the son of Amittai (2 Kg. 14:25), traditionally located at Mašhad three miles north-east of Nazareth. It is uncertain whether Nazareth was included in Zebulun or Naphtali, since it is unmentioned in either, but the specific reference to the easterly trend of the border between Japhia and Gath-hepher suggests that it ran along the ridge east rather than west of the upland depression of Nazareth with its spring. The next point is **Rimmon** (v. 13), Rummāneh, six miles north of Nazareth, and so on to **Hannathon** (v. 14), Hinnatuni of the Amarna Tablets, Khirbet al-Beidāwīyeh, the conspicuous tell that once controlled access to the trunk highway through the upland plain of the Baṭṭūf from the Great Central Plain by the open valleys by Bethlehem ('the brook that is east of Jokneam') and the Wadi 'l-Mālik farther north, the valley of Iphtahel. The western boundary is not defined, but it was no doubt formed by the pass from Hannathon to the wadi by Bethlehem. The five settlements listed in v. 15 may be the remnant of an administrative list from the north kingdom of Israel, or from the Assyrian administration in the late eighth and seventh centuries, or possibly even a redactional expansion from the list of unconquered places in Jg. 1:30, as is suggested by the fact that more places are listed than the twelve of the final enumeration.

17–23. *The Lot of Issachar*, north of Manasseh, east of Asher, south of Naphtali and south-east of Zebulun. On the original significance of Issachar, see above, pp. 12f.

Owing to the vagueness of the northern boundary of Manasseh (17:10f.) and of the borders of the neighbouring Galilean tribes the boundaries of Issachar are also vague. The position of **Jezreel** (Arab Zer'in) (v. 18) and **En-gannim** (Arab Janīn) (v. 21) indicates that the lists of places in vv. 18–22 does not describe a boundary. Only v. 22 from Tabor to Jordan describes a boundary, and here the significance of **Shahazuma** and **Beth-shemesh** is not clear owing to the uncertainty of the locations. The source of the town-list in Issachar is uncertain.

24–31. *The Lot of Asher*, contiguous with Manasseh on the south (17:10f.) and with Zebulun and Naphtali on the east. Here there is a bewildering combination of incomplete boundary-points and groups of settlements. Many places cannot be precisely located, even where they are mentioned in the Karnak inscriptions of Thothmes III, such as **Helkath** (v. 25), with which the list begins, so that it is impossible to tell if this is a boundary-point on the southern edge of the Great Central Plain (so Noth, *op. cit.*, pp. 118f.), or simply a settlement within Asher, possibly at Tell al-Harbaj at the south-east extremity of the Plain of Acco (so Alt, *PJB* 25, 1929, pp. 38ff.). The deficiency of the source material is indicated by the fact that the compiler does not, as in the southern areas, repeat contiguous boundary-points in contiguous tribal territories; thus it is impossible to tell how far **Asher** extended into the hills of Galilee. Another complication is, we suspect, that the term **Asher** is ambiguous, an ethnic term referring to the tribe, but perhaps primarily a geographical term describing a physical region, from which this component of Israel took its name; cf. *Asaru* as a place-name in the Egyptian Papyrus Anastasi I (late thirteenth century BC). See further, above, pp. 13f. This theory is supported by the fact that in v. 29 the northern boundary apparently terminates at **Achzib** (Arab ez-Zīb, nine miles north of Acco), whereas in v. 29 the area is stated to include Tyre and Sidon, being bounded in the south by **Shihor-libnath** (v. 26), which drains from Carmel, and may be the Nahr az-Zarqā, which flows into the Mediterranean *c.* three miles north of Caesarea, thus including **Dor** (Khirbet Burj aṭ-Ṭanṭūra) some five miles north of this, which is reckoned to Manasseh in 17:10. In the tribal territory of Asher so described from the western slopes of Carmel to the Plain of Acco with its numerous tells, conspicuous though not certainly identified, and the western foothills of lower and upper Galilee to Achzib, it is noteworthy that in the list of conquered kings in ch. 12 only **Achshaph** is mentioned (probably Tell Keisān; but see on 12:1). This seems to suggest the limitation we have suggested for the settlement of Asher as part of an aggressive Israel. The extension to **Sidon**, with the addition of place-names in this direction in vv. 28–29*a*, may be the work of a late redactor, who has in mind the geographic rather than the ethnic significance of 'Asher'. But here, as in the Blessing of Zebulun in Gen. 49:13, **Sidon** may refer to the northern coast of Palestine as far south as Carmel, where the harbours were controlled by the Phoenicians (Mowinckel, *Israels opphav*, p. 130). According to Dt. 33:18ff., Issachar and Zebulun profited from trade in this region along the long-established trade-routes to the interior, while Jg. 5:17, the reference to Asher's association with the coastal inlets, implies the people's involvement with the Phoenicians.

29. In the region of **Achzib: Mahalab** should almost certainly be read for MT *Mehebel*, with LXX; cf. Jg. 1:31, where Ahlab and Helbah are mentioned. This might be Arab Maḥālib, just south of the mouth of the Litani (Maḫalibu of Assyrian records). On the other hand, Mehebel of MT might mean 'mooring-place' (of Achzib). **Ummah** (Acco, after LXX; cf. Jg. 1:31), **Aphek** and **Rehob** are part of a town-list, which, from the enumeration in v. 31, is incomplete. The association with Acco (Tell al-Fukhār, just east of the modern town) suggests that **Aphek** and **Rehob** are to be identified with conspicuous tells in the Plain of Acco, the former with Tell Kurdāneh at the source (Hebrew *'ᵃpēq*) of the River Na'mīn, and **Rehob** possibly with Tell al-Bīr al-Gharbi, by al-Birweh, seven miles east of Acco.

32–39. *The Lot of Naphtali*: contiguous on the south-east with Issachar, on the south-west with **Zebulun** (v. 34) and on the west with **Asher** (v. 34), reaching the upper **Jordan** (v. 33) and where the river flowed out of the Sea of Galilee, and contiguous with Dan on the north-east. On the original significance of **Naphtali**, see above, p. 14.

The compiler conforms here most closely to his pattern in his description of the southern territories, with the boundary-points first, followed by a list of settlements. The significance of the first five places in v. 33 is uncertain, but **the oak of Za-anannim** suggests not a settlement but a landmark, and so a boundary-point. *ṣa'ᵃnānîm* probably means 'caravaneers', derived from *ṣā'an* ('to pack up and travel'; cf. Isa. 33:20) with an Arabic cognate (so Soggin, *Judges*, 1981, p. 66). The place was probably on the ancient caravan route through the Great Central Plain to Damascus. The mention of the **Jordan** suggests that the south-east boundary was being defined, and here **Adami-nekeb** ('Adami the Pass'), probably Adamal mentioned in Egyptian inscriptions from the fifteenth to the thirteenth century, is identical with Khirbet ad-Dāmiyeh south-west of the southern end of the Sea of Galilee. **Jabneel** is probably an Iron Age site in the vicinity, the name being revived in a recent Jewish settlement. The unknown **Lakkum** would then be between this point and the Jordan on the high ground south of the Wādī Fajjās, coinciding with the north-east boundary of Issachar (v. 22), which is not named here. **Heleph** (v. 33) then will be between **Adami-nekeb** and the foot of Tabor (**Aznoth-tabor**, v. 34), south-west of which **Hukkok** must lie. Thereafter, it is vaguely stated that the border was with **Asher on the west**. In the repetition of the border towards 'Jordan and Judah' is absurd and is omitted in LXX. It may be the corruption of a gloss to the effect that 'Naphtali touched Jordan where it flows out of the Sea of Galilee for a few miles, just as Judah touches the lower Jordan before it flows into the Dead Sea.'

The town-list (vv. 35–39) describes the settlement from south to north. A few towns north of the Sea of Galilee, **Adamah** (possibly Ḥajar ad-Damm, *c.* three miles north-west of the debouchement of the Jordan into the Sea of Galilee, **Hazor** (see on 11:1) and possibly **Kedesh**, **Edrei** and **En-hazor**, mark the boundary with Dan to the north-east. The northern limit would seem to be **Yiron**, **Migdal-el**, **Horem**, **Beth-anath** and **Beth-shemesh**, the first located at Yārūn at the present frontier between Israel and Lebanon, **Beth-anath** possibly 'Ainetha, six miles north of Qedeis (**Kedesh**), as the context suggests, and **Beth-shemesh** possibly Ḥāris (cf. Hebrew *ḥeres*, 'the sun', which *šemeš* also means), south-west of Arab Tibnīn in the same locality. The last two places, by their names, were sanctuaries respectively of the Canaanite goddess Anat and the Sun, both of whom play a conspicuous part in the Rās Shamra myths of the fertility-cult.

40–48. *The Lot of Dan.* On the origins of Dan, see above, p. 11. The group of **Dan** never properly settled in the Shephelah (Jg. 18:1), from which they had to migrate to the Upper Jordan. Mowinckel (*Israels opphav*, pp. 128, 157) feasibly proposed that the southern locality of Dan south-west of Ephraim indicates their affinity with Ephraim of the Rachel group, acknowledged by the tradition of the descent of Dan from Rachel's maid Bilhah, together with Dan's Galilean neighbour Naphtali. Here the geographical associations are primary and the genealogy secondary. The Deuteronomist assuming the southern location of Dan cannot even pretend to describe a boundary, but, prompted by a note on the difficulties of the settlement of Dan in the northern Shephelah in

Jg. 1:34f., he utilises the town-list for the second administrative district of Judah (15:33–36), supplemented by the Amorite settlements of **Aijalon** and **Sha-albim** (Jg. 1:35). The extension to **Aijalon** (Arab Yālū; see on 10:12) indicates the administrative division of Solomon, the district being retained by Judah after the Disruption, when Rehoboam fortified Aijalon (2 Chr. 11:10). This is suggested by the fact that the district farther south to Gezer was comprehended in the territory of 'Joseph' (16:3).

The inclusion of **Ekron** (v. 43) and localities such as **Eltekeh** (v. 44), **Bene-berak** (v. 45) and **Me-jarkon** towards **Joppa** (Arab Jaffa; v. 46) indicates the provisional organisation of the Philistine area by Josiah on the decline of Assyria, who had administered this region from Ashdod. The localities in vv. 43f. are probably a fuller draft of the note on the fifth administrative district of Judah in 15:45f., which mentions only the centres Ekron and Ashdod; cf. 1 Kg. 4:9 in Solomon's administration. The omission of important centres in this area, however, notably Lydda and Gezer, indicates that the source material was incomplete. It is not said that Jaffa was included. The section is concluded by a note on the migration of Dan to the upper Jordan after Jg. 18. The text is uncertain. For **When the territory of the Danites was lost to them**, LXX reads 'For the territory of the Danites was too restricted for them.' The reason for the migration seems more realistically given in Jg. 18:1, that they had not been able to effect a settlement in the northern Shephelah, being confined to the hills by the Amorites (Jg. 1:34). The settlement of Dan both east and west of the upper Jordan, of which the Deuteronomistic Historian was fully aware, may account for the fact that in his description of the settlement of Naphtali the boundary is not explicitly taken to the upper Jordan.

49–51. *Conclusion* (v. 49*a*), *with redactional notes of the inheritance of Joshua* (vv. 49*b*f.), elaborated from the note on his grave in 24:30 and Jg. 2:9, *and of the end of the transaction* under Eleazar and Joshua at Shiloh (v. 51). On literary analysis, see Introduction to chs 18–19, p. 151.

50. Timnath-serah: lit. 'the portion of that which is left over', cf. *seraḥ* ('overlap') in Exod. 26:12. The place is so named also in 24:30; cf. Timnath-heres in LXX[B] and the Old Latin versions and in Jg. 2:9, which means 'the Portion of the Sun'. The pagan implications occasioned the modification of the name. The location at Khirbet Tibneh, ten miles north-west of Bethel and of Joshua's burial-place here has a peculiar significance for the actual historicity of Joshua in the tradition of the Gibeonite campaign in chapter 9.

CITIES OF REFUGE

20:1–8

On the question of the date and relation to similar prescriptions in Dt. 4:41–43; 19:1–13; Num. 35:9–34, see Introduction, pp. 46f.

The prescription is the development of a well-established institution in Semitic life and exemplified in more recent times among the Arab tribes of the desert, where every tent is a potential asylum apart from any sacred associations. Sanctuaries were also asylums from rough justice, which was not always nice in its discrimination between murder and accidental homicide, as in the Book of the Covenant (Exod. 21:13f.) and in the time of Solomon (1 Kg. 1:50–53). Of the six cities in Jos. 20:7f., the three west of Jordan were certainly sanctuaries, though in the role of the cities and their elders (v. 4) the institution is already being secularised. This may be the specific contribution of the Deuteronomist, reflecting the suppression of local sanctuaries in the time of Josiah. The regularisation of the tribal rites of sanctuary, however, was probably necessitated earlier in the settlement of the various elements of Israel in a limited area. The complications of tribal sanctuary are well illustrated by the famous War of al-Basūs in Arab tradition, when the accidental wounding of a refugee's camel and the punctilio of vengeance by those who sheltered the man led to a forty years' war!

2. cities of refuge: (Hebrew *'ārê hammiqlāṭ*) The definite article indicates that the subject had already been introduced, e.g. in vv. 7–9*a*, where the language is less technical. Verses 1–9 are strongly impregnated with the phraseology of P, e.g. in the technical term 'city of refuge', which is not used in Dt. 4:41–43; 19:1–13 (which refer explicitly to the institution), but in Num. 35:9–34 (P).

3. manslayer: (*rôṣēaḥ*) from the same root as the verb in Exod. 20:13, denoting murder or killing in the blood-feud, but usually with the connotation of wanton killing, where the subject takes the law into his own hands.

without intent: (*bišᵉgāgāh*), so Num. 35:10; carried beyond intent by passion.

unwittingly: so Dt. 19:4; cf. 4:42. LXX omits the phrase as tautological after 'without intent'.

the avenger of blood: blood here defines one of the duties of the kinsman (*gô'ēl*), preferably the nearest kinsman, whose general duty it was to sustain the right of his kinsman; here to avenge his death (cf. 2 Sam. 14:11). The present institution, allowing blood-revenge only for premeditated murder, modifies the custom, though not abolishing it. Modification within the sanction of blood-revenge was also provided by Muhammad in Islam, and was probably also implied in the Decalogue (Exod. 20:13).

4. **at the entrance of the gate:** not at the sanctuary or altar, the deliberate secularisation of an older custom. See Introduction to ch. 20. The role of the elders may also indicate the custom as envisaged by the Deuteronomist, apart from the secondary elaboration of v. 6; see Introduction to ch. 20.

6. **until he has stood before the congregation:** this belongs to v. 3 (so Num. 35:12 and LXX, which omits vv. 4f. and reads v. 6*a*, influenced by Num. 35:12, immediately after v. 3.). This indicates that vv. 2f. are elaborations on Dt. 19:1–13.

until the death of the high priest: redactional after Num. 35:9–34 (P). This reflects the unique status of **the high priest**, on whom many of the functions of the king devolved after the Exile, a situation well illustrated by the respective positions of Zerubbabel and the high priest Joshua in Zech. 4 and 6.

7. **set apart:** the verb denotes consecration, and certainly **Kedesh in Galilee**, **Shechem** and **Hebron** were sanctuaries, as were probably the three places east of the Jordan. In the Deuteronomistic context, where a secularisation of the institution is intended, the primary meaning 'sanctification' has given way to the secondary meaning **set apart**. All those cities are listed as Levitical settlements in ch. 21. The regional rather than tribal distribution of the cities of refuge is noteworthy. In so far as the arrangement reflects, as it probably does ultimately, conditions of the settlement, this regional arrangement was necessary to obviate local and inter-tribal complications in exercise of the right of sanctuary (see Introduction to ch. 20). In this context, though **Naphtali**, **Ephraim** and **Judah** are familiar as the names of tribes, their significance here and probably, we think, originally was to physical geographical features.

8. The Transjordanian cities are also located in primarily geographical regions, the **wilderness**, or 'steppe', at the edge of **the tableland**, **Gilead**, 'the hard', rocky 'land' (see on 12:1) in the mountains east of Jordan, and **Bashan** in the north, 'the soft, fertile land' (see on 12:4), where the district al-Jaulān preserves the name of **Golan**. Here the tribal locations are added secondarily through the misunderstanding of Naphtali, Ephraim and Judah in v. 7.

THE LEVITICAL CITIES

21:1–45

This is apparently a detailed specification of the arrangement for Levitical settlements in Num. 35:1–8 (P) as in the case of the cities of refuge in ch. 20 (cf. Num. 35:9–34). Wellhausen (*Prolegomena to the History of Ancient Israel*, E.T. rep. 1957, pp. 159ff.) indeed regarded the whole of Jos. 21 as dependent on Num. 35:1–8, and a late Priestly reconstruction, which may nevertheless have had as a historical basis the provision for Levites of provincial sanctuaries after Josiah's reformation. But more recent scholarship has treated the tradition as genuinely historical as early as the reign of David. See General Introduction, pp. 47ff.; and for the text, cf. 1 Chr. 6:54–81 (MT vv. 39–66). The Levites are assumed here, as in the Blessing of Jacob (Gen. 49) and Moses (Dt. 33) to be a full tribe, or at least a full member of the twelve-tribe community and a priestly caste. This conception is no earlier than the time of David. On the Levites, see further, on Jg. 17:7.

The list of settlements by tribes in vv. 4–7 is secondary, as the extraordinary arrangement of the tribes indicates, this being superimposed on a primary geographical distribution. The repetition of v. 3 and v. 8*a* also indicates the secondary nature of vv. 4–7, like the apportionment of the settlements of Levitical families by lot, which is artificially brought into conformity with the tribal apportionment by Eleazar the priest, Joshua and 'the heads of the fathers' houses of the tribes of the people of Israel' at Shiloh (vv. 1f.; see on 18:1). The secondary character of vv. 4–7 is confirmed by the fact that in the lists of the actual settlements in vv. 9–40 the arrangement is primarily geographical, the tribal distribution within the various regional areas being obviously artificial.

The peculiar geographical division of the four main Levitical families, if these are original, is hard to understand unless on the assumption that they had been deliberately settled as part of a regular policy in the organisation of the kingdom under David and Solomon, into which Canaanite regions were incorporated. Thus, the Levites are thickly settled in the plains and on the frontiers (vv. 21–25, 28–31, 34f.), with settlements beyond Jordan in what might be a frontier area (vv. 36–39). From their strategic posting, the Levites may have had a military function, though 1 Chr. 26:30 implies a fiscal function. Places with former local sanctuaries like Gibeon (v. 32) may have been settled with Levites to counteract native religious influences; cf. Noth (*op. cit.*, p. 127), who regards the cities, which are all cities of refuge, as secondary additions. Geba, Anathoth and Almon in Benjamin (vv. 17f.) may have been settled to counteract the influence of Saul's kindred, and the country south-east and south-west of Hebron was a Kenizzite area, Hebron probably being a common sanctuary for the Kenizzites Kenites and Judah. The Levites of Hebron were vital for David's administration, according to 1 Chr. 26:29–32; but it is not certain whether Hebron was the chief centre of the Levites before David's employment of them, as 1 Chr. 26:29–32 describes, or whether they were settled there by him first to make Israelite influence dominant there and possibly to re-establish his influence after Absalom's revolt, and were subsequently settled elsewhere late in his reign, as 1 Chr. 26:31 suggests and as Jos. 21:8–40 may describe. We have to reckon moreover with the further possibility that Jos. 21:8–40 reflects a later settlement of Levites by Rehoboam, apparently with a strategic purpose (2 Chr. 11:13–17, esp. v. 17), and possibly also a similar settlement by Josiah after he recovered the southern part of Judah, which had been lost to Assyria in the time of Hezekiah, as Alt proposed (*KS* II, 1953, pp. 310–15). Alt notes the correspondence between the Levitical settlements in Judah and the extent of the land covered by the fortresses ascribed to Rehoboam in 2 Chr. 11:6–10, those in the Shephelah being in areas of doubtful loyalty, which would be even more so after the truncation of the kingdom under Hezekiah. Thus, whatever the origin of Levitical settlements, which may feasibly go back to David, the policy was probably continued under Rehoboam and after Hezekiah's reign, being attributed to Joshua by the Deuteronomistic Historian or the later redactor.

The particular Levitical families, which are apparently unknown to the Chronicler in Ezr. 2:40–Neh. 7:43, but are mentioned in 1 Chr. 6:1, may be secondary in Jos. 21 and late.

The general allotment of settlements to the four Levitical families in particular tribes **21:1–7**

1. the heads of the fathers' houses: a phrase characteristic of P in the description of the assembly of the sacral confederacy.

2. at Shiloh in the land of Canaan: in this peculiar post-Exilic addition **the land of Canaan** may mean the Promised Land, specifically west of Jordan.

the LORD commanded through Moses: cf. Num. 35:2 (P).

pasture lands: lit. 'places for driving out'; cf. the outfield of former British land economy.

4–7. Part of the introduction by a post-Exilic, probably Priestly redactor, who assumes the priestly families familiar in later times, Gershon, Kohath and Merari with the Aaronids, who were a branch of the family of Kohath (cf. Exod. 6:16: Num. 3:17; 26:57; all P) and evidently an élite, since their allotment is represented as being in Judah with **Simeon** and **Benjamin**, where the Temple was in

Jerusalem in later times, and where the ancient sanctuaries of Hebron (v. 11) and Gibeon (v. 17) are mentioned among their settlements. No actual settlement in **Simeon** is named, though in the period of the kingdom of Judah two important sanctuaries were here, both attested by archaeology, namely, Arad and Beer-sheba. Simeon and Judah are treated as a unit implying the situation in the Solomonic administration, as in the reckoning of Simeon as the first district in Judah in 15:29–32; cf. 19:1–9. Owing to their affinity with the Aaronid élite, Kohath is listed before the oldest family Gershon. Here the redactor superimposes the tribal system on the geographical distribution of the Levites in vv. 9–30. The association of the family of Gershon with the north (v. 6; cf. v. 32) is significant in view of their association with the sanctuary of Dan in Jg. 18:30, though this place is not associated in Jos. 21 with Gershon, being occupied by the Israelite group Dan only as the end of the settlement (Jg. 18).

The Particular Settlements of the Levites **21:8–40**

The Aaronids in Judah and Benjamin **21:8–19**

This may reflect the settlement of **Levites** to strengthen the standing of David in areas dominated by the Kenizzites in and around Hebron and in Benjamin, where opposition might have been expected from the kinsmen of Saul (2 Sam. 16:5–14; 20:1–21). It is possible also that in David's unification of the kingdom there was a strategic posting of Levites in places in those regions where there were Canaanite sanctuaries, e.g. **Gibeon** (v. 17), **Beth-shemesh** (v. 16), the name of which indicates a sanctuary of the sun-cult, possibly **Eshtemoa** (v. 14), the name of which suggests an oracle-sanctuary, and certainly **Hebron** (vv. 11, 13), the first of the Levitical settlements to be named. This supports Mazar's feasible view, which we have adopted with modification (see Introduction, pp. 49f.), that the Levitical establishment at Hebron was the basis of the whole system of David's strategic posting of the Levites. Besides, points in the west of the Shephelah, e.g. **Libnah** (v. 13) and **Beth-shemesh** (v. 16) were occupied possibly for strategic purposes, and the whole settlement may have subserved David's fiscal system. On the various localities in Judah, see on 10:38f.; 15:15 (**Kiriath-sepher**), 14:15 (**Hebron**), 15:33–36 (**Beth-shemesh**), 10:29; 15:42–44*a* (**Libnah**); and for other districts, where **Jattir**, **Holon** and **Eshtemoa** were, see 15:48–51; and for **Juttah**, see 15:55–57. On **Gibeon**, see 9:3.

The Rest of the Kohathites **21:20–26**

In the hill country of **Ephraim** (vv. 20–22), not primarily the tribe (see on 20:7), as the inclusion of **Shechem** (actually in Manasseh) indicates, and in the original southern district of **Dan** (vv. 20–24) and **Manasseh** west of the Jordan (v. 25).

21. The settlement at **Shechem** may have been designed to safeguard the interest of David at a sanctuary where the old tradition of the sacral confederacy of the groups of north Israel was strong and where the development of Jerusalem, the crown-possession of David, as a new religious centre might well have been resented. It was here in effect that the democratic spirit of Israel asserted itself against the house of David under Rehoboam (1 Kg. 12). Moreover Canaanite influence was strong enough to assert itself against Israel in the time of Abimelech (Jg. 9). Of the other settlements, **Beth-horon** (v. 22; see on 16:3), by its name, had been a sanctuary of the Canaanite god (probably of the underworld) Ḥoron, known as such from mythological texts from Rās Shamra. It was, moreover, of strategic significance on its famous 'ascent' from the Philistine Plain like **Aijalon** (v. 24; see on 10:12), **Gezer** (v. 21; see on 10:33), **Elteke, Gibbethon** (v. 23) and **Gath-rimmon** (v. 24). The last three places are feasibly located respectively near Tell al-Muqanna', Tell al-Malāt, and possibly Tell Jerīsheh on the River 'Aujā (Jarkon), just north of Jaffa.

25. Taanach: the sudden appearance of this place so far north of the places in the plain between Jaffa and the foothills of Judah is suspect, and the repetition of **Gath-rimmon** increases suspicion of the text. 1 Chr. 6:70 (MT, v. 55) reads 'Aner' for Taanach and 'Bileam' (Ible-am) for Gath-rimmon of the present passage. Taanach and Ible-am had a strategic significance as Canaanite strongholds covering passes from the Great Central Plain to the coastal plain, and so we consider Taanach in the district of Manasseh feasible and would seriously consider reading Ible-am for Gath-rimmon after 1 Chr. 6:70 (MT, v. 55), **Gath-rimmon** in v. 25 being possibly a copyist's error of homoeoteleuton.

The Settlements of Gershon in North Transjordan **21:27**

Two places are mentioned in East Manasseh in north Transjordan, with other settlements in the Great Central Plain in Issachar and in Galilee in Asher and Naphtali.

27. Be-eshterah is probably an abbreviation or corruption of Beth-eshterah, taken as Ashtaroth in this region in 1 Chr. 6:71 (MT

v. 56). The name suggests that it had been a pagan sanctuary of the fertility goddess Astarte.

Golan is also listed as a city of refuge in 20:8, and was thus probably also a sanctuary.

Besides the association with two sanctuaries, it may be noted that the Levites are also settled in a frontier area, as in the Shephelah.

The Settlements of Gershon in Galilee and the Northern Part of the Great Central Plain **21:28–33**

28. Kishion: in Issachar (19:20) may be connected with the source of the River Kishon; but the text is in doubt; cf. Kadesh, 1 Chr. 6:57.

Daberath: at the foot of Tabor (see on 19:10–16).

29. Jarmuth: cf. the mention of 'the mountain(s) of Yarmuth' in the stele of Seti I from Bethshan, dated 1313 BC (Albright, *BASOR* 125, 1952, pp. 25ff.). Jarmuth is probably to be located at or near Jabbūl north of Beisān.

En-gannim: listed in Issachar (19:21), Arab Jenīn (see on 19:17–23). 1 Chr. 6:73 (MT, v. 58) reads Aner.

31. On **Helkath** and **Rehob** in Asher, in the vicinity of Acco, see respectively on 19:25 and 19:24–31.

32. **Kedesh** in Naphtali was another sanctuary, as the name implies (see on 12:19–23).

Hammoth-dor . . . and Kartan: for the first, read possibly 'Hammath' (by the hot springs south of Tiberias), after LXX and 19:35, and for **Kartan**, which is not mentioned in the settlements of Naphtali in 19:35–38, read 'Rakkath' (19:35).

The comparatively thick settlement of Levites in the Central Plain and the foothills of Galilee may have been intended to strengthen the influence of Israel in the incorporation of the Canaanite cities here under David and Solomon.

The Settlement of Merari in the West of the Great Central Plain and South Transjordan **21:34–40**

This wide distribution of the Levites of the family of Merari is unnatural except on the assumption of a deliberate policy of settlement, such as has been associated with David. On the settlements in Zebulun, see on 19:10–16.

35. **Dimnah** is possibly the result of scribal corruption of Rimmon (cf. 19:13; 1 Chr. 6:77 (MT, v. 62)).

36. Jahaz: cf. 13:18; located in the inscription of Mesha north of Dibon and by Eusebius south of Medeba.

37. Kedemoth: on the upper course of the Arnon, according to Dt. 2:26, hence a border settlement.

38f. On the settlements of Gad, see on 13:24–28.

Here LXX expands with the statement that 'Israel (cf. MT 19:49, 'Joshua') completed the partition of the land and gave Joshua his portion in Timnath-serah, which he built', after 19:49f., adding the antiquarian gloss that Joshua took the flint blades used at Gilgal in the circumcision of those born in the wilderness and deposited them in Timnath-serah.

Concluding Summary, with Enumeration of Levitical Settlements
21:41–42

Conclusion to the Deuteronomist's presentation of the Occupation
21:43–45

Cf. the programme according to the Deuteronomist in 1:15. The statement **not one of all their enemies had withstood them** ignores the incomplete nature of the occupation, as noted in Jg. 1:21f., and indicates that the general subject of this part of the Deuteronomistic History is the realisation of the promise rather than a detailed factual history. The long struggle to occupy the land in face of reverses was known to the Deuteronomist, but was reserved as the subject of the next two parts of his work in Jg. and Sam.

3. CONCLUSION **22–24**

The account of the occupation of the Promised Land in the Deuteronomistic History in Jos. is rounded out with the statement of the fulfilment of the promise (21:43–45), the dismissal of the Transjordan groups to their homes (22), recalling the theme and indeed the language of 1:12–18 (cf. Dt. 3:18–20), and Joshua's formal farewell (23:1–16), which is a homiletic elaboration of the older tradition of the sacrament of the covenant at the assembly of the sacral community, which emerges clearly in ch. 24; or, rather, this is the elaboration of the paraenetic address which concluded this ceremony, of which Dt. 28ff. is the best example. In 24:1–28, as distinct from 21:43–45, the occupation is admitted to be incomplete. Assimilation to the Canaanites is forbidden, and the discipline and favour of God conditional upon the reaction to the Canaanite way of life accords with the homiletic purpose of the Deuteronomistic History. The section chs 22–24 has secondary expansions in the note on the dismissal and settlement of eastern Manasseh (22:7f.) and in the controversy over the altar by Jordan (22:10–34), which, whatever its historical origin (see above, p. 52) is an elaboration reflecting Priestly influence. Also secondary is the description of the covenant at Shechem (24:1–28), which elaborated 8:30–35 and gives the context of Joshua's paraenesis in ch. 23, reflecting however, a genuine ancient tradition and probably even an important moment in the development of the Israel of ten groups, which we encounter in Jg. 5:13–18 (see above, pp. 17f). Also possibly redactional is the note on the burial of the bones of Joseph (24:32) and the death and burial of Eleazar (24:33), which is prompted by the note on the death and burial of Joshua (24:29f.). The last passage is repeated in Jg. 2:8f., somewhat oddly after Jg. 1:1, which begins 'After the death of Joshua', and must therefore be secondary in Jg. 2:8f. The statement of the fidelity of Israel during Joshua's life and 'all the days of the elders who outlived Joshua who had known all the great work that the Lord had done for Israel' is substantially repeated in Jg. 2:7, serving as fitting conclusion to the theme of Jos. and as introduction to the theme of the Deuteronomist in Jg.

THE RETURN OF THE TRANSJORDANIAN TRIBES

22:1–9

This is part of the historical framework of the Deuteronomistic History, which resumes at 23:1. Verses 7f. are probably redactional elaborations, and v. 9 the introduction to the post-exilic redactional passage on the controversy with the Transjordan tribes over the altar in the Jordan Valley. The dismissal with the solemn injunction to 'observe the commandment and the law' (v. 5) reflects for the Deuteronomist an element in the ceremony of the sacrament of the covenant, which is envisaged as the *Sitz im Leben* of chs 23 and 24.

4. **has given rest:** cf. Dt. 3:20; Jos. 1:15 (promise); 21:44 (fulfilment).

to your home: lit. 'tents'; cf. Jg. 19:9, a survival from Israel's past. The present passage indicates that it refers to the several homes of the people and not to the warriors' tents, as is sometimes supposed, in 1 Kg. 12:16.

5. Though the epitome of the faith of Israel, which emphasises the free and devoted response to the personal approach of God (**to love the LORD your God . . . to serve him with all your heart**

and with all your soul) as well as the pragmatic keeping of the law is in the characteristic terms and homiletic style of the Deuteronomist, it may still reflect an earlier formula of dismissal in the context of the paraenetic address in the covenant sacrament at the sacral assembly in the days of the settlement.

6. blessed them: formally secured them in the experience of God's favour by the renewal of the covenant. The blessing, whereby one is associated with a subject known to possess the favour of God, often signifies either welcome or dismissal, and was held to be automatically effective. So Joshua takes leave of Caleb (14:13).

The Dismissal of East Manasseh and the Division of the Spoils 22:7–9

The specific mention of this element apart from Reuben and Gad is suspect as a redactional expansion suggested by the secondary insertion of east Manasseh in the narrative in vv. 9–31, which originally concerned only Reuben and Gad of the Transjordanian tribes (vv. 25, 32–34; cf. Num. 32). The note on the division of the spoils of war (v. 8) may be a further expansion in respect of the principle attributed to David in 1 Sam. 30:24.

9. This verse, which is somewhat tautological after v. 7, is possibly a later expansion. The qualification of **Shiloh** as **in the land of Canaan** seems to imply the limitation of 'the land of Canaan' to western Palestine, as indicated by the reference to **the land of Gilead** in Transjordan (see on v. 11).

THE CONTROVERSY OVER THE ALTAR IN THE JORDAN VALLEY

22:10–34

On the Deuteronomistic and Priestly character of this passage and on the possibility of the reflection of an earlier historical situation, see above, p. 52.

10. the region about the Jordan: Hebrew *gᵉlîlôt*, lit. 'circles', is a geographical term; cf. 18:17 (between Benjamin and Judah); cf. 13:2. LXX and Syriac have 'Gilgal', but v. 19*b* states that the altar was built on the actual bank of the Jordan.

an altar of great size: (lit. 'great in appearance'), anticipating the claim that it was simply monumental (cf. v. 27).

11. at the frontier of the land of Canaan: so LXX for MT 'opposite . . .'. Throughout this chapter 'the land of Canaan', denoting Palestine as distinct from Transjordan, characterises passages which are by other indications suspect as late and redactional, e.g. 'Shiloh which is in the land of Canaan' (v. 9).

on the side that belongs to the people of Israel surely indicates a date not earlier than the time of Josiah and probably after the Exile, where the actual apportionment is confined to west of the Jordan; e.g. Ezek. 47:15–48:7.

in the region about the Jordan: see on v. 10. The Syriac reads 'Gilgal' here for *gelîlôt*, but LXX[B] reads, wrongly, 'Gilead'.

12. to make war against them: lit. 'to go up against them to war'. The Jordan valley was much lower than Shiloh, which indicates that 'to go up' is a technical term meaning 'to go to war', as here (cf. Jg. 1:1; 6:3; 12:3; 15:10; 18:9; 20:9).

13. Phinehas: cf. Exod. 6:25; Num. 25:7, 31, his grandfather; represented as active on this mission as befitted his age, his father **Eleazar** being represented in the redaction on the apportionment as still alive.

14. ten chiefs: on **chiefs**, lit. 'those raised up', as representatives of the tribes in the assembly in the conception of P, see above, on 8:15.

families: possibly 'thousands', referring to the number theoretically provided by each clan within the tribe (see de Vaux, *Ancient Israel*, 1961, p. 216).

16. the whole congregation of the LORD: a characteristically Priestly term; but on the general significance of Hebrew *'ēdâh* (**congregation**), see on 18:1.

treachery: (Hebrew *ma'al*) characteristically P (see on 7:1).

17. the sin at Peor: see Num. 25:1–9; Dt. 4:3. For the **plague**, see Num. 25:3, 8, 9. The role of Phineas in this incident must be emphasised, and probably suggested his role in the present passage.

18. angry with the whole congregation: this emphasises the conception of the solidarity of the society; see on 7:1, where the whole 'congregation' was involved in the sin of Achan, which is explicitly cited here (v. 20).

19. This may reflect an independent tradition of the allegation by the Transjordanian groups that they had built an altar east of the river to hallow the land. It may, on the other hand, be a reconstruction by the Priestly redactor, for whom the land west of the Jordan was properly the holy land (see above, on v. 11, hallowed by the one legitimate sanctuary, here described as **the LORD's land where the LORD's tabernacle stands**. Apart from 'the tent of meeting' (Hebrew *'ōhel hammô'ēd*) at Shiloh (18:1), this is the only mention of the tent-sanctuary (*miškān*) in Joshua, where the symbol of God's presence is the ark. The tent of meeting, associated properly with the oracle (Exod. 33:7–11, E), belongs to the desert tradition, and seems originally independent of the ark. The **tabernacle** (*miškān*) is a Priestly modification of the conception of the Temple as God's dwelling-place, which is accommodated to the theology of P, where God occasionally condescends to meet man at his own discretion (so von Rad, 'Zelt und Lade', *Gesammelte Studien zum Alten Testament*, 1958, pp. 109–29).

22. The Mighty One, God, the LORD: the triplication of divine titles is repeated as the preface to an adjuration. El (**God**) was the name of the high God of the patriarchs and known to the Canaanites as supreme over gods and men. Used of the God of Israel, apart from patriarchal religion, it is late and poetic. Here *RSV* emphasises the possible root meaning of 'strength' (*'ālāh*), though the root of El may rather be *'ûl* ('foremost'). We prefer to regard the first name (*'ēl*) as the proper name of the High God, the second (*'ᵉlôhîm*) as the generic term and the third (*yhwh*) as the peculiar name of the God of the sacral community of Israel, who assimilated the universal status and functions of the High God, particularly through the development of the cult at Jerusalem (H. Schmid, 'Yahweh und die Kulttraditionen von Jerusalem', *ZAW*, N.F. 26, 1955, pp. 168–97; W. Schmidt, *Königtum Gottes in Ugarit und Israel*, BZAW 80, 1961).

23. burnt-offerings . . . cereal offerings . . . peace-offerings: the first term (*'ôlôt*) denotes offerings made wholly over to God, of which the worshipper did not partake, as distinct from the last type of offering, *RSV* **peace-offerings**, better 'communion-offerings' (*šᵉlāmîm*), where the worshippers, partaking of the same victim as had been partially offered to God, effected solidarity with him and with one another. The second category (*minḥâh*), is obviously the bloodless offering in the present context, as distinct from *'ôlôt* and *šᵉlāmîm*. In earlier usage, *minḥâh* may also denote the sacrifice of a slaughtered beast (1 Kg. 18:29), hence the present usage indicates the sacrificial system of P (e.g. Lev. 1; 2; 3).

24. from fear: better 'from anxiety', implied in v. 19, where it is implied that the altar was built to hallow the land where the Transjordanian tribes were settled. *RSV*, after the Syriac version, omits the following word *middābār* (*AV*, 'and of purpose'). This phrase might be translated 'on account of a particular thing'; but there may be a nuance of an Arabic cognate in *dābār*, which means in the Intensive of the verbal root 'to pre-arrange'.

26. The lack of an object after the transitive verb 'to make' indicates a lacuna of at least one word.

27. a witness: cf. the stone set up by Joshua as an inanimate witness of the covenant of the assembly of the sacral community (24:26f., on which see) and 'the cairn of witness' in the popular etymology of 'Gilead' in Gen. 31:48 (JE). **Witness** was evidently one element in the name of the feature, as indicated in v. 34, where unfortunately the name has dropped out. It has been plausibly conjectured that the name was 'Gilead', and that the tradition was perhaps a variant of the popular etymology in Gen. 31:47ff. (F. O. Garcia-Treto, 'Genesis 31:34 and "Gilead", a possible solution', *ZAW* 79, 1967, pp. 13–17). The treaty implications of *'ēd*, as well as 'witness', are indicated by the Aramaic treaties of Sujīn.

28. copy: better, 'pattern' or 'construction' (cf. Dt. 4:16).

29. Far be it from us: lit. 'Unholy to us' (cf. *ad profanum*).

34. Witness: so *RSV*, after the Syriac version. In MT the name of the altar has dropped out.

JOSHUA'S FAREWELL ADDRESS

23:1–16

The conclusion to the book of Joshua in the Deuteronomistic History, is continued from 22:1–6, interrupted by the redactional 22:7–34, and supplemented by the redactional ch. 24. The passage is modelled on the admonition of the conditional nature of God's grace to Israel in the sacrament of the covenant, as the late redactional ch. 24 makes explicit. This therefore serves the same literary purpose in marking a period in the occupation of the Promised Land as Moses' speech in Dt. 1–11 and 29–30 on the eve of the fulfilment of the promise, which is also related by the Deuteronomist to the sacrament of the covenant in anticipation of the assembly of the sacral community at Shechem. It resumes the Deuteronomist's theme of God's grace in the fulfilment of the promise conditional upon the keeping of the law expressed in the Deuteronomistic introduction to Jos. in ch. 1, the language of which it re-echoes. The homiletic tone emphasises that those are not so much the words of Joshua to his contemporaries as the words of the Deuteronomistic Historian addressed to Israel of all time, and particularly to his contemporaries at the end of the Monarchy. This is in fact an adumbration of the whole Deuteronomistic History from the settlement to the Exile on the major theme of the operation of the word of God (the blessing and the curse in the sacrament of the covenant) in the history of Israel. The reference to the Exile in vv. 15f. and the warning against assimilation to the peoples of Palestine in vv. 11–13 may reflect the problems present to the mind of the Exilic redactor; but see below, on v. 3.

1. A long time afterward, when the LORD had given rest . . .: implies the struggle for occupation, which is the theme of Jg. rather than Jos.

rest: the keynote of the conclusion to Jos., but also of the pattern of the settlement in Jg., according to the Deuteronomistic framework, where repeated conflicts secure temporary 'rest'.

2. all Israel: envisaged by the Deuteronomist as represented at the general assembly by various representatives, all of whom, except **the heads**, are explicitly mentioned in the sacrament of the covenant in the assembly at Shechem in 8:33, which is probably a redactional interpolation in its context suggested by the present passage, like ch. 24; cf. Dt. 28:1ff., relating to the same occasion, when all categories except 'the heads' are explicitly mentioned. On **officers** and their role in mustering the people, see on 1:10.

3. it is the LORD, your God who has fought for you: cf. 'the nations that remain' (v. 4). Here again, in contrast to 21:44, there emerges the paradox between faith and history, the theme of God's complete victory in the occupation of the Promised Land, which faith asserted in the cult (e.g. Ps. 44:1–3) and the sober fact that the supremacy of Israel in the land was not realised until the time of David. Various attempts are made by the Deuteronomistic theologian to resolve this paradox, the one favoured here being that the potential menace of the unconquered Canaanites accentuated the conditional grace of God in the covenant (vv. 5ff.). This occasion subserves the purpose of the Deuteronomist at the end of the Monarchy, when the deportations from North Israel were a *fait accompli* and the deportations from Judah at least an imminent possibility and indeed a fact since 597 BC (cf. vv. 13–16).

4. those nations that remain: implies the particularist tendency among the natives of Palestine, largely originating in their ethnic diversity, e.g. Canaanites, 'Hittites' etc., and fostered by regional and climatic diversity.

with all the nations that I have already cut off: probably a later addition, which has upset the original text.

to the Great Sea: should be inserted into MT; so *RSV*.

6. be very steadfast: lit. 'hold firm', a characteristic phrase of Deuteronomistic exhortation (cf. 1:6, 7, 9, 18).

the book of the law of Moses: another late Deuteronomistic conception (see on 1:7).

7. make mention of the names: pronounce **the names** and so realise the presence, or at least admit the reality of, the gods invoked (cf. Exod. 23:13).

swear: so *RSV* correctly, with the Syriac version and the Targums, with a change of the vowels of MT. The various prohibitions, including intermarriage with its implication of recognition of the way of life and faith of the other party and the influence of the mothers on the children of the union (Neh. 13:24), reflect the strenuous efforts to assert the distinctively nationalist faith of Israel at the end of the Monarchy, of which Josiah's reformation was the expression. In the growth and consolidation of Israel in the days of the settlement also, however, precautions were no doubt taken against the same dangers in the sacrament of the covenant, the tradition behind the present passage. In this context **serve** (strange gods) and **bow down to them** (cf. v. 16) significantly re-echo the commandment in the Decalogue (Exod. 20:5), which is relevant to the same occasion. The negative particle and mood of the verb are those of solemn divine prohibition proper to such an occasion.

10. puts to flight a thousand: note the frequentative tense. For the hyperbole, cf. the psalm in Dt. 32:30.

12. turn back: the Hebrew *šûb* means both 'to return to God' and 'to apostatise', the latter being the meaning here.

13. snare . . . trap: on peculiar dangers from mixed marriages, see on v. 7.

scourge: better 'scourges', with a slight change of the last Hebrew consonant and vowels.

thorns in your eyes is a conventional description of the continued vexation of alien elements aggravated by toleration.

14. to go the way of all the earth: so David speaks of his death to Solomon (1 Kg. 2:2).

16. quickly vanish: As Soggin suggests (p. 162), the verb *'ābad*, which means 'perish', and means also 'to be lost' or 'stray aimlessly', like the asses of Saul's father or Jacob as a nomad in Israel's 'historical creed' in Dt. 26:5, may be used by the Deuteronomist with conscious reference to Dt. 26:5.

APPENDIX

24:1–33

The Pledge to serve the L*ORD alone in the Context of the Covenant in the Assembly of the Sacral Confederacy at Shechem* **21:1–28**

The regular practice on that occasion is reflected. It has been contended (Sellin, Noth) that the passage relates to the foundation of the twelve-tribe 'amphictyony' including the older elements of the Hebrew kinship, with whom the new-comers now united on the basis of the experience of the great deliverance and the covenant, now sacramentally communicated to the older groups. The emphasis on the renunciation of elements of worship foreign to Yahwism might seem to support this view with respect to the older groups which had not actual experience of Yahweh which was the genesis of the vital, even aggressive, faith of the dynamic Rachel group. Though the passage is coloured by the later, regular celebration of the covenant sacrament, the commitment to the worship of Yahweh, not as a demand but as an option indicates that there is some reminiscence here of a decisive phase in the foundation of the sacral assembly, which we should, however, limit to the ten-member community of Israel in Jg. 5:13–18 (see above, pp. 17f). This passage, which includes such elements of the covenant sacrament as in vv. 24–27, together with a free construction of the historical prelude to the covenant (see above, p. 53) on the basis of all main strands of the Pentateuch, is elaborated to support the Deuteronomistic compiler's conclusion with Joshua's address in ch. 23 in order to put this more explicitly in the context of the covenant sacrament, the paraenetic elaboration of the final adjurations of which (cf. Dt. 27:15–26) and the immediate sequel (Dt. 28–30) it reflects. For details of literary analysis and traditio-historical affinity, see Introduction, pp. 52ff. Formally the alternation between 'you' and 'your fathers' in the recapitulation of the Exodus theme has been taken as evidence of parallel sources, respectively the older southern, or L (lay) source and of E (so Eissfeldt, *Hexateuch-Synopse*, 1922, pp. 79ff.); but this may reflect rather the repetition of the well-known theme and its sacramental appropriation by succeeding generations.

The Calling of the Assembly of the Sacral Community **24:1**

The sanctuary ('before Yahweh') is **Shechem** in the country of Manasseh and formerly Machir, on the significance of which as a boundary sanctuary between Ephraim and her southern associate Benjamin and Machir/Manasseh and the sanctuary where the sacral confederacy of the ten groups of Israel in the north may have been inaugurated, see above, pp. 16ff. The note on **the elders, the heads, the judges and the officers of Israel** may be a Deuteronomistic expansion after 23:1; cf. 8:33, on which see. For **officers**, see on 1:10.

The Historic Prelude **24:2–13**

As in Hittite vassal-treaties of the fourteenth and thirteenth centuries, this cites God's grace and power as the basis of his claim to exclusive allegiance (v. 14). See Introduction, p. 53.

2. Thus says the LORD, the God of Israel: this was eventually the title of Yahweh ('**the LORD**') in the assembly of the sacral community (C. Steuernagel, *Jahweh der Gott Israel*, BZAW 27, 1914, pp. 329ff.). It implies the rededication of the sacral community to Yahweh and the formal renunciation of strange gods, which was a feature of this occasion (vv. 14–24; cf. Gen. 35:2–4, located at Shechem), and is an essential element in the apodictic law (e.g. Exod. 20:3–5), which related to the sacrament of the covenant (so Alt, 'The Origins of Israelite Law', *Essays on O.T. History and Religion*, E.T. 1966, pp. 79ff.). The prophetic introduction **Thus says the LORD** reflects the sacramental significance of what followed. The title in the present passage may reflect the real significance of the occasion reflected in Jos. 24, the mediation of the cult of Yahweh, the Deliverer from Egypt, by the Rachel group, who had hitherto worshipped Yahweh, whose social concern and that of the 'God of the Fathers' facilitated assimilation with the worship of the older Hebrew groups of the centre and north, as the social concerns of El facilitated the assimilation of the older Hebrew groups of the centre of the country with the sedentary natives of the district, suggested by Jacob's altar to El the God of Israel in Gen. 33:20.

Terah, the father of Abraham and of Nahor: cf. Gen. 11:27ff. (J and P). Perhaps **Terah** and **Nahor** are mentioned to except Abraham from the charge of worship of strange gods.

served other gods: In the Pentateuch the only implication of strange gods after Abraham is the mention of Rachel's *t^erāpîm* (Gen. 31:19), described as 'gods' (*'^elôhîm*) in Gen. 31:32.

3. **I took your father Abraham . . . and made his offspring many:** a direct reference to the tradition of the call of Abraham (Gen. 12:1–4*a*, J).

4. The mention of **Isaac, Jacob and Esau** implies the emphasis on the election of Israel. Esau's possession of **Mount Seir** is possibly introduced to emphasise by contrast the bondage of the house of Jacob in Egypt and the special grace of God in their deliverance. Mount Seir, though occasionally referring to the western escarpment of the Arabah (11:17), also refers to the highlands of Edom proper east of the Arabah, modern Jebel aš-Šera', in the heart of which lay the capital of Edom, The Rock (*haṣṣela'*).

5. The mention of **Moses and Aaron** together in the deliverance from Egypt is evidently borrowed from the narrative sources of the Pentateuch in their literary form; but the omission of v. 5*a* in LXX makes the verse suspect as a later expansion.

I plagued Egypt: an essential motif in the deliverance from Egypt in J, E and P. The plagues, intensifying until the last fatal visitation, traditionally on the night of the deliverance, are feasibly taken by Pedersen ('Passafest und Passalegende', *ZAW* N.F. 11, 1934, pp. 161–75) as belonging to the legend of the cult-drama of the Passover in the context of the drama of salvation. In the certainly dramatic arrangement of this tradition cult-drama and popular saga have influenced each other, and the tradition thus developed has become the basis of Exod. 1–15, particularly in the J version, which culminates in the psalm in Exod. 15, which is probably from the early Monarchy.

6. to the Red Sea: actually 'the Sea of (Papyrus) Reeds' (Hebrew *yam sûp*; cf. Egyptian *twfi*, 'papyrus'). This, as the name indicates, was a fresh-water lagoon in the east of the Delta, the region of the Bitter Lakes at the eastern end of the Wādī Ṭumeilāt to Lake Manzāleh, south-east of Tanis (Zoan), also called Pi-Rammesse (Ramses), modern Ṣān al-Ḥagar in the north-east of the Delta. This is the culmination of the great deliverance.

7. darkness between you and the Egyptians: it is noteworthy that the most sober tradition of the great deliverance at the Reed Sea (Exod. 14:10–14, 19–20; J) is used here, where the miracle is confined to the element of coincidence. The chariots and horsemen play a conspicuous part in the psalm in Exod. 15:1, 4. The alternation between narrative in the third person ('your fathers') and direct address ('you came to the sea') in this passage (v. 6) reflects Israel's sacramental experience of the drama of salvation in the cult. In view of the covenant mediated by Joshua at Shechem the total omission of any reference to the Sinai covenant is surprising, affording strong support to von Rad's theory that the traditions of the Exodus and desert wandering and occupation of the land and that of the Sinai covenant were originally distinct. The combination of the traditions in J and E in the early Monarchy strongly suggests that despite Deuteronomistic redaction, a genuine tradition from the pre-Monarchic period underlies Jos. 24.

8. the land of the Amorites: here specified as east of Jordan, as in the campaign against Moab (v. 9) and against Sihon and Og (Num. 21:23–25; 22–24; Dt. 1:44; 2:24; 3:9). The occupation of the Promised Land is the culmination of the great deliverance and the desert wandering. The use of the term **Amorites** to denote all the inhabitants of Palestine encountered by Israel, as distinct from one part of them, is unique in Jos. and in the older narrative sources of the Pentateuch. In what seems like a citation from the liturgy of the covenant sacrament, adapted in the convention of the divine controversy (*rîb*) with his people, Am. (2:9–10) uses 'Amorite' in the same sense as Jos. 24:8.

I gave them into your hand: the conception recurs with variation in vv. 10*b* and 11*b*, re-echoing the oracle of reassurance in the tradition of the Holy War (cf. 6:2).

I destroyed them from before you: after 'I gave them into your hand', this is probably a redactional expansion.

9. Balak . . . king of Moab . . . fought against Israel: unless the verb means 'began to fight' (so E. Nielsen, *Shechem*, 1955, p. 95), this is a notable divergence from Pentateuchal tradition (cf. Dt. 2:9; Jg. 11:25). The redactor seems to be conscious of this in adding the note on **Balaam** (vv. 9*b*–10*a*) from Num. 22:5ff. (JE), which re-echoes the language of Dt. 23:5.

10. blessed you: actually MT means 'went on blessing you', a reference to the series of blessings in the oracles of **Balaam** in Num. 23:7–10, 18–24 (E) and 24:3–9, 15–19 (J) and the oracle against Israel's enemies the Amalekites (Num. 24:20, J) and the later oracles against the Kenites (Num. 24:21f.) and Assyria (Num. 24:24). The emphasis on the blessings and on the occupation of the land by the sole power and grace of God independently of human endeavour in vv. 11–13 reflects the suzerain's pointed reminder to the vassal of the benefits he has received in the vassal-treaties of the fourteenth and thirteenth centuries BC.

11–13. The occupation of the Promised Land, as in chs 2–11, though in general terms, the only particular event referred to being the defeat of the men of Jericho *in battle*, which significantly disagrees with ch. 6. Here only v. 11*a* to 'fought against you' and 'gave them into your hand' in v. 11*b*, and possibly v. 13, are original, and the rest redactional expansion. 'Even the kings of the Amorites' may be a secondary gloss on the indefinite 'them' in v. 12*a*. Here LXX has an interesting reading 'the twelve kings of the Amorites' for MT 'the two . . .', perhaps a stylisation of the enemies defeated west of the Jordan (cf. ch. 12). In view of the correspondence of the description of the Promised Land in v. 13 with Dt. 6:10f., Noth (*op. cit.*, p. 135) takes this as a Deuteronomistic expansion. But those details may reflect the definition of boundaries and territories in the convention of vassal-treaties.

13. hornet: Hebrew *ṣir'âh*, only here and in Exod. 23:28 (E) and in Dt. 7:20, the meaning being suggested by LXX. Garstang took this as a reference to the Egyptian expeditions to Palestine in the XIXth Dynasty, which weakened native opposition, the bee being the symbol of Lower Egypt (*Joshua and Judges*, 1931, pp. 259f., with illustration, Pl. I). Actually the word probably means 'enervation'; cf. Arabic *ḍara'a*, 'to submit' (L. Koehler, *ZAW* N.F. 13, 1936, p. 291), divinely inspired panic being a regular feature of the holy war.

God's Claim to the Sole Allegiance of His Beneficiaries **24:14**

Again, as in vassal-treaties.
and in Egypt: probably a redactional gloss, unless this is related to the ceremony of discarding amulets with a pagan significance, like figurines of hippopotamus, cat, ape, the grotesque dwarf Bes, Horus and the Horus eye, familiar in archaeological sites in Syria and Palestine in the Late Bronze and early Iron Age. Such a rite is referred to in the burial of such objects under the oak at Shechem in Gen. 35:4 (E); cf. the discarding of ornaments also in the context of the covenant, in Exod. 35:5f. (E).

Joshua's Personal Challenge to Decision **24:15**

A significant departure from the established pattern in the covenant ceremony, and as such possibly reflecting the leading role of Joshua's group Ephraim, his house, in the inauguration of the larger sacral community at Shechem. Alternatively this may, as G. Widengren has suggested ('King and Covenant', *JSS* 2, 1957, pp. 12ff.), be a Deuteronomistic reflection of King Josiah's role in the renewal of the covenant in 2 Kg. 23:1–3. Fohrer (*History of Israelite Religion*, E.T., 1973, p. 88) takes **my house** more literally, relating the occasion at Shechem to Joshua's bringing in of the *whole* of his group in central Palestine to the worship of Yahweh. But it is more likely that Ephraim and their southern associates Benjamin were already worshippers of Yahweh, and that those brought in were the older groups of the Hebrews to the north, as the reference to the worship of the patriarchal God of Israel indicates. The reference to the Exodus and the occupation indicates a larger group than the family of Joshua.

The Appropriation of the Covenant **24:16–24**

16–18. Historical Credo, with summary recapitulation of the historical preamble in the formal tradition of the vassal-treaty.

19–24. This passage, where Joshua again brings the people to the point of decision for God, is generally taken to be tautological after their decision in v. 18, and is thought to be redactional. Ancient literary and oral narrative knew the convention of accentuating a point by making it controversial and suspending agreement, e.g. Moses' controversy with the Pharaoh before deliverance and, in the Rās Shamra myth of Baal, Baal's controversy with the divine craftsman over the installation of a roof-shutter in the temple of Baal, which was a vital element in a rite of imitative magic to induce rain. Moreover, this opens the way for Joshua's admonition with its implication of blessing and curse and the solemn citation of witnesses, all of which were essential elements in the vassal-treaty to which Jos. 24 formally corresponds.

22. You are witnesses against yourselves: this corresponds to the invocation in the vassal-treaty of various gods as witnesses. In Israel heaven and earth are invoked as witnesses (e.g. Is. 1:2); cf. the stone set up as a witness in v. 27.

And they said, 'We are witnesses', which interrupts the speech of Joshua, is almost certainly a later interpolation, and is omitted in LXX.

24. his voice will we obey: together with exclusive service (i.e. worship), on which the passage repeatedly insists, obedience to God's categorical demands is required, such as conserved not only the purity of worship, but the distinctive nature and integrity of the sacral community, as in the Decalogue and other fragments of apodictic law in the Book of the Covenant and the Twelve Adjurations (Dt. 27:15–26); so Alt, 'The Origins of Israelite Law', *Essays on Old Testament History and Religion*, E.T. 1966, pp. 79ff., *KS* I, 1953.

The Making of the Covenant 24:25

This is, in our opinion, between the Rachel group and the northern groups and Yahweh through Joshua; cf. the role of Moses as mediator of the covenant, and of Josiah in 2 Kg. 23:3.

covenant: see on 9:7.

statutes and ordinances: singular in MT. The plural, possibly suggested to *RSV* translators by 'these words' in the sequel, naturally suggests both apodictic laws (*ḥôq*) and casuistic laws (*mišpāṭ*) declared by the mediator of the covenant in the name of God (cf. Exod. 24:3ff.), which crystallised into the Book of the Covenant (Exod. 20:22–23:33) in the Sinai tradition. The Hebrew means simply that he made the covenant binding as a decree (*ḥôq*) and a decision (*mišpāṭ*). The terms (lit. 'words') of the covenant are the redactional importation of the conception of decrees (*ḥuqqîm*), the apodictic obligations of the covenant, and casuistic laws (*mišpāṭîm*), declared by the mediator of the covenant. In view of the silence of the passage on the Sinai tradition, however, the original situation was the significance of the covenant for the parties concerned and their commitment to the worship of Yahweh, however that was expressed.

The Written Record of the Covenant **24:26–28**

Also its deposit at the sanctuary, as in vassal treaties of the Late Bronze Age, which were invalid without such written record.

The conception of the book of the law of God is probably late, but may be suggested by the Book of the Covenant (Exod. 20:22–23:33). The original record at the sanctuary was more probably a short series of apodictic laws on a standing stone (cf. Dt. 27:2–4; Jos. 8:32), which may have been the source of the tradition of the two stone tablets of the law at Sinai.

the oak (Hebrew *he'allâh*): the form is peculiar to this passage; cf. Gen. 35:4 (*'ēlâh*), which also refers to Shechem. Gen. 12:6; Dt. 11:30; Jg. 9:37 refer to an oracle-terebinth (*'ēlôn*) at Shechem, which, apart from vowels, differs from the Hebrew word only in the last consonant. This tree may be envisaged in the sanctuary (so *RSV*), which would be a large bounded precinct rather than a built shrine, in the fashion of the Muslim Sacred Area (*Ḥaram aš-Šarīf*) in Jerusalem, though on a much smaller scale.

a great stone, and set it up there under the oak . . .: cf. the twelve standing stones for the same purpose in Exod. 24:4 (E). The '*twelve* stones' is possibly a secondary tradition developed from the single stone of witness at the sanctuary at Shechem, cf. Jg. 9:6, reflecting the twelve-tribe Israel of the early monarchic period. On the stone as witness of the covenant, see above, on v. 22.

The Tradition of the Graves **24:29–33**

The graves of **Joseph** and **Eleazar** (v. 33) were near **Shechem**, reflecting the interest of pilgrims, like similar topographical traditions near or on the way to Gilgal in chs 2–8. The grave of **Joshua** (vv. 29–30) in his patrimony in his native Ephraim is probably a better attested historical tradition.

30. Timnath-serah: see above on 19:50. Joshua's grave was visited in the time of Eusebius at Thamna (Onomasticon, 70.20ff.), modern Khirbet Tibneh, *c.* twelve miles north-east of Lydda (H. W. Hertzberg, *PJB* 22, 1926, pp. 89ff.).

31. had known all the work which the LORD did for Israel: 'known' might signify personal experience, but the verb *yāda'* has convenantal implications, meaning the acknowledgement of the benefits from the suzerain, in the covenant in Israel, the acknowledgement of Israel's total debt to God for his saving work in the great deliverance, the basis of his sovereign claim in the obligations of the covenant, e.g. as in the Decalogue with its historical prelude, as recognised by H. B. Huffmon, *BASOR* 181, 1966, pp. 31–7.

32. **the bones of Joseph:** cf. Gen. 50:25; Exod. 13:19 (both E). This was a well-established tradition localised at Shechem and projected back to Egypt when the drama of the great deliverance (*Heilsgeschichte*) became an element in the covenant-sacrament at Shechem, the boundary sanctuary of Ephraim and Machir/Manasseh and the central sanctuary of the larger group of the Israel of Jg. 5:13–18. The local association of the grave of Joseph at Shechem, actually in Manasseh, may support de Vaux's theory that Joseph was specifically associated with Machir (*Histoire ancienne* I, pp. 595–8). **a hundred pieces of money:** the precise significance of 'piece of money' (Hebrew *qᵉśîṭâh*) is unknown.

33. **Gibeah, the town of Phinehas** is quite unknown. The Egyptian name (*pe-neḥesi*, 'the Negro') indicates affinity with Hebrew elements who had come out of Egypt. It is uncertain whether the *RSV* translation is correct here. MT might simply denote 'the hill', but it could also signify a town Gibeah, characterised as 'Gibeah of Phinehas' to differentiate it from, for instance, Gibeah of Saul. *RSV* follows LXX. **Phinehas** recurs as the name of the son of Eli, the priest at Shiloh (1 Sam. 1:3), the family with the custody of the ark there; cf. the active role assigned to Phinehas in 22:13.

INTRODUCTION
to
Judges

1. TITLE, SCOPE AND PLACE IN THE CANON

Judges (Hebrew *šôpᵉṭîm*), the title of the book in the Hebrew Bible and the versions, relates to its scope, the bulk of which (3:7–16:31) deals with the struggles of the various elements of Israel in the settlement of Palestine under the leadership of dynamic men of sagacity and personal authority before the institution of the Monarchy. Not all those heroes are designated 'judges'. Ehud, Barak and Gideon, for instance, are not so called, while, beyond the book of Judges, Eli (1 Sam. 4:18) and Samuel (1 Sam. 7:15) are said to have acted as 'judges'. Though certain figures, who are generally termed 'the minor judges', such as Tola, Jair, Ibzan, Elah and Abdon, of whom no stirring exploit is recorded, are included, together with Abimelech, who made an abortive attempt at kingship, the book is dominated by the heroic exploits of such as Ehud, Deborah and Barak, Jephthah and Gideon, who are envisaged in 2:16, which states that 'the Lord raised up judges who saved them out of the power of those who plundered them', a verse which may have suggested the title of the book. On the connotation of the verb *šāpaṭ* in Jg. with relation to the major and minor 'judges', some of both of whom were termed rather 'deliverers' (*môšîʿîm*), see above, pp. 22f.

The scope of Jg. is the period when such order as there was actually in the Israel of Jg. 5:13–18 and, in the assumption of the Deuteronomistic Historian, of the twelve-tribe community of Israel, was considered in retrospect to have been upheld by those 'judges' and 'deliverers' before a regular centralised government under the Monarchy, with which the older order is contrasted in Jg. 18:1; 19:1 and 21:25. The last verse in Jg., like the historical introduction, emphasises the local nature of the struggle for settlement and the local significance of the 'judges' despite the impression which the Deuteronomistic Historian and his predecessor, the compiler of the traditions of the great 'judges', sought to convey that the authority of the personalities he mentions extended to all Israel.

Though the priest Eli and Samuel are regarded as 'judges' the figure of Samuel is inseparably associated with the inauguration of the Monarchy, so that Jewish tradition has included his activity in the First Book of Sam., which deals with the immediate prelude to the establishment of the Monarchy and the reigns of Saul and David. This is emphasised more strongly in LXX, which terms 1 and 2 Sam. '1 and 2 Dynasties' (*Basileiai*).

Jewish tradition included Jg. as the second part of 'the Former Prophets' (Jos.–Kg.), the Deuteronomistic History from the occupation of the Promised Land to the end of the Monarchy. The essentially theological character of this study of the operation of the word of God declared in blessing and curse in Dt. 27ff. in the history of Israel confirms the soundness of the Jewish assessment of the book of Jg. as the second part of 'the Former Prophets'. Like Jos. it deals with the settlement, but, whereas the account of the settlement in Jos. 2–12 mainly bears the impress of the occupation as the theme of the cult, the object of faith at the sanctuaries, particularly at Gilgal, and is therefore unrealistically schematised, even before the Deuteronomistic History, Jg. is based ultimately on local, more secular, traditions of the settlement, which, without being literal or annalistic, are much more sober and factual, being safeguarded in the families and communities of those involved. Both books, however, subserve the purpose of the Deuteronomistic philosophy of history. Jos. emphasises the favour of God in the occupation of the land when the people under the guidance of Joshua, the associate and successor of Moses, 'served the Lord . . . and acknowledged all the work which he did for Israel' (Jos. 24:31), serving at the same time notice of the conditional grace of God (Jos. 23:15f.; 24:20); Jg. illustrates God's discipline of his people (2:10–15; 3:1ff., etc.), of which the Deuteronomistic conclusion to Jos. (ch. 23) had served due notice.

In spite of the fact that with Eli and Samuel the period of the judges strictly extends to the introduction of the Monarchy (1 Sam. 8ff.), Sam. even in its early chapters is sharply demarcated from Jg. Whereas in Jg. local traditions are used, generally with great respect, the sources in Sam. are quite different in character. Eli, in spite of the statement in 1 Sam. 4:18 that he was a judge, plays no independent part in Sam. He is introduced in anticipation of the fall of his house; the ark tradition in 1 Sam. 1–4 anticipates David's restoration of the ancient palladium to hallow Jerusalem as the new religious centre of his Israel; and the prophetic tradition of Samuel—a source used for the first time in the history of Israel—is drawn upon to emphasise the role of the prophet behind the throne. The selection and treatment of the traditions of Samuel are ultimately conditioned by interest in the Davidic house, so that, with justice, Jewish tradition makes a division in the Former Prophets between Jg. and Sam.

2. CONTENTS

The book of Judges consists of three main sections:

INTRODUCTION TO THE MAIN THEME **1:1–3:6**
NARRATIVES OF THE JUDGES **3:7–16:31**
APPENDICES
THE ORIGIN OF THE PRE-MONARCHIC SANCTUARY OF DAN **17–18**
THE BENJAMIN WAR: ITS CAUSE AND SEQUEL **19–21**

INTRODUCTION TO THE MAIN THEME

1:1–3:6

The Deuteronomistic History in Jg. properly begins at 2:6–9 with Joshua's dismissal of the people after his farewell address (Jos. 23), a note of his death and burial (v. 9) and of his contemporaries' fidelity to the purpose of God (v. 7), which a redactor repeats, though in a different order, in Jos. 24:28–31. The Deuteronomistic Historian prefaces his main theme in Jg. by contrasting the infidelity of the next generation with the faith of Joshua and his contemporaries (v. 10), which he elaborates in vv. 11–19, outlining the pattern of his work in 3:7–16:31. At this point, in more general terms, the post-exilic redactor adds a note on the failure of Israel to effect a complete conquest, admitting that 'So the Lord left those nations, not driving them out at once, and he did not give them into the power of Joshua' (v. 23). This he related to the failure to keep the covenant (vv. 20f.), with the apologetic note that the nations were left to test Israel's fidelity (v. 22). He elaborates this theme in 3:1–6, the further explanation being given that the nations were left to give the new generation of Israel experience in war against the peoples in Palestine (vv. 1f.), specifying those in general Deuteronomistic terms and particularising the Philistines (vv. 3–5), the last enemy to be mentioned in Jg., in the Samson cycle (chs 13–16), and alleging intermarriage and apostasy (v. 6). In ch. 1 the redactor pursues the theme of the incomplete conquest in his account of the piecemeal and partial settlement of the various tribes of Israel, though the Deuteronomistic image of Joshua is conserved in agreement with 2:6f., the situation being dated 'after the death of Joshua (1:1)'; cf. the Deuteronomistic introduction, which represents Joshua as still alive (2:7f.). In 1:2–21 the redactor draws upon older historical traditions which, with the exception of Caleb's occupation of Hebron (v. 20; cf. Jos. 14:6–15) and Othniel's occupation of Kiriath-sepher (vv. 11–15 = Jos. 15:16, 19), had not been used in Jos., while in the account of the partial occupation of the various tribal territories represented as assigned by Joshua in Jos. 16–19 conditions just before the organisation of the kingdom of David are remembered.

Also redactional is the incident of the angel at Bochim ('Weepers') by Bethel (2:1–5), where the place-name is related in the fashion of aetiological myth to public lamentation on the solemn reminder of the infringement of covenant obligations which had as its consequence the failure to dislodge the Canaanites (cf. 2:20f.).

NARRATIVES OF THE GREAT JUDGES

3:7–16:31

The judges are twelve in number, reckoning either Deborah or Barak as a judge and omitting Abimelech, whose status in fact depended wholly on his descent from Gideon, and who was in effect not a 'deliverer', and a 'judge' only in the sense of a local ruler on his own account.

Among those are six figures whose charismatic leadership involved them and their followers in significant political incidents which, though primarily local for the most part and involving only their own groups or their immediate neighbours, contributed to the progress of the settlement and the growth and eventual consolidation of Israel. This is interpreted as divinely-granted relief to the people, who by their indifference to their status as the people of Yahweh had merited the oppression of their various adversaries. Thus the Deuteronomistic Historian introduces the exploit of each divinely-inspired leader, enumerating the years of suffering and ending with the statement that 'the land had rest' for so many years, usually a multiple or half of forty. These are termed 'the great judges', and include Ehud of Benjamin, the sequel of whose exploit in the valley of the lower Jordan involved at least some of the Ephraimite neighbours of his group (3:12–30), Deborah, who is associated with Barak from Naphtali (chs 4–5), with Zebulun and possibly Issachar (4:6, 10; 5:14f.), Gideon from Abiezer a clan of Manasseh (chs 6–8), which is followed by the episode of the abortive attempt at kingship by Abimelech (ch. 9), Jephthah from Gilead (10:6–12:7), Samson from Dan in the northern Shephelah (chs 13–16) and Othniel from the Kenizzites south of Hebron, who were affiliated to Judah (3:7–11). Also reckoned as a judge in virtue of an obscure martial exploit is Shamgar ben Anath (possibly, 'Shamgar the man of Beth-Anath'), of whom it was related that he 'killed six hundred of the Philistines with an ox-goad' (3:31).

Of all those local heroes concrete exploits are related, and their obvious political significance for the settlement and consolidation of Israel makes it possible to regard them, in spite of the primarily local nature of their exploits, as vindicators ('judges') of Israel and as 'deliverers' (*môšî'îm*), an assessment which is related to the ultimate result of their exploit rather than any regular office during their lifetime. The possession of the divine favour (*berākâh*) signalised by their success in arms authenticated their initial impulse to leadership and probably secured popular esteem beyond the local scene during their lifetime, so that the Deuteronomistic statement that they 'judged' Israel until their death may well reflect an element of historical fact.

The traditions of those 'judges' vary from the detailed and circumstantial, such as the exploits of Ehud, to the bare statement of a single fact, as in the case of Othniel or Shamgar; from the simple tradition of a single action and its sequel, as again in the case of Ehud, to a complexity of traditions regarding the main action of a 'judge', as in the passages on Deborah and Barak, or they may include a variety of traditions which have nothing directly to do with the main action, as in the case of Gideon, where the traditions of the battle against the Midianites and the pursuit of the enemy and those of the establishment of the cult of Yahweh are complex and probably independent, as is certainly the Abimelech tradition, which is nevertheless a natural sequel to the end of the Gideon tradition. Again, the traditions so transmitted vary in character and treatment from the transmission in saga of matter of obviously political moment, such as the exploits of Ehud, Shamgar, Deborah and Barak, Gideon, Jephthah and Othniel, vague as the exploit of the last is, to the hero-legend of Samson, where, whatever the ultimate political significance of his exploits may have been, the focus of attention is rather on the hero than on the significance of his actions.

There is a great variety too in the sources of the traditions and in the media whereby they were conserved and shaped to the form in which they were taken up and worked into the Deuteronomic History. Those of Ehud, Gideon, Jephthah and Othniel, though they do not minimise the role of the hero, were sober historical traditions conserved locally, possibly in saga form, among those who had been involved in the events narrated. The exploits of Samson, and probably also of Shamgar, were pure hero-legend, and in the case of Samson, whose home was near Beth-shemesh ('the Shrine of the Sun'), may have been influenced by motifs from the mythology of the local sanctuary, which may or may not have been divorced from their cultic context in the two centuries of Israelite settlement before the Monarchy. In the victory of Barak under the inspiration of Deborah, on the other hand, though the subject of secular saga, the theme of song and story 'at the watering-places' (5:11), the extant poetic version, the famous Song of Deborah (ch. 5), is transmitted as a hymn on the subject of Yahweh's vindication (*ṣidᵉqôt yhwh*) of his purpose and his people in the assembly of the sacral community, probably on the occasion of the sacrament of the covenant (cf. Dt. 26–27; Jos. 24), when the recounting of God's grace and power in history, which is the prelude to, and basis of, God's claim on his people in the covenant, is carried forward to current history (A. Weiser, 'Das Deboralied, eine gattungs- und traditionsgeschichtliche Studie', *ZAW* N.F. 30, 1959, pp. 67–97). There are also aetiological traditions, particularly in the Gideon cycle in the origin of the name Jerubba'al (6:25–32) and the establishment of the altar 'The Lord is Peace' (6:19–24) and in the association of the incident of Jephthah's vow with the women's annual mourning rite (11:37–40).

Within this section (3:7–16:31) directly on the judges, there is evidence of an earlier collection of narratives of the great judges, which is given coherence in a framework which may be discerned at 3:7–11, 12–15*a* and 30; 4:1*a*, 2*a*, 3*a* and 23f.; 5:31*c*; 6:1–2*a*, 7–10; 8:28, 33–35; 10:6–16; 11:33*b*. This framework is recognised by W. Beyerlin ('Gattung und Herkunft des Rahmens im Richterbuch', in *Tradition und Situation*, eds. E. Würthwein and O. Kaiser, 1963, pp. 1–29) as a direct reflection of the liturgy of the divine contention in the public fast and penitence in the context of the sacrament of the covenant in the assembly of the sacral community (cf. 1 Sam. 7:3–8). Beyerlin goes on to argue that the flexibility of the language in which the liturgical formula is expressed at those points indicates oral tradition rather than literary composition (*op. cit.*, p. 28). But it might be argued that oral tradition, so obviously conscious of the original *Sitz im Leben* of the formula, would be more punctilious than a later literary tradition which would be content to reproduce the theme rather than the stereotyped form of the liturgy. However that may be, the liturgy in question supplied an admirable framework to comprise the local exploits of the great deliverers in a unified theme which had a relevance to the community of all Israel.

Here then we have a unified body of tradition and conceivably a literary compilation corresponding to the collection of the traditions of the settlement in Jos. 2–11. As the difference in language and content between the framework and the Deuteronomistic introduction in 2:11–19 indicates, the compilation of the traditions of the great deliverers in 3:7–16:31 antedated the Deuteronomistic History (so Budde, *Die Bücher Richter und Samuel*, 1890; and most later scholars, e.g. W. Richter, *Traditionsgeschichtliche Untersuchungen zum Richterbuch*, BBB 18, 1963: *Die Bearbeitung des 'Retterbuches' in der deuteronomischen Epoche*, 1964). In the latter work, Richter would distinguish an original Book of Deliverers (*môsîʿîm*) comprising the exploits of Ehud in 3:15*b*–26, of Jael in 4:17*a*, 18–21, and of Gideon in 7:11*b*, 13–21; 8:5–9, 14–21*a*, concluding perhaps with 9:56. This, according to Richter, was later expanded to elevate the exploits of those local heroes into wars of Yahweh. This was further expanded to include the exploits of Othniel, Deborah and Barak, probably reckoned severally, and Jephthah, with Ehud and Gideon a total of six. The Samson cycle (chs 13–16), so different in theme from the rest of the narratives of the great judges, and without the same introduction and conclusion, was probably later included owing to its immense popularity and because of the resistance to the Philistines, otherwise, except for the passage on Shamgar, not represented. The passage on Shamgar, too, is probably a comparatively late accretion, introduced as it is in a brief notice of one unrelated exploit in one verse without introduction. This view is supported by the fact that in the immediate sequel the exploit of Deborah and Barak is introduced after the note on the death of Ehud (4:1f.), Shamgar being totally ignored. This pre-Deuteronomistic compilation within its framework suggested by the liturgy of the divine contention, the public repentance and the ensuing grace of God, agreed so admirably with the general theme of the Deuteronomist that he could incorporate it *en bloc* with few modifications except his schematic chronology, the material on Shamgar and Samson and the lists of the 'minor judges'.

With the 'great judges' in the Deuteronomistic History, subsuming Barak under the figure of Deborah and admitting Shamgar, the complement of twelve is made up by the inclusion of five figures, Tola of Issachar (10:1f.), Jaïr from Gilead (10:3–5), Ibzan from Zebulun (12:8–10), Elon from Zebulun (12:11f.) and Abdon from Ephraim (12:13–15). They are associated with no great exploit in events of external politics, though in the case of Tola, there is a hint of this in the statement that he arose 'to deliver Israel'. Only their family affinities and consequence are recorded; all are said to have 'judged Israel', and the place of their burial is noted, which is not always so in the case of the 'great judges'. This would seem to indicate their significance, or at least repute, beyond their own kindred or locality. Furthermore, in contrast to the 'great judges', who in the fashion of saga and stylised Deuteronomistic chronology, secured rest for the land for forty years or double that period, the fact that the duration of the authority of the 'minor judges' is more particularly specified, together with the invariable note on their burial-place, indicates a well-established tradition, if not the record of a regularly-established office, that of accredited expounders of the law and arbiters in disputes, as Alt and Noth contended. On this and other possibilities regarding the actual significance of the 'minor judges', see above, pp. 22ff.

Now the same statistical detail is given in the case of Jephthah alone of all the 'great judges', of whom alone of all the 'great judges' it is not said that after his exploit the land had rest for forty or eighty years. The fact that the tradition of Jephthah including his exploit in arms and its tragic sequel (11:1–12:6) immediately follows the notices of the 'minor judges' Tola and Jair (10:1–5) and immediately precedes the notices of the other 'minor judges' Ibzan, Elon and Abdon (12:8–15) is basic to the view of Noth, *The Deuteronomistic History*, E.T. 1981, pp. 46ff., that Jephthah was a 'minor judge', in the juridical sense in his opinion, who by coincidence was also a 'great judge', or charismatic leader, who performed an act of vindication in arms. According to Noth, this coincidence of charisma and office in the case of Jephthah contributed to the view that the charismatic leaders who signalised themselves by a great exploit in the days of the Israelite settlement were also 'judges' of Israel in the juridical sense. We have noticed that the verb *šāpaṭ* in the case of the 'minor judges' may have had the connotation rather of local rulers (see above, p. 22f.), Jephthah being the only one the circumstances of whose rise, in his exploit against the Ammonites, is recorded. However this may be, it was probably Jephthah's function as 'judge' (*šôpēṭ*) that suggested the same designation for the great leaders.

APPENDIX A. *The Origin of the Pre-monarchic Sanctuary of Dan* 17–18

This section has a peculiar interest since it transmits, without apparent inhibition, the tradition of an iconic cult at Dan served by a Levitical priesthood which claimed descent from Moses and survived until 'the captivity of the land' (18:30), by which we should probably understand the incorporation of Galilee as a province in the Assyrian empire under Tiglath-pileser III in 734–732 BC (2 Kg. 15:29). This violates Deuteronomic principles so much that it obviously represents a genuine old tradition too well established to be suppressed. This seems to be confirmed by the admission of the regulative influence of the king in the cult (17:6; cf. 18:1), the aspersions on the Levitical priesthood, which suggest the viewpoint of the north Israelite priesthood of Bethel established by Jeroboam I (1 Kg. 28–30). Moreover, the fact that this section, unlike chs. 1–16, contains no saving act or personality and stands outside the chronological scheme of the Deuteronomistic History indicate that, whatever its origin, it is a redactional appendix.

APPENDIX B. *The Benjaminite War: Its Cause and Sequel* **19–21**

Like Appendix A this section on the outrage on the Levite's concubine by the men of Gibeah (ch. 19), the consequent war against the Benjaminites (ch. 20) and the provision of wives for the survivors of Benjamin (ch. 21) lacks any saving act or saviour-figure and stands outside the chronological scheme of the Deuteronomistic History. Though developed from a historical tradition in the struggle of Ephraim's southern associate Benjamin to assert its independence, it has probably been included in Jg. by the Exilic redactor of the Deuteronomistic History. See further, below, pp. 347.

3. SOURCES AND COMPOSITION

A. INTRODUCTION TO THE MAIN THEME

PREFATORY RECAPITULATION OF THE SETTLEMENT, USING LOCAL HISTORICAL TRADITIONS

1:1–2:5

In contrast to Jos., which represents the occupation of Palestine as a sweeping conquest in two main campaigns under Joshua, Jg. presents a much more sober account. Jg. emphasises the local activity of independent communities, sometimes less and sometimes more than a tribe, but never all Israel, though the Deuteronomist and his predecessor in the narratives of the great judges represent the judges and their followers as acting on behalf of all Israel, in which their authority was subsequently recognised. Here the role of local leaders is emphasised, and the whole gives the impression of sober history, which is generally corroborated by archaeology, in contrast to the representation of the 'conquest' in Jos. The main body of Jg. is in fact based on local tradition which was so well known and so well preserved by the descendants of the groups involved as to demand serious respect by any compiler. Those traditions of the various elements of Israel in their long struggle to settle in Palestine were presented by the pre-Deuteronomistic compiler in the framework of assimilation to the Canaanite way of life, and even apostasy, and Divine discipline and subsequent repentance and renewal of grace. This accorded with the Deuteronomist's presentation of the history of Israel and was therefore incorporated practically *en bloc*, being introduced by a recapitulation on the situation in the settlement of Israel in ch. 1.

This passage, relating events **after the death of Joshua** (1:1), seems an interpolation after the continuation of the Deuteronomistic History from Joshua's farewell speech (Jos. 23) to his dismissal of the tribes to their several territories and his death and burial (2:6–10). Jg. 1 assumes the allotment of the land to the several groups, beginning with **Judah** (1:1ff.) and **the house of Joseph** (vv. 22–26). The priority of Judah in this passage indicates the origin of the tradition at the earliest in the early Monarchy and probably later, and the statement that certain **Canaanites** were not dislodged by the various elements of Israel, but put to the corvée (1:28, 30, 33, 35) implies familiarity with Solomon's administration. The statement, however, that Judah took and destroyed **Jerusalem** and reduced **Hebron**, **Gaza**, **Askelon** and **Ekron**, indicates the Exilic redactor. The unrealistic account of the occupation of the south is qualified by the admission that **Debir** and, it is implied, **Hebron**, was the operation of the Kenizzites independently (1:11–15; cf. Jos. 15:13ff.).

Another possibly genuine historical tradition incorporated by the redactor is the taking of **Bethel**, formerly called **Luz**, by **the house of Joseph** (1:22–26), though what precisely he understood by 'the house of Joseph' is uncertain. We consider it likely that, in view of the reflection of conditions in the Monarchy in the priority of Judah in 1:1–10, 'the house of Joseph' signifies Ephraim as the chief element in the Joseph group and also in the northern Kingdom of Israel, which was designated 'Ephraim' in Hos. and 'the house of Joseph' in Am. 5:6. In view of the association of the ark as the symbol of the presence of Yahweh with Ephraim and the tradition of its association with Bethel (20:27), this might be supported by the tradition of the angel of the Lord at **Bochim** by Bethel (2:1–5), and so reflect, at least in germ, the decisive step in the settlement of the Rachel group on the plateau north of Jerusalem. But, as it stands, 2:1–5 is an aetiological myth of the significance of **Bochim** ('weepers'; cf. vv. 4f.), which is adapted by the redactor of the Deuteronomistic History to emphasise the divine warning that his grace to Israel was conditional upon faithfulness to covenant obligations, a characteristic Deuteronomistic theme.

The statement that the gradual occupation of Palestine was **after the death of Joshua** (1:1) is the redactor's reconciliation of faith and fact. Faith is represented in the Deuteronomist's depiction of the occupation of the Promised Land by God's grace to his faithful people under Joshua, despite the known fact that throughout the whole of the pre-monarchic period the occupation was incomplete. The consciousness of the paradox between faith and fact emerges at various points in the framework of Jg., where various answers are proposed, e.g. that the Canaanites were left as a convenient labour force (1:28, 30, 33, 35), or to test Israel's faith (2:21f.), or to keep Israel in training for war (3:1f.).

DEUTERONOMISTIC INTRODUCTION

2:6–3:6

As is indicated by the reference to the apportionment to the tribes and their dismissal by Joshua (2:6; cf. Jos. 24:28) and the notice of the death and burial of Joshua and his generation in 2:7–9, which agrees practically verbatim, if not in order, with Jos. 24:29–31, this is the direct continuation of the Deuteronomistic History from Jos. 23:16.

Here the Deuteronomist adumbrates the theme of the main body of Jg., apostasy, or at least easy tolerance and conformity with the Canaanite way of life, discipline under local oppression, repentance, grace and deliverance by means of the 'great judges'. As in 1:1, the precarious situation of Israel in Canaan is deliberately divorced from the occupation of the land as the culmination of the *Heilsgeschichte* which was ideally represented as the conquest under Joshua. Apostasy and reversals of fortune are represented as beginning after the death of Joshua and his generation (2:7–10), the Deuteronomist thus conserving his representation of the success of Israel when held to the divine purpose by the hand of Joshua, the faithful successor of Moses. The essentially theological character of the Deuteronomistic History is thus emphasised afresh, and more particularly the paraenetic character of that work. We are here forcibly reminded that the history of Israel to be presented in Jg. and the rest of the Deuteronomistic History is 'preached history' (Hertzberg, *op. cit.*, p. 162). In typical homiletic style, though reflecting the liturgy of the divine contention and public fast and penitence, which was the framework of the pre-Deuteronomistic story of the great judges (3:7–12:7), the Deuteronomist, especially in 2:16–20 emphasises his main theme, the operation of the word of God in the curse on the infringement of the principles of the covenant (cf. Dt. 27:15–26). He insists, moreover, that such progress as Israel was able to make in the settlement was by the grace and forbearance of God, and even if he admits human courage and resource in the work of the 'great judges' for the survival and growth of Israel, he emphasises the special grace and divine favour, or charisma, of the leaders as the result of the possession of the spirit of God, which made them executives of his will, in which the Deuteronomist agrees with his predecessor the compiler of the stories of the 'great judges'.

B. NARRATIVES OF THE 'GREAT JUDGES'

3:7–16:31

Othniel 3:7–11

The first instance of deliverance in Jg. is exceptional in that it is in the nature of a summary with scant detail. The passage, giving the apostasy of Israel (v. 7) as the occasion for oppression (v. 8), their appeal to God and his relief through a **deliverer** (v. 9), who was invested with **the spirit of the LORD** as vindicator (**and he judged Israel**) into whose hand God delivered the enemy (v. 10), after which **the land had rest forty years** is probably editorial. The last verse is part of the Deuteronomistic framework of the book, but the rest is the familiar framework of the fast-liturgy in the earlier collection of narratives of the great judges. The details of the historical situation have been lost, but the eight years of oppression does not suggest a merely conventional figure, and may contain, along with the name of the deliverer and the enemy, the germ of historical truth. Nevertheless, as the present text stands, the passage has all the appearance of artificiality. **Cushan-rishathaim** ('Cushan of the Double Iniquity') does not sound historical, and it seems quite improbable that a **king of Mesopotamia**, again a vague term, should have oppressed Israel for **eight years**, to say nothing of the fact that an Israel embracing Judah and her Kenizzite neighbours was non-existent as a political force in the time of the judges. Even granted that the oppressor was no more than an Aramaean chief from north Mesopotamia who raided periodically, such raids, if not actually impossible, in view of the far-ranging raids of Awda Abū Ṭai a generation ago from the hinterland of Aqaba to the Euphrates, are unlikely.

It is even more unlikely that **Othniel** the Kenizzite, whose significance was limited to districts south of Hebron, should have headed resistance to the attack, even granted that it came through Transjordan by way of Jericho. In view of the association of the Kenizzites with Judah, it is suggested (J. L. McKenzie, *The World of the Judges*, 1966, p. 122) that the inclusion of Othniel among the great judges reflects the work of a redactor from Judah to include a representative of Judah among the great judges, who were all from the north. We do not doubt this, but question if the 'redactor' of the traditions of the great judges was other than the compiler from Judah in the early Monarchy. It would be odd if Othniel, a Kenizzite from remote Kiriath-sepher, should be selected without being associated with some significant incident.

In **Cushan-rishathaim king of** Aram-Naharaim (*RSV*, **Mesopotamia**) we may suspect in 'Aram' the scribal corruption of an original 'Edom', first proposed by Klostermann (*Geschichte des Volkes Israel*, 1896, p. 119), 'Naharaim', which particularises the locality in Mesopotamia, being a later addition. Now in view of the coppermines in the escarpment of the Arabah, which were worked at this time (B. Rothenberg, 'Ancient Copper Industries in the Western Arabah', *PEQ*, 1962, pp. 5–71) and were probably the inducement to David's conquest of Edom, it is most likely that Edom, already a kingdom, was settled at this time west of the Araba and may well have resented the occupation of south-eastern Palestine by new and aggressive elements. Moreover, the Kenizzites had also an Edomite affinity, and the establishment of Othniel's group in Palestine may have suggested that there was room for further occupation. Certainly the Edomites would be interested in the movements of the Kenizzites in Palestine and in the new political alignments they made. The identity of the enemy with the Edomites suggests a feasible original for the name **Cushan-rishathaim**. For the last element, Klostermann suggested *rô'š hattêmānî* ('chief of the Temanites'); cf. 'Husham of the land of the Temanites' (Gen. 36:34). Alternatively Cushan, which is parallel to Midian in Hab. 3:7, may be a district, and the original text may have been 'Cushan and the Temanites and the king of Edom'. In any case the recognition of Edom in the passages makes the tradition of Kenizzite resistance to the eight-year menace historically probable, though Othniel may be cited by the pre-Deuteronomistic compiler as a traditionally active Kenizzite from Jos. 15:16–19// Jg. 1:12–15.

Ehud 3:12–30

Within the editorial framework (vv. 12–15*a*, 30) the exploit of **Ehud** of Benjamin and those who followed him from 'the hill country of Ephraim' is described. Here the circumstantial narrative indicates a well-established local Benjaminite tradition. Moore (*Judges*, ICC, 1908, p. 90) and Burney (*The Book of Judges*, 1930, p. 67) found traces of two versions of the tradition; e.g. in v. 19*b* Ehud secures his private interview with the king after returning from Gilgal and coming before him among his courtiers, whom the king on Ehud's request dismissed, while in v. 20 Ehud apparently comes directly to the king in his private roof-chamber and announces that he has a message from God. Those statements, however, are not mutually exclusive, as the king after dismissing his retainers may have withdrawn for his private audience with Ehud to the roof-chamber. Ehud's dismissal of his followers (v. 18), apparently at the court, and his return alone from the vicinity of **Gilgal** (v. 19*a*), reads somewhat awkwardly, but the immediate dismissal was calculated to allay suspicion, and his visit to Gilgal may have been to communicate his final plan to his followers, who might congregate there without exciting suspicion, since it was an Israelite sanctuary. Thus we find no compelling evidence of variant sources in this brief, though lively and circumstantial, account of Ehud's exploit and the sequel in the successful onslaught of the people from the hill country of Ephraim, the Benjaminites and their immediate neighbours Ephraim, which Ehud's bold stroke inspired.

Shamgar 3:31

The exploit of **Shamgar the son of Anath** has every appearance of an adventitious introduction into the narratives of the great judges, perhaps by the Deuteronomistic Historian after the incorporation of the five 'minor judges' in order to make up the round number of twelve judges, subsuming Barak under Deborah. This is indicated by the fact that the notice of Shamgar is inserted actually *before* the end of the notice of Ehud's work in the statement of the apostasy on his death (4:1), nor does the passage agree stylistically with the context. Actually in certain MSS of LXX it is grouped with the Samson cycle after 16:31; the call or rise of Shamgar is not noted as in the case of the charismatic liberators; nor is the length of his rule, the place of his burial or his tribal affinities, as in the case of the 'minor judges'. He is introduced as **Shamgar the son of Anath**, by which is meant probably 'Shamgar the man of Beth-Anath', and there is no note of the district in which this place may be located. The name itself, if genuine, is probably not Hebrew, but rather Hurrian, and the person may be one of the non-Semitic elements which the Amarna Tablets attest in Palestine in the fourteenth century BC.

In the uncertainty of the local affinity of Shamgar, it is not easy to determine the capacity in which he acted, but in view of the possibly Hurrian name he may have been a mercenary commandant of the Egyptians who took part in the resistance to the 'Sea-peoples' including the Philistines who invaded the coastal plain of Palestine in the first half of the twelfth century BC, as Alt proposed ('Megiddo im Übergang vom kanaanäischen zum israelitischen Zeitalter', *KS* I, 1953, p. 261). His actual historical role may have been confused in popular tradition with that of Samson, of whose exploit with the jawbone of an ass Shamgar's feat with the ox-goad is reminiscent, if indeed 'ox-goad' is not the result of scribal corruption (see below, on 3:31). It may further be noted that Shamgar is not actually called a judge, and the words **and he too delivered Israel**, with which the passage ends, further suggests that the passage is secondary. The figure is probably suggested by the passing — and ambiguous — reference to Shamgar in the Song of Deborah (5:6).

Deborah and Barak 4–5

The exploit of **Deborah** and **Barak** and the miserable end of their adversary **Sisera** by the hand of **Jael** is transmitted in prose (ch. 4) and poetry (5:19–30). The latter is a simple tradition, though, being in poetry, it is both more and less full than the prose account. The former is more complex, and is further complicated by the apparent affinity with the tradition of the defeat of Jabin of Hazor in Jos. 11:1–11. Here we must remember that a prose narrative is always more open to secondary additions and adjustments than a poetic version, which by its very nature demands to be incorporated as it stands. Hence, in the reconstruction of the prose account in ch. 4, it is the poetic version in 5:19–30 which is the key to the solution, though to be sure poetry raises its own problems by expressions which may be figurative rather than literal.

The discrepancies between the prose version of the exploit of Deborah and Barak and the poetic version are at once apparent. In the former, the enemy is **Jabin** of Hazor in the extant text, who is not mentioned in the Song of Deborah, where the enemy was quite definitely **Sisera** of Harosheth of the Gentiles (*RSV*, **Harosheth-ha-goiim**) at the north-west end of the Great Central Plain, or perhaps the south-east end of the Plain of Acco. Here Sisera was evidently acting on his own initiative, and is in fact regarded as a king (5:28–30), whereas in 4:2 he is said to be simply the officer of Jabin king of Hazor. Thus, whatever common tradition may underlie the prose and poetic versions of the campaign against Sisera, the two have developed independently.

The source of the complication is the mention of Jabin of Hazor in ch. 4, who according to Jos. 11:1–11 was already defeated by Joshua and his city destroyed. Assuming that the same king really belonged to the tradition of the victory of Deborah and Barak in ch. 4 and to the tradition of the victory at the Waters of Merom in Jos. 11:1–11, Hertzberg proposes that Jos. 11:1–11 and Jg. 4–5 are variant traditions of the same event, a difficult hypothesis since Sisera is not mentioned in Joshua and the location of the action is quite different.

Kedesh also, where Sisera was killed in the tent of Jael the wife of Heber the Kenite, and which is associated in Jg. 4:17 with an alliance between Heber and Jabin of Hazor, poses a further problem. Kedesh of Upper Galilee, which this verse envisages, was too remote from the battlefield where Sisera was defeated near Megiddo, and the same applies to Kedesh, the muster-place for the battle against Sisera (Jg. 4:10), which Jg. 4:11 locates in south-east Galilee (cf. Jos. 19:33). Accordingly it is suggested that two traditions known to different sources have been fused here, that of the defeat of Jabin of Hazor (cf. Jos. 11:1–11), where the Kedesh envisaged was in Upper Galilee, and the battle against Sisera in the Great Central Plain. It is suggested that the former tradition knew the heroine as the wife of Heber the Kenite and the latter knew her as Jael, the confusion arising from the role of a leader from Naphtali, the tribe of Barak (Jg. 4:6), in both actions (so Moore, Budde, Nowack, Gressmann, Burney, Eissfeldt and Simpson).

Noth, who did not subscribe to the documentary hypothesis of those scholars, saw also the source of the confusion of the two traditions in an unnamed leader of Naphtali against Jabin in Jos. 11:1–11, identified with Barak in Jg. 4 and 5. This is a probable solution of the difficulty, though we should share Noth's reserve with regard to documentary sources before the pre-Deuteronomistic compilation in Jos. 2–11, which accredits the defeat of Jabin of Hazor to Joshua.

We subscribe to the view of Wellhausen and Lagrange that Jael's encampment where Sisera was killed was at Tell Abū Qadis near Megiddo and Taanach, where the battle was (Jg. 5:19), which may be the Kedesh which was reckoned to Issachar in 1 Chr. 6:72 (MT, v. 57). On this view, the muster in Jg. 4–5 may have been at Kedesh in south-east Galilee (Khirbet Qadīsa, suggested by the mention of the **oak in Za-anannim** (Jg. 4:11; cf. Jos. 19:33). The redactional note on the peace between Heber the Kenite and Jabin of Hazor evidently envisages the place of Sisera's death at Kedesh in Upper Galilee, an impression encouraged by the role that a leader of Naphtali played both in the action against Jabin of Hazor in Jos. 11:1–11 and against Sisera in Jg. 4–5, though the scenes of the action and the times are widely different.

In the question of the Israelites who were engaged in the action too there is apparent discrepancy besides essential agreement. It is generally held that although the prose version names only **Zebulun and Naphtali** (vv. 6 and 10), the poetic version names **Ephraim**, **Benjamin**, **Machir** and **Issachar** besides. Here, however, the appreciation of the relevance of ch. 5 to the cultic occasion of the sacrament of the covenant (Weiser, *op. cit.*), to which we subscribe, limits the reference to the battle to vv. 18–30, where, significantly, only Zebulun and Naphtali are mentioned in this connection (v. 18). When this is appreciated, outstanding discrepancies between the prose and poetic versions disappear.

A further discrepancy between chs 4 and 5 is the figure of **Deborah**. Both passages agree in regarding her as a charismatic inspiring **Barak** and his warriors to heroic action in vindication of God's cause (4:6–10, 14; and apparently also 5:15), a role which she shared with the 'great judges'. On the other hand, 4:4 states that she was a judge, or arbiter, in Israel, associating her with the palm-tree **of Deborah between Ramah and Bethel in the hill country of Ephraim**. In the case of the 'great judges' we have seen how the combination of the role of ruler, including arbitration and jurisdiction, in the case of Jephthah suggested the characterisation of the great charismatic leaders as national figures with a similar office. In the case of **Deborah** the process was probably reversed. Her role as charismatic prophetess (4:4*a*), inspired and inspiring, suggested the tradition that she held also the office of a 'minor judge', a tradition encouraged by the probably oracular significance of the **palm of Deborah between Ramah and Bethel**, where tradition knew a sacred oak associated with another Deborah, the nurse of Rebecca (Gen. 35:8); or as Richter prefers (*op. cit.*, pp. 39f.), the oak of Tabor in the same locality in 1 Sam. 10:3, a possibility considered, but rejected by Lagrange (*Le Livre de Juges*, 1903, p. 67). Such conspicuous trees associated with a worthy of the past who has possessed the divine favour (*b^erākâh*) are often associated with oracles, decisions, pledges and oaths among the Arabs, and this may have been the tradition in the case of the sacred tree in question, whether oak or palm, which suggested the secondary tradition that Deborah had also the office of a 'minor judge'. The relevant passage, however, is a rather obvious parenthesis, an editorial expansion, and once this is discounted as secondary, further agreement between chs 4 and 5 is established.

Thus in the charismatic leadership of **Deborah**, with **Barak**, the participation of **Zebulun** and **Naphtali**, and particularly in the end of **Sisera** at the hand of **Jael** (4:18–22 and 5:24–30), there is striking agreement in the two accounts of the conflict against Sisera. In the presentation, however, the two accounts differ, apart from the obvious difference of presentation in prose and poetry, and discounting Jabin of Hazor and the much wider historical perspective which his inclusion would imply. The fact remains that in its account of the muster at **Tabor** (4:6, 12, 14) or **Kedesh** (4:9f.) under Barak at the stimulus of Deborah (a conflation of two different versions, as Richter, *Traditionsgeschichtliche Untersuchungen*, p. 55, has recognised) and that of the battle in a locality unspecified, but certainly east of **Harosheth** of the Gentiles (4:16) and by the **Kishon** (4:7), and that of the death of Sisera by the hand of Jael, the prose version relates the incident with much fuller historical appreciation, and this is indeed its sole object.

The poetic version by contrast is concerned with the incident as the subject of praise to Yahweh for the vindication of his purpose through Israel. This, according to the most feasible view of Weiser, was fittingly expressed in a hymn in the assembly of the sacral community when the incident was still fresh in the memory. According to this interpretation, the enumeration of the various elements of Israel in 5:14–18 does not relate to the campaign, except perhaps in the case of **Issachar** and certainly in the case of **Zebulun** and **Naphtali**, though the reference to their part in the battle is not the primary purpose for which they were mentioned. This passage is primarily a tribal roll-call, where all members of the sacral community of the ten groups of northern Israel, whether present or absent, were named to preserve the solidarity of the community. The mention in this context of **Zebulun** and **Naphtali** (v. 18), significantly mentioned last of the ten groups, suggests the campaign in which they had so lately distinguished themselves, which from this point becomes the subject of a hymn of praise (vv. 19–30). This, and the reference to the part of Zebulun and Naphtali in v. 18, is properly the verse account of the battle and its sequel. The campaign, however, is not described in detail nor set in the wide historical perspective of the prose account. Instead, certain details of the battle are highlighted, and here, in the fashion of poetry, details are given which are omitted in the prose account. Thus the battle is localised **at Taanach by the waters of Megiddo** (v. 19), an exceedingly important detail for the understanding of the course of the battle, and the discomfiture of the enemy's chariotry in the Kishon, probably in consequence of a rainstorm, when **the stars . . . fought against Sisera** (v. 20; see below, ad loc.). The death of **Sisera** is described in detail in both accounts, though the poetic version naturally dramatises the incident in praise of **Jael**. Likewise, the poem dramatises the miserable end of Sisera by depicting at length, and in graphic detail in the literary convention of the taunt-song, the sanguine yet vain expectancy of his mother and his harem (vv. 28–30).

Thus there is sufficient common matter in both versions to indicate a very reliable tradition, the poetic version being the more reliable in the tradition of the actual battle, retaining the freshest impressions of the incident, though for this very reason the prose account presents the campaign in wider historical perspective, discounting the figure of the already defunct Jabin of Hazor.

The poetic version of the battle, significant as that is, is but one element in a liturgical complex relative to the assembly of the sacral community of the ten groups of Israel as the people of Yahweh. This consists of various literary elements. Chapter 5, presented as the Song of Deborah, opens with the call to praise (vv. 2*c*, 9*c*) and continues with the declaration of devotion in praise (v. 3), to which v. 2*ab* relates, as an indication of the cultic occasion of rededication to which the sequel is relevant, the renewal of the sacral solidarity of the people of Yahweh (v. 13), doubtless at Mount Tabor. There the territories of Zebulun, Issachar and Naphtali met and there was their boundary-sanctuary of Yahweh, where the three groups might express their solidarity as the people of Yahweh and at which groups of worshippers of Yahweh from beyond Jordan, in western Galilee and in the centre of the country might realise their solidarity as the people of Yahweh (Dt. 33:18f.; Jg. 5:11), the 'Israel' of vv. 13–18 (Eissfeldt, *ARW* 1934, pp. 14f.). The psalm of praise (vv. 4f.; cf. Ps. 68:7ff., MT, vv. 8ff.) assures the community of the presence of God, recalling the theophany at the first occasion of the covenant at Sinai (cf. Pss. 18:7ff. (MT, vv. 8ff.); 50:2ff.; 68:7ff. (MT, vv. 8ff.); 77:16ff. (MT, vv. 17ff.); Dt. 33:2; Mic. 1:3ff.; Nah. 1:3; Hab. 3:3ff.). This is followed by a confession of apostasy, which is related to the sufferings of Israel (vv. 6–8), which is an essential element in the sacrament of the covenant (cf. Jos. 24:19). The theme of the psalm of praise (vv. 19–30) is introduced proleptically in vv. 10–11*ab*, but is followed by the description of the gathering of the various members of the sacral community on the occasion, absent members being named in the muster-roll of the tribes (vv. 11*c*–18). This culminates in the honourable mention of **Zebulun** and **Naphtali** (v. 18), which, as we have seen, leads naturally to the hymnic celebration of the victory over **Sisera** as the latest of God's acts of vindication (*ṣidᵉqot yhwh*) (v. 11*b*). This corresponds to the historical prelude to the covenant recounting the mercies of God to his people, which was the basis of his claim to their absolute allegiance, the genesis of the sacral community and the grounds of its hope; cf. Ps. 44, where, however, the drama of salvation points a contrast to the disaster experienced. In the psalm of praise in the Song of Deborah, the recent victory actualises Yahweh's vindication of his people and his purpose.

The recognition of the relation of the hymnic celebration of Barak's exploit to this particular cultic occasion suggests that other exploits of the 'great judges', of which we have now only the prose version, may also have been the theme of a hymn in such a context. This of course is a pure conjecture, and we should emphasise rather independent tribal saga as the primary source of the traditions of the judges transmitted to us. The public acknowledgement of the exploit of Deborah and Barak, however, in the liturgy of the sacrament of the covenant just described suggests that the significance of local exploits of the judges to the rehabilitation of the people of God was appreciated long before the schematic presentation of the Deuteronomist, and had motivated the earlier collection of the traditions of the 'great judges' under the theme of discipline and divine grace within the framework of the divine contention with his unfaithful people and their repentance.

Gideon **6–8**

Here, and particularly in the story of Gideon, an exceptional number and variety of sources have been used, tribal and local historical traditions, cultic and topographical aetiological sagas and of course the hero-saga of Gideon himself. There may be in addition, as de Vaux suggested (*op. cit.* II, p. 109), a fusion of the tradition of the great judge Gideon of Ophrah and that of Jerubba'al the father of Abimelech, also of Ophrah, who, like his son Abimelech, had once authority in Shechem as a kind of protectorate, to which a precedent has been claimed in Labaiyah and his sons in the Amarna Age (H. Reviv, 'The Government of Shechem in the El-Amarna Period and in the Days of Abimelech', *IEJ* 16, 1966, pp. 252–7). Those various sources are combined to emphasise the theme of apostasy and its consequences and the over-ruling power and grace of God in choosing and endowing his agent Gideon and effecting his purpose almost independently of human agency in the crisis. Here the work of the earlier compiler of the traditions of the judges could be simply incorporated into the Deuteronomistic History, but the Deuteronomist has made one very important contribution, that on the subject of the kingship. The tradition of a limited kingship by Gideon/Jerubba'al is used by the Deuteronomist to emphasise the kingship of God by the reply he puts into the mouth of Gideon (8:23). The grim interlude of Abimelech's abortive *coup d'état* and Jotham's parable (ch. 9) are given prominence in trenchant criticism of the institution of kingship, which recurs in the antimonarchic passages in 1 Sam. 8:6ff.; 10:18f.; 12:12.

The components of the Gideon story are as follows:

6:1, 2*a*, 6*a*, stereotyped introduction to the pre-Deuteronomistic narratives of the judges, introducing a new phase of oppression and eventual deliverance.

2*b*–5, historical elaboration of the oppression.

6*b*–10, a prophetic rebuke, emphasising the reason for the oppression.

This is in the literary form of God's contention with his people at a fast and public lamentation at the assembly of the sacral community, when God charges his people with infringement of his suzerain rights to exclusive worship on the basis of his great deliverance; cf. Isa. 1:2f., 10–20. This, after the introduction in vv. 1, 2*a*, 6*a*, sounds like a secondary insertion by the Deuteronomist to emphasise the reason for the oppression; but it may well be the Deuteronomistic elaboration of this formal introduction to the exploit of the judge in the pre-Deuteronomistic compiler. In view of this first emergence of the prophet, it is uncertain whether this also was a contribution of the Deuteronomist; but even if this is so, the prophet may reflect the role of the spokesman for God in the pre-Deuteronomistic introduction in the form of the divine contention.

11–24, deliverance anticipated by the call of Gideon.

One source of the passage is the aetiological saga of the foundation of the **altar** of **the LORD is peace** at **Ophrah**, authenticated as a cult-site by the theophany to Gideon, as indicated by **unto this day**. The fact that the holy site so authenticated was apparently on virgin rock indicates an original foundation. It may be the later adaptation of the original foundation of the Baal-altar of Ophrah. That vv. 11–17 and 19–24 represent two distinct traditions is indicated by the fact that in vv. 14, 15 and 16 Gideon's interlocutor is known and addressed as **the angel** of God, whereas in vv. 19–24 he is known as God only when fire consumed Gideon's food-offering (vv. 21f.). It is difficult to tell whether v. 18 belongs to the former passage or the latter. Formally it belongs to vv. 11–17, but in content to vv. 19–24, and in view of the editorial combination of both traditions it may be assigned to the editor. In any case, vv. 19–24 are an aetiological legend of the foundation of the altar of **the LORD is peace**, which possibly derived from the local priesthood of Ophrah; and vv. 11–17 are from the hero-saga of **Gideon** describing his call, which has its immediate sequel and conclusion not in vv. 19–24, but in vv. 36–40 (the sign of the dew and the fleece). The unity of vv. 11–16 and 36–40 is corroborated by the pattern of the divine call and subsequent confirmation by a sign in the case of Moses (Exod. 3:10–12, E), cf. Jeremiah (Jer. 1:5–19), aptly cited by E. Kutsch ('Gideons Berufung und Altarbau, Jg. 6:11–24', *ThLZ*

81, 1956, cols. 79f.). This belongs, with the story of Gideon's victory over the Midianites, to the hero-saga of Gideon from the tradition of his clan Abiezer, though in the present form of the tradition the call to deliver 'Israel' indicates that it had been already incorporated in the pre-Deuteronomistic compilation of the narratives of the great judges.

25–32. Whatever historical fact may be in the tradition of Gideon's destruction of the altar of Baal at his native Ophrah, to be replaced by one of Yahweh, it has been turned to account to give a popular explanation of the name Jerubba'al. Jerubba'al may have been another prominent man of Ophrah, notable for the protectorate he exercised over Shechem (9:1), whom tradition had confused with Gideon (see below, pp. 210f.). The popular etymology is indicated by the fact that the verb 'to plead', which it assumes, is not *rûb*, which the name Jerubba'al demands, but *rîb* (6:31f.). The verbal element in the name is more likely a by-form of that in Jeroboam, meaning possibly 'May Baal be great'. So adapted, the episode provides an appropriate prelude to the saving exploit of Gideon, suiting the theme of the pre-Deuteronomistic compiler of deliverance following due penitence. From 6:32 until the Abimelech incident (ch. 9) Gideon is equated with Jerubba'al in explicit parenthesis (6:32; 7:1; 8:29, 35).

6:33–35; 7:1–25, from the hero-saga of Gideon, preserved in the tradition of his clan Abie-zer. The power and grace of God are emphasised by the prominence given to the panic of the Midianites (7:22); cf. the collapse of the walls of Jericho (Jos. 6) and the panic of the Amorites at Gibeon (Jos. 10:10) in the pre-Deuteronomistic compilation of the tradition of the occupation in Jos. 2–11. The victory over the Midianites in the Great Central Plain was probably the achievement of Gideon's own clan of Abie-zer, as 8:2, probably from an independent Ephraimite tradition, indicates. In this case Gideon's appeal to the rest of **Manasseh** and the neighbouring tribes **Asher**, **Zebulun** and **Naphtali**, all of which except Zebulun are mentioned in the pursuit of the defeated Midianites (7:23), while natural in view of the field of campaign between Gilboa and the Hill of Moreh, was probably simply an alert in view of the rout of the Midianites, like the appeal to Ephraim to man the fords of the Jordan (7:24). The tradition of the selection of Gideon's three hundred from 32,000 may be a compromise between the historical tradition of the exploit of Gideon and the men of Abie-zer and that of the part played by the other groups in the sequel. Alternatively, the role of the other tribes may be suggested by hymnic celebration of this instance of 'God's vindications' at the sanctuary common to all the groups in question, like the victory of Deborah and Barak and Zebulun, Naphtali and possibly Issachar in Jg. 5. On the whole we prefer the former explanation.

In the account of the battle itself, the mention of the jars and torches and the trumpets, as well as the weapons of Gideon's commandos, are generally taken as evidence of two sources, though we do not regard this as compelling evidence. Probably the equipment of *all* with **jars** and horns (7:16) is a redactional elaboration; but in the two war-cries **For the LORD and for Gideon** (v. 18) and **A sword for the LORD and for Gideon** (v. 20) two variant traditions seem clearly indicated. Those, however, are both of the category of hero-sagas and are not different in kind.

8:1–3, the incident of the *contretemps* between Gideon and **Ephraim**, who claimed that they had been insulted in not being called to action in the beginning of the campaign. This has no obvious reason for its inclusion within the liturgical framework of the pre-Deuteronomistic compilation of traditions of the judges or the Deuteronomistic History. It is an accretion to the tradition of Gideon's exploit, but soundly based in history, reflecting the known pre-eminence in early Israel of Ephraim. The tradition may owe its preservation to the famous figurative reply of Gideon, **Is not the gleaning of the grapes of Ephraim better than the vintage of Abiezer?** (8:2). This reply, which resounded to the honour of both parties, was probably preserved in the traditions of both. 8:1–3, however, is probably part of the Ephraimite tradition of the cutting off of the Midianites at the fords of the Jordan, of which 7:24f. is the version current in Abi-ezer, probably a genuine historical tradition in all but the names, which are the basis of an aetiological legend explaining the place-names the Rock of Oreb (Raven) and the Winepress of Zeeb (H.-J. Wolf).

8:4–21, Gideon's raid on the Midianites in Transjordan. This is probably a genuine historical tradition, of which the introduction has probably been lost. Its independence of 7:24f. is implied not so much by the names of the Midianite chiefs **Zebah and Zalmunna** as by the fact that the Midianites were apparently undefeated, as is suggested by the confident reply of the men of **Penuel** and **Succoth** (8:6, 8). Gideon's motive of personal blood-revenge moreover is different from his pursuit of the defeated Midianites, so completely routed that one could speak of the vintage of Abi-ezer and the gleanings of Ephraim (8:2). Those considerations must militate against Hertzberg's view that those are the Ephraimite and Manassite versions of the same raid (op. cit., p. 197). Gressmann's view that those were two of many raids with which Gideon was associated (*SAT* I, 2, p. 209) is much more feasible. Hertzberg's suggestion that the incident involving Succoth and Penuel may be a Transjordan tradition has much more to recommend it, and we should emphasise the precise topographical note of the place where Gideon met the youth of **Succoth** (8:13f.). From the incident itself, it is not possible to tell if the tradition is inimical to Gideon, as we might expect after his savage reprisals on the men of **Penuel** and **Succoth** (vv. 16f.). If the making of the ephod in the sequel, however, is really associated as closely with this tradition as the present collocation suggests in stating that it was made from the spoils of the Midianites (var. 'Ishmaelites', v. 24), both passages, 4:21 and 22–27, may be coloured by Transjordanian tradition.

8:22–27, the tradition of the local kingship of Gideon (vv. 22f.) and the ephod (vv. 24–27). Here it must be noticed that kingship, which was exercised briefly by Abimelech (ch. 9) is not explicitly mentioned in the tradition of Gideon, but simply 'rule' (*māšal*). Formally, Gideon rejects the proferred rule with an authority beyond that of the judges, as that is represented in the pre-Deuteronomistic compilation. The older critics (Moore, Budde, Nowack, Burney) took the grounds of Gideon's apparent refusal as secondary, reflecting the bitter experience of the Monarchy towards the end of the kingdom of north Israel by a prophetic reviser of the northern Israelite tradition of Gideon ('E^2'), whose sentiments recall those of Hosea. This antipathy to monarchy as an infringement of theocracy may reflect the spirit of the sacral community in north Israel, which was realised in Jg. 5:13–18, especially if we accept that the authority of Yahweh in the covenant-formula was regarded as analogous to that of a suzerain over his vassals as in imperial vassal-treaties of the fourteenth–thirteenth centuries BC, see above, pp. 53f. (so M. Buber, *Königtum Gottes*, 3rd ed. 1956, pp. 3ff.; Noth, *History of Israel*, ET, 2nd ed. 1958, pp. 92ff.; de Vaux, *Ancient Israel*, 1961, pp. 92ff.). Hertzberg (*op. cit.*, p. 199) would see in Gideon's reply to the offer the contrast between the *ad hoc* authority of the charismatic leader, which by possession by the spirit of Yahweh is an extension of the authority of Yahweh, and permanent hereditary monarchy, where authority passed on automatically independent of the spirit of God and irrespective of any call to meet a specific crisis. Lagrange (*op. cit.*, p. 149) saw in Gideon's apparent refusal in deference to the rule of God an acceptance of the power, though with the rejection of the title of king. Since there is no mention of the title of king, though that appears to be implied in the offer of hereditary rule, it seems safer to follow Hertzberg. But the passage is highly ambiguous.

G. H. Davies (*VT* 13, 1963, pp. 151–7) argues that Gideon's refusal, where the emphatic use of the personal pronoun points the contrast with divine rule, cannot be literally pressed, but, like the instances he cites from Gen. 23 and 2 Sam. 24:21ff., is simply a dialectic convention implying his acceptance, albeit with scruples. We may cite in support of this view the same literary convention of dialectic controversy to emphasise the controversial point in the discussion between Baal and the craftsman god in the Baal-myth of Rās Shamra over the installation of a roof-shutter in the 'house of Baal', which the sequel shows to have been a vital element in a rite of imitative magic, yet Baal is for long obdurate against the proposal for the installation. Again, the tradition in Jg. 8:22f. is not necessarily the whole tradition. Possibly this is only the beginning of the transaction, the eventual acquiescence of Gideon being omitted by the compiler of the traditions of the great judges or even by the Deuteronomist. If Gideon was identical with Jerubba'al the father of Abimelech, 9:2 would indicate that he did accept the monarchy, though that is not explicitly stated of Gideon in 8:22f., nor elaborated. The identity of Gideon with Jerubba'al, however, may seriously be questioned.

De Vaux has feasibly suggested (*The Early History of Israel*, E.T. 1978, II, pp. 772ff.) that the tradition of Abimelech may have been associated with that of Gideon owing to the fact that the father of Abimelech, Jerubba'al, also came from Ophrah, which may possibly account for the variant of the name of Gideon in repeated parenthesis (6:32; 7:1; 8:29, 35). However this may be, Jerubba'al exercised a kind of protectorate over Shechem such as was evidently exercised in the Amarna Age by Labaiyah (H. Reviv, *IEJ* 16, 1966, pp. 252–7). The short reign of Abimelech was evidently similarly limited. Gideon, who had defeated the Midianites with three commandos from his own clan of Abi-ezer, possibly supported by detachments from the rest of Manasseh and their neighbours to the north Asher, Zebulun and Naphtali, and had pursued his private vengeance successfully over Jordan, is not likely to have been invited to rule over all the north Israelite confederacy without the support of Ephraim, whom he had offended. This being so, we understand the passage on the offer of rule more permanent than the *ad hoc* authority of a judge, which Gideon is represented probably as rejecting, to be developed by the Deuteronomist or his source the pre-Deuteronomistic compiler to point the contrast with the unsavoury Abimelech and his father Jerubba'al.

As for the incident of the **ephod** for the sanctuary of **Ophrah**, the historical kernel of the tradition may be that this object, in the form of a sheet-metal or brocade robe (see below, on 8:7), may have represented simply the dedication of spoils to Yahweh (cf. 2 Sam. 8:11), the allegation that **all Israel played the harlot after it** (8:27) being a Deuteronomistic comment. We take also as Deuteronomistic the statement that the ephod was a snare to Gideon and his family, this introducing the miserable fate of Jerubba'al's family in ch. 9. It is with this in view that the incident of the ephod, itself probably historical, is associated with the offer of rule to Gideon by the Deuteronomist or his predecessor, the compiler of the traditions of the great judges.

8:30–32, obituary on Gideon (v. 32), preceded by a note on his large family, though used in the Deuteronomistic History to introduce the Abimelech incident (v. 31; ch. 9), mentions his large harem (v. 30). This belongs to the tradition of one who affected kingship, however local, but may belong to the tradition of Jerubba'al if he was really distinct from Gideon. The note on his burial-place may associate Gideon with the 'minor judges', whose burial-places are regularly noted. If those men were local rulers rather than accredited custodians of the law, the collocation of the tradition of the rule of Gideon or Jerubba'al and his son Abimelech with the notice of the activity of the 'minor judges' (10:1–5; 12:8–15), including that on Jephthah (11:4–11; 12:7), is significant.

Abimelech 9

Abimelech, though not classified as a judge, is the subject of one whole chapter. The account of his abortive rule is so circumstantial as to indicate a genuine historical tradition incorporated in the pre-Deuteronomistic compilation, perhaps after considerable telescoping of independent traditions, though Abimelech is in no sense one of the great judges. The inclusion is probably determined by the association of Abimelech with **Ophrah**, whether he exploited the prestige of Gideon or was a member of a rival local family, that possibly of Jerubba'al, who is named as father of Abimelech to the exclusion of Gideon in ch. 9. If Jerubba'al was really distinct from Gideon, with whom he has been confused in the tradition rendered in the pre-Deuteronomistic compilation, this may represent, as the name suggests, the Canaanising element in Abi-ezer in contrast to the Yahwistic party of Gideon.

The presence of an active militant group, such as Gideon had been able to muster in his clan of Abi-ezer, might well be employed to protect the interests of a city-state like Shechem, with which the Israelite community at Ophrah had social relations (8:31). Such a situation at Shechem would have a precedent in the exploitation by its ruler Labaya in the Amarna Age of local *ḫabiru* (Knudtzon, **Die el-Amatna Tafeln,** 1905-1915, pp. 289, ll. 22f.). This might result in a protectorate such as the family of Jerubba'al evidently exercised over Shechem (v. 2). It was a situation ripe for exploitation by an ambitious individual like Abimelech. He did not assume rule by a personal *coup d'état*, however, but worked to this end through **the whole clan of his mother's family** in Shechem, who enlisted the support of the ruling elements in the city (*baʿalê šekem*) (vv. 2, 6). Meanwhile, Abimelech's kinsmen in Shechem provided him with funds to recruit a private army (v. 4), with which he eliminated **his brothers** in Ophrah, possibly the rival family of Gideon (v. 5), of whom only **Jotham** escaped (v. 5). So Abimelech was accepted as king (v. 6), though he evidently did not reside at **Shechem**, but probably at Arumah some distance to the south-east (vv. 31, 34), with a deputy (*pāqîd*), **Zebul**, in Shechem (vv. 28, 30). Eventually the ruling class in Shechem found that Abimelech had exceeded his commission as their protector (v. 28) and their dissatisfaction was exploited by **Gaal** (v. 26) and **his kinsmen**, who were able to maintain themselves in Shechem while Abimelech's deputy Zebul was still there. This suggests the presence of two fairly balanced parties in Shechem, the influential class (*baʿalê šekem*) and those who had persuaded them at the outset to accept the protectorate of Abimelech (vv. 1ff.). Täubler (*Biblische Studien: die Epoche der Richter*, ed. H.-J. Zobel, 1959, pp. 271f.) regarded those parties as the native Semites, or Canaanites in his terminology, and the non-Semitic 'Hivites' (Gen. 34:2), or Hurrians (see above, p. 100), as possibly the survivors of the ruling class in the city under Egyptian administration. However this may be, Abimelech asserted himself at Shechem, though indicating his sense of permanent insecurity there by razing the city (vv. 34–35) and the **Tower of Shechem** with its temple of **El-berith** ('God, or El, of the covenant', vv. 46–49; see below, on v. 6). The account of Abimelech's career is closed with a passage on his end in a campaign against nearby **Thebez** (vv. 50ff.), the connection, if any, of which with the events at Shechem is not clear.

Nor is it clear to what extent the swift succession of events conveyed in ch. 9 is a foreshortening by the pre-Deuteronomistic compiler of several situations developing over the whole of Abimelech's career. The statement that he **ruled** (*māšal*) **over Israel** for **three years** (v. 22) is ambiguous. That he ruled *over Israel* is the uncritical assumption either of the pre-Deuteronomistic compiler or the Deuteronomist. Coming immediately after his acceptance by the rulers of Shechem, it may refer to the period before the revolt of Gaal in the immediate sequel; but it probably refers to the whole career of Abimelech in the chronology of the Deuteronomistic Historian, whose theology of sin and retribution is expressed in vv. 23f.

Included in the complex is the protest of **Jotham**, the survivor of Abimelech's massacre at Ophrah (v. 5), in the form of the fable of the trees (vv. 8–15). The fable, cast in the rhythm almost of regular poetry, has probably an independent origin, though it may well have been cited, possibly in a shorter form, by some opponent of Abimelech at Shechem, the citation of the full fable in its rhythmic measure and its attribution to Jotham in a dramatic appearance at Shechem being the result of free treatment of the tradition by the compiler, who knew the original. The literary category of the beast- or plant-fable, so well known in Greek through Aesop's fables, was already well established in the east in Mesopotamia (E. Ebeling, *JCS* 4, 1950, pp. 215–22), Egypt (Erman-Ranke, *Ägypten*, 1923, pp. 429, 474) and in Aramaic literature (A. E. Cowley, *Aramaic Papyri of the Fifth Century BC*, 1923, pp. 216, 224), and was developed in Hebrew literature, e.g. Joash's fable of the cedar and the thistle in 2 Kg. 14:9, the allegory of the eagle, cedar and vine in Ezek. 17:3–10 and possibly the discourses on plants and animals in the tradition of Solomon's wisdom (1 Kg. 4:32, MT 5:13). Jotham's fable recalls particularly the altercation between the palm and the tamarisk on their respective merits in the Babylonian wisdom text cited in W. G. Lambert, *Babylonian Wisdom Literature*, 1960, pp. 151–67. The appearance of Jotham, sole survivor of Abimelech's massacre, at Shechem, which had already accepted Abimelech, is unlikely, even **at the top of Mount Gerizim**, and here there is every appearance of the fusion of two independent traditions, that of the survival of Jotham (9:5) and his escape to Edom (v. 21) and that of some local protest against Abimelech's designs at Shechem, citing the gist of the parable. The secondary character of the whole episode as related in 9:7–21 is indicated by its evident intrusion between 6 and 22ff., as Richter and Soggin conclude. Thus the compiler, by creating this dramatic scene, intensifies the suspense in the narrative (so Budde) and sharpens his criticism of the kingship solely by human initiative, and for the same reason he amplifies the tradition of the fall of Abimelech.

In the context of the Deuteronomistic History the abortive rule of Abimelech, one instance of local rule, such as that of Jephthah (11:4–11; 12:7) and possibly of the 'minor judges' (10:1–5; 12:8–15), is presented in anticipation of the kingship of Saul and David under divine direction and as a consequence of seduction to the ephod introduced by Gideon (8:27).

Jephthah 10:6–12:7

On the historical tradition of Jephthah, inserted between notices of the 'minor judges' (10:1–5; 12:8–15), with whom he is associated by a similar notice (12:7), see above, pp. 24f., 193.

The historical conditions connected with Jephthah's exploit against the Ammonites are introduced in the framework of the divine contention, *rîb* (10:11–14), on Israel's apostasy (10:6) and the public penitence (10:10, 15f.). In this introduction (vv. 6–16), all the regular elements of the convention are described, though much more expansively than usual. Thus, in the apostasy that provoked the divine wrath there is a similar expansive treatment (v. 6) as well as in the enemies that afflicted Israel (vv. 8, 11*b*, 12), both probably the subject of later elaboration. The introduction to the exploit of Jephthah, moreover, deviates from the normal introduction to the exploits of the great judges, not stating, for instance, that God responded to the contrition of the people by immediately raising him up as a deliverer invested with the spirit. This has suggested to Richter (*Traditionsgeschichtliche Untersuchungen zum Richterbuch*, p. 328; so also Soggin, *Judges*, pp. 205–7) that the whole section on Jephthah was secondarily admitted into the work on the great deliverers. In support of this view we may note the emergence of Jephthah as deliverer from the Ammonites primarily as a result of his proven ability and authority with his private army in the marginal land north of Gilead (11:3) and, after deliberation and on the initiative of the elders of Gilead (11:5f.) and practical negotiation between them and Jephthah (vv. 7–11), the agreement being confirmed at the sanctuary of Yahweh at Mizpah (v. 11). By the same token this and the diplomatic correspondence between Jephthah and the king of Ammon, details apart (vv. 12–18), suggests an independent historical tradition, supported by the precise duration of Jephthah's rule as *šôpēṭ* (12:7) in contrast to that ascribed to the other great judges in terms of decades. The secondary admission of this distinctive historical tradition into the work on the exploits of the great judges is indicated, moreover, by the fact that Jephthah is said to have been invested with the spirit of Yahweh in 11:29 only after the foregoing negotiations and with the actual campaign against the Ammonites.

The appointment of Jephthah **10:17–11:11**

The Ammonites take the field and encamp in Gilead, which brings the Israelite inhabitants of the hill-country of Gilead together at Mizpah, which from 11:10 was evidently a sanctuary of Yahweh. Here the statement that **the people of Israel came together** indicates the compiler, but **the leaders of Gilead** as well as the human initiative in the appointment of Jephthah indicate an earlier local source. Those local notables ask: 'Who is the man who will strike the first blow?' This may be a public deliberation or a challenge; it may even be an enquiry of the oracle. However this may be, the community undertakes to make that man **leader** (*qāṣîn*) against the Ammonites. In response to this question, Jephthah was obviously the one most prepared to strike the blow, if indeed he had not already done so, as Täubler considered (*op. cit.*, p. 285), with his band of semi-nomad Aramaeans from Tob beyond the Jabbok north-east of Gilead. This is not explicitly stated, but may be inferred from the passage on Jephthah's origins and present circumstances in 11:1–3, and from the invitation to Jephthah in vv. 5f.

In 11:1–3 and 4–11 we have in historical narrative local source-material used by the pre-Deuteronomistic compiler, who has assumed that the Ammonites made war on Israel rather than on the Gileadites (10:17; 11:4f.), despite the fact that the action was strictly local (cf. the statement that the Ammonites crossed the Jordan to fight against Judah, Benjamin and Ephraim, in the elaboration of the introduction to Jephthah's exploit in 10:9). The strictly local significance of the Ammonite war and the involvement only of Gilead is indicated by the fact that Jephthah was made head (*rō'š*) over the inhabitants of Gilead (11:8–11). There are two exceptional features here in the narratives of the judges: Jephthah is not initially called by God nor yet invested with the spirit of God; and the biographical note (11:1–3) and account of his appointment by the notables of Gilead is far more prgamatic than the call of any judge. This points to an ancient historical tradition relating to Jephthah as a local ruler rather than a charismatic distinguished by one exploit, and indeed 12:7 implies as much. This early historical narrative continues with Jephthah's campaign against the Ammonites in 11:29 and 32f., where the hand of the pre-Deuteronomistic compiler is indicated in the attribution of the victory to Israel (v. 33) and probably the note on the investment of Jephthah with the spirit of the Lord (11:29*a*). This historical source-material is elaborated by certain accretions, the diplomatic exchanges between Jephthah and the king of Ammon (11:12–28), which is secondary, being based on Num. 20–24, and by Jephthah's vow (11:30f.) and its tragic consequences, his sacrifice of his daughter (11:34–40), and the contretemps with the Ephraimites (12:1–6).

Diplomatic exchanges with Ammon **11:12–28**

The interruption of the factual historical narrative by diplomatic exchanges, with an argument which recapitulates the theme of Num. 20–24 (JE), with special reference to the overthrow of the Amorite realm of Sihon, which stretched from the Arnon to the Jabbok (Num. 21:21ff.; cf. Dt. 2), is obviously a secondary literary elaboration. Moore (*op. cit.*, p. 291) suggested that it reflects Ammonite aggression east of Jordan at the end of the Monarchy (Jer. 49:1–6), but, whatever the source of Jer. 49:1–6 may have been, it is difficult to appreciate the relevance of Ammonite expansion there to Judah, who had made no claim to Gilead, or the north part of Moab, since the time of Solomon. On the other hand, from the inscription of Mesha of Moab it is certain that Omri (885–874 BC) did successfully make such a claim, and to this period Täubler (*op. cit.*, p. 292) dated the passage, which in this case would coincide in time with the crystallisation of the tradition of Israel's occupation of Sihon's kingdom in E.

Jephthah's vow and its consequences **11:30–40**

Jephthah's vow, which accentuates the activity of God in his campaign, is here associated with an aetiological legend, which offers an explanation of an annual rite of mourning by young women, probably a rite in the fertility cult, the mythological prototype of which is the mourning by the virgin Anat for the dead Baal, later called Hadad-Rimmon (Zech. 12:11); cf. the women's lamentation for Tammuz in Jerusalem (Ezek. 8:14). The rite is here divested of its association with the fertility cult through its association with a historical incident. The virgin daughter of Jephthah is the connecting link, and while it is impossible to demonstrate the historicity of the tragic incident as it is described here, neither is there any compelling reason to doubt it.

Jephthah's contretemps with the Ephraimites **12:1–6**

This seems at first sight a tradition influenced by the incident of the reaction of the Ephraimites to Gideon's exploit against the Midianites beyond Jordan (7:24–8:3). As there, the Ephraimites object to the independent action of the principal and they are involved in an incident at the crossing of the Jordan (7:24; cf. 12:5f.). But while Gideon placates the Ephraimites and has actually called on them to man the fords of the Jordan to cut off the Midianites (7:24) before the contretemps (8:1), Jephthah asserts his independence by force of arms (12:4ff.) and the Ephraimites are discomfited at the fords of the Jordan (12:5f.). Here as in 10:18f.; 11:4–11 we notice the involvement not of Israel but only of the Gileadites (12:4f.), which seems to indicate a genuine ancient tradition. The statement in 12:4, **You are fugitives of Ephraim, you Gileadites, in the midst of Ephraim and Manasseh**, seems the clue to the situation, though the passage is omitted in certain MSS of LXX, followed by *NEB* (see below, p. 321, ad loc.). In view of the close affinity between Ephraim and Manasseh in the Jordan Valley and later in Transjordan, Ephraim may have been sensitive to the possible assertion of independence by their associates beyond Jordan, as to Benjamin's assertion of independence in Jg. 19–21. The tradition obviously goes back to the days of the settlement, when Ephraim exercised practical hegemony among the groups in north Israel and Transjordan listed in Jg. 5:13–18, which seems to be implied in Jephthah's initial appeal for help from Ephraim (12:2f.), if this, mentioned here for the first time, is not suggested by Gideon's appeal to the Ephraimites in 7:23f. The reaction of Ephraim was probably to the established local rule of Jephthah as 'head' (*rô'š*) of the inhabitants of Gilead including settlers from Ephraim and Manasseh who had accepted him, the substance of their animadversion **You are fugitives from Ephraim . . .** (12:4), if that passage is genuine. In those circumstances the association of the incident with Jephthah's Ammonite campaign might be secondary, suggested to the pre-Deuteronomistic compiler by the incident of Gideon and the Ephraimites in the same region.

Notice of Jephthah's period as 'judge' and of his death and burial 12:7

The section on Jephthah ends with a similar notice to that on the 'minor judges', but differs in the omission of his local affinity, of which there is no need after the passage on his origins and rise to power in 11:1–11, 29, 32f.

Samson 13–16

Though the story of Samson is introduced by the statement that **Israel did what was evil in the sight of the LORD, and the LORD gave them into the hand of the Philistines for forty years**, this is not set in the context of the divine contention with Israel, public repentance and divine mercy as in the pre-Deuteronomistic collection of the narratives of the great judges. Nor does the sequel deal with the single successful exploit of a charismatic liberator, but with a series of miscellaneous exploits from a hero-legend, some ostensibly serious, as Samson's mighty exploit at Ramath-lehi

(15:14–17), actually an aetiological legend, but usually rather clumsy practical jokes on a heroic scale, which are in the nature either of hero-legend or aetiological legend, and perhaps even the historification of local nature-myth. The Deuteronomistic narrator knew full well that what he incorporated was no self-contained narrative of liberation from the oppressor as in the case of the other 'great judges'. The introduction to the Samson cycle notes that the Lord gave Israel into the hand of the Philistines for forty years (13:1), double the twenty years ascribed to Samson's activity (15:20; 16:31). It is in fact said that Samson should only *begin* **to deliver Israel from the hand of the Philistines** (13:5). The involvement of Samson, moreover, with Philistine women, the woman of Timnah (ch. 14), with its sequel in his revenge for the loss of his *ṣadîqa* wife (15:1–8), with the harlot of Gaza and its sequel in the removal of the gates of Gaza (16:1–3) and with Delilah and its grim consequence in the captivity and death of the hero (16:4–31), removes Samson from the category of the great charismatics devoted wholly to the high enterprise of the deliverance of the people of God and successful in the enterprise. The figure of Samson is in fact so unlikely among the judges that it has been taken to have been included by the Deuteronomistic Historian as a tragic example of the abuse of a high calling. That, however, is rather the reflection of modern homiletics, and it is not supported by any Deuteronomistic comment in the entirely neutral presentation of the Samson tradition. Those considerations seem to confirm the view that the Samson cycle represents a well-established local folk-tradition in the Shephelah, and particularly about Beth-shemesh, of a local Danite strong man and colourful leader in frontier exploits with the Philistines, both more and less hostile.

Despite the difference between Samson's exploits and the acts of deliverance of the great judges, those traditions were incorporated into the pre-Deuteronomistic compilation since Samson was the only figure to be associated with the Philistines, the last and most formidable enemy of Israel which was overcome only under the Monarchy. He was the first figure to be so engaged before Samuel, whom tradition associated with more sustained and serious resistance, and with David (1 Sam. 16:6–13). The known fact that the Philistines were not seriously checked until the first quarter of David's reign, which is recognised by the statement that Samson only began resistance to them (13:5), possibly accounts for the lack of the regular introduction to the stories of the great judges in the pre-Deuteronomistic compilation. The recognition of the more, though not completely, effectual power of Samuel and Ephraim in their sustained struggle against the Philistines seems to us, following the suggestion of de Vaux (*The Early History of Israel*, II, p. 686), to account for certain similarities in the accounts of the birth and dedication of Samson and Samuel (ch. 13; cf. 1 Sam. 1), both born to evidently barren women and both dedicated before they were born, while the lapses and ultimate failure of Samson may be presented as a contrast to the steady application of Samuel and the final liberation from the Philistines under David. The statement that **the Spirit of the LORD began to stir** Samson (13:25) before the account of his exploits is probably the contribution of the pre-Deuteronomistic compiler. This, however, was not associated with his call or his response, but with personal exploits of exceptional strength, perhaps the sense in which the source-tradition of the pre-Deuteronomistic compilation understood Samson's possession by the spirit of the Lord, as when he mangles the lion with his bare hands (14:6), slays thirty Philistines of Askalon for their garments to pay his wager to the Philistines of Timnah (14:19) or frees himself from bonds at Lehi (15:14).

Combined with hero-saga is aetiological legend explaining the sanctity of the rock-altar at **Zorah** (13:9ff.) and local place-names, **Ramath-lehi** (15:9–17), the Partridge (lit. 'Caller') Spring in the same vicinity (15:18–20) and possibly 'the Gates of Gaza' near Hebron, possibly at the head of the Wadi 'l-Afranj, north-west of Hebron, from which the coast near Ashkelon and Gaza is visible. The interest in the Samson cycle in the region about Beth-shemesh, from which the tribe of Dan migrated in the time of the judges (ch. 18), reflects either a tenacious determination to conserve local traditions which might otherwise have died out with the Danite migration or else renewed interest in the locality under David and Solomon and the early Monarchy, when Zorah was fortified by Rehoboam (2 Chr. 11:10) and Beth-shemesh (probably) by David or Solomon (Y. Aharoni, 'The Date of the Casemate Walls in Judah and Israel and their Purpose', *BASOR* 154, 1959, pp. 35–9; cf. G. E. Wright and F. M. Cross, 'The Boundary Lists of the Kingdom of Judah', *JBL* 75, 1956, pp. 215–17).

Apart from local aetiological traditions, the tradition of Samson's birth and designation as a Nazirite (ch. 13), aside from possibly conscious assimilation to the tradition of the birth of Samuel, is elaborated in the hero-legend to emphasise an important element in the conservation of primitive Yahwism and the distinctive Israelite way of life (13:7; cf. Am. 2:11f.). Samson's relations with Philistine women, however, indicates the complexity of traditions in the Samson cycle.

It is difficult quite to dissociate the Samson-cycle from cult-legend of the shrine of Beth-shemesh ('the shrine of the Sun') *c.* three miles south-south-east of Zorah, Samson's reputed home. The role of the hero with the sun-name as the upholder of God's order against the enemies of his people is reminiscent of the Sun as the protagonist of Cosmos against Chaos in the Egyptian myth of the Sun-god nightly menaced by Apophis the serpent of darkness. The theme was also known in the sun-mythology of Canaan and is explicitly expressed in a hymn appended to the Baal-myth of Rās Shamra (C. H. Gordon, *Ugaritic Handbook*, 1947, 62; 11:42–52; A. Caquot, 'La divinite solaire ougaritique', *Syria* 36, 1959, pp. 90–101). Samson, who has been in his prime vigour in the summer (ch. 15), ends his days in the darkness (ch. 16), which suggests winter. He grinds, repeating the weary round of daily toil under external compulsion. It has been suggested that the end of Samson between the pillars amid the ruins of the Philistine building is a mythologisation of the setting sun, but that is not a view that can be well controlled, and for that matter there is no independent evidence of the cult-myth of Beth-shemesh.

Features in the Samson cycle which are common to the myth of Heracles have also been noticed, e.g. the killing of a lion with the hero's bare hands, betrayal by a woman, the hero deciding his own death, the descent to the darkness, Samson blind to the prison and Heracles to the underworld. Samson's menial labour in the prison for the Philistines he has so often discomfited has suggested the labours of Heracles at the order of the weaker Eurystheus. The incident of the gates of Gaza has been compared to the setting up of the Pillars of Heracles. The question of motifs of Greek mythology in Palestine resolves itself into one of date. Older criticism pointed to the assimilation of Heracles to Phoenician Melqart, whose cult is attested in the north part of the coastal plain in the third century BC. But there were much earlier contacts between Palestine and the Aegean, with strong Aegean influence in art and architecture in Mycenaean settlement at Minet al-Beidā, the maritime quarter of ancient Ugarit, and a Greek commercial settlement is actually attested at Meṣad Hashavyahu, some fifteen miles south of Jaffa (J. Naveh, 'The Excavations at Meṣad Hashavyahu', *IEJ* 12, 1962, pp. 89–113). The local association of the myth of Perseus and Andromeda, the Canaanite original of which is extant in an Egyptian version (A. H. Gardiner, 'The Astarte Papyrus', *Studies presented to F.Ll. Griffiths*, 1932, pp. 74–85), with Jaffa may indicate another such settlement there in the Late Bronze Age, some twenty-five miles from Samson's home.

Both the Heracles tradition in the Levant and the Samson tradition, however, may have been influenced by the Mesopotamian Gilgamesh epic, as Burney suggested (*op. cit.*, pp. 391ff.). That this was known in Palestine, apart from its probable transmission by the popular story-teller, like the Arabi *rāwī* of more recent times, is indicated by a fragment of a fourteenth-century version in Babylonian cuneiform found near Megiddo (A. Goetze and S. Levy, 'A Fragment of the Gilgamesh Epic from Megiddo', *Atiqot* II, 1959, pp. 121–8). The most notable analogy in the Samson tradition to the Gilgamesh epic is the part played by females; cf. the opposition of Ishtar to Gilgamesh and the taming of the wild man Enkidu by the harlot.

Whatever significance there may be in such literary analogies, or in the possibility that the Samson tradition retains traces of the solar mythology of Beth-shemesh, the tradition has been historicised in its transmission. The introduction is firmly related to the institution of the nazirate, and the tradition of the grave 'between Zorah and Eshtaol' persisted.

The essentially local independence of the tradition of Samson, as distinct from the traditions of the other great judges, is further indicated by the local, sporadic and often trivial nature of the hero's exploits, which are so often motivated by his personal whims and impulses. Here is no charismatic, quickened and directed by the spirit of God to a sober end, but a reckless and irresponsible practical joker, whose phenomenal physical strength rather than his single-minded devotion to the will of God and the welfare of his people is taken as evidence of his possession by the spirit of God. His 'case' is presented not so much as a devoted charismatic cooperating with God but as the over-ruling divine exploitation of human ineptitude. In the association of the intercourse of Samson with the Philistine woman of Timnah with his slaughter of the Philistines and burning of their corn (14:1–15:8) and of his affair with Delilah (16:4ff.) with his suicidal slaying of more Philistines in his death than in his life (16:30), we may see the theological justification of the inclusion of Samson among the great judges in the pre-Deuteronomistic compilation.

With the exception of Gideon (8:32) and Joshua (Jg. 2:9), the only great leaders among the Israelites in the time of the settlement whose tombs are localised are the 'minor judges', Tola (10:2), Jair (10:5), Jephthah (12:7), Ibzan (12:10), Elon (12:12) and Abdon (12:15). It is therefore suggested that Samson, whose tomb is also located, was a 'minor judge' like those figures, whatever that may have involved. Unlike them, however, no specific period is mentioned during which he exercised office except the obviously conventional twenty years (15:20; 16:31), which is not convincing. Samson's exploits and authority, moreover, were not of the order of, for instance, those of Jephthah *qua* 'great' or 'minor judge'. He was rather a figure of picaresque legend, the heroic scale of his strength, daring and exploits suggesting the possession of divine favour to popular imagination. Now the grave of such figures as the centre of tradition and indeed the object of pilgrimage is well known in Palestine through the ages, and it may well have been pilgrimage to the tomb of Samson which conserved his memory and promoted the development of his tradition, occasioning also the aetiological traditions of localities in the vicinity.

The last act of the drama of Samson from his intercourse with Delilah to his end at Gaza exhibits the art and stylisation of the hero-saga. The tension of his betrayal is sustained by his threefold prevarication, with verbal repetition characteristic of popular saga, until he finally divulges the secret of his strength. After his downfall, the phenomenal strength of the hero, which has hitherto been invincible, is now employed on the work of an ass or menial, even a slave-girl (Exod. 11:5). Rather naïvely representing the return of Samson's strength as the concomitant to the regrowth of his hair, the saga rehabilitates the hero, while at the same time emphasising the agency of God, who throughout has made possible the spectacular achievements of Samson.

APPENDIX A. THE ORIGIN OF THE PRE-MONARCHIC SANCTUARY OF DAN

17–18

See above, pp. 193f.

In this section, which describes the local cult of the Ephraimite Micah served by the Levite from Bethlehem who was to become the ministrant of the sanctuary of Dan (ch. 17), and goes on to describe the migration of six hundred men of Dan to the upper Jordan, taking with them the Levite and his cult objects (ch. 18), certain variations are to be noted, which have been taken by some to indicate two main sources and by others later elaboration of an original tradition. This, however, does not impair the progress of the narrative in its almost novelistic movement.

The name of Micah is spelt in the longer form *mîcāyᵉhû* in 17:1–4 and in the shorter form elsewhere; 18:30ff. mentions one graven image, which seems to be envisaged in 17:4*c*, while 17:3, 4*ab* mentions a graven and a molten image and 18:18 envisages certainly two distinct images. It has been suggested that the ephod and teraphim (17:5; 18:14, 17ff. and 20) are variants of the image, but they are probably rather accessories to it. Further, the Levite is variously a youth who happens to be sojourning in Micah's community (17:7) and a man who sets out from Bethlehem to sojourn where he may find employment and, chancing to come to Micah, is engaged as a priest (17:8). The status of the Levite as 'father' to Micah (17:10), though it may refer to office rather than seniority or personal status, probably belongs to the latter tradition, while the description of the Levite 'as one of his sons' (17:11) probably belongs to the former. These variants might indicate not two different sources, but later elaborations of an original source-tradition, the molten image being suggested to a redactor or glossator by the fact that the silver was handed over to a metal-caster (17:4), as maintained by Kuenen, Lagrange and Gressmann, but probably they represent variant sources (so Budde, Moore, Burney).

If we may hazard a conjecture regarding the respective sources of those variant traditions, we may suggest that one was from the Levitical priesthood of the tribal cult at Dan and the other from the non-Levitical priesthood of the royal cult established by Jeroboam I at Dan or Bethel (1 Kg. 12:28–30), with which, on the evidence of 18:30, the cult at Dan with its symbols and Levitical priesthood survived till the destruction of Dan, probably in 734 BC. This cult was perhaps specifically associated with oracles, as the association with ephod and teraphim suggests (cf. 2 Sam. 20:18, LXX). Noticing that the phrase 'everyone did what was right in his own eyes', which is found in conjunction with the statement that there was no king in Israel (17:6; 21:25; cf. 18:1; 19:1), is found in Dt. 12:8 in conjunction with the centralisation of the cult, Soggin (*Judges*, p. 265), after T. Veijola (*Das Königtum in der Beurteilung der deuteronomischen Historiographie, Acta Academiae Scientiarum Fennicae* B, 1977, pp. 24–9) would see here a reflection of the reformation of Josiah, ascribing the appendices to the Deuteronomistic History. But, as Soggin has already admitted (*op. cit.*, pp. 263, 269), they do not exhibit the characteristic features of the Deuteronomistic History in the rest of Jg. In our opinion the derivation of a composite tradition from the two sanctuaries at Dan would admirably account at once for the lack of explicit condemnation of the iconic cult and the quiet, subtle mockery of the tribal cult, which Nötscher (*Das Buch der Richter*, Echter Bibel, AT I, 1955, ad loc.) and Noth ('The Background of Judges 17–18', *Israel's Prophetic Heritage*, eds. B. W. Anderson and W. Harrelson, 1962, pp. 68–85) have noticed. A measure of such literary unity as the section presents was possibly given to the compilation by the royal priests of Bethel or Dan as distinct from the oracle-priests of the tribal sanctuary at Dan who were descended from Micah's Levite. This is doubtless the source of the mild ridicule of the origin of the cult-symbols in money stolen and cursed, of the priesthood of a vagabond and disloyal Levite and of the high-handed appropriation of both by the Danites in their occupation of the defenceless settlement of Laish. Further, the note on the regulative influence of the king in the cult (17:6; cf. 18:1) is more readily explicable in the context of tradition from the priesthood of the royal sanctuaries of Dan or Bethel than from any other source, and certainly precludes the Deuteronomist. The occasion for the literary composition of the traditions of the origin of the tribal cult at Dan may have been the destruction of the settlement in Tiglath-pileser's campaigns in 734–732 BC, when survivors of the priesthood of Dan may have taken refuge at Bethel when their district became an Assyrian province and the northern kingdom of Israel was limited to Samaria and district.

Containing no saving act or any saviour-figure and without the introductory framework of lapse, oppression, penitence and grace, neither this passage nor Appendix B was part of the pre-Deutero nomistic compilation of the traditions of the great judges. The absence of positive censure on cultic unorthodoxy and the significant fact that it stands outside the chronological scheme of the Deuteronomistic History indicate that those appendices were no part of the Deuteronomistic History. The implication of the regular government of the king indicates, as we have noticed, source-material from the monarchy of north Israel before or about 732 BC. On the clue of the statement that there was yet no king in Israel as well as of the origin of the cult of Dan in the settlement of the region by the Danites this matter was added by the redactor of the Deuteronomistic History as an appendix to that part of the Deuteronomistic History dealing with the judges. The redactor dates the premonarchic cult at Dan before that at Shiloh (18:31) probably to explain his insertion of Appendix A before the next phase of the Deuteronomistic History, which is set at Shiloh (1 Sam. 1ff.), assumed to be the sanctuary of all Israel.

APPENDIX B. THE BENJAMINITE OUTRAGE AT GIBEAH AND THE WAR

19–21

The story of the outrage on the Levite's concubine by certain louts of Gibeah in Benjamin, with the consequent war of the rest of the tribes on a defiant Benjamin and the measures whereby the depleted tribe was subsequently rehabilitated, shows elements both old and new.

The initiative of Judah in response to the oracle at Bethel, **Which of us shall go up first against the Benjaminites?** (20:18), the only reference to the involvement of Judah in Jg. except in a similar response to an oracle in 1:1f., suggested to Gudemann in 1869 and Graetz in 1874 that a historical tradition of the period of the judges was worked over by a Judaean hand in the reign either of David or Solomon in the interests of the house of David and in disparagement of Saul's community of Gibeah and Jabesh-gilead which had supported him. Wellhausen (*Prolegomena to the History of Ancient Israel*, pp. 232ff.) doubted if there was any historical nucleus at all in the passage, which in his opinion was an artificial creation in condemnation of the role of Benjamin as Saul's tribe and in particular of Gibeah, his home town, on the basis of Hosea's reference to 'the day of Gibeah' (Hos. 10:9). The relation between Jg. 19–21 and Hos. 10:9, however, is hard to determine, the more especially since in Hos. 10:9 it is Israel who had sinned and not, as in Jg. 19–21, only Benjamin. Notwithstanding, the reference in Hos. rather supports a genuine historical nucleus in Jg. 19–21, however that may have been understood or misunderstood by the prophet. However this may be, the question of the historical relevance of Jg. 19–21 to the period of the judges has divided scholars ever since.

Noth accepted as historical the tradition of the punishment of the Benjaminite outrage by all Israel as a sacral community, or, in his own terminology, the 'amphictyony', though he admitted that it has reached us through the Deuteronomistic Historian and the redactor (*Das System*, 1939, pp. 100–6, 168–70). We would question the evidence for the sacral community of twelve tribes including Judah (20:18) in the period of the judges, finding that conception a reflection of David's unification of his realm. For us the question is whether the tradition of the action of the sacral community was from the Deuteronomistic Historian or from the later redactor or from a pre-Deuteronomistic compiler, though a different one from the compiler of the traditions of the great judges in 3:7–16:31. The anti-Benjaminite tone of the passage might suggest a pre-Deuteronomistic compiler comparatively early in the Monarchy. But this bias against Saul and his people is the hall-mark also of the Deuteronomistic History and later of Chronicles. Indeed, if we may discount the hypothesis of the bias against Saul, the action of his native Gibeah being simply a coincidence, the anti-Benjaminite tone of Jg. 19–21 might simply reflect the resentment of Ephraim at the attempt of her southern neighbour and confederate Benjamin to assert their independence. Late redaction is certainly indicated in the *inclusio* we have noticed in the initiative of Judah in response to the oracle in 1:1–15 and 20:18 and in certain other features which we shall point out; we have already noted that 19–21, like 17–18, stood outside the pre-Deuteronomistic compilation in 3:7–16:31; from the collocation with 17–18, which is not part of the Deuteronomistic History (see above, p. 224), we may fairly regard 19–21 as a redactional insertion in the Deuteronomistic History, like Jos. 24, after Jos. 23, with which the first part of the Deuteronomistic History ends. This of course is not to say that the redactor had not earlier tradition at his disposal.

Eissfeldt ('Der geschichtliche Hintergrund der Erzählung von Gibeas Schandtat', *Festschrift Georg Beer*, 1935, pp. 19–40; *KS* II, 1953, pp. 65–79, esp. 70–9) found the historical nucleus in the assertion by Benjaminite Gibeah and neighbouring towns, so far under the dominance of the power and pretensions of Ephraim, of independence, out of which Benjamin emerged. This is supported by the fact that the parties directly involved were Ephraim, from which the outraged Levite and his host in Gibeah came, and Gibeah and the rest of Benjamin. In view of the independent status of Benjamin in the sacral community in 5:13–18, *c.* 1150 BC, and the depletion and near elimination of the group in 20:44ff., when, according to Schunck (*op. cit.*, pp. 69ff.), Benjamin lost their independence, the event in 19–21 might be dated either before 5:13–18, in which case we must suppose that Benjamin had been rehabilitated, or after 1150 BC, when the growing power of Benjamin encouraged the assertion of independence of their powerful northern neighbour Ephraim. In this case Benjamin would seem to have recovered their status since it was from this group, and indeed from Gibeah, that Saul emerged as the first king in Israel. It might, of course, be argued that Saul of Benjamin was invested with this authority on the initiative of Ephraim as permanent commander of a striking force at the strategic point of resistance to Philistine penetration of the plateau north of Jerusalem, and that in effect he shared power with Samuel of Ephraim, who, according to tradition promoted him (1 Sam. 10:1), so that the reduction of Benjamin to subordination to Ephraim, for which Schunck contends in 19–21, may be dated after *c.* 1150 BC, at the end of the period of the judges.

Thus we may accept the substance of ch. 19 as genuine tradition from that period, though in the extent and diffusion of the circumstantial narrative we would admit free composition at a much later date under the literary influence of the story of the sexual outrage threatened at Sodom in Gen. 19:1–11 (J) and of the incident of Saul's summons of Israel by sending pieces of his dismembered oxen 'all through Israel' (1 Sam. 11:7) from the Deuteronomistic History. Thus it may fairly be assumed that ch. 19 in its present form is an elaboration of an earlier historical tradition by the redactor of the Deuteronomistic History.

Chapter 20 has undergone a similar development. The historical nucleus of the narrative was probably Ephraim's reprisal and the tough Benjaminite resistance, which, indeed, is only explicable if the opposition was only Ephraim rather than **all the Israelites, the whole community** (*'ēdâh*) **from Dan to Beersheba and out of Gilead, as one man** (20:1). As this passage indicates, this is gross exaggeration. The artificiality of the assembly of **the whole community of Israel from Dan to Beersheba** is indicated by the statement that the assembly had to send men **through all the tribe of Benjamin** to convey the assembly's demand for retribution (20:12ff.). The numbers stated to have been involved in the attack on Gibeah are quite preposterous: 400,000 against 26,000 Benjaminites, with the impossible problem of commissariat, to which 20:9f. is sensitive. Here again we notice the hall-mark of the redactor of the Deuteronomistic History in the literary *inclusio* on Judah's initiative in response to the oracle in 20:18; cf. 1:1, the only places in Jg. where Judah is represented as active.

This late date and hand are further indicated by the conception of the involvement of **all Israel** including Judah and Simeon (**from Dan to Beersheba**) and its designation as **the congregation**, or community (*qāhāl* and *'ēdâh*), which is characteristic of P in the Pentateuch. Other peculiarities of language which indicate a late hand are **the country of the inheritance of Israel** (20:6), which has its only parallel in the post-Exilic Isa. 58:14; *zimmâh*, 'lewdness' (*RSV*, **abomination**) (20:6), is peculiar to late sources, e.g. Ezekiel, the Holiness Code (Lev. 17–26) and Job, and is no earlier than Jeremiah (13:27), and **to put away the evil** (*bi'ēr hārā'âh*) (v. 13) is Deuteronomic and so probably from the post-Exilic redactor.

Another indication of the free composition of the redactor is the fact that in reporting the outrage to the assembly the Levite presents it as a personal injury. The redactor has lost sight of the important fact that it was an outrage on the part of the Benjaminites of Gibeah against Ephraim, to which the Levite and his host belonged. In the vain appeal of the assembly to Benjamin to punish the miscreants the redactor has obscured the point of the original tradition that the incident and the refusal of the guilty community to give satisfaction to Ephraim as the injured party were symptomatic of the assertion of Benjaminite independence from Ephraim. Again, just as the outrage on the Levite guest recalls the incident of Lot at Sodom in Gen. 19:1–11, we notice in the final defeat of the Benjaminites by Gibeah (20:30–42) a striking replica of the stratagem in the attack on Ai in Jos. 8:1–22. While this passage may be the elaboration of an earlier tradition of the victory of Ephraim over Benjamin, as Malamat suggests (*Encyclopaedia Judaica Yearbook 1975*, 1977,

p. 176), the redactor's utilisation of the Pentateuchal tradition of the Sodom incident in ch. 19 strongly suggests that 20:30–42 is the redactor's elaboration of the tradition of the attack on Ai from the Deuteronomistic History and its early monarchic source.

In ch. 20 there is clear indication of a composite narrative. First, after the notice of the assembly at Mizpah (vv. 1f.), which included **the people of Israel** to a man, it is stated that **the Benjaminites heard that the people of Israel had gone up to Mizpah** (v. 3). The natural sequel is the muster of 'the Benjaminites' to war with 'the people of Israel' (v. 14). The sequence is broken, however, by a fresh statement of the rally of 'the men of Israel' against Gibeah 'united as one man' (v. 11). This is the outbreak of hostilities, hence the appeal to the Benjaminites and its rejection (vv. 12f.) must have preceded this step, being in place before v. 11 in the tradition to which it belongs. There are two statements of the opening of hostilities at Gibeah (v. 19 and v. 20). The account of the second day's fighting is related in v. 22 actually *before* the lamentation of Israel after the first day's reverse and the consulting of the oracle regarding a second attack (v. 23), and the successful ambush on the third day is detailed in vv. 36*b*–ff. *after* the action has already been described in vv. 29–36 from the setting of the ambush to the final casualties of the Benjaminites. It has been noticed that Israel is spoken of variously in this chapter as 'the children of Israel', *RSV* 'the people of Israel' (*bᵉnê yiśrā'ēl*) (vv. 1, 3, 7, 13, 14, 18, 23, 24, 25, 26, 27, 30 and 35) and 'the men of Israel' (*'iš yiśrā'ēl*) and this has been taken as the criterion of two parallel traditions; and certainly by this standard two accounts of the event can be reconstructed which are free from the outstanding discrepancies.

Thus in vv. 1–7 'the people of Israel' meet and deliberate the case in assembly at Mizpah; they appeal to the Benjaminites for redress, but the Benjaminites are defiant and muster for resistance (vv. 12–16). Here we notice a certain discrepancy in that 'all the tribes of Israel' have already concluded that Benjamin will not yield and they beset Gibeah, ready for action (vv. 8–10). Evidently after the appeal of 'the people of Israel' had been rejected, which is not actually mentioned, they consult the oracle at Bethel, and at the response Judah takes the initiative and they besiege Gibeah. Here it may be noticed that 'the men of Israel', with no mention of the initiative of Judah, beset Gibeah with hostile intent (v. 20). On the clue of the initiative of Judah in response to the oracle (cf. 1:1), this suggests that the passages characterised by 'the people of Judah' are redactional, unless the mention of Judah is a redactional gloss. To continue, evidently after a defeat on the first day, which is mentioned in v. 21, 'the people of Israel' abase themselves at Bethel and enquire of the oracle if they should renew their attack. On the response they attack on the second day, are again defeated and again fast at Bethel and ask the oracle if they should attack for the third time (23–28); they do so, this time taking the precaution to set an ambush; the main force feigns flight (31–32*a*). In what follows 'the men of Israel' decide to feign flight, the men in ambush attack and the Benjaminites were finally defeated (vv. 32*b*–36). In this section for details the redactor evidently used the tradition characterised by 'the people of Israel', which we have taken as later. From this point, however, to the end of the chapter (vv. 36*b*–48) the ambush and final victory of 'the men of Israel' is again described, this time in more detail. It is here that the influence of the tradition of the fall of Ai (Jos. 8:19–21) is evident. The fact that this repeats what had already been recorded more summarily of 'the men of Israel' suggests to us that it is a redactional elaboration in the light of the Ai incident according to the Deuteronomistic History.

In the passage characterised by 'the men of Israel', they decide to attack Gibeah, for which they muster (vv. 8–11), the respective numbers of Israel and Benjamin in v. 17 being probably secondary; they attack the town (v. 20), are defeated and rally for the second attack (v. 21f.), with no mention of retiring to Bethel for fast and oracle. Without specific mention of fast and oracle at Bethel for the second time or, for that matter of a second defeat, 'the men of Israel' decide on the ambush (v. 32*b*), and the final battle and victory is described (vv. 33–36). The battle is elaborated secondarily under the literary influence of the fall of Ai in the Deuteronomistic History (vv. 36*b*–43). The statement in v. 35 that 'the men of Israel destroyed 25,100 men of Benjamin that day' (i.e. at their final victory) is elaborated in the account of the casualties in the main battle (v. 44), in the pursuit in two stages (v. 44) to the total round number of 25,000 (cf. 25,100 in v. 35). The passage closes with the notice of six hundred Benjaminites who found refuge to the east at the Rock of Rimmon for four months (v. 47) and of further slaughter and devastation throughout Benjamin by 'the men of Israel' (v. 48).

It has been suggested that duplicate sources in chs 20 and 21 are indicated by the two places, sanctuaries, Mizpah and Bethel. According to 20:1, 'the people of Israel' assembled 'before the Lord' to hear the Levite's complaint and to decide what steps to take for redress. At Bethel they sought an oracle on further steps against Benjamin (vv. 18, 23, 24) and fasted after defeat (vv. 23, 26). The significance of Bethel as a sanctuary is in no doubt. In view of its association with Ephraim in one tradition of the occupation of Palestine (1:22–26), it was probably the chief Ephraimite sanctuary before Shiloh and the boundary sanctuary between Ephraim and

Benjamin (see above, pp. 15f.), so that the note in 20:27f., though probably redactional, is true to fact, the ark being specifically associated with Ephraim. In 20:27f. 'the ark of the covenant' reflects the redactor of the Deuteronomistic circle, who, in view of the ill repute of Bethel in the northern Kingdom and under Assyria, is not likely to have gratuitously noted the sanctity of the place unless it was a well-established tradition in his source-material. Mizpah, if identical with the Mizpah of 1 Sam. 7:5–12; 10:17ff., was a sanctuary, which we now consider to have been located at Tell an-Naṣbeh, *c.* four miles north-north-west of Gibeah (Tell al-Fûl) and the same distance south-south-west of Bethel (Beitīn). Such close proximity of two sanctuaries might indicate two different sources, as Noth suggested. This, however, in our opinion, does not follow. Bethel, though a boundary-sanctuary near the border with Benjamin, was specifically associated with Ephraim (1:22–26), while Mizpah, though also a boundary-sanctuary in Ephraim, as the description of the boundary of Benjamin in Jos. 18:13–20 indicates in contrast to the later, anachronistic town-list in Jos. 18:21–26, esp. v. 26, had a more local, and perhaps minor, significance. For this reason, while matters were still open to negotiation, the injured party may have stated his case there, while the community, or, in the original, Ephraim, resorted to the Ephraimite sanctuary of Bethel for oracular direction after conciliation had failed and when war had broken out. Thus, while two main variant traditions are represented in ch. 20, or rather two stages of the post-Deuteronomistic redaction of an ancient tradition from the time of the judges, it is most unlikely that there are two ancient traditions, one from the sanctuary of Mizpah and the other from that of Bethel, as we suggested in our earlier edition. In ch. 21 there is the same association with sanctuaries at Mizpah (vv. 1, 5, 8) and Bethel (v. 2) as in ch. 20. But after the reduction of Benjamin it is very unlikely that the sacral confederacy or, as we think, Ephraim, should meet and take an oath at a minor sanctuary. Thus we agree with Schunck (after A. Jepsen, *Die Quellen des Königsbuches*, 2nd ed., 1956, p. 99) that Mizpah in Jg. 20 and 21 is adventitious, stemming from a post-Exilic redactor whose home was at Mizpah (Tell an-Naṣbeh); cf. 2 Kg. 22:23.

Chapter 21 deals with the rehabilitation of Benjamin. This begins with an awkward association of Mizpah and Bethel. At the former, the community of Israel takes an oath not to permit intermarriage with Benjamin (v. 1) and continues with their fast and remorse at Bethel (v. 2). This is the redactor's introduction to provision for the restoration of Benjamin within the restrictions of the oath by the extraordinary expedient of the massacre of Jabesh-gilead (vv. 8–15) and the rape of the girls at the vintage festival at Shiloh (vv.

16–23). We are prepared to admit with Eissfeldt (*op. cit.*, p. 78) the historicity of the refusal, at least by Ephraim, of intermarriage with the refractory Benjamin, perhaps rather as a temporary sanction. But this has been enormously elaborated in the highly artificial story of the extermination of the inhabitants of Jabesh-gilead, from which the required brides were excepted, on the grounds that they had not been present at the general assembly of Israel when the oath was taken. The involvement of all Israel is the redactor's fancy, as is the absence of only one community of 'all Israel' from the assembly, to say nothing of the solution of the problem of the extinction of one tribe from Israel by such crudity. Jabesh-gilead is singled out in the redactor's story owing to the community's evident affinity with Benjamin which is reflected in 1 Sam. 31:11–13. If there is any historical kernel in the redactor's elaboration, this may be some incident in the eastward expansion of Ephraim's confederate Manasseh which had made women of Jabesh-gilead available for a depleted community among Ephraim's associates, possibly Benjamin, during Ephraim's ban on intermarriage. Here again, however, as in the striking parallels in 19:22ff. compared with Gen. 19:1–11, and in 20:36*b*ff. compared with Jos. 8:19–21, the redactor may have combined the known tradition of the affinity of Jabesh-gilead with Benjamin with the literary motif of the massacre of Baal-peor, from which nubile girls were excepted (Num. 31:16–18, P), the phraseology of which strikingly recalls 21:11f.

That the events in ch. 21 really concerned only Ephraim and their southern neighbours and associates, Benjamin, is indicated by the parallel or supplementary tradition of the provision of wives for the survivors of Benjamin from the girls who danced at the annual vintage festival at Shiloh, which was at that time a local Ephraimite sanctuary. This may be the historification of a rite of the vintage festival, the last and most significant festival in the peasant's year, which was both harvest and new year festival, as in Israel before the great autumn festival of the Ingathering in the middle of the month of Tishri was staggered in post-Exilic times into the New Year on the first day of Tishri, the Day of Atonement on the tenth, and the Feast of Tabernacles, the harvest festival proper, from the fifteenth to the twenty-second. Here we may notice the practice in late Judaism of the acquisition of brides from girls dancing in vineyards on the Day of Atonement (*Mishnah Taanith* 4.8). The association of such a practice with the most solemn Day of Atonement surely indicates the survival of a rite in the earlier autumn festival, probably going back to the Canaanite fertility cult. If, as seems likely, the incident of Gibeah is to be dated from a time when Bethel was the chief sanctuary of Ephraim and Shiloh not yet the sanctuary housing the ark, the point of the incident of the rape of the girls of Shiloh may be that Shiloh was still associated with local Canaanite agrarian rites which Israelites and Canaanites shared, so that wives could be secured for Benjamin from Canaanite *metoikoi* by connivance of Ephraim without breach of the oath. But here the motif of the incident of the girls of Beth-peor (Num. 31:16–18), which we have noticed in 21:10–12 may indicate the literary influence of the association of Israelites with local girls in the fertility rites at Beth-peor (Num. 25:1f., J) in the redactor's version.

Whatever historical conditions may be reflected in the incidents of Jabesh-gilead and Shiloh, the hand of the post-Exilic redactor is plainly visible in the conception of the involvement of all Israel as a unity in which any breach was intolerable (vv. 3, 6, 15). So also in reference to 'the congregation' (*hā'ēdâh* in vv. 10, 13, 16; *qāhāl* in v. 5), in the schematised and grossly exaggerated number of twelve thousand men against Jabesh-gilead (v. 10) and in the learned antiquarian's location of Shiloh 'in the land of Canaan', that is, west of the Jordan (v. 12). This is, prematurely in the period of the Judges, depicted as the central sanctuary of 'the congregation' of all Israel. To the same hand also belongs the reference to 'north of Bethel, on the east of the highway that goes up from Bethel to Shechem, and south of Lebonah' (v. 19).

COMMENTARY
on
Judges

INTRODUCTION TO THE MAIN THEME

1:1–3:6

REDACTIONAL RECAPITULATION OF THE SETTLEMENT

1:1–2:5

On components, content and sequence of thought, see above, pp. 188f.

A CONSPECTUS OF THE OCCUPATION AND ITS LIMITATIONS

1:1–36

This gives fuller details of the occupation of the south by Simeon and Judah (vv. 1–7), vv. 5–7 being possibly an earlier independent tradition of Simeon in the central highlands (see on v. 4) confused with some incident in Judah's clash with Jerusalem, the occupation of Hebron (v. 10), Othniel's occupation of Kiriath-sepher/Debir (vv. 11–15), the penetration of the south-east by Judah and Simeon (17, var. the Kenites, v. 16) and the occupation of Bethel by 'the house of Joseph' (vv. 22–26). The limitations of the settlements of Benjamin (v. 21), Manasseh (v. 27), Ephraim (v. 29), Zebulun (v. 30), Asher (vv. 31f.), Naphtali (v. 33) and Dan (v. 34) are noted, agreeing in the case of Manasseh and Ephraim with statements in Jos. 17:11–13 and 16:10, while vv. 21 and 31 agree respectively with Jos. 15:63 (with 'Judah' for 'Benjamin') and Jos. 19:24–31, where Acco is omitted. The tradition of the occupation of Hebron and Kiriath-sepher/Debir (vv. 10–15) is here obviously secondarily related to Judah, being actually a Kenizzite operation (so Jos. 15:13–19; cf. Jos. 14:13–15). Here Jg. 1:11–15 agrees practically verbatim with Jos. 15:15–19. The other matter, however, is not found in Jos. Here are independent local historical traditions of considerable value, which were not integrated with the Deuteronomistic History in Jos. and Jg. in its first draft, but, emphasising the incomplete and piecemeal nature of the occupation, suggested to the post-Exilic redactor a suitable introduction to the story of Israel's vicissitudes in Jg.

The Occupation of the South, subsumed under the advance of Judah and Simeon **1:1–9**

1. **After the death of Joshua:** not recorded until 2:8 in the

Deuteronomistic introduction proper. The admission of the struggle to effect settlement and the vicissitudes of the tribes, the subject of Jg., demand such an apologetic note from the redactor to conserve the Deuteronomist's representation of Joshua and his generation as entirely successful in Jos. and Jg. 2:6f.

inquired of the LORD: consulted the oracle; cf. 20:18, also redactional, on the same question of initiative in battle and with the same response regarding Judah, a significant *inclusio*. The sanctuary envisaged is either Gilgal, after Jos. 2–11, or Shiloh, after Jos. 18ff.; probably the former, after Jos. 14:6. The oracle is envisaged as given by the sacred lots, the Urim and Thummin, as in the case of Achan (Jos. 7:14).

go up: may refer to the contour of the land, Gilgal being *c*. 600 feet below sea-level; but the term is also a technical one for going to battle (see on Jos. 22:12).

Canaanites: here the inhabitants of Palestine generally, as in post-Exilic usage; see on Jos. 22:11. On the particular significance and development of the term, see on Jos. 3:10.

2. **Judah shall go up** (*sc.* first) . . . **behold I have given the land into his hand:** oracular response with divine assurance in the declaratory, or prophetic, perfect. On the response of Judah to the oracle as to who should take the initiative as an indication of redaction here and in 20:18, see on v. 1. The subsuming of the activities of Simeon in the Negeb (v. 3) and the Kenizzites (vv. 10, 11–15; cf. Jos. 14:13–15; 15:13–19) and the Kenites (v. 16) under the occupation by Judah, reflects Solomon's administrative division familiar to the redactor through its reflection in the territorial apportionment to Judah in the Deuteronomistic History in Jos. 15.

3. **Simeon:** located in historical times in the far south with its local sanctuary probably at Beersheba, its status relative to Judah, as here, being indicated by the enumeration of its settlements, detailed in Jos. 19:1–9, as the settlements of Judah in the Negeb in Jos. 15:21–32.

the territory allotted to me: lit. 'my lot', envisaging the apportionment by lot in Jos. 14:2ff.

4. **Perizzites:** generally listed among the seven peoples of pre-Israelite Palestine, but whether as a genuine ethnic term or an appellative, 'dwellers in open settlements', is uncertain (see on Jos. 3:10).

Bezek: the only **Bezek** known in the Old Testament, apart from this passage, is where Saul mustered his force before marching to the relief of Jabesh-gilead (1 Sam. 11:8), probably by way of Shechem and the Wadi Far'a. Thus it may be located at Khirbet Ibzîq, on the hill-road between Nablus and Beisān (so Eusebius,

Onomasticon). This seems not to accord with the southern location of Simeon, the associate of Judah, and other incidents described in 1:1–21. But Hertzberg (*JPOS* 6, 1926, pp. 213–21) rightly emphasises the earlier aggressive activity of Simeon in the vicinity of Shechem before their expulsion to the far south (Gen. 34; 49:5–7), so that the incident of Adoni-bezek of Bezek may be a peculiarly Simeonite tradition from this period, which survived their migration to the south and is here erroneously associated with Judah. The mention of Jerusalem (v. 7) may not be original, but suggested to the redactor either by confusion of names and traditions of Adoni-bezek of Bezek and Adoni-zedek of Jerusalem, who headed the Amorite alliance against Israel at the battle of Gibeon (Jos. 10:1ff.), though to be sure he was hanged, according to Jos. 10:23–27, by the Cave of Makkedah, or by the assumption that if Judah and Simeon went to Hebron and the south (v. 10) from Gilgal, Jerusalem might be a natural obstacle. This secondary and unhistorical mention of Jerusalem and the fate of its assumed king suggests the note on the destruction of the city in v. 8 (on which see), which as it stands is a direct contradiction of v. 21 and Jos. 15:63.

6. cut off his thumbs: a practical disablement for military service, once recorded of prisoners taken by the Athenians at Aegina.

and his great toes: so Hannibal once treated prisoners of war. A further significance of this mutilation may perhaps be inferred from the fact that the right thumb, big toe and tip of the right ear were the points at which Aaron and his sons were said to be touched with the blood of consecration (Exod. 29:20f., P). In view of the sacral function of the king in Canaan, now attested in the royal legends from Rās Shamra, this peculiar mutilation may have been designed also to invalidate the consecration of the king, if there is any historical basis of the story recorded by the post-Exilic redactor.

7. seventy: this is an excellent example of the use of this number as the indefinite large number in saga; cf. the seventy sons of Jerubba'al slain by Abimelech (9:5) and the seventy sons of Ahab slain by command of Jehu (2 Kg. 10:7), where the number indicates totality.

Jerusalem: see above, on Jos. 10:1.

8. set the city on fire: lit. 'let the city go in fire', or perhaps, if the Hebrew verb *šālaḥ* is cognate with Arabic *salaḫa*, 'to strip, skin' (Moore, *op. cit.*, ad loc.), 'stripped the city with fire'. This is possibly the reflection of an old tradition of Judah of some incident in the occupation of the land of Jerusalem as apart from the actual fortified city on the south-east hill, implied in the description of the territory of Judah in Jos. 15:7–9, which included all the cultivable land of Jerusalem (so Hertzberg, *op. cit.*, p. 150). Conceivably, if historical, it may refer to the devastation of unfortified settlements on the south-west hill, which was not fortified until the time of Hezekiah (N. Avigad, 'Excavations in the Jewish Quarter of the Old City, 1969–71', *Jerusalem Revealed*, ed. Y. Yadin, 1975, pp. 41f.).

9. in the hill country, in the Negeb, and in the Lowland: the hills of Judah, which rise to just over 3,000 feet north of Hebron, the semi-arid steppe in the south, and the Judaean foothills in the south-west (see on Jos. 10:40).

The Kenizzite occupation of Hebron and Debir/Kiriath-sepher **1:10–15**

Parallel to Jos. 15:13–19, with certain trifling textual differences, which are greater in v. 10, which attributes the taking of Hebron to Judah; cf. Jos. 14:6ff., where it is taken by Caleb. The redactor in Jg. 1 subsumes the Kenizzite occupation of this region under that of Judah (see on v. 2; and for details, see on Jos. 15:13–19 and introduction to Jos. 14).

The Kenite Occupation of the south-east **1:16–17**

Subsumed under the occupation by Judah and Simeon.

16. the descendants of the Kenite, Moses' father-in-law: the name of a Kenite clan may have dropped out, hence LXX (Vaticanus, Sinaiticus) reads the name 'Jethro', the father-in-law (*ḥôtēn*) of Moses. In 4:11 Hobab is named as Moses' *ḥôtēn*, which elsewhere in the Old Testament means 'father-in-law', though the Arabic cognate denotes both 'father-in-law' and 'brother-in-law', and indeed any of a man's relations through his wife. Another difficulty is the lack of the definite article with **Kenite**, which would indicate in Hebrew idiom the eponymous ancestor, and not a contemporary individual. We might suppose that 'the father-in-law of Moses' was a gloss, but in this case we should have to account for the fact that the verbs in the sequel are singular. The simplest solution is to follow LXX and read the definite article with **Kenite**. The Kenites were an itinerant smith caste, as the name implies, whose eponymous ancestor was in Hebrew tradition Cain (Num. 24:22), whose itinerant habits and immunity among the peoples are the subject of a well-known aetiological tradition in Gen. 4:9–15. Their occupation of the wilderness of Judah, which lies in the Negeb near Arad (Tell 'Arad, *c*. seventeen miles south-south-east of Hebron), suggests an advance from the Arabah, where they had been involved in the mining and working of copper, which is attested east and west of the depression since the middle of the third millennium BC. They had been associated with the Hebrews since the time of Moses, Exod. 18:12, probably reflecting a covenant between the two groups at Kadesh. Apart from elements of the Kenite faith, which the Hebrews possibly adopted and developed, and their knowledge of the desert (Num. 10:29–31), their understanding of metallurgy was of great importance for a group about to fight for a new home in the settled land.

the city of palms: denotes Jericho in Dt. 34:3, Jg. 3:13 and in 2 Chr. 28:15, and here also for the redactor in agreement with the advance, according to the oracle from the sanctuary, probably of Gilgal (see on v. 1). But here the redactor may have misunderstood a specifically Kenite tradition of an advance by way of another place Tamar ('Palm'), that 'Tamar (MT *Kᵉre*, Tadmor) in the wilderness', i.e. of Judah (1 Kg. 9:18; Ezek. 47:19; 48:28), Thamara, located by Eusebius one day's journey from Mampsis (modern Kurnub) on the way from Elath on the Gulf of Akaba to Hebron. This is probably the same tradition as in Num. 21:1–3 (J), where the opposition of the king of Arad is broken and his cities put to the ban, one being called Hormah (see on v. 17). Also contributing to the confusion was the association of the penetration from the neighbourhood of Jericho through the Buqei'a towards Bethlehem and Hebron by elements of Judah associated with Achan in the occupation-tradition of Gilgal by Jericho (Jos. 7:16–26).

the wilderness of Judah, which lies in the Negeb near Arad: LXX (Vaticanus) reads: 'the desert which was in the south of Judah, which was by the descent of Arad'. This is obviously a conflation of two variants. MT is viable, **Negeb** usually being further defined, here by **Arad**. The site of **Arad** is now identified through the excavations of Aharoni and others at Tell 'Arad, *c.* twenty miles east-north-east of Beersheba, thanks to ostraca of the eighth century BC which name the place (Aharoni, *IEJ* 16, 1966, pp. 1–7). Derelict between the Early Bronze Age and the nineteenth century, its sanctity is attested by a small temple to Yahweh from the tenth century BC, which may perpetuate the tradition of a primitive sacred area (Arabic *ḥaram*) dedicated to Yahweh during a pre-Israelite Kenite occupation, as B. Mazar has proposed (*JNES* 24, 1965, pp. 298–303).

17. **Hormah:** identified with Arad in Num. 21:1–3, where the name is explained by the ban (Hebrew *ḥerem*) laid on the place after the victory of Israel. This popular etymology of Hormah is contradicted by the mention of Hormah in the Negeb in Egyptian texts from the nineteenth century BC. If Num. 21:1–3 and Jg. 1:17 reflect the same tradition, as may be, **Zephath** may be identical with Arad, and indeed the construct form Zephath suggests that it was a common noun 'watch-tower' of some place unnamed, a variant in

fact of Mizpah. **Hormah** is mentioned again in connection with a defeat of Israel, in their attack from the south (Num. 14:45). But, as in Arabic, Hormah may denote a cult-place (so. A. von Gall, *Altisraëlitische Kultstätten*, BZAW 3, 1898, p. 37). If the tradition of the victory at Arad-Zephath-Hormah, after the attack from the south, is genuine, it may refer to the Calebite (Kenizzite) occupation of the south as far as Hebron independently, or with Judah and Simeon and the Kenites (so C. Steuernagel, *Die Einwanderung der Israëliten in Kanaan*, 1901, pp. 70ff.; and W. Nowack, *Richter*, Handkommentar zum AT, 1902, p. 7); but cf. Möhlenbrink, 'Josua im Pentateuch' (*ZAW* N.F. 18, 1942, pp. 45f.), who regards the penetration by Caleb from the south as independent, the association with Judah being effected in the Monarchy. The association of Jg. 1:17 with Num. 21:1–3 is indicated by the advance on Arad 'by way of Atharim' (Num. 21:1), which is possibly a corruption of *t^e^mārîm* ('palms').

utterly destroyed: laid under the ban (*ḥerem*), involving total destruction as an act of dedication or renunciation in the holy war (see on Jos. 6:17).

SUMMARY OF THE OCCUPATION BY THE TRIBES

1:18–36

Judah 1:18–20

18. Gaza . . . Ashkelon . . . Ekron: three of the great commands of the Philistine in the coastal plain. If the text is sound, this would indicate an anachronistic note reflecting the incorporation of that region in the realm of Josiah (*c.* 621–610 BC), which is recently attested by a Hebrew ostracon from the seaward settlement of Ashdod (J. Naveh, 'A Hebrew Letter from the Seventh Century BC', *EIJ* 10, 1960, pp. 129–39); so also Jos. 15:45–47. But the reading of LXX and V should be noted: 'Judah did not take Gaza . . . Askalon . . . Ekron', which would accord with vv. 19*b*, 21, 27, 29–35.

19. chariots of iron: see on Jos. 17:16.

20. Displaced from before v. 11, where 'Caleb' occurs for 'Judah' at v. 10.

Benjamin 1:21

Note the close association with Judah in the text, indicating the association of the two since David. Conditions in the late monarchy are reflected even more faithfully in Jos. 15:63, where the settlement of Judah in Jerusalem is described in the same words except for 'Judah' instead of 'Benjamin'.

'The house of Joseph' 1:22–26

22. Bethel: on the tradition, see above, p. 85. On the view that **the house of Joseph** in the redactor's terminology refers actually to those of the Rachel group who emerged as Ephraim, see above, p. 10. It may be noticed that the fall of Bethel is not mentioned in Jos. except in the redactional 12:16.

23. Luz: perhaps cognate with Arabic *lūz* ('almond'), is given as the former name of **Bethel** (Gen. 28:19); but in Jos. 16:2 the two names denote separate places. These are probably Burj Beitīn, *c.* two miles south-south-east of Beitīn, which may have been the sanctuary (*bēt 'ēl*) of the place Bethel (modern Beitīn), which was formerly called Luz.

24. deal kindly with: better 'deal loyally with', a conception native to the covenant relationship (see on Jos. 2:12).

26. the land of the Hittites: probably north Syria, the inland parts of which, as far as Kadesh on the Orontes, had been vassal states of the Hittites in the Late Bronze Age, whose empire was based on Anatolia. Diplomatic texts from the palace at Rās Shamra document this relationship from the middle of the fourteenth century BC to the beginning of the twelfth century, and attest that Carchemish was ruled by a Hittite viceroy of the royal family. On the collapse of the Hittite empire, those states asserted their independence, absorbing Aramaean tribal invaders from the Syrian steppe, but providing the ruling class. Hence in Assyrian records this is termed 'the Hittite land', a term which was extended by the Assyrians to denote Palestine as well as Syria. In view of this wide application of the term, the statement in v. 26 is uncertain, nor may a northern Luz be identified.

The Limitations of the Occupation West of the Jordan 1:27–36

27. Manasseh: cf. Jos. 17:11–13. See ad loc., with notes on locations.

The fact that there is no mention of Egypt in Jos. or Jg. does not mean that there was no vestige of Egyptian power in Palestine, as is indicated by inscriptions of Ramses III (1184–1153 BC) and a statue-base of Ramses VI (*c.* 1140 BC) at Megiddo. The explanation is rather that the presence of Egypt was limited to strategic cities on the trunk highways, such as those cities in vv. 27–34, where the Israelites made no impression, as proposed by de Vaux (*op. cit.*, I, 1971, p. 462). **Beth-shean**, **Taanach**, **Megiddo** and **Ible-am** were significantly the fortress towns commanding the passes to the Great Central Plain, and **Dor** the west end of the most northerly pass. Possibly the five towns constituted a league, like the five Amorite towns in Jos. 10, or Hazor and her four allies in Jos. 11:1–11.

28. forced labour: Hebrew *mas*, 'labour-conscription', a characteristic Canaanite institution, now admirably illustrated in administrative texts from the palace at Rās Shamra (see on Jos. 16:10). It is highly questionable if the new settlers had any occasion for forced labour or the means of organising it. It was a feature of the administration of Solomon and possibly of David *vis-à-vis* their Canaanite subjects and so is probably an anachronism of the redactor in Jg.

29. Ephraim: cf. Jos. 16:4–10, with note on the name Ephraim in Jos. 20:7.

30. Zebulun: cf. Jos. 19:10–16, where, however, **Nahalol** (var. Nahalal) is noted as a settlement in Zebulun and one of the Levitical cities (Jos. 21:35), and **Kitron** is not mentioned at all.

31f. Asher: cf. Jos. 19:24–31, where no such exceptions are made. On the name Asher, with the apparent omission of Acco, see on Jos. 19:24–31 and 19:29. **Acco**, **Sidon** and **Achzib** are on the coast, of vital importance for **the Canaanites** (Phoenicians), who could provision them by sea, and **Rehob** and **Aphik** guarded the east of the Plain of Acco, confining the settlement of the Israelites to the hills of Galilee. Again, a local league may be implied as in v. 27.

33. Naphtali: cf. Jos. 19:32–39, where no exceptions are made (see notes, ad loc.).

34f. Dan: Yadin has proposed (*The Australian Journal of Biblical Archaeology* 1, 1968, pp. 9–23) that **Dan** was the Danuna, one of the 'Sea Peoples' associated with the Zakkala about Dor and the Pulusatu south of Jaffa, who had thrown in their lot with the sacral community of Israel. See further, on Jg. 5:17. On the district of Dan in the foothills of Judah, see Jos. 19:40–48, where **Aijalon** and **Sha-albim** (see note, ad loc.) are given as Danite settlements, in an artificial reconstruction from Solomon's fiscal organisation. The passage in Jg. does not mention the northern migration and occupation of Laish in ch. 18, and it is feasibly proposed that v. 34 is actually the introduction to ch. 18 (so Täubler, *op. cit.*, pp. 70f.). The specification of **Aijalon**, **Sha-albim** and **Har-heres** indicates that the low ground that Dan failed to occupy was the Wādī 'ṣ-Ṣurār, where it crosses the depression of the Shephelah and its northern extension. **Har-heres** ('the Mountain of the Sun') may be either Beth-shemesh or the hills about Timnath-heres, the home of Joshua (see on Jos. 19:50; cf. 24:30; Jg. 2:9).

In view of the tradition of the conflict between the Danite Samson and the Philistines in the Wādī 'ṣ-Ṣurār, we should expect those rather than **the Amorites** to be the oppressors of Dan. The explanation of the role of the Amorites, specifically of **Har-heres, Aijalon** and **Sha-albim** may be that, hindered by the Philistines in the Wādī 'ṣ-Ṣurār, the Danites sought a settlement in the northern extension of the Shephelah, where they were hindered by the Amorites, as Täubler proposed (*op. cit.*, pp. 70ff.).

36. the border of the Amorites: read 'Edomites', with LXX (cf. Jos. 15:1ff.). The border from **the ascent of Akrabbim** ('Scorpion Pass') from the Arabah to the steppe south-east of Beersheba certainly supports this reading (see on Jos. 15:3).
Sela: ('the Rock'). Not the capital of Edom, often so called, but a strategic point south-south-west of the Dead Sea, on the way to the Arabah with its copper-beds (2 Kg. 14:7).

THE INCIDENT AT BOCHIM (LXX, *Bethel*)

2:1–5

Formally this is a self-contained aetiological narrative giving the popular explanation of the place-name **Bochim** ('Weepers'), possibly Allon-bacuth 'the Oak of Weeping') near Bethel (Gen. 35:8), but otherwise unknown. It may be a feature by the sanctuary of Bethel connected with ritual mourning. This may have been concerned with mourning rites for the dead vegetation deity Baal-Hadad; cf. Zech. 12:11; Ezek. 8:14 (Tammuz); cf. the weeping of the goddess Anat for the dead Baal in the fertility myth from Rās Shamra (Gordon, *Ugaritic Textbook* 67, VI, 25–31; J. Gray, *The Legacy of Canaan*, 2nd ed., 1965, pp. 62ff.), or some other fast-rite. However that may be, the redactor has utilised the aetiological legend to supplement the introduction proper to Jg. in the Deuteronomistic History (2:6–19), relating the weeping to the dismay of Israel at the divine rebuke for their infidelity to the covenant and the consequences in the vicissitudes which is the theme of Jg. The aetiological legend concerning the place-name, however, seems to be fused with one authenticating a cult-place, suggested by the statement that the angel of the Lord went up from Gilgal to Bochim, if we understand the ark as the symbol of the presence of God, his 'angel', as in Exod. 32:34; 33:14 (E). If there is any reflection of actual history in the transference of the ark to Bethel from Gilgal, this may refer to the decisive occupation of the interior by Ephraim; or it may have been occasioned by the Moabite menace about Jericho and Gilgal before the resistance of Benjamin and Ephraim inaugurated by Ehud (3:12ff.). But such a historical nucleus, if any, has been obscured by the aetiology of Bochim, by the redactor's aplication of the convention of the fast-liturgy to provide a theological supplementation of the Deuteronomistic introduction and by his assumption that the incident was a pan-Israelite occasion. An important sanctuary of Ephraim and their boundary-sanctuary with Benjamin, the assumption that Bethel had from this early period a pan-Israelite significance may have arisen in view of the emergence of those elements to hegemony with Samuel and Saul, though in the traditions of neither is Bethel mentioned.

1. **the angel** (Hebrew *mal'āk*, 'emissary') **of the LORD:** usually the extension of the divine personality in a human agent, e.g. a prophet, or of his presence symbolised by the ark. The theophany here indicated was the regular means of the authentication of a cult-site; cf. the theophany to Jacob at Bethel, also through the medium of angels, in Gen. 28:11ff. Behind the present passage there may be the tradition of the occupation of the settlement and sanctuary of Bethel by 'the House of Joseph' (cf. 1:22–26). *RSV* disguises the fact that MT 'and I brought you up' indicates a lacuna.
Gilgal: on location and significance as a sanctuary, see above, on Jos. 1:12–18.

2. The dangers of assimilation to the amoral nature-cult of the Canaanites and covenant-fellowship with them, implying recognition of their gods, is a recurring theme in the Deuteronomistic History. But here the redactor was re-echoing also the language and thought of an earlier period, which characterised the Ritual Code in Exod. 34:10–26 (J), with its insistence on the celebration of the three main festivals of the peasant's year at the sanctuary of Yahweh ('before the Lord'), with the artificial relation of these to Israel's experience of the grace and power of Yahweh in the great deliverance from Egypt as a deliberate antidote to Canaanite influence where it was strongest.

3. **adversaries:** (Hebrew *ṣārîm*), so *RSV*, after LXX, for MT *ṣiddîm*; cf. *AV* '(thorns in) your sides' (*ṣiddîm*). 'But shall be a snare to you' in the sequel supports the view that *ṣiddîm* is a cognate of Assyrian *ṣaddu* ('trap'), as assumed in *NEB*, 'will decoy you'. The same language and context in the covenant-sacrament is reflected in Jos. 23:3 and in the Ritual Code (Exod. 34:12).

DEUTERONOMISTIC INTRODUCTION TO JUDGES

2:6–19

See Introduction, p. 188.

6. When Joshua dismissed the people: the abrupt statement in the present context, connecting directly with Jos. 23:16 in the Deuteronomistic History and 24:28 in the redaction, indicates that Jg. 1:1–2:5 is redactional. Here **the people** (Hebrew *hā'ām*) means the sacral assembly.

7. the elders who outlived Joshua: lit. 'who prolonged days . . .', a common Deuteronomic expression (cf. Dt. 4:40; 5:33 etc.). **who had seen:** cf. the parallel passage in Jos. 24:31, 'had known', i.e. 'had personal experience of', as in 'know the Lord' in v. 10.

9. within the bounds: possible, but the Hebrew *g^ebûl* may mean also 'territory' allotted to Joshua in Jos. 19:45–50. There it is 'Timnath-serah' (Khirbet Tibneh), an orthodox adaptation of **Timnath-heres** ('Portion of the Sun'), where a solar cult is implied (see on Jos. 19:51 and 24:29, 30).

11ff. The assimilation of the Israelites to the life and worship of Canaan was more than a chauvinistic and general objection of the Deuteronomist and the redactor. It was a natural consequence of the settlement of nomads to the sedentary life of Palestine with its new social involvements and its agricultural techniques and rituals. In the seasonal migrations of nomads to the customary grazing-grounds in the settled land, social ties are made and intermarriage may take place, with agreements and oaths at local sanctuaries. Older groups of the later Israel, settled in the land since patriarchal times, and other under-privileged inhabitants who became Israelites, would be to a great extent thus assimilated. So the Israelites may have assimilated the Canaanite version of common Oriental law exemplified in the casuistic laws in the Book of the Covenant (Exod. 20:22–23:33). Prophylactic and homoeopathic rites at seasonal crises were also of vital importance in local agriculture, together with the myths which accompanied them, and the extent to which Israel assimilated those is evidenced by the ideology and imagery of the kingship of God in the psalms relevant to the autumn festival in the Old Testament, which reflect the theme of the struggle against the powers of chaos and the establishment of order, as in the Baal-myth from Rās Shamra (J. Gray, 'The Kingship of God in the Prophets and Psalms', *VT* 11, 1961, pp. 1–29; *The Biblical Doctrine of the Reign of God*, 1979, pp. 15–116). The extent and menace of the Canaanite fertility-cult is reflected in the insistence in the Ritual Code that the three chief agricultural festivals should be kept by

Israel at the sanctuary of Yahweh, even though that should involve pilgrimage. The significance of those in the fertility cult was further counteracted by association with phases in Israel's drama of salvation.

11. the Baals: local manifestations of the fertility-god, primarily manifest in the thunder, lightning and rain of late autumn and winter, and secondarily in the dying-and-rising god identified with the vegetation he stimulated. His proper name was Hadad, Baal being his title, as is known from the myth from Rās Shamra relating the perpetual struggle of the god for kingship, which guarantees order in nature against the perpetual menace of chaos, identified with the turbulent waters, and against drought and sterility.

12. The amoral nature-cult of Canaan is here set in sharp contrast to the historical faith of Israel (see on vv. 11, 13ff.).

13. The Ashtaroth: local manifestations of the fertility-goddess Astarte, known from the Rās Shamra texts and from late Phoenician inscriptions. In extant Rās Shamra texts she is not so prominent as the goddess Anat, the sister of Baal and the goddess of love and war, but the two were closely associated, and, while Astarte is less prominent than Anat in the Rās Shamra texts, the situation is reversed in the Old Testament.

14. could no longer withstand their enemies: apart from the possibly enervating influence of the Canaanite nature-cult, the alleged excesses of which, incidentally, are not attested in the Rās Shamra texts, the assimilation to the Canaanites and their cult was a disintegrating force in Israel, if substituted for the cult at the sanctuaries of Yahweh which preserved the solidarity of Israel in the sacramental experience of the drama of salvation and the social discipline of the covenant and its obligations.

15. marched out: so *RSV*, rightly, for 'went out', a technical term (cf. Dt. 28:7; 2 Sam. 11:1; Jg. 11:3, etc.).

as the LORD had sworn: the reference is to the admonitory address which followed the final adjurations in the covenant ceremony, exemplified in the twelve adjurations of Dt. 27:15–26, with the following elaboration in Dt. 28.

16. judges: see Introduction, pp. 189f.

16–19. Verses 16 and 18f. state that after the striking deliverance by each 'judge', Israel remained faithful till after his death. Hence v. 17, in asserting apostasy even in the lifetime of the judges, is probably redactional, prompted perhaps as an afterthought by the recollection of Gideon's ephod, which was regarded as idolatrous (8:27).

17. played the harlot: possibly putting themselves beyond the pale of the society of the sacral community, like the harlot (lit.

'strange woman') in Prov. 2:16; 5:3, 20 etc., or reflecting ritual prostitution as a rite of imitative magic in the Canaanite fertility cult.

18. was moved to pity: 'relented'; the reflexive of the same verb is used in the active (Intensive with Causative sense) in Isa. 40:1 ('Comfort . . . my people').

REDACTIONAL ELABORATION OF DEUTERONOMISTIC INTRODUCTION

2:20–3:6

20. my covenant: note the emphasis on the conditional grace of God expressed in the context of the covenant in 2:1–5 and Jos. 23–24, the major theme of the Deuteronomist, developed from the liturgy of the sacrament of the covenant (cf. Dt. 27ff.). The possessive pronoun puts the covenant formally into the category of a vassal-treaty, known from Hittite prototypes (see above, pp. 53f.), where the suzerain gives his treaty with its security and conditions as a favour.

22. that by them I may test Israel: here the redactor expresses Israel's consciousness of the paradox between faith in the triumphant climax to the drama of salvation in the occupation of the Promised Land, Israel's historical credo (cf. Dt. 26:5ff.), and the realistic fact of her political limitations, and offers one solution in suggesting that the opposition was maintained as a challenge to Israel's faith. Other explanations, which reflect the same theological embarrassment, are that the land would otherwise have been overrun by wild beasts (Exod. 23:29ff., E; Dt. 7:22) and that the Canaanites were left so that the Israelites might be trained in war (3:2). The various answers reflect the measure of theological embarrassment.

23. and he did not give them into the power of Joshua: the redactor indicates his awareness of the limitations to the Deuteronomistic representation of the 'conquest' of Joshua, admitted in Jos. 13:13; 15:63; 17:11–13, 16–18; and Jg. 1:19, 27–34.

The Unconquered Peoples and Israel's Relation to them 3:1–6

1. to test Israel . . . all in Israel who had no experience of any war in Canaan: see on 2:22; cf. the more realistic answer to the problem of the local resistance to Israel in 1:19, 27–34, that Israel could make no headway against the Canaanites in their fortifications and in the plains where they could deploy their chariots.

3. the five lords of the Philistines: see on Jos. 13:2 and 3.

Canaanites: the association with **Sidonians** indicates that 'Canaanites' may be used in the narrower sense, as in Num. 13:29, where they are located by the sea and in the plains, that is to say, in regions open to the influence of Canaan proper, the coast of Lebanon and north Palestine. See further, on Jos. 3:19.

Sidonians: probably denotes the Phoenicians of the coastal strip from Acco northwards (cf. Jos. 13:4), who limited the settlement of Asher according to 1:31f.

Hivites: probably non-Semites from the north (cf. Jos. 11:3). Often, though not here, LXX reads Chorraioi (Hurrians) for 'Hivites' (see on Jos. 3:10).

Lebanon: generally agrees with Jos. 13:5, which locates the 'Hivites' under Mount Hermon, the southern culmination of the Antilebanon range.

Mount Baal-hermon: cf. in a similar context 'Baal-gad below Mount Hermon' in Jos. 13:5 and 11:17, on which see.

the entrance of Hamath: probably reflecting the actual limit of David's empire; see on Jos. 13:5.

5–6. On the conventional list of inhabitants of pre-Israelite Palestine, here omitting Girgashites, see on Jos. 3:10.

NARRATIVES OF THE JUDGES

3:7–16:31

On sources and composition, see above, pp. 197ff.

OTHNIEL AS DELIVERER

3:7–11

Possibly a historical tradition of the Kenizzites presented in the framework of God's contention against his apostate people, their repentance, appeal in extremity and the divine mercy particularised in the exploit of the judge. The details of the tradition have been all but lost, so that only the fact of deliverance by Othniel from an Edomite menace, and possibly the name of his opponent, have survived (see further, Introduction, pp. 197ff.).

The characteristic details of the framework introducing the passages on the great judges are here incomplete, suggesting that the tradition may have been adapted from a fuller Kenizzite tradition to complete the quota of the 'judges of Israel', or even freely composed from such a tradition, by the Deuteronomist on the model of the pre-Deuteronomistic collection (so Richter, *Die Bearbeitung des 'Retterbuches'*, ad loc.).

Introductory Formula 7–8a

7. **Baals:** see on 2:11.
Asheroth: probably local manifestations of the fertility-goddess Asherah, now known from the Rās Shamra texts as the consort of the senior god El and the mother of the divine family. She was frequently represented as the tree of life, which is often depicted in Canaanite art as flanked by caprids which reach up to its fruit. A variant of this motif is the fertility-goddess who offers ears of corn to two rampant caprids in the celebrated ivory unguent box from Minet al-Beidā by Rās Shamra (C.F.A. Schaeffer, *Ugaritica* I, 1939, Pl. I). The tree of life is stylised in Canaanite art, and in the fertility cult was represented either by a natural tree, which was planted in the sanctuary, or by a stylised wooden pole, the *'ᵃšērah*.

8. **Cushan-rishathaim:** 'Cushan-of-the-Double-Evil', a scribal parody, possibly originally 'Cushan the chief of the Temanites' (*kûšān rô'š hattêmānî*), as Klostermann proposed, or 'Cushan and the Temanites' (*kûšān wᵉhattêmānî*); see Introduction to Jg., p. 198.
Mesopotamia: Hebrew *'ᵃram nahᵃrayim*. On the reading *'ᵉdôm* (Edom) corrupted to *'ᵃram*, which was qualified by *nahᵃrayim*, denoting Upper Mesopotamia, and on the historical probability of Edomite pressure on the Kenizzites in south-eastern Palestine and on the alignment of the Kenizzites with the later Israel, see Introduction to Jg., p. 198.

9. **deliverer:** lit. 'one who makes room', according to the Arabic cognate. The meaning of the verb develops from the physical sense (e.g. 1 Sam. 14:45) to the spiritual one, which has still the connotation of freedom from limitations. Here the physical connotation prevails.
Othni-el: note that he is a Kenizzite. The Kenizzites in south-eastern Palestine were also affiliated with the Edomites (Gen. 36:10f., 42; cf. 1 Chr. 1:35f.), hence the resentment of Edom at their present alignment. On Othni-el and his association with Caleb, see further, on Jos. 15:13–19, introduction to Jos. 14, and p. 198.

10. **The Spirit of the LORD came upon him:** this expresses in the Old Testament the invasive influence which transforms a man, either in physical or spiritual potential, e.g. poet, sage, prophet, artist, craftsman, warrior or leader. Saul's madness was said to be caused by the withdrawal of the Lord's spirit and the invasive influence of an evil spirit (1 Sam. 16:14). Thus is explained the

physical strength of Samson (14:6, 19; 15:14) and here and in the story of Gideon (6:34) and Jephthah (11:29) the resolution and courage to commit oneself in a hazardous venture.
judged: (Hebrew *šāpaṭ*), maintained the order (*mišpāt*), i.e. of God for his people against the menace of dissolution, hence 'vindicated'.
11. forty years: part of the Deuteronomistic chronology (see General Introduction, pp. 4f.). As distinct from the conventional general number **forty,** the eight years of oppression (v. 8) seems a realistic tradition, but this may also be conventional 'seven, yea eight', which occurs in the Rās Shamra myths.

EHUD AS DELIVERER

3:12–30

A local Benjaminite hero-sage. For historical reconstruction and source-analysis, see Introduction, pp. 198f.
12. Eglon: otherwise unknown.
Moab: the surface exploration by Glueck in Transjordan has demonstrated the consolidation of territorial states from *c.* 1250 BC, demarcated by frontier fortresses at strategic points over the deep ravines of the Wādī 'l-Ḥesā (the Brook Zered) and the Wādī Mūjib (Brook Arnon) and on heights towards the desert in the east (*Explorations in Eastern Palestine I–IV*; *AASOR* 14, 1934, pp. 1–113; 15, 1935, pp. 1–202; 18–19, 1939, pp. 1–288; 25–27, 1951, pp. 1–711). Moab had been deprived of land north of the Arnon by the Amorites (Num. 21:26), which was occupied by Reuben and Gad after the defeat of Sihon of Heshbon, according to J. This was evidently the beginning of a Moabite revival (Num. 21–23) which resulted in their eventual occupation of the oasis of Jericho, 'the city of palms' (v. 13; cf. 1:16, and see note), which was probably the administrative centre where tribute was collected from the people west of the Jordan, though this is not explicitly stated. The land north of the Arnon was disputed territory between Israel and Moab, who were always ready to recover it, as the inscription of Mesha indicates, and were ever ready to raid west of Jordan (2 Kg. 13:20).
13. Ammonites: lit. 'the sons of Ammon', always designated by the tribal title in the Old Testament, even after they had a king. They were the northern neighbours of Moab, their name surviving in 'Ammān. They evidently kept their tribal constitution, which is reflected by the fact that, except at 'Ammān, archaeology has attested no fortified city of the Ammonites, but only open villages with fortified watchtowers.
the Amalekites: usually located in north Sinai, being bitterly hostile

to Israel. The term here may be loosely applied to hostile Bedouin, either from east of the Jordan or from the desert west of the Dead Sea, who might have been the more easily enlisted against Israel since the loss of seasonal grazing rights in the settlement of the Israelites.

city of palms: Jericho (see on v. 12 and 1:16). Kathleen Kenyon's excavations at Jericho (*Digging up Jericho*, 1957, pp. 263ff.) attest a considerable Iron Age occupation at Tell as-Sulṭān on the evidence mainly of artifacts washed off the tell; but those are mainly from the seventh century BC and later. Besides the statement of Ahab's rebuilding of Jericho in 1 Kg. 16:34, 2 Sam. 19:5 implies a settlement in the time of David, though not necessarily a fortified one. The tradition of a Moabite palace at Jericho need imply no more than a mansion or a small fort. De Vaux (*The Early History of Israel*, II, p. 809) made the interesting suggestion that, in view of the general dereliction of Jericho in the Early Iron Age, its designation here as 'the city of palms' refers to the oasis rather than a city.

15. Ehud . . . Gera: Ehud in 1 Chr. 7:10 and **Gera** in 1 Chr. 8:3, Gen. 46:21 and 2 Sam. 16:5 are clan names. Gera was probably the clan of Ehud, but as the clan Ehud was probably named after an individual ancestor, there is no objection to an individual being named after the eponymous ancestor. The details of the tradition are too circumstantial and locally based in Benjamin not to relate to an individual exploit.

a left-handed man: Hebrew *'iṭṭēr yad-yᵉmînô*. 'restricted in his right hand', also the description of the left-handed slingers of Benjamin in 20:16, but for which the phrase might have been taken here as describing a bodily defect, as the form *'iṭṭēr* might suggest (R. Meyer, *Hebraïsche Grammatik* II, 1969, §38.3), which would have allayed suspicion of the assassin. The meaning, however, is simply 'left-handed', which would in itself deceive the guards, who would naturally look for a weapon on the left side. Ehud would thus surprise his victim. The phrase 'restricted in his right hand' might refer to the training of boys for left-handed fighting, which was the more effective since the shield of the antagonist was normally carried on the left arm. A clan of Scottish Borderers, the Kerrs, had this tradition.

tribute: (Hebrew *minḥâh*). Elsewhere the word means 'present' or 'offering, sacrifice', but also 'tribute', as in 2 Sam. 8:2 and in administrative texts from Rās Shamra. Agricultural produce is no doubt denoted, as the reference to bearers may indicate (v. 18).

16. a cubit: Hebrew *gōmed* is unique here in the Old Testament, and is explained in the Talmud as the length of the forearm (the standard cubit) minus the fingers.

19. sculptured stones: (Hebrew *pᵉsîlîm*; *RV* margin, 'graven images'). Perhaps inscribed stones recording the dominion of Moab and the terms imposed on her subjects, and possibly carved with a figure of the god guaranteeing the validity of a vassal-treaty, as in the Aramaean vassal-treaties at Sūjīn. The location of the stones in question at **Gilgal** has suggested that they were the standing-stones of the sanctuary (see on Jos. 4:19). But we think it more likely that they were the stones recording a vassal-treaty, erected by Gilgal, where the Israelites for their part swore by Yahweh.

a secret message: the public announcement has been contrasted with Ehud's coming to the king in private on the pretext of a message from God (v. 20), and taken as evidence of variant traditions, but, we think, on insufficient grounds (see Introduction, pp. 198f.).

20. cool roof chamber: on the flat roof, such as is still used in Arab villages for lodging a guest (cf. 1 Kg. 17:19; 2 Kg. 4:10), or for parties. The place was well adapted for the secret business that Ehud alleged (cf. the business of Samuel and Saul on the roof-top, 1 Sam. 9:25). These are usually simple shelters, but this one was more elaborate, having folding doors that bolted (v. 23), and apparently a separate chamber that served as a lavatory (v. 24), through which Ehud may have escaped (v. 23).

arose from his seat: Eglon's rising on the announcement of a message from God may have been in deference to the mention of the holy name, as Rabbinic commentators suggest. He may have expected an oracle (Nötscher, *op. cit.*, p. 16). This probably gave Ehud his chance for his sudden fatal thrust.

22. the blade: Hebrew *lahab*, which means 'flame', possibly referring to the gleam.

and the dirt came out: reading *wayyēṣē' happereš* (so Moore, Budde, Gressmann) for MT *wayyēṣē' happaršᵉdônâh*, the last word of which is unattested in the Old Testament. The phrase is omitted in LXX, which might suggest that it is the corruption of a gloss on the next phrase noting the way of Ehud's exit. Thus it perhaps indicates an original gloss *ša'ar happinnâh* ('the door in the corner'), as suggested in Kittel's critical apparatus. The difficulty here is that *ša'ar* ('gate') would not apply to the door of a comparatively flimsy roof-chamber. Koehler-Baumgartner (*Lexicon in Veteris Testamenti Libros*, p. 783) suggests that *paršᵉdônâh* is cognate with Akkadian *parašdinnu* ('hole'), thinking of an architectural feature. G. R. Driver, cited in C. A. Simpson (*Composition of the Book of Judges*, 1957, p. 11) takes it to refer to the anus, the subject of the verb being 'the blade'.

23. the vestibule: Hebrew *hammisdᵉrônâh* (final *h* local), unattested elsewhere in the Old Testament, 'vestibule' being suggested by LXX. The ending is probably locative, indicating a feature outside the cool upper chamber as the place to which Ehud went out. The root of the word *sdr* suggests 'order, row or gradation', so a portico or, more probably we think, an outside stairway may be indicated. **and locked them:** the Hebrew conjunction with the perfect of the verb indicates a late interpolation; but in the earlier unvocalised Hebrew text the verb may have been an infinitive absolute with the significance of the perfect active.

24. relieving himself: lit. 'covering his feet', a well-known euphemism (cf. 1 Sam. 24:3).

25. till they were utterly at a loss: Hebrew *'ad bôš*. The verb is probably akin to Arabic *bāṯa* ('to scatter'), hence 'till their wits were scattered'. Alternatively, with the more regular meaning of *bôš* in Hebrew, it may mean 'as long as shame demanded'. The verb (MT, *wayyāḥîlû*, lit. 'and they writhed') is almost certainly a corruption of *wayyôḥîlû* or *wayᵉyaḥᵃlû*, 'and they waited'.

26. escaped: the root of the verb is the same as in 'Malta', a refuge in the days of Phoenician coasting navigation in the dangerous long hop between Crete, Sicily and North Africa. The escape of Ehud, presumably to his own hills of Benjamin, by way of Gilgal, was taken by older commentators as evidence that his exploit was east of Jordan, because they accepted the traditional ecclesiastical location of Gilgal south-east of Jericho. But with the location of Gilgal north-north-east of Jericho, the scene of the exploit is certainly Jericho, which is specifically noted in v. 14. In this context *haśśᵉ'îrāthāh* cannot mean 'to Seir' in Edom. The definite article denotes a common noun, 'the rough scrub' country; cf. Arabic *ša'ār* ('well-wooded').

27. sounded the trumpet: the ram's horn, the conventional means of rallying forces in Jg. (cf. 6:34).
in the hill-country of Ephraim: a geographical rather than a strictly tribal term, possibly signifying the vegetation west of the watershed contrasting with the arid eastern slopes; see on Jos. 20:7. The action was probably a local one, but we should not on that account unduly doubt its relevance to 'the people of Israel', specifically at least Ephraim and her confederate Benjamin, the nucleus of the ten-tribe 'Israel' of Jg. 5:13–18 (see above pp. 9ff.).

28. Follow after me: Hebrew *ridᵉpû*, generally in Hebrew 'pursue'. LXX reads 'Come down . . .' (Hebrew *rᵉdû*), which should probably be accepted; cf. 'so they went down' (v. 28*b*). The Arabic adjective *radīf* ('riding pillion'), however, suggests that the Hebrew cognate may also mean 'come after' in the sense of 'accompany'.
for the LORD has given your enemies . . . into your hand: here

the hero-saga has probably borrowed the language of the reassuring oracle from the tradition of the war of Yahweh (cf. 1:2).

seized the fords of the Jordan against the Moabites: the interception of the Moabites, disconcerted by the death of their king, at the fords of the Jordan is a further argument for the location of Ehud's exploit at Jericho.

29. about ten thousand men: unrealistic, but not necessarily Deuteronomistic, as the older critics suggest, but rather the hyperbole of saga, as is certainly the statement that **not a man escaped**.

30. On the Deuteronomistic chronology, see General Introduction, pp. 4f.

SHAMGAR THE SON OF ANATH

3:31

A brief note, without the customary introduction or conclusion, on an obscure figure and incident. On the secondary nature of the passage between the consequences of Ehud's exploit (v. 30) and the note of his death (4:1), the identity of Shamgar and his possible significance, see above, pp. 199f.

with an ox-goad: Hebrew *b^{e}malmad habbāqār*; cf. LXX^{A}: 'apart from the cattle' (Hebrew *mill^{e}bad habbāqār*). The exploit with an iron-tipped plough-staff matches Samson's exploit with the jaw-bone of an ass, which, however, is obviously an aetiological topographical legend suggested by the place Lehi, which as a common noun in Hebrew means also 'jaw-bone'. This incidentally was the scene of a single-handed victory over the Philistines by Shammah the son of Agee in a lentil field (2 Sam. 23:11).

DEBORAH AND BARAK

4:1–24

Prose version, with unhistoric editorial reference to Jabin, king of Hazor (vv. 2, 7, 17, 23, 24); cf. Jos. 11:1–11. For critical analysis and relationship with Jos. 1:1–11 and Jg. 5:18–30, see Introduction pp. 200f.

Introductory Framework 4:1–3

The apostasy of Israel, the wrath of God, public appeal in distress and divine relief in the sequel. This phase of apostasy and deliverance is dated after the death of Ehud, Shamgar being ignored, which indicates that the passage on Shamgar was inserted in the narratives of the judges only secondarily, possibly suggested by the mention of Shamgar son of Anath with Jael in 5:6. It is significant that it is only in the editorial introduction (v. 2) and epilogue (vv. 23f.) and editorial glosses at vv. 7 and 17 that Jabin of Hazor is mentioned and he does not appear at all in the poetic version of the culmination of the campaign under Deborah and Barak against Sisera (5:18; 19–30); see Introduction, pp. 200f.

2. Jabin king of Canaan, who reigned in Hazor: here an anachronism (see Introduction, pp. 200f.). On the destruction of **Hazor,** *c.* 1225, some 75 years before the probable date of the campaign against Sisera, in the light of archaeological evidence, see on Jos. 11:1–11.

Sisera: the actual enemy of the Israelites in the time of Deborah and Barak, and the protagonist against them throughout ch. 4 and in 5:19–30. He was certainly independent of Hazor, which had already been destroyed. The ethnic affinity of Sisera is uncertain. The name seems certainly non-Semitic, occurring in the Old Testament only of Temple menials in Ezr. 2:53; Neh. 7:55, who may have been foreign, possibly of Hurrian descent, from the region of Gibeon (see on Jos. 9:3). Sisera may have been descended from a Hurrian chief of a hereditary fief of Egypt, or even of Hazor at the height of her power, Hurrian names being attested among Egyptian vassals in Palestine in the Amarna Tablets and among chiefs of hereditary fiefs in administrative tablets from the palaces at Rās Shamra and Atchanah (Alalakh) in the fourteenth and twelfth centuries BC. Alternatively, Sisera may have been a chief of the 'Sea-peoples' who had invaded Palestine in the twelfth century and whom Ramses III claimed to have settled as his vassals in fortresses in the land. His seat, Harosheth of the *Gentiles*, may indicate so much. This place is not certainly identified. The name suggests al-Ḥārithīyeh, a modern village in the vicinity of Tell al-'Amār, an Iron Age site which may be the location. Alternatively, Harosheth of the Gentiles may be located at the much larger Bronze Age site of Tell al-Harbaj some three miles north-west of al-Ḥārithīyeh (Garstang, *Joshua and Judges*, 1931, pp. 297f.) at the bottle-neck between Carmel and the foothills of Galilee, and between the Plain of Acco and the Great Central Plain.

3. nine hundred chariots of iron: this would involve at least 1,800 horses, an extravagant claim considering that even in the monarchy under Solomon and Ahab the stables of Megiddo accommodated only 450 horses, and Solomon is accredited with no more than 1,400 chariots in the whole realm (1 Kg. 10:26).

Digression on Deborah 4:4–5

The assertion that Deborah was judge in Israel (v. 4*b*), together with the statement that the Israelites went to her for justice at the palm-tree of Deborah between Ramah and Bethel (v. 5), is a Deuteronomistic or redactional gloss, a parenthesis which interrupts the narrative between vv. 4*a* and 6. It seems to confuse Rachel's nurse Deborah, who was buried at the Oak of Weeping near Bethel (Gen. 35:8), with Deborah who inspired Barak in the campaign of the Kishon. The palm-tree between Bethel and Ramah was probably one of those prominent trees associated with oracles, like the Diviner's Oak of Gen. 12:8 and Jg. 9:37, which gave rise to the tradition that here Deborah exercised judgment. The obviously parenthetic character of vv. 4*b*f. and the fact that no notice of Deborah as judge appears in the list of 'minor judges' in 10:1–5; 11:7–15, supports the view that this passage is redactional.

4. **Deborah:** ('Bee'). Her prophetic power or charismatic enthusiasm is noted, in virtue of which she was able to inspire Barak to raise his men. The role of Deborah in this action and in the actual campaign has many parallels among the Arabs, both in ancient times and more recently among the Ruwalla in the north Syrian desert (A. Musil, *In the Arabian Desert*, 1931, pp. 141ff.). The genuineness of this tradition is corroborated by her acclamation in the ancient poem (5:7) as 'a mother in Israel'. It may be more than coincidence that the name of Deborah's husband is given as Lappidoth ('torches' or 'lightning-flashes'; Exod. 20:18) and that the leader she inspired was Barak ('lightning'). A number of scholars since Wellhausen have held that Lappidoth and Barak were one and the same. Our opinion is rather that the unknown husband of Deborah was named Lappidoth by tradition, suggested by the well-known Barak. This is supported by the fact that, as distinct from Barak, Lappidoth's father is not named.

5. **the hill country of Ephraim:** the location of the sacred tree **between Ramah and Bethel**, actually in Benjamin, confirms the view that 'Ephraim' here, as in certain other passages (e.g. 3:27) and probably originally was a geographical term (see on Jos. 20:7).

The Historical Tradition of the Campaign: the Rally under Barak 4:6–10

This seems the conflation of two traditions, one (vv. 6–9) possibly conserved at the sanctuary of Tabor, and one (vv. 9*b*f.) current in

Zebulun and particularly in Naphtali, the tribe of Barak (see further, Introduction, pp. 201–205).

6. Barak: possibly appears as Bedan in the list of judges in 1 Sam. 12:11, where LXX and Syriac read Barak.

Kedesh in Naphtali: the name implies a sanctuary. There were possibly two places of this name in Naphtali, the better known being *c.* seven miles north-north-west of Hazor and the other possibly identical with Khirbet Qadīsa on the high ground west of the southern end of the Sea of Galilee, which seems to be envisaged in the location of the Oak of Za-anannim near Kedesh (v. 11); see on Jos. 19:33, where the Oak of Za-anannim ('Caravaneers') is located in this region. The latter site, further suggested by the association of Issachar with Barak in the Song of Deborah (5:15), may have been the home of Barak, the linking of the unnamed chief of Naphtali in the victory over Jabin of Hazor in Jos. 11:1–11 with the better known Kedesh in Upper Galilee being the possible source of the introduction of Jabin of Hazor in the present narrative.

Mount Tabor: Jebel aṭ-Ṭūr, the conspicuous limestone dome, well characterised by Polybius as 'like a breast', which dominated the central part of the Great Central Plain from the north. It was apparently a sanctuary from the early days of the settlement of Israel (Dt. 33:19) until Hosea (Hos. 5:1, *EVV* 4:5). Tabor and the foothills of Galilee are comparatively well wooded, and would mask the muster of the Israelites, being at the same time ground unfavourable to attack by chariots.

gather your men: the verb in MT is without an object, and means lit. 'draw out'. It is apparently a technical term meaning 'march'; cf. 20:37, where it might mean 'deploy'. The verb *māšak* is used of broadcasting seed (Ps. 126:6), and in the present context the word may signify the rally to Tabor in small, staggered parties to evade suspicion.

ten thousand: seems rather a round number and exaggerated, but the mention of Zebulun and Naphtali appears to be a sober historical tradition, as also the omission of Issachar, which inhabited the vicinity of Tabor. This account of the campaign makes no mention of any other tribes, which corroborates the view of Weiser that in ch. 5 the listing of the tribes in 5:13–18 relates to the assembly of the sacral community for a cultic occasion and only vv. 19ff. and the citation of Zebulun and Naphtali in v. 18 refer to the battle of the Kishon.

7. draw: (Hebrew *māšak*; cf. v. 6). The verb is transitive according to MT, with Sisera as object; in which case we should probably understand that Deborah had her own plan for causing a diversion to lure Sisera to unfavourable ground by the Kishon. But we should expect the same idiom as in v. 6, where the same verb is used but without an object. LXX and Syriac read 'against Sisera', taking the verb as intransitive as in v. 6.

the river Kishon: played an important part in the strategy of the campaign (see on 5:19–21), restricting the movement of Sisera's chariots at a decisive juncture of the battle, or sweeping them away in sudden flood (see on 5:20f.). Unfortunately, the locus of the battle is not specified in the prose version, and the strategy might be inconclusively debated; but we believe that the poetic version in 5:19–21 gives sufficient specification. The **Kishon**, though draining the whole western half of the Great Central Plain, is a quite insignificant stream, dry for much of the year, except from the bottleneck between Carmel and the foothills of Galilee near al-Ḥārithīyeh, where, fed by the springs from Carmel, it is a deep, though not broad, stream with a muddy bed, dammed back by a sandbar at its mouth. Here it would be a formidable barrier, but it is unlikely that the Israelites would venture so near Sisera's base, and the action must be located further east. Immediately west of the bottleneck there is a marshy area, and again about four miles south-east of Megiddo, and so near Taanach, a belt of basalt provides a natural causeway over the Kishon basin (D. Baly, *Geography of the Bible*, 1957, p. 152), which, at the same time it dams in the rainy season, and causes marshes long after. The latter location is suggested as the site of the battle by the explicit reference in the poem to 'Taanach by the waters of Megiddo' (5:19). See further, below, ad loc.

and I will give him into your hand: the oracle through the prophetess, probably in the traditional language of the war of Yahweh (cf. 1:2).

9f. Kedesh: the muster of 10,000 men of Zebulun and Naphtali at Kedesh (Khirbet Qadīsa; see on v. 6) seems a doublet of the muster of the same number from the same tribes at Tabor (v. 6), which may reflect a variant tribal tradition. On the other hand, the site of Tell Abū Qadīs, *c.* three miles south-east of Megiddo, may have been confused in tradition with the place of the muster. The encampment of Heber the Kenite so near the scene of the battle would admirably suit the incident of the refuge and death of Sisera (so Nötscher, *op. cit.*, p. 20). Here again, in the location of this encampment at Kedesh by the Oak of Za-anannim (v. 11), the tradition of an encampment near Megiddo seems to be confused with that of the muster at Khirbet Qadīsa, west of the south end of the Sea of Galilee.

Digression on Heber the Kenite (secondary) **4:11**

Heber the Kenite: The segholate form *ḥeber* is suspect as a proper name, and is certainly more natural as a common noun 'group', as Soggin (*VT* 31, 1981, pp. 89–92) has argued. But his rendering, on this assumption, of *'ēšet ḥeber haqqēnî* (4:17) as 'a woman of the Kenite group' (*Judges*, 1981, ad loc.) does violence to the Hebrew. The abrupt introduction of v. 11 indicates a secondary expansion suggested by Kedesh and in anticipation of the role of Jael the wife of Heber in v. 17. It may still, however, preserve a genuine tradition, the Kenites being itinerant smiths, whose presence near military action is natural. The name Heber may be genuine; but certainly secondary is the detail that Heber had separated from the Kenites, the descendants of Hobab the father-in-law of Moses (cf. 1:16 and Num. 10:29, J, where Hobab is said to be the son of Reuel or Jethro, the father-in-law of Moses). On *ḥôtēn*, any kinsman by marriage, see on 1:16.

The Battle **4:12–16**

12. Tabor: the muster-place of the Israelites reported to Sisera, who now heads for the Kishon (v. 13). This movement, involving a detour to the river, is hard to understand unless a diversion had been created to lure Sisera into chosen terrain, for which we have argued in our note on v. 7. Perhaps a rumour was disseminated that the Israelites intended to attack Megiddo or Taanach, to divert Sisera south of the Kishon between the river and the Carmel range and so to restrict the movement of his chariots. Some such advantage to the Israelites is suggested by v. 14 by Deborah's order to advance **for this is the day in which the LORD has given Sisera into your hand.**

15. the LORD routed Sisera: or 'threw Sisera into confusion', conceivably the unexpected resistance of the Israelites, which enabled them to exploit the marshy terrain. The account of the battle, as so often in the Old Testament, is laconic. The poetic version is more explicit, stating that 'the stars in their courses fought against Sisera', and adding that 'the river Kishon swept them away' or perhaps 'headed them off' (5:20f.). A passage in the Rās Shamra texts refers to the stars as the source of rain, so that a sudden rainstorm seems to be indicated as the efficient cause of Sisera's sudden discomfiture, which is directly referred to God in the poetic version. The marshes of the Kishon near Megiddo might account for the initial difficulties of the chariotry of the too confident Sisera;

but the flood of the lower Kishon, which the writer has seen between Haifa and Megiddo as a strong-flowing current of liquid mud, unapproachable on vague banks which had become a quagmire, would head off the fugitives from their base at Harosheth (v. 16), or sweep them away headlong if they were rash enough to attempt to cross. **Sisera alighted from his chariot:** perhaps to facilitate his flight in the mud, but also possibly to evade detection. It was something which saga would not fail to stress as emphasising the humiliation of Sisera.

The Death of Sisera in the Tent of Jael **4:17–22**

On the location of the Kenite encampment where Sisera was killed at Tell Abū Qadīs, near Taanach and Megiddo, see Introduction to Jg., p. 201. The Kenites, as itinerant smiths, would always have business about the Canaanite cities, in the neighbourhood of which they encamped, like the nomad tinkers, the Nawwār and Ṣulayb, at the present time. Their proximity to the combatants, too, is not unnatural. It is noteworthy that Sisera reached the tent of Jael on foot and was killed apparently not long before Barak arrived at the tent (v. 22), probably after his pursuit of the fugitive chariotry westwards towards Harosheth (v. 16).

17. the tent of Jael: we should expect it to be termed the tent of her husband Heber. It may refer to the screened harem section of the long Bedouin tent, which would be more secure. In this case Jael, true to the desert tradition, would be caught between the horns of a dilemma; to grant the conventional sanctuary and hospitality to the refugee and at the same time to vindicate her honour from suspicion, which she did in the drastic way described. Alternatively, the specific mention of her tent may indicate that she was an older, discarded wife of Heber.
there was peace between Jabin . . . and the house of Heber: we regard this as a gloss by an editor, who has mistaken the Kedesh of v. 11 (see on v. 9) for the city of the same name in Upper Galilee; cf. the view of Hertzberg (*op. cit.*, p. 176, after Moore, Budde, Nowack, Gressman, Burney, Eissfeldt, Simpson) that there is a conflation of two traditions, one of Heber, a Kenite, who had revoked his allegiance to Jabin of Hazor to throw in his lot with the Israelites in the campaign of Jos. 11:1–11, and another of Jael, a Kenite woman who slew Sisera much later. Actually, the relation between Jabin of Hazor and a Kenite family is quite feasible, especially if the Kenites were itinerant smiths who had special immunities (Gen. 4:15).

18. Jael came out to meet Sisera: if this is not meant to emphasise the initiative of Jael in anticipation of the slaughter of Sisera, it may indicate the nomad convention of sanctuary claimed within a set distance from the tent, in certain cases, in recent times in Transjordan, as far as a man could throw a camel-stick (A. Jaussen, *Coûtumes des Arabes au Pays de Moab*, 1908, p. 214).

a rug: the Hebrew word here (*śᵉmîkâh*) is used only here in the Old Testament and its etymology is uncertain. LXX translates variously as 'covering', 'screen' and 'leather covering', using a word which generally means 'tent-curtain', which is also understood by the Syriac Hexapla. The reference is probably to the screened quarter of the women, which would give Sisera a false sense of security and, from Jael's point of view, hide an embarrassing guest.

19. The request for **water**, apart from being natural, was designed to establish the link of hospitality, which would normally guarantee security, as in the case of the notorious Renauld de Châtillon in the tent of Ṣalāḥ ad-Dīn after the battle of Hattin in 1187, which, however, the Sultan was careful not to give personally, thus reserving the right of revenge.

a skin of milk: the well-known article of furniture in a Bedouin tent, the **skin**, which serves as a churn, as 5:25 indicates in referring to butter-milk (Hebrew *ḥem'âh*, Arabic *libn*), a most refreshing drink and the regular refreshment offered on arrival at a Bedouin encampment.

21. tent peg: much longer and sharper than is necessary on our soft turf, and in a smith's family probably of metal.

a hammer: possibly for driving in the tent-pegs. Among modern Bedouin, pitching the tent and striking camp is women's work, so that Jael would not be awkward with the hammer. In the poetic version (5:26), the hammer is 'the workman's mallet'. Here it is explicitly stated that Jael killed Sisera in his sleep, which would be more natural if she used a tent-peg and a hammer. This is not contradicted in the poem, but the statement that 'she crushed his head' (5:26) and 'he fell . . . at her feet' (5:27) rather suggests a variant tradition that she felled him with a hammer as he drank while still standing, this being conflated with the prose version.

into his temple: Hebrew *rakkātô*. Possibly attested in this sense only in Ca. 4:3; 6:7 (*RSV*, 'cheeks'). G. R. Driver (private communication, cited by Simpson, *op. cit.*, p. 16) suggested that *rakkâh* ('soft part') may signify 'brain'. Driver suggested further that the following verb *wattiṣnaḥ*, apparently attested in the Old Testament only in Jos. 15:18 and Jg. 1:14, meaning possibly 'beat', 'struck' (see on Jos. 15:18), may be a homonym, cognate with

Akkadian *ṣanâḫu* ('to discharge', of mucus), so describing Sisera's brains as running out on the ground (so *NEB*).
for weariness: (Hebrew *wayya'ap*) was taken by Driver, following LXX, as 'and he twitched convulsively', after a possible Syriac cognate.

22. as Barak pursued Sisera: possibly having first chased the enemy westwards towards Harosheth (v. 16), and then, not finding Sisera, having come back eastwards.

Editorial Epilogue 4:23–24

Introducing Jabin of Hazor, of whom the original tradition, as in the poetic version, knew nothing: see Introductory Framework, vv. 1–3.

THE SONG OF DEBORAH

5:1–31

The date of the action in vv. 18ff. is probably *c.* 1150 BC, before the Philistine war of 1 Sam. 4ff. (so A. D. H. Mayes, 'The Historical Context of the Battle against Sisera', *VT* 19, 1969, pp. 353–60). The poem has been claimed to reflect the rough vigour of the action and the poetic form and language of the twelfth century BC (so F. M. Cross and D. N. Freedman, *Studies in Ancient Yahwistic Poetry*, 1950, pp. 27–42). J. A. Soggin (*Judges*, 1981, pp. 80f.) cites G. Garbini ('Il cantico di Debora', *La parola del passato* 178, 1978, pp. 5–31) for the view that the language indicates a period after the tenth century BC, but before classical Hebrew of the eighth century. This would pertain to the literary crystallisation of the poem and does not militate against an oral version soon after the action, *c.* 1150 BC. For our presentation of the view of Weiser that the account of the battle is limited to vv. 19–30, introduced by the reference to Zebulun and Naphtali in the roll-call of the member-groups in the general assembly of the sacral community (v. 18), and that vv. 19–30 are a hymn of praise to Yahweh for the latest vindication of his purpose and his people in the liturgy of the renewal of the covenant soon after the victory, see Introduction, pp. 204f.

The liturgy begins with a note on the occasion (v. 2; see note for our interpretation, which differs from *RSV*) and continues with a hymn on the theophany of Yahweh God of Sinai (vv. 3–5), the reminiscence of recent sufferings (vv. 6–8), with the transition to the theme of God's renewed grace (vv. 9–11), which incidentally reflects the declaration of Israel's apostasy and degradation (cf. v. 8*a*) and the mercy of God in the fast-liturgy, which is the framework giving coherence to the pre-Deuteronomistic collection of the traditions of the great judges and to Jg. as a whole in the Deuteronomistic History. The apostrophe to Deborah (v. 12*a*) leads to the introduction of Barak and other notables, the representatives of the various groups of the sacral community, in a festal procession (vv. 12*b*–15*a*), the integrity of the people thus symbolised being palpable evidence of God's vindication of his cause (*RSV*, 'the triumphs of the Lord', v. 11; see note). In vv. 14–18 the various members of the sacral community are named, whether present or absent, in what we regard as the roll-call of the ten members, an assertion of the integrity of the community. Here dramatically Zebulun and Naphtali are kept to the end (v. 18), their honourable mention leading to the hymn of praise for the victory over Sisera (vv. 19–30), specifically their exploit, with the result that Yahweh's people are vindicated and the present assembly was possible.

Though the hymnal elements are strictly limited to the hymn on the theophany (vv. 3–5) and the description of the battle and its sequel (vv. 19–30), the other liturgical elements, usually more prosaic in character, were on this occasion transformed by the mood of Deborah, who, in virtue of her prophetic elation is given the leading part in the direction of the liturgy of the sacrament of the covenant. No element in the chapter, however, not even the hymn, in vv. 19–30 may be divorced from the cultic occasion. The relevance of the fragmentary hymn on the theophany (vv. 3–5) to such an occasion is obvious. The relevance of the triumph song (vv. 19–30) to the sacrament of the covenant is also apparent from the exclusion of Meroz from the fellowship by curse (v. 23) and the final curse and blessing (v. 31), which should probably be considered apart from the hymn, and which have an analogy in the blessings and curses in Dt. 27:11f. in the context of the sacrament of the covenant.

Editorial Introduction 5:1

Ascribing the hymnic elements to **Deborah**, with the secondary addition of **and Barak the son of Abinoam**.

The Occasion 5:2

That the leaders took the lead . . .: after LXX[A], understood after **bless . . .** (v. 2*c*). This is not the natural translation of the Hebrew, but is based on the assumption that the verb is cognate with Arabic *fara'a* ('to be lofty'). It is more likely to be cognate with Arabic *faragha* ('to be free, unrestrained'). The phrase *bip^e^rôa' p^e^rā'ôt* may mean rather 'when the flowing hair was let loose' (cf. Dt. 32:42; Num. 6:5; Ezek. 44:20). The last two passages refer to the hair of the Nazirite unshorn in consequence of the vow of consecration, and the first refers to the long hair of warriors, who in ancient times were consecrated for war (M. Weber, *Ancient Judaism*, 1952, p. 95). The infinitive construct introduced by the preposition *b^e^* could refer to the past or the present. In the past, it could refer to vows and volunteering (*hitnaddēb*) for the recent campaign. In the present, it could refer to a renewal of vows of 'the people' (v. 2), i.e. the sacral community, possibly omitting 'bless . . .' as a misplaced rubric or a late insertion, as the parallelism in the couplet demands. The long hair might symbolise a reversion to desert conditions; cf. the long 'lovelocks' (*nuwās*) of the Bedouin, the loss of which was a particular disgrace. Arabic *faragha* means also 'to be free to devote one's whole attention to something', and in the Xth Form, 'to spend oneself in a great effort', which P. C. Craigie has in mind in rendering: 'When . . . men were dedicated unconditionally' ('A Note on Judges V 2', *VT* 18, 1968, pp. 397–9). If this is the meaning, *p^e^rā'ôt* would be an internal accusative, and the phrase a close parallel with *b^e^hitnaddēb* . . ., though the alternative, 'when the flowing hair was let loose', in the sense we have proposed, would still preserve the parallelism. If we are to understand MT *bip^e^rôa' p^e^rā'ôt* as Craigie proposes, the preposition would rather signify 'Because', as Soggin (*Judges*, ad loc.) assumes, taking 'bless the Lord' as original and rendering:

> Because the people in Israel have regained liberty,
> because the people offered themselves willingly,
> bless the Lord!

Israel has a peculiar significance as the religious community, realised at the assembly at the sacramental renewal of the covenant, which is also the significance of 'the people of Yahweh' (*'am yhwh*) in v. 2*bc*, reading *'am yhwh* and omitting MT *bār^e^kû* ('bless'). The people (*hā'ām*) is generally a kinship group, used of a people together with its eponymous forefather (also *'am*) or its god, who is often considered as a kinsman, as in the Egyptian Execration Texts naming Amorite tribesmen in Palestine, *c*. 1850–1800 BC. In Israel also it denotes the people with its God, and so comes to denote often the religious community in solemn assembly, where that solidarity between people and God was specifically realised.

Introduction to the Hymn on the Theophany 5:3

kings . . . princes: (better 'kings . . . rulers'). The conventional antagonists to the sovereignty of God are cited to listen to the account of his triumph and to acknowledge his sovereignty. This is a conventional motif in passages on the kingship of God, e.g. Ps. 2:2; Isa. 52:15; and Hab. 1:10; cf. Ps. 68:32 (MT, v. 33), which is strongly influenced by the Song of Deborah, and indeed is almost certainly a development of it (so Mowinckel, *Der achtunsechszigste Psalm*, Avhandlinger utgitt av Det Norse Videnskaps-Akademiei Oslo II, Hist.-Filo. Klasse, 1953, No. 1, pp. 10, 56–9; H. J. Kraus, *Die Psalmen* I, BK XV, 1960, pp. 164–468; J. Gray, 'A Cantata of the Autumn Festival: Psalm LXVIII', *JSS* 22, 1977, pp. 5ff.).
I will sing: the conventional introduction to a hymn, as also in the Rās Shamra texts. Deborah, a prototype here of later cultic prophets (Mowinckel, *The Psalms in Israel's Worship*, E.T. 1967, II, pp. 53ff.), gives expression to the praises of the assembly.
to the LORD: in MT the personal pronoun 'I' is repeated, which makes it uncertain whether the meaning is 'I, even I, will sing to the Lord', or, as Weiser maintains (*op. cit.*, p. 73), is a cultic interjection 'I am for Yahweh'; cf. 'As for me and my house we will serve the Lord' in the context of the covenant sacrament (Jos. 24:15). The parallel with the following line suggests that the second pronoun is a dittograph, as indicated by its omission in certain MSS.
I will make melody: the verb literally means 'to pluck the strings' (cf. Am. 5:23), and is an early reference to instrumental music in psalmody.

Invocation of Yahweh in Terms of the Sinai Theophany 5:4–5

The close affinity in language and conception with Dt. 33:2ff. and Ps. 68:7f. (MT, vv. 8f.) (cf. Ps. 77:17f., MT, vv. 18f.; Mic. 1:3f., Hab. 3:3, etc.) indicates the stereotyped language of the liturgy, and relates not to the coming of Yahweh to the particular battle with Sisera, but, as the above passages indicate, to his presence in the sacrament of the covenant (Weiser, *op. cit.*, p. 74). 'The LORD, the God of Israel' (v. 3*b*) is specifically the title of Yahweh in the assembly of his people on this occasion, whereby the various groups of Israel who made common cause with the Rachel group expressed their solidarity as the people of Yahweh in the sacramental experience of the Exodus and covenant (cf. Jos. 24; see above, pp. 16, 52).

The specific reference to the theophany on the occasion of the covenant in the desert and the association of Yahweh with Sinai reflect the theological difficulty for early Israel of a God who was attached to a certain locality being present with his community in new localities and of the validity of his worship at new cult-sites. This is obviously reflected in the question of the presence of God when Israel was to leave Sinai (Exod. 32:34; 33:12–16, J) and in the practice of pilgrimage to Sinai-Horeb (1 Kg. 19:8), which is possibly the source of the itinerary of the Exodus and desert wandering (Noth, 'Der Wallfahrtsweg zum Sinai', *PJB* 36, 1940, pp. 7ff.).

4. **didst go forth . . . didst march:** similarly paired in the description of the theophany in Ps. 68:7 (MT, v. 8) and Hab. 3:12f., also referring to the Sinai theophany.

Seir: specifically associated, as here, with **Edom** in Gen. 35:8 and Dt. 2:5, latterly east of the Arabah, is somewhat vaguely understood and occasionally refers to the escarpment west of the Arabah (see on Jos. 11:17).

the heavens dropped: (Hebrew *nāṭāpû*, 'dripped'). The Aramaic and Greek translations indicate doubt in this reading, suggesting variously 'declined' (*nāṭāyû*), 'were disturbed' and 'were removed' (*namôṭû*), imagery which recalls 2 Sam. 22:8. 'Dripped' is possibly a scribal corruption suggested by the verb in the immediate sequel 'the clouds dripped water'. Up to this point the LORD is addressed in the second person, as distinct from the statements about him in the third person in v. 5. The function of the singer is to invoke and address God on behalf of the community (v. 4) and to reassure the community of the divine presence (v. 5). He, or she, is the mediator representing the community before God and the channel of God's communication to the community.

5. **the mountains quaked:** (reading Hebrew *nāzōllû* for MT *nāzelû*, 'flowed down', after LXX). Both readings are possible in the context, but in view of the probable chiastic arrangement of the parallelism the former is almost certainly correct.

yon Sinai: not a correct translation of the Hebrew; nor must we assume here and in Ps. 68:8 (MT, v. 9) that this is a late gloss, 'this is Sinai'. The word, taken as a demonstrative (*zeh*), is actually an older form of the relative particle *de* in Aramaic and Ugaritic (cf. Arabic *dhū*, lit. 'master of . . .'. Qualifying Yahweh, it means 'He of Sinai'.

the LORD, the God of Israel: repeated emphatically at the end of the invocation of the presence of Yahweh in the assembly of the sacral community in emphasis of the invocation and assurance of his presence.

The Recent Suffering and Degradation of Israel recalled as a Prelude to the Divine Deliverance **5:6–8**

Note the different literary form, and possibly also a different voice; cf. 7, 12.

6. Shamgar, the son of Anath: the reference possibly suggested the mention of Shamgar in 3:31, where he is included, probably secondarily, among the judges (see ad loc.). The present passage would naturally suggest that Shamgar was regarded as an oppressor of Israel (see Introduction to Jg., pp. 199f.). The reference to **Jael** is also at first sight strange in this context, since, if the same person as the assassin of Sisera is indicated, she was not active until the time of Deborah (v. 7). Suggested emendations are *bîmê yā'îr*, 'in the days of Jair'; cf. 10:3 (Ewald); *bîmê 'ôlām*, 'in the days of old' (Burney, *op. cit.*, p. 114, after C. J. Ball) and *bîmê 'ôl*, 'in the days of the yoke' (Sellin, Grether, Soggin). As those are conjectural emendations, unsupported by the versions, the assumed corruption must have been relatively early in the Hebrew text. Weiser, on the other hand, proposed that Shamgar's time marked the beginning and Jael's the end of the oppression of Israel. The association with Jael here suggested to the author of 3:31 that Shamgar was a champion of Israel, hence to be included among the judges (see Introduction to Jg., pp. 199f., and on 3:31).

caravans ceased: so *RSV* correctly, reading *'ôr^{e}ḥôt* for MT *'^{o}rāḥôt* ('highways'). This implies a reversion to local anarchy, so graphically illustrated in the Amarna Tablets, which attest the robbery of a Babylonian caravan at Ḫinnatuni (Khirbet al-Beidāwīyeh at the western end of the Plain of the Baṭṭūf, north-east of Haifa). The local independence of Canaanite chiefs, nominally vassals of Egypt, and their private wars and depredations, which made traffic unsafe, also prevented the cohesion of the various elements of the later Israel, even single wayfarers being obliged to use byways (v. 6*c*, *d*, omitting MT *'^{o}rāhôt* as a dittograph). In a wider historical context, this was the result of the relaxation of Egyptian control in Palestine and possibly of the disruption caused by the invasion of the Philistines and other 'Sea-peoples', which may have been the proper context of Shamgar, a local commandant in Egyptian service, according to Alt. In those circumstances the periodic sacrament of the covenant at the assembly of the sacral community of vv. 13–18 may have been suspended. This would account for the absence of so many groups, which is noted without censure in vv. 15*b*–17.

7. The peasantry ceased: Hebrew *ḥād^{e}lû p^{e}rāzôn*, treating the latter word as a collective singular; but possibly *p^{e}razîm* should be read in strict agreement with the verb, or *p^{e}rāzôt* ('open villages'), as in Ezek. 38:11; Zech. 2:4 (MT, v. 8); Est. 9:19, with certain MSS. LXX, however, suggests the reading *rôz^e^nîm* ('rulers'), the chief scribal variant being dittography of *r* in MT, which closely resembles *p* in the archaic Hebrew script. This is supported by the reference to the authority of Deborah in the parallel colon, with whose effective resistance Sellin saw a contrast in the inactivity of the leading classes before her (so Weiser and Soggin). *p^e^rāzîm*, however, cognate with Arabic *barrāz* ('champion in single combat'), admits this contrast.

until you arose: the verbal afformative is ambiguous (cf. *AV*, 'until I arose'). But it is probably an archaic form of the second person singular, as *RSV* reads, and is supported by the direct address to Deborah in v. 12. LXX, reading the third person feminine singular, indicates doubt in the Hebrew text.

a mother in Israel: a title implying respect and authority; cf. 'father' (2 Kg. 2:12; 13:14), also of prophets. Weiser, rightly in our opinion, emphasises the role of Deborah in the convocation of the assembly of the sacral community after a considerable lapse. The primary relation of ch. 5 to this occasion rather than to the battle thus explains the reference to her rather than to Barak, the actual victor in the battle, who, even when he does appear, is second to Deborah.

8. When new gods were chosen: if the text is correct, the literal meaning is 'they (singular of indefinite subject) chose new gods'. The text is also in doubt in the following parallel colon, nor do the versions give any material help. In the parallel colon (*RSV*, 'when war was in the gates'), Budde (*Das Buch der Richter*, 1897, ad loc.), after LXX and the Syriac version, proposes with a minimum of emendation:

God's sacrifices ceased,
Barley bread was spent,
zib^e^ḥê '^e^lōhîm ḥād^e^lû
'āzal leḥem ś^e^'ōrîm

This involves the reading *zib'ḥê* for *yibḥar* ('one chose'), which is not a drastic emendation of the archaic Hebrew text, and the assumption of *l* after *'az* ('then'), quite a natural scribal error (haplography) before *l* of the following word *leḥem*. This is feasible, giving a good parallel between the due of God and the daily food of men.

Equally feasible, though involving a greater change of text, is the suggestion of Ball, incorporated by Burney (*op. cit.*, pp. 117, 119):

They had no armourers,
Armed men failed from the cities,
ḥās^e^rû lāhem ḥārāšîm
'āz^e^lû ḥ^a^mûšîm me'îr

Retaining MT *ḥād^e^lû* for Burney's *ḥās^e^rû*, which seems to us a gratuitous emendation and not graphically feasible, this would accord with the following couplet, which refers to the lack of arms among the Israelites; cf. conditions before Saul's revolt, when the Israelites had to rely on the Philistines to set even their agricultural implements (1 Sam. 13:19–21).

Another conjectural emendation to the same effect, and with the merit of agreeing with the immediate context, but much nearer MT, is that of Zapletal, adopted by Hertzberg (*op. cit.*, p. 171):

Deaf were the young warriors of God (*sc.* to the call to arms),
At an end was war before the gates (i.e. warlike exercises).
b^e^ḥûrê 'elôhîm ḥēr^e^šîm
'āzal leḥem baššeʿārîm.

Weiser, however (*op. cit.*, pp. 75f.), would retain the Hebrew text, agreeing with *RSV* in the rendering 'They chose strange gods', and continuing with 'Gods whom formerly they had not known', for which his easiest reading is *'āz* (or *mē'āz*) *'elôhîm lō' šā'arû*. With little drastic emendation of MT, this re-echoes the words of Dt. 32:17 and touches upon a vital feature of the covenant sacrament. This then is the element of confession of sin in relation to the disasters of Israel; cf. the curses in Dt. 28:15ff., which include weakness before the enemy (vv. 25ff.). On the other hand, the couplet as understood by Weiser interrupts the sequence of thought and may be a theological gloss after Dt. 32:17. Budde's reading agrees with what precedes in vv. 6f., if we read *perāzîm* or *perāzôt* ('open villages'); Burney's reading agrees with the rest of v. 8 and with *pārāzîm* ('champions') in v. 7.

Anticipation of the Hymn on God's Vindication (*RSV* 'the triumphs of God', v. 11) *in the Assembly, with notice of the Assembly of 'the People of Yahweh'* (v. 22*b*) *and their Representatives* (vv. 9f.) **5:9–11**

Without specifying any cultic occasion, Nötscher (*op. cit.*, p. 23) also conjectured a reference to a festal procession in vv. 9–11.

9. My heart goes out to the commanders of Israel: (Hebrew *libbî leḥôqeqê yiśrā'ēl*, lit. 'my heart to the commanders . . .'. If the text is correct, the sense would be 'I animadvert upon . . .', the **heart** being for the ancient Hebrew the seat of cognition. Burney, however (*op. cit.*, p. 122), adopted Ball's suggestion *lekû* for *libbî*, translating 'Come, ye governors . . .', the vocative particle *le* being now attested in the Rās Shamra texts.

commanders: Hebrew *ḥôqeqê* (lit. 'those who impose statutes'); perhaps better *meḥôqeqê*, as proposed by Ball.

who offered themselves willingly: possibly present tense, in which

case it would refer to the representatives of Israel voluntarily offering themselves in a renewal of allegiance to Yahweh in the covenant; cf. Jos. 24:15: 'As for me and my house we will serve the LORD'.
among the people (*bā'ām*): Perhaps we should rather render 'as the people' (*sc.* 'of Yahweh'), the preposition expressing the capacity in which the leaders freely dedicated themselves.
Bless the LORD: not to be omitted as a meaningless repetition of the exclamation in v. 2, as many commentators suggest. After the catalogue of the degradation of Israel (vv. 6–9), it strikes an auspicious note in anticipation of the freedom to renew the covenant and of the hymn on the victory which made that possible.

10. you who ride on tawny asses: The reference is to the more dignified members of society (cf. the families of the 'minor judges', Jair (10:4) and Abdon (12:14)), as **you who walk by the way** refers to humble persons.
you who sit on rich carpets: something of a paraphrase, the Hebrew word rendered 'carpets' (*middîn*) meaning 'what is stretched out'. The phrase disrupts the metric system, and it is feasibly suggested that it should be emended, with less disturbance of MT than the translation suggests: 'Let them consider it' (*yāšîbu 'al-libbām*). We consider the phrase more likely to be a gloss on the dignitaries, meaning 'those who sit in judgment' (so LXX).

11. To the sound of musicians at the watering-places: so *RSV*, after LXX. Weiser is possibly right in connecting Hebrew *meḥaṣeṣîm* (*RSV*, 'musicians') with the Hebrew word for 'half' (*ḥaṣî*), the reference being to antiphonal singing; in which case we might amend the masculine of the participle to the femine, rendering:

> At the voice of the women singing antiphonally (as indicated in LXX) as they draw water,
> Let them repeat in response Yahweh's acts of vindication.

In support of this rendering we may cite the verb *ṯnn* in Ugaritic, meaning 'to be double', hence 'repeat'. We should note E. F. C. Rosenmüller's suggestion (*Scholia in Vetus Testamentum – Judices et Ruth*, 1835, ad loc.) to retain the Hebrew text, but to take the participle *meḥaseṣîm* as referring to the shepherds dividing their flocks, as the writer has seen Arab shepherds do by the sound of the voice, sheep separating from goats at the troughs by the wells. Hence the rendering may be:

> At the voice of the (shepherds) shedding out the flocks as they draw water,
> Let them repeat in response Yahweh's acts of vindication.

Weiser's further proposal (*op. cit.*, p. 80) should also be noted, that the initial preposition suggests the comparative particle *min*:

Louder than the voice of those that distribute water among the well-channels
Let them repeat . . .

Our preference is for Weiser's first suggestion.

triumphs: *ṣidᵉqôt*, lit. acts 'right' rather than 'righteous', which is a secondary meaning. The feminine plural, however, may indicate the abstract, hence 'vindication'. The primary meaning of Hebrew *ṣedeq* is 'that which is right or proper with relation to a given object', e.g. 'right paths' (*magᵉlê ṣedeq*) in Ps. 23:3, and right offerings (*zibᵉḥe ṣedeq*) in Dt. 33:19; or what measures up to a norm, e.g. right weight (*'eben ṣedeq*) in Dt. 25:15. It may also mean 'legitimate', as in Phoenician inscriptions, when a king claims he is *melek ṣedeq*, 'a legitimate king' and not a usurper; cf. in the Legend of King Krt in the Rās Shamra texts, where the mother of a dynasty is termed *'ātt ṣdq*, 'a proper wife', 'a legitimate queen'. In the present context *ṣidᵉqot yhwh*, if it means acts which are *ṣedeq*, would mean the acts which vindicate God's purpose and his people, and if an abstract, denotes 'vindication'. *RSV* 'triumphs' in this passage is prompted by *ṣedeq* in parallelism with *yᵉšû'âh* ('deliverance') in Isa. 62:1. This does not invalidate our meaning 'vindication' as being nearer the basic meaning of *ṣedeq*, even in Isa. 62:1.

his peasantry: (Hebrew *pirᵉzônô*). Collective singular, possibly the inhabitants of open villages (see on v. 7). There may be a dittograph in the case of initial *p*, however, the original reading being *rozᵉnô* ('his rule'), *p* and *r* closely resembling each other in archaic Hebrew script. The vindication of God's rule would have point here in view of the summons in v. 3: 'Hear, O kings; give ear, O princes' (actually *rôzᵉnîm*).

Then down to the gates marched the people of the LORD: not *to* the gates, or, by synecdoche 'cities' of the enemy (so Burney, Grether), which was not Israelite strategy, but, in view of the preposition *lᵉ*, meaning 'from' regularly in Ugaritic, '*from* the gates' of the Israelite settlements. The preposition should be similarly understood in 2:9; 19:30; 21:19. The verb may be the perfect, or, with change of pointing, jussive, which we prefer.

the people of the LORD (*'am yhwh*) is the technical description of the sacral community of Israel.

Apostrophe to Deborah and Barak **5:12**

awake, utter a song: Hebrew *'ûrî dabbᵉrî šîr*, *'ûrî* being better translated 'rouse thee'. According to *RSV*, this might seem an interjection of the devotees, encouraging Deborah to sing the hymn of praise for the recent victory (vv. 19–30). But as this does not begin immediately we may question the translation and the text. 'Speak a song' would be a unique expression in the Old Testament. Actually, certain families of LXX and the Syriac translation of one Greek version read 'rouse the tens of thousands of thy people' (*hāʿîrî ribᵉbôt ʿammēk*), 'song' being possibly a later adjustment after the corruption of *ribᵉbôt* to *dabbᵉrî*. We propose a much simpler emendation, which is, admittedly, conjectural: *ʿûrî, dabbᵉrî ʾāśîr* ('rouse thee, lead the prisoners behind thee!'). Deborah and Barak lead the procession of the groups of the sacral community or their representatives, with the captives of the recent battle. Our emendation, which posits the meaning of *dabbēr*, a denominative verb cognate with Arabic *dubr* ('back'), envisages an arrangement like the tow-rafts of timber (*dôbᵉrôt*) in 1 Kg. 5:9 (MT, v. 23). The emendation has the merit of restoring the parallelism with the following colon with the minimum of disturbance of MT.

lead away your captives: rather 'parade your captives'; cf. Syriac, 'lead captive those who would take thee captive' (cf. Isa. 14:2). For a parade of captives by a triumphant king from the palace of Megiddo (*c.* 1350–1150 BC), see *ANEP*, Fig. 332.

The Roll-call of the Tribes 5:13–18

Even those absent are named to preserve the integrity of the community of the ten northern groups, according to the ancient Hebrew conception of the substantial significance of the name. The absence of certain tribes is probably owing to the lapse of the assembly due to the stiffening of Canaanite resistance, this being the first occasion of its resumption. The absence of Asher may indicate that Harosheth, Sisera's fortress, was still an effective barrier, and the border groups, Reuben, Gad (MT Gilead) and Dan in the far north had too precarious a foothold to attend in force, if indeed at all. On the growth of the sacral community Israel of ten groups, as in vv. 13–18, see above, pp. 11ff.

13. Then down marched the remnant of the noble; the people of the LORD marched down for him against the mighty.

This is the general sense though not the translation of MT, which as it stands is not patient of satisfactory translation. Jewish tradition suggests that the word rendered 'marched down' (MT *yᵉrad*) should be read 'may he cause to have dominion over', which, with slight emendation, is possible but unlikely. LXX read:

Then came down a remnant to the strong ones;
The people of God came down to him among the mighty ones.

This is a feasible translation, differing from MT only in the vowel change in MT *yerad*, and in the reading 'to him' for 'to me'. We might further suggest that for MT *śārîd le'addîrîm* we should read *yiśrā'ēl bā'addîrîm*, which involves less of a disturbance of the text than is at first sight apparent, *d* in MT *śārîd* being an easy corruption of ' in the archaic Hebrew script and initial *y* of our reading *yiśrā'ēl* being misplaced to the second syllable of *śārîd* after the corruption. This would restore the parallelism with *yiśrā'ēl . . . 'am yhwh*. We further suggest that the preposition in *baggibbôrîm* signifies not 'against', as in *RSV*, but 'in the person of'; hence we translate:

Then Israel came down in the person of the notables,
The people of Yahweh came down to him in the person of their men of substance.

The reference is not to the muster for the battle, but to the gathering of the sacral community, the people of Yahweh, through their representatives to the assembly. Our proposed emendation and translation notwithstanding, we admit that *śārîd* ('survivors') and *gibbôrîm* ('mighty men, warriors') in MT might have a particular point, especially after the mention of Deborah and Barak with the prisoners at the head of the procession. The participants and survivors might then follow, together with the representatives of the various groups (vv. 14–15*a*).

Weiser (*op. cit.*, pp. 85f.) notes the significant fact that in vv. 9, 13–15*a*, the notables of the various tribes are mentioned as present, whereas in vv. 15*b*–17 the tribes which are absent are referred to in the mass. Obviously the notables are representing their tribes at the cultic occasion for which he argues. On the other hand, when the warlike exploit of Zebulun and Naphtali is mentioned (v. 18), those tribes as a whole are mentioned, despite the fact that the representatives of Zebulun at least have already been mentioned in MT (v. 14*d*). Obviously then, vv. 18ff. relates to the battle and vv. 13–17 to the tribal assembly.

14. From Ephraim they set out thither into the valley: reading *minni 'eprayim šārû šām bā'ēmeq* for MT *minnî 'eprayim šoršām bā'amāleq* ('from Ephraim their root in Amalek'), meaningless and obviously corrupt. LXX 'Ephraim eradicated them in Amalek' indicates MT, except for *minnî*, pointing MT *šoršām* as *šērešām*, which is still not satisfactory so far as MT *minnî* and *ba'amālēq* are concerned, though LXX understands *minnî* as *mimmennî* ('from me', i.e. 'with my authority'). *RSV* 'into the valley' (*bā'ēmeq* after LXX[A], Lucian's recension and Theodotion) for *ba'amālēq* is surely correct, referring to the assembly in the Great Central Plain at Tabor (so Weiser, *op. cit.*, p. 86). MT *šoršām* ('their root') must be the corruption of a verb, either *šārû* ('they came forth') or possibly *me'aššerîm* ('they marched out in order'). For the location of Ephraim and the other groups, see on Jos. 16:4–10 and, generally, Jos. 15–19. Notice the priority of **Ephraim**, indicated by the fact that though the groups are listed from north to south, Ephraim is mentioned before her southern neighbour Benjamin, as K. D. Schunck emphasises (*op. cit.*, p. 54). On the Rachel group, particularly the later Ephraim, as the dynamic force in the settlement of Palestine and in the growth of the ten-group sacral community Israel of vv. 13–18, see above, pp. 10f.

Following you, Benjamin, with your kinsmen: the text has been suspected, but in view of the battle-cry of Benjamin in Hos. 5:8 (G. A. Smith, *The Twelve Prophets*, 1927, on Hos. 5:8), the reading should be retained. The slogan may refer to the role of Benjamin with Ephraim the militant element in the emergent Israel, and particularly to their significance as long-range slingers and archers, shock-troops, which was given recognition in the election of Saul of Benjamin as the first king of Israel, or head of a permanent striking force. Their warlike nature is expressed in the Blessing of Jacob (Gen. 49:27) and in the initiative of Ehud of Benjamin against Moabite aggression in Jg. 3:12ff., which in fact may have given rise to the slogan. *RSV* is certainly right in reading 'thy kinsmen' for *AV* 'with thee' (cf. LXX^A and Lucian's recension). For *ʿamāmekā* ('thy clansmen', or better 'the heads of thy clans'), cf. Gen. 25:8. *ʿam* denotes a tribal ancestor (see above, on v. 2) or senior relative, and is also a term of respect in Arabic. We would explain the preposition *bᵉ* in *baʿamāmekā* as 'represented by' (your clan heads).
Machir: On the settlement of Machir east and, as here, west of Jordan, their origin, affinities and warlike character, see above, pp. 11f., 14, and on Jos. 13:31. The antiquity of the group (and of Jg. 5) is indicated by the fact that here it takes the place of the later Manasseh of the Blessing of Jacob (Gen. 49, J) and of Moses (Dt. 33, E) in western Palestine and is located east of Jordan in Jos. 13:31.
commanders: better, 'law-givers' (see on v. 9).
those who bear the marshal's staff: the Hebrew verb *māšak* in this context is probably cognate with Arabic *masaka*, 'to grasp, hold'. Here *sôpēr* is genuine, but in the same sense as in 2 Kg. 25:19, where it denotes the scribe who was concerned with conscription. Qualification for military service may have been necessary for membership of the sacral community.

15. **the princes of Issachar came with Deborah:** so *RSV* after the Targum for MT, 'and my princes among Issachar with Deborah'. From this it appears that Deborah was from Issachar, which indi-

cates the secondary nature of the tradition which connects her with 'the palm of Deborah' in Benjamin in the hill-country of Ephraim (4:5).

and Issachar faithful to Barak: reading *kēn lebārāq* for MT *ken bārāq*, taking *kēn* as an adjective 'true', as in Gen. 42:11, 19, 31, 33, 34; 2 Kg. 27:9; Prov. 15:7. The verse seems to contradict the tradition which associates Barak with Naphtali (4:6), and probably Naphtali should be read here, otherwise the tribe is not mentioned at all in connection with its representative at the assembly of the sacral community (so S. R. Driver, G. A. Cooke, Gressmann and Burney). Hertzberg (*op. cit.*, p. 172) after Täubler suggests the reading 'As Deborah so Barak' and further that 'Naphtali' was inadvertently omitted at the end of the next clause owing to its resemblance to the first word of the next sentence, *bipelaggôt*. We prefer to read 'Naphtali' for 'Issachar' with *RSV*, 'Issachar' being repeated possibly as a scribal inadvertency.

into the valley they rushed forth at his heels: better 'they streamed forth following him into the valley'—to the sacral assembly, not to the battle, as *RSV* implies. This seems an odd colon wanting a parallel (which may have dropped out), but the versions give no clue to reconstruction.

Among the clans of Reuben: 'clans' (cf. 2 Chr. 35:5) is certainly to be preferred to *AV* 'watercourses' (cf. Ps. 1:3; Isa. 30:25; Job. 20:17), the high plateau round Heshbon occupied by Reuben being particularly scarce in running water.

great searchings of heart: reading *ḥiqerê lēb* (for MT *ḥiqeqê lēb*). According to the feasible view of Weiser, the mention of the absent members was designed to preserve the integrity of the sacral community notwithstanding. **Reuben** is not, as is usually held, censured for absence, but excused. Exposed as they were, like their neighbours Gad (Gen. 49:19) to raiders from the desert, they might well be excused, though their absence was not without serious debate.

16. among the sheepfolds: (Hebrew *bên hammišpetayim*) actually 'between the converging fold-walls', as the dual *mišpetayim* indicates. This feature is well illustrated in Transjordan in ancient drystone sheepfolds with converging fold-walls to facilitate the corralling of flocks in the event of sudden raids from the desert (A. S. Kirkbride, 'Desert Kites', *JPOS* 20, 1946, pp. 1–5); cf. the figurative description of Issachar 'between converging fold-walls', i.e. the bottleneck of the hills of Lower Galilee and Gilboa, in Gen. 49:14 (Eissfeldt, 'Gabelhürden im Ostjordanland', *F. und F.* 25, 1949, pp. 9–11). The feature is depicted on the early Egyptian Dynastic palette of Narmer, where two Semitic enemies of the Pharaoh flee naked, one from a walled perimeter with redoubts and the other from a circular corral with converging entry-walls (*ANEP*, p. 296). The preoccupation with the defence of the marginal lands which prevented the semi-nomadic Reubenites from effective participation with the rest of the sacral community in Jg. 5 accords with their diminished numbers noticed in the Blessing of Moses (Gen. 49:3f.). The event(s) which led to this are unknown, but from Dt. 33:20f. we may fairly conclude that in Transjordan Gad had become the stronger party in an alliance with Reuben, which was practically absorbed (so H.-J. Zobel, *Stammesspruch und Geschichte*, BZAW 95, 1965, p. 65). This situation of Reuben in Transjordan is, we consider, explicable if Reuben had been forced out of an earlier settlement west of Jordan (see above, on Jos. 1:12 and 15:6). Their membership of the sacral confederacy, notwithstanding their numerical and effective weakness, may be explained by their early adherence to the militant Rachel group east of the lower Jordan, with whom, with Gad, they maintained their solidarity, possibly at the sanctuary of Gilgal.

the piping for the flocks: the 'whistling' (*šᵉrîqôt*) may denote the controlling of the flock, which is still done by voice among Arab shepherds (cf. Jn. 10:3f.) or a signal to gather it into safety (cf. Zech. 10:8). Weiser's explanation notwithstanding, there is probably a gentle censure of Reuben and other absentees, with which the conduct of Naphtali and Zebulun in v. 18 is a marked contrast.

17. **Gilead:** in the list of tribes we should expect Gad (so the Syriac version), as in the Blessings of Jacob and Moses. 'Gilead', like Ephraim, Asher and Naphtali is actually a geographical term, but like them comes to denote the members of the sacral community Israel settled in the region, in this case Gad. 'Gilead' here as a designation of the group rather than the region recalls 'Gilead' with a tribal connotation in Jg. 11:2. The absence of Gad from the tribes in Jg. 5:13–18 is supported by its absence from Jg. 1:27ff., and Zobel (*op. cit.*, p. 99) significantly notes that the first datable mention of Gad is in the time of Saul (1 Sam. 13:7), where it is located in 'the district of Gad and Gilead'. On Gad and Gilead, see further, above, p. 12.

and Dan, why did he abide by the ships?: this is a very questionable reading. Two Hebrew MSS and the Vulgate omit 'why?'; but the main problem is the reference to ships. Nötscher (*op. cit.*, p. 24) explains it as indicating the employment of men of Dan, while still in the Shephelah, in ships or about the port of Jaffa. Täubler (*op. cit.*, pp. 91f.), citing the supply of his subjects as dockers at Jaffa by a king of a Canaanite city in the Amarna Tablets (Kn. 294.18ff.), proposed that the reference was to *seasonal* employment of able-

bodied young Danites from Laish/Dan in the Phoenician ports of Tyre or Sidon, or, perhaps, we might suggest, to the employment of men of Dan to transport or escort merchandise overland to those ports, which might necessitate their temporary residence there, as *gāt* might suggest, always assuming that *'ᵒnîyyôt* means 'ships'. On this assumption, Yadin's view that Dan was a group of the 'Sea-peoples' which had made common cause with Israel in the Shephelah (see above, p. 241) might gain credibility. But still the phrase *yāgûr 'ᵒnîyyôt* without the preposition before *'ᵒnîyyôt* is suspect, though to be sure the omission of *b* by haplography after *r* in the archaic Hebrew script would not be surprising. We consider that the Rās Shamra Legend of King Krt has suggested the solution. There in a passage describing delay in attacking a city, it is said of the hero *gr 'an 'rm*, where we have taken *gr* as cognate with Hebrew *gûr* and *'an* as cognate with Arabic *'āna* ('to be at ease') (J. Gray, *The Krt Text in the Literature of Rās Shamra*, 2nd ed. 1964, p. 46), translating 'He abode, he remained at ease at the city' (*op. cit.*, p. 16). Hence we propose the translation of the present passage 'and Dan abode at ease', omitting 'Why?' and taking *'ᵒnîyyôt*, perhaps vocalised differently, as an adverbial accusative.
Asher sat still at the coast of the sea: i.e. in the coastal plain of north Palestine. Settled precariously in a restricted area where they were far outnumbered by the Canaanites (1:31f.), with whom they had evidently good relationships, Asher was probably not a militant group, but rather early *ḫabiru* who were employed as peasants, sharing the rich produce of the land of the Canaanite cities that they cultivated (Gen. 49:10) and being employed about the harbours, as the present passage suggests. Such, according to Mendenhall's feasible view of the emergence of Israel as the result of a social revolution in Palestine triggered off by the penetration of the nucleus of the Covenant-community Israel, were a not inconsiderable element of the later sacral confederacy Israel. Thus, despite being part of Israel in this sense, Asher was not able effectively to participate in the assembly after the defeat of Sisera, whose fortress Harosheth stood between them and Tabor.
by his landings: better 'bights', like the mouth of the River Na'mīn near Acco, or bights in the broken, rocky coast from Acco northwards.

18. Zebulun . . . Naphtali: though the former and probably also the latter have already been mentioned in the roll-call of the sacral assembly at vv. 14 and 15 respectively (reading 'Naphtali' for 'Issachar' in v. 15*b*, on which see), they are singled out again for special commendation in view of the transition to the hymn of praise celebrating the victory over Sisera (vv. 19–30). Their courage is strik-

ingly described as 'contempt of their life even to death' (*RSV*, **jeoparded their lives to the death**). The verb *ḥērēp* signifies 'reproach' or 'belittling'. The expression, if possible, is strange, and Ball's suggested emendation of *ḥērēp* to *heḥᵉrîm* ('devoted') may be seriously considered.
on the heights of the field: if the battle was fought on the slightly raised belt of basalt between the winter marshes of the Kishon near Megiddo (see on 4:7), the reference is perfectly intelligible. Alternatively, if the reference here is general, it may refer to the exploits of Naphtali in the hills of Galilee, specifically to the earlier victory over Jabin of Hazor at the Waters of Merom (Jos. 11:1–11).

The Hymn of Praise for the Victory over Sisera 5:19–30

Naturally less circumstantial than the prose version in the general account of the campaign, the hymn admirably supplements that account by emphasising certain important details in the actual battle, such as the location 'at Taanach, by the Waters of Megiddo' (see on 4:7). In five staccato couplets (vv. 19–22) the battle is described and the important fact emphasised that the rain and the flood of the Kishon was a vital factor in the defeat and rout of the enemy. A curse on an unco-operative locality Meroz (v. 23) introduces the blessing on Jael (v. 24), leading to the account of her assassination of Sisera (vv. 25–27), which at the same time is a taunt-song (a feature of primitive Semitic war poetry) on the fall of the enemy by the hand of a woman. The taunt element is accentuated in vv. 28–30, with a dramatic description of the vain expectation of Sisera's mother and the harem.

The Battle 5:19–22

19. the kings: probably refers to Sisera and his allies, the local rulers of the neighbouring Canaanite cities, who are, however, unnamed; but it is at the same time a familiar motif in later liturgical poetry, which similarly poses the antithesis between human and divine authority (see on v. 3).
at Taanach, by the waters of Megiddo: better 'by Taanach', a precise location of the battle (see on 4:7). After this statement Albright would date the battle and the poem rather precisely, assuming that Taanach was occupied and Megiddo was not, which generally accords with the history of those sites as demonstrated by archaeology, one being occupied while the other was abandoned

(*The Archaeology of Palestine*, 1949, pp. 117f.). This is not strictly accurate, and in any case Albright surely presses a poetic statement too far, considering the exigencies of parallelism, though to his general conclusion that the battle and the poem date to *c.* 1150 BC (*Yahweh and the Gods of Canaan*, 1968, p. 11, n. 82) we have little objection.

they got no spoils of silver: Hebrew *beṣa'* means 'unlawful gain violently extorted'. The *RSV* interpretation is probably right; but it may be a contemptuous reference to the exactions of the Canaanites from their Israelite neighbours, who were treated as *ḫabiru*, or underprivileged alien sojourners who were open to exploitation or conscription, a status which the Israelites still had in the time of Saul (1 Sam. 14:11).

20. From heaven fought the stars,
from their courses they fought against Sisera.

So *RSV*, rightly arranging the couplet. The reference is to a rainstorm, **the stars** being a source of rain in the Rās Shamra myths. Albright found a further reference to the 'eternal courses' of the stars, the disruption of which causes rainstorms, in his feasible emendation of Hab. 3:6 ('The Psalm of Habakkuk', *Studies in Old Testament Prophecy*, ed. H. H. Rowley, 1950, pp. 11, 12, 14, 15).

21. the torrent Kishon: *RSV* rightly renders **torrent** (Hebrew *naḥal*), the **Kishon** in its upper course being indeed a seasonal wādī, which, however, rises quickly and strongly in its lower course, swollen by flash floods from the slopes of Carmel and the hills of Lower Galilee as they converge upon it near Harosheth. In such conditions the current of heavy mud-laden water was strong enough to sweep away or head off Sisera's chariotry, which was at a hopeless disadvantage in the marshy ground which then welled up by the basalt dam near Megiddo, and in flight westwards where eventually the flooded Kishon 'headed them off' (so, with a change of vowels, for *RSV* **the onrushing torrent**). For the verb *qiddēm* in the sense 'to intercept', cf. Job. 3:12.

March on, my soul, with might: lit. 'Thou shalt stamp, my soul, mightily', the final noun being adverbial accusative. The language is so strange as to warrant emendation; cf. Burney (*op. cit.*, p. 148), 'Bless the might of Yahweh, O my soul', taking Yahweh as expressed by the single *yod* in abbreviation, after 'strength', and reading *bārᵉkî* for MT *tidrᵉkî*. Weiser, however (*op. cit.*, p. 91) defends MT, aptly citing the stamping of the feet as a gesture in the curse in Ezek. 6:11. The purpose also might be to accentuate the hoof-beats of the horses of the enemy in flight, which is onomatopoeically expressed in the sequel.

22. loudly beat the horses' hoofs: in MT the final *m* of *sûsîm* has

been inadvertently omitted before the initial *m* of the following word (haplography).
galloping: the repetition of the trisyllabic noun with the accent on the final syllable produces a striking onomatopoeic effect, while the repetition conveys a quantitative impression.
his steeds: *'abbîrāyw*, better 'stallions', from a root cognate with Arabic *'abara*, 'to impregnate'. It is used of bulls in the Rās Shamra texts, but of chariot horses in Jer. 8:16; 47:3 and 50:11.

The Curse on Meroz 5:23

Suggested by the blessing on Jael, which introduces the latter part of the poem. **Meroz** is unknown, possibly because it was a small Hebrew settlement like the peasant settlements of the Early Iron Age, noticed by Y. Aharoni in Lower Galilee (*Antiquity and Survival* II, 1957, pp. 142–50), which did not survive the curse laid upon it and all who should settle there (*RSV*, **its inhabitants**). The fact that it was expected to co-operate with the Israelites has been taken to indicate that it was an Israelite settlement (so O. Grether, *Das Deboralied*, 1914, p. 47). Alt, however ('Meroz', *KS* I, 1953, p. 275) suggested that it was a Canaanite settlement bordering on the Great Central Plain near Taanach, possibly identical with *mrḏḥky* of the Egyptian Execration Texts, *c.* 1800 BC (G. Posener, *Princes et pays d'Asie et de la Nubie. Textes hiératiques sur des figurines d'envoûtement du Nouveau Empire*, 1940).

23. Curse Meroz, says the angel of the LORD: (Hebrew *'ôrû mērôz 'āmar mal'ak yhwh*). Here *'āmar mal'ak yhwh* disrupts the metre, indicating scribal corruption, possibly of an original *'ôr mērôz 'ᵃlātᵉkā yhwh* ('Curse Meroz with Thy Curse, O Lord').
to the help of the LORD: in the 'war of Yahweh,' in which the sacral community expressed its faith and solidarity. The curse on those who ignore the call to war is cited in Jer. 48:10.

Blessing pronounced on Jael 5:24

Jael . . . the wife of Heber the Kenite: see on 4:11, 17.

Jael's Assassination of Sisera **5:25–27**

For similarities and divergences of detail, see on prose version, 4:17–22. The haste of Sisera and quick response of Jael are well expressed in two couplets, each of two stressed syllables, with an economy of conjunctions and subordinate clauses, which are used in a predominant 3:3 metre for the same effect in the final 'showdown' between Baal and Mot in the Baal-myth from Rās Shamra; cf. the advance of the Assyrian armies on Jerusalem in Isa. 10:28–32.

25. curds: the regular drink of the shepherd (cf. Isa. 7:15–22; and see above, on 4:19).
a lordly bowl: lit. 'a shallow bowl fit for nobles'. A similar qualification is found in the Baal-myth of Rās Shamra.

26. workmen's mallet: (Hebrew *halmût*; cf. *makkebet*, 4:21). The Targum is probably right in taking it as a smith's implement, the Kenites being itinerant smiths. There may be an intended contrast between this tool and a warrior's weapon, which would have made a more dignified end for Sisera. The verb *tišlaḥnāh* (third or second feminine plural) is taken as singular by *RSV*, pointing, probably rightly, *tišlāḥennāh*, 'she stretched it (*sc.* her hand) forth'. The form, however, may be the energetic form of the imperfect, common in the Rās Shamra texts, here misunderstood, as often, by late Jewish scribes.
shattered: (Hebrew *māḥ^{a}ṣāh*), common in this sense in the Rās Shamra myths. The verse reflects the fusion of two variant traditions, that Jael felled Sisera while he stood stooping and drinking the curds and the other that she drove the tent-peg through his temples while he lay asleep.
pierced: cf. Job 20:24; 'passed on from one side to another'. The verb *ḥālap* is cognate with Arabic *ḫalafa* ('to succeed'), hence Khalīf (Caliph, lit. 'Successor').

27. he sank: (Hebrew *kāra'*), envisaging the knees giving; cf. *birkayim kôr^e'ôt* ('tottering knees'), Job. 4:4. Here Sisera is represented as struck while he was still on his feet, as also by 'he fell'.
dead: (Hebrew *šādûd*), lit. 'devastated'; so Driver's 'undone'. The repetition of the words indicates the finality of the action.

The Taunt Song **5:28–30**

Here the writer adapts the theme of the women who welcome back the victor with triumph songs (e.g. 1 Sam. 18:6f.; cf. Exod. 15:20–22).

28. the mother of Sisera: as in the Israelite monarchy, the mother of the king, and not one of his many wives, was the first lady (Hebrew *haggᵉbîrâh*; cf. 1 Kg. 15:13; 2 Kg. 10:13. This seems also to have been the convention among the Canaanites and Amorites in north Syria in the fourteenth century BC, where a princess of the house of Amurru is termed 'the Great Lady' (*rabitu*), and the mother of the king of Ugarit evidently acts as regent in his absence in royal correspondence in the Rās Shamra texts.

gazed: i.e. 'looked attentively'; so *RSV* after LXX^A and Lucian's recension and the Hexapla Syriac, assuming the reading *wattābēṭ*. *AV* 'cried', as a rendering of the verb *yābab*, unattested in the Old Testament, might claim the support of the Aramaic and Syriac verb *yᵉbab* ('to sound the trumpet' or 'cry'). The parallelism supports *RSV* and *NEB* ('peered').

lattice: to admit air without too much light, and to preserve the privacy of the harem.

hoofbeats: (Hebrew *paʿᵃmê*) so correctly *RSV* (cf. *AV* 'wheels', and, better, *NEB* 'clatter').

29. her wisest ladies: better 'the wisest of her princesses', either plural as in MT or singular as in the Syriac and Vulgate versions. The 'princesses' (*śārôt*) are the harem of Sisera under the surveillance of the queen-mother, Sisera being thus a king and not a mere lieutenant of Jabin of Hazor. 'Wise' here, as often in Hebrew, means 'shrewd'.

30*a*. Are they not finding and dividing the spoil?': note the descriptive imperfect, used in the dramatic Rās Shamra myths and legends. 'Find' (*māṣā'*) often means 'light upon' in the Old Testament. The imperfect and staccato arrangement of eight words in four couplets, each of two stressed syllables, as in v. 25, conveys the urgency and excitement of the questions and the vivid imagination of the speaker, as well as the swift, ruthless action of the spoilers, which from the point of view of the speaker was not yet completed.

A maiden or two for every man: lit. 'a womb, two wombs to (each) head of a man'. The allusion is to the fate of captive girls, which was concubinage. The inscription of Mesha of Moab employs the same figure (G. A. Cooke, *NSI* 1, 17).

30*b*–*c*. The couplet probably contains dittographs and displacements and subsequent corruptions, and the most feasible reconstruction out of the component parts may be that of Budde:

šᵉlal ṣᵉbāʿîm lᵉsîsᵉrā'
riqmâh riqmātayim lᵉṣawwārî
Spoil of pieces of dyed stuff for Sisera,
A piece or two of embroidery for my neck.

Alternatively we might suggest retaining the second *ṣᵉbā'îm* of MT, the repetition indicating abundance, and reading with Ewald *lᵉṣawwᵉrê šēgāl* ('for the neck of the queen') for MT *lᵉsawwᵉrê šālāl*:

šᵉlal ṣᵉba'îm ṣᵉbā'îm lᵉsîsᵉrā'
riqmâh riqmātayim lᵉṣawwᵉrê šēgāl
Spoil of much dyed stuff for Sisera,
A piece or two of embroidery for the neck of the queen.

Final Imprecation and Blessing **5:31a**

Note the sudden address to Yahweh, indicating that v. 31 is independent of the poem in vv. 19–30. The passage reflects the consciousness of the consequences in blessing and curse of being in or out of the sacral community, more strikingly expressed in the Decalogue (Exod. 20:5f.).

31*b*. Deuteronomistic chronological note, withheld from the end of the prose account of the campaign in ch. 4.

THE GIDEON CYCLE

6:1–8:32

For literary analysis, see Introduction, pp. 205–211. The episode may be dated after the campaign of Deborah and Barak, since Manasseh has now emerged as a consolidated tribe as distinct from one element Machir in 5:14. The mass incursions into the Great Central Plain suggest a time after the Egyptian occupation of Bethshan, which lasted until the latter part of the twelfth century BC (W. A. Ward and F. W. James, *The Iron Age at Bethshan*, 1966, pp. 172–9).

1. Midian: the designation both of a people akin to the Hebrews (Gen. 25:1f.) and a locality in the hinterland of 'Aqaba (1 Kg. 11:18), where the name survived in a settlement noted by the Arab geographer Idrisi five days' journey from 'Aqaba. This region may have been the proper home and cult-centre of the Midianites, but they ranged into Sinai, where Moses and his people were associated with one of their clans (Exod. 3:18). Their aggression in the time of Gideon may have been connected with the domestication of the camel (cf. v. 5), unattested in the Assyrian inscriptions before the twelfth century BC, as Albright noted (*Archaeology of Palestine*, 1949, pp. 296f.), and with the general Aramaean influx from the north Arabian desert to Syria, as seems implied in 'the people of the east' (v. 3). De Vaux (*The Early History of Israel*, II, pp. 815ff.) raised the question whether the Midianite menace was seasonal incursions of nomads in transhumance, as 6:4 may imply, or razzias by highly mobile warlike bands. He doubts if 'camels' was an element in the original tradition, objecting that the Israelites could never have caught up with camels. The encumbrance of booty, however, would make this possible, and the concentration of Midianites in Gideon's decisive attack suggests that the incursions were more than transhumance for seasonal grazing after harvest, according to the age-long Bedouin custom. Midianite aggression in Transjordan is reflected in Gen. 36:35 and in Num. 22:4, 7; 25:6–18.

2. dens: (Hebrew *minhārôt*). This is a *hapax legomenon* in the Old Testament, and is possibly explained in the following word **caves,** in which case it may be cognate with the Arabic *minhāra*, 'a place hollowed out by water', though this denotes a water-course (*nahr*) rather than stagnant water. Another possibility is that the word is connected with Hebrew *nāhar* ('to shine') (Ps. 34:5, MT, v. 6; Isa. 60:5; Job 3:4) and denotes beacon-posts. In this case the situation would be paralleled in periodic Bedouin raids into Palestine till as late as the early days of the British Mandate, in face of which there were regular watchers of crops and signal stations on prominent hills. **The mountains** imply by contrast cultivable plains and valleys, which were often at some distance from the hill-top villages.

3. Note the frequentative tense of the verbs.

the Amalekites: see on 3:13.

4. as far as the neighbourhood of Gaza: if this is related to the Israelite settlement, it denoted in the original tradition rather the western foothills of Israel and Judah flanking the road through the coastal plain to Gaza, as MT suggests by 'until thou comest to Gaza'. But, in view of the action of Gideon in the Great Central Plain, it is probably an anachronism of the Deuteronomist or the pre-Deuteronomistic compiler.

5. like locusts for number: a common hyperbole in the Old Testament (cf. 7:12). C. S. Jarvis has described a locust swarm in Sinai 'ten miles deep, length unknown, but definitely over twenty miles' (*Three Deserts*, 1936, p. 217). In respect of the origin of locusts in the desert as well as in their disastrous effect (cf. Jl 2:3) and the black goat-hair tents of the Midianites covering the land, this was an apt description.

6. The entirely helpless and defensive attitude of the Israelites introduces the manifestation of the power and grace of God in the sequel.

7–10. A prophetic rebuke reflecting the framework of the pre-Deuteronomistic collection of the narratives of the judges in the pattern of God's contention (Hebrew *rîb*) with the sacral community on the grounds of their infringement of his sovereign claims to their exclusive allegiance, to which his great deliverance entitles him. This passage is a late insertion in the Gideon tradition, as is indicated by the repetition of v. 6*b* at 7*a* and by the irrelevance of the assurance not to fear the gods of the Amorites (v. 10) to the context of the Midianite situation (see further, W. Beyerlin, 'Geschichte und Heilsgeschichtliche Traditionsbildung im Alten Testament', *VT* 13, 1963, pp. 10ff.; and Introduction, pp. 206f.). The passage is significantly wanting in 4Q Judges [a], which indicates that it was recognised as redactional in a text still current in the first century AD (F. M. Cross, 'The Contribution of the Qumran Discoveries to the Study of the Biblical Text', *IEJ* 16, 1966, pp. 81–95).

8. a prophet: lit. 'a man, a prophet', envisages such a figure as Elijah was in Ahab's time. It is the first appearance of such a figure in the history of Israel, and may be a fiction of the Deuteronomist, as God's agent in his contention, which he elaborates (but see Introduction, p. 206).

The Call of Gideon 6:11–24

This is a composite narrative, consisting of the tradition of Gideon's call (vv. 11–17, continued at vv. 19–40) and the aetiological legend of the foundation of the altar of 'the Lord is Peace' (v. 24) at Ophrah (vv. 19–24), v. 18 being editorial. Common to both and facilitating the fusion is the element of the theophany. See further, Introduction, pp. 206f.

11. the angel of the LORD: cf. vv. 14, 16, 23, where Gideon's interlocutor is Yahweh himself. The angel (Hebrew *mal'āk*), or bearer of God's message, was here in human form and was not immediately recognised by Gideon. Doubtless human associates who raised scruples and were instrumental in nerving a man's holy resolve were so understood, and the encounter with the angel of God might even be the personification of a man's conscience when faced by what he recognised as the divine challenge.

the oak: (Hebrew *'ēlâh*). Actually terebinth, a conspicuous tree, which, like so many in Syria and Palestine, was anciently regarded as the abode of a local numen, Arabic *wālī*.

which belonged to Joash: Joash being possibly the custodian of the sacred tree.

Ophrah: qualified in v. 24 as 'of Abiezer', to distinguish it from Ophrah in Jos. 18:23, given there as in Benjamin, but probably originally in Ephraim (see above, ad loc.). The name is probably originally a common noun, signifying, as the Arabic cognate suggests, 'ash-coloured'. Aharoni (*The Land of the Bible*, pp. 240ff.)

proposed ʿAffuleh in the Great Central Plain, which would suit the location in Manasseh; cf. Abel (*op. cit.*, II, p. 403), who located it at Ṭayibeh, known in the Middle Ages as ʿAfrabala (Ophrah of Baʿal?), Forbelet of the Crusaders, *c.* seven miles north of Bethshan, which, with its villages was reckoned to Manasseh in Jos. 17:11.

the Abiezrite: Abiezer is given as a clan of Manasseh in Jos. 17:2.

beating out wheat in the wine-press: i.e. with a flail, or even a bent stick (Arabic *maḥbaṭ*), which was used for threshing out small quantities (cf. Ru. 2:17) when the normal threshing with ox and sledge on the exposed threshing-floor in a high, airy situation would have been too conspicuous. If *gāt* has the usual meaning 'wine-press', a rock-cut depression is envisaged for trampling the grapes, communicating with a deeper vat (*yeqeb*) for collecting the juice. But in administrative texts from the palace at Rās Shamra, *gt* signifies a piece of land, probably a feudal holding, so the present passage may mean that Gideon was threshing on his own plot and not on the public threshing-floor. This, however, is uncertain, and the meaning is probably that Gideon was threshing his corn in small quantities not *in* but *by* the wine-press, where he might hide what he had threshed.

to hide: lit. 'to cause to flee', with an Arabic cognate 'to escape, shun or move away', so 'to shift it out of the way of' the marauders; cf. R. G. Boling (*Judges*, Anchor Bible, 1975, ad loc.), 'to whisk away'.

12. **The LORD is with you:** benediction in the name of God is still an Arab greeting. In his reply Gideon shows his concern for present problems in his awareness of the paradox—which is shared by the Deuteronomistic Historian—between what was asserted in the historical credo of deliverance from Egypt and the inheritance of the land and the forfeited favour of God (cf. Ps. 44).

mighty man of valour: a technical term for a freeman of substance whose status made him liable for military service or for supplying a substitute; hence it often means 'a warrior'. It has secondarily a moral connotation and has been comprehensively defined as 'a gentleman and one expected to behave as such'.

13. **Pray, sir:** lit. 'by thy leave, my lord!'. Hebrew *bî* is possibly the imperative of *'ābāh* ('to be willing'), with the survival of the original final consonant (A. M. Honeyman, *JAOS* 64, 1944, pp. 81f.); cf. Gen. 44:18; Num. 12:11; 1 Sam. 1:26, etc., for the same formula of respectful entreaty.

14. **the LORD turned to him:** cf. LXX 'the angel of the Lord . . .' (see on v. 11).

in this might of yours: possibly refers to the courage of Gideon in having secured a harvest in spite of Midianite raids, and in venturing to thresh it, or it may refer to his strength of character in questioning the conventional greeting and showing his awareness that the troubles indicated an estrangement between God and the Israelites according to the solemn warning in the adjurations to the covenant-sacrament. Gideon was thus, in the view of the pre-Deuteronomistic compiler, a fit agent in the rehabilitation of the people of God. The apparently ungrammatical *bekoḥakā zeh*, where we should expect the definite article before the demonstrative adjective, is paralleled in Gen. 24:8; Dt. 5:26; 21:20; Jos. 2:14, 20; Dan. 10:11, 2 Chr. 24:18, etc.; and in the inscription of Mesha of Moab, e.g. *hbmh z't* ('this cult-place').

deliver: (Hebrew *wehôša'tā*). The verb is here used in its original physical sense 'to make room for; relieve from restrictions', as the Arabic cognate suggests.

do not I sent you?: better 'Have not I sent you?'. This surely discloses the Lord as the speaker, as is appreciated by the Massoretes, who depict Gideon as now addressing his interlocutor not now as 'Sir' (*'adônî*) but as 'My Lord' (*'adônay*) (v. 15); cf. the topographical tradition in vv. 19–24, where Gideon recognises the presence of God only after the phenomenon of the fire (v. 22).

15. my clan; it is the weakest in Manasseh, and I am the least in my father's family: the word translated by clan is *'elep*, which here obviously denotes the *mišpāḥâh* as distinct from the tribe (*šēbet*) and family (*bêt 'āb*). Since *'elep* also means 'a thousand', the word is ambiguous in notes of military strength and casualties, especially in oral tradition rendered in late redaction. A thousand may have been the ideal number of the clan, which was actually either more or, more frequently, less, which must be borne in mind when we study traditions of military action. That the saviour should be of such unpromising origins is a common motif of saga and folk-tale. In the collection of the traditions of the judges, it enhances the power and grace of God in his deliverance.

16. But I will be with you: so God reassures Moses (Exod. 3:12, E). Note the adversative particle in response to Gideon's diffidence.

17. show me a sign: this anticipates the passage vv. 36–40 (the fleece and the dew), which also belongs to the tradition of Gideon's call (cf. the authenticating signs at Moses' call, Exod. 4). The 'sign', or manifestation of the ultimate power of God in the world of sensible phenomena, authenticates a practical divine command. The phenomenon was often quite natural, miraculous only in respect of coincidence with man's need and the action of God, but in view of the supernatural power so authenticated it tended to be related, especially in saga, as also supernatural.

18. This connects with the incident of the food-offering in the

tradition of the theophany which authenticates the cult-place of 'the Lord is Peace' at Ophrah (vv. 19–24), and is probably editorial.
my present: (Hebrew *minḥātî*). This is ambiguous, the noun signifying both a present (Gen. 32:13, 18, 20, 21; MT, vv. 14, 19, 21, 22; 33:10; 43:11–15, 25, 26), whereby two parties are associated, and a sacrificial offering. Here the term is probably intentionally ambiguous at this stage, the meal becoming a sacrifice in v. 21.

The Theophany authenticating the Cult-place of 'the Lord is Peace' **6:19–24**

19. a kid: lit. 'a kid of the goats', cf. Manoah's offering at the theophany at Zorah, with which the present theophany (13:15, 19) has affinities.
unleavened cakes: possibly secondary, definitely implying a sacrifice, indicated by the large quantity of flour, **an ephah**, i.e. about a bushel, by the Levitical prescription of unleavened bread with sacrifice (Lev. 2:4) and by the final verb (*wayyaggēš*), which has the connotation of offering sacrifice (var. lect. LXX[A], 'he did obeisance' (*wayyiggaš*).

21. fire from the rock: fire is the conventional token of the theophany (cf. Exod. 3:1–6; Lev. 9:24; 2 Kg. 18:24).

22. Alas, O LORD GOD! For now I have seen the angel of the LORD face to face: a common conception in ancient Israel (cf. 13:22; Exod. 3:6, the theophany to Moses; 33:20, 23), which probably suggested the use of incense to preserve the conception of the *deus absconditus* in the Temple (Isa. 6:4; Lev. 16:12f.).

24. The LORD is peace: the name of the altar at Ophrah is suggested by the words of divine assurance (v. 23), or rather the story of the divine assurance was prompted in explanation of the name of the cult-place.
To this day: indicates the nature of the tradition as aetiological legend.

The Destruction of the Altar of Baal in Ophrah **6:25–32**

An aetiological legend, perhaps reflecting the appropriation of a Canaanite cult-place for Yahweh (see Introduction, p. 207). It may also be designed to explain the name Jerubba'al, which the pre-Deuteronomistic compiler assumed to be Gideon's byname. Originally Gideon and Jerubba'al may have been two distinct persons, the latter being a kinsman, perhaps even a brother (the son of Joash) of Gideon, who affected the Canaanite way of life. The reply of Gideon in vv. 32f., 'Let him' (*sc*. Baal) 'contend (*yāreb*) for himself' may animadvert on the opposition of Jerubba'al, perhaps as priest or custodian of the Canaanite sanctuary.

25. That night: it is impossible to determine whether this is editorial or part of the original tradition.

Take your father's bull, the second bull seven years old: the text here is awkward and possibly corrupt. Gideon is bidden: *qaḥ 'et-par-haššôr 'ašer le'ābîkā ûpar haššēnî šeba' šānîm* and in v. 26 *welāqaḥtā 'et-happār haššenî*, and in v. 27 he 'took seven men of his slaves and carried out God's instructions'. The phrase *par haššôr*, where both nouns mean 'ox', and the ungrammatical *par haššēnî* in v. 25, are suspect. We propose to solve the first problem by reading *'et-pûrâh haśśākîr 'ašer le'ābîkā* ('Purah your father's hired man') for *'et par-haššôr*; and for the ungrammatical *par haššēnî*, in the same verse, *pārah šemenâh* ('a fat cow'), and *'et-happārâh hašemēnâh* ('the fat cow') for *'et-happār haššēnî* ('the second bull') in v. 26, assuming scribal corruption in the archaic Hebrew script, which involved less emendation that at first sight appears. The reading *šāmēn* ('fat') for *šēnî* ('second') is assumed by LXX[A], which translates *siteuton* ('fattened'). Alternatively, MT *par šēnî* might mean 'an ox with his second teeth' (i.e. 'full-grown'), as A. Guillaume proposed (*JTS* 50, 1949, p. 52f.), citing Arabic *ṯinî* with this meaning. In v. 27 Gideon carries out those instructions, taking with him ten of his (or his father's) servants. They were required for the demolition of the altar of Baal and for the sacrifice on the new altar and perhaps for his protection. In the association with Purah, his father's hired servant, according to our reading, we may have a variant tradition to that in v. 27. But there may be point in the personal association with Purah in addition to the ten servants, he being a hired servant and so of a higher status. Purah is further associated with Gideon in his decisive attack on the Midianites (7:10ff.).

the altar of Baal which your father has: grammatically either the altar or the baal might pertain to the hero's father. If the former, he might be the custodian, as of the sacred terebinth in v. 11, and this is more probable. In view of the public interest in this hill-top sanctuary, it is unlikely that the reference is to a private cult of a local numen by the father of Gideon, the example of Micah (ch. 17) notwithstanding. On the other hand, we suspect that 'which your father has' (*'ašer le'ābîkā*) is a dittograph of the phrase earlier in the verse. The altar and cult of Baal at Ophrah would be a concern of the community and not of an individual.

cut down the Asherah: the verb indicates that **the Asherah** was a standing wooden object, a tree natural or stylised, representing the tree of life, symbolising the mother-goddess Asherah, as in Canaanite art (see on 3:7).

26. the stronghold: a prominent feature, possibly a high rock; cf. 'a fortress-rock' in Isa. 17:10; Ps. 31:2 (MT, v. 3), which served as a citadel of the settlement. A different cult-place is envisaged from the holy rock in the less conspicuous vineyard (vv. 11–24).
in due order: the language is technical (cf. Num. 23:4), here referring to the courses of stones, which, rather than a casual agglomeration of stones and earth, would indicate Gideon's *fait accompli* of the destruction of the altar of Baal and his dedication of an entirely new one.

31. Will you contend for Baal? Or will you defend his cause?: the specific use of the personal pronouns in MT emphasise them. The challenge of Joash with the threat of death to any who **contend for Baal**, if this is original, indicates his local authority and also the fact that, though the traditional Canaanite fertility cult was practised, it was incompatible with the official Yahweh cult of the sacral community of Israel. *RSV* **defend his cause** might better be translated 'effect relief for' (*tôšî'ûn*): see on v. 14.
If he is a god, let him contend for himself: cf. the irony of Elijah at a similar juncture. On the relevance of this to the name Jerubba'al only in popular etymology, see above, p. 207.

Gideon's Rally against the Midianites 6:33–35

This is in the Great Central Plain and forms a historical narrative (see Introduction, pp. 207f).

This was primarily, and perhaps solely, addressed to Gideon's own clan of Abi-ezer. The association of Asher, Zebulun and Naphtali may be secondary, but in view of the action in their vicinity, they may have been notified with a view to provisioning Gideon's force and exploiting the victory (see further, below, Introduction to 7:2–8 and 7:23). The involvement, in whatever degree, of Asher in contrast to their absence from the sacral assembly after the victory over Sisera (5:17) may well indicate a date for Gideon's exploit after that event, Asher's freedom of movement being partly thus explained and partly through the decline of the coastal cities of Canaan after the coming of the Philistines and their associates 'Sea-peoples'. The aggression of Zebulun and Naphtali is readily understood as in defence of what they had won by their initiative in the campaign against Sisera (4:9f.; 5:18ff.). The narrative is continued in 7:1. Gideon's moment of decision to act is marked by his investment with the spirit of Yahweh, on which see 3:10. The particular verb 'clothed' (v. 34) is rare in connection with possession by the spirit (cf. 2 Chr. 24:20), and may imply general recognition of Gideon's authority as the distinctive robes or armour of the kings of Israel in 1 Kg. 22:10, where the passive participle of the same verb is used absolutely.

The Sign of the Fleece and the Dew **6:36–40**

The conclusion of the narrative of the call of Gideon (vv. 11–17); see Introduction, pp. 206f.

This does not concern the moment opportune for attack as the present context implies, but the authentication of Gideon's call (vv. 11–17). It may be compared with the signs of the serpent and the leprosy in the call of Moses (Exod. 4:1–7), and here too the phenomenon and its reverse constitute the sign.

36. God: rather than 'Yahweh', is distinctive of this passage, and may indicate a different version of Gideon's call from the theophany in vv. 11–17, where the angel of God is evidently addressed as 'my Lord'.

37. a fleece of wool: lit. 'a clipping of wool', but a single fleece as the bowlful of water indicates. The dew would soon evaporate from the rock or beaten earth, and this is no miracle. But the reverse would be a miracle, belonging to the very stuff of saga, and so serving the purpose of the collector to emphasise the power of God independent of human ability in Gideon's enterprise.

GIDEON'S CAMPAIGN AGAINST MIDIAN

7:1–25

A historical tradition, continued from 6:33–35.

1. the spring of Harod: mentioned in the Old Testament only here, it is one of the springs of Nahr Jalūd at the foot of the north slope of Mount Gilboa, probably 'Ain Jalūd itself.

the hill of Moreh: ('the Hill of the Oracle'), probably Jebel ad-Dāhī, an outlier of the Galilean foothills, *c.* four miles north of 'Ain Jalūd.

The Selection of Gideon's Force **7:2–8**

Either an expedient to discard all but his picked commandos without giving offence, or a literary device to reconcile the original tradition of the exploit of Gideon and his followers from Abiezer (cf. 8:2) with the later tradition of the victory of all Israel (see Introduction, pp. 207). It presupposes, however, Gideon's summons to the groups about the Great Central Plain (vv. 34f.), which was a practical measure in the event of failure of his commando raid and for provisioning of his men and pursuit in the event of success. From the dream of the Midianite (v. 13), it is apparent that Gideon's concentration was no secret to the enemy. Even though he had determined on a night attack with a small commando force, it would still have been good tactics to keep the enemy apprehensive of hostility and potential attack from all directions.

2. lest Israel vaunt themselves: probably a theologoumenon of the collector.

3. trembling: (Hebrew *ḥārēd*), perhaps the relic of a popular etymology of the place-name Harod.

And Gideon tested them: so *RSV*, reading *wayyiṣrᵉpēm gidʿôn* for MT *wᵉyiṣpôr mēhar haggilʿād* (*AV*, 'and let him depart early from Mount Gilead'), which is highly suspect. If a mountain is denoted, Gilboa rather than Gilead in Transjordan would be most natural. Alternatively, we might suggest the reading *wᵉyiṣpeh mēhar haggilbôaʿ* ('and let him keep watch from Mount Gilboa'); or, closer to MT, *wᵉyiṣṣābēr bᵉhar haggilbôaʿ* ('and let him concentrate on Mount Gilboa'). If Gilead of MT must be read, the reference, assuming one of the last two alternatives, may have been to anticipate the sequel to the rout of the Midianites by the east, as actually materialised (vv. 24f.).

4–7. The test is generally taken as designed to test the vigilance of those who scooped up water with their hand as they knelt; but the difficulty is that in vv. 6 and 7 it is stated that those chosen were those who lapped and it is specifically stated that the majority knelt. The matter is complicated by the statement that those who lapped, like a dog (v. 5), put their hand to their mouth (v. 6). 'With their hand to their mouth' seems obviously displaced from the end of v. 7 ('. . . knelt down to drink water'). The test, we submit, was not to determine something that Gideon did not already know. We suggest that he had already determined upon tactics such as he actually employed, and had picked his commandos of three groups of a hundred (v. 16) from his own clan of Abi-ezer (cf. 8:2). The 'test' then, probably preconcerted, was designed to obviate inconveniently large numbers and to reserve volunteers from other groups without giving offence, which in such circumstances was too easily taken (cf. vv. 24ff.; 12:1–6). Those who drank, or apparently intended to, in the more unusual manner were chosen. That was lying down and drinking directly from the water as a dog drinks.

J. N. Schofield (*Peake's Commentary*, revised ed., 1962, p. 309) emphasises the danger of leeches, and in drinking directly from a stream the writer has often followed his Arab companions in sucking water through the folds of a head-cloth. Practically, this 'test' solved Gideon's problem; theologically, it served the compiler's purpose in minimising the part of man in the victory, which was God's.

4. and I will test them: better 'that I may sort them out' (*w*e*'eṣr*e*pēm*), i.e. as a goldsmith assays pure metal.

8. So he took the jars of the people from their hands: so *RSV*, reading *wayyiqqaḥ 'et-kaddê-hā'ām miyyādām* for MT *wayyiq*e*ḥû 'et-ṣēdâh hā'am b*e*yādām* (*AV*, 'and the people took provisions in their hand'). MT signifies that the main body ('the people') played the part that Gideon had determined, to supply provisions for his commandos; the *RSV* reading, which is conjectural, explains how the striking force had so many jars. The collocation of 'the trumpets' indicates that this is the correct reading.

Gideon's Reconnaissance 7:9–14

10. But if you fear to go down: Gideon's 'fear' was rather anxiety as to whether the moment or the mood of his men was opportune for the night attack he had planned. By his reconnaissance of the psychological rather than the tactical disposition of the enemy, he confirms his own resolution and secures an auspicious sign (cf. 1 Sam. 14:9f.) to strengthen the morale of his commandos and authenticate the divine oracle which had prompted him to attack (v. 9).

11. the outposts of the armed men: lit. 'the extremity . . .', to test the adequacy of the armed guard in view of the distribution of his striking force.

13. a cake: (Hebrew *ṣ*e*lîl*, a *hapax legomenon* in the Old Testament). It is possibly cognate with an Arabic word *ṣalla*, signifying a dry, consistent substance, like leather or baked earth; an apt description of bread baked in the ashes, as the Old Latin versions render.

tumbled: 'came turning over'.

14. Taking the barley bread as emblematic of the Israelite peasantry and the tent of the nomad Midianites, the Midianite betrays his apprehension and the disposition of the enemy to leave the initiative to the Israelites, and gives the latter the auspicious sign that they require. **Into his hand God** (LXX^{A} 'Yahweh') **has given Midian** . . . rather reflects the free narrative of the compiler than the actual speech of the Midianite.

Gideon's Preparation for Action **7:15–18**

Apparently a composite tradition, to judge from the narrative of the action in vv. 15–18. In vv. 15–18, when Gideon blows the trumpet, the others are to sound a blast and shout 'For the Lord and Gideon!' But in v. 18 there is no reference to the jars and torches mentioned in v. 16, which play an essential part in the night attack in vv. 19f., where another indication of the composite tradition is the war-cry 'A sword for the Lord and for Gideon!' It may be that vv. 15–18 originally knew nothing of the stratagem of the torches and jars, which were mentioned secondarily in v. 16 by a harmonising editor.

15. Worshipped: rather 'did obeisance', accepting the divine oracle communicated in the conventional form of the oracle in the tradition of the holy war (cf. 1:2; 4:7).

16. three companies: lit. 'heads', distributed round the enemy, as explicitly stated in v. 18; cf. Saul's strategy against the Ammonites, also in a night attack (1 Sam. 11:11). The torches would be of a smouldering substance which would blaze out when waved in the air. For a precise analogy, see Burney (*op. cit.*, p. 216), cited from Lane, *Manners and Customs of the Modern Egyptians*, 1890, p. 120).

The Assault, a Composite Tradition **7:19–22** (*see on vv. 15–18*)

19. at the beginning of the middle watch: cf. 'the morning watch', when Saul with his three columns attacked the Ammonites (1 Sam. 11:11). The night was divided into three watches of four hours each, so that the attack was made between 10 and 11 p.m., before the relief sentries became accustomed to local features in the darkness.

21–22. Apart from the war-cry, the only mention of weapons refers to the swords of the enemy. The original tradition probably implied that the Israelites drew their swords after the alarm with the jars and torches and/or the trumpets; but in the extant version only the tumult and shouting and the panic of the Midianites is mentioned; the Israelites **stood every man in his place round about the camp**. The activity of God is thus emphasised, as in the fall of Jericho.

21. all the army ran: perhaps, with a slight change of consonants, 'awoke' (*wayyîqaṣ*, for MT *wayyārоṣ*) (so Moore).
they cried and fled: so *RSV*, after *Qᵉre*, LXX, Syriac and Targum, for *Kᵉtib*, 'They put (them) to flight'.

22. Beth-shittah: 'the House of the Acacia', may have left its name in the small Arab village of Shaṭṭah, *c.* five miles north-west of Bethshan. **Abel-meholah** is probably Tell Abū Sifrī, *c.* ten miles south of Bethshan (1 Kg. 4:12). **Zererah** (MT, *ṣᵉrērātāh*, 'to Zererah') may be a corruption of Zarethan in the Jordan Valley (1 Kg. 7:46), just beyond Abel-meholah. **Tabbath** is quite unknown; but in view of Gideon's pursuit beyond Jordan (v. 25), a locality *Rās Abū Ṭābāt* below Ajlun is not excluded.

The Pursuit **7:23–25**

23. Naphtali . . . Asher . . . and Manasseh join in the rout; cf. 6:33–35, where Zebulun is included.

24f. Ephraim is enlisted to seize the watering-places on the Midianite line of flight.

Beth-barah may possibly be located where the Wādī Far'a joins the Jordan. As Gideon was already over Jordan in pursuit, the Ephraimite exploit (vv. 24f.), though historical, seems to represent an independent Ephraimite tradition concerning **the rock of Oreb** ('Raven') and **the wine-press of Zeeb** ('Wolf').

Gideon's Controversy with Ephraim **8:1–3**

Possibly prompted by the folk-saying, 'Is not the gleaning of the grapes of Ephraim better than the vintage of Abi-ezer?' (v. 2), this may be the Abiezrite version of the incident, and suggested in this context by the local Ephraimite tradition of the place-names, the Rock of Oreb and the Wine-press of Zeeb. Ephraim, the dynamic element in the growth of Israel of the ten groups in 5:13–18 and exercising hegemony under Samuel, already resented the assumption of leadership or independent action by any other group, as later in the case of Jephthah (12:1–6), by which time they had colonists beyond Jordan.

2. gleanings: (Hebrew *'ôlᵉlôt*), used specifically of grapes, summer fruits and olives (Mic. 7:1; Isa. 17:6; 24:13; Jer. 49:9), but not of grain. The allusion is to the capture of the chiefs. The reference to the victory as the exploit of **Abi-ezer** is noteworthy in view of our interpretation of Gideon's campaign (see on 7:2–8).

3. their anger: lit. 'their spirit', expressive of the invasive influence which altered a man, e.g. in prophetic inspiration, poetic exaltation, phenomenal physical strength, madness, or, as here, and in Prov. 15:32; 25:28; Job 15:13; Ec. 10:4, hot temper.

Gideon in Transjordan **8:4–21**

A tradition independent of 7:24f. (See Introduction, pp. 208f.).

4. and passed over: so *RSV* after LXX, Syriac and the Vulgate for MT participle, which is barely possible.

the three hundred men: if this were part of the same tradition as in ch. 7, we should expect many more in the pursuit. This is a different exploit by a permanent striking force, or a body of Gideon's clansmen, on a mission of vengeance. The definite article indicates harmonisation with ch. 7.

faint yet pursuing: a possible translation, but doubtful; cf. LXX[A], Hexapla Syriac and Old Latin versions: 'exhausted and hungry' (*ʿᵃyēpîm ûrᵉʿēbîm*).

5. Succoth: (lit. 'bivouacs'). Possibly Khirbet Deir ʿAllā, or one of several adjacent tells just north of the mouth of the Jabboq, where H.-J. Franken discovered evidence of metallurgy (cf. 1 Kg. 7:46); the name may signify temporary dwellings of itinerant smiths. This is the nature of the settlement as Franken's excavations indicate, and the reluctance of the inhabitants and their 'chief men' to co-operate with Gideon may indicate their affinity as Kenites with the Midianites, rather than that they were men of Machir or Benjamin or Gadites not yet integrated with Israel and in apprehension of Midianite reprisals, as de Vaux suggested (*The Early History of Israel*, II, pp. 771ff.). Contributing to their reluctance may also have been the fact that Gideon was bent on a mission of private vengeance.

Zebah and Zalmunna: ('Sacrifice' and possibly 'Refuge Refused') are either Hebrew word-plays on actual names, or artificial names given to unnamed chiefs in the light of the sequel. The fact that the chiefs are termed not 'princes' or 'leaders', as in 7:25, but **kings** corroborates the latter suggestion.

Are Zebah and Zalmunna already in your hand?: so *RSV*, reading *ha'ap*, the interrogative particle ('Yes, and . . .?') for MT *hᵃkap* ('are the hands . . .?'). *ha'ap* often introduces a dramatic question, but MT may be retained here, the hand of the enemy in the victor's hand either signifying submission or a trophy of victory, cut off from the vanquished enemy according to Egyptian practice (so Nötscher, *op. cit.*, p. 35), now further attested in the Baal-myth of Rās Shamra, where *kp* is actually used.

officials: (Hebrew *śārîm*). Probably active leaders appointed by the elders, who are mentioned also in v. 13. The defiant reply of the men of Succoth does not suggest the sequel to the victory and rout of 7:19ff., but a separate exploit at some considerable interval.

7. I will flail your flesh with the thorns of the wilderness and

with briars: the verb *dûš* denotes threshing, either by trampling beasts, or by threshing-sledges shod with sharp stones or metal points. Thus we consider that the preposition should be translated 'together with' (actually, MT *'et*, 'together with') and not taken as instrumental, the sense being that Gideon would trample down the bodies of the men of Succoth with as little ceremony as he would trample down the thorns and briars of the wilderness. In v. 16 the thorns are actually the instruments of chastisement (see ad loc.), but this verse may be a redactional gloss. The word rendered 'briars' (*barqᵉnîm*) is unknown except here and in v. 16.

8. Penuel: possibly Tulūl adh-Dhahab ('the Mounds of Gold'), so called from the yellow sandstone of which they are composed, standing on the Jabboq about five miles from its junction with the Jordan (so Albright and Glueck, after Merrill). Glueck located Penuel more particularly at the eastern mound, where he found Early Iron Age potsherds, and there is no reason to doubt this location. The first specific indication of Israelite occupation is the statement that Jeroboam 'built' (*bānāh*), perhaps 'rebuilt' or 'fortified', Penuel (1 Kg. 12:25).

9. in peace: better 'safe and sound', 'peace' being a secondary meaning of Hebrew *šālôm*, which means primarily, as here, a state of wholeness. The tower may have been a redoubt attached to an unwalled settlement such as those noticed as a feature of Ammonite settlement west of 'Ammān (G. M. Landes, 'The Material Civilization of the Ammonites', *BA* 24, 1961, pp. 68–74, fig. 3).

10. Karkor: unknown. It is probably a common noun, 'waterholes', 'wells' or 'springs' (cf. *qr* in the Rās Shamra texts). It may indicate some oasis in the north Arabian steppe, like Qorāqir, which played a vital part in the dramatic switch of Khalid ibn al-Walīd from Iraq to Damascus in the Muslim Conquest in AD 632.

all who were left . . .: connects the incident with the action in chapter 7, but this may be a redactional gloss: cf. Nötscher (*op. cit.*, p. 35), who suspects two sources here.

11. by the caravan route: rather a paraphrase for MT, 'by way of those who dwelt in tents', or 'by way of the tent-settlements'; i.e. the marginal land, possibly in the northern part of Transjordan towards the Hauran, where **Nobah**, also an element in the kinship of Manasseh, is noted among the tent-agglomerations of Jair (Num. 32:40–42), though the mention of **Jogbehah**, south of Penuel, seems to rule this out here.

Jogbehah: noted among the settlements of Gad (Num. 32:35), west of 'Ammān. Here Khirbet Jubeihāt, *c.* twenty miles south-east of the Jordan at ad-Dāmiyeh, may preserve the name. If **Nobah** is towards the Hauran, the distance between those two sites either describes a much longer campaign than is at first apparent or is a telescoping of different punitive expeditions of Gideon and his striking-force.

12. threw into a panic: (Hebrew *heḥ^e^rîd*). Not the expected description of the culmination of the expedition. The word may be a corruption of *heḥ^e^rîm* ('devoted to destruction') or *heḥ^e^rîb* ('destroyed'), which is nearer MT in the archaic Hebrew script.

13. by the ascent of Heres: a locality unknown, but familiar to the inhabitants of Succoth, and indicative of local tradition. The Greek and Syriac versions indicate uncertainty in the reading Heres. Aquila (*c.* AD 130), with a change of the sibilant, reads 'forest', which may be correct, MT being possibly a scribal corruption suggested by the similar word ending the previous verse. The element *l* in *mil^e^ma'^a^lēh* is now known from the Rās Shamra texts to mean 'from' as well as 'to', thus here amplifying the preposition *min*.

14. wrote down: already by the twelfth century the linear alphabet of twenty-two signs had been developed in Palestine. This was easily mastered even by minds less retentive than those of the ancient Oriental, which was so well trained in oral tradition, so that the ability of a young lad encountered by chance need surprise us no more than the alphabetic inscriptions left by Canaanite slaves in the turquoise mines of Sinai. On the local government of **Succoth** by **elders** and younger, more active executives ('**officials**'), see on v. 6.

seventy-seven: probably the indefinite number of saga; cf. the seventy sons of Ahab (2 Kg. 10:1), of Gideon (v. 30 and 9:2), the seventy souls who went down with Jacob to Egypt (Gen. 46:27), the seventy 'brothers' of the Aramaean king Panammu, slain by a usurper, and the seventy brothers slain by Baal in the Rās Shamra myth (Gordon, *UT* 75, II, 47–50). In such a context the number usually indicates totality.

16. taught: lit. 'caused to know' (Hebrew *wayyôda'*), or, assuming that the verb *yāda'* is cognate with Arabic *wada'a*, 'made them meek'. LXX and the Syriac version, with the change of one consonant of MT read 'and he threshed them' (*wayyādoš*), using the same verb as in v. 7, on which see. But v. 16 may be a redactional gloss.

18–21. The vengeance motif suddenly emerges. The killing of Gideon's brothers at Tabor cannot refer to the action against the Midianites at Moreh, since that was not a battle, but a rout. If there is any connection, it must refer to some unrecorded incident before this action, but it probably represents some different tradition from the narrative in ch. 7. For **Where . . . at Tabor?** (*'ēpōh . . . b^e^tābôr*) we may read, with comparatively little emendation, 'How . . . in appearance?' (*'ēkāh . . . b^e^tô'ār*). This is suggested by the Syriac version and the Vulgate, and agrees with the answer in v. 18.

18. every one: reading *'eḥād 'eḥād* for MT *'eḥād*.

19. the sons of my mother: perhaps in parallelism with 'my brothers', which would indicate the poetic cadence of oral tradition; but in a polygamous society it was practical to define one's brother more closely either as a half-brother or uterine brother.

20. Jether: a variant of Jethro, the truncated form of a theophoric name. The social duty of blood-revenge is given to Jether, the eldest son of Gideon, who thus thought to initiate the lad into the responsibilities of an adult in the community. The boy, however, shrinks from slaughter in cold blood.

21. crescents: (Hebrew *śah^a^rônîm*), cognate with Arabic for 'month', 'new moon'. The **crescents**, perhaps indicative of an astral cult, were used as amulets or ornaments or both on the camels, as today beads of blue glass are often hung on children, animals and even on motor buses among the simpler Arabs to avert the influence of the evil eye. Gold crescents (cf. v. 26) have been found in excavations at Tell al-Ajjul and other sites.

The Affair of the Kingship 8:22–23

This passage, with Gideon's rejection of the offer of rule (*mšl*) in the interests of the theocracy, betrays the hand of the Deuteronomist or his predecessor, the compiler of the traditions of the judges in the early Monarchy, who uses it as an introduction to the episode of Abimelech (ch. 9). Underlying the passage there may be the tradition of a local attempt at permanent rule by Jerubba'al the father of Abimelech, a local rival and kinsman of Gideon, with whom he has been confused (see above, pp. 207, 210.). The hand of the pre-Deuteronomistic compiler is evident in the invitation to Gideon to assume rule by 'the men of Israel', which is unlikely in view of Ephraim's resentment of the local initiative of Gideon (8:1–3) and Jephthah (12:1–6).

22. The title 'king' (*melek*) of Gideon or of Yahweh is not actually used in this passage, though it is implied in the hereditary principle mentioned here, and cited by Abimelech in 9:2ff. The conception of the kingship of God is generally particularised in the Old Testament in Psalms and the Prophets in the context of the conflict between Cosmos and Chaos, with its antecedents in the myth of the Autumn, or New Year, festival in the fertility cult of Canaan and the adaptation of the theme in the religion of Israel. It is expressed much later than the time of Gideon, when the assimilation of this cult and its ideology was in its early stages.

23. On the altercation here, its possible truncation and its ambiguity, see Introduction, pp. 209f. As it stands, it reflects the effort of the pre-Deuteronomistic compiler and the Deuteronomistic Historian to safeguard the reputation of Gideon and maintain the theological conception of Israel as a theocracy.

The Spoils of Midian and the Ephod of Ophrah 8:24–28

Verses 27*b* and 28*c* at least indicate Deuteronomistic comment, and the incident, possibly Gideon's dedication of spoils to Yahweh at Ophrah, is adapted to serve, with the incident of the attempt to establish permanent rule at Ophrah (vv. 22f.), as an introduction to the episode of Abimelech (ch. 9). See further, above, pp. 210f.

24. earrings: the Hebrew *nezem* signifies both ear-ring (Gen. 35:4; Exod. 32:2f., etc.) and nose-ring (Gen. 24:47; Isa. 3:21; Prov. 11:22). In the present context, the former is the meaning. **Ishmaelites:** note the variant to Midianites, as in the J and E versions of the story of Joseph. Hebrew tradition derives the former from Abraham through Hagar (Gen. 16:16) and the latter from him through his second wife Keturah (Gen. 25:1–6).

26. one thousand seven hundred shekels of gold: i.e. between 40 and 75 lbs, according as the shekel was the light or heavy one. The number is conventional 'a thousand' and '*seven* hundred), and the verse may be a redactional expansion, as Wellhausen suggested (so also Moore).

27. ephod: (Akkadian *epadatu*, 'a garment'). As distinct from the priest's loincloth (1 Sam. 2:18; 2 Sam. 6:14), this was a garment or similar covering to be laid over some symbol of the divine presence at a shrine, or worn by a priest. It was used for divination (1 Sam. 23:6; 30:7), and probably contained pockets for the sacred lots, the Urim and Thummim (Exod. 28:28–30, P). It survived as a relic in the high priest's pectoral, set with its twelve precious and semi-precious stones. The weight of metal in Gideon's ephod, if literal, would indicate an image; but v. 26 may be a redactional expansion and the tradition exaggerated or distorted through later theological bias. In congruity with the root meaning of **ephod**, we read it as the covering for the symbol of the divine presence either in sheet metal or in metal brocade, such as is attested in texts from the palace at Rās Shamra, and as such it may have represented the dedication of spoils in the sanctuary of Yahweh (the Lord is Peace), established at **Ophrah** by Gideon (6:24).

27*b*. The language indicates Deuteronomistic comment.

28*c*. This is also from the Deuteronomistic Historian, the forty years rest being part of his chronological framework.

Summary of the End of Gideon's Life and his Obituary **8:29–32**

In stating that 'Jerubba'al . . . went and dwelt in his own house' the compiler is obviously interested only in the deliverance effected by Gideon as a charismatic leader within the general pattern of his compilation. This is naturally followed by the notice of the hero's death and burial (v. 32). The statement about his 'seventy sons' and Shechemite concubine is secondary, prompted by Abimelech's slaughter of the seventy sons of Jerubba'al (9:5), which has led also to his introduction of 'Jerubba'al' for 'Gideon' in v. 29.

31. his concubine: (Hebrew *pîlagšô*). The designation may not be strictly accurate in view of Abimelech's status in Abi-ezer and his influence among the notables of Shechem. She was probably a *ṣadīqa* wife, who continued to live in her father's house (see W. R. Smith, *Kinship and Marriage in Early Arabia*, 1887, pp. 75ff.). The situation reflected the intimate and long-standing relations between Shechem and Machir, later Manasseh (Jos. 17:1f.), to which Abi-ezer belonged. Jotham's description of the woman as his 'father's maidservant' may be a case of the compiler's free rendering of the conflated traditions of Gideon and Jerubba'al.

Editorial Transition from the Story of Gideon to that of Abimelech **8:33–35**

In this transition from the story of the charismatic Gideon, divinely called and equipped for his act of deliverance, to that of the abortive attempt of Abimelech the son of Jerubba'al to establish permanent rule by intrigue and with the support of his Canaanite associates and the rulers of Shechem, the next phase of the history of Israel according to the pre-Deuteronomistic compiler begins. It is introduced, like the exploits of the great judges, with a statement of Israel's apostasy (v. 33), but that is set out in terms which indicate the Deuteronomistic Historian: **Israel turned again and played the harlot after the Baals**. The sequel in the Shechemite incident and the bloody coup of Abimelech is anticipated by the specification of the cult of **Baal-berith**, which was particularly associated with Shechem, and by the statement that (Israel) **did not show kindness to the family of Jerubba'al (that is, Gideon) in return for all the**

good that he had done to Israel (v. 35). The parenthesis 'that is Gideon' may indicate the fusion of two separate, though related, traditions, that of Gideon in what precedes and that of Jerubba'al the father of Abimelech, both from Ophrah and kinsmen, and possibly even brothers; see above, pp. 207, 210f.

33. Baal-berith: ('Lord of the covenant') reflects long-standing relations between elements of the later Israel and the people of Shechem, of which the first evidence appears in Gen. 34.

THE REIGN OF ABIMELECH

9:1–57

On this incident in the plan of the pre-Deuteronomistic compilation and of the Deuteronomistic History and its original political significance, see Introduction, pp. 211f. Note the animadversion on the attempt at permanent personal rule by a half-Canaanite with the support of the Canaanites of Shechem, and particularly by the garrison of the local fortress, backed by a personal force of desperadoes hired with funds from the local sanctuary of Baal-berith and effected by fratricide (vv. 1–5), which supports the condemnation of personal rule as distinct from the spontaneous response of the judges to the call of God and unlimited by the characteristic features of the Davidic Monarchy.

Abimelech's Coup and the Massacre at Ophrah 9:1–6

1. Note that Abimelech of his own initiative and, neither moved by the challenge of God nor motivated by any generous impulse interpreted as the spirit of God, nor indeed invited to rule, began his intrigues to that end through his kinspeople in Shechem, probably the local Canaanite element there as distinct from the traditional ruling class, 'all the citizens of Shechem', whom they succeed in persuading (vv. 2–4, 6).
Shechem: Tell Balāṭa, just east of modern Nablus in the pass between Ebal and Gerizim from the coastal plain to the Jordan Valley and commanding the hill roads south to Bethel and Jerusalem and north to east of the Great Central Plain, was traditionally associated with the Hebrews from patriarchal times (Gen. 34; 48:22), when there was a holy site in the vicinity (Gen. 33:18–20) and the traditional burial-place of Joseph (Jos. 24:32). Hebrew relations may go back to the fourteenth century BC, when one of the Amarna Tablets alleges that *ḫabiru* were admitted into the district by Labaya,

either a local ruler or a chief of the *ḫabiru* who, like Abimelech, exercised a local protectorate over Shechem (so H. Reviv, *IEJ* 16, 1966, pp. 282–7; de Vaux, *Histoire ancienne*, II, 1973, p. 109). This may connect with the association of Hebrews and the ruler of Shechem in Gen. 34, which was probably established by covenant at the local sanctuary of Baal-berith, 'the Lord of the Covenant'.
his mother's kinsmen: the influence of the family of Abimelech's mother in Shechem is assumed, which reflects on her status as a *ṣadīqa* wife (see above, on 8:31) rather than as a concubine.

4. seventy pieces of silver: a conventional large sum (see on the seventy sons of Gideon, etc., 8:14).
the house of Baal-berith: 'house' here, as in the Rās Shamra texts, means 'temple'. Temples were also treasuries, repositories of votive gifts, as in the Rās Shamra Legend of King Krt, and of spoils of war, like Solomon's Temple (1 Kg. 7:51). This temple at Shechem is identified by G. E. Wright (*Shechem*, 1965, pp. 80–102) after Sellin, with the large building, once double-storeyed, at the summit of the city site, which was built in the seventeenth century BC and destroyed after its third reconstruction in the twelfth century.
hired worthless and reckless fellows: personal retainers engaged in Abimelech's private enterprise, in contrast to the spontaneous following of the great judges. *RSV* **worthless** means literally 'empty', without visible evidence of material success, as the destitute and desperate who joined David in the cave of Adullam (1 Sam. 22:2). This for the ancient Semite, who believed that material success was a concomitant of moral worth, reflected on the character, which was 'hasty' (*AV*, 'light').

5. upon one stone: this was possibly hollow, to concentrate the blood, the baneful effect of which on the land (cf. Gen. 4:10–12) was apprehended by the ancients; cf. Abimelech's sowing of Shechem with salt (v. 45), possibly to neutralise the effect of the blood shed (A. M. Honeyman, *VT* 3, 1953, pp. 192–5), or as the ritual accompanying the curse of infertility.

6. Beth-millo: is distinguished from Shechem, as the Tower of Shechem is distinguished from the city (vv. 46ff.). Millo, from the verb *mālē'*, 'to be full', is a common noun, the Akkadian cognate of which denotes an artificial earthwork, terrace or embankment. At Jerusalem (2 Sam. 5:9; 1 Kg. 9:15, 24; 11:27; 2 Chr. 32:5) it may denote the 'filling out' by terrace and buttress of the steep slope and particularly the depression to the east between the ancient settlement on the south-east hill and the north-east, or Temple, hill in Solomon's time. Wright has established that the temple at Shechem (probably that of El-berith) and its precinct stood on an artificial 'fill' or esplanade (*op. cit.*, pp. 80ff.), which was a *millô'*.

Thus the people of Shechem and of Beth-millo may denote, not two distinct settlements, but rather the people of the town in general and an upper stratum, perhaps descended from the class of professional soldiers so characteristic of the city-states of Syro-Palestine in the Amarna Age (fifteenth and fourteenth centuries BC); cf. the Ḥara ('downtown') and Qaṣba ('citadel') in north African towns. An alternative name for Beth-millo may have been, as Wright suggested (*op. cit.*, pp. 126ff.), 'the Tower of Shechem', so called after the first temple on the site, which was sufficiently massive to have served also as a citadel. This would accord with the statement in vv. 46ff. that after the destruction of the town of Shechem the inhabitants of the Tower of Shechem took refuge in the Temple of El-berith. At Shechem it possibly means a redoubt, perhaps so called because of its revetted defences.

made Abimelech king, by the oak of the pillar at Shechem: so *RSV* after Moore, Nowack, Burney and Gressmann, with slight, and probably correct, emendation of MT. This may suggest the sacred tree of Gen. 35:4, respected by the Hebrew patriarchs, which, however, was not an oak (*'allôn*), but a terebinth (*'ēlâh*), and the standing stone (*maṣṣēbâh*), which was witness of the covenant (Jos. 24:27); but in view of the significance of the transaction for the men of Shechem, it probably indicates the tree and stone familiar in any Canaanite sanctuary. G. R. Driver (*JTS* 35, 1934, p. 390) would retain MT *'ēlôn muṣṣāb*, regarding it as the sacred oak which was 'propped up' through age.

Jotham 9:7–21

Jotham's protest in fable (vv. 8–15) and prose imprecation (vv. 16–20), introduced in v. 7 and concluded with his escape (v. 21). For the literary affinities of the fable and the fusion of two independent traditions, see Introduction, pp. 212f.

7. **the top of Mount Gerizim:** possibly an elaboration by the compiler, like the introduction of Jotham, to give dramatic expression to his criticism of the monarchy of Abimelech. If an incident on Gerizim is historical, some lower spur of the mountain dominating Shechem may be indicated.

8–15. *Jotham's fable.* Fruitful trees are too content and preoccupied with fruit production to seek pre-eminence. Only the low straggling buckthorn, which has a potential only to choke other growth and, through friction in dry summer, to start a forest fire, accepts the honour on its own terms. So the kingship sought and secured by personal ambition, without call, gift or sense of responsibility, but for one's own sole advantage, bodes only ill.

8. to anoint a king: the regular means of investiture with the royal office in the ancient Near East. Olive oil had healing and strengthening properties, and in the royal investiture special power was probably considered thus to be conferred. But administrative texts from the palace at Rās Shamra attest anointing as a rite of emancipation. In Egypt and among the Hittites, it was a rite in marriage and betrothal, and among the Amorites at Mari in the eighteenth century BC, it was practised in business transactions and conveyance of property. It signifies severance from former associations and initiation into a new status. Thus a priest through anointing is set apart for the exclusive service of, and association with, God, as indicated by the use of *qiddēš* as a synonym for anointing (*mšḥ*) in Exod. 28:41; 30:30; 40:13 (all P), *qiddēš* meaning 'to remove from the sphere of the profane to the sacred'. By this rite a king was removed from secular to sacral status, as the dedicated executive of God. Though initiation into a new status is the dominating idea, it should be noted that the special authority of the king was delegated by anointing, as in the case of Egyptian nobles with a special commission and certain Canaanite vassals of the Pharaoh in the Amarna Tablets (E. Kutsch, *Salbung als Rechtsakt im Alten Testament und im Alten Orient*, BZAW 87, 1963, pp. 1–78). In Jotham's fable the emphasis is on being set apart.

9. the olive: like the fig and the vine, specially mentioned in the description of Palestine or Syria in the Egyptian Tale of Sinuhe (twentieth century BC). All are admirably cultivated on the terraced hillsides exposed to the Mediterranean climate.
my fatness, by which gods and men are honoured: So *RSV*, after LXX[B]. The reference is to the use of oil in sacrifice with meal and in entertainment, e.g. Ps. 23:5, in the anointing of a guest with oil, where the verb (*diššēn*) is of the same root as 'fatness' in the present passage. Included in the honouring of men with olive oil is also of course the anointment of a king.
to sway over: derogatory and even ridiculous, mere posturing in contrast to fruitful contribution, and bending to the wind instead of standing firm and stately.

13. wine: actually new wine, the ferment of the must, which is also so denoted (*tîrôš*), being checked at an early stage.
which cheers gods and men: in libations (to gods) and, for men, at the Autumn festival, when wine flowed freely (v. 27; Amos 2:8), and in other convivialities.

14. bramble: (Hebrew *'āṭād*) *Lycium europaicum*, a quick-burning fuel, understood by Sa'adya as Arabic *'awsāj* ('buckthorn'), the low thorn-scrub, which, though it may rise to the height of a tree, affords a meagre shade and is fruitless.

15. shade: (Hebrew *ṣēl*). The word has a *double entendre*, 'protection' and 'shade', of which the buckthorn with its thin foliage has practically none. The *double entendre* of the word is familiar in the conception of kingship in Mesopotamia, Canaan and Egypt, e.g. in the account of the experience of the Egyptian envoy Wen-Amon at Byblos (*ANET*³, p. 28a).

the cedars of Lebanon: the acme of stature and majesty among plants and the antithesis of the scrub (cf. 2 Kg. 14:9).

16–20. *Jotham's imprecation* has the form of two long conditional sentences; the first (vv. 16–19) with three protases, the last repeated (v. 29*a*) after a long parenthesis (vv. 17f.) and the second (v. 20) quite simple.

16. in good faith and honour: (Hebrew *be'emet ûbᵉtāmîm*, 'in good faith and in all sincerity'). The second and third protases might be paraphrased 'assuming that you have done well by Jerubba'al, etc.'

17. risked his life: a good paraphrase of the Hebrew; lit. 'cast his life before (him)', or 'far (from him)'.

18. his maidservant: see on 18:31.

19. rejoice in Abimelech: it is noteworthy that Jotham's objection is personal, the name, or possibly nickname, **Abimelech** being an animadversion on kingship as such.

20*b*. Jotham gives an additional turn to the application of the fable. While warning of the fatal consequences of association with Abimelech, he drops a shrewd hint that the men of Shechem had the power to destroy him.

21. to Beer: this element ('well') is so common in place-names as to be quite undeterminable. MT *bᵉ'ērāh* may be a scribal corruption of *be'ᵉdôm* ('in Edom').

Deuteronomistic introduction to Abimelech's rule 9:22

The assumption of the pre-Deuteronomistic compiler or the Deuteronomistic Historian that **Abimelech ruled over Israel** (*wayyāśar 'al-yiśrā'ēl*; cf. *śārîm* of the notables of Succoth, 8:6) is unhistorical, since the sequel indicates that he exercised a precarious protectorate only over Shechem for a very brief period, and had come to power by the bloody suppression of local opposition in his native Ophrah. His three years rule in *Shechem*, however, is probably historical.

Revolt against Abimelech **9:23–25** (continued in vv. 42*b*–49, v. 42*a* being redactional).

On the possible telescoping of the events in vv. 23–49, see Introduction, p. 212.
Verses 23–25 are a general introduction freely adapted by the Deuteronomist, who in v. 24 emphasises the retribution for the fratricide of Abimelech. In vv. 25ff. the circumstancial detail indicates a genuine local historical tradition. The fact that Zebul held his place as Abimelech's city-commandant and was able to expel Gaal and his party from Shechem (vv. 26–41) indicates that the people of Shechem were not bitterly hostile to Abimelech, though in their own interest not willing to support his full authority. This encouraged Gaal's attempt, which obviously fell within Abimelech's period of rule, but was not part of the action of the Shechemites in v. 25 or of Abimelech's reduction of Shechem (vv. 42*b*–49), though his drastic treatment of Shechem was probably not unconnected with their relative complacency in the affair of Gaal. The whole is probably compiled from a general Israelite version, especially vv. 23–25 and 42*b*–49, and vv. 26–41 from a local Shechemite version.

Anarchy in Shechem **22–25**, the beginning of retribution for Abimelech; continued in vv. 42*b*–49.

23. God sent an evil spirit: the invasive influence which thwarted the purpose of Abimelech and disrupted the union which the parties themselves had willingly contracted. 'Evil' means here rather 'disastrous', describing the effect of the supernatural influence. A rough analogy is the lying spirit by which God animated the prophets to lead Ahab to his doom (1 Kg. 22:19–23).

25. The strategic position of **Shechem** and the narrow pass by two main cross-roads (see on v. 1; 8:30–35) gave great opportunities for brigandage. Nablus, Tulkarm and Jenin formed the notorious 'Triangle of Terror' in the British Mandate. The mountain-tops were occupied not as ambushes, but to alert parties in ambush of approaching caravans, the dative of disadvantage *lô* indicating the intention to prevent Abimelech's security measures or to undermine his authority. Possibly, as J. L. Mackenzie has suggested (*op. cit.*, p. 142), the rulers of Shechem resented Abimelech's claim on tolls from caravans which passed through their territory, which they had traditionally enjoyed.

Gaal's Rising **9:26–41**, possibly interrupting vv. 23–25 and 42*b*–49.

See Introduction, p. 212.
The sudden introduction of **Gaal** indicates perhaps a local tradition elaborated as an explanation of the main narrative of Abimelech's conflict with Shechem (vv. 23, 25) and his reduction and destruction of the city (vv. 42*b*–49).

26. Gaal the son of Ebed: possibly Go'el, but in any case a curious name; cf. *gō'al* ('loathing'), which may suggest a parody of his real name. **Ebed** occurs as an element in theophoric names, but not absolutely as a proper name. The form 'Obed is more likely, MT giving a wilful perversion of the name: 'Loathing, the son of a slave'. The identity and status of this man and his 'brothers' is unknown. But for the statement that he **moved into Shechem**, we might have thought that he and his 'brothers' were an influential family of Shechem; but 'brothers' in this case probably means 'party', of uncertain identity.

27. held festival: (Hebrew *hillûlîm*), properly a festival of praise, showing appreciation of the bounty of nature by uninhibited joy and shouting and liberal eating and drinking (cf. Isa. 9:3, MT, v. 2; Ps. 4:7, MT, v. 8). The fruit of trees in their fourth year, which was dedicated to God in thanks, was termed 'a holy thing of praise' (*qōdeš hillûlîm*). The verbal root probably denotes the exuberant licence of the marriage song in Ps. 78:63. In such a mood, local feeling against the half-Israelite Abimelech, who was not even resident in Shechem, asserted itself in the general cursing of him.

28. who are we of Shechem?: so *RSV*, reading, probably correctly, *mî b^e^nê š^e^kem*, as indicated by the following verb in the first person plural for MT 'Who is Shechem?'.
Did not the son of Jerubbaal . . . serve the men of Hamor the father of Shechem?: so *RSV*, reading *'ăb^e^dû* for MT imperative *'ib^e^dû*, indicating that Abimelech and his officer were put in office by the Hamor clan of Shechem. Another possibility is suggested by certain MSS of LXX: 'Are not the son of Jerubba'al and Zebul . . . holding the men of Hamor in servitude?'
Hamor the father of Shechem: cf. the apparently personal narrative of the relations between the family of Jacob and these Shechemites (Gen. 34). The men of Hamor in the present passage may be the dominant native clan in Shechem, **the father of Shechem** being a redactional expansion, after Gen. 34.

29. I would say: so *RSV*, after LXX, for MT 'and he said', which is not appropriate in Abimelech's absence.

31. at Arumah: (Hebrew *'^a^rûmâh*) so *RSV*, after v. 41 for MT *b^e^tormâh*; *AV*, 'craftily', which is just possible.

stirring up: so *RSV*, reading *me'îrîm* for MT *ṣārîm* ('besieging'), which, however, is not unintelligible in view of the fact that Zebul was in a city at least partially hostile, and is actually read, followed by the appropriate preposition *'al*, in a fragment of Jg. from Qumran (see General Introduction, p. 44). But Zebul had evidently freedom of movement and continued to have free communication with Gaal (vv. 36ff.).

33. rush upon: actually 'deploy', attack in open formation from concentration in ambush (cf. 20:37), and of a general attack, with the implication of deploying from concentrated formation (1 Sam. 23:27; 30:1, 14).

35. went out and stood in the entrance of the gate: not 'marched out', as he did not expect the enemy, who were in ambush (vv. 35f.), but simply 'went out' to the place of common gathering.

36. from the mountain tops: i.e. Ebal and Gerizim.

37. the centre of the land: Hebrew *ṭabbûr hā'āreṣ*, lit. 'the navel of the land'; cf. Ezek. 38:12 and Aramaic; so understood by LXX and the Vulgate. This was either a small hill, which would be east of Shechem, as the rabbinic commentators Rashi and Kimchi suggest, or more probably, in our opinion, the point east of Shechem where the roads north, south, east and west crossed.

the Diviners' Oak: (Hebrew *'elôn me'ônenîm*), an oracle oak near Shechem, possibly 'the oak of Moreh' ('the oak of the oracle-giver'). The verb *'ānan* is found of augury also in 2 Kg. 21:6, being possibly cognate with the Arabic verb *'anna* ('to hum', of insects or persons).

42*a*. This clause is possibly editorial, linking two separate narratives, vv. 23–25, 42*b*–49 and vv. 26–41.

The Reduction of Shechem 9:42b–49

Continued from v. 25. Gaal's expulsion with his party by Zebul indicates perhaps that the Shechemites were glad to make them the scapegoats, while Abimelech was at Arumah, possibly Jebel 'Urmah five miles south-east of Shechem.

44. rushed forward: 'deployed' (see on v. 33).

45. sowed it with salt: perhaps symbolic of irrevocable destruction. So the Carthaginians did in the Punic wars. The custom is otherwise unknown in the Old Testament. It may have been a prophylactic rite to neutralise the influence of blood shed violently (see on v. 5); or, more probably in view of the significance of salt as 'unproductive seed', to curse the survivors with barrenness and so obviate blood-revenge.

The finality of the note on the sowing of Shechem with salt in v.

45 indicates that vv. 46–49 refer to an incident before this and simultaneous with the actual destruction of the lower town. It is therefore from a variant source; so E. Nielsen (*Shechem, a Traditio-Historical Investigation*, 1955, p. 131). However this may be, this marks an end of Shechem as an independent community confederate with elements in Israel. It re-emerges in the tenth century as an Israelite town in the reign of Jeroboam I (1 Kg. 12:25).

46. the Tower of Shechem: see on v. 6.

stronghold: so *RSV* after LXX[A]. The word *ṣ*[e]*riaḥ* is known in the Old Testament only here and in 1 Sam. 13:6, where it is a place of hiding associated with caves and cisterns. In Nabataean funerary inscriptions it denotes a rock-hewn tomb. This might suggest a crypt over which the temple at Shechem was built, but there is no such feature in the temple at Shechem. The word in the present passage is rather cognate with Arabic *ṣarḥ*, meaning 'tower', as Wright suggested (*op. cit.*, p. 127).

48. Mount Zalmon: i.e. 'Shady', not otherwise known in this locality; possibly another name for Gerizim on the south side of Shechem with a northern exposure, hence more shaded than Ebal, which is reflected in a heavier vegetation.

an axe: actually in MT 'the axes', for which the singular should probably be read, the definite article indicating the object understood in the situation (GK, §126s).

The Death of Abimelech 9:50–55

The siege of Thebez is introduced to explain the death of Abimelech in fulfilment of just retribution (vv. 56ff., which are probably editorial). The motive for Abimelech's attack on Thebez is not specified. It might be an effort to extend the effective occupation of Manasseh (so de Vaux, *Histoire ancienne*, p. 113). But if Abimelech was, as we consider, throughout promoting only his own interests, it would represent an effort to counterbalance the loss of the support of the people of Shechem by the occupation of a considerable Canaanite town with similar strategic and commercial advantages, such as Tirṣah in the same locality (see on v. 50).

50. Thebez: located by Eusebius thirteen Roman miles from Neapolis (Nāblus), on the road to Scythopolis (Beisān), where Ṭubas is situated, though de Vaux (*op. cit.* II, p. 111) doubts this in view of the discrepancy in the initial consonants, following Malamat's suggestion that *tebeṣ* is a corruption of *tirṣâh* in the same locality.

51. strong tower: a redoubt either attached to the wall or, as here, independent, was a feature of Canaanite fortifications in the

Late Bronze and Early Iron Ages. It was surmounted generally by a battlemented platform projecting by corbelling, which gave the defenders the same advantage as machicolation (*ANEP*, Fig. 329).

53. upper millstone: lit. 'riding millstone', as distinct from the lower millstone, than which it is lighter, was either a cylinder of hard stone, usually black basalt, about a foot in diameter and several inches thick, turned by two women, by a handle on a central pivot, or a long ovoid stone rubber. The verb 'threw' (*wattašlēk*) points to the latter.

54. armour-bearer: for armour on the march or for spare weapons in combat (cf. 1 Sam. 14:6; 31:4ff.).
kill me: better 'dispatch me', in view of the intensive form of the verb, as in 1 Sam. 14:13.

55. Surely editorial, assuming Abimelech's authority over all Israel instead of a protectorate over Shechem with the support of a private army of mercenaries (9:4–6).

Editorial Conclusion **9:56–57**

Associating the incident of Jotham with Abimelech's reign and death and evincing theological interest in the principle of sin and retribution.

LIST OF 'MINOR JUDGES'

10:1–5 (*continued in 12:8–15*)

On the significance of the 'minor judges', see General Introduction, p. 22ff.

The passages on the 'minor judges' do not conform to the editorial plan of the stories of the 'great judges', or to that of Jg. as a whole. Hence it would seem that they have been included, perhaps selectively, simply to supplement the number of the judges to the conventional number of twelve, thus possibly to make the judges as representative of all Israel.

Tola of Issachar **10:1–2**

1. After Abimelech: it is uncertain whether the authority of Abimelech is here recognised among the 'minor judges', as the Vulgate assumes in regarding **Tola** as the son of the uncle of Abimelech (MT, *ben dôdô*). The association of Tola with Abimelech may indicate that some, if not all, of the 'minor judges' came to rule through acquisition of local power as in the case of Abimelech and the 'kings' of the small city-states of Palestine and Syria in the Amarna period. The notice that Tola 'arose to *save* Israel' **after Abimelech** may be editorial, the rule of Abimelech being regarded as a symptom of public backsliding (cf. 8:33–35) from which deliverance was necessary.

Tola the son of Puah, son of Dodo, a man of Issachar: Tola (Hebrew *tôlaʿ*, 'cochineal worm') and **Puah** (Hebrew *pûʾâh*, 'red madder dye') are names of clans of Issachar (Gen. 46:13; Num. 26:23; 1 Chr. 7:1); but clans were often called by the name of a reputed ancestor, whose names might recur in individuals of the clan; cf. Jair (v. 3), Elon (12:11) and Ehud (3:15). **Dodo** means literally 'his uncle' (so LXX and the Vulgate) and is often used as the predicate in a theophoric name. This may be the significance here, the divine element having dropped out, as not infrequently. **Shamir**, the seat of Tola, was in the hill-country of Ephraim, which is here probably a geographical term rather than an ethnic one (see on Jos. 20:7), since Tola was a man of Issachar.

Jair the Gileadite 10:3–5

Jair is given as a clan of Manasseh (Num. 32:41), and is probably another case of an individual named after the eponym of his clan. He lives in Gilead and may therefore be of East Manasseh, where his tomb is noted at Kamon (v. 5), possibly the Kamon which Polybius notes with Pella (v.lxx.12) in his account of the Seleucid wars, the name possibly surviving in Qamūn, *c.* two miles west of Irbid in north Transjordan.

4. **thirty sons:** suggestive of his substance, reflected in his large harem, which may indicate his influence beyond his own community (see on 12:9).

thirty asses: indicative of the dignity of each son (cf. 5:10; 12:14), which may be further indicated by their thirty cities (so correctly *RSV*, reading MT *ʿᵃyārîm* ('ass-colts') as *ʿārîm* ('cities'). 'City' may mean in this context no more than a settlement with a watchtower; see below, on v. 17. The **thirty cities**, however, may be a gloss suggested by **Havvoth-jair** ('the tent-agglomerations of Jair'; see on Jos. 13:30). If, however, there is actually a connection between the 'minor judge' Jair and 'the tent-agglomerations of Jair' that would indicate Jair's rise to power by his influence in the frontier area of north Transjordan, like Jephthah in the same region and David in Judah. But the correspondence of the name Jair may be fortuitous.

THE JEPHTHAH TRADITIONS

10:6–12:7

On the historical tradition of Jephthah, inserted between notices of the 'minor judges' (10:1–5 and 12:8–15), with whom he is associated by a similar notice (12:7), see above, pp. 24, 193; for literary analysis of the section, see above, pp. 214ff.

Editorial introduction 10:6–16

As the traditions of the other great judges notable for a spectacular act of deliverance, the exploit of Jephthah is introduced by the pre-Deuteronomistic compiler by a note in the conventional formula of the apostasy of Israel (v. 6), the wrath of God (v. 7), particularised in the attacks of Ammon for eighteen years (v. 8), the repentance of Israel and appeal to God (v. 10), the divine contention, *rîb* (vv. 11–14), the reiterated confession and appeal (v. 15), and the relenting of God (v. 16*b*).

The conventional introductory framework, however, is complicated by many accretions, e.g. the particularisation of the gods of the various peoples to whom Israel apostatised (v. 6*b*), the extent of the Ammonite raids west of the Jordan, and the expanded list of the enemies from whom God in his contention claims to have delivered Israel, e.g. the Ammonites and the Philistines. The double menace of Ammonites and Philistines may correspond to historical fact. But deliverance from Ammonites and Philistines and others (vv. 11f.) in the introduction to Jephthah's deliverance from Ammon, before God has even consented to the deliverance, is proleptic and betrays the hand of the Deuteronomistic Historian or the later redactor. Here, the restrained pre-Deuteronomistic framework to the collection of narratives of deliverance is expanded to Deuteronomistic homily.

6. Baals . . . Ashtaroth: see on 2:11 and 13.
the gods of Syria: better 'Aram', the Aramaean tribes of the north Arabian steppe, who were penetrating the settled land of inland Syria about this time. From inscriptions from the Aramaean states of Syria in the eighth century BC, they seem to have adopted Canaanite deities, their own contribution being possibly the cult of the Venus star Athtar. The reference, however, to the gods of Ammon and Moab, both perhaps astral deities, respectively Melek-ma (parodied Milcom), and Chemosh (see below, p. 313), and to **the gods of the Philistines** is vague and redactional generalisation.

the gods of Sidon: the gods of the Canaanite fertility cult, Baal, Astarte, Anat and Asherah the Mother-goddess, principally, but also El, the head of the Canaanite pantheon, whose province was order among the gods and, as in the patriarchal narratives, among men, on the evidence of the Rās Shamra texts. **Sidon** is probably singled out as a metropolis typical of Canaanite culture.
the gods of Moab: besides the fertility gods familiar among the Canaanites, only one god is specifically associated with Moab, Chemosh (1 Kg. 11:33; see on 11:24), associated with Ashtar the Venus star in the compound title 'Ashtar-Kemosh in the inscription of Mesha of Moab (line 17). Among the gods of Ugarit one *kmṯ* is named, but of him nothing but the name is known.
the gods of the Philistines: this is a loose reference, nothing being known of those, except Dagon (1 Sam. 5:1–7) and Baal-zebub (2 Kg. 1:2), probably Baal-zebul, both Canaanite fertility gods adopted by the Philistines on their settlement in Palestine.

7. **Philistines:** see on Jos. 13:2.

8. **crushed:** better 'shattered'. The word *rā'aṣ* closely resembles the following *rāṣaṣ*, and dittography is suspected, but *r'aṣ* is attested in glosses in the Canaanite dialect in the Amarna Tablets, in Aramaic, and occurs in the Old Testament, though only in one other place, Exod. 15:6.
that year: may reflect the regular office of Jephthah to be described in the sequel, with perhaps annalistic records. 'Year' (*šānâh*), however, may be a dittograph of 'years' (*šānâh*) in the following phrase 'eighteen years', or a scribal corruption of '(that) time', lit. 'hour' (*šā'âh*) which LXX[B] read here.
the land of the Amorites, which is in Gilead: i.e. that reputedly taken from Sihon, the Amorite king of Heshbon.

9. **the Ammonites,** like the Moabites on occasion (3:13ff. and 2 Kg. 13:20) raid west of the Jordan against Judah by al-Buqei'a (Plain of Achor; see on Jos. 7:24) and against Benjamin and Ephraim, north and west of Jericho.

11. **Did I not deliver you from the Egyptians and from the Amorites, from the Ammonites and from the Philistines?:** *RSV* supplies the verb, which is lacking in MT. The deliverance from the Ammonites and the Philistines is another difficulty, being in the future. Thus corruption of the text may be suspected, with redactional expansion. We suggest that the required verb was *hiṣṣaltîkem*, which *RSV* evidently assumes. This might then have been corrupted to *ṣîdônîm* (Sidonians), the first word in v. 12, which is also suspect, since the Sidonians are not known in Jg. or elsewhere as the enemies of Israel at this early time. Lagrange (*Le livre des Juges*, 1903, p. 190) suggested that the original text re-echoed the drama of

salvation in reading *he'elētî 'etekem* ('[did I not] bring you up?') after 'from the Egyptians', the rest of the verse with the mention of the various oppressors in v. 12 being redactional. The mention of the Philistines and the Amalekites anticipates the theme of Sam. **Maonites** may be a scribal corruption of 'Midianites' (so LXX), though 2 Chr. 26:7 mentions 'Meunites' together with the Arabs as enemies of Uzziah, and Assyrian inscriptions mention 'Magan' in north Hejaz, of which Ma'an in Transjordan may be a survival.

Prelude to the Story of Jephthah's Deliverance **10:17–18**

Anticipating Jephthah's appointment at the sanctuary of Mizpah (11:4–11).

17. the Ammonites . . . encamped in Gilead: a definite locality as distinct from a district seems to be envisaged, possibly Jebel Jal'ud, *c.* sixteen miles north-west of 'Ammān, or Khirbet Jal'ad north-east of as-Salṭ. The Ammonites were apprehensive of the expansion of Israelite colonisation (cf. 12:4) from the west to the fertile upland plain of the Biq'a, which they valued, as is indicated by their village settlements and watch-towers on the eastern edge of this plain (G. Landes, *op. cit.*).

Mizpah: a sanctuary of the Israelites in Transjordan (v. 18; 11:4–11), but unidentified.

Parenthetic Digression of Jephthah's Origins **11:1–3**

Perhaps cited from a hero-saga of Jephthah, but showing later influence; cf. the popular genealogy, which depicts Jephthah as the son of an individual Gilead (vv. 1*b*f.).

1. the Gileadite: as the following genealogy indicates, this is taken as an ethnic rather than a geographical term, as in v. 8*a* (cf. 5:17, where, however, the Syriac version read 'Gad').

a mighty warrior: this early mention of Jephthah's prowess may hint that fear of his domination was the motive for his expulsion.

a harlot: not a concubine, a regular member of his family (cf. 19:1; Exod. 21:7f.) or a *ṣadîqa* wife (see on 8:31), but a public prostitute (*'iššâh zônâh*), hence Jephthah had no legal standing.

Gilead was the father of Jephthah (*wayyôled gil'ād 'et-yiptaḥ*): evidently amplifies the statement that Jephthah's father was unknown. Perhaps we should read 'a Gileadite' (*gil'ādî*) for Gilead, final *y* having been omitted before the following ' in the archaic

Hebrew script. LXX[L] and the Hexapla Syriac read 'and she bore him to Gilead' (*wattēled legil'ād*).

3. the land of Tob: possibly the steppes north-east of the eastern edge of the plateau of north Transjordan, occupied by Armaean tribesmen, who were called in by the Ammonites against David (2 Sam. 10:6, 8). But a locality not so far north of the Jabboq may be here denoted (Noth, *Geschichte Israels*, 3rd ed., p. 246, n. 2). J. L. McKenzie (*op. cit.*, p. 145) has aptly drawn the analogy between Jephthah and his private army and Abimelech with his band (see above, p. 211f.), in virtue of which they were able to extend their authority, Abimelech on his own initiative and Jephthah by invitation, a situation which, incidentally, may support the view that the 'minor' judges mentioned together with Abimelech (10:1–5) and Jephthah (12:8–15) 'judged' in the sense of exercising local political rule (see above, pp. 22ff.). However this may be, the careers of Abimelech and Jephthah were the shape of things to come in Israel, foreshadowing David's career as the leader of a similar band to Jephthah's (1 Sam. 22:1f.), then a vassal of Achish of Gath with personal retainers (1 Sam. 27:1–6), then accepted as king in Hebron, a sanctuary of Judah and the Kenizzites, and eventually over north Israel also by a covenant 'before the Lord' (2 Sam. 5:3; cf. Jg. 11:11).

worthless: lit. 'empty'; better 'destitute' (see on 9:4).

The Appointment of Jephthah 11:4–11

A historical tradition, continued after the parenthesis of vv. 1–3 from 10:17f., v. 4 being an editorial introduction after the parenthesis. The sober and circumstantial narrative indicates a well-established historical tradition, possibly preserved at the sanctuary of Mizpah. The appointment of Jephthah, like his negotiations with Ammon (apart from details) indicates a straightforward account of his being given regular authority to meet an emergency, if not to more regular rule, rather than the divine call to an act of deliverance. It is only on the eve of action that he receives an access of the spirit (v. 29), probably the contribution of the pre-Deuteronomistic compiler as distinct from his source, and in vv. 4–11 his call to leadership comes not from God but from the tribal elders of Gilead, and with them he firmly stipulates for the recognition of his authority. Jephthah must safeguard his authority in view of his social disadvantage. The transaction is ratified at the sanctuary ('before the Lord at Mizpah', vv. 10f.), the regular authority of Jephthah being recognised as 'head' (*ro'š*) and 'leader' (*qāṣîn*, 'military commander'; see on Jos. 10:24), titles which are applied only to Jephthah in Jg.

6. leader: Hebrew *qāṣîn*, here in a military sense, as of the commanders of Israel in the battle of Gibeon and its sequel; see on Jos. 10:24.

8. the inhabitants of Gilead: the wider district, the name of which survives in Kh. Jil'ad, just south of the middle course of the Jabboq.

11. spoke all his words before the LORD at Mizpah: Mizpah was thus a central sanctuary of the various groups worshipping Yahweh east of Jordan, which gave the agreement its validity. The transaction is somewhat reminiscent of the regularisation of Saul's kingly office at the sanctuary of Gilgal (1 Sam. 11:14f.), and of the adoption of David as king of Israel by covenant 'before the Lord' at Hebron (2 Sam. 5:3). **all his words** refers to Jephthah's stipulation in v. 9 and the elders' agreement in v. 10. **Mizpah**, with its sanctuary of Yahweh in Gilead, is not certainly identified. The place and its significance is noticed in the covenant between Jacob and Laban in Gen. 31:49, where it was identified with Gilead, explained popularly as 'the Cairn of Witness', suggesting a specific place in the district Gilead, as possibly in 10:17.

Diplomatic exchanges with Ammon 11:12–28

It has been noticed that the localities mentioned in the alleged correspondence were not in Ammon, but in Moab, and that the reference to 'Chemosh your God' (v. 24) indicates that Jephthah was dealing with Moab. It is thus argued that he was involved in a war with Moab as well as the better known war with Ammon, with which the sequel is concerned, but that the details of the Moabite campaign have been lost (so Eissfeldt, *Die Quellen des Richterbuches*, 1925, p. 283). Nötscher (*op. cit.*, p. 48) found it natural that Moab should have supported Ammon against the Israelites. It is very doubtful, however, if more than the bare fact of Jephthah's negotiations with the Ammonite king is part of the historical tradition. The appeal to the occupation of the former Amorite kingdom of Sihon by right of the sword and the strong reflection of the tradition of the occupation of the Promised Land (cf. Num. 14–22; Dt. 2) indicate free adaptation by the Deuteronomistic Historian, though the 'three hundred years' occupation of the kingdom of Sihon agrees only very broadly with the schematic chronology of the Deuteronomist (see General Introduction, pp. 4f.).

12. my land: Jephthah adopts the language best understood by the king of Ammon, making clear at the same time that the Israelites in Transjordan had a regular representative and leader.

13. From the Arnon to the Jabbok and to the Jordan: the Amorite kingdom of Sihon, reputedly conquered from Moab before the Israelite settlement of Reuben and Gad (Jos. 13:15–28); cf. Num. 21:27–30; Jer. 48:45, and other passages *passim*, which incorporate laments from Moab from this earlier period. On Arnon (Wādī Mūjib) and Jabbok (Nahr az-Zarqā), *c.* fifty miles further north, see on Jos. 12:1–6. The Ammonites, always referred to by their tribal designation 'sons of Ammon', were settled generally east of this region, though they claimed the fertile upland plain of the Biq'a, north of the modern village of Suweileḥ, having settlements of open villages protected by watchtowers of dry stone walling on the higher ground along the eastern edge of this depression (G. M. Landes, *op. cit.*).

19. Heshbon: modern Ḥesbān, or the adjacent mound of al-'al (see on Jos. 9:10).

20. did not trust Israel to pass through his territory: perhaps rather, on the analogy of Arabic, 'did not give Israel safe-conduct . . .' (G. R. Driver, cited by C. A. Simpson, *op. cit.*, p. 48). **Jahaz:** see on Jos. 21:36.

24. Chemosh: the national god of Moab; see on 10:6. This is a classic expression of Israelite henotheism, the recognition and worship of Yahweh only in Israel and the admission of the existence and authority of other gods among their worshippers. The Deuteronomist in his free construction of the situation is trying to reproduce conditions of the times.

26. Aroer: the association with **Heshbon** may indicate the place of that name near 'Ammān (see on Jos. 13:24–28), while the mention of **the Arnon** may indicate Aroer (modern Khirbet 'Arā'ir, just north of the Wādī Mūjib (see on Jos. 12:2).

The Ammonite Campaign, including Jephthah's Vow 11:29–33

29. the Spirit of the LORD came upon Jephthah: his call to leadership (vv. 4–11), though ratified at the sanctuary of Mizpah, and his negotiations with the king of Ammon (vv. 12–28) had been on human initiative. The moment of action is marked for the pre-Deuteronomistic compiler by the divine initiative. In view of his systematic recruiting march before he actually attacked, it seems as if this note on his accession of the spirit is introduced by the compiler to bring the exploits of Jephthah into conformity with his presentation of the traditions of the other great judges.

he passed through Gilead and Manasseh, and . . . Mizpah of Gilead, and . . . to the Ammonites: after regularising his call to leadership at the sanctuary of Mizpah (v. 11), Jephthah may have returned to Ṭob, probably to organise his striking-force, the nucleus of which was doubtless the band of personal retainers he had gathered there, which it would have been indiscreet to bring to the assembly at Mizpah. His return, which is described from the north, is probably a recruiting march.

30. Jephthah made a vow to the LORD: since this was, most naturally, before he proceeded against the Ammonites, and was entered into at the sanctuary at Mizpah, 'to the Ammonites' in v. 29 is proleptic. The vow may have been occasioned by the disappointing response to his recruiting march; but by its specified formula **If thou wilt give the Ammonites into my hand . . .** it serves the purpose of the collector to emphasise the divine aspect in the deliverance. The historical tradition is interwoven with the story of the vow and its discharge (vv. 34–39*a*), which is related aetiologically to the annual mourning of the virgins on the mountains (vv. 39*b*–40). There was probably a historical basis for the tradition of the vow and its tragic discharge (cf. 1 Sam. 1:11); but this tradition was appropriated in explanation of the mourning-rite, which was originally quite independent of such historical associations.

31. whoever: var. 'whatever', but MT (the participle) is patient of both translations. A person of Jephthah's household may be envisaged; cf. Mesha's sacrifice of his eldest son (2 Kg. 3:26f.) as an expression of the total commitment of the subject into the hand of his god.

32. crossed over to the Ammonites: note that Jephthah advanced against the Ammonites *after* his vow (cf. v. 29 and note on v. 30).

33. from Aroer: probably that near 'Amman (Jos. 13:25), and not Aroer on the Arnon.

Minnith: location uncertain, but probably south of 'Ammān, as Eusebius suggests.

Abel-keramim ('Stream of the Vineyards'): location unknown.

twenty cities: it is uncertain whether this refers to places between **Aroer** and **Minnith**, which in this case would be more distant than Eusebius suggests, or to the total number of places captured in the war. In view of the quite small settlements designated as **cities**, this is a limited gain and represents the successful result of a frontier affair. Those **cities** or fortified settlements probably included the Ammonite villages with their round watchtowers on the eastern edge of the Biq'a, which now passed into Israelite hands and were the major acquisition of the war.

The Discharge of Jephthah's Vow, with Aetiological Application
11:34–40

A historical tradition adapted as an aetiological legend explaining a local custom, probably a fertility rite (see on v. 37).

34. his daughter came out to meet him with timbrels and with dances: cf. Miriam and the women in Exod. 15:20, and the women on the triumphant return of Saul and David (1 Sam. 18:6ff.). They sang, probably antiphonally (1 Sam. 18:7). **Timbrels** were properly small drums.

his only child: the Hebrew is very emphatic on this point. With her his name died and he was utterly extinct.

35. rent his clothes: a conventional expression of grief in the ancient Near East, probably a modification of rending the skin, graphically attested as a mourning rite in the Rās Shamra texts.

brought me very low: lit. 'brought me to my knees' (Hebrew *hikra'tînî*), i.e. 'enervated me'. The consonants, however, in a different order, may indicate 'thou hast brought trouble upon me' (*he'ekartînî*).

you have become the cause of great trouble to me: this should probably be retained notwithstanding variant readings in the Greek and Latin versions ('you are a stumbling-block in my eyes'). Jephthah's life had been clouded by the hostility of his kindred, who had forced him to lead a turbulent life among brigands. Now that he is restored with honour, his own daughter is the unwitting cause of his undoing. The Arabic cognate of the Hebrew verb 'to trouble' (*'ākar*, used also in Jos. 7:24–26) means 'to foul with mud'.

37. that I may go and wander upon the mountains: so *RSV* probably correctly for MT 'that I may go and go down . . .', reading *weradtî* for MT *weyāradtî*. The verb *rûd* ('to wander, be restless') is rare, but attested in Jer. 2:31, and probably in Ps. 55:2 (MT, v. 3).

bewail my virginity: in the narrative this implies mourning that she should die before wedding and motherhood. **Virginity**, however, may have been suggested by a fertility rite which had its prototype in the mourning of the goddess Anat, whose stock epithet in the Rās Shamra texts is 'the Virgin', for the dead Baal in the Canaanite fertility cult, which is actually described in the Baal-myth from Rās Shamra:

Anat too goes and ranges
Every mountain in the heart of the land,
Every hill in the midst of the fields . . .

The historification of this fertility rite may be an attempt to gloss it over, or it may be a more artless assimilation after the real significance of the rite had been forgotten. The part of the women in such ritual at transitional seasons may be noted; cf. the role of Anat and other females at such junctures in the myths and legends of Rās Shamra and of the women in Jerusalem who wept for Tammuz (Ezek. 8:14) and of those who mourned for Hadad-Rimmon (Zech. 12:11) where, however, women are not specified.

40. to lament: so LXX and the Vulgate; cf. Hebrew *l^etannôt*. The verb *tānāh* is found in 5:11, where we have suggested that, cognate with Ugaritic *t̠ny* and Arabic *t̠anay*, it may signify repetition or recounting, probably in antiphonal chant. Here it might mean the re-enactment of the weeping of Jephthah's daughter.

The Rivalry of Ephraim and Gilead 12:1–6

The similarity of this incident, at least in the beginning, to the incident in 8:1–3, has suggested to certain scholars since Wellhausen (e.g. more recently Alt and Täubler) that the incident is secondary here, suggested by 8:1–3. The motif of the emulation of Ephraim apart, the two passages are markedly different, especially in their conclusion, and the Shibboleth incident seems too circumstantial not to be genuine, while the saying about the gleaning of Ephraim and the vintage of Abi-ezer (8:2) must surely be related to the aftermath of Gideon's victory over the Midianites. Both surely reflect the aspirations of Ephraim, later realised in their hegemony in the time of Samuel. There may, however, be a fusion of traditions in the ostensible cause of the quarrel, the exclusion of Ephraim from the exploit in Transjordan (v. 1; cf. 8:1). The real reason for the drastic action of Ephraim was possibly the suspicion of a local Israelite ruler in Transjordan (so Hertzberg, *op. cit.*, p. 218), who had already taken independent action, a situation which might disrupt the integrity of the sacral community realised in 5:13–18. This may be an adumbration of the attitude of Ephraim with Samuel to the authority of Saul.

1. were called to arms: lit. 'were called'.

to Zaphon: so *RSV* after certain MSS of LXX and the Old Latin version, which is preferable to *AV* 'northward'. Zaphon was north of Succoth, east of Jordan, near the mouth of the Jabbok, according to Jos. 13:27.

2. my people: better 'my kindred' (Hebrew *'ammî*). See on 5:14.

I called you: this appeal is not previously mentioned, but is possibly implied in the extremity in which Jephthah made his desperate vow (see on 11:29). His recruiting march probably affected settlers from Ephraim in Transjordan (cf. v. 4).

3. took my life in my hand: lit. 'I put my life in my hand', the

regular Hebrew idiom for the supreme risk; but, in view of the ancient Hebrew conception of the survival of a man in his family, this had particular point in Jephthah's sacrifice of his only daughter.
come up: a technical term 'to attack' (see on Jos. 22:12).

4. **gathered:** indicates some time after the end of the Ammonite campaign, when Jephthah had settled in Mizpah (11:34).
because they said, 'You are fugitives from Ephraim, you Gileadites, in the midst of Ephraim and Manasseh': though East Manasseh was settled from the west, there is no reference except here to a settlement of Ephraimites in Transjordan. The omission of the words in certain MSS of LXX suggests that they may be repeated by a scribal error from v. 5, 'when any of the fugitives of Ephraim said', with subsequent adjustment of the corrupt text. The fact that the word translated 'fugitives' (*p^e^lîṭê*) means 'survivors' supports this explanation of the text. Alternatively, if MT is correct, the word might refer to elements of Ephraim who had survived some disaster, such as a famine, by migration to Transjordan.

5. **Against the Ephraimites:** the preposition introduces the dative of disadvantage, as in 3:28 and 7:24.

6. **Shibboleth:** lit. 'ear of corn' or 'stream'. The difference of the pronunciation of the sibilant, which corresponds to the variation in Hebrew and Arabic, indicates the piecemeal nature of the Hebrew settlement and the local independence of the various groups.
forty-two thousand: evident exaggeration. 'Forty' is the conventional indefinite number of Semitic folk-legend and saga and 'two' may be added to give the semblance of verisimilitude. 'Forty-two' has this significance in the story of Elisha and the rude boys of Bethel (2 Kg. 2:24), Jehu's slaughter of the royal family of Judah (2 Kg. 10:14) and is the number of the months of the reign of the beast in Rev. 13:5. The number has the same significance as 'fifty siller bells and nine' in ballad poetry of the Scottish Border.

Death of Jephthah **12:7**

7. On the significance of the obituary of Jephthah, like the rest of the 'minor judges', see Introduction to Jg., pp. 24, 193. The name of the place where he was buried is, surprisingly, omitted, and LXX reads 'in his city in Gilead' (so *RSV*). Josephus evidently knew a reading which was a corruption of 'in Mizpah in Gilead'. MT *b^eʿārê gilʿād*, however, might mean 'in one of the cities of Gilead' (GK §124o).

LIST OF THE 'MINOR JUDGES'

12:8–15 (*continued from 10:1–5; 12:7*)

See above, p. 310.

8. Ibzan: the name is not elsewhere attested, and, as certain MSS of LXX suggest, may be Abiṣan or Abeṣṣan. The tribal affinity of Ibzan is not noted like the other 'minor judges' except Abdon. It is not stated if Bethlehem was the well-known Bethlehem of Judah, or Bethlehem in Zebulun (Jos. 19:15) in the Galilean foothills, *c.* seven miles west-south-west of Nazareth. Josephus understood it to be in Judah, and it may be that a judge of repute or local ruler from Judah was included by the pre-Deuteronomistic compiler to give Judah representation among the 'minor judges' as Othniel was included among the great 'deliverers'. But the predominating interest in the situation in the 'Israel' in the north of 5:13–18 indicates that Bethlehem was in Zebulun.

9. The notice of large families is a notable feature of the passages on the 'minor judges' (cf. 10:4; 12:14). This implies a large harem, betokening the prestige of the 'judge' and probably exogamy to increase his affinities and political influence: cf. David's marriage with Kenizzites (1 Sam. 25:42f.), women of Jerusalem, hitherto outside Israel (2 Sam. 5:13), and with an Aramaean princess of Geshur (2 Sam. 3:3). Ibzan's policy of exogamy for his large family had probably the same significance.

11. Elon: the name of a clan in Zebulun (Gen. 46:14; Num. 26:26); cf. Tola of Issachar (10:1) and Jair of Manasseh (10:3–5), possibly a case of the recurrence of the name of the eponymous ancestor of the clan. The settlement was named after the clan, **Aijalon** being simply a different vocalisation of Elon. This Aijalon in Zebulun in the Great Central Plain or the foothills of south-western Galilee, which incidentally is not mentioned in the description of the territory of Zebulun in Jos. 19:10–16, must be distinguished from Aijalon in the foothills of the hill-country of Ephraim.

13. Abdon . . . the Pirathonite: like Ibzan, Abdon is designated only by his local, and not by tribal affinities. 'The Pir'athonite' suggests the ancient site by the Arab village of Far'ata, *c.* eight miles south-west of Nāblus, as is indicated by its location in Ephraim (v. 14). This would be the one case of an Ephraimite among the 'minor judges'.

14. forty sons and thirty grandsons, who rode on seventy asses: 'forty' and 'seventy' are round numbers and suggest popular amplification of the historical notice. The historical nucleus of the tradition, however, may be the large harem of Abdon; cf. on v. 9 and 10:4. Alternatively the 'forty', 'thirty', or 'seventy' persons given as the judges' families may be persons associated with them in their administration, like the 'sons' of Samuel (1 Sam. 7:15–17; 8:1f.).

15. in the hill country of the Amelekites: almost certainly a corruption. Certain MSS of LXX read 'in the hill country of Ephraim in the land of Sellēm'. LXX Sellēm indicates possibly a scribal corruption of Sha-albim (Selbit) (Jos. 19:42).

THE SAMSON CYCLE

13:1–16:31

For literary analysis and sources, see Introduction, pp. 217ff.

Editorial Introduction 13:1

The Philistine oppression presented as retribution for Israel's 'evil in the sight of the Lord' after the style of the introduction to the exploits of the great judges, but without notice of repentance and divine grace, indicating perhaps that the inclusion of the Samson cycle was secondary to the first pre-Deuteronomistic compilation of the traditions of the judges.

the Philistines: see on Jos. 13:2. In the sequel the Philistines do not appear to have been on the offensive, but their control of the western foothills limited Israelite settlement. It is not certain that such conditions antedate the Danite migration to the north, and the reference to the 'clan', or 'kinship' (*mišpāḥâh*), and not the 'tribe' (*šēbeṭ*) of Dan (v. 2) may indicate that the migration of the tribe had already taken place, leaving behind only such as had admitted intercourse with the Philistines (cf. ch. 14).

forty years: cf. the twenty years of Samson's career (15:20; 16:31), which indicates the awareness that the liberation from the Philistines was not achieved in the lifetime of Samson, and may indicate the point of view of the Deuteronomistic Historian that there was no break between Jg. and Sam., Samuel also being regarded as a judge (see further on v. 5).

The Tradition of Samson's Birth (from the Samson hero-legend) 13:2–8

The motif of the birth of a hero to a hitherto barren woman who is the recipient of special revelation is a familiar one of hero-legend, e.g. Rebekah, Rachel, Sarah, Hannah and Elizabeth. Such special revelation involves the revelation of a special destiny or commission (v. 5); cf. the case of Jeremiah (Jer. 1:5) and the Servant of the Lord in Is. 49:1–3. The tradition of the birth of the hero Samson is elaborated to emphasise the institution of the Nazirites. In the birth of the hero to a hitherto barren woman and his dedication before birth we notice traditions common to Samson and Samuel, the one having probably influenced the other through the involvement of both in resistance to the Philistines, the failure of Samson contrasting with the success of Samuel (see above, pp. 218f.).

2. Zorah: see on Jos. 15:33–36. In view of the connection of the name Samson with Shemesh (the Sun) and the possible historification of a solar myth, at least in part of the Samson cycle, see on 16:21f., and Introduction to Jg., pp. 219f. The proximity of Samson's home to Beth-shemesh ('the Sanctuary of the Sun') is significant.

the tribe of the Danites: so *RSV*; but rather, 'kinship' (*mišpāḥâh*); see on v. 1.

Manoah: this name, which is probably connected with the clan of the Manahathites, associated with Zorah in 1 Chr. 2:54, may be another case of the recurrence of the name of the eponymous ancestor of the clan; cf. Tola (10:1), Elon (12:11) and Ehud (3:15); or it may be the reconstruction of an editor of the tradition on the basis of the association of the Manahathite clan with Zorah. The name of this clan may be reflected in Manḫato in this vicinity in one of the Amarna Tablets (Kn. 292) from the first half of the fourteenth century BC or, as Dhorme proposed (*RB* 5, 1908, p. 516), Wādī 'l-Menāḥ just south-west of Zorah.

4. The dedication of the hero begins in his mother's womb (v. 5; cf. Jer. 1:5; Isa. 49:1), and is signalised by the same abstinence from wine and fermented drink as will be incumbent on the boy when he is born.

unclean: here the application is only to food and not to contact. There is no explicit prohibition of food to Nazirites except grapes, fresh or dried (Num. 6:3); cf. v. 14, 'anything that comes from the vine'. The regulations for Nazirites (Num. 6:1–24) are from P, but probably conserve an earlier tradition. We may note that it is the mother of Samson who observes those regulations. Samson's drinking-feast in 14:10 does not indicate abstinence, though to be sure it is not said that he himself drank.

5. No razor shall come upon his head, for the boy shall be a Nazirite to God: this is a regulation for the Nazirite also in Num. 6:5. In v. 7 it is stated that Samson was to be a Nazirite for life. Num. 6:1–21 prescribes for temporary Naziriteship, after which the hair was cut and burnt in the sanctuary (Num. 6:18). Among the ancient Semites, the hair, as part of the person, was considered to represent him; e.g. in pre-Islamic times the cutting off of the forelock among the Arabs as a substitute for the killing of prisoners of war, who might then be used as slaves. Etymologically Nazirite is connected with *nādar* ('to vow'). On the view that the Nazirite was primarily dedicated for war, see above, on 5:2.

he shall begin to deliver Israel from the hand of the Philistines: this indicates the awareness of the compiler that Samson's work was not conclusive, but merely a prelude to the wars against the Philistines under Samuel, Saul and even David, and, like the assumption that 'all Israel' was involved, is an indication of his hand in the transmission of the tradition.

6. A man of God: actually, in MT, 'the man of God', perhaps a scribal inadvertency under the influence of the definite article in v. 8. The definite article may denote a single person present to the mind under given circumstances (GK §126qff.). The phrase naturally suggests a prophet, who was apprehended as an extension of the divine personality, hence an angel (vv. 9ff.) and God himself (v. 22); see on 6:11. The fact that the woman did not ask him who he was or whence he came indicates her impression that this was a divine visitation.

8. This serves as a bridge between the birth of the hero and the theophany which authenticates the rock-altar of Zorah (vv. 9–23). This is indicated by the fact that no new instructions sought by Manoah are given concerning the hero, and those concerning Manoah's wife are simply reiterated. On the contrary, a sacrifice is demanded (v. 16) on the place of the theophany.

The Tradition of Samson's Birth continued in the Context of the Aetiological Myth of the Rock-altar of Zorah 13:9–24

Cf. 6:11–24.

12. the boy's manner of life: Hebrew *mišpāṭ* denotes the orderly government or training of the boy.

what he is to do: the task for which he was dedicated.

16. burnt offering: Hebrew *'ôlâh*, a sacrifice with effusion of blood offered wholly to God as distinct from communion-offerings (*šᵉlāmîm*), of which both God and the community partake. The occasion here was nothing short of the dedication of the place of the theophany as an altar.

18. The **name**, whereby the presence of God could be invoked, is not disclosed; cf. in the case of Jacob at the Jabbok (Gen. 32:29), and Moses at the burning bush (Exod. 3:13f.). This in itself indicated that the angel represented One whose fullness was never exhausted by any revelation so that he could be controlled by man. God cannot be expressed but only addressed.

18. wonderful: such a passage concerning the declaration of the place of a theophany usually contains the name of the place in terms of the revelation. The repetition of 'wonderful' in v. 19 suggests that the altar at Zorah was dedicated to 'Yahweh who works wondrously' (reading the definite article before the participle in MT instead of the conjunction). 'Wonder' (Hebrew *pele'*) denotes the immediate activity of God to a certain end which seems to transcend the limits of the natural processes, hence understood by man as miraculous.

19. the kid with the cereal offerings: lit. 'the kid and the (cereal) offering'. This may denote the kid as the actual offering, *minḥāh*, which has this general sense in earlier sources (e.g. 1 Sam. 2:17, 19; 26:19), 'and' in this case being explicative (GK §154, n.b), or it may reflect later usage when a *cereal* offering accompanied the bloody offering in the understanding of the Deuteronomistic Historian.

the rock: not so far mentioned; probably a well-known rock-altar at Zorah.

to him who works wonders: so *RSV*, reading *hammaplî' la'ᵃśôt*, the name of the altar (see on v. 18), and omitting MT 'and Manoah and his wife saw', which is inadvertently repeated by the scribe from v. 20.

20. The moment of conviction in the theophany is associated here as in 6:21 with fire (cf. Exod. 3:2–6; Lev. 9:24; 1 Kg. 18:38f.). In 6:21, however, the fire was kindled when the angel's hand touched the food; here it is not said by whom or how the fire was kindled, which is associated with the sudden disappearance of the angel.

22. We shall surely die, for we have seen God: cf. 6:22.

23. and a cereal offering: probably redactional, reflecting the later usage of the cereal offering as the regular concomitant of sacrifice (see on v. 19).

24. Samson: after LXX and the Vulgate; cf. Hebrew *šimšôn*. The name is unique in the Old Testament and is connected with Hebrew *šemeš* ('sun'). The association of Samson with Zorah, two miles from Beth-shemesh ('Sanctuary of the Sun'), is unlikely to be fortuitous. On the possibility of the historification of a solar myth, at least in part of the Samson tradition, see Introduction, pp. 219f., and on 16:21f.

Samson in Action: Samson's Wooing **13:25–14:4**

From the hero-legend of Samson.

25. the Spirit of the LORD began to stir him: the blessing of God, mentioned in the note on Samson's birth and growth in v. 24, is thus specified, and his activity in his life's work thus marked. The verb *piʿēm* is used of the agitation of a man's spirit by a disquieting dream (Gen. 41:8; Dan. 2:1).

Mahaneh-dan: the place is evidently located west of Kiriath-jearim in 18:12, where its name is derived from a station in the northward migration of Dan. Here a different site is envisaged in the valley between Zorah and Eshtaol, which are some two miles apart. The difficulty of two places of the same name, associated with the same folk-group about eight miles apart, suggested to S. A. Cook (*CAH* II, 1926, p. 314) the emendation Manahath-dan (cf. 1 Chr. 2:52, 54; see above on v. 2). The etymology in 18:12 supports the reading 'Mahaneh' ('camp'), and Alt suggested that the two places of this name in the valley by Beth-shemesh and up in the hills west of Kiriath-jearim, may be a relic of the seasonal migrations of the group of Dan in the early days of the settlement when they were semi-nomads ('Erwägungen über die Landnahme der Israeliten in Palästina', *KS* I, 1953, p. 152; so also Täubler, *op. cit.*, pp. 65ff.). Notwithstanding, the vowels similar to Manahathites of 1 Chr. 2:52, 54 and the association of MT Mahaney-dan and Manahathites of 1 Chr. 2:52, 54 with Zorah and Eshtaol and with Kiriath-jearim, suggests that Mahaneh-dan was the corruption of an original gentilic term, the significance of which had been forgotten since the migration of Dan from the district in which they had probably not stayed long.

14:1. Timnah: Khirbet Tibneh, *c.* four miles from Zorah, lower down the Wādī 'ṣ-Ṣurār and, on the south side of the valley; cf. Jos. 15:10; 19:43, where its inclusion in Dan is secondary to its inclusion in Judah in Jos. 15:10, which reflects the administrative divisions of Judah in Solomon's time, with subsequent modifications. LXX[A] adds 'and she was right in his eyes' (*w*[e]*hî' y*[e]*šārâh b*[e]*ʿênāw*), i.e. she seemed suitable to him. The same adjective, which means 'straightening up to a standard', is used of a wife in the royal Legend of King Krt from Rās Shamra.

2. get her for me as my wife: marriage is a matter for arrangement between the respective families, as still in Arab society.

3. and his mother: this may be an addition; cf. MT 'my people', but *RSV* retains and reads **our people** (cf. LXX, Lagarde's ed., and the Syriac version, 'your people').

uncircumcised: a regular stigma of the Philistines in the Old Testament (cf. 15:18; 1 Sam. 14:6, etc.). The practice was general among the Semitic peoples and the Egyptians, possibly originally related to puberty (cf. Exod. 4:25) and ripeness for marriage and military service, hence membership of the sacral community. If we may credit the tradition in Gen. 34:22–24, the inhabitants of Shechem in the patriarchal period had not practised the rite, possibly indicating their Hurrian (so LXX, for 'Hivite' stock), Gen. 34:2.

4. An apologetic note from the compiler, reconciling the tradition of Samson's affiance with the Philistines with that of his exploits against them as one of the champions of Israel.

Samson's Exploit with the Lion and his Riddle at the Marriage Feast **14:5–20**

The occasion was ostensibly that of the betrothal feast, the marriage corresponding to a *ṣadīqa* marriage among the Arabs, where the wife continued to live in her father's house, being visited periodically by her husband with a gift for her maintenance (cf. 15:1). It is hard, however, to imagine the incident of the lion happening without the knowledge of his parents (v. 6*b*) in such open country with no other cover than the trailing vines on the gentle slopes of the Wādī 'ṣ-Ṣurār, and it is therefore likely that the mention of the parents in vv. 5 and 6*b* is secondary and that there is here probably a telescoping of the tradition of the slaying of the lion and that of the betrothal of Samson at which his parents would be present, the two traditions being independent. That of the killing of the lion, or at least the incident of the honey from the carcase, is probably secondary to the tradition of Samson's riddle at the marriage feast.

Samson's Exploit with the Lion **14:5–9**

6. the Spirit of the LORD came mightily upon him: lit. 'leapt upon him', as a lion on its prey. This expresses simply Samson's phenomenal access of physical strength and courage, also considered to be the influence of God beyond the natural force of man, as the heroic impulse to lead and hazard all in God's cause, the wisdom of the sage, the technical insight and skill of the artisan or artist, the insight and courage of the prophet, the frenzy of the dervish and even the madness by which God makes one 'another man'.
lion: lions are familiar in the Old Testament as not uncommon in Palestine (e.g. Amos, Jeremiah, etc.), though rather associated with remoter regions such as the jungle by the immediate banks of the

Jordan. They were found in Syria as late as the Middle Ages when Usāma ibn Munqidh of Shayzār, the contemporary of Salāḥ ad-Dīn, hunted them in the Orontes valley.

he tore the lion asunder as one tears a kid: as a carcase is still divided at an Arab guest-meal. The same verb (*šissa'*) is used of the tearing open of a sacrificial dove by the wings in Lev. 1:17. For this action, Burney (*op. cit.*, p. 401) cites the motif of a bull-man rending a lion by the hind-legs in a Mesopotamian seal (*op. cit.* Pl. II, fig. 4) and the crude figure of a giant, possibly Heracles as Phoenician Melkart, so rending a lion in a piece from Cyprus (*op. cit.*, Pl. VI). The tradition may have been influenced by the motif of Gilgamesh as a tamer of lions, well known in Mesopotamian sculpture; but the myth of Heracles is another possible source, mediated perhaps by Mycenean settlers on the coast by Jaffa at the end of the Bronze Age (see Introduction to Jg., pp. 220f.).

8. he returned to take her: if this is original it envisages the marriage after the betrothal.

And after a while: This note possibly envisages the carcase of the lion being cleaned to a dry skeleton by jackals and flies. The bees must also have had time to build and fill a honeycomb. The word for swarm (*'ēdâh*) is that used technically, particularly in P, for the religious community; *EVV* 'congregation' (see on 20:1).

9. Samson as a Nazirite has no inhibition about contact with a dead body, to say nothing of eating the honey from the carcase of the lion; cf. the prohibition of such contact in the passage on the Nazirites in Num. 6:6 (P). This seems to prompt the statement that Samson did not tell his parents where he had got the honey (v. 9b), which may be secondary.

Samson's Riddle at the Marriage Feast 14:10–20

10. a feast: lit. 'a drinking-party'. LXX and the Syriac version add 'for seven days', which is stated explicitly in v. 12.

for so the young men used to do: possibly introduced to explain the apparent incongruity of Samson, a Nazirite to whom wine was banned, giving a drinking party.

11. when the people saw him: possibly with LXX, with a slight change of consonants 'because they feared him'; but see note following.

they brought thirty companions to be with him: the bridegroom's attendants are a regular feature of peasant marriage in the ancient and modern Semitic world (cf. Mt. 9:15), but are from his own community. In this case the *ṣadīqa* marriage with a Philistine girl may explain why Samson had no attendants from his own community. The abnormally large number may have been complimentary to Samson; but alternatively it may be explained by the LXX reading, 'because they feared him' (Hebrew *beyir'ātām*; cf. MT *kir'ôtām*, 'when they saw'), anticipating the sequel. One of these was especially attached to the bridegroom (v. 20) as chief negotiator and master of ceremonies (cf. Jn. 3:29).

12. put a riddle: the verb is denominative from *ḥîdâh* ('riddle'), used only here and in Ezek. 17:2, where it introduces not a brief figurative saying or a proverb of an enigmatic nature, but a parable. The riddle (*ḥîdâh*) is usually, as here, figurative and was often used as a test of natural ingenuity in diplomatic encounters (1 Kg. 10:1). Such tests of wits are a feature of social life in non-literate societies, as among the Arab peasants and Bedouin and formerly in the crofting communities in the Scottish Highlands.

the seven days of the feast: this is still the statutory duration of the wedding among the Arab peasants (so also Gen. 29:27).

thirty linen garments: these are not further defined, but in conjunction with the sequel denote possibly a light undergarment like the long shirt of the Arabs (*qamīs*).

festal garments: Hebrew *ḥalîpôt begādîm*. The first word means generally 'change' or 'succession', e.g. Job 14:14; cf. Arabic *ḫalīfa* ('Caliph', i.e. successor); in this case the reference might be to changes from working clothing. The word might be cognate, however, with an Akkadian verb 'to cover', and refer to the overcloak (Arabic *'abāya*) of heavier dark cloth, often very fine with embroidery. Such gifts of clothing were valued; cf. 2 Kg. 5:5, where the same term is used.

13. the battle of wits is accentuated by the bet.

14. The riddle is set in the characteristic parallelism of Hebrew poetry. It is a word-play on *'arî*, which means 'lion' in Hebrew and, to assume a Hebrew noun cognate with Arabic *'ary*, 'honey'. The lion was 'the eater' and 'the strong, or fierce' and the honey 'the food' and 'the sweet'. The riddle may have meant, What is both eater and for food and both strong and sweet? the answer: *'arî*. This probably prompted the tradition of the unlikely swarming of bees in the carcase of the lion, if not indeed the tradition of Samson's slaying of the lion. The contest of wits between the bridegroom and the bride's people is probably a modification of an earlier practice of a contest to prove the bridegroom's strength and to conserve the tradition of marriage by force, which survives in the colloquial Arabic phrase for marriage, *ḫaṭfu 'l-bint* ('snatching the girl').

15. on the fourth day: so *RSV*, after LXX and the Syriac version for MT 'seventh'. This punctuation of the seven days may be in the

saga convention; cf. the Rās Shamra Legend of King Krt, where the king on the journey to the home of his bride goes, a day, a second day, a third day, when he breaks his seven days' journey to make a vow at the sanctuary of the Mother-goddess. The succession of seven days thus interrupted sustains the tension of the episode. The threat of arson is the same as in the case of the Ephraimites and Jephthah (12:1).
Entice: the Hebrew verb *pātāh* (intensive-causative), used also of Delilah's wheedling of Samson (16:5), means 'to stultify', 'make a simpleton of', 'circumvent a man's wisdom' (1 Kg. 22:20); or 'to seduce' a woman (Exod. 22:16).
to impoverish: lit. 'to possess by dispossessing'; the verb, here intensive, is regularly used in the causative of the Israelite occupation of Palestine.

18. before the sun went down: this in English seems a natural expression, the new day for ancient Israel beginning at sunset. But it is peculiar Hebrew, meaning literally 'before he came to the sun'. The word for 'sun' too (*ḥeres*) is strange in this context, being archaic and poetic. Thus we should probably read ***haḥadrāh*** for ***haḥarsāh***, translating 'before he entered (the bride-) chamber'. For 'the chamber' in the sense of 'the bride-chamber', cf. 15:1.

In the narrative Samson salvages the position by answering in another couplet, which preserves his ascendancy in the conventional contest. This was probably a familiar by-word in Israel, which is adapted to the Samson-legend.

19. He requites the guile of the Philistines also with open violence, keeping his bargain at the expense of the Philistines of Ashkelon.
the Spirit of the Lord: in this case, as well as nerving Samson for this unusual method of paying his debt in the saga, the access of the Spirit for the pre-Deuteronomistic compiler relates to the proper work of the judge, war with the Philistines.

20. Not unnaturally the father of the lady assumed that relations with Samson were at an end, and she **was given to his companion** (see on v. 11). This might be more easily done in the case of a *ṣadīqa* marriage. Probably after the apparent lapse of the marriage the 'companion', evidently local, was held responsible for the girl's status and maintenance.

Samson and the Burning of the Philistines' Corn 15:1–8

This is in the context of his relations with the woman of Timnah, which seems to be used to connect a number of independent traditions about Samson. On the possible elaboration of the saga from a local agricultural rite, see on v. 4.

1. **at the time of the wheat harvest:** i.e. the second harvest, about the end of May in the Shephelah, anticipating v. 5.

with a kid: indicating a *ṣadīqa* marriage, as in ancient Arab practice (W. R. Smith, *op. cit.*, pp. 75ff.).

3. **blameless:** Hebrew *niqqētî*. Now he has a wrong to avenge. But perhaps, with the addition of one consonant *niqqamtî* ('I shall be avenged') should be read.

4. **three hundred foxes:** possibly jackals, which are more common in Palestine. This may be the round number and exaggeration of saga, but it may suggest a public rite as a factual basis, a prophylactic against rust-fungus in the corn, caused by the sudden strong sun upon the heavy dew which is a feature of the Palestinian summer, particularly in the coastal plain and areas of the Shephelah and the Negeb with a Western exposure. Thus, in the festival of Ceres in Rome in April, foxes with burning torches attached to their tails were hunted about the Circus (Ovid, Fasti, iv.679ff.). On the other hand, the tradition of the foxes, or jackals (*šû'ālîm*) may have developed from the use of firebrands (Arabic *ša'lāt*) in such a rite.

5. **standing grain:** the plural participle used here in MT has been suspected; cf. the sequel, where the singular is used. We should understand the plural as 'fields of standing corn' and the singular as generic 'standing corn' as distinct from *gādîš*, cut corn in heaps (*RSV* **shocks**) which has an Aramaic cognate.

as well as the olive orchards: MT includes 'vineyards' (*kerem*), which no version questions. Soggin (*op. cit.*, ad loc.) regards this as exaggeration since fresh wood is not combustible, but, while admitting that this is saga and not necessarily fact, the trees would be sufficiently scorched to be ruined.

6. **her and her father:** read 'her and her father's house' with some Hebrew MSS and the Greek and Syriac versions (cf. the threat in 14:15).

8. **smote them hip and thigh:** actually 'leg upon thigh', the former (*šôq*) denoting the leg from the knee down. The expression has been taken to be a wrestling term, but that is not readily intelligible, and it may rather denote headlong flight; cf. 'showing a clean pair of heels'.

in the cleft of the rock of Etam: this is probably some unidentified locality in the western escarpment of the mountains of Judah, which abound in large limestone caves.

Samson's Victory at Lehi **15:9–17**

A local aetiological legend.

9. in Judah: see on v. 8.

Lehi: as well as meaning 'jawbone', Lehi is a place-name, the scene of a single-handed victory by one of David's warriors Shammah also over the Philistines (2 Sam. 23:11f.), which may have influenced the present tradition.

10ff. the compliance of the men of Judah with the Philistines' expedition against Samson, though perhaps designed to enhance the personal exploit of the hero, does reflect the historical situation in Jg., when there was only local resistance to the enemies of those who worshipped Yahweh.

13. The single-handed exploit of Samson is accentuated by his submission to be bound by the men of Judah. This, like the specification of new ropes and the large round numbers, 3000 and 1000, is a feature of saga rather than history.

14. the spirit of the LORD: thus his phenomenal strength is explained, but for the compiler it heralded also a victory over the Philistines in the liberation of Israel.

15. a fresh jawbone: hence not brittle.

16. In the poetic couplet:

With the jawbone of an ass,
heaps upon heaps (lit. 'a heap, two heaps'),
with the jawbone of an ass
have I slain a thousand men,

there is a word-play between 'ass' (*ḥ^amôr*) and 'heap' (*ḥōmer*; cf. Exod. 8:14 (MT, v. 10), where the dead frogs are piled up, *ḥ^omārîm ḥ^omārîm*). For 'heaps upon heaps' (*ḥ^amōr ḥ^amōrātayim*), we may read *ḥamôr ḥ^amartîm* ('I have surely heaped them up'); cf. LXX^{BA} and the Old Latin version 'I have certainly destroyed them', understanding in *ḥōmer* the nuance of ruin-heap, as in Aramaic.

17. Ramath-lehi: i.e. 'the Height of Lehi'.

Topographical Aetiological Legend of En-hakkore **15:18–19**

18. the uncircumcised: see on 14:3.

19. the hollow place: (Hebrew *hammaktēš*), lit. 'the mortar' (cf. Prov. 27:22). It is used of a local depression between the Temple hill and the west hill of ancient Jerusalem (Zeph. 1:11), and in modern Hebrew of the great *cirques* in the Negeb.

En-hakkore: *'ên haqqôre'*, lit. 'the Spring of the Caller'. This is the place where Samson called to God; but 'the caller' probably denotes the partridge (1 Sam. 26:20; Jer. 17:11); cf. 'the cheerful chirrup of the rock partridge', so often remarked by C. M. Doughty, *Travels in Arabia Deserta*.

Editorial Note **15:20**

20. The editorial note here on the duration of Samson's work as a judge may be suggested by the fact that this for the compiler was the end of his effective work for Israel. The Deuteronomistic notice of the duration of the 'rest', or peace secured by his efforts as judge is lacking because the editor has already indicated his awareness of the inconclusive work of Samson. Noting that the Philistines oppressed Israel forty years (13:1, on which see note), he thus ascribes twenty years to Samson as judge. The further note on the duration of Samson's activity as judge in 16:31 may be due to a secondary editor.

Samson and the Gates of Gaza **16:1–3**

A local aetiological legend; see Introduction to Jg., p. 219.

1. Gaza: see on Jos. 10:41. Samson's visit to the harlot is narrated without inhibition or stricture, an indication that the Old Testament must be understood in its own context.

2. the Gazites were told: MT, 'to the Gazites saying'. Obviously 'and it was told' has been omitted by scribal error, as indicated by LXX.

3. doors of the gate of the city: the plural rather than the dual suggests a double or triple chambered gateway (*ANEP*, Fig. 713), the gates turning on their pivots in sockets of iron or bronze, and being shut with a bar which held them rigid and fitted into two sockets in the jambs. Gates, jambs and bar are depicted as all carried away bodily. **The hill** overlooking Hebron from the west, probably at the head of the Wādī 'l-Afrānj, which leads down to the coastal plain near Ashkelon and Gaza, some forty miles distant, may have been called 'the Gates of Gaza', indicating a local aetiological myth.

The Betrayal and Imprisonment of Samson **16:4–21**

Here, we consider, a solar myth has influenced the hero-legend; see Introduction, pp. 219f.

4. the valley of Sorek: the Wādī 'ṣ-Ṣurār, which drains from just north-north-west of Jerusalem, past Moṣā, and through the Shephelah, past Zorah on the north, and Bethshemesh and Timnah on the south.

Delilah: the name has been associated with the Arabic verb 'to be languid' or 'to be coquettish', and that is possible. But it may also be cognate with an Akkadian word for 'devotee', the lady being possibly a devotee of the fertility-goddess. She was doubtless Canaanite, since the Philistines 'came up' and suborned her to betray Samson.

5. **lords of the Philistines:** on those feudal lords and their fiefs, see on Jos. 13:2.

Entice: see on 14:15.

wherein his great strength lies: according to MT 'wherein his strength is great'.

eleven hundred pieces of silver: probably shekels are envisaged. This odd number, a thousand and a hundred, and its agreement with the sum stolen by Micah (17:2), may indicate an editorial adjustment. The sum according to the computation of A. R. S. Kennedy (*HDB* III, p. 420a) would be about £150; but with variations of the value of the shekel in time and place this is quite uncertain.

7. **seven fresh bowstrings:** so LXX, correctly translating the Hebrew; cf. *AV*, 'green withs', after Josephus, who specifies 'of vine'. **fresh** indicates 'full of natural sap' (cf. Dt. 34:7). The number **seven** encourages Delilah's belief in the magical source of Samson's strength. The strength and suppleness of the fresh sinews, which made tight knotting possible and by their elasticity frustrated strain, made the communication more credible and at the same time enhances Samson's ability to get free, as in the case of his bonds in new rope in 15:13.

9. **a string of tow:** lit. 'a twisting of tow' (Hebrew *p*ᵉ*tîl han*ᵉ*'ôret*); cf. the figure in 15:14.

when it touches (lit. 'smells') **the fire:** the verb (Hebrew *hērîaḥ*) denotes the first reaction to a stimulating object, e.g. the horse 'scenting battle' (Job. 39:25).

11. **new ropes:** cf. 15:13. Here again there is natural verisimilitude as well as a suggestion of magic in the use of new objects unimpaired by common use; cf. the new dish in Elisha's restoration of the spring at Jericho (2 Kg. 2:20), the new cart on which the ark was transported (1 Sam. 6:7; 2 Sam. 6:3) and possibly Ahijah's new mantle in his rite of prophetic symbolism (1 Kg. 11:29).

13. Certain MSS of LXX indicate that Samson's instructions in the Hebrew text are incomplete and that the verse should read **If you weave the seven locks of my head with the web and make it tight**

with the pin, then I shall become weak, and be like any other man (so *RSV*). A horizontal loom is envisaged, as in Egyptian sculpture (A. R. S. Kennedy, 'Weaving', *EB*, col. 5279), and the simple apparatus of the Bedouin and certain Arab villagers in Palestine (cf. Gustav Dalman, *Arbeit und Sitte in Palästina*, V, 1964, pp. 100ff.).

the seven locks: (Hebrew *maḥl^e pôt.*) Those may be either curls or plaits. The limited number of locks, if not suggested by the 'seven fresh sinews' in the saga-complex, may indicate affinity with the Gilgamesh tradition, as Burney surmised (*op. cit.*, p. 404), citing the representation of Gilgamesh on seals with six curling locks (*op. cit.*, Pl. III, fig. 3). Whatever the origin of the motif, this feature serves to connect the fall of Samson with the abuse of his status as a Nazirite (v. 17), though there is no explicit censure of Samson in the narrative.

14. So while he slept, Delilah took the seven locks of his head and wove them into the web: so *RSV* after LXX, for the obviously incomplete MT, **and she made them tight with the pin**, with which *RSV* continues. **made them tight** means 'beat up firmly' into the web.

pulled away the pin, the loom, and the web: the pointing of **the pin** in MT indicates doubt as to the reading of the text, and if, as the preceding verse indicates, the pin was not for fixing anything, but for beating the weaving up close, it may be that 'the pin' should be omitted here. Alternatively, it should be pointed out that as an absolute and not as a construct (so *RV*, following MT), as the definite article shows, the conjunction 'and' should be read before 'the loom' (*hā'ereg*).

15. your heart is not with me: i.e. you are not sincere with me.

16. his soul was vexed: better perhaps 'his temper was short'. Hebrew *nepeš* does not mean 'soul' in the metaphysical sense, Hebrew knowing no dichotomy of soul and body, as in Greek and Western thought. Meaning primarily 'life', *nepeš* means also 'impulse', as in Prov. 19:2: 'Impulse without knowledge is not good.'

17. If I be shaved, then my strength will leave me: here he refers to his status as a Nazirite. It is noteworthy that in the revelation to his mother that he should be a Nazirite (13:7), there is no mention of his physical strength. This is an accretion to the tradition of Samson as a Nazirite and may indicate homiletic expansion.

20. and shake myself free: Delilah had perhaps bound him in addition as a precaution against the surprise of the Philistines.

the LORD had left him: i.e. the spirit of the Lord as an extension of the divine personality.

21. gouged out his eyes: cf. the blinding of King Zedekiah (2 Kg. 25:7). The resulting darkness may be a feature of solar mythology in the tradition of Samson.
ground at the mill: the work of maid-servants (Exod. 11:5), slaves, prisoners and asses.

The Death of Samson **16:22–31**

22. the regrowth of Samson's hair may be a literary convention to introduce the next episode. Here we are in the realm of magic and folk-lore, perhaps even of mythology with the recurring cycle of the sun.

23. a great sacrifice: (*zebaḥ*) implies also a feast, as in the Rās Shamra texts and Zeph. 1:7.
Dagon their god: Dagon, connected with the word for 'corn' in Hebrew and Ugaritic, is well known as a Semitic deity in Mesopotamia in the Amorite period (early second millennium BC) and at Rās Shamra (fourteenth–thirteenth centuries BC) and in Palestine in theophoric names and in the place-name Beth-dagon, near Jaffa (Jos. 15:41). He was thus a local Semitic deity whose cult was adopted by the Philistines (1 Sam. 5:2ff.) in their settlement of the corn-growing coastal plain, just as the Assyrian colonists in Samaria adopted the cult of Yahweh (2 Kg. 17:26ff.). There is no real foundation for the view of Rabbinic commentators that **Dagon** was a fish-god, which is based on a false etymology (*dāg*, 'fish'), reflected in a corrupt text at 1 Sam. 5:4.

24. Our god has given Samson our enemy into our hand: suggests that the feast was in commemoration of a victory over Samson. But that must have been after some interval, when Samson's hair had grown and his strength had returned, according to the narrator. It seems rather to anticipate the appearance of the captive Samson as the butt of their jests. The exclamation of the Philistines could be resolved into couplets. The recurring rhyme of the first plural pronominal suffix seems hardly fortuitous.

26. their hearts were merry: lit. 'their hearts were good', a regular description of physical satisfaction, contentment and confidence.
that he may make sport for us: lit. 'that he may make us laugh', either in his downfall, or by amusing them with feats of strength or wit in reply to their taunts.

26f. the pillars on which the house rests probably indicates a large hall, like the Greek megaron, with three sides and an open central courtyard (see on v. 29). While spectators are envisaged on the flat roof, it is unlikely that they numbered **about three thousand**

men and women, which is the hyperbole of saga (cf. LXX 'seven hundred').

28. that I may be avenged . . . for one of my two eyes: a better reading is suggested by LXX, the Hexaplar Syriac and Vulgate, 'a single vengeance for my two eyes', reading *wᵉʾinnāqᵉmāh nᵉqāmâh ʾaḥat miššᵉtê ʿênay* for *wᵉʾinnāqᵉmāh nᵉqam ʾaḥat miššᵉtê ʿênay*.

29. the two middle pillars upon which the house rested: The only Philistine temple so far excavated is that at Tell Qasileh, just north of Tel Aviv. This was in the form of a long hall, the roof of which was supported by two pillars (A. Mayer, 'A Philistine Temple at Tell Qasile', *BA* 36, 1973, p. 43). But those are set longitudinally and supported a roof enclosing the whole building. The two pillars in the temple at Gaza are evidently envisaged as supporting the two angles in a three-sided colonnaded building; but in a building of any appreciable dimensions it would be impossible for Samson to reach both. Perhaps this is another case of the hyperbole of saga.

30. Let me die: lit. 'let my life perish'. On 'life' (*nepeš*), see on v. 16; but *nepeš* with the pronominal suffix often means 'self'.

31. The notice of Samson's burial-place may either be suggested by the stereotyped obituary of Jephthah and the 'minor judges', which the Samson narrative immediately follows; or it may originate from the tradition of the reputed tomb of the hero in the valley below Zorah (see on 13:2, 25), which was venerated like an Arab *wālī*, the tomb of one who has possessed the divine favour and who is venerated as an intercessory saint. The 'high places' against which Israelite reformers inveighed so vehemently may have been associated with such tombs (so Albright, 'The High Places in Ancient Palestine', *VT Supplement IV*, Congress Vol., 1957, pp. 242–58.

APPENDIX A
THE ORIGIN OF THE PRE-MONARCHIC SANCTUARY OF DAN
17–18

A literary source, compiled by the priesthood of the royal sanctuary of Dan, possibly at Bethel after 734 BC, from their own traditions and those of the Levitical oracle-priests at the tribal sanctuary at Dan, and later incorporated in the Deuteronomistic History, with a chronological note on the contemporaneity of this local cult at Dan with that at Shiloh. For variations, sources, compilation and redaction, see Introduction to Jg., pp. 222ff.

The Origin of Micah's Cult-Symbols in stolen Silver, on the Thief of which a Curse had been invoked **17:1–6**

The tradition exposes the tribal cult of Dan to the gentle humour of the priesthood of the royal sanctuary, which the Deuteronomist transmits.

1. the hill country of Ephraim: this is perhaps a geographical rather than a tribal designation (see on Jos. 20:7);
Micah: a shortened form of *Mikay^{e}hu* ('Who is like Yahweh'), suggesting that the graven and the molten image in the sequel, however much it contravened the principle in Exod. 34:17 (cf. Exod. 20:4 and Dt. 27:15), was part of the furniture of the cult of Yahweh along with the ephod and the teraphim used in divination, which was probably the speciality of the cult and Levitical priesthood at Dan (2 Sam. 20:18, LXX), if indeed the ephod and the teraphim were not all that was made of the silver. Micah's 'house of gods' gives a false impression, meaning possibly no more than 'a shrine' (sc. of Yahweh).

2. Micah's mother had unwittingly cursed her own son, the unknown thief of **the eleven hundred pieces of silver**. The sum, identical to that paid by each of the lords of the Philistines for Samson's betrayal (16:5), is obviously editorial, the one passage influencing the other.

The **curse**, enlisting the power of the divine and supernatural on the principle of imitative magic in words (e.g. Balaam's oracles), was the effective means of dealing with crime when the agent was not known or where there were no witnesses (Num. 5:19). From the text it is uncertain whether the curse was laid on the unknown thief directly, or indirectly through the stolen goods, as Täubler proposed (*op. cit.*, p. 42). The latter view would make the blessing on Micah more feasible, though the counteracting of a formal curse by a blessing was possible.
which were taken from you: the preposition *l^e* is now to be understood in the light of the Rās Shamra texts as meaning 'from'.

2–4. MT rendered by *RSV* tells how Micah was scared into a confession by his mother's curse. In v. 2 we should normally expect direct speech after 'and also said' (cf. *RSV*, **and also spoke it in my ears** (*w^{e}gam 'āmart b^e'oznay*). Hence it is proposed (so Moore) that the text is upset. With modification of Moore's proposal, we might read from v. 3: 'I had dedicated the silver, O my son, to Yahweh to make a graven and a molten image.' After Micah's confession, **behold, the silver is with me; I took it** (v. 2) we expect **and now therefore I will restore it to you** (v. 3*b*). **So he restored the money to his mother** (v. 3*a*). But this would leave **and his**

mother said in v. 3 superfluous, unless it is a dittograph of the phrase in the previous verse. Alternatively, if we accept the *RSV* and *NEB* assumption that the text is in order, and that *w^e gam 'āmart b^e'oznay* refers to the declaration of the curse in the previous phrase, the sequel might signify that after Micah's confession his mother blessed him (v. 2) and he restored the silver, which, being the subject of the curse, on Täubler's interpretation, Micah's mother then dedicated (in the declaratory perfect), restoring it to Micah (v. 3) in the sense that the cult-objects, on which two hundred pieces of silver were expended (v. 4) were in his keeping, with presumably the rest for the maintenance of the cult, though that is not stated. We would suggest that the admitted difficulty of the verb *'āmart* without direct speech in v. 2 might be solved by assuming scribal corruption of an original *'ārôt* ('and cursed') in the archaic Hebrew script.

The text may be further complicated by the use of two variant sources, as seems to be indicated further by the tradition that the image apparently consisted of *one* cult-object ('and *it* was in the house of Micah'), but is described as both 'graven' and 'molten'. This, however, if not an editorial expansion reflecting the formal language of the Twelve Adjurations (Dt. 27:15), where the two are associated, might refer to a hewn wooden image (*pesel*) with molten metal overlay (*massēkâh*). In 18:17, however, *two* images are envisaged, indicating editorial elaboration if not the fusion of two sources.

4. two hundred: this smaller sum as distinct from the whole which had been dedicated might imply a variant source. But the balance may have provided for the maintenance of the cult.

5. a shrine: lit. 'a house of god'. It is stated that this housed the **ephod** and the **teraphim**, which were, according to this verse, made by Micah over and above the 'graven and the molten image'. Perhaps the making of the ephod and teraphim was the original tradition, that of the graven and molten image being secondary. Alternatively, the tradition of the ephod and teraphim may be an apologetic modification of the tradition of the graven and molten image on the part of the priesthood of the tribal sanctuary of Dan. On the **ephod**, the covering of a cult-symbol with pockets for the sacred lots used in divination, and conceivably of sheet-metal, see on 8:27. The **teraphim** are associated with the ephod and a standing-stone of a sanctuary in Hos. 3:4. The association with the ephod suggests that the teraphim were also used in divination (cf. 1 Sam. 15:23, where 'teraphim' is parallel to 'divination by sorcery'). The question is complicated by the significance of the word as 'household gods' (Gen. 31), perhaps represented by anthropoid masks of favoured ancestors, as 1 Sam. 19:13ff. may suggest. Secondarily, the word may denote a similar mask used to efface the person through whom an oracle was declared, and so to emphasise the divine authority, which may be the significance of Moses' veil or mask in Exod. 34:29–35, especially vv. 34f., omitting 'the skin of Moses' face' with LXX.

installed: lit. 'filled the hand', the technical term for priestly investiture, possibly indicating the filling of the ordinand's hand with the sacred portions of the first sacrifice, which is literally done in Exod. 29:31–34 in the case of 'the ram of installation', lit. 'filling'.

Consecration to the priestly office in this period was not nearly so formal as the Priestly account in Exod. 29 suggests, nor was there an exclusive priestly caste as the consecration of Micah's son indicates (cf. David's consecration of his sons as priests (2 Sam. 8:18); but v. 13 indicates that the Levites had a recognised priestly status, perhaps particularly in the manipulation of the oracle (18:5; cf. Dt. 33:8).

6. in those days there was no king in Israel: probably reflecting the interest of the priesthood of the royal sanctuary at Dan as distinct from the oracle-priests of the tribal sanctuary there descended from Micah's Levite. Perhaps this tradition crystallised after the withdrawal of the priests from the royal sanctuary at Dan to Bethel on the destruction of Dan by Tiglath-pileser III in 734 BC (see Introduction, pp. 223f.).

Micah secures a Levite as Priest 17:7–13

The inadequacy of the first provision that Micah made for the service of the local cult is exposed, and the origin of the priesthood of the pre-monarchic sanctuary at Dan in a vagabond Levite is ridiculed. Later, however, the tradition, probably that of the oracle-priests of Dan themselves, emerges that those priests were descended from Moses through Gershom (18:30).

7. Bethlehem in Judah: as distinct from Bethlehem in Zebulun (Jos. 19:15), still a populous town and still called Beit Laḥm.

of the family of Judah, who was a Levite: in the pre-Deuteronomistic compilation and in the Deuteronomistic History Judah is a tribe (*šēbeṭ*) and not a clan, or family (*mišpāḥâh*), so it is likely that in the consonantal text, if that is original, the plural *mišpeḥôt* should be read, with the partitive *min*, denoting an unspecified item in a certain category (*GK* §124 o); cf. *beʿāre gilʿād* ('in one of the cities of Gilead', possibly in 12:7). So also perhaps for MT *mimmišpaḥat dan* in 13:2 and *mimmišpaḥtām* in 18:2, where LXX and the Targum actually read the plural. It is doubtful if there was a tribe Levi with political status, as Gen. 34:25f. and 49:5–7 assume. The inclusion of Levi among the twelve tribes may reflect rather the representation of the Levites as a priestly caste in the sacral assembly. The description of the Levite here as 'of one of the families of Judah' and Micah's satisfaction in having 'a Levite to priest' (v. 13) support this view of his status, which is noticed in Dt. 33:8ff. Levites were not particularly associated with Bethlehem, but certainly with Hebron (Jos. 21:11; 1 Chr. 26:20–32). This association which the Levites shared with the Kenizzites may indicate a penetration northwards from Kadesh, with which the Levites are associated in Dt. 33:8; cf. their association with Simeon in the reduced circumstances of the latter in north Sinai. The association of Levites at Kadesh (Mowinckel, 'Kadesj, Sinai og Jahwe', *NGT* 9, 1942, pp. 1–32) with the Rachel group Joseph and Benjamin, the dominant element in the settlement of central Palestine and the nucleus of Israel, and their devotion to the cult of Yahweh accounts for the status of the Levites, recognised by Micah. Mowinckel's most recent view (*Israels opphav*, pp. 145f.) is that Simeon and Levi were originally southern groups, the latter the custodians of the sanctuary of Yahweh at Kadesh (cf. Dt. 33:5–12), who were repulsed after the abortive attack on Shechem (Gen. 34; cf. Gen. 49:5–7), which Mowinckel associated with Hebrew/*ḫabiru* pressure there in the Amarna period. This view seems best to allow for the historicity of the tradition in Gen. 34 and for the status of the Levites as individuals socially dependent (*gērîm*) on other tribes and cultic specialists. *lwy* is attested as a common noun in south Arabia, where it signifies one 'attached' to the cult, which is also a feasible etymology in Hebrew.

8. to live: Hebrew *gûr*, i.e. as a *gēr* in a strange community, where his only protection was the recognised sanctity of his status and the convention of hospitality; cf. *jāru 'llāhi*, 'protected alien of Allah' in an Arab tribe. The recurrence of the verb *gûr* (vv. 7, 8, 9) seems to anticipate the tradition of the descent of this Levite and his successors in the tribal cult at Dan from Gershom (18:30) according to popular etymology ('a sojourner there').

10. a father: not indicating seniority here, but a term of authority and respect, as indicated by the fact that the Levite was young (v. 7); cf. Gen. 45:8 (Joseph); 2 Kg. 2:12 (Elijah) and 2 Kg. 13:14 (Elisha). *RSV* omits MT, 'and the Levite went' (*wayyēlek hallēwî*; cf. the Old Latin versions, 'and he constrained the Levite', *wayeʿāś hallēwî*, of which we do not consider MT a graphically feasible corruption). If the consonantal text is correct, it may be read *wayyillōk hallēwî*, as G. R. Driver proposed (*ALUOS* 4, 1964, p. 18), taking the verb as *lākak*, so far not attested in Hebrew; but cf. Arabic *lakka* ('to hesitate'), adopted by Soggin (*op. cit.*, ad loc.).

12. installed: lit. 'filled the hand' (see on v. 5).

13. a Levite as priest: lit. 'the Levite . . .', possibly a case of the definite article with demonstrative force (*GK* §126b). Micah's estimation of the Levite probably reflects the recognition of the association of the Levites with the cult of Yahweh at Kadesh (see on v. 7).

The Danite Migration: the Levite's Oracle 18:1–6

1. In those days there was no king in Israel . . .: on the analogy of 17:6 and 21:25, this statement should end an episode rather than introduce a fresh section.

no inheritance among the tribes of Israel had fallen to them: cf. Jos. 19:40–48, which lists places allocated to Dan in the time of Joshua in the northern foothills of Judah and states that this territory was lost to them. This corroborates the view that the town-list in Jos. 19:41–46 is constructed artificially from the note of the second and fifth administrative districts of the kingdom of Judah in Jos. 15:33–36 and 45f. The mention of Zorah and Eshtaol in vv. 2, 8 and 11 alone in the presumed southern settlement of Dan (cf. 13:25) indicates that the settlement of Dan in that area was quite exiguous. This seems to be supported by the mention of Dan not as a tribe, but as a clan (*mispaḥâh*) in v. 2; cf. 13:2. But cf. LXX and the Targum, which read the plural ('from one of the clans . . .'; see above on 17:7. *RSV* reads the last word of v. 1 *naḥalâh* for MT *benaḥalâh* ('as an inheritance'), taking the subject *naḥalâh* from the previous clause.

2. able men: lit. 'men of substance' (*benê ḥayil*); see on 6:12. The persons in question had to be mature and responsible.

from the whole number of their tribe: (Hebrew *miqeṣôtām*, lit. 'from their extremities', an inclusive term, as in Gen. 47:2).

3. they recognised the voice: they either recognised the dialect as of Judah near their home country, or the voice of the individual, which is less likely, or they may simply have heard him at the service and recognised a priest.

5. Inquire of God: i.e. consult the oracle, which according to Dt. 33:8 was the special province of the Levites, for which the equipment was available in the ephod and teraphim (see on 17:5).

6. under the eye of the LORD: lit. 'in front of Yahweh'; or, in English idiom, 'under his countenance'.

The Danite Migration: the Reconnaissance of Laish **18:7–10**

7. Laish: cf. Leshem in Jos. 19:47, known by this name only here, and later called Dan, conventionally the northernmost settlement in Israel as Beersheba was the southernmost, possibly with reference to the significance of both as cult-centres at the extremities of the land, e.g. Am. 8:14. It is identified with Tell al-Qāḍī ('the Mound of the Judge'), which suggests Dan, this name probably surviving in Nahr Leddān, one of the sources of the Jordan. The site is about thirty miles from Tyre and forty from Damascus. Recent excavations (A. Biran, *IEJ* 19, 1969, pp. 240f.) have revealed a flourishing Middle Bronze settlement, which was destroyed *c.* 1600 BC. Cypriot and Aegean wares in tombs of the Late Bronze settlement support the statement of Phoenician settlement here in the last two centuries of the Late Bronze Age (*c.* 1400–1200 BC).

after the manner of the Sidonians, quiet and unsuspecting: on Sidon, see on 10:6. By the middle of the Early Iron Age (*c.* 1100 BC), in which those events are set, the Phoenicians had been confined to their coastal settlements by the Aramaean settlement in the interior of Syria, hence they impressed the Israelites as a peaceful people. Their occupation of this settlement on the upper Jordan was probably connected with their interest in communications with Damascus, the metropolis of the north Arabian steppe and a great entrepôt of caravan trade with south Arabia and Egypt with Mesopotamia. They probably had a further interest in the Hauran, which was a source of grain for Palestine and the Lebanon until Turkish times.

and had no dealings with any one: (Hebrew *wᵉdābār 'ên lāhem 'im 'ādām*); the last word is possibly a scribal error for *'ᵃram*, 'the Aramaeans' (so Greek versions). Aramaean tribal confederacies had by this time settled in the vicinity. Warlike, like Israel, they might have proved valuable allies to the Phoenicians, and it would be the business of the spies to find out the state of relations between them and the Phoenicians of Laish.

lacking nothing that is in the earth, and possessing wealth: cf. MT, *wᵉ'ên maklîm dābār bā'āreṣ yôrēš 'eṣer* ('and there was none in the land possessing authority that might put them to shame'), a translation literally just possible, but unlikely. The versions give no help, but the text may be restored with the minimum of emendation: *'ên mikkol-dābār bā'āreṣ rēš wā'ōṣer* ('there was no dearth or shortage of a single thing in the land', which is stated in different words in the spies' report in v. 10. Here we may note the partitive preposition *min* with the singular after the negative, which, as in Arabic signifies 'not a single . . .'; cf. 1 Sam. 14:45: 'there shall not fall a single hair of his'.

8. What do you report?: lit. 'What you?' *EVV* feasibly assume haplography of 'say' (*'ômᵉrîm*) before the first word v. 9, 'and they said' (*wayyô'mᵉrû*). The reply is not a factual statement, but a call to aggressive action, so sanguine were the emissaries.

The Danite Migration: the Appropriation of Micah's Levite and Cult Equipment 18:11–27a

11f. Zorah and Eshtaol: again mentioned alone (cf. v. 2) in connection with the association of Dan with the foothills of Judah, indicating the limited settlement of Dan there. The place-names **Mahaneh-dan** (lit. 'camp of Dan') between those places (cf. 13:25), and **Kiriath-jearim** (v. 12), some six miles eastwards, probably relate rather to rallying-places of the scattered elements of Dan than stages in the emigration, as the present passage suggests. It is even possible that Mahaneh-dan in both localities may be a corruption of 'Manahathites', a clan of Dan, who are located near Kiriath-jearim (1 Chr. 2:52, 54); cf. the burial-place of Manoah, whose name indicates the same clan, between Zorah and Eshtaol. See further, on 13:2.

12. Kiriath-Jearim: by Qiryat al-'Ainab, also called Abu Ghōsh; see on Jos. 15:9.

13. The hill country of Ephraim: the route of the migration, like the home of Micah, is not further particularised, but probably followed the Wādī 'ṣ-Ṣurār, as the localities in vv. 11f. indicate, so that 'the hill country of Ephraim' might be the upper course of the wadi, just north of Jerusalem.

14. in these houses: indicates an open village.

15. asked him of his welfare: in Hebrew idiom, 'greeted him'. The mass of the Danites thus diverted the attention of the Levite while the five former spies stole the cult equipment.

16. men of the Danites, armed with their weapons of war: so *RSV* rightly, associating the adjective with the men, the phrase 'men of the Danites' being misplaced in MT by a scribal error.

by the entrance of the gate: this normally suggests a gate in a walled settlement, but here it may indicate a gate in the courtyard of Micah's house, which served also as the precinct of his sanctuary.

17. went up: indicating that the house was on a higher level. On the two images here envisaged, see on 17:2–4. On the **ephod** and **teraphim**, see on v. 5.

18. What are you doing?: the protest is remarkably feeble.

19. a father and a priest: also the terms of Micah's invitation; see on 17:10.
a tribe and a family in Israel: the use of 'family' (*mišpāḥāh*), better, 'clan', *along with* 'tribe' (*šēbeṭ*), suggests that 'tribe' is a secondary gloss, the Danites being better described as a 'clan' (cf. v. 11; 13:2).

21. putting the little ones and the cattle and the goods in front of them: they were apprehensive of pursuit and attack, which suggests that Micah might have had more supporters than the narrative suggests (cf. vv. 22f.).
goods: (Hebrew *hakk^{e}buddāh*; lit. 'weight'); cf. Gen. 31:1; Isa. 10:3, where the masculine form is used.

22. were called out: the regular description of the local rally in Jg. Micah had obviously been able to rally some of his neighbours.

23. that you come with such a company: Burney's translation is better, 'that you are up in arms' (see on v. 22).

24. my gods: the plural is possible, but probably the singular is to be understood.

25. angry fellows: lit. 'acrid of temper' (cf. Moore, *op. cit.*, ad loc.); not 'embittered', but rather 'resentful'. On 'temper' (*nepeš*), see on 16:16.

The Danite Migration: the Capture of Laish, the Founding of Dan, and the Establishment of the Cult **18:27b–31**

28. On the location of the city and its aloofness from Aramaean neighbours, see on v. 7.
in the valley which belongs to Beth-rehob: Beth-rehob is mentioned in connection with the Aramaeans in 2 Sam. 10:6, 8, where it is also associated with Maacah, probably the Aramaean tribe, whose name is preserved in Abel-beth-Maacah (Tell Ibl al-Qamḥ, *c.* four miles west of Dan), and with Zobah about Ba'albek in the Biq'a south of Ḥamā, according to Assyrian inscriptions of the seventh century, and with Ṭob, the steppe north-east of Gilead, where Jephthah took refuge (11:3). In view of the location of Dan **in the valley which belongs to Beth-rehob**, a particular site is envisaged, which may be Bāniās, as proposed by Nötscher (*op. cit.*, p. 70).

29. Dan their ancestor, who was born to Israel: i.e. to the individual Jacob, a reference to the patriarchal history in the narrative of the Pentateuch (Gen. 30:5f.), suggesting literary redaction rather than original tradition.

30. the graven image: note the singular here (cf. vv. 14, 17, 18, 20. See on 17:2–4).

Jonathan the son of Gershom, son of Moses: Jonathan was probably the name of the Levite, reputedly the first priest of the tribal sanctuary of Dan. He is represented as the son of Gershom, the son of Moses (Exod. 2:22; 18:3). If this is intended literally, it surely indicates the redactor. But it may signify that he was of the Gershomite branch of the Levites. 'Moses' is converted in MT to 'Manasseh' with the addition of the letter 'n' above the other consonants. By the use of the name of the apostate king of Judah, the scribes preserve the name of Moses from the taint of idolatry in the cult of Dan.

until the day of the captivity of the land: probably the deportation by Tiglath-pileser III in 734 BC, when all the kingdom of Israel except Samaria and district was reorganised as Assyrian provinces.

31. as long as the house of God was at Shiloh: if the text is to be accepted, this may simply assert the fact that the two cults were contemporary until the cessation of Shiloh as the sanctuary of the ark (1 Sam. 4:11; cf. Jer. 7:12, 14; 26:6, 9; cf. Ps. 78:60ff.). On **Shiloh**, see Jos. 18:1. But 'Shiloh' may be a scribal inversion of the consonants of *hallayiš*, the original name of Dan.

APPENDIX B

THE AFFAIR OF GIBEAH AND THE BENJAMINITE WAR

19–21

For sources and literary affinities, see Introduction, pp. 224ff.

The Levite's Recovery of his Concubine 19:1–10a

Here the reference to the woman as a 'wife' (*'iššâh*) and a 'concubine' (*pîlegeš*) and to her father as 'his father-in-law' (*ḥōtenô*, v. 4, 9) have been taken to indicate duplicate traditions. This, however, does not necessarily follow. Ugaritic usage indicates that *'iššâh* refers to various degrees of marriage, requiring further qualification when it denoted a fully legal wife. The status of *pîlegeš*, on the other hand, as 8:31 and ch. 9 indicate, denotes a regular status like that of a *ṣadīqa* wife in early Arab usage, or a concubine contracted for a certain period (e.g. Hos. 3:3). *ḥôtēn*, rendered here 'father-in-law', may, as in Arabic, denote either the father-in-law or brother-in-law (cf. 1:16; 4:11), or any male relative through marriage, particularly the one assuming responsibility for the rights and duties of the wife. There does seem, however, to be evidence of duplicate sources in v. 9, when it is twice said in different words that the day is declining, and the invitation to stay overnight is given variously in the singular and the plural. Again, though the men of Gibeah demand to abuse the Levite carnally (19:22) and actually abuse his concubine until she dies (v. 25), the Levite's accusation is that they had murderous designs on him (20:5). The host's offer of his own daughter and his guest's concubine to appease the lust of the townsmen (v. 24) would be as much a breach of the convention of hospitality; cf. the accidental killing of a guest's camel in the Arab tribe of al-Basūs, which occasioned a forty-year tribal war. Here, then, we submit, is another trace of the variant tradition, unskilfully joined to the tradition of the offering by the Levite of his concubine. The refusal of the offer of the host's daughter (v. 25*a*) is from a different tradition, which here follows Gen. 19 more closely, and is probably the contribution of the redactor.

The dating of the incident 'in those days, when there was no king in Israel' may be redactional repetition of 18:1, anticipating the establishment of the Monarchy in the next part of the Deuteronomistic History. It is no part of an original tradition like 18:1, which we understand as reflecting the animadversion on the tribal cult at Dan by priests of the royal sanctuary at Dan.

1. sojourning: see on 17:8.

the remote parts of the hill country of Ephraim: from the Levite's return journey this was in the north. The **hill country of Ephraim** may denote the tribal district rather than the geographical region (see on Jos. 20:7), since the affinity of the Levite with the social group Ephraim is a cardinal feature of the passage.

concubine: (Hebrew *pîlegeš*). See introduction to this section.

2. became angry with him: so *RSV* after some MSS of LXX and Old Latin versions. Burney (ad loc.) reads *wattiz'ap* for MT *wattizneh* ('and she played the harlot'); cf. Koehler (*Lexicon*, p. 261), who retains MT, taking the verb as a cognate of Akkadian *zinû* ('to be angry'). The whole transaction in the sequel, presuming MT to be correct, would suggest that there was a regular contract between the Levite and the woman's family; cf. 'many days' in what appears to be such a contract in Hos. 3:3. Koehler's interpretation, on the other hand, is supported by v. 3, which speaks of the Levite speaking kindly to, i.e. soothing, the girl.

some four months: lit. 'days, four months', the latter particularising on the former, which is indefinite. Even so the phrase is peculiar, and may be a corruption of 'many days' (*yāmîm rabbîm*), 'four' being in Hebrew *'arbā'âh*.

3. her husband: this implies a regular contractual association, which would obtain even if the woman were *pîlegeš*. See on v. 2, and Introduction to this section.

and bring her back: so *RSV* with the versions for MT 'to bring it back'.

and he came: so *RSV*, with certain LXX texts, for MT, 'and she brought him in'.

4. his father-in-law, the girl's father: the latter defines the former, which in the Arabic cognate may be father-in-law, brother-in-law or any male relative of the wife. On the relevance of this to source-analysis, see on v. 2, and Introduction to this section.

5. a morsel of bread: note litotes, as in Gen. 18:5–8.

6. let your heart be merry: lit. 'be good', the conventional description of the relaxation at a party (cf. v. 22; 16:25).

8. tarry until the day declines: in view of the fact that in v. 9 the declining of the day (a different phrase) is alleged as a reason for spending the night, the text has been suspected. Certain MSS of LXX read 'and he persuaded him' and 'he/they tarried', for the imperative 'tarry' has been conjectured. The reference may rather be in the first place to the coolness of the afternoon, which is noted by the Arabs (Dalman, *Arbeit und Sitte*, I.2, reprint 1964, p. 613), who use the evening greeting after midday, and the second reference in v. 9, lit. 'the day has drooped to sunset', may be to the quick decline of the day towards the early darkness of those latitudes; cf. 'the sun has declined to setting' in the idiom of the modern Arab peasants, referring to any time after 3 p.m.

9. tarry all night. Behold, the day draws to its close: Hebrew *hinneh ḥanôt hayyôm*, the third different reference to the declining of the day. The imperative is in the masculine plural, and may indicate a variant tradition from v. 6, where the singular of the same verb is used. The following clause is a doublet of 'the day has drooped (*RSV*, **waned**) towards sunset' (*RSV*, **evening**) (*hinneh-nā' rāpāh hayyôm*), which again may indicate a variant source; but cf. note on v. 8. The verb *ḥānāh* is not attested in this sense elsewhere in the Old Testament; but the meaning of the cognate in Arabic and Syriac, 'to bend down', suggests that this is the root meaning of Hebrew *ḥānāh* ('to camp'). Calculating from sunset at Gibeah about 6 pm, the party must have left Bethlehem at about 3 pm, which is reckoned by the Arabs as evening (*'asr*); cf. 2 Kg. 16:15.

10a. Jebus: as in 1 Chr. 11:4f., glossed as **Jerusalem**, which is attested in the Amarna Tablets, *c.* 1400 BC, and the Egyptian Execration Texts from Luxor, *c.* 1850 BC, applies particularly to Jerusalem immediately before David's occupation (2 Sam. 5:6ff.), the name being an artificial reconstruction from the inhabitants, 'the Jebusites'. The first reference to those just before David's occupation may suggest that they were kindred of the Philistines, who garrisoned certain parts of the central highlands at this time, e.g. Gibeah and Michmash, just north of Jerusalem. E. A. Speiser's view that the Jebusites were Hurrian on the evidence of the theophoric name of Abdi-Khepa, the chief of Jerusalem in the Amarna Age, two and a half centuries earlier (*The World History of the Jewish People*, I, 1964, p. 159), is precarious. **Jebus** is used of the city only here and in 1 Chr. 11:4, 5, so that in Jg. 19:10 it probably indicates the redactor of the Deuteronomistic History.

The Journey to Gibeah and the Night's Lodging **19:10b–21**

We find no certain evidence of a duplicate tradition here. The statement that the men of the place were Benjaminites (v. 16*c*) seems obviously a post-Exilic gloss.

11. the day was far spent: lit. 'had gone down', reading *yārad* for *rād* of MT. The phrase is unique, though intelligible, the reference being to the decline of the sun.

12. the city of foreigners: so *RSV*, correctly, for MT, 'a foreigner'. The explicit mention of a settlement of 'the people of Israel' in contrast to 'foreigners' designedly emphasises the breach of hospitality by the men of Gibeah. The reference to foreigners here reflects the 'Hivite', i.e. Hurrian, settlements in the vicinity, such as Gibeon (see on Jos. 9:3).

Gibeah: lit. 'hill', is generally defined as 'Gibeah of Benjamin' (1 Sam. 13:15, etc.) or 'Gibeah of Saul' (1 Sam. 11:4, etc.) to avoid confusion with nearby Geba' (also 'a hill'). Listed as a settlement in Benjamin in Jos. 18:28, it is identified with Tell al-Fūl, *c.* four miles north of Jerusalem, where excavations by Albright in 1922 and 1923 revealed occupation since *c.* 1200 BC, or possibly just before (Albright, *AASOR* 4, 1924, pp. 7f.; 44ff.; *BASOR* 52, 1933, p. 7; L. A. Sinclair, *AASOR* 34–35, 1960, pp. 1ff.), the first settlement being destroyed by fire, *c.* 1100 BC, which Albright related to the destruction of Gibeah in Jg. 20:40. The ancient road to the north evidently followed the dry ridge, as most ancient roads did, just west of the watershed, the same line as was taken by the Roman road and which is still visible between Tell al-Fûl and ar-Rām (Ramah) slightly west of the present road from Jerusalem to Nāblus.

14. the sun went down on them: an important feature in foot-travel in Palestine even in Mandatory times, since scarcely an hour intervenes between sunset and darkness and closed doors.

15. and they turned aside: i.e. from the comparatively level road to the hill-top on which the village, like most in ancient Palestine, was situated for security.

in the open square of the city: lit. 'the broad place'. Such settlements were huddled closely together within their walls. Streets were narrow lanes, but the space within the gate was open, and was in consequence a place of business or social life (cf. Ru. 4:1; Job. 29:7; Prov. 31:23); e.g. the Damascus Gate of modern Jerusalem, with its money-changers, notaries, public scribes and cafés. Here local elders gave arbitration, justice was dispensed (Dt. 22:24; Am. 5:15, etc.) and a man's reputation was sustained or marred (Prov. 31:23). Here the two angels are met and invited by Lot to spend the night (Gen. 19:1, J) in the first of the significant close parallels between the story of Sodom and one variant of the story of the outrage at Gibeah.

16. As in Gen. 19, the hospitality of the sojourner emphasises by contrast the churlishness of the natives.

18. I am going to my home: so *RSV*, after LXX, for MT, 'the house of Yahweh', which is probably a scribal corruption, the pronominal suffix *y* being mistaken for the abbreviation of 'Yahweh', this being suggested to the late scribe by the priestly status of the Levite, probably assumed to be attached to the shrine of Shiloh, which lay further north.

19. straw: Hebrew *teben*, Arabic *tibn*, the straw chopped small by the threshing, still used as fodder.

provender: Hebrew *mispô'*, known as fodder only here and in Gen. 24:32; 42:27; 43:24, from a verbal root attested in Ugaritic, Aramaic and Palmyrene meaning 'to nourish' (G. A. Cooke, *NSI*, no. 121, line 7).

the young man with your servants: possibly better 'the young man with your servant' (i.e. 'me' of deferential address).

20. Peace be to you: after the conventional enquiry 'Whither and whence?', which established that the stranger was not an enemy, the bond of hospitality is established by the greeting.

21. gave provender: lit. 'gave mixed fodder' (Hebrew *wayyābol*, *Q^{e}re*; or *wayyibbôl*, *K^{e}tib*); cf. Arabic *bulla* and Hebrew *bālîl*, 'fodder', 'chopped straw mixed with grain' (Job. 6:5; 24:6) from the root *bālal* ('to mix').

The Outrage at Gibeah 19:22–28

22. base fellows: (Hebrew *b^{e}nê b^{e}lîya'al*). According to the pointing of MT, this is a compound of a negative particle *b^{e}lî* and a verbal noun *ya'al* ('profit'), hence usually taken as 'worthless'. But the phrase *naḥ^{a}lê b^{e}lîya'al* parallel to *ḥab^{e}lê-māwet* ('the bonds of death') in Ps. 18:6 (*EVV*, v. 5) = 2 Sam. 22:5 suggests that the original phrase may have been *b^{e}nê b^{e}lîa'-l, b^{e}lîa'* or *b^{e}lôa'*, meaning 'ruin',

'perdition', and final *l* being an abbreviation of *'el*, which as a predicate in Hebrew and Ugaritic has a superlative significance, 'awful' or 'vast'. However this may be, *bᵉlîya'al* is personified in intertestamental literature as Belial, or, by phonetic dissimulation, Beliar (cf. 2 Cor. 6:15).
beset the house round about: as the Sodomites in Gen. 19:4.
that we may know him: i.e. carnally (cf. Gen. 19:4). This enormous breach of the convention of hospitality was possible only because the host was a sojourner; but on that account it was doubly odious, since the sojourner (*gēr*, see on 17:8) was under the protection of God.

23. this vile thing: Hebrew *nᵉbālâh* means rather 'wantonness', caring nothing for the restraints of reason, morality or religion.

24. The host's offer of his own daughter (see Introduction to this section) emphasises his punctilio in the law of hospitality and the defence of his guest, which emphasises by contrast the xenophobia of the louts of Gibeah (cf. Gen. 19:8).
ravish them: Hebrew *'innāh* is the technical term for rape (Gen. 34:2; Dt. 21:14; 22:24, 29; 2 Sam. 13:12; 14:22, 32). The pronominal suffix *m* seems at first sight masculine, but it may be a vestigial dual form.

25. abused her: Hebrew *wayyit'allᵉlû bāh*; cf. Exod. 10:2; Num. 22:29, 'to make cruel sport of'.
as the dawn began to break: lit. 'as the dawn went up', the false dawn, a feature of which is faint shafts of light shooting up into the sky before actual sunrise (v. 26).

The Levite's Appeal to the Tribes of Israel 19:29–30

The division of the body recalls Saul's graphic summons in 1 Sam. 11:7, the actual phraseology of which is largely repeated. This suggests that this particular embellishment and the assumption of the twelve-tribe Israel, which is foreign to the sources of Jos.–Jg., is from the Deuteronomistic Historian or the later redactor. In any case, it is one other example of the literary influence here of the Deuteronomistic History as a whole which characterises this section. It will be recalled that Saul's dramatic gesture was also associated with Gibeah.

30. Some MSS of LXX read 'And he charged the men whom he sent saying, Say these words to every man of Israel, Has such a thing as this happened from the day that the children of Israel came up out of the land of Egypt to this day? Consider it, take counsel, speak.' The three last verbs, being in the imperative, are obviously part of the message. The verbs 'was' (*wᵉhāyāh*) and 'said' (*wᵉʾāmar*) in MT could only be frequentative, indicating the repetition of the response of those who at various times were shown the grisly remains.

The War with Benjamin 20:1–48

For historical relevance and literary analysis, see Introduction to Jg., pp. 225ff.

The Assembly 20:1–3

1. came out: probably idiomatic, for war or to the sacral assembly (see on 2:15).
the congregation: (Hebrew *hāʿēdâh*), here essentially a religious community, lit. 'those who keep tryst' (*môʿēd*), characteristic of P, though meaning generally an assembly or gathering in a non-religious sense, e.g. a swarm of bees (see on Jos. 18:1).
was assembled: though used generally in earlier sources, the verb *qāhal* is used characteristically in P in the Pentateuch for the gathering of the religious assembly (*qāhāl*).
Dan to Beersheba: the conventional north and south limits of the land settled by Israel. The specification of those two places may be owing to their significance as sanctuaries and objectives of pilgrimage at the extremities of the historical Israel (Am. 8:14) as Täubler proposed (*Biblische Studien, I. Die Epoche der Richter*, ed. H.-J. Zobel, 1958, p. 41). Such a comprehensive 'Israel', including Judah and Simeon (cf. 5:13–18) in the time of the judges, is unrealistic.
the land of Gilead: this refers generally to the north part of Transjordan.
to the LORD at Mizpah: indicated a sanctuary at Mizpah, Tell an-Naṣbeh, *c.* four miles north-north-west of Gibeah, was in Ephraim, according to the description of the boundary of Benjamin in Jos. 18:13–20, in contrast to the town-list in vv. 21–26, esp. 26, where, like Bethel, it is located in Benjamin, reflecting Josiah's administration. As a boundary sanctuary between Ephraim and Benjamin, but of minor significance than Bethel (see above, p. 271), it may have been the natural resort at the initial stage of proceedings; but it may reflect the home of the Deuteronomistic Historian or/and the redactor (see above, p. 272).

2. the chiefs of all the people: Hebrew *pinnôt* (lit. 'corners'; cf.

1 Sam. 14:38; Isa. 19:13), recalls the Arabic Rukn ad-Dîn ('the Corner-stone of the Faith'), the title of the Mameluke Sultan Baibars. The people (Hebrew *hā'ām*) denotes primarily a kinship unit, and eventually in Israel the religious community (see on 5:2).
four hundred thousand: cf. forty thousand in 5:8. Making the modest allowance for a wife, two children and a parent for each fighting man in Israel, apart from Benjamin, the total would be over two million, if not even more! Even if instead of 'thousand' we regard *'elep* as signifying, as has been suggested, a detachment from each clan numbering either more or less than a thousand, this far exceeds computations based on archaeological data and the statistics of any given period in the history of Palestine, except in the highly technological modern state of Israel, and is plainly redactional.

The Recapitulation of the Outrage 20:4–7

5. **meant to kill me:** lit. 'conceived an image . . .', i.e. formed the intention. There is no mention of this in the narrative in ch. 19.

6. On the post-Exilic affinities of **the country of the inheritance of Israel** and **abomination** (*zimmâh*), see Introduction, p. 227.

The Response of Israel 20:8–11

See Introduction, p. 229.

8. **to his tent:** i.e. home, surviving as an anachronism long after the settlement.

9. **we will go up against it:** so *RSV*, rightly, after LXX, the verb being omitted in MT before similar consonants in 'against it'. The verb has a technical sense 'to attack', *sc.* the town on its elevated mound (see on Jos. 22:12).
by lot: to determine the foraging party (v. 10). Perhaps **a hundred of a thousand**, etc., is a redactional elaboration of the muster of four hundred thousand in v. 2, which raised an impossible problem of provisioning.

10. **so that when they come they may requite Gibeah of Benjamin:** so *RSV* for MT, which reads 'Geba', an easy corruption, since both Geba' and Gib'ah mean 'hill' and are neighbouring villages, though quite distinct, lying respectively east and west of the watershed of Palestine. MT, *la'ᵃśôt lᵉbô'ām lᵉgeba' binyāmîn*, is irregular, and probably corrupt. LXX^{A} and the Syriac version read *labbā'îm la'ᵃśôt lᵉgib'âh* ('for those who come to deal with Gibeah').

11. united as one man: Hebrew *kᵉʾîš ʾeḥād ḥᵃbērîm*; cf. Moore, 'confederates'.

Abortive Negotiations **20:12–13**

Redactional; see Introduction, p. 230.

12. tribe of Benjamin: so, rightly, the versions, for MT plural.

13. Though the sin of the guilty impairs the whole community, here of Benjamin, the assembly would have been content with the capital punishment of only the guilty individuals. It was only after identifying themselves with the guilty persons by their refusal to give them up that Benjamin came collectively under the ban. This is a case of corporate responsibility rather than 'corporate personality'. The incident no doubt reflects a situation not uncommon in the growth of the sacral community, when local solidarity and the honour involved in the protection of the members of each group conflicted with loyalty to the sacral confederacy. An interesting analogy to the attitude of Benjamin in protecting their own tribesmen is the situation among the clans of Mecca at the time of Muhammad, where his clan, the Banū Hāshim, though not cordially supporting him, effectively protected the Prophet against the stronger, more hostile clans in his unpopular mission.

Mobilisation of Benjamin **20:14–17**

On literary analysis, see Introduction, p. 228f.

15. twenty-six thousand men: cf. certain MSS of LXX, 25,000; but cf. v. 35, which gives the casualties of Benjamin as 25,100; cf. v. 46, which gives 25,000 casualties, and v. 47, which gives 600 survivors.

16. picked men who were left-handed: lit. 'restricted in the right hand' (see on 3:15), a *corps élite*, against whom the shield of the antagonist on the left arm was no adequate protection. This seems to have been a speciality of the archers and slingers of Gibeah, who were among David's retainers at Ziklag (1 Chr. 12:2).

The Consultation of the Oracle before the Attack **20:18**

Redactional after 1:1ff., where in reply to a similar consultation Judah takes the initiative in the occupation of the land. This is prefaced by the statement of the muster of four hundred thousand men against Benjamin, as in v. 2. For literary analysis, see Introduction, p. 229f.

18. Bethel: lit. 'the house of God'. Formally, this may be a proper as well as a common noun; but in view of the specific note on Bethel as the sanctuary of Yahweh in v. 28, it is certainly Bethel, Arab Beitīn, envisaged as the scene of the fast in v. 26 and of the public mourning in 2:1–5 (cf. Gen. 35:1–15).

Two Defeats of the Confederacy in Two Days' Fighting; the Oracle for the Third Day's Battle **20:19–28**

The passage is badly edited, and v. 22 is out of place before v. 23. See further, Introduction, p. 228f.

21. felled to the ground: so *RSV*, after Burney and C. J. Ball, who took the verb as cognate with Akkadian *šaḫâtu* ('to fall').

21, 25, 26. There is a definite schematisation in the representation of two full-scale battles with such large casualties before the final battle, and the fast of all Israel with holocausts and communion-offerings at such a juncture is unrealistic. On the other hand, **Bethel** as an important sanctuary of Ephraim and a boundary sanctuary with Benjamin probably played a significant part in the campaign, prompting the redactional gloss on the location there of 'the ark of the covenant' and the Aaronid priesthood in vv. 27*b*–28*a*. Perhaps the fast and sacrifices are an elaboration of the redactor in v. 26, the nucleus of the tradition being the fast and consultation of the oracle on the next steps in the campaign. The representation of the three days' battle, with the heavy casualties and the intervening fasts, sacrifices and consultation of the oracle at Bethel, is probably the editor's stylisation of several stages in a more protracted struggle. See further, Introduction, p. 229.

26. burnt offerings and peace offerings: the former are rendered by LXX 'holocausts', wholly offered to God and expressing total dependence; the latter were communion offerings, effecting a reintegration with God through the convention of a common meal, the blood, fat and vital parts of the victim being the portion of God and the rest being eaten by the community. The present passage, which is relevant to the sacral assembly, probably reflects the reintegration of the community and God through communion-offerings proper to that occasion (cf. Jos. 8:31; Exod. 24:5, which, however, were not in the heat of a campaign).

27. the ark of the covenant of God: a Deuteronomistic phrase, expressing the Deuteronomistic theology of the ark not as the symbol of the presence of God, or the footstool of his throne, but as the receptacle of the covenant tablets. The Deuteronomistic conception notwithstanding, the association of the ark with Bethel before Shiloh may be a genuine ancient tradition of Ephraim.

28. Phinehas the son of Eleazar, the son of Aaron: cf. Exod. 6:25; Num. 25:7, 11 (both P) and Jos. 22:13, a post-Exilic redactional insertion. This assumes a date early in the settlement of Palestine. The association of this family with Ephraim is borne out by the tradition of their association with the ark at the Ephraimite sanctuary of Shiloh (1 Sam. 1–4), and by the burial of Eleazar in the hill-country of Ephraim (Jos. 24:33). The association of Ephraim with Bethel, probably earlier than the establishment of Shiloh as the sanctuary of the ark, may be indicated in the tradition of the occupation of Bethel by 'the house of Joseph' in 1:22–25.

The Third Day's Fighting 20:29–48

The ambush and final defeat of Benjamin, a composite account with redactional harmonisations of the variant traditions of the casualties (vv. 45*a*–46). See Introduction, pp. 228ff.

31. and were drawn away from the city: so *RSV*, apparently reading *wayyontᵉqû* for asyndetic MT *hontᵉqû*, which would be a feasible scribal corruption (so Ehrlich, Burney), rather than a late redactional gloss, as the asyndeton and uncontracted *n* in MT has suggested.

in the highways: lit. 'raised causeways' (*mᵉsillôt*), indicating a much-frequented road (see on 19:12). Two such roads are envisaged, one to Bethel, the great north road, and the other probably to Gibeon (corrupted in MT to 'Gibeah'), and so on to the coastal plain by the Wādī Salmān to the valley of Aijalon, one of the recognised passes from the coastal plain to the central plateau north of Jerusalem. An ambush can scarcely be envisaged in the open country visible from Gibeah towards the west, and we suppose that here a diversion was created by an attack on Gibeah by a relatively small body (as is suggested by thirty casualties) and a withdrawal to where the main body was stationed as a decoy at Baal-tamar, a place not certainly known, but located by Eusebius just north-east of Tell al-Fûl (Gibeah). Meanwhile an ambush had been laid nearer Gibeah, apparently east of the watershed, utilizing the wadis in the bare, rocky country (*maʿᵃreh*) by Gebaʿ, three miles east of Gibeah (v. 33), where *RSV* reads 'west of Geba' (*maʿᵃrab gebaʿ*).

33. rushed out: (Hebrew *mēgîaḥ*); better, 'burst forth'; from the same root as in Gihon ('the Gusher'), the intermittent spring in the Kidron Valley, the source of the water supply of ancient Jerusalem.

37. rushed upon: (Hebrew *wayyipšᵉṭû*); better, 'deployed from ambush', a variant of the tradition 'burst forth' in v. 33.

moved out: (Hebrew *wayyimšôk*); probably also 'deployed', as indicated by the subject 'ambush'; cf. *mešek-hazzera'*, possibly 'prolongation of seed', i.e. seed for broadcasting (Ps. 125:6).

38. the appointed signal: lit. 'the appointment', that which had been agreed upon. This, and the sequel in the variant tradition, were probably influenced by the tradition of the fall of Ai in Jos. 8:19ff., unless Jos. 8:19ff was influenced by that of the campaign in Jg. 20. The sundry features in Jg. 1–20, which indicate the influence on the post-Exilic redactor of earlier literary traditions in the Pentateuch and Deuteronomistic History, however, suggest that the former possibility is the more likely.

39. that . . . the men of Israel should turn in battle: evidently reading *wᵉyahpôk* for MT *wayyahpôk* ('and they turned'), which is supported by LXX^A. LXX^B reads 'and the children of Israel saw that the ambush had already taken Gibeah, they stood in their ranks'. Verse 38 indicates that something like what *RSV* reads should follow.

40. looked behind them: lit. 'turned (and looked) back'.

behold the whole city went up in smoke: better, 'behold the holocaust of the city', after Moore (ad loc.), who cites Dt. 13:16.

42. and those who came out of the cities destroyed them in the midst of them: better '. . . out of the city . . . in the midst', reading *mēhā'îr*, with dittograph of *m* of the preformative of the following word, and *bᵉtāwek* for MT *bᵉtôkô*. The Benjaminites were caught between the main force of the Israelites and the ambush, which had taken the city, from which they then advanced to cut off the Benjaminites.

43. Cutting down: so *RSV* after LXX, reading *kittᵉtû* ('they beat down' or 'crushed'). MT reads *kittᵉrû* ('they surrounded'), which, however, means 'ringed about', and, if not unintelligible, is less fitting than the emendation, which suggests crushing as between the hammer and the anvil.

they pursued them: better, 'and they pursued them', reading *wayyirdᵉpûm* for MT *hirdîpûhû*. *y* is easily corrupted to *h* in the archaic Hebrew script, as is *m* to *w*.

and trod them down: reading *wayyidrᵉkûm* for the asyndetic *hidrîkûhû*. On the particular scribal corruption, see preceding note.

from Nohah: so *RSV*, after LXX^B, for MT *mᵉnûḥâh* ('resting-place'), with a change of vowels only. Noḥah is cited as a clan, hence a settlement, of Benjamin in 1 Chr. 8:2, the location of which is unknown, though the association of Noḥah with Rapha in 1 Chr. 8:2 might suggest the plateau north-west of Gibeah, where a place Irpeel is known (Jos. 18:27), *c.* three miles north-west of Gibeah.

Alternatively, assuming haplography of *m* in MT *m^e^nûḥâh*, we may read *mimm^e^nûḥâh* ('without respite'), as proposed by G. R. Driver (*ALUOS* 4, 1964, pp. 6–25, ad loc.).

45. toward the wilderness: east of the watershed, where the land in the rain-shadow rapidly deteriorates.

Rimmon: Arab Rammān on the rock-spur, *c.* six miles north-east of Gibeah, over the upper part of the Wādī 's-Suweiniṭ. On the numbers here, as in v. 46, see Introduction, p. 229.

to Gidom: no such locality is known. The reading may be either 'Geba', with certain MSS of LXX, or perhaps better 'Gibeon'. The passage is redactional.

48. men: so certain Hebrew MSS, reading *m^e^tîm* and omitting *mēʿîr* of MT *mēʿîr m^e^tôm*.

The Provision of Wives for the Survivors of Benjamin 21:1–25

Verse 17, which is almost certainly to be restored with certain MSS of LXX as 'How shall those of Benjamin who have escaped survive?' or the like, coming after the practical solution of the problem by the provision of girls from the massacre of Jabesh-gilead (vv. 7, 8, 12*a*, *b*), suggests that the sequel, the provision of wives by the rape of the girls at the vintage-festival at Shiloh (vv. 18–23), is a variant tradition, possibly the historification of a local fertility rite at the festival. The two traditions have been combined by the post-Exilic redactor, whose hand is evident in the twice-redundant 'And the people had compassion for Benjamin, because the Lord had made a breach in the tribes of Israel' (v. 15) and the raising again of the question of wives for Benjamin by 'the elders of the congregation' (v. 16) and the same question in v. 17 (according to certain MSS of LXX). Before vv. 15f., 'but they did not suffice for them' may be a redactional harmonization between the two traditions. Further indication of redaction is v. 9, where the statement of the absence of representatives of Jabesh-gilead at the assembly of the sacral community is tautological after v. 8*b* and in vv. 9–11 with its schematised and grossly exaggerated number of twelve thousand armed men against Jabesh-gilead, the conception of Israel as 'the congregation' (*hāʿēḏâh*), the description of Shiloh as 'which is in the land of Canaan' (v. 12*b*), and the language and severely doctrinal theology and possibly the literary influence of the Pentateuchal tradition of the massacre at Beth-peor of all except marriageable virgins (Num. 31:17f., P) in the tradition of the rape of the girls at Shiloh. For literary analysis and historical relevance, see further, Introduction, pp. 230ff.

The Oath Prohibiting Marriage with the Benjaminites **21:1**

A redactional elaboration of the Ephraimite denial of connubium to the Benjaminites; see Introduction, p. 231.

the men of Israel had sworn at Mizpah: the binding force of the oath in the presence of Yahweh could be contravened only by the observation of the *letter* of the oath (cf. v. 22). No reason is given for the absence of the isolated community of Jabesh-gilead from the tribal assembly which is envisaged. There was a peculiar tie between Jabesh-gilead and Gibeah, as indicated by two instances in the history of Saul (1 Sam. 11 and 31:11–13); but whether those instances were the consequences of the association of Benjamin with Jabesh-gilead described in Jg. 21:6–14*a* or, as we consider more likely, this passage is an aetiological tradition to account for that association, is uncertain. The relationship between Benjamin and Jabesh-gilead is possibly to be explained in the context of a local association of Benjamin and her neighbours in Transjordan with Gilgal by Jericho as their boundary sanctuary, as Möhlenbrink suggested *à propos* of Jos. 22:1–8 (*ZAW* N.F. 15, 1938, pp. 248f.), or on the assumption of an earlier settlement of Benjamin east of the Jordan, as Mowinckel proposed (*Israels opphav*, p. 125).

Mourning at Bethel **21:2–5**

Redactional introduction to the incident at Jabesh-gilead (vv. 6–14*a*).

2. Bethel: see on 20:18. After the battle this ceremony, which probably involved a fast, was practicable, and indeed natural after the casualties, even granting the exaggeration of both sources and redaction. The intention to evade the oath would be further occasion for the ceremony. The fast was a ritual imposed *ad hoc* by a crisis in the life of the community, which involved suspension of normal activities, familiar to anthropologists as 'rites of separation'. The people at the sanctuary, for instance, are represented as *sitting* in abasement while they wept, like Job on the kitchen midden (Job 2:8).

4. built an altar: in this passage and in the similar passage describing public lamentation at Bethel (2:2–5), which both describe generally a similar occasion, we may suspect a certain stylisation. The redactional passage on the public lamentation at Bethel in 21:2–5 has probably the local aetiological tradition of Bochim ('weepers' or 'weeping') in mind, where sacrifice is also noted. The redactor may have retained a variant tradition pertaining to an obsolete altar or cult-place near Bethel.

5. they had taken a great oath concerning him who did not come up to the LORD: lit. 'for the great oath had been pronounced concerning him . . .'. The definite article may envisage the most solemn adjuration involving the death penalty or excommunication, familiar in the Twelve Adjurations in the sacrament of the covenant (Dt. 27:15–26) and apodictic laws in the Book of the Covenant (e.g. Exod. 21:12, 15, 16, 17; 22:19f.), which use the formula 'he shall surely be put to death'. More closely analogous, though not related to the assembly, was Saul's curse in 1 Sam. 14:24ff. The tradition of the Shiloh affair, or the redaction, assumed such an adjuration (v. 18), which in form conforms to the terseness of the prohibitions in Dt. 27:15–26.

The Affair of Jabesh-gilead **21:6–14a**

For indications of redaction, see Introduction, pp. 230 and 232.

6. had compassion: the reflexive of the same verb is used in the intensive-causative in Isa. 40:1, 'Comfort ye, comfort ye my people!'
is cut off: lit. 'is lopped off', as a branch from the parent tree.

7. for those who are left: lit. 'for them, for those that remain', the later phrase being a redactional gloss.

8. Jabesh-gilead: a night's march from Bethshan (1 Sam. 31:11–13), which agrees with Eusebius' location in Transjordan, six Roman miles from Pella (Fiḥl) in the hills on the way to Gerasa (Jerāsh). There the name may survive in the Wādī Yābis, though the site cannot be precisely determined. Aharoni (*The Land of the Bible*, pp. 223ff., 254ff.) feasibly proposed Tell al-Maqlūb. On the association of the community of Jabesh-gilead with Gibeah, see on v. 1.
the assembly: here the Hebrew is *qāhāl*, as referring to the sacral assembly characteristic of P in the Pentateuch, though used earlier in a general sense, e.g. Gen. 35:11 (a number of peoples in general) and Ezek. 38:15 (the nations associated with Gog and Magog).

9. mustered: lit. 'reviewed', from the root *pāqad*, used of a review before and after battle and in the spiritual sense, when God notices merit and delinquency and 'visits' his people accordingly. Such a review at the sacral assembly is envisaged in 5:13–18, according to the view of Weiser, which we accept.

11. utterly destroy: lit. 'put to the ban' (*ḥerem*) in consequence of 'the great curse' of v. 5. The occasion is not actually a holy war and the language is figurative, indicating a redactional theologoumenon, as suggested by the inclusion of women and children. See Introduction to ch. 21.

that has lain with a male: lit. 'that has known coitus with a male' cf. Num. 31:17. At the end of the verse we should probably read, with LXX[B] and the Vulgate, 'but the virgins shall ye save alive. And they did so'.

12. at Shiloh, which is in the land of Canaan: a redactional gloss. On the defining clause, see on Jos. 21:1; 22:11 (both part of the post-Exilic redaction of the Deuteronomistic History), where it denotes Palestine west of Jordan, the Promised Land proper. Since it appears in the next phase of the Deuteronomistic History as the sanctuary of the ark, assumed by the Deuteronomistic Historian and his early monarchic source and by the redactor to be the rallying-post of all Israel, it is taken here to have the same significance. It was, however, an Ephraimite sanctuary, the ark being peculiarly associated with Ephraim. It may well be that in view of the determined resistance of Benjamin to Ephraimite dominance which underlies the present passage the ark was shifted from Bethel to Shiloh, which then attained the significance it has in 1 Sam. 1–4.

The Problem of Insufficient Wives for the Benjaminites after the affair of Jabesh-gilead **21:14b–16**

A redactional harmonisation of the tradition of the intermarriage of Benjaminites and the virgins of Jabesh-gilead and that of the rape of the girls of Shiloh.

14. but they did not suffice for them: better, if the MT is correct, 'yet so they did not find enough for them', which has the support of certain MSS of LXX. The general tradition of LXX, however, omits the negative particle. This suggests that the original text may have read 'Thus did they find (wives) for them', which would be the end of the tradition of the affair of Jabesh-gilead.

15. Redactional, adapted after v. 6 as the introduction to the Shiloh affair.

16. the elders of the congregation: (Hebrew *ziqᵉnê hāʿēdâh*); cf. Lev. 4:15 (P), so probably from the post-Exilic redactor.

The Rape of the Maidens of Shiloh **21:17–24**

A variant tradition to the incident at Jabesh-gilead, possibly the historification of a rite in the licence of the vintage festival, combined with the Jabesh-gilead tradition by the post-Exilic redactor. See Introduction, pp. 231f.

17. There must be an inheritance for the survivors of Benjamin: MT is so terse as to be suspect, lit. 'And they said, An inheritance of the survivors.' 'Inheritance' (*y^{e}ruššat*) is generally taken as implying land, but that is not the problem in the sequel, which is concerned with the posterity of the survivors. This, however, may be the meaning of *y^{e}ruššat* in the collective feminine singular; cf. the Ugaritic Legend of King Krt, where the king's posterity is in jeopardy and the cognate *yrṯ* stands in parallelism with 'family' (*špḥ*). Some MSS of LXX read 'How may the survivors of Benjamin survive?' (reading *'ēk tiššā'ēr p^{e}lēṭâh l^{e}binyāmîn* for MT *y^{e}ruššat p^{e}lēṭâh l^{e}binyāmîn*).

19. the yearly feast of the LORD: the **feast** (*ḥag*) implies pilgrimage, and is used specifically of the great occasion in the peasant's year in the festal calendar of Israel at the autumnal New Year, which was a harvest festival after the vintage, and anticipated the new cycle of agriculture. The association with **Shiloh** may indicate a period when the Canaanite fertility-cult predominated at Shiloh, either before or soon after the establishment of the cult of Yahweh by the Israelites of Ephraim, in whose district the place lay. The association of the festival with the cult of Yahweh may be the assumption of the redactor, like the location of **Shiloh, which is north of Bethel, on the east of the highway that goes up from Bethel to Shechem, and south of Lebonah**. The narrative implies that the community at Shiloh was of Israelite worshippers of Yahweh, and if this relates to a historical situation, that may have corresponded to Joseph-el and Jacob-el, who are mentioned in the central highlands in the inscriptions of Thothmes III (fifteenth century BC). Such a community would facilitate the assimilation of the Rachel group and their associates to the life of the settled land with its agricultural festivals, and from them, on the periphery of the community of Israel of 5:13–18, wives might be sought in the present emergency. On the vintage festival, see further, on 9:27; and on the selection of brides from girls dancing in the vineyards on the Day of Atonement in post-Exilic Israel, see Introduction, p. 231.

the highway that goes up from Bethel to Shechem: lit. 'a highway . . .'; see on 19:12f.

Lebonah: Arab al-Lubbān, *c.* three miles north-north-west of Shiloh (Khirbet Seilūn). The grapes of Lebonah were used in the service of the Second Temple, and are still celebrated. The local directions are not part of the original tradition. Such usually indicate the post-Exilic redactor.

21. dances: usually associated with primitive religion, man 'dancing out his religion before thinking it out' (cf. 2 Sam. 6:14;

Ps. 150:4). Here it may have been connected with sexual excitement in a rite of imitative magic in the fertility cult.

22. With LXX we should emend the first plural pronominal afformatives to the preposition and to the verb to second plural, 'to you' and 'you will say'.

Grant them graciously to us: emending one letter (feminine for masculine of the pronominal suffix, 'them'). The argument is twofold. First, it refers to the concession of the assembly to admit the seizure of the surviving girls of Jabesh-gilead and appeals to the Ephraimites of Shiloh to be indulgent to those Benjaminites who had failed to get wives there. Then it emphasises that the Ephraimites of Shiloh had not *offered* their daughters to the Benjaminites, and so by consenting to a *fait accompli* they would not be breaking their oath in the assembly (21:2).

else you would now be guilty: this is obviously the sense, suggesting that MT *kā'ēt* (*tē'šāmû*) should be emended to *kî 'attāh* . . ., 'for in that case . . .' (cf. 13:23).

23. and rebuilt the towns: so, correctly, *RSV*; the verb, which generally means 'to build', often means simply 'repair', in this case after a war of some four months (cf. 20:47).

Concluding Summary **21:25**

The final note on the irregularities of the pre-monarchic period if not supporting the hypothesis of a tradition conserved by the priesthood of the royal sanctuary of Bethel, like chs 17–18, is a note from the redactor, dating the episode before the foundation of the Monarchy, which is the theme of the next part of the Deuteronomistic History.

INTRODUCTION
to
Ruth

1. PLACE IN THE CANON

The book of Ruth is associated in Massoretic tradition neither with the Former Prophets (the Deuteronomistic History) nor with the Law in Israel's drama of salvation. It is included among the Writings, one of the 'five rolls' read at the Jewish festivals at least since the twelfth century AD, Ruth being considered appropriate to the Feast of Weeks (Pentecost), which once celebrated the end of the wheat harvest.

The place of the book in the Writings, however, does not reflect a unanimous Jewish tradition. In LXX, which no less than MT represents a Jewish tradition, Ruth appears after Judges. This was suggested by the setting of the story 'in the days when the judges ruled', and specifically two and a half generations before David, according to the genealogy in Ru. 4:18–20. This was evidently taken at its face value by Jewish tradition, which, as reflected in the Babylonian Talmud (*Baba Bathra* 14b), considered that Samuel wrote the book. The positioning of Ruth after Judges in LXX occasioned the order in the Vulgate and in subsequent Western versions. Its place in MT in the Writings certainly indicates late acceptance as canonical Scripture probably no more than two centuries before Christ. But that does not necessarily mean late composition.

2. DATE

The early composition of Ruth was maintained by Jewish tradition in the Talmud. A number of modern scholars have also contended for a comparatively early date (most recently Myers, Gerleman, Fichtner, Lamparter and Campbell) or some time during the Monarchy (Oettli, S. R. Driver). But until lately the consensus among modern critics favoured a date during or after the Exile. There is nowadays a tendency to date the book during the Monarchy.

On grounds of orthography, morphology, syntax, vocabulary and idiom, J. M. Myers saw an affinity with J and E in the Pentateuch, the book having originated as a nurse's tale, first transmitted orally and finally redacted after the Exile. Gerleman, who sees a reflection of the theology of the Story of the Davidic Succession in the providential preparation for David's reign and dynasty through human agencies and motives (so also Lamparter), proposed composition in three stages: first, as a poetic tale of non-Israelite origin circulated orally, then rendered into prose in the ninth or eighth century, when it was given Israelite colouring, and finally redacted to its present form after the Exile. Campbell also proposes an origin in the early Monarchy, possibly reflecting Jehoshaphat's reforms (2 Chr. 17:1–9; 19:4–11).

A date later in the Monarchy, perhaps as late as the time of Jeremiah, has also been suggested (Gunkel, Gressmann, Rudolph, Haller, Hertzberg). The view of the comparatively late composition of Ruth (Eissfeldt, Weiser, Rost-Sellin) is usually supported by reference to social conventions in the book which are held to post-date the legal part of Dt., to alleged Aramaisms, and to the spirit of tolerance and universalism voiced in the Servant Songs in Deutero-Isaiah and in the book of Jonah and contravened by the rigorist policy of Nehemiah and particularly Ezra in the matter of mixed marriages. Since those criteria, however, have been seriously questioned, they may be considered in more detail.

The explanation of the custom of the transfer of a sandal in the transaction of redemption (4:7) has been related to such a custom in connection with the renunciation by a brother-in-law of the right and duty of levirate marriage in Dt. 25:5–10 (Gressmann, p. 274, with comparative material from India, Egypt and among the Arabs). It has been argued that Ruth must post-date the legal part of Dt. in the late seventh century by a considerable time.

But it must be noted that there are significant differences in the transactions in Dt. and Ruth, though both are concerned with levirate marriage. In the former, only a brother-in-law is involved, and that a minor still living in his father's house. There is no mention of the acquisition of property. In divesting the defaulting kinsman of his sandal, the rejected widow publicly spits in his face. In Ruth there is no mention of this rite, and in that of the sandal only the kinsman and Boaz are involved. The rite in Ruth thus betokened renunciation of the kinsman's levirate obligation and his proprietary right which that included (4:7). In Ruth neither the kinsman nor Boaz was a brother of Ruth's dead husband; hence Gressmann (p. 268) supposed that levirate marriage in Ruth reflected wider application in an earlier usage than in Dt. (so also L. M. Epstein, Rowley, Rudolph). The laws in Dt., as C. M. Carmichael has observed on this subject (*JBL* 96, 1977, pp. 321–36) represent a regularisation of procedure after a survey of existing local customs and the rejection of certain of these. It is therefore questionable whether we may date Ruth relative to Dt. 25:5–10 on the grounds of the discrepancy of Ru. 4:7. This passage may be one of the instances of historical verisimilitude in the story, which is set in the time of the judges. But the fact that it is presented as a custom not only ancient but obsolete, since it required explanation, indicates a late date of composition.

Apart from the fact that Aramaisms could indicate an early origin before the development of classical Hebrew or a provincial dialect, as we have proposed in the anecdotes of Elisha in 2 Kg. 4:1–37 (J. Gray, *I & II Kings*, 3rd ed., 1977, p. 467), as well as during the Exilic and post-Exilic period, the Aramaisms in Ruth are now thought to be few. Thus Joüon considers only four were beyond doubt: the verb *śibbēr* in 1:13, the expression *nāśā' nāšîm* ('to take wives') in 1:4, and the verbs *qiyyēm* and *šālap* in 4:7. In his monograph on Aramaisms in the *OT* (*Die Lexikalischen und grammatikalischen Aramaismen in alttestamentlichen Hebräisch*, 1966), M. Wagner admits only *śibbēr* and *ne'ᵉgan*, both in 1:13. In addition, *lāhēn*, taken in the sense 'therefore', is claimed as an Aramaism on the evidence of Dan. 2:6, 9; 4:21, though LXX and the Syriac version understood it as meaning 'for them' (*lāhem*). Since it is unlikely that the Syriac version in an Aramaic dialect would have failed to recognise the Aramaic *lāhēn*, as Rudolph has argued, MT *lāhēn* is probably a scribal corruption of *lāhem* in the archaic Hebrew script. Actually, the expression *nāśā' nāšîm*, in the sense of marriage, is used in the *OT* only in Ru. 1:4 and in the post-Exilic Ezr. 9:2, 12; 10:44, Neh. 13:25; 2 Chr. 11:21; 34:3. Thus, while it may reflect late Aramaic, it may also be a late Hebrew idiom independent of Aramaic, like *'āgan* in 1:13, a *hapax legomenon* in the *OT*. This verb is used in the Mishnah of the compulsion on a woman, whose husband has disappeared and whose death is uncertain, to remain continent (Joüon, p. 40). Here it may be an Aramaism, though this is not certain.

While on the subject of language as a possible indication of the date of the composition of Ruth, we may note that the supporters of an early date adduce such forms as the paragogic *nun* in the 2nd feminine singular and 3rd masculine plural of the imperfect respectively in 2:8, 21; 3:4, 18, and in 2:9; and the 2nd feminine singular of the perfect *yrdty* in 3:3, and *škbty* in 3:4. In the last two instances the final *y* of MT may be cases of dittography in the archaic Hebrew script. The paragogic *nun* might be Aramaic, but could also be archaic Hebrew, or a feature of the local dialect retained by the narrator (as its incidence in the direct speech of Naomi of Bethlehem suggests), or it may be conscious archaising. Modern scholarship is increasingly sceptical about such linguistic features as a criterion of a very early or a post-Exilic date for the composition of Ru. For the most part, the book is in good classical Hebrew narrative prose with a certain poetic cadence, recalling, especially in direct speech, the narrative sources of the Pentateuch J and E and the Story of the Davidic Succession. This, however, need not indicate that Ruth was composed between the tenth and eighth centuries BC, but simply that the prose of this period was the model followed.

It is true that the book of Ruth, free from prejudice and ready to acknowledge true worth wherever it was evinced, reflects the liberal spirit of the Servant Songs in Deutero-Isaiah and in the book of Jonah after the Exile, though without the consciousness of mission which characterises those works. This limitation might reflect rather the confidence of the age of David or Solomon, whose modest empire was cemented by marriages with foreign women, including women from Moab (1 Kg. 11:1), the paternalism of which may be reflected in Boaz' blessing to Ruth in the name of Yahweh, the God of Israel 'under whose wings you have come to take refuge' (2:12). But this is no conclusive argument. While it is true that the appreciation of Ruth the Moabitess, the ancestress of David, contrasts sharply with the rigorous nationalism of Ezra and Nehemiah in the matter of mixed marriages, it may be argued that, if intended as a protest, Ruth would have shown much more evidence of the controversy. Hertzberg is probably right in his view that this issue had not yet been raised in Israel. We believe, nevertheless, that the liberal tone of Ruth is related to practical issues of the time of its composition, notably to the resettlement of the returning exiles, who found it not so easy to reoccupy their ancestral lands (Ezek. 33:24; Zech. 5:1–4; Neh. 5:1–13). So we find that the definitive composition of Ruth is relevant to the post-Exilic period before Ezra and perhaps also before Nehemiah.

The book consciously adapts several of the traditions of the J source of the Pentateuch in Genesis, particularly the stories of Rebekah, Tamar and Joseph, and the story of the wise woman of Tekoa in the Story of the Davidic Succession in general. This, however, proves no more than that the short story in graphic, direct narrative style, with due appraisal of human factors rather than resort to the *deus ex machina* or the miraculous, was known as early as the early Monarchy and could thus be used as a model, as for instance in the book of Jonah, at any subsequent period. In recognising this affinity of Ruth, with the J narratives of the Pentateuch, Eissfeldt has adduced a cogent argument for the late date of Ruth in the refinement of the motifs of Gen. 19:30ff. (Lot and his daughters) and Gen. 38 (Judah and Tamar). A comparison of the characterisation in Ruth with that in Judges leads to the same conclusion. In the latter, outstanding characteristics in the figures are portrayed, often inconsistent with other traits in their character, the figures being strictly subordinate to the theological plan of the history in which they were involved. Ruth, Boaz and Naomi are in themselves character-studies. In them the outstanding social virtues are increasingly refined. If Orpah and the defaulting kinsman fall far short of Ruth and Boaz, they serve as foils to the principal characters. The high degree of literary elaboration and the interest in individual character suggests the late composition of Ruth, though admittedly those are also features of the Story of the Davidic Succession in the tenth century BC.

3. PURPOSE

The date of the book is bound up with the question of its purpose. We have already rejected its primary relevance to the nationalist policy of Nehemiah and Ezra on mixed marriages, though we admit that in extolling the loyalty of Ruth in the family of worshippers of Yahweh, 'under whose wings' she had sought refuge (2:12), the author may have been encouraging foreign women whom Jews had married, before this issue became controversial in the time of Nehemiah and Ezra.

Gunkel (*RGG* V, 1913, col. 107) and Gressmann (p. 284) took the view that Ruth was simply a short story praising the loyalty and worth of Ruth. This, however, is to confuse purpose with form, which is undoubtedly that of the short story or novel, like the Joseph story in Gen.

Rudolph rightly emphasised the significance of 2:12: 'The Lord recompense you for what you have done, and a full reward be given you by the Lord, the God of Israel, under whose wings you have come to take refuge.' This might be taken as encouragement to proselytes. But in view of the affinity in general motif between the story of Ruth and the stories of Rebekah and Joseph, the passage strikes the keynote of the whole book of Ruth as a short story, like that of Joseph in Jewish and Muslim tradition, or like the book of Tobit (Fichtner, *RGG*, 3rd ed., V, 1961, col. 1254), designed to emphasise the power of Providence (so too, Hertzberg, p. 259; Vincent, p. 275). But, while this analogy in form and content is valid, a book in the Old Testament is generally addressed to a more particular situation.

We find the clue to the situation in the question of redemption. This is opened by the statement in 2:1 that Naomi had a substantial kinsman, Boaz. Naomi does not direct Ruth to Boaz' harvest field, but this is the writer's way of sustaining suspense in the development of his major theme. The next stage is the favour shown by Boaz to

Ruth in the harvest field (2:4ff.). Then on the threshing-floor Ruth makes her direct appeal for redemption (3:9). Boaz admits responsibility (3:11f.), but suspense is intensified by his disclosure that there is another kinsman who has priority (3:13). In the scene at the city-gate tension mounts with Boaz' confrontation of the nearer kinsman. It is increased by this man's admission of his right and responsibility to redeem the land to keep it in the family (4:5). Finally, the full responsibility of redemption is disclosed and, with the nearer kinsman's refusal to accept this, Boaz assumes responsibility (4:6–10), with the blessing of the community (4:11f.), the fruition of which sets the seal on Boaz' loyalty to the sound social values. Sustained suspense and controversy is a literary device in Semitic literature to accentuate the main theme. The installation of a roof-shutter in 'the house of Baal' in connection with a rite of imitative magic to induce the seasonal rains is a matter of altercation between Baal and the divine craftsman in the Ugaritic Baal-myth, and the mercy of God and the enormity of the sin of Sodom and Gomorrah is similarly emphasised in Abraham's importunity of God (Gen. 18:23ff.).

Thus the main issue in Ruth is that of rehabilitation, and here we may note the recurrence in the book of the verb *šûb* ('to return' or 'be rehabilitated'). This was the main issue soon after the fall of Jerusalem in 586 BC for those who had taken refuge beyond Jordan (Jer. 40:1) and were returning, like Naomi, after a comparatively short absence and in 'the day of small things' in the next half-century. Then great faith in God was required of those returning from the Exile and great charity and loyalty to the good old social standards on the part of substantial peasants like Boaz. Many of them, less worthy than he, congratulated themselves that 'Abraham was only one man, yet he got possession of the land; but we are many; the land is surely given to us to possess' (Ezek. 33:24). Addressed primarily, we believe, to this situation in the exilic and post-Exilic period, the book states the case of destitution in its most extreme degree in citing the situation of Naomi. By its selection of the Moabite woman Ruth as its central figure, it also seems to reflect sensitivity to the problem of the admission of alien women to the Jewish community, though this problem had not yet, we suggest, become so acute as in the time of Nehemiah and Ezra.

4. COMPOSITION

We find no reason for regarding the rhythmic prose of much of Ruth, especially the direct speech, as evidence of an earlier poetic version, as Myers (p. 2) proposed, or for regarding the work, apart from the summary genealogy in 4:17*b* and the more formal and longer one in 4:18–22, as other than a unity.

Intimately related to the purpose of the book and to its date is the question of the originality of David in the literary complex. The view that the Davidic genealogy is integral to the original book of Ruth was held by Wellhausen (*Einleitung in das Alte Testament*, ed. Bleek, 4th ed., 1878, pp. 204ff.) and has recently been maintained by Gerleman, so far at least as concerns the Israelite version of what he regarded as an original non-Israelite poetic tale; so also Lamparter (pp. 16ff.), who finds the book relatively early and regards it as an apologetic for a presumed Moabite strain in David's ancestry. Fichtner also (*op. cit.*, col. 1253), while rejecting 4:18ff. as a redactional addition after the genealogy in 1 Chr. 2:4–14, admits the summary genealogy in 4:17*b*, recalling that at a time of stress David sent his parents for safety to the king of Moab (1 Sam. 22:3), though we may observe that if David's family really had had natural ties of kinship in Moab, he would have sent his parents quietly to the family and locality where they were related, and this would have been sufficient security without his special request to the king. If Ruth is to be dated in Solomon's reign, the emphasis on the presumed Moabite origin of David would be strange at a time when the narrative J was probably written, emphasising as it does the hostility of Moab to Israel at the end of the desert wandering and condemning the association with Moabite women at Beth-peor (Num. 25:1*b*f.). But it be argued in support of the Solomonic date of the book, including at least 4:17*b*, that Ruth might have been written, in face of the anti-Moabite attitude of J, in justification of Solomon's admission of a Moabite wife to his harem (1 Kg. 11:1). There are, however, strong grounds for doubting this early date and purpose of the book of Ruth. The Davidic genealogy is assumed as integral to the book also by May, (*JRAS*, 1939, pp. 75ff.) who regards it as relatively early in the Monarchy, being an authentication of David as the divine king sprung from a *hieros gamos* at the 'high place' at Bethlehem, Naomi and Ruth being sacred prostitutes representing the mother-goddess. In its present state, on this view the book would represent a historification of this theme. But that is surely a gratuitous fiction which would deceive no one in Israel. The divine sonship claimed by the Davidic line was more surely based on the specifically Israelite ideas of covenant and adoption as expressed in the Story of the Davidic Succession from the time of Solomon. May's thesis requires more positive support than the problematic nocturnal encounter of Boaz and Ruth at the threshing-floor, which he couples with Hosea's reference to sacred prostitution on threshing-floors (Hos. 9:1), which is to be admitted as a rite of imitative magic. It is not thus that the originality of David in Ruth may be established.

At the other extreme, Gunkel (*op. cit.*, col. 107) rejected all of 4:17*b*–22 as a later addition. Bentzen (p. 183) and Hertzberg (pp. 258f.), on the other hand, maintained that 4:18–22, which by its introduction, content and affinity with 1 Chr. 2:4–15 seems indeed to be an appendix (so Campbell, Witzenrath), must have been suggested by some previous reference to David. This they find in 4:17*b*, which Witzenrath regards as the culmination of Ruth. Würthwein (p. 2) regards David as secondary in Ruth, added after Boaz of Ruth had been identified with Boaz of the Davidic genealogy in 1 Chr. 2:3ff. The majority of modern scholars would thus agree that 4:18–22 is a late appendix in Ruth. The problem is whether the summary genealogy from Boaz to David in 4:17*b* is also a secondary addition.

If, as Würthwein proposes, David in Ruth is suggested by the secondary identification of Boaz in Ruth with Boaz of the Davidic genealogy in Chr., the assumption is that the hero in Ruth is independent of Boaz of Chr. In that case, the fuller genealogy in 4:18–22, suggested by 1 Chr. 2:4–15, or its source, may have been actually earlier than the summary one in 4:17*b*, the secondary character of which is indicated by the name of Ruth's son as Obed instead of the compound of *nʿm* which 4:17*a* leads us to expect. But the identification of Boaz of Ruth with David's great-grandfather, according to the genealogy of Chr., may be the creation of the original author, in this case late, and not of the redactor. This may have been suggested by the setting of Ruth in the days of the judges, that is, two generations before David. In this case, David might well be original in Ruth, mention of the great king being reserved until the final dramatic *dénouement*, the fulfilment of the blessing that the dutiful Boaz might win repute (lit. 'a name') in Bethlehem (4:11). This view might be supported by the setting of the story in Bethlehem. If this is so, the whole of the book, the genealogy in 4:18–22 and the rest, might be a unity and a post-Exilic composition. This we consider more likely than Myers' proposal that 4:18–22 is, like the rest of Ruth, early monarchic, being drawn from palace records, the source of 1 Chr. 2:4–15 (*1 Chronicles*, AB, 1965, ad loc. so also Campbell and Sasson). Actually ten generations from Perez to David with Boaz in the prestigious seventh place, as noticed by Sasson (*ZAW* 90, 1978, pp. 171–85) seems artificially foreshortened, being suggested, we believe, by the citation of Perez in the local marriage blessing (4:12), the culmination of the genealogy in David being prompted by the wish that Boaz might acquire a name in Bethlehem (4:11).

Here Eissfeldt (pp. 589ff.) contributes to the debate, applying form-criticism to 4:17, on the analogy of the birth narratives of Gen. 25 and 38, with the latter of which Ruth has peculiar affinities. He notices that the naming of the child (with which, according to him, Ruth culminated) differs markedly from the prototype, in that the name has no relation to the circumstances of the birth. The declaration 'a son has been born to Naomi' demands a name like *Ben-nō'am*, *Na'mān*, or possibly *Ebed-nō'am*, or the like; with this, according to Eissfeldt, the original book ended. Certainly, the name *'Obed* in 4:17*b* is quite unexpected. It may, on the assumption of an original book which ended here independent of David, be *Ebed-nō'am* or *Ebed-na'îm*, with the suppression of the latter element, which had traditional associations with Baal in the Canaanite fertility cult. But in any case it seems a secondary attempt to bring David into the book after the genealogy in 1 Chr. 2:4–15 or its source.

Bearing in mind that the main theme of Ruth is redemption, there is substance in the objection that the omission of Mahlon, Chilion, the dead husband of Ruth, and Elimelech from the genealogy contradicts the whole theme of the book of leviratic marriage, whereby the name and lineage of the deceased was preserved. Rowley (pp. 184–6) proposed to overcome this difficulty by supposing that Boaz was old and without a son, so that Ruth was actually rehabilitating his house also (4:12). This is possible, though, with Boaz' obvious potency, it is unlikely in a society which so strongly emphasised progeny and permitted polygamy. Campbell (p. 172) has contended that the son of a leviratic marriage could be reckoned both as the son of the deceased and of his natural parent, and thus in Ruth the name of his more illustrious natural parent might be preferred. But, as Boaz himself emphasised (4:5), the primary purpose of the transaction, which we should expect to be expressed in the genealogy if that were original, is 'to restore the name of the dead to his inheritance'. Here we should do well to remember that, whatever historical verisimilitude there may be in Ruth, it is still to a large extent fiction, particularly in the names Mahlon ('Weakness') and Chilion ('Consumption'), which could hardly win a place in genealogy. For this reason, we regard the historicising Davidic genealogy through Obed as secondary, both in 4:18–22 and later in 4:17*b*.

5. LITERARY FORM AND SOURCES

It is now generally agreed that the original book of Ruth is the short story, as in the book of Jonah and that of Tobit. But Ruth clearly reflects the influence of stories in the narrative sources of the Pentateuch, particularly J. Thus the story of God's providence in the guiding of the poor and destitute suggests the Joseph story. In the colourful and circumstantial detail, the ethical tone and the idyll of simple family piety, the book reflects the influence of the patriarchal narratives, to which in fact there is explicit reference in Ru. 4:11f. The analogy with Tamar (Gen. 38) is particularly important, not only in view of the broad community of motif, but in the local significance of that tradition in Bethlehem.

The source of the story could be a popular local saga from Bethlehem (so Eissfeldt, p. 592), perhaps a family tradition of the return of a widow from a temporary sojourn abroad during one of the periodic droughts and her rehabilitation (so Gressmann, p. 592) like the woman of Shunem in 2 Kg. 8:1–6. However that may be, it has been elaborated under the influence of patriarchal narratives, particularly the story of Tamar the mother of Perez in Gen. 38, who is cited in the marriage blessing in Ru. 4:12, which may well reecho the traditional marriage blessing in Bethlehem. The reference to Leah, the mother of Judah, and to Rachel, whose burial-place was traditionally associated with the vicinity of Bethlehem (Gen. 35:19) further indicates the influence of patriarchal narratives.

But the combination of the names Mahlon and Chilion suggests fiction rather than history. Ruth and Orpah are not attested as proper names in Semitic antiquity. It is usually suggested that Ruth is an elided form of *reʿût* ('companionship'), which is certainly read by the Syriac version and would accord with Ruth's famous declaration of loyalty to Naomi in 1:16. But the elision of the strong middle guttural is unlikely. Orpah is connected by most with *ʿōrep* ('the back of the neck'), and taken to signify 'she who turned her back'. If the names, as is probable, are fictitious, Ruth might better, we suggest, be connected with the verb *rāwāh* ('to be saturated' or 'abundant in water'); Orpah might mean 'a cloud' (cf. *ʿrpt* in the Rās Shamra texts), such as excites hopes only to disappoint like the morning cloud in Hos. 6:4. The name Elimelech, however, though attested in the *OT* only in Ruth, like Naomi and Boaz, which are cited from 1 Chr. 2:4–15, is quite a likely name, and is the name of one of the scribes in the longer literary texts from Rās Shamra. W. E. Staples ('The Book of Ruth', *AJSL* 53, 1937, pp. 157ff.) saw here a designation of Tammuz; but *melek* ('king') was the title of any god. Boaz, it is suggested, may be a conflation of *baʿal ʿaz*

('Baal is strong'), which occurs, probably as a cultic response, in a certain passage in the Baal-myth of Rās Shamra celebrating the triumph of Baal the god of fertility over Mot, sterility and death; but that is conjectural. The name might be fictitious, the name of one of the free-standing pillars at the door of Solomon's temple being used to denote the stability of the subject in his society. But the incidence of the name in David's genealogy in 1 Chr. 2:5–15 indicates that it was realistic, possibly a modification of Baal-'az. Naomi ('my favour'), or, with an Aramaic ending, a form of Na'amah (cf. Gen. 4:22; 1 Kg. 14:21) has also been claimed as connected with the title of Tammuz. But Staples' thesis of a source in the myth of the fertility cult of Canaan, modified by M. Haller (*HAT*) and recently revived by J. F. X. Sheehan ('The Word of God as Myth: the Book of Ruth', *Word in the World: Essays in Honor of Frederick L. Moriarty, S.J.*, 1973, pp. 40–3) cannot be consistently worked out.

We must abandon the attempt to recover the source through the names of the protagonists. The one certain clue, in our opinion, is the citation of Perez in the blessing of Boaz' marriage (4:12). This is a clear reference to the story of Judah and Tamar on the same theme of rehabilitation by leviratic marriage, of which Ruth is a refined version, with a more particular and constructive end in view. Ruth preserves what Tamar had founded. Further echoes of the Pentateuchal narratives of Rebekah, Leah and Rachel, familiar in oral and literary tradition, point clearly to the dominant influence of those patriarchal traditions as the expressions of the social values, which the author of Ruth emphasises. The theory of a source in cult-drama is quite gratuitous.

In our rejection of Staples' theory of the mythology of the fertility cult as a source of Ruth, we ought in justice to recognise that he came very near the truth in discerning that the purpose of the book was to encourage Jews to return from refuge and exile. In support of this view, he might have cited the recurrence of the verb *šûb* ('to return'; but also 'to be rehabilitated') twelve times in ch. 1. In our opinion, however, the situation to which the book is addressed is after the return of exiles and refugees rather than before. Facing the problem of poverty and disillusionment after the liquidation of the state in 586 BC, the author points the way to rehabilitation through the practice of simple piety and loyalty to the family and to the local community; in short, *ḥesed*, loyal love in fulfilling the obligations of the covenant which expresses the *ḥesed* of God to his people and guarantees social stability whatever may hap. Illustrative of such loyalty is the ancient custom of leviratic marriage and redemption. In the presentation of the generous Boaz, the writer is obviously appealing to the better instincts of the more substantial and fortunate among the remanent Jews, many of whom were too content with their material prosperity to show much sympathy to their less fortunate compatriots returning destitute from refuge and exile.

But as the book has reached us it has acquired yet more meaning. With the addition of the genealogy of David, the final editor emphasises that God's daily providence, which vindicates the faith and obedience of simple men and women, not only builds up the family but relates the faithful to his higher order once symbolised by the dynasty of David and yet to be consummated by the Davidic Messiah (Hertzberg, p. 260). That the whole was so understood is indicated by the citation of Boaz, Ruth, Obed, Jesse and Perez in the genealogy of Jesus Christ in Christian apologetic in Mt. 1 and Lk. 3.

6. TEXT

For general considerations on MT and the versions, see above, pp. 34ff.

The earliest Hebrew text of Ruth is attested in eight fragments of four MSS from Qumran, two from Cave 2 (M. Baillet, J. T. Milik and R. de Vaux, 'Les "petites grottes" de Qumran', *Discoveries in the Judean Desert*, III, 1962, pp. 71–5, and Pls. XIV and XV) and two from Cave 4 (so far unpublished; cited by Campbell, pp. 40f., by courtesy of F. M. Cross). Of those, fragments of one MS from Cave 2 (2QRuth[a]) and another from Cave 4 (4QRuth[a]), from the first half of the first century AD, vary very little from MT. But a fragment of another MS, 2QRuth[b], containing parts of 3:13–18, shows more divergence; e.g.

3:14, 'she came to the threshing-floor' (*bā'āh haggōren*); cf. MT, 'the woman came to the threshing-floor' (*bā'āh ha'iššâh haggōren*),

3:15, 'and he measured out there and then six measures of barley' (*wayyāmod šēš-śe'ōrîm šām*); cf. MT, 'and he measured out six measures of barley' (*wayyāmod šēš śe'ōrîm*), and

3:16, *māh-a'tt* for MT *my-'att* ('in what condition are you?'; see below ad loc.), where the Qumran variation may derive from a scribal corruption of *y* in the archaic Hebrew script.

On this evidence, the variation from MT is minimal; any variation attested does not substantially affect the meaning of the text. The versions, however, exhibit greater differences.

The two main versions of significance for the text of Ruth are the Greek (LXX) and the Syriac, the Peshitta and the Syriac Hexapla. Generally, the variants from MT are not substantial. The Syriac has minor explicatory amplifications, from which LXX is free. But in two instances both have slightly longer texts, where MT is rather too terse and probably deficient. Thus in 1:9, where, according to MT, Naomi says to Orpah and Ruth (in hardly possible Hebrew) 'the Lord grant that you may find a resting-place', LXX and the Syriac read 'the Lord grant you mercy: May you find a resting place!' Another passage, where the Syriac version either corrects the grammar of MT or indicates a more correct variant of the Hebrew text, is in 4:1, where to MT *haggô'ēl . . . 'ᵃšer dibbēr bô'āz* ('the kinsman . . . of whom Boaz had spoken') the Syriac adds the resumptive pronoun with the preposition *'al* ('concerning'). In 4:7, with reference to the rite of the sandal in redemption or conveyance of property, MT seems deficient in the statement *wᵉzô't lᵉpānîm* (lit. 'and this beforetime'). The matter is made explicit in LXX, Syriac and the Vulgate, which have 'and this *was the custom* beforetime'), probably reading *wᵉzeh hammišpāṭ lᵉpānîm*.

In the unvocalised text of the Hebrew MSS, the imperfect indicative is implied in 1:8, where the *Qᵉre* understood the optative. This is supported by LXX, which reads the optative in 1:17 where MT has the imperfect indicative. In 1:13, LXX and the Syriac version understood MT *lāhēn* as *lāhem* ('for them'), which would give good sense in the context. *lāhēn*, however, if correct, would be an Aramaism ('on that account'), which is feasible. With the possibility of the confusion of *m* and *n* in the archaic Hebrew script, however, MT *lāhēn* may be a corruption of an original *lāhem*, as read by LXX and the Peshitta.

There are a dozen or so cases where the versions give a meaning different from MT. Some we may ignore. The LXX statement in 1:14 that when Orpah left Naomi, Ruth 'followed', *ēkolouthēsen*, is an obvious corruption of Greek *ēkollēthē*, 'cleaved to' (Naomi), Hebrew *dābᵉqāh*. Another is 'tribe' (Greek *phylē*) for MT 'gate' (Greek *pylē*) in 3:11 and 4:10. But other variations merit more serious consideration.

In 1:21, MT *'ānāh bî*, '(the Lord) has testified (lit. answered) against me' is understood by LXX and the Peshitta as *'innāh bî* ('has brought me low'). This verb is certainly apposite in Naomi's case, but it would take the direct object, so that it may be ruled out in favour of *'ānāh bî* in MT, which is well attested as a forensic term in Exod. 20:16; Dt. 5:20; 2 Sam. 1:16, and is not unapt in its context, where Naomi voices the same sentiment as Job, who uses forensic language throughout the book. In MT 2:13, in Ruth's expression of gratitude to Boaz, 'though she is not as one of his maid-servants', LXX and the Peshitta omit the negative. This would indicate an original statement that Ruth will relate to Boaz with the same obligations and privileges as one of his maid-servants. In MT, *l'*, there pointed as the negative particle, may have been understood by the versions as the particle *lû'* introducing the optative: 'May I be as one of your maid-servants.' In 2:14, where Boaz proffers Ruth parched corn, the verb in MT, *ṣābaṭ*, is a *hapax legomenon*. LXX reads 'he heaped up', which implies Hebrew *ṣābar*, attested in this sense in Gen. 41:35, 49 and Exod. 8:10, and which may be supported by the statement that Ruth had more than she could eat. The participle of the same verb is understood by LXX in 2:16, which is generally understood as '(pull out some for her from) the handfuls' (*sc.* what is grasped with one hand to be reaped by a stroke of the sickle). 'Handfuls' renders MT *ṣᵉbāṭîm*. The implication is that LXX read the same Hebrew root in both places. Both *ṣābaṭ* and *ṣᵉbāṭîm* are *hapax legomena* in the Old Testament, but the latter may be supported by the Akkadian *ṣabâtu* ('to grasp'), while the former is attested in Late Hebrew *bêt ṣᵉbāṭîm* ('jar-handle') and in Ugaritic *mṣbṭm* ('tongs'), by which an article is lifted and 'reached over', the sense of *ṣābaṭ* generally understood in 2:14. Here it would seem that LXX indicates a scribal emendation to substitute a well-known term for one unfamiliar or perhaps obsolete.

In 4:5 in Boaz' disclosure to the nearer kinsman of the obligation to take Ruth to wife with the property to be redeemed the consonantal text of MT reads *qnyty* ('I shall acquire'). Here *Qᵉre* is *qānîtā* ('you will have acquired'), which was understood also by LXX and the Hexapla Syriac. The Peshitta and the Vulgate read the imperative *qᵉnēh*. In the blessing on Boaz' union with Ruth in 4:11, 'May Yahweh make the wife who now enters your house like Rachel and Leah, who between them built up the house of Israel', MT continues: *wa'ᵃśēh-ḥayil bᵉ'eprātâh* ('and be worthy/procreative in Ephrathah'). LXX reads 'and they effected strength in Ephrathah'. Here the verb in the third masculine plural cannot refer to Rachel and Leah, but must be understood to indicate their progeny, 'the house of Israel'. But LXX ignores the parallelism in the end of the verse:

wa'ᵃśēh-ḥayil bᵉ'eprātâh
ûqᵉrā' šēm bᵉbêt lāhem,

which confirms MT. For MT, *ûqᵉrā' šēm* (and 'proclaim a name'), LXX[BA] reads *kai estai onoma*, 'and there shall be a name'. The version is not helpful and the peculiar *ûqᵉrā' šēm* might be the scribal corruption in the archaic Hebrew script of an original *ûniqrā' šimᵉkā* ('and may your name/fame be proclaimed'), which is agreeable with the parallelism. In 4:14, in the women's blessing of Naomi: 'Blessed be the Lord who has not let you lack a redeemer, so that his name shall be proclaimed in Israel', LXX reads 'you (*sc.* Naomi) will proclaim your name in Israel', thus understanding *šᵉmēk* for MT *šᵉmô*, which is graphically feasible archaic Hebrew script. But the object of leviratic marriage was to perpetuate the name of the father through the son (A the son of B) and not the mother or, in this case, grandmother, so that there is no reason to question MT. In 4:5, in Boaz' declaration that the nearer kinsman in acquiring the land from Naomi will be obliged also to acquire Ruth, MT reads *ûmē'ēt rût* ('and from Ruth'), which is followed by LXX. The Peshitta and the Old Latin versions and the Vulgate indicate the obvious original *wᵉgam 'et-rût* ('and Ruth also'), of which MT is obviously a scribal omission by haplography of *g* between *w* and *m* in the archaic Hebrew script.

The most awkward passage in Ruth is 2:7, where MT *watta'ᵃmōd mē'āz habbōqer wᵉ'ad-'attāh zeh šibtāh habbayit mᵉ'āṭ* ('and she has stood from the earliest [the morning] until now, this her sitting [in] the house a little'). LXX reads 'and she has stood from early (in the morning) until evening; she has not rested (even) for a little in the field'. The Vulgate reads '. . . from morning until now and has not returned home (*wᵉlō' šābāh habbayit*), while the Peshitta reads '. . . from morning until she is sitting', with nothing corresponding to the rest of MT. Straightway 'until evening' of LXX may be rejected, since the context is the mid-day break. In the context 'the house' (*habbayit*) is admissable only if MT *šibtāh* is taken as a corruption of *šābāh*, which the Syriac version implies. 'She has stood', however, suggests a contrast with 'sitting' (*šibtāh*) or resting (*šābᵉtāh*) with LXX. Thus MT *habbayit* may be understood as a dittograph and a corruption of *bth* in *šbth*, perhaps facilitated by the similarity of *h* and *y* in the archaic Hebrew script. The negative in LXX should surely be seriously considered, and this in turn points to the indicative *šābᵉtāh* ('she has stopped work, or rested'), which LXX read. MT *mē'āz* is conjecturally emended to *mē'ôr* (*habbōqer*) ('from morning light'), which assumes a scribal corruption of *r* to *z*; but there is no evidence for this in the versions, and in any case this is graphically feasible only in the last stage of the development of the Hebrew script when the text was all but standardised. Two solutions present themselves, both assuming that *mē'āz* means 'from the earliest', as in Pss. 76:8 and possibly in 46:2 (*EV*, v. 1), where *me'ôd* may be a dialectic form of *mē'āz*. We propose that *habbōqer* is either a variant reading, eventually fused with *mē'āz* in this sense, or is a gloss on this expression which has crept into the MT. Thus we propose the following restoration of the text: *watta'ᵃmōd mē'āz* *w^{e}‘ad-hā’ēt hazzeh w^{e}lō’ šāb^{e}tāh m^{e}‘āṭ* (‘and she has stood from the earliest until this present time and she has not stopped work [even] a little’).

COMMENTARY
on
Ruth

ELIMELECH'S FAMILY AT THE NADIR OF THEIR FORTUNES

1:1–5

1. In the days when the judges ruled: in view of the probably late composition of Ruth (see above, pp. 366ff.), this might refer to that section of the Deuteronomistic History, but it may also reflect the tradition of the judges in the pre-monarchic period.
a famine: the cause is not stated. It was probably drought, which is depicted as lasting for a long time, occasioning the family of Elimelech to live in the plains of Moab 'about ten years' (v. 4); cf. the seven years famine in 2 Kg. 8:1. Famine might also be the result of war. The Palestinian farmer lived so near subsistence level that one or two bad harvests brought him near to ruin.
Bethlehem in Judah: here so designated to distinguish it from Bethlehem in Zebulun. This was a place which might be influenced sooner than many places by drought since it is on the eastern side of the watershed of south Palestine, being still the metropolis of the Wilderness of Judah towards the Dead Sea and the lower Jordan Valley, where the first of the Dead Sea Scrolls were brought to market.
to sojourn: Hebrew *lāgûr* denotes the status of an alien who is nevertheless protected by his hosts. Such a person is *gēr*, Arabic *jāru 'llāhi*. Elimelech's case recalls the migration of the patriarchs to Egypt in time of famine.
the country of Moab: (Hebrew *śᵉdê mô'āb*). The phrase recalls Num. 22:1; 33:48ff., where the locality is specified as 'by the Jordan at Jericho'. It is thus not the rolling plains on the plateau east of the Dead Sea, as Campbell supposes (*op. cit.*, ad loc.), preferring the singular *śᵉdēh*, as in 1:6f. and 2:6, which is read at 1:1 by certain Hebrew MSS and in LXX, the Peshitta and Vulgate and in an unpublished fragment of Ruth from Qumran, Cave 4 (cited by Campbell from a communication by Cross). This reading, however, and the singular in 1:6f. and 2:6 of MT, may be an early scribal corruption of *y* to *h* in the archaic Hebrew script. Reading the plural, we understand it to refer to the foothills and plains north-east of the Dead Sea, which are watered by little perennial wadis, a natural place of refuge in time of drought, especially for the marginal lands of Judah between Bethlehem and the Dead Sea. This association may go back to the penetration of the region of Bethlehem by immigrants from the country beyond the lower

Jordan, which seems to be indicated by 'the Stone of Bohan the son of Reuben' south-west of Jericho (Jos. 15:6; 18:17; see above, p. 135). In more recent times, the Ta'amira Arabs by Bethlehem and Tekoa with grazings north-east towards the lower Jordan entered Palestine in their migration from the Hejaz, after a sojourn in the valley east of the lower Jordan (B. Couroyer, 'Histoire d'une tribu semi-nomade de Palestine', *RB* 58, 1951, pp. 75–91). There was probably an age-long relationship between the two regions, with rights of intermarriage, which made it natural for people of Bethlehem to find refuge there. David, himself of Bethlehem, sent his parents for safety to Moab (1 Sam. 22:3).

2. **Elimelech . . . Naomi** (cf. v. 20) **. . . Mahlon . . . Chilion:** see Introduction, pp. 374, 375.

Ephrathites: Ephrathah is parallel to Bethlehem in 4:11, and was evidently the district in which Bethlehem was situated (Mic. 5:2, MT, v. 1; cf. Gen. 35:16–19; 48:7), probably so named after the clan which had settled there, perhaps specifically in the region of richer vegetation (see above, p. 10), just west of the watershed at Bethlehem. Since 'Ephrathite' denotes 'Ephraimite' in Jg. 12:5 and 1 Sam. 1:1, Reuss proposed that the purpose of Ruth was to demonstrate that David was descended both from Ephraim (through Mahlon) and Judah (through Boaz), and was therefore entitled to rule the united kingdom.

and remained there: undoubtedly the sense of MT *wayyihyû* ('and they were'), for which two late Hebrew MSS and 4QRuth[a] read *wayyēšᵉbû* ('and they settled').

4. **took Moabite wives:** on the phrase *nāśā' nāšîm*, attested in post-Exilic sources in the Old Testament, see above, p. 368. The explicit exclusion of Moabites and Ammonites from the religious community of Israel in Dt. 23:3ff. may indicate that intermarriage with those neighbouring peoples in the circumstances indicated in 1:1 was not uncommon before the end of the seventh century BC. The practice analogous to Arab *ṣadīqa* marriage, where the wife continued to live with her parents and was visited occasionally by her husband (see on Jg. 14:5–20), may have been in use here, though in the ten years sojourn of Naomi's family in Moab the unions in this case were envisaged as more permanent.

Orpah . . . Ruth: on the names, see Introduction, p. 375.

5. **was bereft of her two sons:** lit. 'was left from . . .', a pregnant construction, the preposition being privative. Since leviratic marriage provided primarily for children, the situation of a widow too old to have children was a desperate one in her own community; abroad, where she had no kindred, it was hopeless. Even in her

own country, apart from the sale of her husband's property, only charity remained.

THE RETURN OF THE WIDOWS

1:6–22

Naomi's destitution is expressed in her reply to the women of Bethlehem in vv. 19–21. The arrival of Naomi and Ruth at the beginning of the barley harvest (v. 22) provides for their relief in gleaning and prepares the way for Boaz' recognition of Ruth and ultimate redemption.

6. had visited his people: the verb *pāqad* means primarily 'to review' and so 'to take note of' and secondarily 'to make a visitation' for relief or for punishment according to deserving need or delinquency discovered in the review (see above, on Jg. 21:9).

7. from the place where she was: the resumptive preposition in the relative clause, where we should expect *šām*, is *šammāh*, which regularly means 'thither'. *šām* may be a later form of an original *šammāh*, which means 'there' with emphasis in Ezek. 32:29, 30, varying with *šām* in vv. 22, 24, 26 in the same passage.

8. her mother's house: the father's house might be expected; but this may be an anachronism, alluding originally to the part of the tent reserved for the women (Arabic *ḥarīm*) and presided over by the mother (cf. Ca. 3:4).

deal kindly with you: better, 'deal loyally with . . .', a phrase which is originally related to covenant obligations (see on Jos. 2:12), where the phrase is used in its original connotation. In *'immākem* ('with you'), the pronominal suffix in *m* is probably not masculine, a scribal corruption of *n* in the archaic Hebrew script, but a dual, as in Gen. 31:9 (of Rachel and Leah), 1 Sam. 6:7, 10 (of two cows) and Exod. 1:21 (of two midwives) and in Ugaritic (Gordon, *UT* §6:12). In the present context Naomi, mindful of her own distress, may urge on the girls their duty to their own mothers in the event of similar need.

9. they lifted up their voices and wept: for MT *qôlān* ('their [fem.] voices'), 4QRuth[a] (cited by Campbell, *op. cit.*, ad loc.) reads *qôlām*. Though this may be a scribal inadvertancy or corruption of *n* to *m* in the archaic Hebrew script, it could be feminine dual, as in v. 8.

10. And they said to her, "No, we will return . . .": (Hebrew *kî . . . nāšûb*), understanding *kî* in its adversative sense. *lāh* ('to her') might be a scribal corruption of *lō'* in the archaic Hebrew script; but though *kî* adversative is usually reinforced by the negative particle, it may be used without it.

11–13. The destitution and hopeless prospect of Naomi is emphasised, and at the same time the question of leviratic marriage, so fundamental to the book, is touched upon. The practice of marriage with the widow of a brother or kinsman who had died childless was not confined to Israel. On the discrepancy between 3:12 and Dt. 25:5–10, which limits leviratic marriage to a brother of the deceased living still in his father's house, as in Gen. 38, and its relevance to the date of Ruth, see Introduction, p. 367. The child was reckoned as the son of the dead man, whose name, status and property he maintained (4:10). But the status of the wife to her original husband and his brother was posed as an academic question by the Sadducees in Mt. 22:23ff., ignoring the real point of the convention.

13. would you therefore wait . . . would you therefore refrain?: on the Aramaisms *śibbēr* and *lāhēn* and the late Hebrew or Aramaic *'āgan* and the relevance to the date of Ruth, see Introduction, p. 368.

No, my daughters: the negative particle *'al* generally introduces a prohibition in Hebrew, with the imperfect jussive of the verb, and we may understand a prohibition here in contradiction of what the girls have offered in v. 10*a*, as in Jg. 19:23, where *'al* is used, first absolutely then with the imperfect jussive.

it is exceedingly bitter to me for your sake that the hand of the LORD has gone forth against me: so *RSV*, understanding *mikkem*, lit. 'from you' (dual), as the cause of Naomi's bitterness (cf. Ps. 119:53), which is possible in the sense that their involvement in her destitution is the cause of her bitterness. Naomi appears to resign herself to the fact that she has evidently lost the *beràkâh*, or divine favour, and is a baneful influence to all associated with her, according to the primitive Semitic conception of the cumulative and infectious effect of blessing or curse. The author intensifies the literally hopeless situation of Naomi, and may be animadverting upon the lack of faith among Jews after the collapse of the state in 586 BC. Alternatively, as the Peshitta recognises, *min* may be comparative, Naomi declaring that her bitterness is much more than that of her daughters-in-law, who after all, with youth and kindred, had some hope. This is the meaning assumed by Joüon, *op. cit.*, ad loc. Rudolph (*op. cit.*, ad loc.) in the sense 'my bitter condition is too grave for you to bear' (so more recently, H. C. Brichto, 'Kin, Cult, Land and Afterlife', *HUCA* 44, 1973, pp. 12ff.) and 'for things go far more bitterly for me than for you' (Campbell, *op. cit.*, ad loc.).

14. Orpah kissed her mother-in-law: LXX adds 'and she returned to her people', her first reaction having been to be willing to go with Naomi (v. 10). The long parting is a literary convention to emphasise the destitution of Naomi and the sacrifice of Ruth, who by her return apparently sacrifices the prospect of security and marriage.

15. to her gods: or 'god'; *sc*. Chemosh of Moab (see on Jg. 10:6; 11:24). It is implied that the return of Orpah to her people involves the worship of the national god, who stands in a kindred relation to his people (Hebrew *'am*) (see on Jg. 12:2). The same is implied in Ruth's reply 'your people shall be my people, and your God my God' (v. 16).

return after your sister-in-law: LXX and the Peshitta read '(return) you, too' (*gam-'att*).

your sister-in-law: (Hebrew *y^ebimtēk*). *y^ebāmâh* is used in Gen. 38:8 and Dt. 25:5–10 of a widow *vis-à-vis* her dead husband's brother, who had the duty of marrying her in the convention of leviratic marriage, and thus being his sister-in-law. Here Ruth's *y^ebāmâh* Orpah is a young widow as a similar liability, which is evidently understood by LXX, which translates *synnymphos* ('fellow-bride', presumably in prospect). In the Rās Shamra myths Anat, the sister of Baal, is termed *ybmt l'imm* ('the sister of the Mighty One'), from which we have reasoned that Hebrew *y^ebāmâh* and its Ugaritic cognate denote an unattached female who was the responsibility of her next of kin, brother or brother-in-law.

16. I will lodge: Hebrew *'ālîn* (lit. 'spend the night') refers to the stages of the journey immediately in prospect and possibly in the uncertain future (so Sasson, *Ruth*, 1979, p. 30). In Ruth's classical reply, where the dramatic climax is marked by poetic rhythm, Ruth sacrifices all that an ancient Semite could—home, kindred, her native religion; in short, all guarantees of protection, and even burial with her own people, and that for a destitute and aging widow who had nothing to offer her.

17. May the LORD so do to me and more also if . . .: the regular oath-formula. Originally, and especially in the case of another than the person who made the adjuration, disabilities would be specified; but when one involved himself in the adjuration, he may have refrained from actual enumeration of these, using instead the general 'thus', possibly accompanied by a gesture, equating himself with the animal severed in the covenant ritual in Gen. 15:7–17 and Jer. 34:18–20.

18. was determined: Hebrew *mit'ammeṣet*, 'having rallied herself'.

19. the whole town was stirred: Hebrew *wattēhōm* is probably the Niphal imperfect of *hûm*, rather than the secondary form of the Qal imperfect of *hāmam*. The latter verb expresses confusion of noise and/or motion, distraction or discomfiture, *hûm* also expresses excited noise and motion, distraction or discomfiture, as notably in the derived noun *m^ehûmâh* (e.g. Am. 3:9). But in 1 Sam. 4:5 it expresses the glad excitement on the appearance of the ark in the Israelite camp and of Jerusalem at the anointment of Solomon (1 Kg. 1:45), where, as in Ru. 1:19, it is said *wattēhōm hā'îr*. Thus, Campbell is right in understanding the expression to refer to the local women's glad excitement at the return of Naomi, which is modified by Naomi's reply, 'Call me not Naomi ("Sweet") . . .'.

the women said: the subject is not specifically mentioned in MT, but is indicated by the preformative and afformative of the verb.

20. Do not call me Naomi, call me Mara: note the word-play on the names, respectively 'Pleasant' or 'Sweet' and 'Bitter', reflecting the common practice of expressing gratitude for, or in anticipation of, divine favour in a name. The MT spelling of Mara with final ' is unusual as the feminine singular of the adjective *mar*, and may be an early scribal corruption of *mārâh* in the archaic Hebrew script.

21. has afflicted me: so *RSV*, with LXX, the Peshitta and the Vulgate, reading *'innāh bî* for *'ānāh bî* ('has testified', lit. 'answered, against me', which we prefer); see Introduction, p. 378. MT implies that Naomi accepts the conventional conception of suffering as the consequence of sin, albeit unknown, which the Lord had now made explicit.

the Almighty: Hebrew *šadday*, though attested in early monarchic sources, either as *šadday* or *'ēl šadday* (e.g. Gen. 49:25, J; Num. 24:4, JE; Ps. 68:14, MT, v. 15), is generally late and post-exilic (Gen. 17:1; 28:13; 35:11; 48:3; and especially Exod. 6:3, all P; Ezek. 10:5; and forty times in Job, where it is a conscious archaising. The translation **Almighty** is prompted by the Vulgate *omnipotens*, after LXX *pantokratōr*. This might suggest a connection with Arabic *šadda* (VIIIth Form, 'to be strong'), which, however, would not be otherwise attested in Hebrew. The fanciful Rabbinic interpretation, 'He who is sufficient' (*ša day*), was known to the early Jewish translators, but cannot be seriously considered. The most probable etymological explanation is that the word is an old Aramaic form from a root cognate with Akkadian *šadu* ('mountain'), possibly surviving from patriarchal times when the Aramaic forebears of Israel worshipped their God in the north Arabian steppe and the highland of the Jebel Bishri, between Damascus and the Euphrates.

22. who returned: according to the pointing of MT the verb is perfect, the article in this case having the same force as the relative pronoun, as in 2:6 and 4:3.

and they came: (Hebrew *bā'û*). If *hēmmāh* is a pronoun, as it may be, it is a feminine dual (see above, on 1:8).

22. at the beginning of the barley harvest: this was associated with the desacralisation rite of Unleavened Bread, and in turn linked with the Passover, which it immediately followed, for seven days from the fourteenth of the month Abib, later called Nisan (March–April) (Exod. 12:1–20, P); cf. Exod. 13:3–10 (J), which does not specify the date in Abib. The harvest would naturally vary from district to district in such a widely diversified land as Palestine. At Bethlehem it would be about the end of April or beginning of May. The writer thus prepares us for the next act, where Ruth is introduced to Boaz in the harvest field.

RUTH'S ENCOUNTER WITH BOAZ AT HARVEST

2:1–23

Boaz is attracted by Ruth's industry in gleaning and by her fidelity to Naomi, which is already known to him (v. 11). The next scene, with Boaz' admission of a kinsman's responsibility (3:11–13), is thus anticipated, especially in v. 12: 'The Lord recompense you for what you have done, and a full reward be given you by the Lord, the God of Israel, under whose wings you have come to take refuge.' The scene is emphasised by Hertzberg (*op. cit.*, p. 267) as a struggle for existence rather than as a delightful idyll. This view, however, must be modified by the blessing of Boaz in v. 12, and what it presages in the main theme of the book.

1. a kinsman: *myd'*, lit. 'one known', which MT reads as the Hophal participle *môdā'*; cf. *môdā'tānû* ('our kindred') in 3:2. But *m^{e}yuddā'* may be read; cf. 2 Kg. 10:11. The term means one known to another, probably with the more pregnant sense of mutual *acknowledgement* of social obligations as between kinsmen, as indicated in 2:20, where Naomi describes Boaz as *qārôb*, 'a kinsman' (cf. *q^{e}rôbay* in parallelism with *m^{e}yuddā'ay* in Job 19:14) and as *miggô'^{a}lēnû*, *sc.* probably *miggô'^{a}lēynû*. Possibly *m^{e}yuddā'* or *môdā'* was of wider application in view of the nearer kinsman mentioned in 3:12, who was properly the *gô'el* ('redeemer') with the first duty and option.

a man of wealth: better, 'a mighty man of substance', socially, materially and morally, a term also, and perhaps originally, related to military service (see on Jg. 6:12).

Boaz: on the name, see Introduction, p. 375f.

2. glean: this right was a convention of poor relief provided for in Dt. 24:19ff.; Lev. 19:9ff.; 23:22ff., and in the Talmud (Mishnah, *Peah*, 'Corner'). Till recently in some Arab villages, a corner of a field was left unreaped for this purpose, though the regular alms-contribution levied in Islam tended to modify this humane custom.

3. the part of the field: i.e. the strip of the cultivable land of the family, which was often allotted annually by lot or rotation among the Palestinian peasants, and, even where farmed permanently by an individual, was unfenced from other parts of the cultivable land.

4. The LORD be with you . . . the LORD bless you: the greeting has its modern Arab parallel. Dalman cited the harvest greeting 'The blessing of the Lord be upon you' and the response 'We bless you in the name of the Lord' in Ps. 129:8 (*Arbeit und Sitte in Palästina*, III, reprint, 1964, p. 43).

5. Whose maiden is this?: in ancient Israel, as in modern Islam, direct interest in a member of the family, especially a female, is suspicious; hence Boaz enquires not directly of Ruth but of her family.

7. and gather among the sheaves: in view of the special concession to glean among the sheaves (v. 15), the phrase is suspect here, and in fact is omitted in the Peshitta and Vulgate. The reapers reaped their handfuls with the sickle, which were left to be gathered into bundles and bound in sheaves, usually by women (cf. v. 8). Only after those might the gleaners come. Boaz' order to the reapers is probably a rather pregnant injunction not to reprimand Ruth for gleaning too near the women binding the sheaves.
from early morning until now, without resting even for a moment: on textual difficulties, and on our reading 'from the earliest until this present time and she has not stopped work (even) a little', see Introduction, p. 380f. This assumes that *bayit* ('house') is inappropriate in the harvest field. Alternatively, Campbell (*op. cit.*, ad loc.) has proposed that Ruth had stood in the field from early (morning) until the time of Boaz' arrival, without returning home (so the Vulgate) even for a little, waiting for his permission to glean. Gleaning, however, was an acknowledged right that would hardly have required explicit permission from the owner; and in any case Ruth had already begun to glean (v. 3).

8–9. This is the first instance of Boaz' appreciation of the character of Ruth, further disclosed in v. 11, and of his paternal care for her. Though the poor might glean, evidently they might be churlishly handled, especially if the owner and his people thought that they approached the reapers and binders too closely; cf. our note on v. 7. Ruth is pressed to glean in Boaz' field for the whole harvest, even among the sheaves, and even to drink the water which was reserved for the workers.

10. she fell on her face, bowing to the ground: a gesture of respect, not of worship as Staples claimed in support of his thesis of the mythological motif in the book. Thus Abigail appeared before David (1 Sam. 25:23).

a foreigner: Hebrew *nokrîyâh*, lit. 'recognised', i.e. conspicuous. Note the word-play between *nokrîyâh* and *lᵉhakkîrēnî* ('to take notice of').

12. recompense: 'pay in full'.

under whose wings you have come to take refuge: though 'wings' is a possible translation of *kᵉnāpayim* or *kᵉnāpîm*, 'skirts' is also possible, and probably better, an anthropomorphism which reflects the spreading of the skirts of one's mantle over a person as a guarantee of protection and, in the case of an unattached female, of marriage (so 3:9); cf. the covering of the bride's head with part of the husband's clothing as a marriage rite in certain Arab communities. A closer analogy is the custom of a kinsman putting part of his garment over a widow, attested by J. Lewy (*RHR* 110, 1934, pp. 31ff.).

13. spoken kindly to: lit. 'spoken upon the heart of . . .', i.e. comforted, a synonym of the verb *niḥam* (so also in Isa. 40:1f.).

your maidservant . . . my lord: conventional terms of respectful address for 'I' and 'you'.

14. Another mark of the simple kindness of Boaz was the invitation to join the workers at their meal. Vinegar (*ḥomeṣ*; *RSV*, 'wine') was the by-product of wine-making, not always intentional. It was an effective thirst-quencher and relish.

passed to her parched grain: on the verb *ṣābaṭ*, a *hapax legomenon* in the Old Testament, see Introduction, p. 379. Parched grain (*qālî*, here barley) was roasted on an iron plate, like that brought by Abigail (1 Sam. 25:18) and Barzillai (2 Sam. 17:28) to David and his men as field rations.

15. even among the sheaves: better 'bundles'; see on v. 7.

16. pull out some bundles: Hebrew *ṣᵉbatîm*, better 'handfuls'; see on v. 7. The verb *šālal* in this sense is not attested elsewhere in the Old Testament. It is probably cognate with Arabic *salla*, 'to draw' a sword out of the scabbard or 'to deliver a child'.

do not rebuke her: Jewish custom, though admitting rights of gleaning, was somewhat punctilious, allowing the gleaners only what was left by chance and not what fell when the reaper's hand was pricked by a thorn or stung by a scorpion (Mishnah, *Peah* 4.10).

17. beat out: Hebrew *wattaḥbōṭ*. Small quantities of corn were beaten out with a curved stick (Arabic *maḥbaṭ*); see on Jg. 6:11. Verse 18 indicates that Ruth beat the corn outside the town, probably on the threshing-floor.

an ephah: the measure of capacity, an Egyptian loanword, was one tenth of a homer ('ass-load'), about 29 lbs, according to R. B. Y. Scott (*Peake's Commentary*, 2nd ed., 1962, p. 341). The standard may have varied locally, like weights in the various districts of Arab Palestine up till the British Mandate, and with passage of time.

18. she showed her mother-in-law . . .: so *RSV* after LXX and Vulgate, with emendation of the vowels of MT, which reads 'and her mother-in-law saw . . .'.

she also brought out and gave her what food she had left over after being satisfied: this probably denotes the parched grain mentioned in v. 14.

20. Naomi's blessing, in mentioning God's loyalty (*RSV*, **kindness**) to the living and the dead, anticipates rehabilitation through Boaz, who, if not himself the nearest kinsman, was sufficiently well-disposed and influential to see that the kinsman's duty of redemption should be fulfilled. The theme of the next scene is thus anticipated.

21. all my harvest: including the wheat harvest about a month later than the barley harvest, ending conventionally at the Feast of Weeks (Pentecost), seven weeks after the inauguration of the barley harvest at the Feast of Unleavened Bread (cf. 1:22).

22. lest . . . you be molested: the verb (*pāga'*) means 'to meet or accost', denoting the uncertainties and hazards to which a defenceless female like Ruth, with no local ties other than through her mother-in-law, the widow Naomi, might be exposed.

ON THE THRESHING FLOOR: A DETERMINED AND SUCCESSFUL APPEAL

3:1–18

1. a home: Hebrew *mānôaḥ*, lit. 'a resting-place'; see on 1:9. As Naomi wished for her daughters-in-law, so now she contrives for Ruth.

that it may be well with you (*'ašer yîṭab lāk*), a final clause as in Dt. 4:40; 6:3.

2. is not Boaz our kinsman?: lit. 'our acquaintance', or kinsman, more general than *gô'ēl*; see on 2:1. *môda'tānû* (cf. *m^e^yuddā'*, 2:1) is the feminine singular collective and abstract, which is occasionally used for the masculine plural participle both in Hebrew (e.g. *yôšebet y^e^rûšālayim* ('inhabitants of Jerusalem') and in Ugaritic (e.g. *t'dt ṯpṭ nhr*, 'the accredited agents of River'. Here it is used for the masculine singular, unless the partitive *m* is omitted by dittography before the preformative *m*.

he is winnowing barley tonight at the threshing-floor: lit. 'he is, or will be, winnowing the threshing-floor of barley . . .'; i.e. the barley which has been threshed and is still on the threshing-floor. The **threshing-floor** (Hebrew *gōren*, lit. the space 'rubbed clear', as the Arabic cognate indicates) was an open space on rock or hard-beaten earth clear of the village (cf. 2:17f.). It was not the most exposed place, but was still open to the breeze, which is necessary for cleaning out the straw and chaff from the grain, the whole being tossed up after threshing with a flat-pronged wooden fork. The grain is finally sieved. The operation, which exploits the prevailing south-west wind in Palestine, which springs up about 3 pm., is done by preference when the wind is steady but not boisterous in the evening and early morning.

Tonight may denote this operation at both favourable times, including for the narrators and probably also for Naomi the night spent by Boaz on the threshing-floor.

3. wash therefore: Hebrew *wᵉraḥaṣt*, with *waw* consecutive with the perfect as an imperative, normally after the imperative, but here after the participle 'is/will be winnowing' (*zôreh*) of continuous action.

4. uncover his feet: lit. 'the place of his legs', a euphemism for sexual parts (cf. Exod. 4:25; Isa. 6:2). This word, like 'lie down', which has often the sexual sense, poses the problem of what actually happened on the threshing-floor. May (*JRAS*, 1939, pp. 75ff.) and Staples (*op. cit.*, pp. 153ff.) boldly declared that this was an instance of sacred prostitution at the 'high place' at Bethlehem, the six measures of barley (v. 15) being the hire of the sacred prostitute (cf. Hos. 2:5; 9:1). In this case the precaution for Ruth's unobtrusive return (v. 14) and the fundamental question of the leviratic marriage is meaningless. We do not deny the sexual innuendo; but that may simply be a refinement of the motif of the Tamar story (Gen. 38), which from this point onwards and possibly in the intention of Naomi, is the prototype for Ruth. The situation, with its admittedly equivocal language, admirably sustains suspense towards the crisis of the story. Arab peasants used still to sleep by the corn on the threshing-floor, usually in tents or light shelters, as a precaution against theft and to take advantage of the early morning breeze for winnowing.

6. went down to the threshing-floor: at some distance therefore from the village; see on v. 2. The threshing-floor at Bethlehem was obviously lower than the village, which like most Palestinian villages, occupied the hill-top.

7. his heart was merry: cf. Jg. 19:6. This may indicate, though it need not, excess. All that may be meant, however, was that he was well satisfied.

at the end of the heap: the cognate of *'ᵃrēmâh* is still used in Arabic for a heap of grain on the threshing-floor.

8. and he turned over: Hebrew *wayyillāpēt*. The Arabic cognate indicates that Boaz turned over rather than that he bent forward. In consequence he discovered Ruth lying beside him and not at his feet (see on v. 4).

9. spread your skirt over your maidservant: see on 2:12. This was a gesture of protection, as is indicated by Ruth's appeal to her dead husband's kinsman (*gô'ēl*) with special reference to marriage (cf. Dt. 22:30, MT 23:1; 27:20; Ezek. 16:8). The *gô'el* is specifically the kinsman on whom lies the obligation of redemption or of blood-revenge (*gô'ēl haddām*) (see on Jos. 20:3). Figuratively, the word is applied to God in the sense of rehabilitator, e.g. of Israel after bondage in Egypt (Exod. 6:6; 15:13; Ps. 74:2, etc.) or after the Exile (e.g. Isa. 43:1; 44:22, 23; 48:20; 52:9; 63:9, etc.).

10. you have made this last kindness greater than the first: the first alludes to Ruth's loyalty in casting her lot with Naomi in her destitution, which Boaz had already acknowledged (2:11), and in supporting her by her gleaning; now she has given further demonstration of her loyalty to Naomi and her late husband by claiming the right of leviratic marriage, like Tamar in Gen. 38, seeking out Boaz and so demonstrating that duty to the family was her motive rather than fancy or fortune in seeking to attract any young man for her own personal advantage. In addition, Boaz, probably no longer young, may have been personally flattered by Ruth's trust.

11. all my fellow-townsmen: lit. 'the whole gate of my people', 'gate' being used for 'city' by synecdoche, here with particular reference to the gate and open space within and without as the place of business and gossip.

a woman of worth: Hebrew *'ēšet ḥayil*, a woman of strength of character, and as such worthy to be the wife of a *gibbôr ḥayil* (see on 2:1) and to share his substance, like the *'ēšet ḥayil* in Prov. 31:10ff.

12. and now it is true that I am a near kinsman: Hebrew *wᵉʿattāh kî 'omnām kî 'im gô'ēl ānōkî*. MT, while including *'im*, omits vowel points, thus recognising a scribal error, *'im* having probably been mistakenly written after *kî* after *kî 'omnām* in the previous phrase. The second *kî* may have been introduced by the same inadvertency. But *kî* after *'omnām* may be recitative; or, if the first *kî* is the Massoretic interpretation of the emphatic *k*, which occurs in Ugaritic, usually emphasising the final word or phrase (cf. Gen. 18:20; Ps. 49:16, MT), it may be concessive. In this case, the sense would be 'and now though, it is true that I am a near kinsman . . .'. In stating that he is *gô'ēl*, Boaz admits not only his consanguinity in the broader sense indicated by *mᵉyuddāʿ* or *môdaʿat* (see above, on 2:1 and 3:2), but also his kinsman's duty; he declares, however, that there is one who has a prior obligation, and, if he cares to exercise it, a prior claim. This claim is often jealously guarded by first cousins among the Arabs. This declaration surely absolves Boaz from the imputation of improper relations with Ruth, since, if the other kinsman had accepted, his own good name and hers among his own kin would have been irrevocably damaged, and perhaps their lives forfeited.

13. Remain this night: since she might have been taken for a public prostitute (cf. Ca. 5:7), and would possibly encounter unprincipled persons, either thieves watching for an opportunity at the threshing-floors or men drunk at that season of harvest.

14. before one could recognise another: a woman stirring in the early morning would attract less suspicion, since work traditionally began before daylight in the Arab villages. The first task of the day being grinding, Ruth, with her load of barley, would be a natural figure.

15. the mantle: lit. 'what is spread out' (cf. Isa. 3:22), perhaps the large white kerchief of the fellahin women among the Arabs, which can be drawn over the face or held in the teeth as a partial veil (so *AV*).

six measures of barley: the actual measure is unspecified. This could hardly be the ephah, which, on the lowest computation (R. B. Y. Scott, *op. cit.*; see on 2:17), would be 174 lbs, too much for Ruth to carry. It has been suggested that the measure was the omer, one tenth of an ephah. But this would have been actually less than 'about an ephah' which Ruth beat out of her day's gleanings (2:17). Hence Jouon (*op. cit.*, ad loc.) and Rudolph (*op. cit.*, ad loc.) proposed the se'ah, one third of an ephah, six of which (*c.* 58 lbs on Scott's reckoning) would be both generous and a possible burden for Ruth.

16. How did you fare, my daughter?: Hebrew *mî naṯabittî*, lit. 'Who are you, my daughter? If literally meant, this might be designed by Naomi, in the event of the woman not being Ruth, to conceal the fact of Ruth's absence. But, as in the Rās Shamra texts, the interrogative pronoun may mean 'in what condition?', i.e. 'How have you fared?'; cf. *b'l mt . . . my hmlt*, 'Baal is dead . . . What of the multitudes?'; and in Hebrew, Am. 7:2, 5: *mî yāqûm ya'ᵃqōb kî qāṭôn hû*, 'How (*sc.* in what condition) shall Jacob stand, for he is insignificant?'

18. rest: lit. 'be silent'.

REDEMPTION EFFECTED

4:1–17

The drama of the rehabilitation of Naomi's family, undertaken by Boaz (3:12f.), a man of substance and standing (*gibbôr ḥayil*, 2:1), is played out in public 'in the gate' (v. 1), tension being sustained by Boaz' gradual statement of the full implications of redemption to the nearer kinsman, who in declining to marry Ruth cedes his right to acquire the property and leaves Boaz to acquire both. His action is publicly attested (v. 11) with the addition of a blessing on the marriage and a wish for the happy issue of progeny, which was the purpose of marriage (vv. 11f.). Local colour is lent by the citation in the blessing of rehabilitation effected by the resource of Tamar in patriarchal times (v. 12), the mother of Perez, a notable ancestor in Judah and perhaps in Bethlehem. With the reference to this patriarchal tradition, the analogy with Gen. 38, which is implicit in Ruth, is now explicit. The episode closes with the realisation of this blessing (v. 13). Emphasis is laid on the rehabilitation of the widow Naomi, symbolised by her taking of the child into her bosom (v. 16) and the declaration of the women who had assisted at the birth, 'A son has been born to Naomi', who was probably named accordingly in what may have been the culmination of Ruth before the Davidic genealogy in vv. 17*b* and 18–22 (see Introduction, p. 374ff.).

1. the gate: see on 3:11. The **gate**, as well as being the natural place of business frequented by elderly men of leisure, like 'the elders' (v. 2), who were available as custodians of local social conventions and as witnesses, was the obvious place to intercept the kinsman on his way to work in the fields.

friend: Hebrew *p^elônî 'almônî*. The narrator has no particular interest in preserving the name, if indeed there was any historical tradition in his story. In such a case, or through haste, a Palestinian Arab will address one, *yā fūlānī* or *shū 'smuk* ('What's-your-name?').

2. the elders of the city: the heads and representatives of the leading families, who are envisaged as judges in domestic cases in Dt. 21:2ff. and 18ff.; 22:15f. etc.

3. is selling: actually in MT 'has sold'; but cf. v. 9, where Boaz buys the land from Naomi, in view of which we might expect the participle *môk^erâh*. The phrase, however, may be a legal idiom, indicating that a party has resolved or offered to sell, *sc.* to the nearest kinsman. The fact that Naomi had a plot of land to sell is here divulged for the first time, which is at first sight surprising in view of the emphasis on her utter destitution on her return. The plot, however, was probably cultivated in her absence, the crop being the property of the cultivator. A destitute woman was not likely to forget the property she had temporarily vacated, like the Shunammite woman in 2 Kg. 4:8–37, who returned to claim her land after seven years' absence in time of famine. The failure to mention Naomi's property before 4:3 may be owing to the narrator's economy; but is probably deliberately reserved until now in order not to impair the impression of Naomi's destitution and Ruth's loyalty to her without hope of material reward.

the parcel of land: see on 2:3.

4. I would tell you of it: lit. 'uncover your ear', i.e. drawing back the long hair.

if you will not redeem it: what precedes and follows indicates that this is the correct reading, though MT has 'If he will not redeem it'. The second person of the verb is supported by certain Hebrew MSS and by all the versions.

5. you are also buying Ruth: *Qᵉre qānîtā* is supported against *Kᵉtib qānîtî* ('I acquired . . .') by the reading *gam 'ēt rût* ('Ruth also'), and by the general sense of the context (on text, see Introduction, p. 379). The verb *qānāh* means 'to buy', but is never used in the Old Testament of acquiring a wife by paying the bride-price. It has definite overtones of redemption in Exod. 15:16: 'the people you have purchased' (*'am-zû qānîtā*); cf. Exod. 15:13: 'the people you have redeemed' (*'am-zû gā'altā*). In the texts on redemption of property in the Old Testament, Lev. 25:25–28 regulates the redemption of a kinsman's property, as in Jer. 23:6–8, but makes no provision for leviratic marriage, while Dt. 25:5–10, in dealing with leviratic marriage, does not explicitly include redemption of the property of the deceased brother, since this was a transaction strictly within the household, the whole purpose of which was to maintain the inheritance of the deceased member of the family through the son of the leviratic marriage, as is certainly recognised by Boaz, who states the purpose of marriage with Ruth as 'in order to restore the name of the dead to his inheritance' (4:10). The present case is complicated by the liability for Naomi, and Sasson has feasibly suggested (*op. cit.*, pp. 123–5) that the verb signifies compensation to Naomi for the release of Ruth from obligation to her mother-in-law, which Ruth had assumed (1:16f.). The qualification of Ruth as **the Moabitess** in this context emphasises that loyalty to wholesome social principles is a matter of principle and not to be modified by strict adherence to the letter. The **Moabitess** underlines the generous disposition of Boaz, as it emphasises the selfless loyalty of Ruth in 1:22; 2:2, 6, 21.

the widow of the dead, in order to restore the name of the dead to his inheritance: the purpose of leviratic marriage, which is, however, ignored in the genealogy in 4:18–22, indicating that this is a later addendum (see Introduction, p. 372ff.).

to restore: lit. 'cause to stand'; i.e. not allow to fall, or lapse.

the name: the realisation of the person; see on Jos. 7:9.

6. To the kinsman's declining to redeem the family of the dead, the Peshitta version adds, 'through lack of faith'. This, visualising the Davidic genealogy in vv. 17*b* and 18–22, and probably also the genealogy of Jesus in Mt. 1:2–16, is a Christian gloss. The refusal of the option was probably through reasonable prudence. In redeeming the property the kinsman would have provided for Naomi, a terminable responsibility. But Ruth, young enough to bear children, was a further, and greater, liability, which was aggravated by the fact that the property would revert to her offspring, the heirs of Elimelech. In buying the property with such liabilities, thereby reducing his own capital to maintain his land, the kinsman might well **impair his own inheritance**. In the declining of the kinsman to marry Ruth, and so rehabilitate the family of his kinsman Elimelech, we have a further analogy with the Tamar tradition in Gen. 38, where Judah's son Onan, for selfish reasons, refused to 'give offspring to his brother' (Gen. 38:9). Campbell has done well to notice that in the kinsman who was disposed to go reasonably far in discharging his responsibilities, but not far enough, there is a correspondence with Orpah, affectionate but not to the point of self-sacrifice, both being foils to the selfless commitment of Boaz and Ruth. This is but one element in the skilfully constructed novelistic book of Ruth.

7. **this was the custom in former times:** so *RSV* after LXX, the Peshitta and the Targums; see Introduction, p. 367.

the one drew off his sandal: we should expect the frequentative of the verb, and not, as in MT, the perfect. This may be obtained by reading *wᵉšālap* (so Campbell, *op. cit.*, ad loc.), assuming the omission of *w* by haplography after *r* of the preceding word *dābār* in the archaic Hebrew script.

and gave it to the other: this is formally ambiguous. A tradition of LXX^{L}, the Targum and Vulgate assume that the kinsman's sandal was given to Boaz, presumably to signify the kinsman's renunciation of his prior duty and claim, as in Dt. 25:9, where the rejected widow removes the sandal and spits in the face of her brother-in-law. In Ruth, however, the case is complicated since it involved also the conveyance of property (Hebrew *tᵉmûrâh*). Here, too, renunciation on the part of the kinsman who refused his kinsman's duty was involved, and the handing over of his sandal to Boaz might correspond to the convention of sasine in Scots law, where the vendor of land hands over a sod. Midrash Rabbah Ruth 7.11 debates the question and decides that Boaz gave his sandal as a pledge. This would have an analogy in the law of Nuzu, *c.* 1400 BC, where a creditor is formally adopted by a debtor, thus being entitled to acquire heritable property otherwise inalienable, handing over clothes or shoes to his adoptive 'father' in token of his 'filial' duty (E. A. Speiser, 'Of Shoes and Shekels', *BASOR* 77, 1940, pp. 15–26). The setting of the shoe upon land, another legal convention at Nuzu, also symbolised legal possession (L. P. Lachemann, *JBL* 56, 1937, pp. 53ff.), like the casting of a shoe over land in Pss. 60:8 (MT, v. 10); 108:9 (MT, v. 10). The explicit statement 'and gave it to him' in v. 8, which LXX and Aquila's version add to MT, would indicate that the sandal was taken off and given to Boaz by the kinsman, who thus renounces his duty and claim. Though betokening renunciation both in Dt. 25:9 and in Ru. 4:7f., there is no indication that it was a gesture of insult in Ruth as it was it Dt. For the author of Ruth, it had a wider significance, indicated by its use in commercial transactions (v. 7*a*), probably both before and after Dt., which has therefore no implication in determining the relative date of Ru.

11. We should expect **the elders** only to declare that they were witnesses of the transaction. If MT is not a case of free composition, the writer may have intended to convey the unanimity of the response, the whole transaction in the gate being public, and **the people** endorsing the attestation of their elders and representatives. Their cordiality is expressed in the double blessing on Ruth, for whom a patriarchal blessing is wished, and for Boaz. The rhythm of the former blessing (v. 11*a*) becomes the parallelism of poetry in the latter (v. 11*b*). The reference to **Rachel and Leah**, in that order, as the mothers of Israel is particularly appropriate in the case of Ruth, through whom the family of Elimelech was to be rehabilitated. The tradition of Rachel was particularly associated with Bethlehem, her tomb being traditionally sited 'on the way to Ephra(tha)h, that is Bethlehem' (Gen. 35:19f., E).; cf. the Arab shrine in the northern outskirts of Bethlehem and the site Ramat Raḥel, on the highest point between Jerusalem and Bethlehem.

prosper: Hebrew *'ᵃśēh ḥayil* may have the pregnant material sense suggested by *RSV*, as in Dt. 8:17. *ḥayil*, however, has the nuance of 'increase' or 'fruitfulness' (Jl 2:20, and possibly Job 21:7f. and Prov. 31:3) (so C. J. Labuschagne, 'The Crux in Ruth 4:11', *ZAW* 79, 1967, pp. 364–7), which would be particularly appropriate in the blessing on Boaz' union and would accord with the purpose of perpetuating the name of Elimelech and his son by a son of his leviratic marriage. The author, however, may use *ḥayil* in its whole range of meaning in his blessing of the union of Boaz, a *gibbôr ḥayil* (2:1) and Ruth, herself an *'ēšet ḥayil* (3:11). In rendering the phrase *'ᵃśēh ḥayil* as 'engender procreative power', Labuschagne suggests that Boaz, like Judah in Gen. 38, was old.

be renowned: possibly reading *niqrā' šimᵉkā*, of which MT *qᵉrā' šēm* may be a scribal corruption in the archaic Hebrew script (see Introduction, p. 379), or *qᵉnēh šēm*. In the latter, *šēm* would mean 'renown'; in the former, it could mean 'renown' but also 'name', *sc.* the name of the son of the leviratic marriage which would include that of the husband of Ruth, thus 'perpetuated in his inheritance' (v. 10). **Ephrathah:** associated with **Bethlehem** in Mic. 5:2; Gen. 35:19, and 48:7, is a locality, perhaps the better wooded western side of the watershed of Judah by Bethlehem, after which the clan of Boaz and Elimelech (1:2) may have been named.

12. On the local significance of the blessing, cf. the story of the birth of Perez, also by a substitute for leviratic marriage, which had been promised, in Gen. 38, which is so strikingly reflected in Ruth. In the blessing of the family of Boaz by Ruth, the narrator seems momentarily to have lost sight of the fact that by the convention of leviratic marriage the first male offspring of the union would be reckoned to Ruth's deceased husband and not to Boaz. Here, Parker has noted that the blessing on Boaz' marriage has a parallel in that of Keret in the royal legend on that king in the Rās Shamra texts. Both recall notable ancestors, Perez, the ancestor of Boaz, and the *rp'um*, who we now know as deified royal ancestors; both blessings include progeny. In the Keret text, the senior god El wishes, or assures, the king of a progeny of 'seven, yea, eight sons' and a like number of daughters. Those include his heir, so designated by being fostered by the fertility goddesses, and the eighth daughter, who shall be given the birthright. Parker concluded that the name or renown promised in Boaz' blessing entitles us on this analogy to regard the Davidic genealogy in vv. 17*b* and 18–22 as original. This, we consider, does not follow. In the *Krt* text a continuity of royalty between Krt's illustrious predecessors and his heirs is natural. But Boaz' marriage is a leviratic marriage to perpetuate the line of the defunct, who, at best, would only be indirectly the ancestor of David. If, indeed, Ruth's son by Boaz were the ancestor of David, we should expect her defunct husband and Elimelech to be mentioned in the Davidic genealogy. In both blessings we have the reflection of a common marriage custom in ancient Semitic society adapted to suit the circumstances of the bridegrooms. The solidarity of the clan associated Boaz with his dead kinsman, both begin Ephrathites and of the clan of Perez. Furthermore, the line of Boaz would be doubly secure by his issue by Ruth and by his previous children, which he probably had. In any case, it must be remembered that this was a personal blessing to Boaz in appreciation of his magnanimity.

14. The women are here again introduced, like the chorus in a Greek drama, heralding Naomi's hope, as they had witnessed her destitution in 1:19.

may his name be renowned in Israel: on the text, see Introduction,

p. 380. Boaz, the redeemer, should gain renown for his generous loyalty to his social duty. This blessing may have suggested to a redactor that he should be blessed in the lineage to David; see Introduction, p. 373.

15. a restorer of life: Hebrew *mēšîb nepeš*, recalling the phrase in Ps. 23:3.

seven sons: the conventional ‘seven’ of folklore and saga; cf. 1 Sam. 2:5: ‘the barren woman has borne seven’; and Job’s seven sons, the perfect family (Job 1:2).

16. laid him in her bosom: it has been suggested that this is a rite of adoption; cf. ‘a son has been born to Naomi’ (v. 17*b*); cf. also Sarah, who bore a son to Abraham through her surrogate Hagar (Gen. 16), a convention well attested in Mesopotamian and Hurrian law in the second millennium BC. But the gesture may have been one of simple affection, as in 2 Sam. 12:3; 1 Kg. 3:20 and Isa. 40:11, where there is no question of a legal gesture.

nurse: Hebrew *’ōmenet*, not wet-nurse, but rather guardian, like the guardians, or tutors (*’ōm^{e}nîm*), of Ahab’s sons in 2 Kg. 10:1, 5, and Mordecai, who brought up Esther (Est. 2:7). Thus, Naomi’s personal status and claim in the community was preserved.

17. gave him a name: if this is the sense of MT *wattiqre’nāh lô šēm*, we should expect the name to have some relation to the declaration, ‘there is a son born to Naomi’, which **Obed** has not. Attempts to get over this difficulty regard Obed, perhaps originally Ebed, as the hypocoristicon of *Ebed-nō‘am* or *Ebed-nā‘îm* (‘Servant/Worshipper of Favour/the Gracious One’), or render the Hebrew phrase ‘and they rejoiced over him’ (Campbell, *op. cit.*, ad loc.), which we think unlikely, or ‘and they established his reputation’, with reference to the blessing in v. 13, which we consider more feasible. If *šēm* does not mean literally ‘a name’, we might suggest that a better translation might be ‘and they declared his significance’, i.e. to be a son to Naomi. In this connection we note the significance in the Rās Shamra texts of the naming of the weapons with which Baal was to overcome Sea-and-Ocean Current, according to their purpose, ‘Driver’ and ‘Expeller’:

k̠tr ṣmdm ynḥt	The Skilful One reaches down a double lightning-bolt
wyp‘r šmthm	And declares its purpose (cf. Akkadian *simtu*, ‘destiny’)
šmk ’at ’aymr	Thy name is ‘Expeller’.
’aymr mr ym	Expeller, expel Sea,
mr ym lks’ih	Expel Sea from his throne,
nhr lkḥṯ drkth	Even Ocean-Current from the seat of his sovereignty.

Nevertheless, we favour Eissfeldt's form-critical argument and conclude that the genealogy in 17*b* is secondary, like vv. 18–22 after 1 Chr. 2:4–15 or its source; see Introduction, pp. 374f.

GENEALOGICAL APPENDIX

4:18–22

This we consider to be inspired by the mention of the house of Perez in the blessing of Boaz in v. 12 and with the identification of Boaz of Ru. with Boaz of Chr. The genealogy of David, artificially foreshortened to ten generations, may be paralleled by king-lists from the Old Babylonian period, as noticed by A. Malamat (*JAOS* 88, 1968, pp. 170–3), the prestigious seventh place reserved for Boaz.

18. Perez: evidently, according to the author of Ru., the ancestor of the clan of Boaz and of the husband of Naomi, and probably of most of the community of Bethlehem. According to Gen. 38, he was the son of Judah by Tamar by the substitute for regular leviratic marriage which Tamar contrived (Gen. 38:29).

Hezron: a son, or clan, of Perez (Gen. 46:12; 1 Chr. 2:5); cf. 1 Chr. 4:1, where he is given as a son of Judah. As Num. 26:21 indicates, this is tribal genealogy, which is still reckoned according to actual or putative ancestors of families among the Arabs.

19. Ram: the grandson apparently of Hezron in 1 Chr. 2:25; cf. 1 Chr. 2:9, where he is given as the son of Hezron. This seeming contradiction is explicable when it is recognised that this is tribal, and not individual family, genealogy. In the genealogy of Jesus in Lk. 3:33, Ram of Mt. 1:3 is given as Arni, after LXX on Ru. 4:19 (*Arran*).

20. Amminadab: the son of Ram (1 Chr. 2:10).

Nahshon: the son of Amminadab (1 Chr. 2:10; also perhaps Num. 1:7; 2:3; 10:14).

Salmon: cf. Salma, the son of Nahshon and father of Boaz, in 1 Chr. 2:11 (cf. 1 Chr. 2:54, where he is connected with Bethlehem). Christian apologetic makes the interesting introduction of Rahab into the Messianic genealogy as the wife of Salmon and mother of Boaz (Mt. 1:5), Rahab (Jos. 2) in Christian thought being symbolic of faith as 'the assurance of things hoped for, the conviction of things not seen' (Heb. 11:31), an interpretation of the Old Testament which is apparent in the addendum to Ru. 4:6 in the Peshitta that the kinsman refused to take Ruth 'through lack of faith'.

INDEX OF MODERN AUTHORS

GENERAL INDEX